WONDERING ABOUT GOD TOGETHER

RESEARCH-LED LEARNING & TEACHING
IN THEOLOGICAL EDUCATION

**Edited by
Les Ball and Peter G. Bolt**

Wondering About God Together
Research-Led Learning & Teaching in Theological Education
Edited by Les Ball and Peter G. Bolt

SCD Press
PO Box 1882
Macquarie Park NSW 2113
scdpress@scd.edu.au

© SCD Press and Contributors 2018

ISBN-13: 978-1-925730-02-9 (Paperback)
ISBN-13: 978-1-925730-03-6 (E-book)

Internal layout and design: Lankshear Design Pty Ltd.
Cover design based on design by: ben taylor creative enterprises, btce.com.au

WONDERING ABOUT GOD TOGETHER

RESEARCH-LED LEARNING & TEACHING
IN THEOLOGICAL EDUCATION

**Edited by
Les Ball and Peter G. Bolt**

**SCD Press
2018**

Publications associated with SCD Learning & Teaching Theology Conferences

1. Les Ball, *Transforming Theology. Student Experience and Transformative Learning in Undergraduate Theological Education* (Preston, Vic.: Mosaic, 2012).
2. Les Ball & James R. Harrison (eds.), *Learning & Teaching Theology. Some Ways Ahead* (Northcote, Vic: Morning Start, 2014).
3. Yvette Debergue & James R. Harrison (eds.), *Teaching Theology in a Technological Age* (Cambridge: Cambridge Scholars Publishing, 2015).
4. Les Ball & Peter G. Bolt (eds.), *Wondering About God Together. Research-Led Learning & Teaching in Theological Education* (Macquarie Park, NSW: SCD Press, 2018).

CONTENTS

Introduction

    1 *Wondering about God: The Conversation Continues.* Les Ball   ix

Part 1: **The Role of Research in Theological Education**

    2 *Remembering the Future: The Contribution of Historical Research to Innovation in Theological Education.* Andrew Dutney   1

    3 *Reflections on the Practice of Research-Led Teaching in a Small College Context.* Willis Salier   19

    4 *Moving from Instruction to Inquiry: How Complexity Theory Informs Work-Integrated Learning.* Stephen Smith   35

    5 *Reflections on the Experience of Wonder In Research-Led Learning—in Company with Nietzsche and Girard.* Nikolai Blaskow   52

    6 *'Unite the Pair So Long Disjoined, Knowledge and Vital Piety': What is the Role of Research in This Process?* David McEwan   71

    7 *Researching the Future: the Implications of Activist Research for Theological Scholarship in Teaching and Learning.* Steve Taylor and Rosemary Dewerse   87

Part 2: **The Telos of Theological Education**

    8 *'To Take You Where You Do Not Wish to Go': Extending the Telos of Online Theological Education—The 'Who' of the Teacher Who Teaches.* Peter Mudge and Dan Fleming   106

9 *'To Take You Where You Do Not Wish To Go': Extending the Telos of Online Theological Education—The 'What' of the Institution That Teaches.* Peter Mudge and Dan Fleming ... 123

10 *Vision for The Good Life.* Bruce Hulme ... 140

11 *Education, Ministry and the New Covenant.* Peter Carblis ... 162

Part 3: **Academic Freedom in Theological Education**

12 *Academic Freedom in the Thought-Policed University: Challenges for Christian Educators Today.* Barry Spurr ... 189

13 *Exploring the Nexus between Academic Freedom and Ecclesial Expectations.* Dean Smith and Rob Fringer ... 203

14 *The Perils of Academic Freedom: the Australian College of Theology as an Australian University of Specialisation.* Geoff Treloar ... 220

Part 4: **Pedagogical Approaches to Deep Learning**

15 *Windows, Mirrors and Icons as Ways into the Context, Content and Call of Sacred Narratives.* Debra Snoddy ... 237

16 *In My Father's House: the Place of Wonder in Proverbs' Vision of Education.* A. J. Culp ... 254

17 *Text and Interpretation: from Classical Music to Biblical Studies.* Sarah Hart ... 270

18 *The Pedagogy of Biblical Fiction: Where Research and Creativity Collide.* Ben Chenoweth ... 284

19 *Is the God of the Bible an Ugly Bully? Helping Bible Students Come to Terms with Violence in the Biblical Text.* Andrew Jaensch ... 303

20 *An Approach for Deep Theological Learning in Research Methodologies.* Denise Goodwin ... 317

21 *The Relational Teacher: Sharing Life as Vocational Essence.* Darren Cronshaw ... 338

22 *Deep Learning from a Shallow Surface? Encouraging Good Research in the Internet Age.* Peter Bolt ... 352

23 *Making Good Practice Affordable: Understanding your Students with Learning Analytics.* Martin Olmos — 373

24 *Theological Education in Context: Exploring the Delivery of Theological Education in a Multi-cultural Setting.* Bruce Allder — 393

25 *Integrating Theology in a Questioning Age.* Les Ball — 410

26 *Curiosity and Doubt in Researching the Future: the Contribution of Flipped Learning to Sociality in Theological Innovation.* Steve Taylor and Rosemary Dewerse — 426

Epilogue Peter Bolt — 453

INTRODUCTION
1 | WONDERING ABOUT GOD

THE CONVERSATION CONTINUES

In the period 2007-2012, the Australian Council of Deans of Theology sponsored a number of research initiatives which led to the publication of two important works, *Uncovering Theology* and *Transforming Theology*. This process quickly gave rise to an earnest discussion of learning and teaching of theology in Australia. The Sydney College of Divinity has since been at the vanguard of this discussion, in its promotion of a series of scholarly conferences and publications. This book is the third in the SCD series of Learning and Teaching publications which seek to further the conversation within the academy.

This volume of essays advances the conversation by somewhat boldly confronting a number of increasingly vital issues for contemporary Australian theological education. The essays proceed from prior conversations and add further dimensions in delving more deeply into four general areas, where much has been said before but where the depth of discussion has stopped short of tackling heavy issues in a front-on manner. The areas addressed include a continuing scholarly dialogue around the increasing recognition of the nexus between *research* and effective teaching; further philosophical pondering on the *telos* of theological education, with probing thoughts on questions of ultimacy in the process; a frank discussion on the significance for learning and teaching of institutional *academic freedom* as it increasingly affects tertiary theological education; and the earnest quest to develop innovative *pedagogical approaches to deep learning*.

Part 1 of this volume explores the role of research in theological education. In the lead essay, 'Remembering the Future: The Contribution of Historical Research to Innovation in Theological Education', Andrew Dutney relates the story of South Australia's Uniting College for Leadership & Theology, showing how a major project of historical research released forces for change and innovation that have given theological education a place at the centre of the emergent 21st century church, and describing what he has learned about being a change leader in theological education. The findings of this research are grounded in a particular case, yet the principles arising from it are eminently transferable to many other institutions. As a personal outcome, he notes how the research led him from being 'the dispassionate researcher' to 'being led by my research into the hands of the living God'.

The following two essays provide further accounts of principles adduced from research applied to specific institutional cases, narrated by the principal actors in the process. Willis Salier's essay, 'Reflections on the Practice of Research-Led Teaching in a Small College Context', proposes a greater focus on the research of teaching and learning as a complement to research in subject disciplines and posits a taxonomy of research led teaching practice. The three planks of such a proposal are encouraging familiarization with books about teaching and learning by initiating faculty discussion; engaging in scholarly teaching, drawing on the abundant data commonly available within teaching institutions; and reflecting on and contributing to the scholarship of teaching and learning. Significantly, the essay concludes with a report on 'a venture into the world of the scholarship of teaching and learning', to illustrate how these principles can be applied even to a small college. In the second of these two essays, 'Moving from Instruction to Inquiry: How Complexity Theory Informs Work-integrated Learning', Stephen Smith engages with research in Complex Living Systems as a platform for developing a dynamic model of theological education. From his background in health science, Smith extrapolates principles of complex systems that have been applied to his own theological institution to develop a heuristic model of *sensemaking* in educational systems, which distinguishes between *simple* or *chaotic* contextual domains of education (where *a teaching culture of instruction* is effective), and the *complicated* or *complex* contextual domains (where *a learning culture of inquiry* is effective). Throughout, Smith discusses the relative merits of classroom based instruction and workplace based learning, with the emphasis always on the most effective arena for the attainment of specified learning outcomes rather than a philosophical polarisation of the two contexts. This exploration of the various domains of Complex Living Systems is as challenging (to conventional models) as it is informative (for innovative learning).

A very different specific study is presented in Nikolai Blaskow's essay, 'Reflections on the Experience of Wonder In Research-led Learning—in Company with Nietzsche and Girard'. This essay presents an analysis not of an institution's experiment in teaching, but of two controversial thinkers from whom we may learn much about the process of theological research and inquiry. Blaskow asks the question: 'What can be learned from Nietzsche—and from Girard—about the wonder and the marvel of research-led learning as opposed to dogmatics and systematics?' It is these characteristics of wonder and marvel, emerging from inquiry untrammeled by conventions and systems, that are at the core of a sometimes chaotic but always energising journey of enlightenment and discovery. With Nietzsche and Girard, Blaskow advocates self-examination and 'the provocation of the truth... [with a] relentless commitment to authenticity—an authenticity that will not be compromised' in the conduct of theological research. He notes further that the person of the researcher cannot be separated from the research, which demands a rigorous accountability of both systems and self in testing their assumptions. Ultimately, research requires a sense of humility and vulnerability in approaching mystery.

David McEwan writes as a practical theologian in his essay, '"Unite the Pair So Long Disjoined, Knowledge and Vital Piety": What is the Role of Research in This Process?' Within a Wesleyan context, he explores the challenges of research-led practical theology to current educational practices in the light of received heritage. The integration of knowledge and piety is at the heart of the Wesleyan educational tradition and is becoming increasingly sought by other traditions. McEwan asks: what role can research play in developing vital transformative outcomes, and to dispel the false (but common) dichotomy between faith and academy. This requires a thorough understanding of the inter-relationship of knowledge and piety. The complexities of contemporary life present challenges to traditional methods, as 'we are unable to *solve* the problems we have created with the *same*... practices that have created them'. McEwan affirms an obligation to create a questioning generation that will do research and develop, rather than be content with themselves and their inherited systems. The basic thesis is that full-scale intellectual engagement is not incompatible with Christian belief and pietistic practice—in fact, the integrated embodiment of knowledge and piety demands rigorous and authentic research.

Part 1 concludes with the hortatory essay, 'Researching the Future: the Implications of Activist Research for Theological Scholarship in Teaching and Learning', by Steve Taylor and Rosemary Dewerse. This essay brings us back to the pivotal role of research in the progressive development of teaching practice. It applies insights of activist research as a theoretical framework to explore the theological educator's identity as theologian (speaking of God's Kingdom) and teacher (wanting to impact students). While the sector has traditionally prioritised research in the domain of theological discovery, this essay calls for more focused attention to the generally *ad hoc* domain of research in teaching and learning. The essay centres around four elements of activist research which can be profitably applied to theological education: (i) clarifying identity and motivation by examining the assumptions we bring to our researching practice; (ii) clarifying research outputs to shift away from a sole priority on the discovery of new knowledge to one that also values knowledge forged in the study of teaching and learning processes; (iii) seizing opportunities for activist research in teaching and learning trends in Higher Education, especially those generated by emergent contextual factors and aided by developments in thinking and technology; and (iv) to consider the various investments being made in the theological education sector, involving learners, teachers, denominational identity, and vocational pathways. These various domains are fertile opportunities for dynamic, relevant and significant activist research. In the midst of massive social change, the essay presents the invitation, and the imperative, for the theological sector to wonder together by researching our teaching practice.

Part 2 comprises three essays offering differently nuanced approaches to the philosophical question of the ultimate end—the *telos*—of theological education. In two thematically related essays, Peter Mudge and Dan Fleming go beyond the more common 'what, how and why' dimensions of theological education to explore the deeper issue of the ultimate purpose—the 'so what'—of theological education, with particular reference to online education. The two essays, entitled collectively '"To Take You Where You Do Not Wish To Go": Extending The Telos Of Online Theological Education', adopt a life journey motif which states the issue as a challenging and discomfiting experience, which may well take travellers to places they may not foresee or wish to reach. Yet it is in such challenge and discomfiture that genuine growth occurs. Ultimately, the t*elos* of theological education is seen as the 'end persons' involved in the process.

The first of the essays, 'The "Who" of the Teacher Who Teaches', posits the aim as the nurture of students who are seekers of truth, endowed with appropriate attitudes and critical skills. While the application to learners is obvious, the special focus of this paper is on the teacher, who is also on a journey which may lead to unwanted and discomfiting places. The tension for the teacher is set in terms of two complementary paths—an easier one that is *chosen by* and a more challenging one that is *chosen for* the teacher. While theological teaching can involve satisfying self-fulfilment, it is disturbing in its demands of '"death", suffering, resilience, sacrifice and discipleship'. The primary requirement for a theological teacher is to be the embodiment of the qualities being sought, which takes priority over other considerations of content knowledge and pedagogical methods. The nexus between a teacher's psyche and practice is as significant as it is inseparable. The second of the two essays, 'The "What" of the Institution That Teaches', follows a similar philosophical approach with reference to the overall theological institution. The institution itself needs to have and to live out consistently a coherent practice of the *telos* of its mission, in its search 'for truth, beauty and goodness, all guided by the premise of a "connected theology"'. The essay embraces Newman's idea of the university as promoting more than knowledge and vocational skill; it extends to the concept of Christ as the *telos* of Christian life and education; and it ends with the ultimate institutional goal of leading people to flourish in the quest for such ultimate ends, in a lived 'connected theology'. The two essays lead finally to a statement of radical and mature theological praxis and wisdom with regard to how teachers teach and how students learn. Together, they present a rigorous discussion of *telos* not only as philosophical speculation, but also for the practical import it will have.

Bruce Hulme's essay, 'A Vision for The Good Life', adopts a similar journey-to-an-end motif but with a different emphasis. While Mudge and Fleming focused on the praxis of teacher and institution, Hulme looks directly at the goal of formation of the learner. His stated goal and implied approach are expressed in the essay's sub-title, '*Shalom* as a *Telos* for Christian Formation in Teaching Theological Reflection'. In advocating the method of Theological Reflection as an operational approach to goal attainment, the essay discusses various elements of both reflection and *shalom*. It explores what dimensions of formation might be considered in theological reflection, how these dimensions relate, and what Christian formation in these dimensions is headed towards. The last element leads to the focal issue of the essay, '"The Walk Towards Shalom" as a *Telos* for Christian Formation'. *Shalom* is presented as a multifaceted term denoting more than conventional tranquil peace or absence of conflict. The term also incorporates the notion of wholeness, with connotations of health, security, well-being, and salvation. As with Mudge and Fleming, 'flourishing' is offered as a useful equivalent concept. Importantly for this essay, while *shalom* can be experienced by individuals, the more predominant use of the word is communal and relational rather than individual—where there are fractured relationships, there can be no peace. The need for communal reflection on and implementation of the principles of *shalom* is therefore developed in some detail. The essay concludes with some observations on pedagogical implications for theological reflection as an effective vehicle for pursuing the goal of *shalom*.

Peter Carblis focuses on the development of personal virtues as the ultimate educational goal. He marries biblical interpretation and teaching outcomes in his essay 'Education, Ministry and the New Covenant'. In an extensive review of biblical and educational literature, the essay argues that, within the context of both ancient and modern discourses, the New Covenant of Hebrews 8:10–11 and the law embedded in it can be interpreted in virtue-based terms and hence relate to the character required to live virtuously. From this premise, Carblis extrapolates a learning outcomes framework for Christian education, personal development, and spiritual formation. Commencing with an excursus on the biblical teaching on covenant, the essay proceeds to the identification of desirable personal virtues as legitimate outcomes pertinent to Christian education. Such learning outcomes are then located within the various cognitive, affective, and conative domains of learning. In this way, the essay provides a means by which frameworks can be developed to guide and evaluate Christian ministry, identify outcomes to be attained, and assess the attainment of the outcomes thus identified.

Part 3 tackles the emerging and critical issue of academic freedom as it increasingly impinges on tertiary theological education. Barry Spurr's essay, 'Academic Freedom In the Thought-Policed University: Challenges for Christian Educators Today', is as passionate as it is provocative. From a well-versed background of the classics of literature and history, Spurr executes a trenchant criticism of what he terms the 'degradation of what a university should be', with a particularly pointed reference to the political ideology which has invaded the humanities arena of many modern universities. The essay analyses how such anti-Western ideology has undermined classical cultural exploration, including the contribution of Christian literary masterpieces, with the substitution of more ephemeral but ideologically driven revisionist works. The punitive gagging of academic opponents of such ideology and the censoring of unacceptable or inappropriate ideas that might be confronting for students are highlighted as an alarming warning to those would resist the political correctness of the prevailing regime. Perhaps not surprisingly, Spurr lauds George Orwell as an 'acute visionary and hammer of tyranny' while roundly castigating the 'predictable barrage of personal and foul abuse of anti-social media and the nitwits of the Twittersphere'. But it is not only secular universities that the political tentacles threaten. For Christian educators in general—and, we may well extrapolate, for theological educators in particular—the threat is ever encroaching on their domains. As Spurr relates, 'Educators committed to advancing the understanding of and a degree of empathy towards texts of Christian provenance are, by that very commitment, set in opposition to all that the contemporary ideologically-driven secular academy stands for and would enforce'. Given the anti-Western propagandist alliance between academy and media that Spurr claims, this essay presents a mordant but timely signal of an impending crisis for all institutions with strong Christian tendencies.

That such a threat is already present n theological institutions is exemplified in the essay 'Exploring the Nexus between Academic Freedom and Ecclesial Expectations', by Dean Smith and Rob Fringer. The essay presents a case study, not of external secular pressure, but of imposed denominational constraints exercised politically within an American Christian University. The specific focus of the conflict is the expression of confessional freedom—a professor's espousal of a doctrinal view not sanctioned by the university President—where the spectre of 'heresy' looms large. While the case is located in USA, the local parallel is potential in Australia, especially in light of the nation-wide trend to having theological education—and its commonly associated ministerial education—often delivered by denominationally aligned and owned colleges accredited as higher education institutions. The tension between denominational control and loyalty and higher educational liberty of thought and critique of practice is constant and increasing. This essay is written from the perspective of college leaders, who are most commonly presented with this issue, as they are the ones charged with giving direction to the institution. However, while highlighting the explosive tension in this particular case, the authors conclude that confessional formation and training need not be at odds with a policy of academic freedom. Indeed, if critique is understood to be constantly necessary and freedom is understood to be inevitably constrained, and if managed well at the level of leadership, the tension involved can facilitate deeper formation and enhanced denominational commitment.

Geoff Treloar's essay, 'The Perils of Academic Freedom: the Australian College of Theology as an Australian University of Specialisation', offers an analysis of the way in which the tensions surrounding academic freedom need to be negotiated by theological institutions in dealing with external officialdom. This case study is based on the Australian College of Theology, the largest private provider of theological higher education in Australia, and its process of seeking accreditation as a university, a rare and lofty status in the Australian scene. A particular strength of the essay is the sensitive balance between institutional rights (often lamented as necessary sacrifices in the quest for accreditation) and institutional responsibilities (not as commonly recognised as advantages by those same institutions). The essay offers practical insights and principled wisdom drawn from direct recent experience and a comprehensive knowledge of the Australian Higher Education accreditation regime. It analyses the nature and variable understandings of academic freedom and applies its tenets and different levels of operation to an Australian context, noting specifically that 'the exercise of academic freedom is risky'. In doing so, it echoes the note of 'an anti-Christian turn in our day which seeks to silence the Christian voice… [and] to limit the enunciation of the Christian standpoint'. This recognition was a significant reservation for the College in its decision to pursue university status, especially in light of the College's being a consortium of numerous institutions holding to a diversity of confessional perspectives. The essay details the strategy crafted by the College and a number of proposals for reconciling academic freedom with institutional integrity, which are informative for all other institutions, regardless of governmental accreditation status. The essay stands as an insightful case study of a theological provider navigating the requirements of the regulatory system while seeking to maintain its institutional integrity and academic freedom as it prepares for a higher level of official recognition.

Part 4 concludes the volume by presenting a set of creative pedagogical approaches to deep learning as a practical contribution to the overall conversation about how we teach theology. The first group of essays focuses on the familiar territory of biblical studies, but they offer fresh ways of engaging with texts. These are followed by several essays advocating a variety of perspectives on teaching theology in general. The final two essays provide a case for a grounded and active process in all teaching of theology.

Debra Snoddy presents a case for a new and challenging approach to the broad field of biblical studies in her essay, 'Windows, Mirrors and Icons as Ways into the Context, Content and Call of Sacred Narratives'. Leaving behind the familiar territory of synchronic and diachronic studies, the essay takes up the approach of meta-chronic analysis as proposed by Reimund Bierenger. Snoddy shapes the essay around the combined theories of Paul Ricœur and Sandra Schneiders, as it allies Bierenger's proposal with the work of the German educationist Wolfgang Klafki to devise a method to engage learners in this meta-chronic process. The basic metaphor is that of viewing the several worlds of the text through three associated yet distinct windows: the past, the present, and the future. By extending interpretation to incorporate a future-oriented eschatology, the interpretive task forms a living bridge between the past, the present, and the future.

A. J. Culp's essay, 'In My Father's House: the Place of Wonder in Proverbs' Vision of Education', brings the motif of 'wonder' into engagement with the wisdom of Proverbs to explore a biblical vision of education. By focusing on salient poetic metaphors of Proverbs, Culp evocatively sparks the imagination of the reader, a process that is integral to such learning. The essay locates this vision of education within the wisdom tradition of Israel, with its fundamental aim of producing wise learners, not only skilled to navigate life, but also imbued with a coherent worldview that makes sense of the wondrous world of human existence. Such wisdom contemplates the wonder of God as creator and draws the learner into the mysteries of that creation and the mighty salvific deeds of that God. Therein lies the core of deep theological learning.

Sarah Hart, an orchestral violinist and teacher of Hebrew Bible, applies the paradigm of 'practising musician' to the practice of biblical studies in her essay, 'Text and Interpretation: from Classical Music to Biblical Studies'. The essay creatively parallels the requirements of musical practice and performance with the components of textual study, namely, facility in basic techniques followed by interpretative skills. It draws largely on direct personal experience of how a musician came to be a biblical teacher, with the musical training a shaping factor in the approach to that teaching. This essay thus spells out the application of the elements of technique, immersion, and encounter with major concepts. It provides demonstrative examples of how students can receive an experience of the Bible, which privileges the direct 'practice' of engaging with the biblical text over the learned scholarship of secondary literature. Such personal absorption into the text is posited as a conduit to deep theological learning.

Ben Chenoweth enters the realm of literary fiction as a means of creative engagement of biblical texts in 'The Pedagogy of Biblical Fiction: Where Research and Creativity Collide'. The approach derives from the concept of fan fiction, whereby a reader of a text provides a creative in-filling of stories and so establishes a more engaged personal investment in the overall narrative. While the creative viewpoint developed by the reader is fictional, the process of engagement is valid, in that it draws a learner more deeply into the world of the biblical text. It is derived from the text as the starting point, it requires coherence with the biblical text and fidelity to the historical and cultural context of the text, and so has the capacity to engage both cognitively and affectively. The essay presents suggestions for the incorporation of various fictional story type useful for biblical studies, such as recontextualisation (based on missing scenes), refocalisation (providing alternative perspectives), genre emulation (creative examples of non-historical narrative), and expansion (creative sequels). Significantly, Chenoweth cogently links this process with the pedagogical elements of Bloom's taxonomy to show how such creative synthesis is both a deep learning experience and a high order of creative operation.

From the musical and literary, the essays proceed to a topical approach in Andrew Jaensch's 'Is the God of the Bible an Ugly Bully? Helping Bible Students Come to Terms with Violence in the Biblical Text'. That violence pervades the Bible, especially the Old Testament, is indisputable; that violence is largely unpalatable to Christians (and theological students) is axiomatic. So, while the topic is inherently ugly, it needs to be confronted honestly, and teachers have a responsibility to lead students intentionally in ways of wholesome management of such a study, rather than turn a blind eye to its unpleasantness. In this essay, Jaensch details a module used in an introductory biblical studies unit which addresses the issue of a violent God in the Bible, followed by a critical reflection on its value and effectiveness. The goal is the fostering of resilient faith and spiritual health. The essay presents principles and methods for effective learning around biblical violence as a case study, which has clear transferability to deep learning around other confronting topics.

Denise Goodwin presents a discussion based on a wider range of theological disciplines in the essay 'An Approach for Deep Theological Learning in Research Methodologies'. The essay focuses on research-led learning via learners' research into the nature of research itself. It provides an informed theoretical commentary on deep learning coupled with a practical case study of teaching a unit in Research Methods to two diverse groups of students embracing the disciplines of biblical study, systematics, church history, and pastoral ministry. In doing so, it describes in detail the processes involved and offers an analytical review of students' growing learnings in both face-to-face and online groups. Helpfully, the essay reviews errors in those learnings which needed rectification, it extrapolates lessons learned from the delivery of the unit, and concludes by offering recommendations for learning and teaching to promote deep learning in research methodologies.

The group of essays presenting perspectives on teaching approaches commences with Darren Cronshaw's 'The Relational Teacher: Sharing Life as Vocational Essence'. This essay adopts the position that individualism is contrary to authentic ministry and that Christianity is at its core relational. Building on this premise, Cronshaw applies the concepts of relationality not to the church in general, but to the person of the theological teacher. The essay is an exercise in critical reflective practice, as it analyses the ways in which theological teaching is understood as relational sharing of one's life in various directions—sharing of that life with God, with colleagues, with students, and with the world. This involves intimacy and openness, with its concomitant vulnerability; it requires management of 'busyness' to make space for relationships; it incorporates discipline in personal spiritual practices; it dwells in mutuality with colleagues and students but avoids narcissistic imposition; and it involves sharing in missional activity in one's own neighbourhood. These are the tenets of relational teaching that pervade this essay, with the overarching goal of fostering deep and dynamic learning in authentic Christianity.

If such community is at the heart of deep and dynamic learning, what then can be achieved in an online mode? Peter Bolt reviews the challenges and pitfalls posed by technology in the quest for deep learning in research in his essay 'Deep Learning from a Shallow Surface? Encouraging Good Research in the Internet Age'. The essay draws an important distinction between deep learning and worthwhile deep learning, the difference being necessary to appreciate when it comes to the popularity of online learning. Bolt lists challenges to both the quality of information and the reliability of conversations, both of which have infinite quantitative dimensions but with no guarantee of quality assurance. In fact, such over-supply of information and conversation partners paradoxically can be a serious impediment to depth or value of learning. The over-reliance on peer group engagement lacking in established expertise in content or methods can produce the 'confidence of the dumb', with consequent decline in deep research and transformative learning, both of which are essential for learning that benefits both the individual and society. An emergent theme in the essay is the pressing need for theological educators to provide reliable guides, in both information and conversations, to ensure technology-driven learning is indeed deep and worthwhile learning.

In a different vein, Martin Olmos also discusses the online format in his empirical study of an evolving approach to distance learning in 'Making Good Practice Affordable: Understanding your Students with Learning Analytics'. Starting from the premise that the optimal educational model is a combination of mastery learning and one-to-one tutoring, the essay relates how the application of technology-driven learning analytics has generated a new business model, with significantly enhanced results in student performance. By the astute use of such analytics, his college changed the economics of educational delivery by 'unbundling' its previously uniformly packaged programs to provide more tailored yet cost-effective offerings. While initial production costs remain significant, dissemination costs are radically reduced, thus affording greater diversity in delivery, and so helping students to learn more deeply in a flexible way. In the process, learning analytics is used to keep students informed and engaged and to identify and cater for particular student needs, which changes the nature of a distance student's experience from transactional to relational. The essay provides an informed quantitative analysis of several areas of implementation, with observations on strategies employed and lessons learned, not the least of which is the technological liberation of teachers rather than the mere replacement of them.

Bruce Allder explores the issue of multi-cultural delivery of theological education in his essay, 'Theological Education in Context: Exploring the Delivery of Theological Education in a Multi-cultural Setting'. The essay is based on the application and extension of Rupen Das's approaches to theological education in *Connecting Curriculum with Context* in engagement with his college's adoption of a 'Jerusalem' or 'Missional' model of preparation of clergy. Specifically, the essay reviews the experience of delivering a formally accredited program in a Culturally and Linguistically Diverse (CALD) context in Fiji, where the issues of local contextuality and higher education accreditation merge. Allders' global church mandate includes educational statements such as 'the variety of cultural contexts around the world makes one curriculum unsuited for all global areas' and 'cultural sensitivity and flexibility will characterize regional provisions for the educational foundations for ministry', which he acknowledges are often more aspirational than actual. Accordingly, his essay analyses how his college attempts to bring context into the ordinary milieu of the education conversation. In doing so, it delineates a practical commitment to bringing both subject content and personal formation into authentic contextual engagement, with its implications for both curriculum development and pedagogy in an often confusing array of contextual diversity.

The two essays that conclude the volume return the focus to the core issue of engaging the learner realistically and dynamically in the learning process. Such engagement needs to take cognizance of the realities of the contemporary world in which theological education and theological learners exist and it needs to involve adult learners in mature activity shaped by and related to their own life context and needs. Les Ball's essay 'Integrating Theology in a Questioning Age' begins with the recognition of the willingness of individuals, including theology students, to challenge received authority and the resultant need for education to address such questioning. It then develops an approach to learning and teaching based on the tenets of practical theology as a means of generating the meaningful integration of knowledge, skills, and values with a coherent correlation between tradition (theology) and experience (practice). Starting from supervise field education, the essay applies more broadly the basic principles of Browning and Osmer's practical theology to a dialogical approach to learning. It concludes with some general pedagogical approaches to theological integration based on Problem Based Learning, Inquiry Based Learning, and Group Project Based Learning as illustrative examples of how such integrative goals may be achieved.

Steve Taylor and Rosemary Dewerse's 'Curiosity and Doubt in Researching the Future: The Contribution of Flipped Learning to Sociality in Theological Innovation' puts the learner front and centre in the educative process: a worthy *conclusio* to the overall conversation. A major concern in theological education is the disengagement of learners from the teaching process, occasioned by the inhibiting limitations of available class time, used mainly for content delivery with a consequent shortage of active student involvement. Such an approach reduces the sociality of learning, which is fundamental to the theological education of mature and heavily invested adult learners. While the phenomenon of flipped learning has been with us for a decade or more as a means to redress this issue, this essay goes more deeply than usual into the conceptual and practical bases of such active learning with incisive insights into the role of technology in increasing student participation and the sociality of learning, with a focus on innovative strategies to increase such active student participation. The incorporation of Bloom's taxonomy not simply as a means of describing the process but actively as an agent in the learning process is skillfully demonstrated, with the incorporation of categories from the taxonomy providing for the learners evidence of a depth of reflection on their own role in learning. A useful appendix, 'Learner-Centred Principles in Action', warrants close and repeated attention. As a finale to this volume, Taylor and Dewerse cogently continue the conversation in pressing the case for ongoing reform towards student-centred curricula, which employs technological tools alongside sound pedagogies.

In the past decade, there has been significant research in Australia into the field of learning and teaching theology. Much of the literature promulgated from this research has expressed growing commitment to curricular and pedagogical reform, with a vital concern for holistic development of graduates. Yet much of that literature reported on earnest aspiration and inchoate strategies. What is particularly heartening about this current volume is the growing report of active implementation and initial attainment, a sense of: 'This is now actually happening'. As we look forward to continuing the conversation, perhaps in another five years we will receive reports of a further stage, that of demonstrable achievements. Then, and only then, will we be able to pause for a while, sit back, and say: 'Job well done'. In the meantime, we commend this present volume as rich fare for sustaining and enriching the conversation.

2 | REMEMBERING THE FUTURE: THE CONTRIBUTION OF HISTORICAL RESEARCH TO INNOVATION IN THEOLOGICAL EDUCATION

ANDREW DUTNEY

Part 1: Historical Research as a Change Agent

In 2001 I was appointed as Principal of Parkin-Wesley College, the South Australian theological college of the Uniting Church in Australia (UCA). It was not a position that I aspired to, and it was one that I only agreed to apply for with real misgivings. I loved teaching. I was good at teaching. Becoming a Principal would take me in a different direction.

In the following year I enrolled in the Doctor of Education course at Flinders University designed for educational administrators and managers—the kind of person I had reluctantly become. It was one of the best decisions I have taken. The course enabled me to acquire the insights, skills and confidence that I needed to fully engage with the challenging new role that the church had given me. I still love teaching, but now I also love leading this learning community. I completed the Flinders University program early in 2007, having taken five coursework options and three major research projects. The program was designed to be tailored to the particular professional needs of the participants so my research projects (as well as most of my coursework assignments) focused on particular aspects of theological education in the UCA. This was just as well, because at the same time as I finished the course I found myself being called upon to lead the college through a process of significant 'organizational and cultural change'.[1]

I have seen that process described as 'the Adelaide experiment' by one of the UCA academics who have done me the honour of critiquing my work.[2] In the neutral territory of this conference,[3] I will take the opportunity to tell the story of 'the Adelaide experiment', focusing especially on how two major historical research projects released forces for change and innovation that have given theological education a place at the centre of the emergent 21st century church, and describing what I have learned about being a change leader in theological education.

But first, I need to make a couple of contextual observations. The first is that Parkin-Wesley College was a denominational college. Although it delivered courses provided by the Adelaide College of Divinity and Flinders University, the college itself was entirely funded, staffed and governed by the Uniting Church in Australia—and expected to deliver theological education which would meet the needs of that denomination. The second contextual observation is that I was 'the Basis of Union guy'. The relevance of that lies in the way I came to be that guy, and what it taught me about historical research.[4]

Becoming 'the Basis of Union guy'

On completing the Uniting Church's prescribed course of training for the ordained ministry I was directed into 'secular employment'. That was the church's way of saying, 'You're dropped'. It was November 1980, little more than three years since the inauguration of the Uniting Church in Australia.[5] I was twenty-two and devastated. How could I have been so wrong about my sense of call to the ministry? How could the church be so wrongheaded in its management of my vocation? What is 'ministry' anyway beyond this stupid, pointless, soul-destroying system? I was very hurt and very angry.

---

1 Decision of the Standing Committee of the Presbytery and Synod of South Australia, quote in Dutney, *A Genuinely Educated Ministry*, 7.
2 Burns, 'Ministry', 67.
3 Sydney College of Divinity Learning & Teaching Conference, *Wondering About God Together—Research-Led Learning and Teaching in Theological Education*, 28-29 April 2017.
4 The following story is from the Introduction to Dutney, *Manifesto for Renewal*, 4-6.
5 The Uniting Church in Australia was inaugurated on June 22, 1977. It was a union between the Congregational, Methodist and Presbyterian churches in Australia. The process and character of that union is described in Dutney, *Manifesto for Renewal*.

In the course of that final year at theological college I had ended up in deep conflict with the Synod Settlements Committee. It was not that I had performed poorly as a candidate for ministry. On the contrary. It had been decided that since I was still very young, and a promising student, I would benefit from the experience of a year of postgraduate study overseas. I had managed to get a place at St Andrews University in Scotland doing a postgraduate Diploma in Ecumenical Studies. However, because the academic years in the northern and southern hemispheres do not coincide, I could not begin at St Andrews until September 1981. The Settlements Committee did not know what to do with me during that awkward nine month hiatus.

I did not see why they had to 'do' anything with me. I was quite happy to find a job to save some money, or to serve in a ministry if there was one that took account of the plans I had worked out with the church. I could not see the problem. But there was a problem—a big one—that no one could explain to me. The deeply held but contrasting assumptions about the relationship between candidates for ministry and the church that had been brought into the Uniting Church from the three previous denominations were present in the Settlements Committee, turning my situation into a test case. As the months went by with no resolution, my uncertainty and anxiety turned to frustration and anger at the process. I became a difficult person to deal with and I felt progressively more alienated from the church's systems and practices.

By the time the letter arrived, officially advising me to 'get a job', I was already working as a clerk in a legal firm. I was happy—regular hours, regular income, regular people my own age—and with the prospect of a career in the sensible field of Law, once I returned from Scotland having completed the Diploma. That adventure had already been planned and saved for and my wife and I were going ahead with it. Three terms of study were to be followed by a few months' backpacking around Europe. We were young after all, with plenty of time to get started on the new career when we came back.

But that is not how things unfolded. It turned out that, away from the distractions and commitments of our life in Brisbane and with no other duty to fulfil than to attend my classes, write my essays and sit my exams, I was quite good at academic theology. My examiners recommended that I be encouraged to go on to doctoral research and I was invited to continue at St Andrews working on a PhD. That appealed to us. We were very happy in Scotland and were beginning to wonder if there might be a way that we could make our life there—far away from the painful associations that Australia held for us.

Having worked out how to finance an extended stay in Scotland with support from our families and part-time and casual work for each of us, the only question remaining was what I would research. That was easy. I was still angry and hurt about what had happened to me as a candidate for the ministry in the UCA. I wanted to expose the stupidity and duplicity of this new church and the way it approached ministry. And I wanted to do a root and branch job of it, starting with the negotiations for church union and uncovering the compromises and mistakes behind the system that had derailed my life and undermined my faith. Staying motivated is half the race in completing a PhD, and my supervisor thought that the thirst for revenge would be a reliable ally in getting me to the finish line. So it was agreed. I would research 'The development of the understanding of ministry in the Australian church union negotiations 1957-1971'[6]—and then watch them squirm.

But once again, that is not how things unfolded. Within a few months, my attitude had been completely transformed. As I investigated the long history of the church union movement in Australia, and especially what was so distinctive about the work of the Joint Commission on Church Union, the body which negotiated the union, I became increasingly convinced that I was dealing with an authentically Spirit-led process—one that challenged the tired denominationalism and unimaginative institutionalism that I despised. And when I eventually arrived at a close study of the final version of the Basis of Union I was simply captivated. The vision within its eighteen short paragraphs crystallised what I had been looking for—a vision that could guide me as a disciple and servant of Jesus and renew the community that gathered around him. All I wanted to do was to share what I had discovered with my peers—my own generation which was the first generation of the Uniting Church in Australia. I did not know it then, but I had found my life's work.

I completed that PhD thesis towards the end of 1984. In the years since then I have written many articles and several books on different aspects of the Basis of Union.[7] I teach courses on the history, theology and polity of the Uniting Church and regularly make presentations on the ethos of the Uniting Church to the boards and staff of UCA agencies.

And over and over again, I have seen how people are empowered by hearing

---

6   Dutney, *The Development of the Understanding of Ministry*.
7   The most widely used are the short works such as, *Where Did the Joy Come From? Revisiting the Basis of Union*, *Introducing the Uniting Church in Australia*, and *The Basis of Union: A Commentary by J. Davis McCaughey*.

and knowing their own story. In particular I see people encouraged to embrace change and inspired towards innovation by the vision of the Basis of Union. I do not have time to explain it now, but those who framed the Basis of Union in the 1960s 'were convinced that God was calling the church away from that nailed-down, sewn-up, nothing-to-learn illusion of "church"' that was so unresponsive to the challenges and opportunities of mission.[8] For the last thirty years, I have seen repeatedly how a simple history lesson—about a community's own history—can release the energy and resources for significant, positive change. But someone has to do the historical research first.

Becoming the Principal

So twenty years after being told to 'get a job', there I was, 'the Basis of Union guy' installed (improbably) as the Principal of one of the UCA's seven theological colleges. And something was clearly not right with Parkin-Wesley College, but not as far as the other six colleges or the national Ministerial Education Commission (MEC) were concerned. Parkin-Wesley was doing what UCA theological colleges did, in the way that they all agreed it should be done. But something was not right.

While overall student enrolments were strong, the numbers of ordination candidates had plummeted. Since union in 1977, the numbers of candidates at Parkin-Wesley had been maintained, roughly, at between 35 and 45. But as the new century began, these numbers settled into the teens. With a striking fall in the number of applications for candidature, together with the increasing average age of applicants, it was clear the church was not replenishing its ministerial leadership and had no prospect of doing so.

As I began moving around the church as the new Principal, I soon became acutely aware of the number of ministers who had specific and deep-felt complaints about their experience as candidates studying at Parkin-Wesley College. I also found that few of the thriving congregations looked to the college for their theological education and training needs. Consequently Parkin-Wesley College, and the prospect of ordained ministry itself, was not really on the radar of the emerging young leaders in those congregations, and the college was at best marginal to the centres of energy in the church.

---

8   Dutney, 'Flexible and Free', 15.

Something was not right with Parkin-Wesley College. I was offered dozens of diagnoses as people became aware that I was actually interested in what they thought about their college—and just as many cures. But it felt premature. I needed to understand in a deeper way what a theological college is in the life of the UCA. So, with the support of the Flinders Doctor of Education program, I once again chose historical research as a way to find that out.

I designed and conducted two historical research projects. The first investigated the place of theological education in the inherited traditions of the Uniting Church. The Congregational and Presbyterian churches represented the Reformed tradition of theological education and the Methodist church owed more to the Evangelical educational tradition. I examined each of these traditions from their roots in the Reformation and in the Evangelical Awakening to identify their key emphases and characteristic expressions. I then studied the history of theological education in each of the Congregational, Methodist and Presbyterian churches in Australia, to see how stable those emphases and expressions were in this context. I then wrote a short history of Parkin-Wesley College as an historical case study of a united Congregational-Methodist college that was supposed to fulfil the expectations of both traditions.

The second historical project investigated the place of theological education within the Uniting Church from its inauguration in 1977 to 2005. There was plenty of material to work with. In less than three decades there had been five national reviews of theological education by different Assembly task groups. In addition, every Synod which had a college had undertaken one or more reviews of its own. Surrounding all of those reviews were reports, discussion papers, minutes and correspondence. As I analysed that material I was able to identify patterns in the way change happened in the UCA, in stakeholder responses, and in the interaction between UCA culture and changes in the surrounding context—religious, educational and social.

Through these two historical studies I learned some of the key the things I needed to know in order to begin to address what was not right at Parkin-Wesley College. I learned what were the core, non-negotiable values of theological education in the UCA. I understood why theological education was such a lightning rod for disaffection in the UCA. I identified opportunities for genuine reform in our approach to theological education. And, incidentally, I came to understand for the first time what had happened to me in 1980—why the conflict with the Settlements Committee was so visceral and wounding on every side.

With these studies completed and with a range of findings before me, I conducted a final study—a mixed-methods study of UCA ministers in South Australia including a survey of all the candidates for ordination accepted in the South Australia Synod between 1995 and 2005. Again, this turned out to be a rich, surprising and very fruitful investigation. On the back of the historical research which I had already completed, this engagement with ministers, many of whom were my former students, became personally transformative of me as a minister, a teacher, and a Principal. I had not expected that. But it also gave me numbers and patterns to add to the narrative I had developed through the historical studies which then became transformative for Parkin-Wesley College. I *had* hoped for that.

What I found

First, I found that a system of theological education is integral to the UCA *as a religion*—it is part of our culture and one of the things that makes us who we are. It is why we do it ourselves rather than outsource to other denominations or para-church agencies or universities. It is why we are willing to dedicate so much of our budget to theological education. It is why we have a college in every Synod—and why the Synods are unable to contemplate forgoing their college for the sake of establishing a national college. It is why, when there is a perceived problem, Synod and Assembly decisions will routinely include the request for action from the colleges. It is why ten of the fifteen Presidents of the Assembly have come from college faculties. Any suggestion that we could walk away from the ideal of what Davis McCaughey called 'a genuinely educated ministry'[9]—and sustaining a system of theological colleges to reassure ourselves that we are pursuing that ideal—is absurd.

Second, I found that although the UCA has this common commitment to theological education, we actually inherited two traditions of theological education, with two ways of valuing and delivering this core activity. They are like each other in some ways, but in very important respects contrast with, or even contradict, each other. I have tried to represent the two traditions of theological education in the table below.

---

9   McCaughey, 'The Uniting Church in Australia: Hopes and Fears', 19.

	Reformed	**Evangelical**
Doctrine of 'Church'	Word of God; true belief	Living faith; authentic experience
Doctrine of 'Ministry'	Preaching: didactic; exposition of Scripture; 'teaching elder'	Preaching: prophetic; proclamation of the Gospel; 'travelling preacher'
Doctrine of 'Call'	Outward	Inward: 'Resist as long as you can'
Active agents in placement process	Congregation and minister	Conference
Method of placement	Call	Appointment
Dominant value	Personal Responsibility	Obedience: 'Go where you are sent'
Catechesis	Minister-led; Didactic; Confessional	Lay-led; Experiential; Sung and lived
Theological Education	Essential ↓ Authentic Christian faith and life	Useful ↓ Authentic Christian faith and life

Third, I found that while both traditions have a valid place in the life of the UCA, and both are consistent with the Basis of Union, only the Reformed tradition is explicitly legitimated (and implicitly mandated) in the Basis—with which the UCA Constitution and Regulations must be consistent.

Fourth, I found that Parkin-Wesley College was the site of a fault line in the UCA when it came to theological education—that was at the core of what was not right. It was a combined Congregational (Parkin) and Methodist (Wesley) college, united at a time when the Parkin College Principal was pioneering a more practical, pastoral emphasis in ministerial training while the Wesley College Principal was actively pursuing a project of 'raising academic standards'. The union seemed obvious and natural at the time, but it did not take into account the contrasting traditions and the contrasting expectations of the two constituencies. For as long as the Wesley College Principal maintained his project, Congregational candidates were fulfilling the expectations of their church. And for as long as Methodist candidates were under the jurisdiction of the Conference and its President, the Methodist church's expectations were being fulfilled. But at the time of union, the authority of the Conference and its President was transferred to the faculty of Parkin-Wesley College—reflecting the way the Reformed tradition had been unintentionally privileged over the Evangelical tradition in relation to theological education in the plan for church union. In South Australia, an overwhelmingly Methodist Synod in the new UCA, the new arrangements were fine for a while. No one noticed really. But over time it broke down, as expectations were disappointed again and again. This was not the only thing that was not right with Parkin-Wesley College, but it was at the core of it. And here the final, mixed-methods study brought things into focus for me.

Fifth, I found that the Reformed tradition, which had been privileged in the Basis of Union and which was oriented towards the formation of professional, teaching pastors, had been overtaken by social change. As Gary Bouma put it, 'Many institutions that train clergy still produce graduates suited to a society and culture that has now passed for more than a quarter-century'.[10]

But, sixth, I found something I had not gone looking for. I was interested in candidates' pathways into theological education—and I found out about that. But what I heard from them primarily—all of them—was their story of being called by God to ordained ministry. And without any correlation to their place on the theological spectrum—fundamentalist, liberal, charismatic, progressive, evangelical—more than two thirds of them described their experience of call in supernatural terms, frequently a disruptive, frightening, unwelcome intervention into what they thought was a reasonably organised life. That is, I found that *God is* calling women and men to ministry and Parkin-Wesley College was supposed to be the place where they were encouraged and equipped to respond to that call. As this became clearer and clearer in the data I was gathering, I found I was not just the dispassionate researcher here any more, but I was being led by my research into the hands of the living God. If God is calling women and men to ministry today, why are they not turning up in the college established and maintained specifically for them?

Having outlined what I learned through historical research, in the next section I want to relate what we did with that—how historical research released

---

10   Bouma, *Australian Soul,* 105.

me and others from the inertia of denominational systems and processes, and what I learned about change leadership through this experience.

Part 2: What We Did and What I learned

What Needed to be Done?

Even as I was conducting the research projects that I described earlier, from 2002 onwards, pieces of the puzzle started falling into place. It was beginning to become clear, in broad terms, what needed to be done. Unfortunately, dauntingly, the thing that obviously needed to be done was a major change-management exercise—including culture change in the church and in the college.

What needed to happen was to find a way to put theological education and Parkin-Wesley College back where it belonged—at the heart of the church's life and mission. Deep down, that is where the church wanted it too—but not in the college's current condition.

Of course, we had students who were studying with us simply because they wanted to—members of other denominations, and lay people and ministers of our own who had chosen our courses over other alternatives for reasons of their own. In fact, by the early 2000s most of our student body was made up of this kind of student. We loved teaching these highly motivated learners, and their satisfaction with what we did and the way we did it kept reinforcing our culture and practices. But our real bread-and-butter—the students for the sake of whom the UCA was willing to maintain a college—was ordination candidates. And, in terms of motivation, they were a very mixed group—I had been wrestling with the challenge they posed for quite a while.

Back in the early nineties, I had published an article entitled 'Disillusionment: Reflections on the Experience of Theological Education', which was a kind of theological pedagogy emerging from my early experience as a teacher—at a time when almost all our students were ordination candidates.[11] A few years later I had conducted a small research project that was published under the title 'Don't Let Them Change You: Psychological Reactance and Theological Education'.[12] It was an explanation of the challenges facing teachers of mandated students—who were there because they had to be there, but who actually did

---

11 *Pacifica* 4 (1991), 137–147.
12 *Uniting Church Studies* 5.2 (August 1999), 1–14.

not really want to be there—using the theory of psychological reactance, and developing a set of strategies that were intended to make everyone's life a bit more tolerable, even if transformative learning proved elusive. Most of our students were still ordination candidates at that stage too.

Later I took this interest further in another project in educational psychology called 'How Made Up Minds Learn: A Pilot Study in Understanding Conceptual Change in Theological Students'. (This was a project within my EdD program, and I never developed the report for publication.) In that study I was trying to understand better that 'significant minority of the people who study at Parkin-Wesley College [but] do not want to study theology and/or do not want to study theology at this college'—in particular, whether and how their 'made up minds' could still learn. By then only a small minority of our students were ordination candidates.

What needed to happen was to find a way to put theological education and Parkin-Wesley College back where they belonged—at the heart of the church's life and mission. The college needed to become a learning community that women and men sensing a call to ministry in the church would *long* to connect with, would make sacrifices to join, and would engage with unreservedly when they became part of it. And deep down, that is what the church wanted its college to be too—but Parkin-Wesley College was just not that kind of college.

So the change process was going to have to start on the edges, with the thriving but disaffected congregations: building relationships and trust with the ministers and key leaders of those congregations; listening to their perceptions of the college, their experiences with it, and their aspirations and needs in theological education and training.

Equipped with what I then knew about theological education and the UCA from the research projects I have described in part 1, I could begin to find ways to reform our processes and structures, and redesign our curriculum that would honour the core values of our tradition while accommodating the aspirations and needs of those parts of the church from which the college had become alienated.

In diagrammatic form, organizational change looks quite simple. A standard way of representing it is in Kurt Lewin's three stage process of change development: 'Unfreezing' (making sure everyone understands and is ready for change); 'Changing' (implementing planned changes); 'Refreezing' (making sure that the new practices, systems or procedures become normative).[13] The trouble with this is that you are supposed to have a *strategy* to take each of these steps.

The unfreezing stage alone is daunting. Management manuals will tell you that, 'People are more likely to accept change if they feel there is a need for it […] Those who plan the change will need to make the case that there is an external or internal threat to the organization's competitiveness, reputation, or sometimes even its survival'.[14] I could probably manage that. But the manuals also tell you that, 'When [people] know what is going to happen, when, and why, they may feel more comfortable'.[15] And working out precisely what the changes to Parkin-Wesley College needed to be was going to take a long time and involve negotiation with a lot of stakeholders. At the beginning to 2007, when I completed my last research project, the only thing I was sure of was that change had to happen and that leveraging South Australia's strikingly resilient memory of Methodism was probably the way to make it happen.

Something Unforeseen Happened

At the end of 2006, while I was taking some study leave and long service leave to finalise the EdD research projects, the South Australia Synod adopted a new Strategic Plan. It involved six Key Directions, the second of which was, 'Raising Leaders: Develop ministers and lay leaders to lead the church to be the best it can be'. Five goals were identified to give substance to that intention:

1. Establish a Leadership Institute;
2. Identify future leadership needs and develop strategies to meet those needs;
3. Develop a strategy for recruitment based on giftedness and passion;
4. Improve the way we value an affirm current leaders;
5. Raise the bar with respect to the continuing education, supervision, performance; expectations and accountability of Ministers.

When the Strategic Plan was adopted by the Synod there was no assumption that the five goals associated with leadership would involve Parkin-Wesley

---

13 Lewin, *Field Theory*; Carpenter et al, *Management Principles v 1.0*, 334; Lussier and Achua, *Leadership*, 486-489.
14 Carpenter et al, *Management Principles v1.0*, 335.
15 Carpenter et al, *Management Principles v1.0*, 335.

College at all. What did it know about leadership? It was an academic institution. Those goals were all related to the 'Leadership Institute' that the Synod had resolved to establish—undefined and not costed (such was the depth of longing for something different in the area of leadership development). In fact, I learned when I returned from leave, many members of the Synod believed that the intention of this initiative was to create an *alternative* to the college. The strength of that view is evident in that even though as early as February 2007 the Synod Standing Committee had determined that the college would undergo 'organizational and cultural change' consistent with the new Strategic Plan, through most of that year it was not clear whether the Leadership Institute would be completely separate from the college, or sit alongside a smaller, more narrowly focused theological college—taking responsibility from the college for any parts of the curriculum that could conceivably be related to 'leadership'. There was no suggestion that the Leadership Institute and the college could be one institution, a 'centre for leadership development', until the following year.

During 2008, the Assembly wound up its national distance education provider, Coolamon College, and requested Parkin-Wesley College to take responsibility for Coolamon's students. This required Parkin-Wesley College to make a stronger commitment to distance education and brought it into relationship with students throughout Australia (and a small number in the Pacific). Then, early in 2009, Parkin-Wesley College was finally replaced by the new Leadership Institute, which would be called Uniting College for Leadership & Theology. Uniting College was purpose-built to 'develop effective leaders for a healthy missional church' while, at the same time, fulfilling the UCA's requirements for a college suitable for the education of candidates for ordained ministry.

What We Did

To get to this point an enormous amount of organisational change had to be managed.
- As a member of the small core team guiding the implementation of the 'Leadership' element of the strategic plan, I was able to have a hands-on role in working out 'what is going to happen, when, and why' in theological education in South Australia.
- Through 2007 different models for the new shape of theological education were presented to three Synod meetings for discussion and feedback.

- The faculty of Parkin-Wesley College was consulted as the models evolved. Not surprisingly, this was a difficult, frequently conflictual process.
- The board that oversaw ministerial education was reviewed, thanked and discharged and a very different kind of board was put in place, the Leadership Development Council (which was replaced in January 2017 by the Mission and Leadership Development Board).
- The traditional shape of the curriculum—Biblical Studies, Historical and Systematic Theology, and Pastoral Care—was set aside and a new curriculum was formed around Biblical Studies, Missiology, Leadership and Discipleship.
- Correspondingly, in 2008, new Position Descriptions for the faculty of the new entity were developed. Instead of simply terminating all positions and recruiting the new team from scratch, as some of the core team proposed, my arguments were accepted and all current faculty could work to the end of their contracted appointments. Faculty members whose current position corresponded closely to one of the new positions would be entitled to a preferential interview for the new position.
- Responsibility for the oversight of the formation of ordination candidates was shifted from the faculty to teams of effective practising ministers (Formation Panels).
- The new network of relationships that we had been building with the ministers and leaders of the thriving churches started to bear fruit as it became evident the college was serious about responding to their aspirations and needs, and the numbers of candidates were soon back into the mid-twenties.
- Candidates' individual experiences of a call to ministry were listened to and study programs and ministry practice placements were shaped around them.
- Candidates' course plans were redesigned to reduce the amount of pre-ordination study and to incorporate three years of planned continuing education after ordination.

In the UCA at that time, theological colleges were overseen by the Ministerial Education Commission (MEC)—essentially a self-regulating 'industry' group, in which the Principals of the then six theological colleges had a powerful influence. When I explained the changes that had happened in South Australia in 2009 to the MEC, as I was required to do, I used this table to simplify the discussion.

New Model	Familiar Model
Forming focussed missional practitioners	Forming general practitioners
Learning context—placement in congregation, faith community, agency or school	Learning context—college community
Learning mode—reflection on ministry practice	Learning mode—academic
Learning focus—the person's passion, gifts and potential capacity	Learning focus—the college course
SFE—the centre of the course, 15 hours per week for 2-4 years	FE—the climax of the course (7 months full-time)
Formation—overseen and delivered by practitioners with support from college faculty	Formation—overseen and delivered by college faculty with support from practitioners
Theological Studies—36-72 units in Core Phase—initial part of an tntegrated continuing education plan	Theological Studies—108 units in Core Phase—not reliant on continuing education

One of the tasks of the MEC was to maintain a regular schedule of college 'visitations' of UCA theological colleges, with a view to confirming their suitability as institutions for the training of UCA ministers. The South Australian college was due for an MEC Visitation later that year. So I said in my 2009 report to the MEC:

> Clearly, we are still at a very early stage in the life of this model of education and are still establishing the administrative and resourcing measures that will enable it to function well. The MEC Visitation brings fresh eyes to the project to give us objective feedback and will also give stakeholders an opportunity to give feedback to an independent body. We are very pleased about the timing of the Visitation, therefore, and eager to receive its report. [16]

But the Visitation produced a report that questioned the validity of the new direction taken by the South Australian Synod and its college and its accreditation remained unresolved until 2011, leading to three years of uncertainty over whether ministers being educated in the South Australian college could really be

---

16   The report is held in the records of Uniting College for Leadership & Theology, MEC, 2009, Principal's Report. It may be made available on application.

recognised as UCA ministers. I had always expected that what we had done in South Australia would have an impact nationally in the UCA, but I thought that it would not happen until after we had had a few years of experience with the new model. Instead, almost immediately, our new college was caught up in a national controversy about the future of theological education in the UCA—celebrated by most as an example of the way ahead and condemned by others as an example of what can go wrong if you let people who are not directly involved in theological education interfere.

What have I learned about change leadership?

I have learned that books on management and leadership really do help—not one in particular, but lots of them in different ways (although I did find myself going back to Mark Gerzon's *Leading Through Conflict* quite regularly).[17] Sometimes dropping in and out of that literature was useful just as a reminder that leadership needs to be conscious and reflective. And that is the second thing I learned: Leadership can be learned and it needs to be cultivated—my own leadership and the leadership of my team members.

I learned that the cliché is true, culture *is* everything after all. And culture needs to be attended to consciously and strategically if it is not going to sabotage innovation. Teams are *also* everything—not least because in theological education it is the faculty, the discipline subgroups, and the administration officers who will embody the culture, either the new culture or the old, in their individual behaviours and corporate practices. So another of my go-to resources was Graham Winter's *Think One Team*.[18] I learned especially that God is up to something in every situation and in every person's life. Working out what that is and then cooperating with it uncovers resources and opportunities for change at the same time as it grows quality relationships.

And I have learned that research releases energy for change, even historical research.

In the two Parts of this essay, I have tried to show how historical research can resource and empower innovation in theological education. The main example I have been using has been 'the Adelaide experiment' of Uniting College

---

17 Gerzon, *Leading Through Conflict*.
18 Winter, *Think One Team*.

for Leadership & Theology. But the same body of research into the heritage, theology and polity and the UCA has also had an impact in a variety of other ways. I described earlier how, when I began the research journey that turned me into 'the Basis of Union guy', the historical research released me personally from the inertia of the UCA's systems and processes. Along the way, that research has also enabled me to resource the church to effect change in other ways too. In South Australia I was not only involved in the formation of Uniting College, but also in a process that led to a major restructuring of the Synod from a system of seven Presbyteries to a single Presbytery with multiple 'mission networks' within it. Nationally, the energy for change expressed in 'the Adelaide experiment' also saw the replacement of the Ministerial Education Commission with a very different Education For Ministry Working Group and, from January 2017, a new set of national Standards for ministerial education and formation that not only permit, but actually encourage and require, much greater flexibility and student-centred education than had ever been possible before. This story of 'the Adelaide experiment' shows how two major historical research projects released forces for change and innovation that have given theological education a place back where it belongs: at the heart of the church's life and mission.

Bibliography

Bouma, G. *Australian Soul: Religion and Spirituality in the Twenty-First Century* (Melbourne: Cambridge University Press, 2006).

Burns, S. 'Ministry', in William W. Emilsen (ed.), *An Informed Faith: The Uniting Church at the Beginning of the 21st Century* (Preston, Vic.: Mosaic Press, 2014), 37–68.

Carpenter, M., T. Bauer and B. Erdogan. *Management Principles v 1.0* (2012) https://2012books.lardbucket.org/pdfs/management-principles-v1.0.pdf [accessed 28 April 2017].

Dutney, A.F. *The Basis of Union: A Commentary by J. Davis McCaughey, Introduced and Edited by Andrew Dutney* (Sydney: The Assembly of the Uniting Church in Australia, 2016).

Dutney, A.F. *The Development of the Understanding of Ministry in the Australian Church Union Negotiations, 1957-1971* (PhD Thesis, University of St Andrews, 1985).

Dutney, A.F. 'Disillusionment: Reflections on the Experience of Theological Education', *Pacifica* 4 (1991), 137–147.

Dutney, A.F. 'Don't Let Them Change You: Psychological Reactance and Theological Education', *Uniting Church Studies* 5.2 (August 1999), 1–14.

Dutney, A.F. 'Flexible and Free: An Ecclesiology of Change', *Uniting Church Studies*, 21.1 (June 2017), 9–18.

Dutney, A.F. *'A Genuinely Educated Ministry': Three Studies on Theological Education in the Uniting Church in Australia* (Sydney: The Assembly of the Uniting Church in Australia, 2011).

Dutney, A.F. *Introducing the Uniting Church in Australia* (Sydney: The Assembly of the Uniting Church in Australia, 2008).

Dutney, A.F. *Manifesto for Renewal: The Shaping of a New Church* (Unley, SA: MediaCom Education, ²2016).

Dutney, A.F. *Where Did the Joy Come From? Revisiting the Basis of Union* (Melbourne: Uniting Church Press, 2001).

Gerzon, M. *Leading Through Conflict: How Successful Leaders Transform Differences into Opportunities* (Boston: Harvard Business School Press, 2006).

Lewin, K. *Field Theory in Social Science* (New York: Harper & Row, 1951).

Lussier, R.N., and C.F. Achua. *Leadership: Theory, Application, Skill Development* (Mason, Ohio: Thomson South-Western, ³2007).

McCaughey, J.D. 'The Uniting Church in Australia: Hopes and Fears', *St Mark's Review*, 89 (1977) 18-22.

Winter, G. *Think One Team: An Inspiring Fable and Practical Guide for Managers, Employees & Jelly Bean Lovers* (Milton, Queensland: Jossey-Bass, 2008).

Andrew Dutney
Flinders University/Uniting College for Leadership & Theology, Adelaide
andrew.dutney@flinders.edu.au

3 | REFLECTIONS ON THE PRACTICE OF RESEARCH-LED TEACHING IN A SMALL COLLEGE CONTEXT

Abstract

The essay reflects on the practice of research-led teaching in small colleges. The discussion is placed in a brief historical context, a helpful taxonomy is surveyed and the various points for and against implementation are outlined. The essay also outlines and reflects on an experiment in the scholarship of teaching and learning that arose from the author's own practice in collaboration with colleagues. It concludes with some personal reflections.

It is suggested that colleges ought to take seriously the necessity of research-led teaching and that there is merit in thinking along the lines of the taxonomy outlined to conceptualise the various possible levels of faculty development in this area.

It is further suggested that there are ample opportunities for development of scholarly teaching arising out of normal practice, but that the pressures of resources and small staff numbers along with the demands of research in the relevant field of knowledge all conspire to frustrate attempts at the level of the scholarship of teaching and learning.

Introduction

When the phrase research-led teaching' is mentioned in a tertiary context, the suspicion is that it is primarily (if not exclusively) in relation to one's discipline. The notion that teaching at a tertiary level (indeed any level) ought to be informed by deep research and insight into the field of inquiry is uncontroversial.

Professional development is aimed at providing opportunity for growth of knowledge and expertise with respect to practice in the discipline and, anecdotally at least, the caricature of the teacher at a tertiary institution bearing with their teaching load in order to pursue their research is still occasionally portrayed.

Without diminishing the importance of discipline research, this essay will consider another aspect of research-led teaching—the activity of teaching itself being informed by research, whether one's own or the research of others. It is suggested that this has been a relatively neglected area in theological education, though it is starting to receive more sustained attention. This essay will consider the concept of research-led teaching, survey a useful taxonomy, suggest some benefits and then consider the practice of research-led teaching. Finally there will be a series of reflections on the author's own experience in a small college context.

A Concept and A Short History: The Scholarship of Teaching and Learning

Before considering the practice of research-led teaching, it is useful to recount briefly the history and some of the discussion swirling around the concept. While there has always been a steady stream of educational research concerning teaching and learning in the primary and secondary sectors, what is being spoken about in the tertiary context really traces its roots from the publication in 1990 of *Scholarship Reconsidered* by Ernest Boyer. Boyer argued that the tertiary sector needed to move past the older teaching/research divide and that the definition of scholarship ought to be expanded to include not only research (the scholarship of discovery) but also what he called the scholarship of integration, the scholarship of application, and the scholarship of teaching. This was developed after research amongst teachers in tertiary institutions revealed a desire for ways other than publications to measure faculty performance, with a special focus on quality of teaching in the mix. The meanings of these four forms of scholarship are separate yet overlapping. Glassick observes that of these four, the scholarship of teaching and learning (Boyer's 'scholarship of teaching') was the most difficult to develop and implement.[1] There are a number of definitions or conceptions of this term in play.

---

1   Glassick, 'Expanded Definitions', p. 879.

Hutchings and Shulman explain that:

> a scholarship of teaching (and learning) is not synonymous with excellent teaching. It requires a kind of 'going meta', in which faculty frame and systematically investigate questions related to student learning—the conditions under which it occurs, what it looks like, how to deepen it, and so forth—and do so with an eye not only to improving their own classroom but to advancing practice beyond it.[2]

Cambridge offers the following definition: 'problem posing about an issue of teaching or learning, study of the problem through methods appropriate to the disciplinary epistemologies, applications of results to practice, communication of results, self-reflection, and peer review'.[3] This definition encapsulates a classic scholarly process of encountering a problem and then finding, enacting, and communicating a solution.

Martin, Benjamin, Prosser, and Trigwell argue that the scholarship of teaching is three related activities: 'engagement with the existing knowledge on teaching and learning, self-reflection on teaching and learning in one's discipline, and public sharing of ideas about teaching and learning within the discipline'.[4] Their definition emphasises the aspect of engagement with existing scholarship and the importance of self-reflection, while retaining the public communication aspect of the concept.

Richlin emphasises the public sharing aspect of the concept but heightens the formality of this sharing when he states, 'The scholarship part of the process involves composing selected portions of the investigation and findings [or integration or reflection] into a manuscript to be submitted to an appropriate journal or conference venue'.[5]

McKinney simply conceptualises the scholarship of teaching and learning as 'the systematic study of teaching and/or learning and the public sharing and review of such work through presentations, publications or performances'.[6]

---

2   Hutchings and Schulman, 'The Scholarship of Teaching', 13.
3   Cited in McKinney, 'Scholarship', n.p.
4   Cited in McKinney, 'Scholarship', n.p.
5   Cited in McKinney, 'Scholarship', n.p.
6   McKinney, 'Scholarship', n.p.

A Useful Taxonomy

While there is much in common amongst these various definitions, there is also vagueness that begs further clarification. This is helpfully provided in a taxonomy proposed by McKinney that distinguishes good teaching from scholarly teaching from the scholarship of teaching and learning.[7]

McKinney suggests that good teaching has at its centre effective teaching that promotes student learning and any other desired outcomes. This can be measured in a variety of ways (student feedback, peer assessment) and it can be developed formally and informally through engagement with peers and the growing body of research.[8]

Scholarly teaching supports good teaching and involves taking a scholarly approach to teaching. Just as a scholarly approach to the subject matter of the discipline taught would be expected, scholarly teaching suggests taking the same approach to teaching practice. This will involve such things as reflective practice, engagement with the literature on teaching, learning, and assessment, and perhaps even engaging with colleagues on teaching and learning issues.[9] The practice of scholarly teaching implies a commitment to teaching and learning as a 'second discipline' in which to develop expertise.

As already noted, the third level, the scholarship of teaching and learning, involves systematic study of teaching and/or learning and the public sharing and review of such work through presentations or publications. It in effect becomes a research area in its own right. While clearly related to the concept of 'scholarly teaching', there is an advance in that the public sharing and review of such work appears to be the defining difference.[10] The public nature of this research means that it is open to critical review, it helps to create new knowledge in the field of teaching and learning, and it enables a community of researchers to respond to, and develop, one another's insights. Clearly there is a feedback loop to both good teaching and scholarly teaching as the results of the scholarship of teaching and learning are made public.

This is a useful taxonomy against which to evaluate practice. College teachers are no doubt familiar with the various forms of feedback on their teaching and hopefully aspire to be good teachers. To this end, the college has the responsibility

---

7   McKinney, 'Scholarship', n.p.
8   Winsomely summarised and presented for example in Bain, *What the Best Teachers Do*.
9   For the importance of reflective practice see Brookfield, *Becoming a Critically Reflective Teacher*.
10 Huber, 'Scholarship', 1. Cf. Glassick, 'Expanded Definition'.

to foster research-led teaching with respect to the other two levels of McKinney's taxonomy, scholarly teaching and the scholarship of teaching and learning. Of the two, it would seem that there is ample opportunity for scholarly teaching in most small college contexts and this ought to be encouraged. The more difficult step is the public nature of the scholarship of teaching and learning and the effort required to produce work in this aspect.

The Advantages of Faculty Involvement in Research-led Teaching

There are a number of reasons for faculties to engage in sustained thinking and effort with respect to at least the first two levels of McKinney's taxonomy and at least to contemplate the third.

a) A Regulatory Requirement

The first reason (though not necessarily the most important) is that in the Australian context, from a regulatory perspective, this is required. Under Section 3 of the Provider Accreditation Standards of Higher Education Standards Framework (Threshold Standards) 2015, entitled 'Teaching', this expectation is implied.[11] In paragraph 2 of Section 3.1 Course Design the expectation is stated:

> The content and learning activities of each course of study engage with advanced knowledge and inquiry consistent with the level of study and the expected learning outcomes, including:
>
> a. Current knowledge and scholarship in relevant academic disciplines
> b. Study of the underlying theoretical and conceptual frameworks of the academic disciplines or fields of education or research represented by the course, and
> c. emerging concepts that are informed by recent scholarship, current research findings and, where applicable, advances in practice.

---

11   Higher Education Standards Framework (Threshold Standards) 2015.

While this clearly applicable to the content of the disciplinary area, it is relevant also to teaching and learning as every teacher's 'second discipline'.

Section 3.2 Staffing is a little more explicit where it is stated in paragraph 3:

> Staff with responsibilities for academic oversight and those with teaching and supervisory roles in courses or units of study are equipped for their roles, including having:
>
> a. knowledge of contemporary developments in the discipline or field, which is informed by continuing scholarship or research or advances in practice
> b. skills in contemporary teaching and assessment principles relevant to the discipline, their role, modes of delivery and the needs of particular student cohorts…

Again, while the focus lies primarily on the discipline, a commitment to scholarly teaching is implied.

b) Professional Commitment

Second, it could also be argued that a professional commitment and approach to the task of teaching and learning requires such reflection in any case, and that forays into the scholarship of teaching and learning may well be a natural scholarly extension of that professional commitment.

Other fairly obvious benefits include the improvement of both programs and practices from a teaching and learning perspective, the revitalisation of teachers, and the benefits that can accrue from collaboration between colleagues. In a faculty collaboration on teaching and learning ,issues could also lead to cooperation across disciplines on the common ground of the teaching and learning task, realising the possibility of other types of cross-fertilisation.

Engagement in the scholarship of teaching and learning brings with it also the possibility of adding to research output in an era where this is increasingly important.

The Practice of Research—Led Teaching

The distinctions between good teaching, scholarly teaching and the scholarship of teaching and learning are extremely helpful for plotting a trajectory for faculty development in the area of teaching and learning within the college context.

The first step is to include encouraging familiarisation with books about teaching and learning; to initiate discussion about this as part of faculty orientation and development; and to help one another to think about what constitutes good teaching and what facilitates student learning in the light of available research.

The next step is to engage in scholarly teaching. Here we can note that in most educational programs there is ample opportunity to engage, as there is a wealth of data that presents itself for analysis. Student results, student evaluations, examiner's reports, teaching in the classroom, and the minutiae of everyday life in a college context all raise issues of teaching and learning to be investigated. Online courses also provide ample data for analysis through the growing field of data analytics. The important thing is to track this material, and any responses and innovations, as evidence of this level of scholarly teaching within college educational programs. In some larger college contexts this might be recorded through the minutes of a Learning and Teaching Committee or perhaps a Quality Committee; in small colleges it might be through the regular faculty meeting minutes. This wealth of analysis and its implications and actions ought to be recognised as evidence of a college's engagement with, and pursuit of, scholarly teaching. Reflection here can lead to the third level, the scholarship of teaching and learning.

Mary Huber talks about the process of participating in the scholarship of teaching and learning. This typically begins by asking questions about the learning of the students in a teacher's class. This leads to the gathering and analysing of evidence to help answer those questions; to trying out and exploring new insights about learning in one's teaching; and to making what one has found public, so that it can be reviewed, critiqued, and built on by peers.[12]

Like all research it begins with a question: in this case a question about one's practice. This may be a concern about teaching or student learning, something that has worked or that is puzzling and is desirous of being understood more deeply. It begins with questions such as: What works? What is going on? What's possible? What theory, framework or model would be useful in understanding a particular issue?[13] These questions of course may lead to a 'scholarly teaching' investigation but they can also lead on to the final level of scholarship.

Huber notes that there are sensitivities about questions of method and rigour

---

12 Huber, 'Scholarship', p. 3.
13 Huber acknowledges following a typology suggested by Hutchings, *Opening Lines*.

within the larger Scholarship of Teaching and Learning community. Sometimes a teacher doing research will be able to draw on the methodology in their field or discipline, at other times they will need to look outside for new methodologies and become adept at instruments such as pre- and post- questionnaires, close reading of samples of student work, focus groups, and surveys of different kinds.

There also may be ethical issues involved in the kind of inquiry that is to be undertaken.[14] Ethics Committee approval may also be necessary for certain kinds of research and there is a sensitivity required to the ethical implications of using one's own students in this way as an object of research.

Huber notes that 'going public' can mean many things.[15] This can range from the presentation of research at faculty forums, disciplinary and professional society meetings and conferences, through articles for newsletters or websites to publishing in peer-reviewed journals, edited books, or even as monographs.[16]

Huber notes that forays into the Scholarship of Teaching and Learning process can start with modest levels of engagement that lead to small changes whose effectiveness in improving student performance can be tracked. At its most elaborate, larger agendas for enquiry can develop with action taken through multiple iterations of a course or set of courses.

Huber styles her perspective on the area as a 'big tent' view that encompasses both research that looks more broadly at students and learning and research that looks more narrowly at specific programs, courses, and units and their design and implementation. The 'big tent' view means that some will be involved in a small way, while others may start small but soon realise they have a bigger project to hand.[17]

This seems to be an eminently sensible approach which can be illustrated by an example from my own practice. The following section will relate this example and then will follow some reflections.

Applying This in the Local Context

How can a college begin to foster a culture of practice at the three levels described? The initial step will be to acknowledge the necessity of sustained

---

14 Hutchings, *Ethics of Enquiry*.
15 Huber, 'Scholarship', 4.
16 Huber, 'Scholarship', 4.
17 Huber, 'Scholarship, 5.

thought and initiative in the area. This is not always immediately obvious. Members of faculty in the theological college context are normally recruited, quite reasonably, on the basis of discipline expertise with the assumption often unexpressed that they can teach. Where recruitment is from former graduates who have some ministry experience the assumption might be that the public teaching experience associated with a formal ministry role is immediately transferable to the classroom setting. This may make an able communicator but not necessarily a good teacher. The problem can be exacerbated in a context where the graduate is recruited on the basis of their higher degree qualification where the emphasis has been on research. Of course many higher degree programs integrate some teaching and other aspects of the faculty role into the practice via the use of tutors, providing some informal and at times formal development, but it is all a little *ad hoc.*

Further thought ought to be given in college faculties to the specific role of a teaching and learning 'champion' who will develop an interest and expertise in this area. Ideally this will be a faculty member with some educational background, though that is not a necessity. They can then become a catalyst amongst the other faculty and start to 'raise the temperature' on issues of what constitutes good teaching and learning among their peers. This may be as simple as taking some initiative to trawl through some of the literature on effective teaching and learning and feed it into other faculty members and perhaps stimulating research about teaching and learning.

Investment needs to be made at the level of library expenditure so that monographs engaging the scholarship of teaching and learning are accessible. Reading groups can be established to encourage engagement with these books and their ideas.

Professional development needs to be conceived as being broader than development in the particular academic discipline and opportunity taken to join in opportunities for thinking about teaching and learning at conferences such as those run annually by Sydney College of Divinity and Australian College of Theoloogy.

On a personal note, I am grateful for three initiatives I have experienced. First, in a college where I was teaching our growing awareness of inadequacy in this whole area resulted in whole faculty participation in a three day seminar on teaching and learning in a tertiary context, run by the Teaching and Learning Unit of a neighbouring university. The faculty was of sufficient size to be able to engage a member of the T&L unit to present a modified version of what would be presented to newly minted academics in the university context. This has since developed into new faculty being sent along to participate in the university's regular three day seminar at the beginning of each year to orient new staff to teaching and learning in the tertiary context.

Second, this experience led to me to use a period of study leave to complete a Graduate Certificate at the same Teaching and Learning Centre over the course of a year. This enabled at least one staff member to be engaged at a little more depth in the area of teaching and learning and to be stimulated to think though the issues of scholarly teaching, reflective teaching practice and the scholarship of teaching and learning.

Third, more recently the faculty of the college where I currently teach participated in a one day seminar entitled 'Thinking about Teaching and Learning', with the aim of formulating a teaching philosophy statement. This was an extremely useful time together as we discussed the various issues that were raised along the way concerning teaching and learning as we struggled to produce these individual statements. This has proved to be a catalyst for ongoing conversation on teaching and learning.

All of these initiatives feed into the first two levels of the typology outlined above: good teaching and scholarly teaching. So, what of the third level, the scholarship of teaching and learning?

Experimenting with the Scholarship of Teaching and Learning

The following is a report of a venture into the world of the scholarship of teaching and learning. The example comes from an experience where I was involved with other faculty in teaching a Greek exegetical class to a cohort of approximately seventy students. This was in the third year of an undergraduate Bachelor's degree course. The students had already completed three semesters of formal Greek instruction to the intermediate level. During their second year the cohort had also participated in Greek exegetical classes. There were two classes created owing to the size of the cohort and these were randomly allocated and were thus of mixed ability.

The third year cohort continued to be taught in two mixed ability classes. We began to explore as a teaching faculty the idea of creating streamed ability classes in the third year exegetical course because of some perceived differences in facility with the Greek language. This looked like some students were becoming demotivated and disengaged. We wondered whether smaller and streamed classes would enable the advanced students to progress a little further in their exegetical skills, while a smaller and more homogenous group might allow students who were perceived to be struggling to receive more individual attention and also be more inclined to be engaged through the asking of questions in a smaller group. The ultimate goal was to enhance each student's facility with the language so that they would persist in its use beyond the formal learning college context.

On the other hand, we were hesitant to explore this path because of the possible implications for students' perceptions of themselves and others being made visible in this fashion. There were also some concerns expressed for the possible consequences for character formation of the 'stronger' no longer having to bear with the 'weaker', with the consequent loss of some opportunities to serve one another—another character value prized by the college. We commenced a literature search on the area of streaming and tapped in to a body of existing discussion about this, which showed that the concerns we had raised concerning the 'institutional visibility' of differences in academic performance were shared.[18] The research was also not definitive, with some studies showing no effect on high ability students, while other studies showed a significant effect. Studies that were critical of the effects on students with apparently lower ability tended to focus on social inequality rather than academic results/learning. Studies also tended to take a quantitative approach and not focus on process or student experience. However, we also found that a lot of this research was based around primary and secondary education and not tertiary. We were suitably encouraged to proceed as a result of this literature investigation but were also sensitised to further issues in implementation.

One of the major issues we wrestled with was the difficulty or working with a single year group to conduct an educational 'experiment '. It was difficult to establish a control group, other than previous year groups' experiences and our perceptions of outcomes. In order to conduct the experiment we needed to 'innovate' with the whole year group as a trial and there would be no 'going back' for that particular group. This precipitated a useful discussion on the ethical issues involved and we reflected that this issue can, in itself, be an

---

18 Betts & Shkolnik, 'Key difficulties'; Cassidy & Eachus, 'Learning Style'; Hall & Farbrother, 'Ability Grouping'; Lejk, Wyvill, & Farrow, 'Group Assessment'.

inhibiting factor leading to a kind of 'better the devil you know' thinking that can inhibit innovation. At the conclusion of the discussion we felt that we should go ahead, all the while fully informing the students about what we were doing and inviting their consent and ongoing feedback. In order to assess the effectiveness or otherwise we decided to use 'hard data' from student results and to supplement this with data from voluntary student feedback. We developed a questionnaire and administered it over a two-year trial.

We asked students to judge whether they thought the selection process for the groups was fair. This process was to enact a cut-off based on Year 2 Greek results and Year 2 Greek exegetical class results. Following the announcement of the classes (in the end three: two of similar size and one much smaller at the lower end of ability), there was a two week period of adjustment possible if a student felt they had been treated unfairly (interestingly we had students go both ways due to their perceptions of the value of the class and their own ability).

We asked them to gauge the extent to which participation enhanced their learning, to try to isolate the effect of simply having a smaller class size. We probed their perceptions about the relative value of the educational experience in the two classes and their perceptions concerning the quality of teaching/lecturer in the respective classes. We enquired as to whether the provision of all resources from all classes to the whole cohort ameliorated any concerns. We also tried to ascertain the extent to which students perceived the community ethos of the year was overly affected. Finally, we asked whether the students felt the class arrangements encouraged innovation in teaching method and whether the grouping arrangements should be continued in following years.

We devised questions for different cohorts. We asked year 2 students to compare their experience of being taught Greek in two parallel mixed ability classes with their Year 1 experience which was a large group 'all-in' experience (except for a small withdrawal group). We asked the students in Year 3 to compare their experiences between their three streamed classes and the Year 2 parallel experience.

The final proposed development (which we did not get around to) was to ask students in Year 4 how they felt about returning to a single mixed ability stream for the Year 4 New Testament exegesis class.

In a sense, all this enquiry could have been achieved anecdotally but we decided to try to formulate a more 'rigorous' process.

Results

We were able to implement the questionnaire for a single year cohort only. We found little difference in performance in the end of year exegetical exam except for a slight improvement in the smallest class with perceived lowest ability. The students did not appear greatly perturbed by the process and the students in the smallest and lowest ability class reported the most satisfaction with the new arrangements, reporting that they felt they received more individual attention, there was not so much pressure to 'move on' though the material, and that there was greater opportunity to ask questions to clarify understanding. There were no reported concerns with respect to the community ethos of the year, with the move being seen to fulfil other aspects of the college's ethos and the community concerns catered for in other ways. The provision of resources and opportunity to change allocation were also seen as positives in the process that further ameliorated any negative feelings about the initiative. The teachers of the various classes were positive about the development and the opportunity it gave to focus their teaching to a more narrow competency range.

Reflection

Reflection upon this experiment in the scholarship of teaching and learning suggests that it was both a success and a failure.

It was a success from the point of view of collaboration amongst colleagues and the stimulation provided by focusing on an educational problem and attempting to research and generate a solution based on more than simply 'gut-feel'. The research into method took the participating faculty members into new areas of thought with respect to research method and exposed gaps and inadequacies as well as providing stimulus for further development of thinking. The actual outcome for students and their learning was marginally positive for a segment of the student population and neutral for the rest. No damage was done from the point of view of ethos, generally, or the confidence of students specifically. One of the key learnings to emerge was the importance of over-communication with respect to attempted educational innovation.

However, it was a failure as an experiment in the scholarship of teaching and learning as there was no publication at the end. As such, it as an exercise in scholarly teaching and none the worse for that. The failure in the area of the scholarship of teaching and learning was mainly due to resource issues, especially time. The experiment was conducted by a small staff, 'between the cracks' of a myriad of other responsibilities in the small college context. This highlights the time, effort, and resources that need to be allocated if the scholarship of teaching and learning is to be pursued. We also found it difficult to conceive of a public forum for 'publication', which may indicate lack of effort or lack of opportunity in the specifically theological context in Australia. Finally, there was a slight crisis of confidence as we ventured into new territory. Was the method rigorous enough? Were the results valid and reliable? Was this study worthy of publication? Were we 'real' educational researchers or pretenders?

The value of the exercise overall was twofold. We did investigate our teaching practice in a more sustained and rigorous way and enacted and tested an innovation. At the same time, we were further sensitised to the many prospects and opportunities, as well as the significant challenges of engaging in the scholarship of teaching and learning.

Conclusion and Final Personal Reflections

There is a helpful 'breaking up of the field' at play in this discussion. I do not doubt the importance of discipline-based research, the importance of a 'sound understanding of current scholarship and/or professional practice in the discipline'. Tertiary lecturers are only too aware of the requirement to be research active. However, we are still 'playing catch-ups' on Boyer's insights and that 'research of discovery', in his terms, is still front of mind when the word research is mentioned. It would be interesting for our theological institutions to interrogate their research policies to see if this is, in fact, the case. And if it is, ought we work towards acknowledging and doing better in Boyer's other areas of research and give due credit and (with a regulatory hat on) justify this broadening within the research policies of our institutions?

At one level, moves towards research-led teaching in the manner outlined here are simply moves towards more reflective teaching practice, engaged with the rigour appropriate to research in the various disciplines taught. There is nothing controversial about this. The conference this paper was initially presented at is a testimony to the significance and importance of this, for at least the attenders. However, it is still, at least anecdotally, notorious in tertiary contexts that many teachers and lecturers love research and tolerate teaching.

Any impetus to encourage higher quality teaching and learning is to be welcomed in the context of theological education and a typology such as that outlined above provides a pathway for a college to walk in this direction. It should at least be hoped that colleges will aspire to scholarly teaching, if not make occasional forays into the scholarship of teaching and learning.

The discussion encourages us to search for rationale and rigour in our practice. I can recall many changes made in units and programs I have run that have been in response to 'gut-feel' (sometimes boredom/familiarisation) rather than 'harder' evidence as to the benefit. I do not want to underplay the benefit of experience but also am grateful for times when I have been able to substantiate the benefit of an intuitive decision with some solid evidence: either results or, more often, student feedback.

The 'bridge-too-far' in my experience comes with the move to the public aspect of the scholarship of teaching and learning: specifically publication. Some of the barriers have been mentioned above. I am heartened by the wide-ranging definition of publication by Huber and grateful for conferences on teaching and learning that are beginning to appear more regularly in the local, theological context. This gives an opportunity at least to present, if not to publish, and to push as a discipline to pursue with more vigour research-led teaching and learning and perhaps to consider working towards articulating a pedagogy of our theological discipline. This is a concept that has fascinated me ever since I came across it in the Graduate Certificate course mentioned above but which, since then, I have neither time nor energy to pursue!

Bibliography

Bain, K. *What the Best College Teachers Do* (Cambridge, MA: Harvard University, 2004).

Betts, J.R. & Shkolnik. 'Key difficulties in identifying the effects of ability grouping on student achievement', *Economics of Education Review,* 19.1 (2000), 21–26.

Boyer, E. *Scholarship Reconsidered: Priorities of the Professoriate* (Princeton, NJ: The Carnegie Foundation for the Advancement of Teaching, 1990).

Brookfield, S. D. *Becoming a Critically Reflective Teacher (*San Francisco: Jossey-Bass, 1995).

Cassidy, S. & P. Eachus. 'Learning Style, Academic Belief Systems, Self-report Student Proficiency and Academic Achievement in Higher Education', *Educational Psychology,* 20.3 (2000), 307–322.

Cohen, L. et al. *Research Methods in Education* (London: Routledge Falmer, 2000).

Glassick C.E. 'Expanded Definitions of Scholarship, the Standards for Assessing Scholarship, and the Elusiveness of the Scholarship of Teaching', *Academic Medicine* 75 (2000), 877–880.

Hall, Bethany & Crispin Farbrother, 'Ability Grouping In Higher Education: a review of the literature' (n.d.) www.bournemouth.ac.uk/cap/documents/Ability%20Grouping%20Literature%20Review.pdf [accessed 31 Aug, 2017].

Huber, M. 'What is the Scholarship of teaching and Learning?' (2013) https://stanford.app.box.com/s/zdld1krv7sx3w6mldjv6 [accessed 31 Aug. 2017]

Hutchings, P. *Opening Lines: Approaches to the Scholarship of Teaching and Learning* (Menlo Park, CA: The Carnegie Foundation for the Advancement of Teaching, 2000).

Hutchings, P. (ed.). *Ethics of Inquiry: Issues in the Scholarship of Teaching and Learning* (Menlo Park, CA: The Carnegie Foundation for the Advancement of Teaching, 2002).

Hutchings, P., & L. Schulman. 'The Scholarship of Teaching and Learning: New Elaborations, New Developments', *Change*, 31(5) (1999), 10–15.

Lejk, M., M. Wyvill, & S. Farrow. 'Group Assessment in Systems Analysis and Design: a comparison of the performance of streamed and mixed-ability groups', *Assessment and Evaluation in Higher Education*, 24.1 (1999), 5-14.

McKinney, K. 'What is the Scholarship of Teaching and Learning (SoTL) in Higher Education?' (n.d.) http://web.uri.edu/atl/files/definesotl.pdf [accessed 31 Aug, 2017]

Willis Salier
Youthworks College, Sydney
Bill.salier@youthworks.net

4 | MOVING FROM INSTRUCTION TO INQUIRY

HOW COMPLEXITY THEORY INFORMS WORK-INTEGRATED LEARNING

Abstract

For over thirty years the Australian College of Ministries has embedded an *instruction–action–reflection* model into all its learning programs. After continuous experimentation the model has evolved and now focuses simultaneously on action (improving things) and research (understanding things) while building on a solid base of foundational knowledge. The aim is to create a living laboratory where theory integrates with practice (improving knowledge in both areas).

Complex living systems (CLS) theory is introduced as a paradigm useful to students learning about a world moving from the certain truth of modernity to the emerging truth of postmodernity. CLS has been a useful framework for understanding the contexts in which inquiry-based learning is most effective. A heuristic model, *sensemaking in a complex living system*, is introduced to aid discussion, where four contextual domains are described: the *simple* or *chaotic* domains (where *a teaching culture of instruction* is effective), and the *complicated* or *complex* domains (where *a learning culture of inquiry* is effective).

Four types of knowledge are highlighted and the differences are noted between *unordered knowledge* (knowable in retrospect) and *ordered knowledge* (knowable in advance) as well as *tacit* knowledge (highly personalised and experience-based) and *explicit* knowledge (formal and systematic).

The result is a model of adult learning moving from *instruction to inquiry* and from *classroom to workplace*—wherever it can be established that the student learning outcomes will be most effectively achieved.

Introduction

A priority for any educator is to seek ways to improve the quality of the student learning experience. The emphasis, then, is for the teacher to be less focused on what they themselves are doing, but more focused on what learning is occurring in the mind and heart of the student. Perhaps the teacher is less like a master musician focused on their own performance and more like a maestro conductor bringing out the best in their musicians.

For over thirty years the Australian College of Ministries (ACOM) has embedded an *instruction–action–reflection* model into all its learning programs. This essay explores possible next expressions of this model reflecting a shift from a *teacher focus* on instruction to a *learner focus* on inquiry. Work-integrated learning is considered a vital aspect of this next expression.

The use of a complexity framework is introduced as a useful model for sensemaking to identify the context in which *instruction* (teaching) as opposed to *inquiry* (research) may be the better approach to produce improved student learning outcomes. It is hoped this exploration will make a useful contribution to the ongoing discussions regarding better practice in adult learning.

Integrating Academy and Field

In 1990 Keith Farmer and Dennis Nutt[1] wrote a brief proposal for the Sydney College of Divinity entitled 'Integrating academy and field', recognising the need for developing ministers holistically. As a result, ACOM transitioned its learning design from a traditional campus-based teaching model to a hybrid learning approach that involved:

- relating instruction more closely to field work;
- structuring field work more carefully as training;

---

1 Farmer and Nutt, 'Integrating Academy and Field', 2.

- reorganising placement of students in the field; and
- enhancing the role of pastoral supervision.[2]

Since that time, the world has changed and the pastoral skills and critical thinking required of ministry practitioners have shifted. The rise of postmodern and post-Christian worldviews, enhanced by rapid technological and social change, has created a very different environment for ministry. In response, ACOM has continued to assess, adapt and refine the model of learning, with continuous improvement to the student learning experience. As such, the College provides a testing ground, a proof of concept, for innovative processes in deep transformational learning.

In parallel, secular higher education providers are urged to produce graduates who are 'job ready' with skills that are a good match for what potential employers are seeking in suitable employees. As such, *work-integrated learning* is becoming more common in Australian universities and is seen as an effective vehicle to provide a direct link between the academy and professional skills.[3] Work-integrated learning is where the student's learning activities are embedded in the context of the workplace and designed to integrate theory and practice. Students are encouraged to apply previous learning and critically reflect on their actions in a work-related context.

Work-integrated learning sees the workplace as rich in opportunities for contextualised learning. However, the reality of application in the university sector reaps varied results. Cooper et al. found the measures of validity and reliability in assessment are problematic concepts in work-integrated learning as their use is often built on the basis that students will all be assessed in the same way and in the same circumstances, saying, 'In light of the variability of conditions a common response has been to resort to work-required systems in which student performance is not assessed; merely tasks to be completed'.[4] This is also evident in the survey of Australian university studies that found a dearth of policies and processes to deal adequately with work-integrated learning.[5] This results in what Cooper et al. observed as the use of 'non-graded pass' and 'pass/fail' assessments as a symptom of a lack of alignment between course

---

2   Banks, *Reenvisioning Theological Education*, 229–230.
3   See, for example, Abeysekera, 'Issues Relating to Designing a Work-Integrated Learning Program'; Barnett, Parry and Coate, 'Conceptualising Curriculum Change'; Smith, Mackay and Holt, 'Seeking Industry Perspectives'.
4   Cooper, Orrell and Bowden, *Work-Integrated Learning*, 101.
5   Orrell and Parry, 'An assessment policy framework'.

learning outcomes, standards of assessment and expectations of the workplace.[6]

It is not About the Workplace—It is About the Quality of the Learning

It would seem that the development of course units based in a workplace does not necessarily ensure that the learning experience is oriented towards the practical or professional. Educators have the opportunity to ensure the workplace opportunity will support the design of the unit and indeed the course as a whole. This leads to the questions of *when* is it most appropriate for learning to take place in the classroom and *when* is it more effective for learning to take place in the field? What learning outcomes and content are best served with either style of learning?

Research within the University of Sydney's faculty of health science focused on the development of healthy and sustainable leaders found the training of healthcare workers had been enhanced by the application of complexity theory in areas such as aged care, healthcare management, medical education, clinical leadership in mental health, health promotion and nurse management.[7] In applying the findings of this research in ACOM today, the question might be asked, 'What can theological educators learn from best practice thinking in the training of medical practitioners?' In responding to this question, the concept of complexity theory must be considered in the context of the student learning experience.

How Complexity Informs the Approach to Learning

The journey to appreciating complexity involves taking on a new way of thinking,[8] standing back from detailed analysis of system 'parts' and taking 'a

---

6   Cooper et al., *Work Integrated Learning*.
7   For examples of each of these areas, see the following:
    Henriksen and Rosenqvist, 'Contradictions in Elderly Care', 27–35;
    McDaniel and Driebe, 'Complexity Science and Health Care Management';
    Fraser and Greenhalgh, 'Coping With Complexity', 799–803;
    Minas, 'Leadership for Change in Complex Systems', 33–39;
    Wilson and Holt, 'Complexity and Clinical Care', 685–688;
    Clancy and Delaney, 'Complex Nursing Systems', 192–20;.
8   Pina e Cunha, Viera da Cunha and Kamoche, 'The Age of Emergence', 25–29.

crude look at the whole',[9] from analysis to synthesis. Complex systems are non-linear[10] with cause and effect often distant in time and space.[11] Gregoire and Prigogine note that the roots of complexity are found in non-equilibrium physics where the prevalence of instability means small changes may lead to large, amplified changes.[12]

Previously, modern theories (of health, science and management) were, for the most part, built on Newtonian assumptions of a 'clockwork universe'.[13] As Shelton writes:

> Newton's thinking had enormous impact, not only on science, but on organizations as well. The founding fathers of industrialism were greatly influenced by his worldview. Newton frequently characterized the universe as a great clock-like machine and his machine metaphor was transferred to the workplace. Organizational charts were designed to look like the schematics of a great machine and managers attempted to create results by managing employees as if they were mechanistic cogs—parts to be manipulated, controlled, and replaced when broken or worn out. Data were collected and analysed (reductionism); prediction was highly valued (determinism); and what could not be measured simply did not exist (positivism).[14]

Ian Hughes, in the context of action research in healthcare, writes:

> Complex systems include a large number of autonomous agents (who adapt to change) and a larger number of relationships among the agents. Patterns emerge in the interaction of many autonomous agents. Inherent unpredictability and sensitive dependence on initial conditions result in patterns which repeat in time and space, but we cannot be sure whether, or for how long, they will continue, or whether the same patterns may occur at a different place or time. The underlying sources of these patterns are not available to

---

9 Gell-Mann, *The Quark and the Jaguar*.
10 Doolittle, 'Complex Constructivism'.
11 Brodnick and Krafft, 'Chaos and Complexity Theory'.
12 Gregoire and Prigogine, *Exploring Complexity*.
13 Olson and Eoyang, *Facilitating Organizational Change*;
    Plsek and Greenhalgh, 'The Challenge of Complexity in Health Care', 625–628;
    Wheatley, *Leadership and the New Science*
14 Shelton, *Quantum Leaps*, 2.

observation, and observation of the system may itself disrupt the patterns.[15]

Examples of complex systems are the financial market, the human immune system, a colony of termites or any collection of humans.[16] The lessons from complexity science suggest that 'illness and health result from complex, dynamic, unique interactions between different components of the overall system'[17] and these unpredictable agents are (1) within each human body, (2) within the choices made by each individual, (3) affected by (and affecting) the web of relationships between individuals and (4) influencing the wider social, political and cultural systems. As such, there is no simple cause and effect modelling that adequately predicts and solves health-related issues when relying on a system to be 'constant, predictable and independent'.[18]

Moving from 'Linear Mechanistic Thinking' to 'Living Systems Thinking'

As part of the understanding of complexity, the move from 'modern' mechanistic thinking to postmodern adaptive complex thinking may be compared by moving from a view of organisations as *a game of billiards*[19] to *a living swarm*.[20] Wadsworth describes modern research with organisations as 'human inquiry for living systems'. She describes system complexity as being like a woman (complex living system #1) riding a bicycle (complex system #2), who is pregnant (complex living system #3), all interacting in constant motion to ride down the street.[21] Wheatley describes this as follows:

---

15 Hughes, 'Action Research in Health Care', 394.
16 Plsek and Greenhalgh, 'Complexity in Health Care', 625.
17 Wilson and Holt, 'Complexity and Clinical Care', 688.
18 Plsek and Greenhalgh, 'Complexity in Health Care', 625.
19 Holland, *Emergence from Chaos to Order*, 177;
   Wheatley, *Leadership and the New Science*, 152;
   Zohar, *Rewiring the Corporate Brain*, 100–107.
20 Fisher, *The Perfect Storm*.
   Goldstein, *The Unshackled Organization*;
   Holland, *Hidden Order*;
   Plsek and Greenhalgh, 'Complexity in Health Care'.
21 Wadsworth, *Building in Research and Evaluation*.

> Nothing described by Newtonian physics has prepared us to work with the behaviour of living networks. We were taught that change occurs in increments, one person at a time. We not only had to design the steps; we also had to take into account the size of the change object. The force of our efforts had to equal the weight of what we were attempting to change. But now we know something different. We are working with networks, not billiard balls. We do not have to push and pull a system, or bully it to change; we have to participate with colleagues in discovering what is important to us. Then we feed that into our different networks to see if our networks agree. [22]

This billiard-ball type thinking is built on key assumptions about the dynamics of the system: reality is objective; effects are predictable and knowledge is acquired solely through the senses—data collection and analysis.[23] In contrast is the view of an organisation as a CLS, more like a swarm of bees, flock of birds, colony of ants or school of fish.[24] Goldstein, in *The Unshackled Organisation*, discusses this complexity through the image of a school of fish, in that:

- a school does not have a single leader;
- control is distributed through the school;
- each independent agent is capable of responding, learning and adapting;
- the school is able to react to threat (stimulus) faster than any single leader could react;
- if there was a single 'leader' fish, the reaction time would be slower;
- the school, as a whole, has capabilities that are not explainable by the capabilities of any individual fish.[25]

In exploring the way leaders make sense of their surroundings I explored a heuristic model to ignite discussion with stakeholders and research subjects. The diagram, *Sensemaking in a Complex Living System* (Figure 1), was found useful to research participants learning about a world moving from the certain truth of modernity to the emerging truth of postmodernity. This model was

---

22 Wheatley, *Leadership and the New Science*, 152.
23 Shelton and Darling, 'From Theory to Practice', 353.
24 Goldstein, *The Unshackled Organization*;
   Holland, *Hidden Order*;
   Plsek and Greenhalgh, 'Complexity in Health Care'.
25 Goldstein, *The Unshackled Organization*, 88.

designed to ignite discussion, and in consultation with 108 research participants four contextual domains were described: the *simple* or *chaotic* domains (where *a teaching culture of instruction* is effective) and the *complicated* or *complex* domains (where *a learning culture of inquiry* is effective). In the context of this essay it is important to note there are circumstances where inquiry is more effective than instruction (and vice versa) in producing learning outcomes.

In this model the concept of sensemaking is introduced. Sensemaking is a well-established theoretical framework for knowledge creation whereby people give meaning to experience.[26] It is a way we deal with ambiguity and uncertainty. In our personal lives, we all do it intuitively every day. To become a method for formal research, it must be intentional and explicit. As Weick and Sutcliffe found, 'to deal with ambiguity interdependent people search for meaning, settle for plausibility and move on. These are moments of sensemaking'.[27] We use sensemaking in the process of creating understanding and knowledge in situations of high complexity or uncertainty, in order to make decisions.[28]

Figure 1 notes four domains of knowledge within the complex living system, as well as a fifth area, a grey zone, where the unknowable seems to reside. The domains are not shown as neat shapes, as in practice they are not clearly defined like a 2x2 matrix. The lines should be seen as fuzzy. No line is square and no classification is absolute. Rather, it is a device for discussion and mutual learning. As Ian Hughes once noted, 'Every model breaks down. No matter how detailed and accurate a model of a plane you still can't get in it and fly to Los Angeles'.[29] So this model is a device to aid inquiry.

---

26   Gioia and Chittipeddi, 'Sensemaking and Sensegiving', 433–448;
     Patriotta, 'Sensemaking on the Shop Floor',349–376;
     Taylor and Van Every, *The Emergent Organization*;
     Weik, *Sensemaking in Organizations*;
     Weik and Sutcliffe, *Managing the Unexpected*.
27   Weik and Sutcliffe, *Managing the Unexpected* , 419.
28   Klein, Moon and Hoffman, 'Making Sense of Sensemaking', 70–73.
29   Hughes, 'Action Research in Healthcare'.

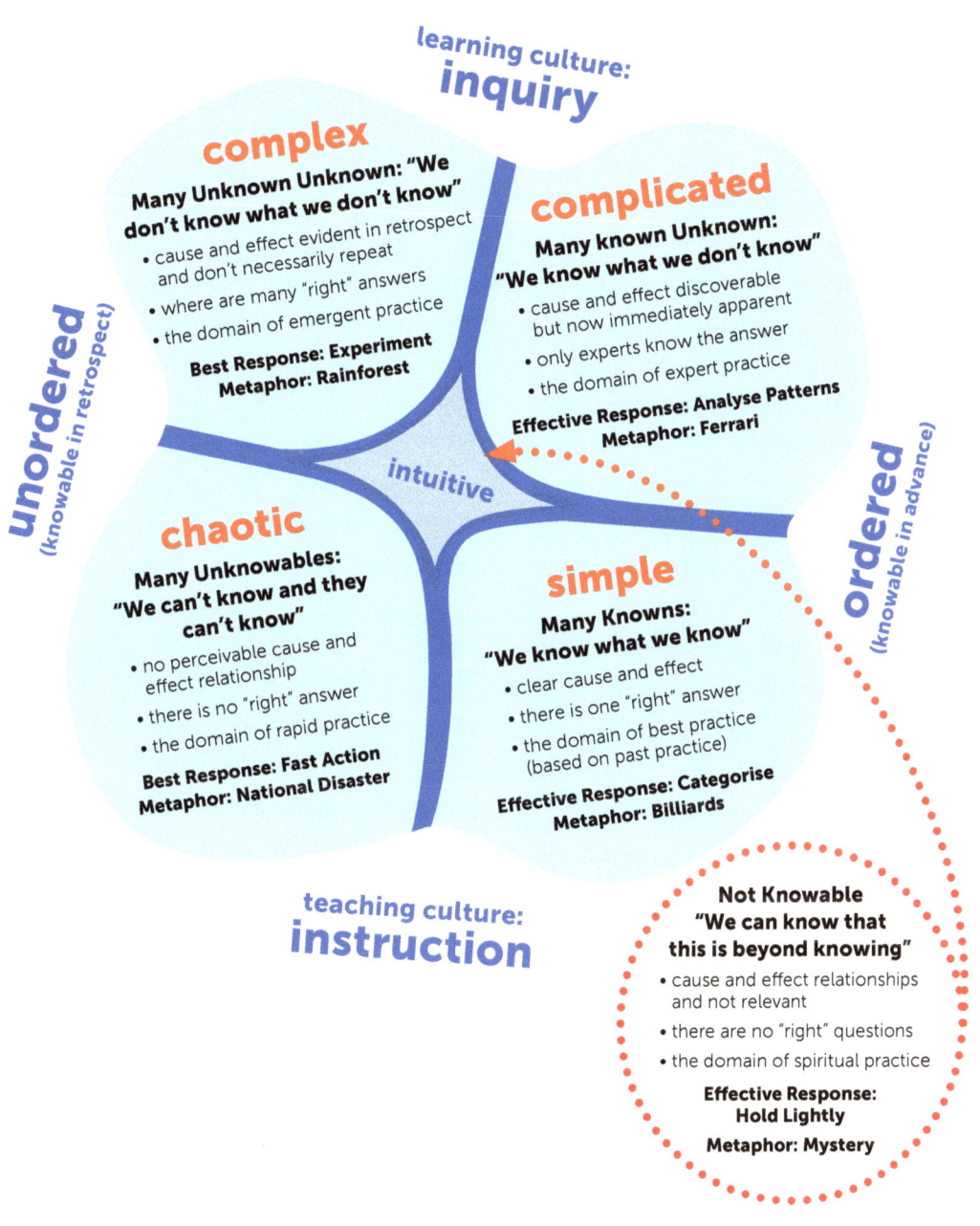

Figure 1: Sensemaking in a complex living system.

The domains of knowledge are:

1. *The simple domain* contains knowledge with many knowns. Cause and effect is understood clearly, and there is one 'right' answer. A metaphor for this is billiards, where simple and accurate mathematical precision will result in the same result every time, as all the relevant variables are knowable in advance. *Effective leadership in this domain is to categorise.* Policy and compliance systems work well because this is the domain of best practice (based on past practice). Teaching and instruction are more effective than exploration or discovery.

2. *The complicated domain* is where we know what we do not know. Here, cause and effect are discoverable but not immediately apparent, and only experts, people with special knowledge skills, know the answer. A metaphor for this is a Ferrari, where all the variables are knowable but an expert mechanic is required as the system is complicated, but still able to be fully described in a manual. *Effective leadership in this domain is to analyse patterns.* Professional consultants work well because this is the domain of expert practice. The most effective learning culture is one of inquiry.

3. *The complex domain* contains many unknown unknowns. In this knowledge domain, cause and effect are discoverable in retrospect but not knowable in advance, and do not necessarily repeat. There are many 'right' and many 'wrong' answers. A metaphor for this is the rainforest, where significant variables are knowable, but only in hindsight. The possible ramifications of any change are unpredictable, as there are living systems within living systems, within living systems—all interconnected and influencing each other. *Effective leadership in this domain is to experiment.* Collaboration and co-creation work well in this domain of emergent practice. Small, leveraging changes may affect the system in unpredictable ways in a web of responding actions and interactions. Experiment, assess, nudge, do more, do less and experiment again. The most effective learning culture is one of inquiry.

4. *The chaotic domain* has many unknowables. Here there are no perceivable cause and effect relationships, and there is no single 'right' or 'wrong' answer. A metaphor for this is a natural disaster, where many variables operate too rapidly for causal analysis to be useful. Change happens quickly, abruptly, surprisingly and unexpectedly, and any attempts at a 'quick fix' may be useless or have unanticipated side effects. *Effective*

leadership in this domain is fast action: taking charge works well, as this is the domain of rapid practice. Doing almost anything decisively is usually better than doing nothing in chaos. The most effective learning culture is instruction (teach the known, providing certainty).

5. **The fifth domain** is drawn in the middle of the two-dimensional diagram but would be better placed above the page or below it. This is the domain of the fundamentals that underpin knowledge as well as transcendent awareness of something bigger than we are. It includes an unknown number of unknowables. Spirituality, theology, and intuitive experiences point to the larger existential meanings of life. This zone is beyond sure knowing, so cause and effect relationships are not relevant. There are no 'right' questions. This is the grey zone of spiritual practice, a mystery. There are many metaphors for this zone, none of which conveys much useful information. *Effective leadership in this domain involves holding assumptions lightly*: observation, curiosity, silence and reflection work well in this zone of suspended judgement. The most effective learning culture is one of intuition and discernment (setting aside assumptions and developing a greater sense of self-awareness, awareness of others and comfort with the uncertainty of not knowing).

These domains provided a framework for discussion and sensemaking with research participants. Complexity was embraced as a paradigm that was helpful to them in their learning about a world moving from certain truth (modernity) to emerging truth (postmodernity). The framework helped them towards deeper understanding and self-awareness in their leadership practice within their organisations.

Of particular use to participants were the implications for leadership action in the different domains. Analysing patterns can be effective in the *complicated zone* (where cause and effect may be discoverable but not immediately apparent) but not the *complex zone* (as cause and effect are discoverable in retrospect but are not usually knowable in advance and do not necessarily repeat). Understanding this distinction was helpful for research participants in managing their personal stress and anxiety when things were happening in their context that were uncertain or ambiguous. Participants found discussing the domains gave them insight into how they might respond: to analyse patterns (complicated domain) or to experiment (complex domain).

This model highlights four types of knowledge and the differences are noted between *unordered knowledge* (knowable in retrospect) and *ordered knowledge* (knowable in advance) as well as *tacit* knowledge (highly personalised and experience-based) and *explicit* knowledge (formal and systematic). Consequently, a teaching culture of *instruction* is deemed more effective in some circumstances and a learning culture of *inquiry* in others. These concepts of knowledge are of particular interest to ACOM as we continue to explore ways to provide transformational learning experiences.

Action Research as Work-Integrated Learning

In seeking to discover the next iteration of ACOM's *instruction–action–reflection* approach, and in the light of what has been said here about complexity and types of knowledge, my research found that 'action research' can be an effective approach to work-integrated learning in complex organisational settings. Action research cannot be neatly put into a box, as it is a 'family of approaches'[30] and has its roots in sociology, social psychology, psychology, organisational studies and education.[31] There is wide support in the literature for this cyclical process of action and reflection leading to further inquiry and action for change.[32] Rapoport described it as follows: 'Action research aims to contribute both to the practical concerns of people in an immediate problematic situation and to the goals of social science by joint collaboration within a mutually acceptable ethical framework'.[33]

Yoland Wadsworth describes the effectiveness of the approach as follows: 'Participatory action research is not just research which it is hoped will be followed by action. It is action which is researched, changed and re-researched, within the research process by participants'.[34] Theories developed using the action research approach are not validated independently and then applied to practice; rather, they are validated through practice.[35] The core validity of an

---

30 Reason and Bradbury, *Handbook of Action Research*, xxii.
31 Hart and Bond, *Action Research for Health and Social Care*, 37.
32 Burns, *Introduction to Research Methods*;
    Kolb, *Experiential Learning*;
    Parkin, *Managing Change in Healthcare Using Action Research*;
    Revans, *Action Learning*;
    Wadsworth, *Building in Research and Evaluation*.
33 Rapoport, 'Three Dilemmas in Action Research', 499.
34 Wadsworth, '"What is Participatory Action Research?' 23.
35 Burns, *Introduction to Research Methods*, 346.

action research project is found in its usefulness to improving practice, as Hughes and colleagues write:

> the key test of validity for action research is not whether research procedures conform to rules established by academics and professional researchers, but whether the knowledge works in practice. Until the knowledge gained in action research is tested in practice, we do not know whether the action research is valid or not. Practical action research projects are not fully completed until the research findings are applied in practice.[36]

At the heart of most action research projects is a question that usually starts with something like, 'How can I (or we) improve…?' The research question may be broad, loosely bound and designed to accommodate emerging perspectives, but it still has three intertwined purposes: action research engages participants as co-inquirers to (1) initiate action designed for organisational change, (2) inspire reflective learning by the researcher and (3) make a unique contribution to the body of knowledge.[37] Lewin's expression, 'there is nothing so practical as a good theory', is still used as a guide by action researchers.[38]

Effective Work-Integrated Learning Should Emphasise Rigorous Inquiry

An appreciation of *Complex Living Systems Theory* (a variation of complexity theory) has been helpful in developing the College's approach to learning not only to understand and improve the ways in which learning can most effectively occur, but also to help prepare for an emergent theology that allows for views of God, church and the human condition that are less simplistic and more nuanced with the unknown. God can be mysterious, unpredictable and complex, yet still be God.

As an organisation that values the quality of its training for ministry practitioners, ACOM has the opportunity to develop graduates who are ready

---

36 Hughes, Ndonko, Ouedraogo, Ngum and Popp, 'International Education for Action Research', 4.
37 Reason and Bradbury, *Handbook of Action Research*
   Wimpenny, 'Participatory Action Research';
   Smith, 'Savouring Life'.
38 Cunningham, 'Strategic Considerations in Using Action Research', 516.

for a ministry environment that is no longer simple, but complex. For this to occur it is no longer enough to have field placements where a student gets out of the classroom and gets their hands dirty. Rather, work-*integrated* learning is perhaps the next step in ensuring that graduates are truly equipped for the roles they seek to pursue. Work-integrated units of study may be vital in that process, but if they are to be effective they will need to have:

- an emphasis on learning through action;
- a clear alignment of the unit learning objectives and assessment to meet the professional skills required of potential employers;
- a focus on inquiry that is adaptive, providing opportunities to explore and experiment;
- an iterative approach where the student can respond to what is observed and take appropriate action;
- opportunities for critical analysis in the light of the literature in the discipline;
- requirements for the rigorous integration of theory and practice, with each informing the other, and identifying knowledge that may be applicable to other contexts.

These elements are essential because they develop graduates who can think and learn for themselves: collecting data, analysing evidence, thinking critically, reflecting personally and adapting iteratively. These are fundamental skills needed for job-readiness. Theoretically, this is not new or insightful. Thirty-five years ago Edgar Schon described what the experience of learning in the field should look like, saying:

> The practitioner allows himself to experience surprise, puzzlement, or confusion in a situation which he finds uncertain or unique. He reflects on the phenomenon before him, and on the prior understandings which have been implicit in his behaviour. He carries out an experiment which serves to generate both a new understanding of the phenomenon and a change in the situation.[39]

However, while every effort should be made by educators to improve the quality of the student learning experience, what is evident is that some course unit learning outcomes are simply better served through instruction. But work-integrated

---

39 Schon, *The Reflective Practitioner*, 68.

learning will be most effective when the learning outcomes are best served through inquiry. The complexity framework introduced in this essay is merely a heuristic vehicle to ignite discussion about *when* instruction or inquiry might be most effective. When educators get this wrong, then learning in the field becomes merely interesting, but not necessarily effective in preparing ministry students to be ambassadors for God in a rapidly changing, postmodern, post-Christian world.

Bibliography

Abeysekera, I. 'Issues Relating to Designing a Work-Integrated Learning Program in an Undergraduate Accounting Degree Program and its Implications for the Curriculum', *Asia-Pacific Journal of Cooperative Education* 7 (2006), 7–15.

Banks, R. *Reenvisioning Theological Education* (Grand Rapids: Eerdmans, 1999).

Barnett, R., G. Parry, & K. Coate. 'Conceptualising Curriculum Change', *Teaching in Higher Education* 6 (2001), 435–449.

Brodnick, R. & L. Krafft. 'Chaos and Complexity Theory: Implications for Research and Planning', Paper presented at the 37th Annual Forum of the Association for Institutional Research, Orlando, Florida, 1997.

Burns, R. B. *Introduction to Research Methods* (Sydney: Addison Wesley Longman, 1996).

Clancy, T. & C. Delaney. 'Complex Nursing Systems', *Journal of Nursing Management* 13 (2005), 192–201.

Cooper, L., J. Orrell, & M. Bowden. *Work-Integrated Learning: A Guide to Effective Practice* (Sydney: Routledge, 2010).

Cunningham, J.B. 'Strategic Considerations in Using Action Research for Improving Personnel Practices', *Public Personnel Management* 24.3 (1995), 515–529.

Doolittle, P. 'Complex Constructivism: A Theoretical Model of Complexity and Cognition', 2002. http://www.tandl.vt.edu/doolittle/research.complex1.html.

Farmer, K.& D. Nutt. 'Integrating Academy and Field', Unpublished paper, Churches of Christ, Sydney, 1991.

Fisher, L. *The Perfect Swarm: The Science of Complexity in Everyday Life* (New York: Basic Books, 2009).

Fraser, S. & T. Greenhalgh. 'Coping with Complexity: Educating for Capability', *British Medical Journal* 323 (2001), 799–803.,

Gell-Mann, M. *The Quark and the Jaguar: Adventures in the Simple and the Complex* (New York: Freeman, 1994).

Gioia, D.A. & K. Chittipeddi. 'Sensemaking and Sensegiving in Strategic Change Initiation', *Strategic*

Management Journal 12. 4 (1991), 433–448.

Goldstein, J. *The Unshackled Organization* (New York: Productivity Press, 1994).

Gregoire, N. & L. Prigogine. *Exploring Complexity* (New York: Freeman, 1989).

Hart, C. 'Pastoral Care and Medical Education', *Journal of Religion and Health* 38.1 (1999), 29–34.

Hart, E. & M. Bond. *Action Research for Health and Social Care: A Guide to Practice* (Buckingham: Open University Press, 1995).

Henriksen, E. & U. Rosenqvist. 'Contradictions in Elderly Care: A Descriptive Study of Politicians' and Managers' Understanding of Elderly Care', *Health and Social Care in the Community* 11 (2003), 27–35.

Holland, J. *Hidden Order: How Adaptation Builds Complexity* (Reading: Addison Wesley, 1995).

Holland, J. *Emergence from Chaos to Order* (New York: Perseus Books, 1998).

Hughes, I. 'Action Research in Healthcare', *Handbook for Action Research: Participative Inquiry and Practice* (P. Reason & H. Bradbury, eds.; London: Sage, 2008), 381–393.

Hughes, I., F. Ndonko, B. Ouedraogo, J. Ngum, & D. Popp. 'International Education for Action Research: The Bamenda Model', *Action Research e-Reports, 020.* www.scribd.com/doc/15494711/International-Education-for-Action-Research-The-Bamenda-Model.

Klein, G., B. Moon, & R. Hoffman. 'Making Sense of Sensemaking: Alternative Perspectives', *Intelligent Systems* 21. 4 (2006), 70–73.

Kolb, D. *Experiential Learning* (New Jersey: Prentice Hall, 1984).

McDaniel R. & J. Driebe. 'Complexity Science and Healthcare Management', *Advances in Healthcare Management* (J. Blair, J. Fottler and G. Savage, eds.; Sydney: Elsevier, 2001), 11–36.

Minas, H. 'Leadership for change in complex systems', *Australasian Psychiatry* 13 (2005), 33–39.

Olson, E. & G. Eoyang. *Facilitating Organizational Change: Lessons from Complexity Science* (San Francisco: Jossey-Bass, 2001).

Orrell, J. & S. Parry. 'An Assessment Policy Framework: A Carrick Institute Study', Presentation to Macquarie University Assessment Working Party, Sydney, 2007.

Parkin, P. *Managing Change in Healthcare Using Action Research* (London: Sage, 2009).

Patriotta, G. 'Sensemaking on the Shop Floor: Narratives of Knowledge in Organizations', *Journal of Management Studies* 40.2 (2003), 349–376.

Pina e Cunha, M., J. Vieira da Cunha, & K. Kamoche. 'The Age of Emergence: Toward a New Organizational Mindset', *S.A.M. Advanced Management Journal* 66.3 (2001), 25–29.

Plsek, P. & T. Greenhalgh. 'The Challenge of Complexity in Health Care', *British Medical Journal* 323 (2001), 625–628.

Plsek, P. & T. Wilson. 'Complexity Science: Complexity, Leadership, and Management in Healthcare Organisations', *British Medical Journal* 323 (2001), 746–749.

Rapoport, R.N. 'Three Dilemmas in Action Research', *Human Relations* 23 (1970), 499–513.

Reason, P. & H. Bradbury, H. *Handbook of Action Research* (London: Sage, 2001).

Revans, R. *Action Learning* (Bromley: Chartwell Bratt, 1982).

Schon, D. *The Reflective Practitioner: How Professionals Think in Action* (Cambridge: Basic Books, 1983).

Shelton, C. *Quantum Leaps* (Boston: Butterworth-Heinemann, 1999).

Shelton, C. & J. Darling. 'From Theory to Practice: Using New Science Concepts to Create Learning Organizations', *The Learning Organization* 10. 6 (2003), 353–360.

Smith, R., D. Mackay, D. Challis, & D. Holt. 'Seeking Industry Perspectives to Enhance Experiential Education in University-Industry Partnerships: Going Beyond Mere Assumptions...', *Asia-Pacific Journal of Cooperative Education* 7 (2006), 1–9.

Smith, S. 'Savouring life: The Leader's Journey to Health, Resilience and Effectiveness', *Spirituality and Human Flourishing* (M. Dowson, M. Miner, & S. Devenish, eds.; Charlotte: Information Age Press, 2012).

Taylor, J. & E. Van Every. *The Emergent Organization* (New Jersey: Lawrence Erlbaum Associates, 2000).

Wadsworth, Y. 'What is Participatory Action Research?', *Action Research International*, Paper 2. Retrieved from www.scu.edu.au/schools/gcm/ar/ari/p-ywadsworth98.html, 1998.

Wadsworth, Y. *Building in Research and Evaluation: Human Inquiry for Living Systems* (Sydney: Allen & Unwin, 2010).

Webster, L. & R. Hackett. 'Burnout and Leadership in Community Mental Health Systems', *Administration and Policy in Mental Health* 26. 6 (1999), 387–399.

Weick, K. *Sensemaking in Organisations* (London: Sage, 1995).

Weick, K. & K. Sutcliffe. *Managing the Unexpected* (San Francisco: Jossey-Bass, 2001).

Weick, K., K.M. Sutcliffe, & D. Obstfeld. 'Organizing and the Process of Sensemaking', *Organization Science* 16. 4 (2005), 409–421.

Wheatley, M. *Leadership and the New Science: Discovering Order in a Chaotic World* (San Francisco: Berrett-Koehler, 1999).

Wilson, T. & T. Holt. 'Complexity and Clinical Care', *British Medical Journal* 323 (2001), 685–688.

Wimpenny, K. 'Participatory Action Research: An Integrated Approach Towards Practice Development', *New Approaches to Qualitative Research: Wisdom and Uncertainty* (M. Savin-Baden & C. Major, eds.; London: Routledge, 2010), 89-99.

Zohar, D. *Rewiring the Corporate Brain: Using the New Science to Rethink How We Structure and Lead Organizations* (San Francisco: Berrett-Koehler, 1997).

Stephen Smith
Australian College of Ministries, Sydney
ssmith@acom.edu.au

5 | REFLECTIONS ON THE EXPERIENCE OF WONDER IN RESEARCH-LED LEARNING

IN COMPANY WITH NIETZSCHE AND GIRARD

Abstract

This essay posits that Friedrich Nietzsche (1844–1900) is as an adventurer, a saint, and a seer. Being driven by the divine passion, there is much to learn from him about the wonder of *undergoing*, *overcoming* and *becoming*, which he, in turn, learned from the Christ of the *Evangel*. It also argues that, understanding Nietzsche's whole project requires a rigorous critical engagement with his provocative aphorisms and story-telling, which ingeniously point towards a self-regulating and self-authenticating research methodology into the darkness of Western culture. This essay is guided by Walter Lippmann's suggestion[1] that the great luminaries of the past, who have made a deep impression on our perception of the world, are those driven by an insatiable, wild curiosity, not always intelligible 'in ordinary terms', and that these are the people who defy the safe 'standards of utility' and disregard the attendant social consequences. Their wonder and passion is often misunderstood as 'useless, brave, divinely foolish', and, more tellingly, it is only barely understood even by themselves. If this is the case, then Nietzsche qualifies as such a luminary. Additionally, if it is true according to the contention that, 'explanation separates us from astonish-

---

1   *The Essential Lippmann: A Political Philosophy for Liberal Democracy.*

ment which is the only gateway to the incomprehensible',[2] then by means of that same astonishment, Nietzsche ushers us into realities that transcend but (ideally) never transgress the reality of the world as it is. In this, Nietzsche is wonderfully complemented by René Girard (1923-2016) whose insights will also briefly be explored.

The path of research-led learning, like any learning, can be compared to the journey that takes you into a far country, a foreign country: full of wonder and adventure, but oftentimes fraught with danger and risk. According to Research Professor in Theology and History from Oxford University, Johannes Zachhuber, academic work at its best and at its core is a risk-taking venture.[3] Research worthy of its name, he affirmed, certainly bears the hallmarks of an academic adventure, but equally constitutes a process that challenges our most cherished beliefs. It is in fact much more than just an intellectual exercise in brinkmanship. Indeed, it is an existentialist one by which long held and cherished beliefs may have to be abandoned. Zachhuber argues that this must always be a real possibility or the research process becomes a sham. Suspension of belief (as opposed to literature's carefree suspension of disbelief) will always be costly.[4]

Nietzsche was taken by many (both in his lifetime and posthumously), as a failed academic, a maverick and gypsy scholar. He was a social recluse, a heretic and in the end a lunatic, who was ignored and overlooked during his active life and later despised as the champion of Anti-Semitism and National Socialism. He has been construed as anti-God and anti-Christ, and as one who hijacked our most treasured values. How could *such* a man turn out to be arguably one of the most influential and inspiring philosophers and teachers for the 20th and 21st century? Or, to put it another way, how could such a one as Nietzsche, be represented as causing us to 'wonder about God together?' What could possibly be gained by consulting such a toxic, sacrilegious, unsystematic thinker who

---

2   Eugène Ionesco, French absurdist dramatist, referred to by Lippmann.
3   Zachhuber made this remark in a master class held at St Mark's Theological College, Charles Sturt University, Canberra, on 2nd August, 2016.
4   Zachhuber's approach to research resonates with that of Nietzsche, also a German speaker and researcher of life, whose thinking is never just cerebral. Theologically speaking we would say his approach is 'incarnational'. For Nietzsche life is an embodied experience, and his philosophy cannot be separated from physiology and psychology—Huskinson, *An Introduction to Nietzsche*, 8. His was the isolated life of an itinerant, stateless scholar whose groundbreaking insights were only universally recognized posthumously.

was shunned by the University after his first work (*The Birth of Tragedy*)[5] because he broke all the rules and to whom is attached such notoriety that to follow him would be to spell one's own academic extinction? How could *such* a man teach us anything about research-led learning?

This essay makes a case for the philosopher/psychologist Nietzsche being a rabbi in the style of Jesus, *Yeshua Rabénu*. In doing so, it draws heavily on Father James Alison's exposition of the Emmaus incident,[6] adding the unique suggestion that reflecting on this incident points to important indications that Girard (whose Mimetic Theory inspires Alison's reading) and Nietzsche's aphoristic critique of modernity, together, create a hermeneutic that opens the way for research-led learning of a quite distinctive quality.

The essay operates with a paradigm inspired by *Ecce Homo*,[7] one of Nietzsche's latest and his most mature works—a unique kind of weird autobiography.[8] The paradigm assumes that Nietzsche deliberately entitled this work after the Vulgate translation of Pilate's admonition to the crowd, *'Behold the man'*, because he wanted to signal the position and perspective from which he was writing: a total identification with that of the accused and innocent Christ. This also intimates that his self-naming as the Anti-Christ brings the two titles (*Ecce Homo* and the *Anti-Christ*) together into the same frame of reference. The combined effect suggests that Nietzsche uses a stratagem designed to test his readers: do they treat him in the same way as the crowd treated Christ that fateful day egged on by provocation, or, having grasped the totality of his project, do they see a man totally identified with the Christ of the *Evangel*—an innocent man whose only crime is to expose false religion and idolatries of all kinds, including the false claims of all knowledge? With Father James Alison, the essay asks: through whose lens do we read when we condemn the Christ— and through whose lens do we see when we condemn Nietzsche? And how might that specific question itself inform research-led learning?

The paradigm promotes the idea that an understanding of Nietzsche's notion

---

5 Nietzsche, *The Birth of Tragedy*.
6 In his four volume set of essays, *Jesus the Forgiving Victim*, particularly Book One, 'Essay 2: Emmaus and Eucharist', 43–79, based on Luke 24:13–35.
7 This paradigm is developed in my PhD thesis, currently being written: RESSENTIMENT: toward a Christology without enemies, Friedrich Nietzsche contra René Girard. Supervisors: Dr Lucy Huskinson Head of Faculty Bangor, UK , for Nietzsche; and Professor Scott Cowdell, CSU, Canberra Australia.
8 *Ecce Homo: How To Become What You Are*, was written in 1888, but not published until 1908.

of *ressentiment*⁹ requires the awareness of at least three points of view embodied and dramatized that morning when the scourged Christ is paraded before a people who just days before had celebrated him as Prophet-King but now clamour for his blood, that of the crowd, Pilate and Jesus himself:

a) the crowd, glad to break free of their impotence and egged on by the religious authorities (leaders who themselves are consumed by *ressentiment*—eaten up with jealousy and anger that Jesus should expose their idols and their bankruptcy), can now only see him as a King of Blasphemy, a God killer—a self-styled Messiah who attempts to displace God;

b) Pilate the Judean Roman Prefect, torn between two loyalties—fear of the Emperor and fear of the crowd—is a man overwhelmed by a feeling of his own personal impotence, which is the tap root of *ressentiment*;

c) Christ on the other hand is (for Nietzsche at least) the epitome of what it means for a human being to be devoid of *ressentiment*. Even in these most dire of circumstances, he is one who affirms life and embraces it, and who, like Dionysus, stands *outside* and *against* the sacrificial order,[10] and exposes its fraudulence.

There is also, of course, the unseen further *personae*—the silent witnesses, if you will, who are *the readers* of the Gospel account in every epoch, and of Nietzsche's unique autobiography, *Ecce Homo*, and *their* interpretation of that same moment.[11]

Neither Nietzsche's notion of *ressentiment*, nor his entire theological/ philosophical/ psychological/ anthropological/ cultural/ political project, can be understood without standing in the place of the total vulnerability which Christ occupied that day before Pilate, an attitude which he carried through to the end at Golgotha. This Christ of the *Evangel* was much admired by Nietzsche as the

---

9   The English word 'resentment' barely does justice to its sense in French and the way Nietzsche used it: in French it means 'to feel over and over again'; for Nietzsche, it was a kind of smoldering real or imagined sense of offence.
10 It is here that the Girardian insight will come into its own. Rowan Williams in his Foreword to *Mimesis and Atonement, René Girard and the Doctrine of Salvation*, xiv, notes that: 'Instead of the cross of Christ being the long-awaited answer to our question about how we might "finally" make the [mimetic scapegoat] mechanism work, it dissolves the entire working of sacral violence and casts the emphasis on the free act of a divine agent beyond all rivalry, negotiation or competition'. How Nietzsche's inclusion of Dionysus works in this context, is convincingly argued by Grant Poettcker, as we shall see.
11 One of the most chilling readings of this moment was the interpretation of: 'let his blood be upon us and our children'. (St Matthew's Gospel, 27:25), which through the ages has been used to justify anti-Semitic behavior, including the Waansee Conference's justification of the 'Final Solution', January 20, 1942.

only one true Christian and the Christ whom he sought to emulate and identify with so strongly all of his life.[12] When Nietzsche declares himself to be the Anti-Christ, he does so, deliberately—provocatively inviting censure, condemnation, and outrage. It is his way of testing whether his project has been understood, or whether the lazy readings of his life work arise from an institutional lynch mob mentality that misperceives Nietzsche in the same way as Christ was misconceived by the 'church' of his day. In effect, if a reading of Nietzsche falters here, it will falter everywhere.

What can be learned from Nietzsche—and from Girard—about the wonder and the marvel of research-led learning as opposed to dogmatics and systematics?[13] And what of Nietzsche's research style, which resembled that of *Yeshua Rabénu*, the rabbi Jesus?

Provocation against anything that robs life of its sacred vitality and integrity brings Nietzsche and Jesus together. Apparently indifferent to a systematic, conventionally learned knowledge, flaunting orthodoxy, the two are equally bent on aphorism, parable, and allegory. These stratagems are designed to force the moment to its crisis—one of self-examination in the light of a truth that has shifted ground.

Such self-examination and the provocation of the truth occurs in the Emmaus event when Cleopas and the unnamed disciple are confronted by the risen Christ with the uncomfortable reality of a violent Jewish religious and cultural history which has consistently persecuted and killed the prophets who expose corruption. Why should they (Cleopas and the unnamed disciple) be surprised that this Jesus was killed and that they and all Jerusalem has been complicit in his death? For this behaviour is deeply rooted in their past. Their shame gives way to joy when the two realise that this Jesus whom they had treated as a stranger and an outsider, has signaled the beginning of the end of this deadly scapegoat mechanism of the 'many' against 'the one' by the power of self-giving love.

While Nietzsche evokes a transcendence firmly rooted in this life and doesn't subscribe to a resurrection in the orthodox sense, he certainly holds fast with great admiration to Christ's legacy, and it is this legacy that informs the method that undergirds his research:

---

12 Kee, *Nietzsche Against The Crucified*, makes a great case for this, though he misunderstands Nietzsche's identification with Dionysus—something elaborated upon below.

13 I think of my early training in 'systematic theology' where we all sat around agreeing with each other—that is, until I encountered Bultmann and Tillich for the first time, and how my heart burned within me as I read them.

> This "bringer of glad tidings" died as he had taught—not to "redeem men" but to show how one must live. This practice is his legacy to mankind: his behavior before the judges [...] before the accusers and all kinds of slander and scorn—his behavior on the cross. He does not resist, he does not defend his right, he takes no step to ward off the worst; on the contrary, he *provokes* it. And he begs, he suffers, he loves with those, in those who do him evil. Not to resist, not to be angry, not to hold responsible but to resist not even the evil one—to love him.[14]

If these claims are true, what might be their implication for research-led learning?

In his Introduction to the volume on Nietzsche in *The International Library of Essays in the History of Social and Political Thought*,[15] Tracy B. Strong offers some helpful insights. Notwithstanding the polarized diversity of interpretations and the bewildering array of self-contradictory pronouncements from the man himself, Nietzsche 'meant something, or was trying to mean something', and that those academic approaches which fail to see Nietzsche's work as a whole, and which deny that, 'Nietzsche's style and rhetoric are centrally important to his philosophical teaching, are seriously wrong'. Strong's advice centres on recognizing that Nietzsche's aphoristic style 'counters' that of 'the treatise as a form of philosophizing'. It is a style which 'broach[es] problems rather than solv[es] them… stimulating insights rather than final truths'. If this is not accounted for, interpreters are likely to draw false conclusions about what Nietzsche is in fact trying to say. Strong highlights, for example, how the philosopher invites his readers into his thought processes by using the German impersonal pronoun 'one' *(man)* in order to jolt the reader into considering whether he or she might 'see yourself that way', as part of this 'one', thus predicating the whole entry into the process of the thinking he proposes, as conditional, negotiable, and certainly not absolute. Thus, the sacrilege of the revolt against life, as Nietzsche sees it, is revealed for what it is: the unwitting oversight of the uselessness, illusiveness, absurdity and mendacity of such a revolt.

Thus, despite the brutal hard edge of Nietzsche's critique and its frequently

---

14 Nietzsche, *The Antichrist*, 35. On November 26, 1888, Nietzsche wrote to Paul Deussen, 'Meine Umwerthung aller Werthe mit dem Haupttitel "Der Antichrist" ist fertig' ['My *Revaluation of Values* under the main title "The Antichrist" is finished']; (*KSB* 8, 492).

15 For the quotations in this paragraph, see Strong, *Friedrich Nietzsche*, xv, xviii, xix, xx.

frustrating, ambiguous, and often self-contradictory tirades, Strong makes a convincing case that Nietzsche's technique is typical of classical rhetoric, which should be respected, since, 'behind the rhetoric there is an argument one can reconstruct'. More importantly, Strong suggests a personalized methodology (under the subheading, 'Producing self-criticality: where is authority?'), that is highly pertinent for how research-led learning might test itself. When reading Nietzsche, for example, in wanting to agree with what he was saying, the reader ought then to ask themselves the question of whether a dissonance might arise between what they want, and what Nietzsche's text says and makes available—or even requires of them—as they read. In other words, the very desire for some kind of resolution to the problem might itself prove to be an idol. Nietzsche constantly invites his readers to 'listen' to the tuning fork which exposes that 'dissonance'—a dissonance between the tone of the fork and the sound that the idol makes when struck.

Strong finishes with this astute observation:

> At best, which is often, Nietzsche forces the reader to come to grips with his or her own unexamined needs and desires: to be self-critical and thus to become his or her own authority. He is trying to make it possible for you to cure yourself, 'to become what you are' in the phrase from Pindar's second Pythian Ode that serves as a touchstone for his enterprise.

As an aside, Strong notes (tellingly) that, 'the multiple understandings of Nietzsche are all, to some degree, understandings of those who have not adequately turned their understanding back on themselves'. This turning of a person's cherished understanding back on itself—will be a most searching and exposing test to take in any research-led learning, with the researcher asking: 'what lens am I looking through when I come to such and such an understanding? And to what degree has it perhaps distorted the reality of the "truth" I am searching for?'.

There are other similarities between Christ and Nietzsche. For, like *Yeshua Rabénu*, in St Luke's account of the Emmaus incident,[16] Nietzsche narrates back to his readers their cultural/moral Western history in such a way that they find their hearts burning within, dismayed as they descend into the depths of the

---

16 Here I am indebted to Alison's take on the Emmaus encounter with the risen Christ; see above, footnote 6.

genealogy of morals into a murkiness which they always suspected was there but whose magnitude was rarely either acknowledged or recognized. Arguably, too, no teacher has been more audacious and insightfully disturbing than Nietzsche's sparring partner René Girard vis à vis the fraught nature of those same cultural origins. For Nietzsche and Girard, pioneers in their respective fields, to use Lippmann's turn of phrase, were 'possessed for a time with an extraordinary passion which is unintelligible in ordinary terms', blazing the trail for innovative strategies in research-led learning, where 'no preconceived theory fits'. In each case, whilst shamelessly straying into a diversity of disciplines (the theologian Michael Kirwan describes Girard's incursions as 'promiscuous'),[17] both these adventurers discover a particularly powerful hermeneutical methodology (though nuanced differently) which effectively serves to reveal the complexity and the wonder and the mystery of God's person, the mystery of the self as moral being and agent and the 'mystery' of the darkness which shadows that self and the culture which nurtures it.

To understand the intricacies of how Nietzsche and Girard's critique of modernity resembles the risen Christ's critique of his own cultural history, an appreciation of the perspectives of the times of Jesus is necessary. According to Father Alison, 'Rabbi', 'teacher', was probably the most common way of addressing Jesus during his ministry. But when *Yeshua Rabénu*, the risen Christ —the dead man walking, the dead man talking—feigns ignorance, draws near to the Emmaus disciples in the midst of their heated argument about the *meaning* of these 'terrible events' which they have undergone, this Rabbi was really asking them: 'How do you read them, these events?'; '*Who* is your rabbi?'; 'Through whose eyes do you read?'. Alison claims that after the destruction of the Temple in AD 70 the answer given would have been: We read these texts through the eyes of Moses our Rabbi—'*Moshe Rabénu*'. And the later New Testament Judaism, which we now call Christianity, he argues, would have given a different answer: 'We read the scriptures through the eyes of Jesus our rabbi, *Yeshua Rabénu*, a rabbi like Moses before him—but much more—a dead, yet living Rabbi, held by life'. This same Jesus, the risen Christ, comes to the disciples, Cleopas and the unnamed one, in the guise of a 'resident alien' a sojourner, like Moses, Abraham, Joseph—someone who lives 'here' but is not from 'here'. Significantly, according to Alison, St Luke fashions his story around a piece of 'theological geography'—which is to say, by being 'not anywhere of

---

17 Kirwan, *Girard and Theology*, 5.

any importance in itself', unlike Jerusalem, Emmaus can, in principle, be anywhere at all, parameters, therefore, of a transferable event, that could happen to anyone. To C.S. Lewis, the atheist, for example, on a bus 'surprised by joy'.[18] And to a Nietzsche, and a Girard, each in his own quite remarkably individual and unique way.

But the Emmaus two, Cleopas and the unnamed one, are party to just fragments, strands of a puzzle story without the hermeneutical key necessary to bring them together into a whole narrative. This is ironic, in as much as *they* think that *he's* the outsider, and *they're* the ones 'in the know'. When he makes as if to go on ahead and they urge him to become their guest, he turns the tables on them by becoming the host, and they become his guests in thrall. In effect, he, the one they thought wasn't quite in the 'know', naïve somehow, suddenly becomes in the re-telling of their scared texts and cultural history, a 'living hermeneutical principle'. And so it is in the moment of the offering of the portions at supper that this 'resident alien' is recognized as Jesus of Nazareth. Suddenly, he—not they—becomes the protagonist, and it is *then*, in the midst of the exegetical discourse, that their eyes are opened—as 'he un-appearing became'. This is a Yahwistic theophany. He is not just a teacher, not just a prophet, not even just a High-priestly figure, but the great I AM. This was a truly immanent transcendent encounter—the kind of metaphysical wonder which Nietzsche could tolerate: one firmly rooted in this world. Nietzsche, too, turns the tables (though he definitely does not aspire to either the godhead or messiahship, claiming that this desire drove him mad).[19] Taking seriously Strong's convincing case that Nietzsche's use of classical rhetoric should be respected and 'behind the rhetoric there is an argument one can reconstruct',[20] it is perilous to ignore the nature and intention of that rhetoric. This is similar to what they did with Jesus' teaching when, a long time before the crucifixion, they wanted to throw this *agent provocateur* (this Socratic gadfly) off a cliff like the scapegoat on Atonement Day. For Jesus was always holding up those as heroes whom the misdirected had learned to hate and despise. So does Nietzsche with his Zarathustra. As Jesus cursed the religious leaders of his day, Nietzsche did his religious leaders for their being embedded with Wilhelmine *Realpolitik,* and its nationalism and colonial imperialism. It was the Church whose founder, Martin

---

18 C.S. Lewis, *Surprised by Joy.*
19 Many Girardian scholars adopt this approach, including Fornari, in *A God Torn to Pieces,* xvi.
20 Strong, 'Introduction', xvii.

Luther (for all of his virtues and insights), taught the hateful anti-Semitic mindset, that Hitler was able to exploit, which Nietzsche has principally in his sights when he names 'Christianity':

> I *condemn* Christianity. I bring against the Christian Church the most dreadful of all indictments that a prosecutor has ever uttered [. By denying life] it has made every value into an un-value, every truth into a lie… draining all blood, all love, all hope for life.

This is Nietzsche's *Wettkampf* (contestation) at its most potent. The passionate language of this contestation is driven by a relentless commitment to authenticity—an authenticity that will not be compromised. For Nietzsche, the person cannot be separated from the research, and claims to partiality are spurious. Because Nietzsche is so conscious of the fact that the teacher and the teaching, the philosopher and his philosophy, are one, he was just as demanding of 'systems' as he was of himself, to test their assumptions.

> The will to a *system*: in a philosopher, morally speaking, a subtle corruption, a disease of the character; amorally speaking, his will to appear more stupid than he is… I am not bigoted enough for a system—and not even for *my* system.[21]

In his July 2014 appraisal *Beyond Nietzsche's War Rhetoric: Ascesis, Sacrifice, and the Recovery of Health*,[22] which follows a similar line of argument to that of Tracy B. Strong, Grant Poettcker concedes that Nietzsche's writings are insightful in unexpected ways and have probably been misunderstood, and not *just* because of their excessive war and madness rhetoric. When taken together, his conclusions open new insights into Nietzsche's teaching and the defence mechanisms designed to expose lacunae in any research led-learning claims:

1) That Nietzsche's writings are replete with masks and excessive rhetoric inviting the sacred misapprehension which is present in Girard's 1976 essay 'Superman in the Underground' where he makes a discursive scapegoat of Nietzsche, portraying himself as out-Freud-ing Freud. Nietzsche,

---

21 Cited by Kaufmann, *Nietzsche*, 80.
22 Poettcker. 'Beyond Nietzsche's War Rhetoric'.

in other words, serves Girard as a means to get to Freud.[23]

2) That Girard misreads the philosopher's apparent individualism as precluding a social anthropology because he assumes that Clausewitz is more dangerous and 'more modern' and has an explicitly social anthropology, whereas Nietzsche does not, rendering Girard's claims highly contestable.[24]

3) That Girard's misunderstanding of Nietzsche's 'slant' on *ressentiment*[25] spills over into mistaking the nature of Nietzsche's identification with Dionysus, which in turn leads to a crucial misreading of that identification.

Nietzsche's identification with Dionysus takes us to the heart of his identification with Christ: its wonder, mystery, and the incredibly powerful hermeneutic that arises from it. This translates into a Girardian hermeneutic which locates the interpretative key with the innocent victim.[26]

The hermeneutical principle undergirding Nietzsche's identification with Dionysus, resembles the risen Christ's strategy with the Emmaus disciples. His recounting of their violent religious-cultural history to explain Jesus of Nazareth's death serves as a shock tactic to throw that history into stark relief. Girard defines identification with Dionysus as being in the grip of, and advocating for sacred violence, and he sees this divinity as a personification of the sacrificial order and an emblem of sacred and sacralising violence. Poettcker argues that, on the other hand, Nietzsche identifies with Dionysus, 'to show how thin the prevailing sacrificial order is—and how violent it is'. It is in the very act of re-valuing values, argues Poettcker, that Nietzsche identifies with Dionysus. In so doing the philosopher highlights the contingency, partiality, and

---

23 I owe this footnote to Dr Poettcker—footnote 7, 2 which explains the *context* of Girard's rivalry with Freud: 'Any effort to make Nietzsche's insanity intelligible will have to focus on those triangular relationships that are at the core of Freud's psychoanalytical theory. This does not mean that we have to be Freudian'. He concludes the essay (p. 1184) by saying that mimetic theory offers 'a far more efficient, more intelligible, and better integrated organization of more data'. In other words, Poettcker convincingly (for me at least) demonstrates how Nietzsche's provocations, his teaching strategies work to expose deficiencies in any proposed critique.

24 Girard, *Battling to the End*, 86—Poettcker continues (7 footnote 30): 'If will to power is, as Deleuze describes it, "not force but the differential element which simultaneously determines the relation of forces (quantity) and the respective qualities of related forces," then the will to power is essentially social'. See Deleuze, *Nietzsche and Philosophy*, 187.

25 *Ressentiment* is a term appropriated by Nietzsche from the French to designate a peevish life-negating attitude so beautifully caught by Feodor Dostoyevsky in his *Notes from the Underground* which inspired Nietzsche and Girard.

26 This is a hermeneutic expertly expounded in Father Alison's writings, most notably in his PhD dissertation, *The Joy of being Wrong, Original Sin Through Easter Eyes*. It accords with the Johannine witness, particularly John 9 where notions of sin and judgement are turned on their head.

fragility of the values enshrined in our cultural/political communities. In this sense, Nietzsche's provocation becomes an iconoclastic and ascetic gesture, aimed at humbling those in authority (in Nietzsche's case—the Wilhelmine regime). Consequently, Nietzsche's war rhetoric serves his Dionysian and iconoclastic purpose: to elicit the greatest possible reaction from those who proclaim, "Peace! Peace!" where there is no peace. In effect, insists Poettcker, 'Nietzsche unmasks the human impulse to appropriate God—to assign God a place within a sacrificial order rather than allowing God to remain sovereign and to allow the Holy Spirit to blow where he will. [...] "A God that one can appropriate is a god that destroys"'.[27]

Nietzsche's philosophy thus strips Christians of the moralised and metaphysicised idol they have made of God—and thereby enables a non-atheistic Christianity.[28] In fact, Nietzsche's philosophy and his madness, claims Jean-Luc Marion,[29] point to an important realization shared by all mystics— that one cannot grant *being* or existence to God. One can only collapse into and lose oneself in the very God whose *yes* creates a world.[30] And *that,* if it is true, in turn must cast Nietzsche's project in a whole new light. Suddenly what seems like madness (*Wahnsinn*) becomes in Poettcker's eyes an ascetic gesture, such that where *"ascesis"* by its very nature appears excessive, it is only to those who are *not* confronted with the kinds of trials and temptations that the ascetic faces who end up misnaming it. And so too, the *'will to power'*, which appears to be a 'quest for self-engineered adversity' (Girard sees it this way), actually becomes, not wanton self-destruction (suggested by Professor Fornari),[31] but something radically different: a purification and the quest for a higher *life.*[32] This ascetic stance attributed to Nietzsche, as Poettcker defines it, is necessary for understanding Nietzsche's project.

This brings us to a two-part concluding observation concerning research-led learning, and the wonder of it: Research-led learning is always overshadowed

---

27 Poettcker citing Girard, *Battling to the End*.
28 That is to say, a Christianity with integrity that is not obligated to go the way of God denial. For Nietzsche that kind of God must be grounded (incarnationally) in this world—otherwise it is a false God of our fantasies and imaginings, rather than the real God in a real world. Nietzsche loves to play with the intrinsically absurd notion that the real God could ever die or be killed. This escapes many commentators who interpret Nietzsche's rhetoric at face value.
29 Marion, *The Idol and Distance*, 65.
30 Marion, *The Idol and Distance*, 55.
31 Fornari, *A God Torn to Pieces*, xvi.
32 Notice Poettcker's emphasis on 'life', highlighting that Nietzsche's project is fundamentally a life affirming project, *not a* death dealing one; Poettcker, 'Beyond Nietzsche's War Rhetoric', 9.

by subjectivity and it can only be truly pursued within an intellectual community that holds itself to account.

Right at the beginning, in the Preface to the *Genealogy of Morals,* Nietzsche makes this stunning observation:

> We remain strange to ourselves out of necessity, we do not understand ourselves, we must confusedly mistake who we are, the motto 'everyone is furthest from himself' applies to us for ever,—we are not 'knowers' when it comes to ourselves.[33]

The darkness thus lies not only in our culture, but also within ourselves—a darkness as deep as the mystery of God, but unlike that mystery, fraught with a willful ignorance against which the research-led adventurer must constantly be alert:

> We are unknown to ourselves, we knowers: and with good reason. We have never looked for ourselves,—so how are we ever supposed to find ourselves? How right is the saying: 'Where your treasure is, there will your heart be also'; our treasure is where the hives of our knowledge are. As born winged-insects and intellectual honey-gatherers we are constantly making for them, concerned at heart with only one thing—to 'bring something home'. As far as the rest of life is concerned, the so-called 'experiences',—who of us ever has enough seriousness for them? or enough time? I fear we have never really been 'with it' in such matters: our heart is simply not in it—and not even our ear![34]

It is in this arena—the *agon*, the Greek notion of the contest—that the researcher is called to compete: one of undergoing, overcoming and of endless becoming. If one is successful here, in the undergoing and the overcoming, one achieves the status of *Übermensch*[35] one who manages to transcend the adversities along the way. But the undergoing and the overcoming are not ends within themselves. It is in the 'becoming', the on-going struggle to discover oneself, to be true to oneself and the reality in which we are immersed, that more truly defines our work as research-led learners.

---

33   Nietzsche, 'Preface', 1.
34   Nietzsche, 'Preface', 1.
35   This term has been so misused and misunderstood. It has nothing to do with the Nazi notion of the superior Aryan. It is a term which Nietzsche uses to designate someone who has 'overcome' adversity, and who strives beyond even that designation to a more superior level of 'becoming'.

Nietzsche, in his ceaseless quest for a paradigm that addresses how we deal with the uncompromising rawness of life with its struggle for survival, and how we cope with our fragile and vulnerable selves (so often pulled this way and that by forces tending in opposite directions), seems to have found in the *agon* a model that not only speaks to us as individuals, but also points to how whole communities can find strength and wholeness through struggle and healthy competition. Indeed, in the *agon* he sees the individual and the community working as one in such a manner that 'individual victories and distinction [strengthen] the bonds between a person and his community rather than further separating him from it'. Also, the *agon* features prominently in Nietzsche's notion of self-overcoming. Fundamentally, the *agon* is based on three assumptions:[36]

> firstly, that human existence is characterized by interminable struggle;
> secondly, that human beings seek meaning in the struggle of existence;
> and thirdly, that such a struggle is 'tolerable, even potentially estimable and affirmable, insofar as it is meaningful'.

The benefits that derive from these particular kinds of contests in their various forms (be they physical, spiritual, religious intellectual) are overwhelmingly positive and include:

- The test of specific qualities such as speed, endurance, creativity, mastery etc.
- The goal of playing well—not necessarily winning.
- The productivity of the outcome: a contest that 'regulates without subjugating the interests of the individual'.
- The exhibition of 'abundance, maximizing value rather the conservation of finite resources'.
- 'A basic orientation toward gratitude, rather than guilt'.
- The re-channeling of 'aggression' into 'productive goals'.
- The acknowledgement that an individual's success reflects the whole community—a case in point being the victory of Hagesidamos, the boys' boxing victor in 476 BCE.

---

[36] The entire section to follow draws heavily on Acampora, *Contesting Nietzsche*, a most helpful introduction to the whole notion of the *agon*, especially pp. 2, 3, 19, 20, 23–34, 38, 201, 202.

Christa Davis Acampora highlights the fact that:

> Hagesidamos's accomplishment is inextricably bound to those who supported and trained him, those who gave him the opportunity to compete for his *polis*, those who founded the games and the poet himself [Pindar] who preserves the victory for others to remember.

Thus, Nietzsche sees the *agon's* great potential for what he later described as the 'revaluation of values', and in its physical forms (like athletics and boxing), as an antidote, possibly even 'a kind of redemption' of war. There is also a sense in which, by tapping into past successes and the reasons for them, human beings are better able to contend with the present, and so effectively prepare for the future. This contesting model, alongside the tragic vision which enabled the Greeks to confront the reality of their deepest fears by reconciling the wild forces of life with the highest aspirations of civilized society, formed the foundation of Nietzsche's insights concerning how we might overcome *ressentiment* and nihilism—two attitudes which if left unchecked, he believed, would lead to a slow decline, followed by decadence and an eventual fall. Niedesh Lawtoo in his final summation observes that, 'Nietzsche ... is warning his posthumous readers that we along with him, may still be implicated in that strange world of phantoms he so deftly dissects, in an age Nietzsche called "the century of the masses" or "the century of enthusiasm"'.[37]

To conclude, when taken together, our two adventurers, Nietzsche and Girard, can refocus the true nature of research-led learning, in an approach following Sarah Bachelard, which serves both academic and existential purposes.[38]

The key to understanding this kind of moral imagination, according to Bachelard, is to visualise a horizon that you are walking towards and that the horizon, while still a mystery yet closed, is opening itself to you as you approach it without preconceptions. You walk humbly, vulnerably towards it and the horizon unveils its mystery—more jaggedly and incrementally, than tidily—for there are no formulas here. So, the start of the journey of discovery is played out in vulnerability and self-confessed ignorance as the imagination allows itself, in Socratic style, to be questioned. Under the insistence of probing questions, from under/within this voluntary ignorance, gradually the truth emerges, the reality

---

37 Lawtoo, *The Phantom of the Ego*, 27–28, and p. 83, reflecting on Nietzsche's expression 'Jahrhundert der Schwärmerei' (Nietzsche, *Daybreak*, "Preface"; 3).
38 Bachelard, *Resurrection and Moral Imagination*.

of the thing observed and wondered about—be it the inscrutability of a situation, an issue, a person or a problem. Indeed, this is the function of the probing question formation—not just to engender bewilderment (*aporia*), but to help align the questioner with reality, truth, goodness, love and justice as they choose to see things through the lens of compassion and unconditional love.

This is more than just a subjective personal truth or reality, which can easily turn out to be a self-delusion or a delusion. No, this is truth, a reality, a goodness which is discoverable to all who are attuned to it. Bachelard affirms that such 'truthfulness' and 'reality' are in fact the lynchpins of the transcendental moral responsive approach, and that they are experiential (lived out), not mere abstractions or theoretical principles. The stakes, moreover, are high: what is at issue is the possibility that one's life might be lived in illusion, that one might fail to be properly oriented towards the real. When that is the case, then moral perception or vision is necessarily distorted, and deep responsiveness to the reality of other people is impossible. Here Bachelard makes the point that if we are not true to ourselves, to life, if we fail to live in the real world as opposed to living in a world of our own making, then the chances of discovering people as they truly are is nigh on impossible. We will see people through a distorted lens—which approximates, perhaps, to what Jesus meant when he said that we can't really take out the splinter from another's eye, if our own is occluded by a timber pole of self-delusion, within which we are then constrained to live. And, finally, the moral transcendent approach invites us to see through the lens of a strong love in the guise of compassion and goodness, which, while never shirking responsibility for the consequences of its own or another's actions, assesses the individual as being of much greater value than his or her own worst actions.

As we have seen, both Friedrich Nietzsche and René Girard, our research led adventurers, bring to their journey a new way of reading our religious and cultural history. For Nietzsche it is the instrumentality of the tuning fork which strikes at the our most precious idols, be they religious, be they our most cherished assumptions about values. For Girard, his Mimetic and scapegoat theory provokes deep self-reflection, exposing the lie of the victors and bringing to light the truth of the innocent victim. And for both that journey is accompanied by a very deep, if provocative spiritual commitment that embraces the beauty and the terror, the joy and the sadness of life.

Near the end of his active intellectual life before his mental collapse, Nietzsche made a heartfelt observation, generated by the deep gratefulness that the agonistic lens accorded him. Despite his lonely, unrecognized life, accompanied by intense physical and mental suffering, he was still able to write in *Ecce Homo* that:

> On this perfect day, when everything is ripening and not only the grape turns brown, the eye of the sun just fell upon my life: I looked forward, I looked backward, and never saw so many good things at once.[39]

And on his own intellectual journey, Girard also allowed himself to be infused with wonder:

> I saw myself as already dead, and all of a sudden, I was resurrected. The most miraculous part for me was that my intellectual and spiritual conviction coincided exactly with the period prescribed by the Church for the penitence of sinners, with three days of grace left over—the most important of all—perhaps to allow me to reconcile with the Church in peace before Easter.[40]

As for my own travail, I constantly stop at the feet of the 13th century Suffi mystic poet, Jelaluddin Rumi, in the field of an imagination that fills me with a profound humility, holy ground:[41]

> Out beyond ideas of wrongdoing and right doing,
> there is a field. I'll meet you there.
> When the soul lies down in that grass,
> the world is too full to talk about.
> Ideas, language, even the phrase "each other"
> doesn't make any sense.

And this invitation to risk and wonder from Christopher Logue:[42]

> 'Come to the edge',
> He said. They Said,
> 'We are afraid'.
> 'Come to the edge',
> He said. They came.
> He pushed them, and
> they flew.

---

39 Cited by Acampora in *Contesting Nietzsche*, xi.
40 Girard, "Quand ces choses commenceront", 190–194, Cited by Palaver, *René Girard's Mimetic Theory*, 7.
41 Rumi, *The Illuminated Rumi*.
42 Logue, *New Numbers*, 65–66.

Bibliography

Acampora, Christa Davis. *Contesting Nietzsche* (Chicago: University of Chicago Press, 2013).

Alison, James. *Jesus the Forgiving Victim, Listening for the Unheard* (Glenview, Il.: Doers Publishing, 2013).

Alison, James. *The Joy of being Wrong, Original Sin Through Easter Eyes* (New York: Cross Road, 1998).

Bachelard, Sarah. *Resurrection and Moral Imagination* (London: Ashgate, 2014; Abingdon: Routledge, 2016).

Deleuze, Gilles. *Nietzsche and Philosophy* (Hugh Tomlinson, trans.; London: Athlone Press, 1983).

Fornari, Giuseppi. *A God Torn to Pieces. The Nietzsche Case* (Studies in Violence, Mimesis, and Culture; K. Buck, transl.; East Lansing, MI.: Michigan State University Press, 2013).

Girard, Rene. *Battling to the End. Conversations with Benoit Chantre* (M. Baker, transl.; East Lansing, MI: Michigan State University Press, 2010 [French: 2007]).

Girard, Rene. *"Quand ces choses commenceront"… Entretiens avec Michel Treguer* (Paris: Arléa, 1994).

Huskinson, Lucy. *An Introduction to Nietzsche* (Grand Rapids: Baker Academic, 2009).

Kaufmann, Walter. *Nietzsche, Philosopher, Psychologist, Antichrist* (Princeton and Oxford: Princeton University Press, 2013 [1950, 1968, 1974]).

Kee, Alistair. *Nietzsche Against The Crucified* (London: SCM, 1999)

Kirwan, Michael. *Girard and Theology* (Edinburgh: T.&T. Clark, 2009).

KSB = Nietzsche, F. Sämtliche Briefe: Kritische Studienausgabe (G. Colli & M. Montinari, eds.; 15 vols.; Berlin & New York/Munich: Walter de Gruyter/Deutscher Taschen-buch Verlag, 1967–1977, 1988).

Lawtoo, Nidesh. *The Phantom of the Ego, Modernism and the Mimetic Unconscious* (East Lansing: Michigan State University Press, 2013).

Lewis, C.S. *Surprised by Joy* (London: Harper Collins, 2012 [Fontana, 1964]).

Lippmann, W. *The Essential Lippmann: A Political Philosophy for Liberal Democracy* (New York: Random House, 1963).

Logue, Christopher. *New Numbers* (London: Jonathan Cape, 1969).

Marion, Jean-Luc. *The Idol and Distance: Five Studies* (Thomas A. Carlson, trans; Perspectives in Continental Philosophy; New York: Fordham University Press, 2001).

Nietzsche, F. *The Antichrist* (H.L. Mencken, transl. & ed.; Pantianos Classics, 2016 [1888]).

Nietzsche, F. *Ecce Homo: How To Become What You Are* (D. Large, transl.; Oxford's World Classics; Oxford: Oxford University Press, 2009 [1908]).

Nietzsche, F. *The Birth of Tragedy: Out of the Spirit of Music* (M. Tanner, ed.; S. Whiteside, transl.;

Harmondsworth: Penguin Classics, 1994 [1872]).

Nietzsche, F. 'Preface', *The Genealogy of Morals* (R. Guess & Q. Skinner, eds.; Cambridge Texts in the History of Political Thought; Cambridge: Cambridge University Press, 2017 [1887]).

Nietzsche, F. *Daybreak. Thoughts on the Prejudices of Morality* (Cambridge Texts in the History of Philosophy; Cambridge: Cambridge University Press, 1997 [1881]).

Nietzsche, F. *Sämtliche Briefe: Kritische Studienausgabe* (G. Colli & M. Montinari, eds.; 15 vols.; Berlin & New York/Munich: Walter de Gruyter/Deutscher Taschen-buch Verlag, 1967–1977, 1988).

Palaver, Wolfgang. *René Girard's Mimetic Theory* (Gabriel Borrud, transl.; East Lansing: Michigan State University Press, 2013).

Poettcker, Grant. 'Beyond Nietzsche's War Rhetoric: Ascesis, Sacrifice, and the Recovery of Health', Colloquium on Violence and Religion, 23 July 2014, Freising, Germany. Unpublished paper, used by permission.

Strong, Tracy B. (ed.) 'Introduction', *Friedrich Nietzche* (The International Library of Essays in the History of Social and Political Thought; London: Routledge, 2009), xi–xxxiii.

Williams, Rowan. 'Foreword', M. Kirwan & S. T. Hidden (eds.), *Mimesis and Atonement, René Girard and the Doctrine of Salvation* (London: Bloomsbury Academic, 2017), xiii–xv.

Zachhuber, J. master class held at St Mark's Theological College, Charles Sturt University, Canberra, on 2nd August, 2016.

Nikolai Blaskow
Bangor University, UK/Charles Sturt University, Canberra
nikolai@nikolaiblaskow.com

6 | 'UNITE THE PAIR SO LONG DISJOINED, KNOWLEDGE AND VITAL PIETY'

WHAT IS THE ROLE OF RESEARCH IN THIS PROCESS?

Abstract

One of the greatest challenges facing theological education is to keep it theologically grounded, rather than being taken captive by the prevailing cultural fads and fashions. Theological faculties need to be instrumental in shaping the life of the church for the future by helping to identify the true nature of the challenges being faced and offering authentic Christian responses. Quality teaching is essential if we are to help produce committed and reflective practitioners who will be ministers, educators and other leaders for the future. Working within a Wesleyan framework, this paper seeks to explore how research-led practical theology challenges us to re-think our current Christian values and practices in the light of the rich heritage of the tradition, our anticipated future in Christ, and the challenges of the present day. Christian theology requires embodiment in the life of the church and the community and the role of research in understanding the interrelationship of 'knowledge' and 'vital piety' is critical if we are to guide students in the task of implementing effective ministry in today's multicultural and multi-faith environment.

Introduction

The church in Australia (along with most Western nations) is faced with many challenges raised by a postmodern, post-Christian, multi-faith, and multicultural society. In such a setting, preparing people for effective ministry (ordained or lay) is an increasingly difficult task because the old assumptions and their associated educational programs are no longer perceived as adequate. Theological faculties need to be instrumental in shaping the life of the church, for both the present day and the future, by helping to identify the true nature of the problems being faced and offering authentic Christian responses. Quality teaching is essential if we are to help produce committed and reflective practitioners who will be the ministers and educators for the future.

This essay is particularly focused on the evangelical Wesleyan churches which are represented in Australia by groups like the Salvation Army, The Wesleyan Methodist Church, and the Church of the Nazarene.[1] Working within a Wesleyan framework, it seeks to explore how research-led practical theology challenges us to re-think our current Christian educational practices in the light of the rich heritage of the tradition. It begins by examining the current context faced by evangelical, pietistic churches in the Wesleyan tradition, before examining the educational framework inherited from John Wesley, particularly the link between knowledge and vital piety. It then moves on to a brief examination of the place of Christian scholarship within higher education and concludes with the role of research in developing transformative practice.

The Current Context and the Challenges We Face

Many evangelical Wesleyan denominations have a strong link with North America, and have been heavily influenced by the education framework of the wider evangelical church in the USA. Octavio Esqueda reminds us that within North American culture (and I believe it would apply equally well to the

---

1 From their websites, the Salvation Army is the largest of the exclusively Wesleyan groups with approximately 52,000 members. It has been in Australia since the late 19th century. The other two groups are much smaller, and both were officially established here just after World War II. The Wesleyan Methodists have less than 3000 full members and the Church of the Nazarene less than 1000 full members. All three Wesleyan groups are part of a global denomination, with much larger total memberships. While the Uniting Church has Methodist roots, it has both Presbyterian and Congregational roots as well.

Australian context) there is a tendency to reduce the Christian faith to mainly religious activities and practices. There is often an assumption that faith and academics are to be kept apart as they represent different spheres of knowledge and practice. Western societies still tend to emphasise individualism as a core value, reducing all religions to a personal, private, and individual faith. The danger here is that the Christian framework is seen to have little direct relationship to learning or to higher education in general.[2] Mark Noll's evaluation of the American evangelical scene in 1994 was that it was not possible to be an evangelical and an intellectual in the USA.[3] Os Guiness believes that evangelicals in the USA have been anti-intellectual since the 1820s and 1830s.[4] In the opinion of Mark Noll, while evangelicals sponsor many seminaries and colleges (which are often now universities), he maintains that they do not maintain a single research university.[5] In evangelical Wesleyan churches, the education focus is often narrowly defined as producing competent practitioners as quickly as possible. Competency is then defined as the ability to perform certain tasks for which the students were trained in a relatively stable environment. Likewise, a practitioner can be understood as one who prioritises doing over being, and methods, techniques, actions, over reflection. Theological education is largely seen in vocational terms as the communication of data and the practices necessary to meet the immediate need. It is little more than providing the student with a toolkit of methods and techniques that enables him or her to be deployed in the minimum time with minimal disruption to personal and congregational life.[6]

These programs of study are usually focused on an activist, populist, pragmatic, and utilitarian ethos, frequently substituting inspiration and zeal for critical analysis and serious reflection.[7] Noll believes that, while 'Evangelicals spend enormous sums on higher education […] the diffusion of resources among hundreds of colleges and seminaries means that almost none can begin to afford a research faculty, theological or otherwise'.[8] In his later (2011) book, he still sees the barriers to productive thinking as substantial in the pietistic and evangelical world. The strong points of evangelicalism (the immediacy of

---

2   Esqueda, 'Biblical Worldview,' 91–92.
3   Noll, *Scandal*, ix. He did not greatly revise this view in his sequel, *Life of the Mind*.
4   Guiness, 'Persuasion for the New World', 15 quoted in Noll, *Scandal*, 23. See also 23–27, particularly his comments on the work of Charles Malik.
5   Noll, *Scandal*, 3. Several Methodist institutions would dispute this claim—see below.
6   McEwan, 'Quality Theological Education'.
7   Noll, *Scandal*, 12
8   Noll, *Scandal*, 16.

conversion, social welfare and populism) also 'pose problems for intellectual life, since serious thinking takes a lot of time, must honor the contributions of past generations, and often relies on the special insights of intellectual elites'.[9] However, in recent years more Christian institutions have 'begun to promote the academic life as a legitimate Christian vocation; more and more are coming to understand that there can be no good teaching without good scholarship'.[10]

Angela Brew is one of many who note the rapid rate of changes in society and the inability to absorb them, let alone respond effectively to them. For example, media can now be accessed on demand rather than at scheduled times decided by others. Such knowledge often comes to us via the internet in sound bites that are chaotic and unplanned, increasing 'the uncertainty and ambiguity of living in a fearful, perplexing and pluralistic world'.[11] Johannes van der Ven sees a range of challenges posed by this increasing complexity in society for the church and its educational institutions. He particularly notes the rapid changes in our culture, the pressure of secularisation, increasing theological pluralism, the impact of postmodernity, and the rapid shifts in education policy.[12] Christian higher education, like Christian ministry itself, is not exempt from the winds of change blowing through our society. It does not exist in some pure, disinterested, ideal form that allows for value-free judgements to be made about the best way to accomplish our goals in the current environment. The task confronting Christian education is to provide the necessary tools for the minister to address and cope with the intricacy of presenting issues in the society, the church and the individual.[13] In his book on the ideal seminary, Carnegie Calian illustrates this through a modified quote from Albert Einstein: 'We are unable to *solve* the problems we have created with the *same* theologizing and church (and seminary) practices that have created them'.[14] In this situation, higher education needs to become more focused on preparing students for our complex and challenging world so that they can offer solutions to a range of currently unimagined and unforeseen problems.[15] In such a multifaceted and uncertain environment, students will need to have developed the skills of critical analysis, enabling them

---

9 Noll, *Life of the Mind*, 152.
10 Noll, *Life of the Mind*, 155.
11 Brew, 'Imperatives and Challenges', 139–40.
12 van der Ven, *Education*, 1–9.
13 van der Ven, *Education*, 45.
14 Calian, *The Ideal Seminary*, Frontispiece (emphasis mine).
15 Brew, 'Imperatives and Challenges', 140.

to judiciously evaluate knowledge and make sound decisions in the light of good evidence.[16] Barbara Zamorski quotes an unnamed university lecturer:

> Universities are concerned with the creation of knowledge and the dissemination of knowledge [...] we all want to develop a better world and a better world is a world of questions and development. And research is a strong part of it [...] it is our moral and even ethical obligation to the younger generation to create a generation that will continue to ask questions and do research and develop, rather than be content with themselves, wherever they are.[17]

This is why the integration of research and teaching is so important, though it is much easier to talk about than to effectively implement.[18] If all of creation comes under God's governorship, then every Christian is involved in integrating faith, learning, and practice.[19] Les Ball believes,

> it is imperative that the academy equip its learners to process analytically and to appropriate in deeply personal ways the information and ideas that they encounter [...] theological delivery needs to embrace creatively the opportunities for deep personal learning presented by the world in which it so strategically exists.[20]

This is reinforced by Noll:

> If what we claim about Jesus Christ is true, then evangelicals should be among the most active, most serious, and most open-minded advocates of general human learning. Evangelical hesitation about scholarship in general or about pursuing learning wholeheartedly is, in other words, antithetical to the Christ-centered basis of the evangelical mind.[21]

In Paul Gould's opinion, the Christian scholar is called to think biblically about how to connect research, teaching, and service in the college or university to the

---

16 Brew, 'Imperatives and Challenges', 141.
17 Zamorski, 'Research-led Teaching and Learning', 421.
18 See, for example, Schapper and Mayson, 'Research-led teaching', 641–651; Malcolm, 'A critical evaluation', 289–301; Brew, 'Teaching and Research', 3–18.
19 Esqueda, 'Biblical Worldview', 94.
20 Ball, 'Where are we Going', 20.
21 Noll, *Life of the Mind*, x.

mission of God in all its dimensions.²² This leads him to uphold a 'transformationist vision (not strategy) as the likely outcome of faithfulness to Christ within the academy'.²³

Knowledge and Vital Piety in the Wesleyan Tradition

Mark Noll is confident that 'the Christian faith contains all the resources, and more, required for full-scale intellectual engagement', and this is not incompatible with Christian belief and practice.²⁴ This approach was clearly demonstrated in the ministry of both John and Charles Wesley, the founders of Methodism in the Eighteenth Century.

> Wesley was deeply convinced that the making of Christians was a process which required devoted and diligent teaching. While never neglecting nor disparaging the importance of preaching, worship and sacraments, and Christian disciplines, Wesley recognized that persons of all ages had to be taught what Christians believe and how Christians live. Such teaching was to be both a cognitive process of didactic learning and a formative process of spiritual nurturing.²⁵

This is captured by the words of Charles Wesley's hymn:

> Unite the pair so long disjoined,
> Knowledge and vital piety:
> Learning and holiness combined,
> And truth and love, let all men see
> In those whom up to thee we give,
> Thine, wholly thine, to die and live.²⁶

Though this was written for children at the opening of the enlarged Kingswood School on 24 June 1748, it has a much wider application. There is a clear link between knowledge and vital piety, learning and holiness, truth and love. As Richard Heitzenrater reminds us, knowledge is not purely an intellectual

---

22 Gould, 'Academic Disciplines', 168.
23 Gould, 'Academic Disciplines', 172.
24 Noll, *The Life of the Mind*, 155.
25 Felton, 'John Wesley and the Teaching Ministry', 92.
26 Wesley, *Works* 7, 644.

attribute but a channel of self-understanding, crucial for salvation. Vital piety is not only a devotional stance based on the love of God but also a social outreach exemplified by love for the neighbour.[27] Michael Austin writes that, 'A Christian academic, who is seeking to bring about shalom in God's creation, will not only engage in implicit and explicit Christian scholarship, but will also seek to exemplify the fruits of the Spirit and a robust Christian character as he loves others in his sphere of influence, especially those who are unloved or appear to be unlovable'.[28] Gayle Felton writes that John Wesley 'viewed education as a means of grace—as an instrument through which the Holy Spirit worked. Much of the ministry of the early Methodist movement was ministry of teaching'.[29] He reaffirmed the ancient injunction that 'Christians are made, not born'. Salvation was 'a lifelong process during which intentional training and nurture in the faith were essential at all ages and stages of spiritual growth'.[30] It was to be a holistic approach to the transformation of people and society.[31] The focus is on character restored by grace, not knowledge for its own sake or for vanity. On the other hand, error and ignorance are not virtues and the later anti-academic stance of those evangelical Protestant churches influenced by pietism is clearly not supported here. The focus is on wisdom, knowledge and truth that are substantial, real, to be lived and not simply intellectually grasped. It is to link with our stewardship of the earth, making use of the knowledge gained in all areas of human life to serve God. It was to be a holistic approach to the transformation of people and society.[32] The focus is on character restored by grace, not knowledge for its own sake or to impress others. According to Felton,

> Wesley must be credited with substantial contributions to English education in general and with helping to foster the later development of universal education in the nation. He understood the potential for education to function as an instrument of social reform and sought to use it for the benefit of the disadvantaged socioeconomic classes.[33]

---

27 Heitzenrater, in Bunge, *The Child*, 289–90. See also Blevins and Sierra, 'Wesleyan Theological Education', 2.
28 Austin, 'Scholarship and Character', 5.
29 Felton, 'Wesley and the Teaching Ministry', 95.
30 Felton, 'Wesley and the Teaching Ministry', 104.
31 Maddix, 'Unite the Pair,' 56.
32 Maddix, 'Unite the Pair', 56.
33 Felton, 'Wesley and the Teaching Ministry', 92–93.

Sam Wells told the students at Duke University:

> "Don't just discover truth, deepen compassion". The extensive time and attention given to the activity of research are at their best a gesture of love. The aspiration to the eternal union of knowledge and religion is the union of knowledge and love. Religion means nothing if it doesn't originate and issue in love. The prayer of true learners should be that their hearts expand with compassion at the same rate as their heads expand with knowledge.[34]

The Wesleyan Education Framework

The tension between knowledge and piety 'signals the classic struggle in graduate theological education: the paideia of Athenian education, with an emphasis on forming character, and the specialization of Berlin University, elevating research as critical study'.[35] Though many of the early Methodists were unschooled in a formal sense, John Wesley knew that they must have an education if they were to be effective. He believed that the fruits of his ministry had to be united with instruction if results were to be permanent.[36] Accordingly, Wesley built the provision of education into the very fabric of Methodism. In fact, 'the entire structure of Methodism' reveals 'a remarkable drive to educate his people in the faith, to identify the heart of the Christian gospel, to teach the faith'.[37] The extensive publication program which he himself undertook was directed to the end of promoting 'reason, knowledge, and wisdom in general' among his followers, as well as at instructing them in Christian doctrine and in the discipline of Christian living. Wesley's conviction was plain: 'Reading Christians will be knowing Christians'.[38] He wrote to George Holder: 'It cannot be that

---

34 Wells, 'Eruditio et Religio', 3.
35 Blevins and Sierra, 'Wesleyan Theological Education', 2, drawing their central idea from Kelsey, *Between Athens and Berlin*.
36 Towns, 'John Wesley', 321. See also Felton, 'Wesley', 93–94; Richey, *University and Church*, 3.
37 Richey, *University and Church*, 3.
38 Wesley, Letters (Telford) VI, 201. Wesley's publishing program was extensive and included not only his own sermons, tracts, treatises, *Journal,* and with brother Charles, books of hymns, but also the fifty-volume *Christian Library*, the *Concise Ecclesiastical History,* the *Concise History of England,* the *Survey of the Wisdom of God in the Creation: Or, A Compendium of Natural Philosophy,* grammars of English, French, Latin, Greek, and Hebrew, an English *Dictionary,* his *Compendium of Logic,* and, in his later years, the *Arminian Magazine*.

the people should grow in grace unless they give themselves to reading. A reading people will always be a knowing people'.[39] The advice to his preachers on this point could be very blunt. For example, he wrote to John Tremblath:

> What has exceedingly hurt you in time past, nay, and I fear to this day, is want of reading. I scarce ever knew a preacher read so little. And perhaps by neglecting it you have lost the taste for it. Hence your talent in preaching does not increase. It is just the same as it was seven years ago. It is lively, but not deep; there is little variety; there is no compass of thought. Reading only can supply this, with meditation and daily prayer. You wrong yourself greatly by omitting this. You can never be a deep preacher without it any more than a thorough Christian [...] It is for your life; there is no other way; else you will be a trifler all your days, and a pretty, superficial preacher.[40]

In *The Large Minutes*, the basic disciplinary plan of Methodism during Wesley's lifetime, he admonished all the preachers in the same vein: 'Read the most useful books, and that regularly and constantly. Steadily spend all the morning in this employ, or, at least, five hours in four-and-twenty'. And if they said they had no taste for it, his advice was uncompromising: 'Contract a taste for it by use, or return to your trade'.[41] If they objected that they had no money to buy the books, Wesley wrote, 'I will give each of you, as fast as you will read them, books to the value of five pounds. And I desire the Assistants would take care that all the large societies provide our Works, or at least the Notes, for the use of the Preachers'.[42] This was a not inconsiderable sum in the Eighteenth Century and it highlights just how much he valued a rigorous program of education for effective ministry. The curriculum which he outlined for the Kingswood School and the course of study which he advocated for all ministers in his 'Address to the Clergy' are both extensive and intensive.[43]

> Ought not a Minister to have, **First, a good understanding, a clear apprehension, a sound judgment, and a capacity of reasoning with some closeness?** [emphasis his] Is not this necessary in an high degree for the work of the ministry? Otherwise, how will he be able

---

39 Wesley, *Letters* (Telford) VIII, 247.
40 Wesley, *Letters* (Telford) IV, 102.
41 Wesley, *Works* (Jackson) VIII, 315.
42 Wesley, *Works* (Jackson) VIII, 315.
43 See Wesley, *Works* (Jackson) XIII, 283–9; *Works* (Jackson) X, 480–500.

to understand the various states of those under his care; or to steer them through a thousand difficulties and dangers, to the haven where they would be?[44]

While this is not formal higher education or academic research, it did underscore the importance of gaining a sound knowledge of ministry, Scriptures, original languages, secular history, the sciences, natural philosophy, geometry, the Fathers, the world and its people (maxims, tempers, manners, in real life), as well as character development. None of this could be attained without considerable effort.[45] Russell Ritchie notes how the USA Methodist General Conference was faithful to Wesley in mandating the establishment of schools, literary institutions and colleges in 1820 and 1824. As the century progressed, Methodism also founded several key research universities: Boston, Northwestern, Vanderbilt, Duke, Southern California, Emory, and Syracuse. Nearly all the theological schools were placed in a university context and a chapel was placed at its heart.[46] Ritchie reminds us that we 'need to be prepared to live and minister faithfully in an ideologically and religiously diverse world'.[47] This requires that 'the theological enterprise needs to stay engaged with the worlds of knowledge and of education as a whole and that candidates should bring a breadth and wealth of wisdom and experience into ministry'.[48]

The Role of Research in Developing Transformative Practice

Angela Brew notes how some think that research is the 'creation or discovery of a body of knowledge which is perceived as detached or separated off from the people who developed it'.[49] This reduces it to a quantifiable reality that can be measured. The other way to view knowledge is as a product of interpretation

---

44 Wesley, *Works* (Jackson) X, 482. The members of the Societies and his personal correspondents were given very similar advice. See, for example, *Letters* (Telford) IV, 272; Letters (Telford) VI, 125–26, 129–30; *Letters* (Telford) VII:78, 81–83, 237; *Letters* (Telford) VIII, 247.
45 Wesley, *Works* (Jackson) X, 483-86.
46 Richey, *University and Church*, 1–11. Richey sees the United Methodists alone in the US facing the challenge of relating to a quality research university among the major Protestant denominations (who prefer to use the college model).
47 Richey, *Formation*, 95.
48 Richey, *Formation*, 94–95.
49 Brew, 'Teaching', 9.

and negotiation that is shaped by its cultural traditions and current context.[50] Theological research in today's world would seem to be more appropriately placed in the second category, while classroom teaching often reflects the first category of 'information transmission'.[51] Looking at the practicalities, Brew is sceptical about the continuing usefulness of the concept of a narrow academic discipline, preferring the idea of academic communities of practice. In such a community, 'students, academics, professionals and indeed anyone else who shares this site of practice, are responsible for the maintenance of the community of practice for inducting newcomers into it, for carrying on the tradition of the past and carrying the community forward to the future'.[52] In this model, knowledge is more likely to be a process of construction, where 'research and teaching are both viewed as activities where individuals and groups negotiate meanings, building knowledge within a social context'.[53] The challenge is to help the community cope with uncertainty and super-complexity in a pluralistic world, as well as being 'ready and able to change (world) views in the light of new information. We know that this is what research is essentially about'.[54]

> This means seeing problems as discrete but interconnected, developing the strategies, techniques, tools, knowledge and experience needed to solve unforeseen problems [...] It means learning which appreciates the importance of context, the significance of different interpretations and revision on the basis of looking again. It also points to teaching which encourages active learning, critical creative thinkers and lifelong learning.[55]

Such a move would promote the integration of personal and professional worlds.[56] Paul Gould notes that 'Christian scholars inhabit two communities: the community of Christians and the community of scholars. Each community has its own distinctive set of beliefs, practices, and criteria for membership'.[57] In his opinion, truth is a unity and the compartmentalisation of our faith commitment and our scholarly discipline is effectively denying God's lordship over all

---

50 Brew, 'Teaching', 9.
51 Brew, 'Teaching', 10.
52 Brew, 'Teaching', 12
53 Brew, 'Teaching', 12. See also Harland, 'Teaching', 461–472.
54 Brew, 'Teaching', 14.
55 Brew, 'Teaching', 14.
56 Brew, 'Teaching', 14.
57 Gould, 'Essay on Academic Disciplines', 167.

of life. The one must surely inform the other. This implies that the scholar is called to think biblically about how to connect research, teaching, and service in the college or university to the mission of God in all its dimensions.[58] This is surely a model that fits Wesleyan churches very well, where the educational institution, the local churches, and the wider community work together, with each contributing their gifts and talents for the benefit of all. Genuine transformation cannot be legislated nor commanded. It comes from working relationships in which all the participants are valued and embraced.

Such an approach fits well with the desire to make the gospel relevant to the cultural context in which it is found. Wesleyan theology emphasises embodiment in the life of the world, but if the need for relevance is over-emphasised, the local community can become captive to the prevailing culture and become little more than the religious veneer on culture. This is a problem that has plagued the church ever since it became a world faith.[59] Esqueda's reminder is timely, that:

> interdisciplinary teaching and research is important to better interact with the complexities of God's creation. This interdisciplinary contact will facilitate faculty and students to perceive the world in a more holistic way that points back to its creator [...] more intentional collaboration with other Christian institutions globally will help faculty members to discern which aspects of their Christian faith are merely cultural rather than truly adhering to a Christian worldview. It is through this kind of interaction that cultural patterns emerge and cause individuals to think more critically about their assumptions and beliefs.[60]

In Gould's opinion, Christian scholars should pursue research that engages their academic discipline as well as engages the needs of the world, helping to meet the tangible needs of the society by transforming both the person and the community.[61] For some, the very notion of being research-led conjures up in their minds the embodiment of irrelevance. While pure research might be constrained to enlarging the frontiers of knowledge, research activity also includes scholarship directly related to teaching and practice. Such research enhances teaching in the academy, practice in the ecclesia and service in the wider community.

---

58 Gould, 'Essay on Academic Disciplines', 168.
59 Brower and McEwan, 'Future Challenges', 10.
60 Esqueda, 'Biblical Worldview', 98.
61 Gould, 'Essay', 168–72.

Research-led practical divinity is a challenge to re-think theological frameworks and how they might be utilised to develop fresh and culturally appropriate practices and expressions. This kind of teaching stimulates in students a hunger for engagement in critical theological reflection and theologically-informed mission because the lecturers themselves are so stimulated. Teaching of this calibre should produce committed and reflective practitioners who will be ministers, educators, and leaders for the future. But this will not happen unless the theological educators—those parts of the body, responsible for engaging in precisely this task—take research seriously.[62] Hemmings and Hill point out that Christian Higher Education Institutions are caught up in the tension between their church world and the established norms of higher education. In this situation, growing a sustainable research culture is a difficult task. It requires faculty and staff 'to alter their thinking about research, including the need for research to inform teaching, the relative value of research compared with teaching, what outcomes might be expected from undertaking research, and the extent to which these outcomes are prized'.[63]

Conclusion

Given the complex and rapidly changing situation facing the western church today, the need for a research-led education program has never been greater. Simply continuing operating in both education and practice as always will result in an ever-growing ineffectiveness in spiritual formation and mission, making the church even more irrelevant to the welfare of the individual and the society.

Whereas John and Charles Wesley faced challenges due to the emerging industrial revolution, present-day Australian Christians face greater change in the new technological age, with the mass migration of disparate peoples, the close interaction between different faiths, and the decline of Christian influence. The educational preparation of Christians (lay and ordained) who can effectively grapple with these complexities in current Australian society is a significant task. Consequently, the role of quality theological education that is research-led can hardly be overstated! It is surely the task of the researcher to help build strong connections between our institutions of higher learning, the local

---

62 Brower and McEwan, 'Future Challenges', 5–6. See also Hemmings and Hill, 'Challenges', 188.
63 Hemmings and Hill, 'Challenges', 185.

churches and the community. These networks must enable and encourage the interweaving of scholarship and spiritual life, providing a solid platform for developing intentional practices of formation, discernment and transformation, both personally and corporately. It is the work of such learning communities that will enable the people of God to provide authentically Christian solutions to the complex issues we face, enabling them to effectively serve the church, the community and the wider world.

Despite some pietist views that tend to denigrate scholarship,[64] John and Charles Wesley both valued and promoted an intimate link between academic scholarship and vital piety, even if subsequent generations were less sure of it. Far from regarding deep spiritual formation as incompatible with rigorous scholarship, the Wesleyan churches have a heritage within their own tradition that can be utilised to grapple effectively with the challenges faced in contemporary Australia.

Bibliography

Austin, M. 'Scholarship and Character as a Christian Academic', Evangelical Philosophy Society (2015), 1–5. www.epsociety.org/userfiles/Austin-Scholarship%20and%20Character%20as%20a%20Christian%20Academic_Edited_DCS.pdf [accessed 27 January 2017].

Blevins, D.G. and R. Sierra. 'What is Wesleyan Theological Education?' *Didache: Faithful Teaching* 6:2 (January 2007), 1-10. http://didache.nazarene.org/index.php/volume-6-2/5-gtiie-blevins-sierra/file [accessed 27 January 2017]

Ball, L. 'Where Are We Going? Questioning the Future of Learning and Teaching Theology' in Les Ball and James R. Harrison (eds.), *Learning and Teaching Theology: Some Ways Ahead* (Northcote: Morning Star, 2014), 11–20.

Brew, A. 'Teaching and Research: New relationships and their implications for inquiry-based teaching and learning in higher education', *Higher Education Research & Development* 22:1 (2003), 3–18.

Brew, A. 'Imperatives and challenges in integrating teaching and research', *Higher Education Research & Development* 29:2 (April 2010), 139–150.

Brower, K. and D.B. McEwan. 'Future Challenges in Wesleyan Theological Education', *Didache: Faithful Teaching* 6:2 (January 2007), 1-10. http://didache.nazarene.org/index.php/volume-6-2/7-gtiie-brower-mcewan/file [accessed 27 January 2017].

---

64 These are an import from a particular pietist stream that flourished in US evangelicalism in the mid-Nineteenth Century and has subsequently impacted the wider Wesleyan church.

Bunge, M.J. *The Child in Christian Thought* (Grand Rapids: Eerdmans, 2000).

Calian, C.S. *The Ideal Seminary: Pursuing Excellence in Theological Education* (Louisville: Westminster John Knox Press, 2002).

Esqueda, O.J. 'Biblical Worldview: The Christian Higher Education Foundation for Learning', *Christian Higher Education* 13:2 (2014), 91–100.

Felton, G.C. 'John Wesley and the Teaching Ministry: Ramifications for Education in the Church Today', *Religious Education* 92:1, (1997), 91–106.

Gould, P. 'An Essay on Academic Disciplines, Faithfulness, and the Christian Scholar', *Christian Higher Education* 13:3 (2014), 167–182.

Harland, T. 'Teaching to enhance research', *Higher Education Research & Development* 35:3 (2016), 461–472.

Hemmings, B. and D. Hill. 'Challenges to Christian Higher Education at a Time of Increasing Emphasis on Research', *Christian Higher Education* 13:3 (2014), 183–198.

McEwan, D.B. 'Quality Theological Education from a Wesleyan Perspective', *The Mediator* 2:2 (April 2001), 94–108.

Maddix, M.A. 'Unite the Pair so Long Disjoined: Justice and Empathy in Moral Development Theory', *Christian Education Journal* 8:1 (Spring 2011), 46–63.

Malcolm, M. 'A critical evaluation of recent progress in understanding the role of the research-teaching link in higher education', *Higher Education* 67 (2014), 289–301.

Noll, M.A. *Jesus Christ and the Life of the Mind* (Grand Rapids: Eerdmans, 2011).

Noll, M.A. *The Scandal of the Evangelical Mind* (Grand Rapids: Eerdmans, 1994).

Richey, R.E. *University and Church: Notes on the Methodist Experience* (Atlanta: Emory University, 2002).

Richey, R.E. *Formation for Ministry in American Methodism: Twenty-first Century Challenges and Two Centuries of Problem-Solving* (USA: General Board of Higher Education and Ministry, The United Methodist Church, 2014).

Schapper, J. and S.E. Mayson. 'Research-led teaching: moving from a fractured engagement to a marriage of convenience', *Higher Education Research & Development* 29:6 (2010), 641–651.

Sherlock, C. *Uncovering Theology: The Depth, Reach and Utility of Australian Theological Education* (Adelaide: ATF Press, 2009).

Towns, E.L. 'John Wesley and Religious Education', *Religious Education* 65:4 (1970), 318–328.

van der Ven, J. A. *Education for Reflective Ministry* (Louvain: Peeters Press, 1998).

Wells, S. '*Eruditio et Religio*', A Sermon preached in Duke University Chapel on 4 October 2009. http://chapel-archives.oit.duke.edu/documents/sermons/Oct4EruditioetReligio.pdf [accessed 27 January 2017].

Wesley, J. *The Bicentennial Edition of the Works of John Wesley*. 35 vols. projected, ed.-in-Chief, Frank Baker. Nashville: Abingdon Press, 1984-. vols. 7, 11, 25, and 26 of this edition originally appeared as the *Oxford Edition of the Works of John Wesley*. [Oxford: Clarendon, 1975-1983].

Wesley, J. *The Letters of the Rev. John Wesley* (8 vols., ed. John Telford; London: Epworth Press, 1931).

Wesley, J. *The Works of John Wesley* (14 vols., 3rd ed., ed. Thomas Jackson; London: Wesleyan Methodist Book Room, 1872 [Reprint, Kansas City: Beacon Hill Press of Kansas City, 1979]).

Zamorski, B. 'Research-led Teaching and Learning in Higher Education: a Case', *Teaching in Higher Education*, 7:4 (2002), 411–427.

David B. McEwan
Nazarene Theological College—Brisbane
dmcewan@ntc.edu.au

7 | RESEARCHING THE FUTURE

THE IMPLICATIONS OF ACTIVIST RESEARCH FOR THEOLOGICAL SCHOLARSHIP IN TEACHING AND LEARNING

Abstract

If we were to apply wonder and research our teaching, what might we discover? Activist research is employed as a theoretical framework to pay attention to our identity as theological (speaking of God's Kingdom) educators (wanting to impact students). Ernest Boyer's domains of scholarship are deployed to analyse the Australasian theological sector. Recent research outputs are clustered around the domain of discovery, with *ad hoc* attention to the domain of research from teaching and learning.

Four theses are proposed that attend to theological educators as activist researchers, the values of our industry (denominational) stakeholders, the research profile of the theological sector in Australasia and in relation to researching our teaching. Concrete next steps in areas of informal research, institutional feedback and researching practice are outlined. In the midst of massive social change, let us wonder together by researching our teaching practice.

Introduction

Come, let us wonder together about researching our teaching. As a noun, 'wonder' speaks to feelings of amazement and admiration, caused by something beautiful. But 'wonder' is also a verb. It speaks to actions, of curiosity and of doubt.[1] This grammatical parsing invites us to consider not only our teaching but also our research. What might research-led teaching, shaped by the researching of our teaching, look like? What are the implications, for teacher, learner, stakeholders and the theological education sector in which we all participate?

In order to address these questions, an approach full of curiosity and doubt will be taken, beginning by defining activist research and pointing to ways it attends to identity and motivation in relation to the investments of teacher and learner in theological education. Outcomes are then considered, involving a survey of research outputs in the area of theological education. The four domains of scholarship are used to analyse recent journals, sector bodies and publications in theological education. What emerges is a sector clustered around research into the domain of discovery, but ad hoc in the domain of teaching and learning. In response, four theses are suggested that apply activist research and the value of all four domains of scholarship to theological education. The essay concludes with some concrete strategies, in areas of individual, institutional, sector wide operation, that allow us to be research-led in our teaching.

Activist research in clarifying identity and motivation

The notion of researching our teaching raises some important identity questions in relation to research. What is research? Who and what can be researched? One way to examine the assumptions we bring to our researching practice is through the approach of activist research.

Activist research is defined by Helen Kara as a distinct approach in which insiders conduct research with the aim of societal transformation.[2] 'Activist' is placed as an adjective in front of the word 'research', in order to qualify and modify research practices, including the ways research is conceived and carried out.[3] Charles Hale argues that activist research is a distinct category, in contrast to research as either pure or applied.[4] As an approach, activist research does not 'replace the theoretically driven quest for understanding of basic processes with

---

1 'Wonder,' www.google.co.nz/search?q=definition+wonder&ie=utf-8&oe=utf-8&client=firefox-b&gfe_rd=cr&dcr=0&ei=clqvWYGjHMHr8Afcuotw [accessed 6 September 2017].
2 Kara, *Creative Research Methods in the Social Sciences*, 41.
3 Hale, 'What is Activist Research?', 13.
4 Hale, 'What is Activist Research?', 13-15.

"applied" problem-solving.'⁵ Rather, activist research is a third category of research. It is research that is theoretically driven yet intended to be put to use.

In using activist as an adjective placed before the word research, Hale does not presume that the researcher or the researched is an activist. Rather, he sees activist research as an invitation. It will:

> put our training and expertise in the hands of an organization, community or group [... to use] a participatory research process to study it [...] and [as a result generate...] research findings [that can be] used to understand and confront problems that I, and those who I have worked closely with, care deeply about resolving.⁶

We will return to this understanding of activist research a number of times, as we continue to wonder together about researching our teaching. What is important here is to note that activist research shapes each stage of the research process, from defining the research question, through data collection, analysis, communication and validation.

Hale articulates three theoretical assumptions in relation to activist research. Each helps us as we consider the identity issues at play when we research our teaching. First, activist research sees no contradiction between an active commitment to resolving a problem and rigorous scholarly research in relation to that problem. Second, activist research is likely to generate better research outcomes. It will enhance empirical knowledge and increase theoretical sensitivity. Third, the inevitable tensions in conducting activist research, if identified and confronted, will actually improve research outcomes.⁷ Activist research thus invites researchers to be agents of change in studying change.

Each of these assumptions is evident in an example provided by Helen Kara, in her book *Creative Research Methods in the Social Sciences*.⁸ Kara groups feminist, activist (which she calls emancipatory), decolonised and participatory research under a heading of transformative research methods. She argues that these methods seek 'to empower disadvantaged people'.⁹ By way of example

---

5   Hale, 'What is Activist Research?', 14.
6   Hale, 'What is Activist Research?', 15.
7   Hale, 'What is Activist Research?', 13.
8   Kara, *Creative Research Methods in the Social Sciences*, 41-2.
9   Kara, *Creative Research Methods in the Social Sciences*, 41. The naming of each of these as transformative is for Kara an inductive move. Each of feminist, activist, decolonised and participatory has a heading, which is then followed by a further heading 'Critiquing transformative research frameworks' in which each of the four types of research is discussed. Kara, 35-54.

she draws on the work of Diana Rose. Rose found that research done by those with no experience of electro-convulsive therapy (ECT) reached different conclusions than research conducted by researchers who had themselves experienced being mental health patients.[10] Her argument was that when researchers had some experience of mental health, either in themselves or their family, they produced research demonstrating much greater sensitivity to the negative impact of electro-convulsive therapy (ECT). Consider this example in light of Hale's three assumptions: first, the value of researchers with a set of active commitments; second, the value of such research in generated more accurate research outcomes; third, the confronting of the tension between pure research and the researchers' 'own experiences'.[11]

In summary, activist research is a distinct way of doing research. It stands in contrast to research as either pure or applied. It shapes every stage of the research process, from defining the research question, through data collection, to analysis, communication and validation. It believes that by engaging the tensions inherent in the interactions between research, researched and researcher, there is the potential to generate more accurate research outcomes.

What does this have to do with teaching theology? My argument is that activist research has significant implications when we decide to wonder together by researching our teaching practice with our students. This becomes clear when Hale's three assumptions about activist research are placed alongside researching our teaching. First, researchers have a set of active commitments. Hence the publication of a book titled *Transforming Theology*, seeking to research 'the claims made by various theological colleges that they provide a transformative educational experience'.[12] An active commitment, to transformation, is central to how theological education understands itself. Second, activist research generates more accurate research outcomes. The actions of our teaching gain theoretical sensitivity and contribute to the gathering of empirical knowledge as we examine the literature and gain feedback from our students. Third, activist research confronts the tension between pure research and the researchers' 'own experiences'.[13] In this case, it involves a willingness to consider the ethical implications inherent in the claims for transforming theology, reflect

---

10 Kara, *Creative Research Methods in the Social Sciences*, 41-2, citing Rose, et. al, 'Review of consumers' perspectives'.
11 Kara, *Creative Research Methods in the Social Sciences*, 42.
12 Ball, *Transforming Theology*, 1.
13 Kara, *Creative Research Methods in the Social Sciences*, 42.

on our actions as a source of research data and participate in the classroom as a research site.

In other words, to apply Hale's invitation to theological education, activist research will:

> put our training (*in theology*) and expertise (*in teaching*) in the hands of an organization (*the church*), community or group (*the student body*) [... to use] a participatory research process (*seeking feedback from students*) [...] and [as a result generate...] research findings... that I, and those who I have worked closely with (*learners*), care deeply about resolving (*to teach theology in ways that impact learners and transform lives and communities*).[14]

Activist research thus attends to a complex set of identity questions inherent in the theological education sector. Activist research provides a theoretical framework by which we can be research-led in our teaching. It attends to our identity as theologians (speaking of God's Kingdom) and as a teacher (wanting to impact students), the investments of students and stakeholders, and the definitional understanding of what research is.

Given this articulation of a research paradigm that enables us to wonder together, full of curiosity and doubt, about our teaching, an analysis of the theological education sector is now offered. This shifts the focus from identity questions in relation to researching our teaching to outcomes in respect to researching our teaching.

Surveying the domains of scholarship in clarifying research outputs[15]

In 1990, Ernest Boyer called for a redefinition of scholarship. This involved a shift away from a priority on the discovery of new knowledge to one that also valued integration through the synthesis of knowledge across time, disciplines or within a discipline; application or engagement, as knowledge was taken beyond the university; and, of most interest in this essay, knowledge forged in

---

14 Hale, 'What is Activist Research?', 15.
15 This research has been made possible by funds form Flinders University, allocated as part of the Vice Chancellor's Award for Excellence in Teaching, which was awarded to Steve Taylor in 2015 and conducted by Rosemary Dewerse.

the study of teaching and learning processes.[16] Thus, using Boyer, the scholarship of research can occur in four domains: discovery; integration; application; and teaching and learning.

What is important for our wondering together about researching our teaching is to consider scholarship in the theological academy in light of these four domains. Our argument is that when Boyer's domains are applied to the research outputs of the theology sector in Australasia, what becomes evident is a marked absence of Boyer's fourth and last category, the scholarship of teaching. We as theological educators are not producing research that takes teaching and learning, and our desires for activist transformation in our students, seriously.[17]

Before we examine the sparsity of scholarship of teaching in Australasia, let us reflect globally. Across the world, theological schools in geographical regions have organised themselves into associations in order to build and resource collegiality for the sake of advancing scholarship and delivering quality education to their students.[18] Few, however, profile a *scholarship of teaching* via publications or dedicated resourcing. There are three exceptions. They are the Association of Theological Schools in North America, the Academy for Evangelism in Theological Education, and the Wabash Center for Teaching and Learning. The latter is a collaboration between a college and an endowment fund for the sake of a wider audience in Theology and Religion.

The Association of Theological Schools (ATS), a key accrediting body for theology across Canada and the United States, provides opportunities for professional development alongside the publication of materials investing in progressing the understanding of and practice in teaching and learning in theological education, and the systems that support those.[19] Since 1964 their journal, *Theological Education,* has profiled and discussed issues, trends, innovations, and challenges.[20] Across the decades, a notable focus has been on the implications of increasing social diversity in regard to race, ethnicity and

---

16   Boyer, *Scholarship Reconsidered*.
17   Boyer, *Scholarship Reconsidered*, 23, 24. For a survey of the impact of Boyer's call to a scholarship of teaching in theology and religion in North America read Killen and Gallagher, 'Sketching the Contours of the Scholarship of Teaching and Learning in Theology and Religion', 107-124.
18   There is also a World Conference of Associations of Theological Institutions, see http://wocati.org/. The last edition of its biannual publication, *Ministerial Formation Bulletin*, that is available is dated November 2008.
19   For more see the Association's website: www.ats.edu/
20   An index of issues from Autumn 1964 through 2015 illustrates something of the scope: 'Theological Education Index: 1964-Present'.

faith for all aspects of pedagogical and institutional life. Committees, commissions and even decades have been devoted by the ATS to scholarly exploration of this.[21] Since the turn of the millennium, other trends in the scholarship of teaching have emerged. These include public theology, the relationship of seminaries to the church, and the impact of technology on teaching, learning and libraries. The last has occasioned a significant shift in ATS-affiliated schools in the delivery of theological education in a time of increasing challenge to viability and sustainability.[22]

Once a year, the Academy for Evangelism in Theological Education meets to 'explore cutting edge issues and trends in evangelism and the teaching of evangelism today'.[23] It produces an online journal, *Witness*, which offers articles on evangelism and also the scholarship of teaching. In recent years, topics have included analysis of the relationship between scholarship and practice (2016), an argument for the role of evangelism when revamping education outcomes (2015), and 'spiritual formation as a hermeneutic for exploring evangelism theologically' (2012).[24]

The Wabash Center, a joint collaboration between Wabash College and the Lilly Endowment Inc, is a significant resource for and investor in the scholarship of teaching. It seeks to support 'teachers of religion and theology in higher education through meetings and workshops, grants, consultants, a journal and other resources to make accessible the scholarship of teaching and learning'.[25] The journal, *Teaching Theology and Religion*, published four times a year, evidences their particular care for pedagogical questions and resources.

The *Journal for Adult Theological Education (JATE)*, formerly the *British Journal of Theological Education*, which does focus more particularly on the

---

21 Cascante, 'A Decade of Racial/Ethnic Diversity in Theological Education', 1-32. A Decade of Globalization was declared across the 1990s. The following issues of *Theological Education* spoke to that: 26.Supplement 1 (Spring 2000); 27.2 (Spring 1991); 29.2 (Spring 1993); 30.Supplement 1 (Autumn 1993), 30.1 (Autumn 1993), 35.2 (Spring 1999); and 36.2 (Spring 2000).
22 A report written by Tom Tanner in February 2017 noted that in a decade 'when overall ATS enrollment declined by 11%, ATS online enrollment grew by 195%'. Tanner, 'Online Learning at ATS Schools', 2. Note: The first online courses began in 1999. Today two-thirds of seminaries within the ATS offer online education to nearly one-third of all theological students. 'If recent trends continue, *a majority of ATS students may be enrolled online within a few years*', 2.
23 'Conference'. The Academy's online journal, *Witness: The Journal of the Academy for Evangelism in Theological Education* is available at http://journals.sfu.ca/witness/index.php/witness/index. In 2014 an article by Australians Stephenson and Cronshaw was published in the Academy's journal: '"Ask Anything"', 53-80.
24 See 'Archives', http://journals.sfu.ca/witness/index.php/witness/issue/archive.
25 See www.wabashcenter.wabash.edu/home/default.aspx.

scholarship of teaching has, in recent years, included articles by theological educators from Australia and New Zealand.[26] A 2016 issue of JATE was edited by members of Broken Bay Institute in Sydney, who provided four of six articles expounding on and responding to the application of Threshold Concepts theory in online and face-to-face theological teaching and learning.[27] Noted participants (repeat offenders) in the last three issues of JATE are Peter Mudge from Broken Bay Institute and Mark Nichols, who worked for a time at Laidlaw College in Auckland.[28] An announcement via Twitter on the 16 March 2017 that *JATE* will be ending removes one key opportunity for rigorous deliberation toward improved processes of teaching and learning.[29] Ironically in the midst of loss—of a journal and of jobs and even institutions across the sector—there is more of a need than ever for us to be actively engaging in and initiating research into the *educational* dimension of theological education for, unless we are privileged with the support of a large trust fund, students are our lifeblood and the classroom our livelihood.[30]

Thus, internationally, there are few journals that attend to Boyer's domain of teaching and learning. In addition, the location and focus for each of these journals is very much on North America and Europe. They remain valuable, given they alert us to trends and offer the opportunity for catholicity in our scholarship. However, for us as scholar-teachers located in Australasia and the South Pacific, they provide limited opportunity for professional development. Nor do they provide spaces for teaching and learning discussions that arise from our local contexts.

So what has been the focus of the journals of local theological associations? Over all, the 'theological' has been prioritised over 'education'. A reading of the

---

26 See particularly: Vol. 9.2 (2012); Vol. 12.1 (2015); Vol 13.1 (2016); and Vol. 13.2 (2016). Dewerse co-wrote an article published in 2010: Nichols and Dewerse, 'Evaluating Transformative Learning in Theological Education', 44-59.
27 Volume 13.2 (2016), coedited by Peter Mudge and Jan H.F. Meyer, with articles by Daniel Fleming, Rachelle Gilmour, Peter Mudge, and Zachariah Duke of Broken Bay Institute.
28 Peter Mudge has articles published in Volume 12.2. and 13.2. Mark Nichols was published in Volume 12.2 and 13.1.
29 https://twitter.com/theonographer/status/842072383976550406, [accessed 21 March 2017].
30 In New Zealand and Australia, anecdotal evidence suggests that financial and government accreditation pressures, as well as the changing demographics of churches, are affecting the future of theological colleges. In the United States, a blog written for *The Huffington Post* in 2016 noted the crisis in theological education there. It also mentioned several initiatives, including 'Reimagining Theological Education' that necessarily lean into a scholarship of teaching and learning to try to address the issues. Clayton, 'Rebooting Theological Education'.

contents pages of the South Pacific Association of Theological Schools (SPATS), the Melanesian Association of Theological Schools, the Asia Theological Association (ATA) and the Australia New Zealand Association of Theological Schools (ANZATS) reveals a weighting toward the scholarship of discovery (Boyer's first category), with occasional consideration of the scholarship of integration and application (Boyer's second and third categories).[31] *Colloquium*, the journal attached to ANZATS, did include five articles on theological education in an issue published in 2015, tackling the topic from conceptual and ideological angles. It was the only issue out of twenty over ten years that specifically engaged the scholarship of teaching.

What, if anything, does this say about the scholarship of teaching? Why are we as a sector privileging the domain of discovery over the domain of teaching? Is this a reflection of time pressures, or values judgements regarding the domains? Whatever the reasons, we would suggest it points to a significant weakness in our sector: a lack of wondering together in the theological education sector about pedagogy.

Having said that, a national research project paying attention to the scholarship of teaching and learning has occurred in Australia in recent years, demonstrating that our sector has the capacity to focus on the domain of teaching and learning. The Transforming Theology project was funded by the (secular) *Australian Learning and Teaching Council (ALTC)* and was conducted across 2010-2012.

It was inspired by the notion of 'transformative learning' that arose from an earlier *ALTC*-funded research project undertaken by Charles Sherlock in 2008-2009 and called *Uncovering Theology*.[32] Les Ball was appointed to research transformative learning in undergraduate theological education. The project produced regular newsletters that offered insights. Opportunities to join workshops were provided and ultimately a book was published, *Transforming Theology*.[33] This was followed by a companion volume, *Learning and Teaching Theology: Some Ways Ahead*, gathered from a 2013 conference hosted by the

---

31 See *Pacific Journal of Theology, Melanesian Journal of Theology, Journal of Asian Evangelical Theology* and the *Journal of Asian Mission*, and *Colloquium*.

32 For the results of the project led by Charles Sherlock, see *Uncovering Theology*.

33 See http://anzats.edu.au/transforming_theology.html. Also Ball, *Transforming Theology*. Eds. note: From 2010 to 2014, SCD actively promoted reflection on Learning and Teaching Theology with a series of newsletters. These can be accessed through the https://scd.edu.au/learning-teaching-theology/.

Sydney College of Divinity.[34] In it, educators from Australia and New Zealand offered creative thinking and practices for theological education going forward.

Beyond the production of these projects, at the 2015 ANZATS conference held at the Sydney College of Divinity, a theological education strand was introduced. The University of Divinity in Melbourne has, in 2017, launched a Graduate Certificate in Theological Education, at this stage 'only open to academic staff of the University of Divinity'.[35] So when we attend in Australasia to the scholarship of teaching and learning, we are working in an area in which there is wide open space for a collaboration and commitment to wonder together about research-led teaching.

Aristotle once said 'teaching is the highest form of understanding' but arguably this is only so if the teacher actively seeks to reflect upon their work and is actively researching to learn and grow in their teaching. While evaluation of teaching that results in improved course offerings and practices is expected in Australia and New Zealand, particularly by governments, of private training providers, rarely does it seem that such reflection results in research outputs in the domain of teaching and learning. But we do the future of theological education a disservice if we neglect to share our discoveries and use them to inspire further depth-work and innovation in regard not only to scholarly discovery, integration and application, but also to the scholarship of teaching and learning, with and amongst our peers.

In sum, when we examine recent research outputs, the theology sector has prioritised the domain of discovery. Our journals show little evidence of research in teaching. The research that is available is resourced by government funding and episodic in nature. Having looked historically across our sector, it is also worthwhile to look forward.

---

34 Eds. Note: Papers from subsequent SCD conferences in 2015 and 2017 are published as Debergue & Harrison, *Teaching Theology*, and in the present volume.

35 For details of the University of Divinity Graduate Certificate see: www.divinity.edu.au/study/our-courses/graduate-certificate-theological-education/
Eds. note: Sydney College of Divinity approved a Graduate Certificate in Theological Education in 2018. https://scd.edu.au/courses/graduate-certificate-in-theological-education/.

Trends in Higher Education: Opportunities for Activist Research in Teaching and Learning

In 2016, Debbie Morrison blogged an article noting three trends she believed would influence teaching and learning in higher education generally.[36] They included 'alternative credentialing', 'experimentation in new teaching models and learning spaces', and a focus on 'student-driven personalized learning'.[37] Her observations noted the momentum generated by particular contextual factors and aided by developments in thinking and technology. They encompassed such innovations as bite-sized professional development course-combinations like Nanodegrees and MicroMasters, harnessing developments in blended learning for empowering student-centred learning, and the possibilities for student-created learning, particularly via smart-phone apps.[38] In 2017, an online article gathering the observations of a number of faculty in higher education furthered momentum, noting trends such as outcomes-based education, the rise of non-traditional students, student video creation, micro-credentialling, and piloting for larger innovation.[39] All of these are fertile fields for research on teaching. What is the impact of changes on student learning? What practices ensure learners feel supported? How are graduate outcomes, including claims for transformation, being embodied?

In theological education, a significant initiative in Canada, accredited by the ATS in 2014, embodies a number of these trends. *Immerse* is a new-look Master of Divinity, developed by Northwest Baptist Seminary in the face of declining MDiv enrolments. Students study mostly *in situ* and are credited not for completing courses *but for mastery of learning outcomes*. Pedagogy is shaped by a commitment to customised learning shaped and best developed, monitored and assessed by a mentor team. This team is made up of an 'academic expert, an on-the-ground pastoral mentor, and a big-picture mentor from the broader network'.[40] The curriculum is integrated, applicants are rigorously assessed before being accepted, and a close relationship is cultivated between the seminary and collaborators on the ground. Such innovations demand to be researched, for the

---

36 In 2012 Morrison began 'Online Learning Insights', a blog and resource including international contributors. https://onlinelearninginsights.wordpress.com/about/.
37 Morrison, 'Three Trends that will Influence Learning and Teaching in 2016'.
38 In the article Morrison sends readers to, among others, Udacity www.udacity.com/nanodegree, Massachusetts Institute of Technology http://news.mit.edu/2015/faqs-mit-new-path-masters-degree-micromasters-1007, and Purdue University and their IMPACT program www.purdue.edu/impact/.
39 Stansbury, '14 Hot Higher Ed Trends for 2017.'
40 See www.nbseminary.ca/programs/immerse.

sake of learners, the wider theological sector and to be accountable for the investment in innovation. *Immerse* has attracted a great deal of interest and take-up already occurring with other organisations.[41] Concepts like activist research allow us to see such innovations as fertile sites for research.

Activist Research and Domains of Teaching and Learning

One way to seek to integrate activist research and domains of teaching and learning is to consider the various investments being made in the theological education sector. My accompanying essay argues that we are dealing in theological education with 'matters of the heart,' to quote singer Tracy Chapman.[42] We noted learners. Those who study theology are invested personally (whether they have faith or none). They come with investments in denominational identity stories (whether positive or negative) and with significant investment in vocational pathways, both lay and ordained. These are the multiple investments of those who learn.

As already argued, we as teachers are also invested. We are teaching in matters of our heart. As we teach, each of us is shaped by denominational identity stories (whether positive or negative). For each of us, our teaching is a vocational pathway (whether adjunct or full-time), in which we are bringing together both theology (content) and education (teaching). We are part of a sector that is making claims for transformation. Teachers, like our students, are deeply invested in multiple ways.

They say you should research what you love. Activist research and Boyer's domains invite us to research what we are invested in both as learners and as teachers. They remind us that for genuine transformation, we teachers will find ourselves learning from our students, as they become our teachers. Such are the methodological pathways and research outputs provided to us by activist research and Boyer's four domains. They summon us to make a priority of wondering together, full of curiosity and doubt, about our actions as teachers.

There is a third area of investment worth pondering. Our denominations are also deeply invested in this sector called theological education. Many of us teach in contexts which rely heavily on that investment, including in the form

---

41   Refer to https://spark.adobe.com/page/WbQBN/.
42   Chapman, *Matters of the Heart*. See also, Taylor and Dewerse, 'Curiosity and Doubt in Researching the Future: the Contribution of Flipped Learning to Sociality in Theological Innovation' in this volume.

of property, brand identity, and regular funding. The primary focus of our denominations is on our teaching.

In my (Steve's) time as Principal of two Colleges, I have faced regular conversations about budget deficits. It is my experience that it is far easier to defend expenditure in areas of teaching than it is to defend expenditure on research. Can we turn this denominational investment into a strength? Why are we not researching our teaching, that which our denominations passionately care about? In a context of rapid change, why is theology not at the forefront of research-led teaching, full of curiosity and doubt, about our actions as teachers?

Let us summarise by nailing—in the Spirit of the 500th anniversary of the Reformation—a set of theses to the wall, then offering some concrete next steps.

1. Theological educators are activist researchers because we care about our content and our communities.
2. Denominational stakeholders value activism, our teaching more than our research.
3. The theological sector in Australasia has been weak in producing research outputs in the domain of teaching and learning.
4. Researching our teaching as activist researchers aligns what we as educators care about with our industry partners and attend to our research weakness as a sector.

Concrete Next Steps

So, what might some concrete next steps look like? Let us offer some suggestions, under headings of informal research, institutional feedback and researching practice.

a) Informal Research
Evaluation is an in-built component of our teaching. How do we as activist teachers go about evaluating ourselves? One way is through informal mechanisms. Often at the midpoint of a class I will ask for feedback: a blank piece of paper and five minutes at the end of class to respond anonymously to three questions: What in this class so far has helped your learning? What has hindered your learning? Any improvements? As part of implementing flipped learning in a 2014 class,[43] I

---

43 For more, see our subsequent essay in this volume, 'Curiosity and Doubt in Researching the Future'.

regularly invited the class to individually address the question, 'What is the most important theological question you still have?' I collected these and while students were working in class on their self-guided activities, I provided short written responses to each question. I also located the responses in relation to Bloom's Taxonomy and provided this as feedback to the class.

Both of these are informal mechanisms for research. They increase our sensitivity as educators to the student experience and allow teaching to be adjusted accordingly. They have a further benefit, related to the cultivation of a community of inquiry. These practices encourage feedback. They signal curiosity, both from the teacher and in relation to independent student learning. The importance of these is magnified in the context of teaching theology. Students can come from more hierarchical religious backgrounds, in which respect is given to teachers in ways that reduce the willingness to ask questions. Regular informal research enhances the development of communities of curious inquiry.

b) Collective Feedback

The standard institutional strategy for evaluating teaching is through Student Evaluation of Teaching (SET) forms. How might these be used in ways that let us wonder together more about our teaching? How might they encourage actions of curiosity and doubt? In order to encourage my wondering about SET results, I have structured a self-reflection process, which involves addressing four questions in response to SET evaluations.[44] This becomes a summative document for reference the next time I teach the course.

These have also become an important tool in Faculty development. As Principal of Uniting College from 2012 to 2015, I invited my Departmental colleagues to use the SET self-reflection process described above. Individually, this became part of regular performance review conversations. Collectively, each semester, every individual self-evaluation was de-identified, summarised and presented for discussion at a Departmental Ministry Studies meeting. Any collective actions were noted and then fed back to students. This provided both individual and collective feedback loops, as student evaluation was considered, reflected and as appropriate, acted upon.

Now, as Principal of Knox Centre for Ministry and Leadership, I have undertaken a similar exercise in regard to block course feedback. Reading the student feedback, I was struck by a range of comments in which students

---

44 Summarise positive responses; student concerns raised; desired improvements; other comments.

identified what enhanced their learning. These included creating a safe place, facilitating content engagement, enabling peer learning, nurturing reality and weaving in diverse cultural perspectives. These were compiled as a lesson plan check list for our Faculty team, who were then invited to structure and evaluate their next block course lectures in light of this feedback. In this way, the research of informal student feedback shaped ongoing teaching.

SET forms can be mechanistic. Equally they can be invitations to wonder together, inviting actions of curiosity and doubt about our teaching. In each of these concrete steps outlined, student feedback has become important data that is shaping an 'activist' teaching institution.

c) Researching Practice

We are in a time of considerable change. As already noted, including in the discussion of *Immerse*, these changes are providing many opportunities for research in our sector. Every innovation we make in our classes is an opportunity for being research-led in our teaching, for wondering together, full of curiosity and doubt about our practice.

Joining a Flinders University Community of Practice in 2014, I was struck with how easy it was to research my teaching. The Community of Practice agreed on four questions, to be asked three times, at the start, middle and end.

- What are you most interested in learning? (What has been the most interesting thing you have learnt so far in this topic?)
- What resources will/have best support your learning in this topic?
- How valuable is it to have choices about what and how you learn in a topic?
- At the outset what aspects of the topic are you initially concerned or worried about (if at all)? (How have your initial concerns been addressed?)

This provided a wealth of data, which has continued to shape my teaching. It has resulted in four conference presentations, three in theology and two in higher education more generally.[45] It has allowed me to be an activist: to take

---

45 'Embodiment and transformation in the context of e-learning', SCD Teaching and Learning Conference (Sydney, September 2013). 'Revaluing the lives we teach: the pedagogies we employ and the Gospel truths they deploy', ANZATS (Sydney, June 29-July 2015). 'Activist research: an examination of lived practices', Ecclesiology and ethnography conference (Durham, Sept 15-17, 2015). 'A class above: Evidence based action research into teaching that is connected, mobile and accessible in a higher education context', HERGA (Adelaide, Sept 22, 2015).

my curiosity and doubt and apply it to my teaching. It has given me confidence to keep innovating.

I am not alone. I am glad of a number of colleagues who are providing leadership in our sector. I note the work of Andrew Dutney and the impact of his Doctor of Education research on Uniting College.[46] I note the work of Rosemary Dewerse and Mark Johnston, both using, with permission, student assignments as the data for considered reflection on their teaching practice.[47] Knox Centre for Ministry and Leadership has appointed a Thornton Blair Research Fellow to enhance delivery of life-long learning that enables the meeting of professional standards and higher education post-graduate requirements. The Research Fellow will research key stakeholders, including the interviewing of fifty-five ministers, in order to ensure an educational design that is both theoretically sensitive and shaped by empirical data.

Each of these is an example of what it means to be research-led in our teaching. They are generated by activist researchers, academics putting their

> training (*in theology*) and expertise (*in teaching*) in the hands of an organization (*the church*), community or group (*the student body*) [… to use] a participatory research process (*seeking feedback from students*) […] and [as a result generate…] research findings… that I, and those who I have worked closely with (*learners*), care deeply about resolving (*to teach theology in ways that impact learners and transform lives and communities*).[48]

Whether formal or informal, they are examples of research-led teaching in theological education.

Conclusion

In this essay, the theme of wonder has been applied to the task of being research-led. Wonder, as a verb, has been employed to explore the action of researching our teaching. Such an approach challenges our teaching, challenges our definitions of research. In order to examine identity and motivation, we have outlined

---

46 See the essay in this volume by Dutney, 'Remembering the Future: the Contribution of Historical Research to Innovation in Theological Education'.
47 Dewerse, 'Whakarongo ki Te Wairua Tapu'; Johnstone, 'The neighbourhood is God's home too'.
48 Hale, 'What is Activist Research?', 15.

the notion of activist research and argued that it is coherent with our investments as theological educators. In order to examine research outputs, we have undertaken a survey of the theological sector, using a framework for scholarship provided by Ernest Boyer.

Theology as a discipline, in its research, has prioritised the domain of discovery; the outputs in the domain of teaching and learning have been minimal and episodic. This is inconsistent with our multiple investments, both as educators and from our key industry partners and so we have instead offered four theses regarding the future of researching our teaching:

1. Theological educators are activist researchers because we care about our content and our communities.
2. Denominational stakeholders value activism, our teaching more than our research.
3. The theological sector in Australasia has been weak in producing research outputs in the domain of teaching and learning.
4. Researching our teaching as activist researchers aligns what we as educators care about with our industry partners and attend to our research weakness as a sector.

To make this concrete, we have suggested some next steps, under headings of informal research, institutional feedback and researching practice.

In the midst of massive social change and in light of the possibilities offered by activist research and the correction inherent in Boyer's four domains of scholarship, we offer the invitation: Come, let us continue to wonder together, in actions of curiosity and doubt, about researching our teaching.

Bibliography

Ball, Les. *Transforming Theology: Student experience and transformative learning in undergraduate theological education* (Preston, Vic: Mosaic Press, 2012).

Boyer, Ernest L. *Scholarship Reconsidered: Priorities of the Professoriate* (A Special Report; The Carnegie Foundation for the Advancement of Teaching, 1990).

Cascante, Fernando A. 'A Decade of Racial/Ethnic Diversity in Theological Education: The Continuous Challenge of Inclusion with Justice', *Journal of Race, Ethnicity and Religion* 1.3 (April 2010).

Chapman, Tracey. *Matters of the Heart* (Album, Elekta, 1992).

Clayton, Philip. 'Rebooting Theological Education', *The Huffington Post* (12 February 2016;

updated 12 February 2017) www.huffingtonpost.com/philip-clayton-phd/rebooting-theological-edu_b_9195678.html [accessed 22 March 2017].

'Conference', https://aete.online/conference/ [accessed 22 March 2017].

Debergue, Y., and J.R. Harrison (eds.), *Teaching Theology in a Technological Age* (Cambridge: Cambridge Scholars, 2015).

Dewerse, Rosemary. 'Whakarongo ki Te Wairua Tapu: Moving Anglican Ordinands from Parish Maintenance to Missional Ministry', *Australian Journal of Mission Studies* 10.1 (June 2016), 3-10.

Hale, Charles. 'What is Activist Research?', *Items and Issues, Social Science Research Council* 2.1-2 (Summer 2001), 13-15.

Kara, Helen. *Creative Research Methods in the Social Sciences: A Practical Guide* (Bristol: Policy Press, 2015).

Killen, Patricia O'Connell & Eugene V. Gallagher. 'Sketching the Contours of the Scholarship of Teaching and Learning in Theology and Religion', *Teaching Theology and Religion* 16.2 (April 2013), 107-124.

Johnstone, Mark. 'The neighbourhood is God's home too', *Australian Association of Mission Studies Conference* (Whitley College, Melbourne 5-7 July 2017).

Morrison, Debbie. 'Three Trends that will Influence Learning and Teaching in 2016', (10 January 2016) <https://onlinelearninginsights.wordpress.com/2016/01/10/three-trends-that-will-influence-learning-and-teaching-in-2016/> [accessed 16 March 2017].

Nichols, Mark & Rosemary Dewerse. 'Evaluating Transformative Learning in Theological Education: A Multifaceted Approach', *JATE* 7.1 (2010), 44-59.

Sherlock, Charles. *Uncovering Theology: The Depth, Reach and Utility of Australian Theological Education* (Adelaide: ATF Press, 2009).

Rose, D., P. Fleischmann, T. Wykes, and J. Bindman, 'Review of consumers' perspectives on electro convulsive therapy.' (London: SURE, 2002).

Stansbury, Meris. '14 Hot Higher Ed Trends for 2017', (2 January 2017) www.ecampusnews.com/disruptions-and-innovations/hot-higher-ed-trends-2017/> [accessed 27 March 2017].

Stephenson, Dale & Darren Cronshaw. '"Ask Anything": Developing a Relational Platform to Mobilise Christians to Share their Faith Through Exploring Questions', *Witness* 28 (2014), 53-80.

Tanner, Tom. 'Online Learning at ATS Schools: Part 1—Looking back at our past', (17 February 2017) www.ats.edu/uploads/resources/publications-presentations/colloquy-online/online-learning-part-1.pdf [accessed 22 March 2017].

Taylor, Steve. 'Embodiment and transformation in the context of e-learning', SCD Teaching and Learning Conference (Sydney, September 2013). Now published in L. Ball & J.R. Harrison (eds.), *Learning & Teaching Theology. Some Ways Ahead* (Northcote, Vic.: Morning Star, 2014).

_____. 'Revaluing the lives we teach: the pedagogies we employ and the Gospel truths they deploy', ANZATS (Sydney, June 29-July 2015).

_____. 'Activist research: an examination of lived practices', Ecclesiology and ethnography conference (Durham, Sept 15-17, 2015).

_____. 'A class above: Evidence based action research into teaching that is connected, mobile and accessible in a higher education context', HERGA (Adelaide, Sept 22, 2015).

'Theological Education Index: 1964-Present', www.ats.edu/uploads/resources/publications/presentations/theological-education/theological-education-index.pdf [accessed 22 March 2017].

'Wonder', www.google.co.nz/search?q=definition+wonder&ie=utf-8&oe=utf-8&client=firefox-b&gfe_rd=cr&dcr=0&ei=clqvWYGjHMHr8Afcuotw [accessed 19 April 2017].

Websites

Association of Theological Schools, www.ats.edu/

Reimagining Theological Education, www.theoedu.org/

Wabash Center, www.wabashcenter.wabash.edu/

Witness: The Journal of the Academy for Evangelism in Theological Education http://journals.sfu.ca/witness/index.php/witness/index

World Conference of Associations of Theological Institutions, http://wocati.org/

Steve Taylor
Knox Centre for Ministry and Leadership, Dunedin/ Flinders University
principal@knoxcentre.ac.nz

Rosemary Dewerse
Knox Centre for Ministry and Leadership, Dunedin
rosemary.dewerse@knoxcentre.ac.nz

8 | 'TO TAKE YOU WHERE YOU DO NOT WISH TO GO': EXTENDING THE TELOS OF ONLINE THEOLOGICAL EDUCATION

PART 1—THE 'WHO' OF THE TEACHER WHO TEACHES

Abstract

Following his resurrection, Jesus counsels Peter that when he was young he was free to do whatever he wanted but 'when you grow old, you will stretch out your hands, and someone else will fasten a belt around you and take you where you do not wish to go' (John 21: 18).[1] Such a predicament is a challenge for younger and older students and teachers alike. Within the context of online theological education (TE) in general, and with a particular focus on Catholic theological education, this essay explores and extends the *telos* or end purpose of teaching and learning. It does so in relation to current practice (being young/going willingly) and a projected more radical and mature reflection and wisdom (growing old/going reluctantly).

It argues that much within the field of TE has been written and discussed about the mechanics of instruction, the 'basics' of learning and essay writing,

---

10   Division of Christian Education, *The Holy Bible*, 116. Hereafter referred to as NRSV.

and the role of technology, or what Palmer[2] refers to as the 'what' and 'how' of teaching. Yet comparatively less attention has been devoted to what this essay argues are more foundational issues and constitute those more challenging places where teachers and students sometimes 'do not wish to go'. These include the deeper *telos* of teaching and learning,[3] the 'who' of the person who teaches,[4] and the 'what' or nature of the theological institution that is engaged in teaching.[5]

This full essay is written in two parts. Following brief sections on *telos* within the context of TE in general, Part 1 explores the 'who' of the person who teaches, while a separate Part 2 examines the 'what' of the theological institution that teaches. Part 1 (this current essay) argues that the online TE teacher should seek to develop students who possess an expansive Catholic Christian vision and thus desire to know the truth. The teacher should also aim to nurture students who are dialogical and inclusive, who cultivate rigour and relevance, and who are educated to think critically, knowledgeably and empathically.

Introduction

Online theological education (TE) can be viewed through many lenses. A possible lens is one that focuses on the discourse of current, traditional practice compared to a projected more radical and mature praxis and wisdom. While current practice might focus on the mechanics of instruction, basic online learning strategies and assessment regimes, a more radical praxis might attend to some deeper theological and methodological questions such as—'what' are the principles guiding the way one teaches or the purpose of that teaching (the *telos*) within a theological institution (online and face to face)?; 'who' is the one that teaches and what therefore are the deeper aims of teaching?; 'what' is the overall philosophy of online learning?; 'what' is the teleological praxis embodied as practical applications in response to the foregoing questions?; and how can the 'what' of the institution that teaches be defined more specifically?

These are some of the issues that this essay seeks to examine. It views them in part as a struggle between two different approaches or mindsets—the younger,

---

2   Palmer, *Courage to Teach*.
3   Madoc-Jones, 'Practices, Narratives'.
4   Palmer, *Courage to Teach*.
5   Garcia, *Academic Freedom*; McDowell, 'God at the end of Higher Education'.

traditional approach in tension with the more mature, dialogical and praxis approach. Such a tension (but one applied to the present era) is evident in the challenge that Jesus issues to Peter in John 21:18-20 (NRSV):

> 'Very truly, I tell you, when you were younger, you used to fasten your own belt and to go wherever you wished. But when you grow old, you will stretch out your hands, and someone else will fasten a belt around you and take you where you do not wish to go'. (He said this to indicate the kind of death by which he would glorify God.) After this he said to him, 'Follow me'.

Viewed within the context of online TE, this passage (and others, such as the predictions of the Passion in the synoptic gospels) implies that there are two complementary paths to that education—an easier one that is *chosen by* and a more challenging one that is *chosen for* the educator. It also implies that the path that is chosen or given is one that involves experiences of 'death', suffering, resilience, sacrifice and discipleship. As Robert Frost famously declared in his 1920 poem 'The Road Not Taken', at different times of life one is offered a choice between the easier and the more difficult pathway. One possible interpretation of Frost's poem, among the many contested, is that the difficult path is more character-building and life-changing:

> I shall be telling this with a sigh
> Somewhere ages and ages hence:
> Two roads diverged in a wood, and I—
> I took the one less traveled by,
> And that has made all the difference.[6]

In order to commence the journey along that more difficult path, we need to make some brief comments about the *telos* of theological institutions, and then explore the *teleology* and *telos* of TE within that *locus* and the broader context.

The goals of theological institutions

It is assumed in what follows that theological institutes share broad goals, which include:

---

6   Frost, 'The Road Not Taken', 270-272, lines 16-20.

1. that they will draw on the intellectual tradition of which they are a part;
2. that they will seek to demonstrate a degree of excellence in teaching and in research according to the disciplines proper to their educational focus;
3. that they will seek to respond to the specific concerns and needs of their student body as well as the world of which they are a part.

These aims strongly suggest certain elements that would be critical in the articulation of any theological institute's *telos* (end point, purpose, ultimate end of that body) but which need to be developed in greater detail to determine their implications for teaching, online study, essay writing, dialogue, and any specific values that underpin the whole enterprise of online learning (for example, service and compassion). In our context, we take our focus within the Catholic tradition,[7] meaning that such elements include Catholic world-view, excellence, human flourishing, intellectual rigour, student centredness, and inclusiveness, among others. Some of these elements and components are explored in more depth below.

It is assumed in what follows that theological institutes exist, not only to cultivate the above characteristics, but primarily to promote actively God's presence in the world, principally through advancement of the mission of God. This mission of God (*missio Dei*) is itself understood as God's work of bringing about the Reign of God through the person of Jesus and his Church within the situation of the contemporary world. In this context Noel Connolly proposes the following definition. Note the manner in which this description solicits a deeper understanding of one's personal *telos* as well as one's group or institutional *telos*:

> The *three Persons of the Trinity* are constantly creating, healing, reconciling, transforming and uniting the world. The mission of the Spirit comes to its fullest expression in Jesus… Caught up in God's mission, *the Church is missionary by nature*. Its particular task is to seek, *uncover and celebrate God's presence in the world*… God is especially active wherever people are inspired to strive creatively for justice, truth, freedom [and other qualities]… Missiology aims at *greater knowledge* of God's purposes but also at *intelligent participation* in them.[8]

---

[7] We assume here that readers not belonging to Catholic or Christian institutions will adapt what follows to their own context and particular tradition.
[8] Connolly, 'Mission: Mother of the Church', presented 1 November 2016, Slide 20, author's emphasis.

The teleology and *telos* of theological education

Teleology is the belief that everything has an inherent or defined purpose. In the context of the abovementioned characteristics and attendant definition of mission, this essay adopts a general definition of teleology that centres on the purpose and existence of TE, rather than its mechanical and pragmatic nature.[9]

Telos is a term with Aristotelian roots employed in this essay to describe the end, purpose or goal of TE. It is the foundation of the aforementioned *teleology*, referring to the study of purposiveness, or the study of objects with a view to their aims, purposes, or intentions. The term is most commonly used in Aristotelian and Thomistic discussions of ethics, as well as in renewed discussions of virtue ethics. In these cases, *telos* refers to the best 'goal' or 'end' for something (for example, an animal), which for both Aristotle and Aquinas was held within the category of flourishing.[10] Such flourishing was understood to be embodied when the animal, to continue with the example, is living to its full potential according to the kind of creature it is. This requires certain external conditions of possibility (such as adequate food, water, warmth and so on) and certain internal dispositions (such as motivation to seek out these things).[11]

In the case of the human person, the category of flourishing takes on a moral quality, because our freedom as individuals and as a species directs (in part, at least) the manner in which we achieve our flourishing. For both Aristotle and Aquinas, flourishing thus becomes the moral goal of human life, and once that is established it is possible to deduce the characteristics (virtues) which best direct one towards that goal.[12] The key difference between this approach to ethics and other approaches (such as deontology) is that ethical dispositions and actions are always considered with reference to the final goal of human life in flourishing, as against being considered in and of themselves. Thus the mediating point of any debate on ethics is reference to a final goal, which provides a context for determining what is good and what is not.[13]

The analogue for our discussion of *telos* in this essay is that, in discussing the optimal goal of education, educational institutions and their staff are much better placed to determine, and debate about, the 'what' and 'how' questions which, as we noted in the introduction, are currently the primary focus of

---

9 McKeown, *Collins Dictionary*, 1711.
10 Porter, *Nature as Reason*, 103. Refer also to Part 2, section 2.4.
11 Porter, *Nature as Reason*, 101.
12 Pope, 'Overview of the Ethics', 33.
13 Pope, 'Overview of the Ethics', 33.

educational discourse. Our argument is, therefore, that a rigorous discussion of this *telos* is needed not only for philosophical speculation, but also for the practical import they will have.

We present a range of arguments here on the *telos* of higher education in general and TE in particular, simply to enlarge the debate and key questions that it raises. For example, John McDowell adjures that even though a single idea of what constitutes a university never truly existed,[14] yet there are worrying signs about the nature of both Western higher education and also theological education. He claims, for example, that a 'culture of self-assertive individualism is generating conditions in which patient reasoned argument and non-competitive conversation are increasingly disregarded'.[15] In this he echoes and cites the writings of David Ford, who laments that universities and public schools 'do not on the whole educate people to engage intelligently in this multi-faith and secular world, nor do they foster the high-quality religion-related study and debate across disciplines necessary to make thoughtful critical and constructive contributions to the public sphere'.[16]

McDowell concludes that a 'well-ordered theology' can prove valuable and resilient in a number of ways. It can, for example, 'enact a witness to the sociology of commitment and responsibility beyond the subjection of the subject to an egological subjectivity that privileges judgments determined by the bare "will to choose"'. It can also 'witness to the healing of the symbiotic relationships between things in the world that moves beyond the fractures of a non-integrative curriculum and the self-interest of intrumentalizing reason'.[17] And finally, evoking significant themes such as flourishing, friendship, the stranger or *other*, some of which are treated elsewhere in this essay:

> [A well-ordered theology] can encourage a commitment to responsibility that labours to keep the question of the justice of common human flourishing on the agenda. Educative activity would then ultimately be directed to those virtues that assist us in our ultimate end—friendship with God enacted in hospitable action to the stranger. In this case, then, our primary theological question would become not that of where is God in higher education, but rather

---

14 McDowell, 'God at the end of Higher Education', 221. Citing Sheldon Rothblatt.
15 McDowell, 'God at the end', 232.
16 Ford, *Christian Wisdom*, 279.
17 McDowell, 'God at the end', 236.

what it is that constitutes higher education *in, with,* and *under* God in Jesus Christ for the renewal of not only specific local contexts but indeed all things.[18]

1. The 'who' of the person who teaches

The God of Christian revelation is One who calls, accompanies, challenges and redeems. As much is assumed throughout this essay. It would be tempting to commence with the nature and *telos* of the theological institution itself. However our argument in this essay is that God, for the person who teaches, is not primarily a God of institutions, élites, political pressure groups, or corporations, but of redemptive, flourishing and life-giving relationships in community. This is evident in texts such as John 10:10—'The thief comes only to steal and kill and destroy. I came that they may have life, and have it abundantly'; and Acts 2:28—'You have made known to me the ways of life; you will make me full of gladness with your presence' (both NRSV; see also the section on 'flourishing' in Part 2, section 2.4).

1.1 The 'who' of the person who teaches

Quaker educator Parker Palmer explores many dimensions of the 'who' of the teacher as one who first of all *is*, and then *teaches*. The first, and perhaps most important dimension, is the actual calling or 'vocation' of the teacher prior to their engagement in the classroom or online. Vocation, argues Palmer, does not evolve from wilfulness or the forcing of the self onto self, others and the world. On the contrary, it 'comes from listening. I must listen to my life and try to understand what it is truly about… or my life will never represent anything real in the world, no matter how earnest my intentions'.[19] Palmer traces this insight from the word *vocation* itself which derives from the Latin word for 'voice':

> Vocation does not mean a goal that I pursue. It means a calling that I hear. Before I can tell my life what I want to do with it, I must listen to my life telling me who I am. I must listen for the truths and values at the heart of my own identity, not the standards by which

---

18   McDowell, 'God at the end', 236. Compare reflections in 'Strategic vision' above on 'mission'.
19   Palmer, *Let your life speak*, 4.

I *must* live—but the standards by which I cannot help but live if I am living my own life.[20]

What then are the implications arising from the 'who' of the teacher for the teachers, students, and institutions in question? Like an epistemological archaeologist, Palmer drills deep down into the psyche and practice of the teacher, in the process unearthing layers and subtleties that continue to elude practitioners and theorists alike. In a deceptively rudimentary schema, he argues convincingly that any aspirations for educational reform are only as good as the questions that drive them. He raises a foundational question about teaching that 'goes unasked in our national dialogue—and often unasked even in the places where teachers are educated and employed… for it honors and challenges the teacher's heart, and it invites a deeper inquiry than our traditional questions do'.[21]

He contends that a seismic shift is required to address the deeper question of the 'who' of the teacher. Hence, he argues, we need consciously to avoid the most commonly asked question—the 'what' question of what subjects shall we teach; the 'how' question of what methods and techniques are required in order to teach effectively; and even the 'why' question of for what purpose and to what ends do we teach (cf. *telos* of teaching). The final frontier of pedagogical questioning and motivation is, rather, this invisible issue:

> But seldom, if ever, do we ask the 'who' question—who is the self that teaches? How does the quality of my selfhood form—or deform—the way I relate to my students, my subject, my colleagues, my world? How can educational institutions sustain and deepen the selfhood from which good teaching comes?[22]

He continues:

> I have no quarrel with the what or how or why questions—except when they are posed as the only questions worth asking. All of them can yield important insights into teaching and learning. But none of them opens up the territory I want to explore… the inner landscape of the teaching self.[23]

---

20 Palmer, *Let your life speak*, 4-5.
21 Palmer, *The Courage to Teach*, 4.
22 Palmer, *The Courage to Teach*, 4.
23 Palmer, *The Courage to Teach*, 5.

1.2 A person with an expansive Catholic Christian vision who desires to know the truth

In the encyclical *Fides et ratio*, St John Paul II noted that: 'God has placed in the human heart a desire to know the truth'[24] which implies that the *telos* of the human journey involves the contemplation of the truth. We assume here that readers not belonging to Catholic or Christian institutions will adapt what follows to their own context and particular tradition.

Christian learning institutions, in general, should be places which freely and courageously engage with the best insights of their day from a variety of academic disciplines, regardless of one's adherence to any religious tradition or belief system. As Thomas Groome also notes, this search for truth goes hand in hand with hospitality, openness and inclusiveness: 'Openness to the truth as an aspect of Catholicity was a frequent theme throughout Augustine's writings. A classic statement is in his text *De Doctrina Christiana:* "All good and true Christians should understand that truth, wherever they may find it, belongs to their God"'.[25] This truism is also echoed by St Ambrose of Milan: '*Omne verum a quocumque dicatur, a Spiritu Sancto est*', which Reilly translates as 'All truth is from the Holy Spirit'.[26]

Within the context of an institution with a specifically Catholic identity, the relationship between the human *telos* and the *telos* of the educational institution is highlighted in Catholicism's dual emphasis on natural revelation and the goodness of reason. On natural revelation, Catholicism shares a position which is found in many Christian thinkers—both Catholic and Protestant—throughout history: that the intelligibility of God is reflected in the good world that God created. Hence, understanding that world better leads to a better understanding of God. There is a motivation internal to these perspectives which spurs on the advancement of knowledge in all fields: wonder and awe in the presence of God's creation provides an impetus for understanding all aspects of that creation as much as possible, and that understanding leads to knowledge of God on the journey to union with God.[27]

Within this world-view, faith and reason are not seen as contradictory, but

---

24   John Paul II, *Fides et ratio*, preface.
25   Groome, *Educating for Life*, 65.
26   Reilly, *Latin Sayings for Spiritual Growth*, 24. This saying is translated elsewhere as: 'Every truth, whoever said it, comes from the Holy Spirit', often cited by St Thomas Aquinas (see Maritain, *Introduction*, 53).
27   Alister McGrath analyses this position in both Thomas Aquinas and John Calvin; McGrath, *Theology*, 49-51.

rather as 'like two wings on which the human spirit rises to the contemplation of truth'.[28] On this view, 'God has placed in the human heart a desire to know the truth',[29] and the *telos* of the human journey involves the contemplation of truth. As such, the good use of reason in the pursuit of truth is seen as part and parcel of the responsible life of individuals and communities. Truth cannot contradict truth, and so Catholic institutions of scholarship and teaching should be places which freely and courageously engage with the best insights of their day from a variety of academic disciplines.[30] This is true regardless of who has these insights—whether of the same faith or not—as Aquinas demonstrated by seeking 'truth wherever it might be found' and in so doing giving 'consummate demonstration of its universality'.[31]

This sense of pedagogical expansiveness is echoed by others such as Pring, who asserts that the one who teaches should seek to cultivate both 'theoretical and propositional knowledge' (*theoria*) as well as 'practical and activity based knowledge' (*techne*).[32] However, Pring also identifies a third, crucial form of knowledge—achieved only through 'reflection, communication with others, the arts, religion, and initiation into communities and their values… It comes through narratives of various kinds—in literature, in religious scriptures, through example and tradition'. He adds: 'Aristotle called it *phronesis*, and it is embedded in particular virtues—particular conceptions of the "good life"'.[33] He names what is perhaps the greatest challenge, but at the same time the greatest privilege, of the teacher—to teach and guide students in what it is to be human: that is, to acquire the above types of knowing and their attendant understandings and capabilities, along with 'a sense of responsibility and moral purpose, and the social skills and virtues for living harmoniously together'.[34]

1.3 A person who is dialogical and inclusive

A part of the 'who' of the teacher is a person who strives to teach in a dialogical and inclusive manner, and who encourages students to cultivate the same qualities. 'Dialogical' carries the sense of to engage in conversation, to discuss,

---

28 John Paul II, *Fides et Ratio*, preface.
29 John Paul II, *Fides et Ratio*, preface.
30 International Theological Commission, *Theology Today*, n.79.
31 John Paul II, *Fides et Ratio*, n.44.
32 Pring, 'Is Religious Education Possible?', 20-21.
33 Pring, 'Is Religious Education Possible?', 21.
34 Pring, 'Is Religious Education Possible?', 22.

exchange opinions, or to explore discourses.[35] 'Inclusive' is more self-explanatory except perhaps for its insinuation of gathering, including in a group, and openness to the *other* or stranger, of anyone the same or different from the person who includes.[36] The need to cultivate dialogue and inclusivity is one of the most formidable challenges facing both teachers and students.

In light of the foregoing insights of Palmer (refer above to section 1.1), it follows that dialogue begins with the internal dialogue or speech of the teacher. In true Socratic style, the teacher must know him/herself, and must engage in deep conversation with him/herself and others on such issues as the nature of the teacher, the purpose of teaching, how best to utilise online learning tools, and so on. This in turn calls to mind the Matthean parable of the two trees (Matt. 7:15-20). This is equally the parable of the two prophets and could be applied to the inner life and integrity of both teacher and student, and the manner of 'fruits' that they produce:

> [Jesus said:] 'Beware of false prophets, who come to you in sheep's clothing but inwardly are ravenous wolves. You will know them by their fruits. Are grapes gathered from thorns, or figs from thistles? In the same way, every good tree bears good fruit, but the bad tree bears bad fruit. A good tree cannot bear bad fruit, nor can a bad tree bear good fruit. Every tree that does not bear good fruit is cut down and thrown into the fire. Thus you will know them by their fruits. (NRSV)

1.4 A person who cultivates rigour and relevance

The inclusion of academic excellence as a goal for theological institutions, both in teaching and research, places an emphasis on rigour and contextualisation as essential to the fulfilment of the *telos* of truth-seeking. In so doing, it points towards the fulfilment of this *telos* as building in individuals the competency to 'scrutinize reality with the methods proper to each academic discipline, and so contribute to the treasury of human knowledge'.[37] This means encouraging courageous scholarship which is not afraid to explore new ways of knowing and understanding, and which delves deeper into the relationships that are uncovered therein. This requires that students are empowered to delve further into the

---

35 Sinclair, *Collins Times English Dictionary & Thesaurus*, 320.
36 Sinclair, *Collins Times English Dictionary & Thesaurus*, 600.
37 John Paul II, *Apostolic Constitution*, n.12.

truths and relationships that we discover through them. Such an approach guarantees that 'each individual discipline is studied in a systematic manner'[38] and so retains its rightful independence from other disciplines, and it also requires that the learning institution sets a context which guarantees 'academic freedom, so long as the rights of the individual person and of the community are preserved within the confines of the truth and the common good'.[39]

Nevertheless, given that all disciplines ultimately find their goals in the common search for truth, the dispositions required to achieve this *telos* move away from the 'rigid compartmentalisation of knowledge within individual academic disciplines'.[40] As against this, it is an approach that brings all disciplines 'into dialogue for their mutual enhancement'.[41] Just as Aquinas made the best use of the new knowledge coming to him in the early days of scientific thinking, whether from Christendom, Judaism, Islam or more widely, or whether from theology, philosophy or emerging new disciplines, so we must be open to receiving new knowledge from wherever it might come to us.

Aquinas's genius was in apprising and critiquing new and old knowledge and, where either passed his scholarly testing, in integrating them into a new approach to theological method. Unlike many who would follow him, taking on new knowledge did not necessarily mean abandoning old knowledge; advances in science did not necessitate the rejection of theology. On the contrary, it meant adapting and re-calibrating theology to take account of it.[42] Similarly, the *telos* of TE should include the pursuit of the fullness of knowledge in the optimal ways available to us, wherever this knowledge is to be found, and to bring forward new theological formulations that embrace it. Clearly such work is always done in a context, and the capacity to understand and apply knowledge-in-context is crucial in the teleological visions of both Aristotle and Aquinas.[43] Hence, the fulfilment of TE also relates to its relevance, both to the context in which it is done and to the person undertaking it.

---

38 John Paul II, *Apostolic Constitution*, n.12.
39 John Paul II, *Apostolic Constitution*, n.12.
40 John Paul II, *Apostolic Constitution*, n.16.
41 John Paul II, *Apostolic Constitution*, n.15.
42 Lovat & Fleming, *What is this thing called Theology*, 73.
43 Porter, *Nature as Reason*, 313.

1.5 A person who is educated to think critically, knowledgably and empathically

The authors concur with the thesis of Martha C. Nussbaum that many in the tertiary and school milieux treat education as though its primary goal were to teach students to be economically productive rather than to think critically and become knowledgeable and empathic citizens. Nussbaum argues that this profit motive suggests the indispensability of science and technology, to which she has no objection, except that certain abilities are getting lost in the competitive flurry: 'These abilities are associated with the humanities and the arts: the ability to think critically;… to transcend local loyalties and to approach world problems as a "citizen of the world"; and, finally, the ability to imagine sympathetically the predicament of another person'. This amounts to a definitive contrast between 'an education for profit-making and an education for a more inclusive type of citizenship',[44] or as Miedema and Biesta express it, a contrast between the instrumental shallowness of *instruction* for 'formalized and decontextualized knowledge' and the imaginative depth of '*education* for life'.[45] The authors continue:

> What does it mean when we proclaim that teachers matter? Should schools be mainly places for training [students] or should they educate as well? Should teachers simply be instructors or is there more to their task? (p. 81)…We will argue that the distinction between 'schooling' and 'education' or between 'instruction' and 'pedagogy' is itself in a sense part of the problem. In order to overcome this problem we will make a case for a transformative conception of education…[where] the pedagogical task is conceived as a concern for the whole person of the student.[46]

Nussbaum also avers that a particular method is well suited to a cultivation of the values that she champions. This method is the 'Socratic pedagogy'. Socrates' life and method is 'central to the theory and practice of liberal education in the Western tradition'.[47] Socratic pedagogy is crucial and to be emulated, not just because it allows an authentic, critical and emancipatory dialogue to transpire between teacher and student, but also because it allows 'truly democratic

---

44 Nussbaum, *Not for profit*, 7.
45 Miedema & Biesta, 'Instruction or educating for life?', 81, our emphasis.
46 Miedema & Biesta, 'Instruction or educating for life?', 83.
47 Nussbaum, *Not for profit*, 47.

vulnerability and humility'[48] and nurtures a particular type of critical thinker—the Socratic arguer:

> The Socratic arguer is a confirmed dissenter because she knows that it is just each person and the argument wrestling things out. The numbers of people who think this or that make no difference. Someone trained to follow argument rather than numbers is a good person for a democracy to have, the sort of person who would stand up against the pressure to say something false or hasty… [a liberal education including a theological one, seeking to inculcate Socratic values and pedagogy, must ensure that] critical thinking [is] infused into the pedagogy of classes of many types, as students learn to probe, to evaluate evidence, to write papers with well-structured arguments, and to analyze the arguments presented to them in other texts.[49]

Conclusions and future directions—Towards a teleological praxis

This essay has argued that while there are traditional practices embedded within TE, perhaps the time has come for a consideration of a more radical and mature praxis and wisdom with regard to how teachers teach and how students learn. It has focused in particular on a deeper and practical understanding of the *telos* of the TE in relation to the 'who' of the person who teaches. It has contextualised its discussion within an expansive understanding of the teleology and *telos* of a typical theological institution.

Reflections on the 'who' of the person who teaches draw on the work of Parker Palmer and others to highlight the (often misunderstood) significance of the 'inner teacher', rather than their teaching as 'product' or what they teach. The same section contends that this 'who' of the teacher requires an expansive 'Catholic Christian' vision of education, guided by a desire to know the truth. It also posits that the 'who' of the teacher must aim to be dialogical and inclusive, to be one who cultivates rigour and relevance, as well as one who thinks critically, knowledgeably and empathically.

---

48 Nussbaum, *Not for profit*, 51.
49 Nussbaum, *Not for profit*, 55.

One of the key challenges implicit in this chapter (and further developed in Part 2) is the centrality of Christ for all discussions about the *telos* of theological education, and for the fundamental orientations of teachers, students, and institutions within that endeavour. For a Catholic institution in particular, any venture into education in general, and theological education in particular, needs to take seriously what Robert Barron calls 'the great principle of Catholicism [which] is the Incarnation, the enfleshment of God... And the Incarnation tells us the most important truth about ourselves: we are destined for divinization'.[50] Barron continues in the same vein with a reflection that assists in concluding Part 1 of this topic, but also in orienting the reader towards some of the rich veins mined in Part 2—including Christ as the *telos* of life and education, and the *telos* of flourishing, meaning the pursuit of truth, beauty and goodness:

> We are called not simply to moral perfection or artistic self-expression or economic liberation but to what the Eastern fathers called *theiosis*, transformation into God... [I want to reveal to the reader] a celebration, in words and imagery, of the God who takes infinite delight in bringing human beings to fullness of life.[51]

Bibliography

Barron, R. *Catholicism: A Journey to the Heart of the Faith* (New York: Image, 2011).

Connolly, N.J. 'Mission: Mother of the Church and Mother of Theology' (Unpublished faculty lecture and power point presentation to BBI staff, 1 November 2016).

Division of Christian Education of the NCCC in the USA. *The Holy Bible: New Revised Standard Version* (London: HarperCollinsPublishers, 1998).

Ford, D. F. *Christian Wisdom: Desiring God and Learning in Love* (Cambridge: CUP, 2007).

Frost, R. (intro. & comm. L. Untermeyer). *The Road Not Taken: A Selection of Robert Frost's Poems* (New York: Henry Holt & Company, 1951).

Garcia, K. *Academic Freedom and the 'Telos' of the Catholic University* (New York: Palgrave MacMillan, 2012).

Groome, T. H. *Educating for Life: A spiritual vision for every teacher and parent* (Allen, TX: Thomas More, 1998).

---

50 Barron, *Catholicism*, 1, 2.
51 Barron, *Catholicism*, 3, 5.

International Theological Commission. *Theology Today: Perspectives, Principles and Criteria (2011)*, Vatican Website, Accessed May 22, 2017: www.vatican.va/roman_curia/congregations/cfaith/cti_documents/rc_cti_doc_20111129_teologia-oggi_en.html.

John Paul II, Pope. *Apostolic Constitution of the Supreme Pontiff John Paul II on Catholic Universities* (Rome: The Holy See, 1990).

John Paul II, Pope. *Encyclical Letter 'Fides et Ratio' (Faith and Reason)* (Rome: The Holy See, 1998).

John Paul II, Pope. *Apostolic Letter 'Novo Millennio Ineunte' (At the beginning of the New Millennium)* (Rome: The Holy See, 2001).

John Paul II, Pope. *Message of the Holy Father John Paul II to the Youth of the World on the Occasion of the XIX World Youth Day* (Rome: The Holy See, 2004).

Lovat, T. & Fleming, D. *What is this thing called Theology? Considering the Spiritual in the Public Square* (Macksville, NSW: David Barlow Publishing, 2014).

Madoc-Jones, G. 'Practices, Narratives, and the *Telos* of Educative Teaching', *Journal of Educational Thought* 38:2 (2004), 171-182.

Maritain, J. *Introduction to Philosophy* (London: A & C Black/ Bloomsbury, 2005).

McDowell, J.C. 'God at the end of Higher Education: Raising the *Telos* of the University Higher', *Colloquium* 47:2 (2015), 221-236.

McGrath, A. *Theology: The Basics* (West Sussex: Wiley-Blackwell, 2012).

McKeown, C. (sen. ed.) *Collins Concise Australian Dictionary* (Glasgow: Collins, 2008).

Miedema, S. & Biesta, G.J.J. 'Instruction or educating for life? On the aims of religiously-affiliated schools and others', *International Journal of Education and Religion* IV:1 (2003), 81-96.

Nussbaum, M.C. *Not for profit: Why democracy needs the humanities* (Princeton & Oxford: Princeton University Press, 2010).

Palmer, P.J. *Let your life speak: Listening for the voice of vocation* (New York: Jossey-Bass, 2000).

Palmer, P.J. *The Courage to Teach: Exploring the Inner Landscape of a Teacher's Life (10th Anniversary Edition)* (San Francisco: John Wiley & Sons, 2007).

Pope, S. 'Overview of the Ethics of Thomas Aquinas,' in Stephen J. Pope (ed.), *The Ethics of Aquinas* (Washington, D.C.: Georgetown University Press, 2002), 30-54.

Porter, J. *Nature as Reason: A Thomistic Theory of the Natural Law* (Grand Rapids: William B. Eerdmans, 2005).

Pring, R. 'Is Religious Education Possible?' in Scherto Gill & Garrett Thomson (eds.), *Redefining Religious Education: Spirituality for Human Flourishing* (New York: Palgrave MacMillan, 2014): 17-28.

Reilly, L. *Latin Sayings for Spiritual Growth* (Huntingdon, IN: Our Sunday Visitor, 2001).

Sinclair, J.M. (gen. consult.). *The Collins Times English Dictionary & Thesaurus: 21st Century edition* (Glasgow: HarperCollinsPublishers & Times Books, 2003).

Peter Mudge
Australian Catholic University (ACU National)
pjpmudge@gmail.com

Dan Fleming
St Vincent's Health Australia
Daniel.fleming@svha.org.au

9 | 'TO TAKE YOU WHERE YOU DO NOT WISH TO GO': EXTENDING THE *TELOS* OF ONLINE THEOLOGICAL EDUCATION

PART 2—THE 'WHAT' OF THE INSTITUTION THAT TEACHES

Abstract

This is the continuation (Part 2) of an essay that explores and extends the *telos* or end purpose of teaching and learning within the ambit of Theological Education (TE). Part 1 focused on both the 'who' of the person who teachers at a TE and the *telos* of the TE *per se*. This second part explores the 'what' dimensions of this same *telos* in relation to the following subtopics—the *telos* of the theological institution, Newman's *The Idea of the University,* Christ as the *telos* of life and education, and the *telos* of flourishing—searching for truth, beauty and goodness, all guided by the premise of a 'connected theology'.

The 'what' of the theological institution that teaches

1 The *telos* of the theological institution

Any effective development of the 'who' of the teacher must of necessity insinuate and flow into the *telos* of the institution and its various sub groups (for example, its faculty) involved in that process of teaching. This section argues that a detailed understanding of its *telos* is crucial for perceiving the theoretical and practical ends of a TE. It commences with an overview of Newman's idea of higher education (the University). It then proposes that this is evidenced through the TE's embracing of Christ as the *telos* of life and education, through the promotion of flourishing as the search for truth, beauty and goodness, and that such stances promote a 'connected theology'.

Langford asserts that the principal theme of John Henry Newman's *The Idea of the University* is:

> both famous and—in a way—surprising. He did not... [argue] for institutions in which theology was supreme—but pleaded instead for the essential integrity and independence of all the intellectual disciplines, including music, in a manner which made education valuable as an end in itself. The very term, 'university', he insists, implies a search for universal knowledge.[1]

2 Newman's *The Idea of the University*

Mike Higton poses the foundational and confronting question: 'Can the university and the church save each other?' He opens his article with a blunt assertion: 'At least at present, the Church and the University need each other in order to regain their right minds'.[2] He laments that the 'mission-shaped' Church is restricted in its almost obsessional fixation on:

> an instrumental vision, in which all its learning—its learning of doctrine, of Scripture, of its own history—is filtered and processed until it becomes fuel for a practical purpose, and the disruptive strangeness of those sources is in danger of being hidden in the rush to use.[3]

This essay takes issue with some views of educators such as Dewey who advocated that humanity has no predetermined, fixed telos or end state. For Dewey, the aim of democracy is democracy itself, just as the aim of growth is

---

1   Langford, 'Newman's *Idea of a University*', 18.
2   Higton, 'Can the University and the Church Save each Other?', 172.
3   Higton, 'Can the University and the Church?', 172.

further growth.[4] This essay asserts, to the contrary, that the telos of TE and Christian higher education is the person, the students and institution, all engaged in an endeavour that is expansive, dialogical, inclusive, flourishing, 'stretching', rigorous and critical, and that advocates Christ as the *telos* of life and education (refer to section 3 below).

In concert with the last statement, Henrie argues that 'the acquisition of useful knowledge is not the primary goal of a university education. While as a practical matter we must keep in mind our career, no human being is defined entirely by his work'.[5] Referencing John Henry Newman's *Idea of a University*, Henrie comments that what should be aimed for in seminaries, monasteries, and Catholic universities alike is:

> not so much mastery of a particular body of knowledge or of a scientific method, but mastery of the passions: training in moral virtue. Such an education is called ascesis. The student aims at a certain disposition of the soul with respect to acts... Certain dispositions of the soul must be achieved in order to study.[6]

Other Newman commentators stress his passionate involvement in the pastoral context of university education—his concern for the availability of wise role models/tutors whose vocation it was to lead their students into a culture of virtue, learning, and selfless service. Teachers, in Newman's purview, were role models, advisors, and cultivators of the good life in their students.[7] Dunne recognises 'breadth' of education, rather than 'instrumentalism', as a key legacy of Newman's thought. In what ways can this broadness be achieved? One method is 'by opening up issues of how the specific goods achieved through that practice fit with the pattern of individual human lives and as the common good of whole communities' and by creating an environment where the various disciplines are 'porous to each other'[8]—suggesting the cultivation of connected knowing between theology, spirituality, biblical studies, philosophy and other subjects.

According to MacIntyre, Newman's view about the *telos* of a university is governed by the belief that 'what matters about an educated individual is not

---

4   Based on Hansen's commentary on Dewey, cited in D'Agnese, 'The Essential Uncertainty of Thinking', 13.
5   Henrie, *The Telos of a University*, 5.
6   Henrie, *The Telos of a University*, 5-6.
7   Shrimpton, *The 'Making of Men'*.
8   Dunne, 'Newman Now: Re-Examining the Concepts of "Philosophical" and "Liberal"', 427.

primarily any set of useful skills that she or he may happen to possess, but her or his capacity for judgment, judgment both in putting these skills to work and in acting as a friend, as a companion, as a citizen, and in domestic life and in the pursuits of leisure'.[9] If the insights of Newman and others are ignored, argues MacIntyre, there is a danger 'that in research universities the ability to think about ends, including the ends [*telos*] of the university, will be lost and with it the ability to engage in radical self-criticism, so that the leadership of those universities will become complacent in their wrongheadedness'.[10]

Scruton observes:

> For Newman a university does not exist simply to convey information or expertise. The university is a society in which the student absorbs the graces and accomplishments of a higher form of life… [and where] the pursuit of truth and the active discussion of its meaning are integrated into a wider culture.[11]

The university of Newman's day was a place in which those in attendance 'lived for scholarship, and arranged their lives around the sacrifice that scholarship requires. It was not simply a repository of knowledge. It was a place where work and leisure occurred side by side, shaping each other, with each playing its part in producing the well-formed and graceful personality'.[12] Elsewhere Scruton asserts: 'Universities exist to provide students with the knowledge, skills, and culture that will prepare them for life, while enhancing the intellectual capital upon which we all depend. Evidently the two purposes are distinct. One concerns the growth of the individual, the other our shared need for knowledge'.[13]

Newman conceived the university as a milieu in which its attendees would accomplish at least four major creative principles, and in so doing refashion their Catholic intelligence and imagination (refer to Part 1, section 1.2). As Imbelli points out, the first of these principles is 'learning to see whole', whereby the student does not become obsessed by a curriculum but cultivates a certain quality of mind (refer to section 2.5 below on 'connected theology'). Imbelli fashions a compelling argument to support his thesis: 'The aim of education is to cultivate a discriminating intelligence, one able to perceive relationships and

---

9   MacIntyre, 'The Very Idea of a University', 15; referring to *The Idea of a University*, Discourse VII, 8, 129.
10 MacIntyre, 'The Very Idea', 18-19.
11 Scruton, 'The Idea of a University', 50.
12 Scruton, 'The Idea of a University', 50.
13 Scruton, 'The End of University', 25.

discern connections'.[14] The second principle is 'learning Christ':

> At the heart of Newman's religious faith and theological vision stands the person of Jesus Christ. Here human yearning finds its consummation, and 'all the providences of God' cohere around this vivifying center. Thus Incarnation is the central idea of principle that grounds and sustains Christian life and imagination... [Newman views Incarnation] as fulfilment of God's creative and sanctifying purpose.[15]

The third principle is 'learning holy living'. Behind this principle is Newman's belief that 'revelation was given not primarily for the sake of notional information, but for the sake of the real transformation of the recipient... [and that, following the Eastern fathers] the salvation won by Christ aimed at the divinization of humanity, a participation in the very life of God through Christ in the Spirit'.[16] Newman's final principle is 'learning to praise', by which he means Christ-centred praise by the person or community in light of the grace bestowed by God and in the form of the entire cosmos.[17]

On a related topic, Jones concludes his assessment on the resurrection of liberal education with the words: 'By centering on the student, rather than the institutional type, the delivery method, or the content area... a broad liberal education is possible and necessary for all and should prepare graduates simultaneously for work, civic participation, and life'.[18] Carol Geary Schneider, former president of the Association of American Colleges and Universities, echoes the same beliefs:

> A liberal education is characterized by enduring goals—fostering broad learning, developing the powers of the mind, cultivating ethical and civic responsibility, preparing learners to put knowledge to use... [in all this it is not static, since] it has constantly adapted its practices to the needs of a changing world... To make excellence inclusive, we must ensure that college learning is collaborative, not solitary.[19]

---

14   Imbelli, 'Refashioning Catholic Imagination, 16.
15   Imbelli, 'Refashioning Catholic Imagination', 16; refer to Section 2.3 below.
16   Imbelli, 'Refashioning Catholic Imagination', 17.
17   Imbelli, 'Refashioning Catholic Imagination', 18.
18   Jones, 'The Continuous Death and Resurrection of the Liberal Arts', 51.
19   Schneider, 'Making Excellence Inclusive: Roots, Branches, Future', 4, 6.

Nevertheless, despite the perceived virtues of a 'liberal education', proponents of this approach need also to be aware of its potential shortcomings. The list of standard charges issued by critics of higher education includes the following—academic work has become too specialised; its materials are often written in a technical language that is opaque to outsiders; the university curriculum has become fragmented and incoherent; and undergraduate education in particular seems adrift without any sense of common purpose (*telos*).[20] On the topic of liberal education, the typical criticisms are: it has become increasingly irrelevant in a world dominated by modern science and technology; it is economically useless; it no longer centres on the arts of language (student essay writing and other skills are deplorable); and while students are being taught to do independent research, they are not taught to think critically for themselves.[21] To this one more could be added: a lack of emphasis on the place of wisdom and philosophical thinking—'Liberal education was once understood as a spiritual discipline devoted to the search for wisdom: "There is only one really liberal study... the study of wisdom"'.[22]

3 Christ as the *telos* of life and education

There are some, both inside and outside the university system, who continue to adhere to beliefs about universities and education in general that have their origins in the evolution of an elite system of higher education initiated some thirty years ago.[23] However, there has been a substantial change during those years in how universities and education are now perceived, namely in their purpose or *telos*:

> There has also been a vast change in society's understanding of the purpose of education since the end of the Second World War. In the past, Australian educators have held one or two competing interpretations of the purpose of education: it would contribute to the emancipation of the industrial working class and reduce the disparity between classes or it would enable less privileged members of society to join the middle classes.[24]

---

20 Arndt, 'Liberal Education in Crisis', 60.
21 Arndt, 'Liberal Education in Crisis', 60.
22 Arndt, 'Liberal Education in Crisis', 82; citing Seneca, *Letters from a Stoic*, 152.
23 Laming, *The New Inheritors*, 3.
24 Laming, *The New Inheritors*, 5-6.

This essay argues that while the aforementioned statements of purpose still hold elements of truth, yet there is a different and deeper understanding of purpose or *telos* at play, especially within a TE or Catholic university. For the Christian TE, Jesus Christ is the *telos* of its life and education. For example, the *telos* of Nazarene Higher Education (guided by Wesleyan beliefs) is focused on principles such as the following—God's Kingdom/Reign of God now, not based on some abstract, future hope; the Holy Spirit's activity in course materials, people and institutions, not simply confined to 'religious' initiatives; the belief that sacred and secular domains are subject to the power of an omnipresent God; co-labouring with God for an optimism of Grace in students [Divine Pedagogy]; and acceptance of the tensions of wide learning, not for mere 'engagement' with knowledge, but Christian maturity.[25] Such principles trace their pedigree through passages such as: 'But these are written so that you may come to believe that Jesus is the Messiah, the Son of God, and that through believing you may have life in his name' (John 20:31).[26] The latter themes will be pursued under the related rubric of 'the Divine Pedagogy' in a future, related paper.

4 The *telos* of flourishing—searching for truth, beauty and goodness and other virtues

The God who accompanies both teacher and student within an institution, a small group, or any other context, is one who at the same time calls all to a life of 'flourishing'. Here we include a comparatively longer section on this topic, given its preeminent importance for the *telos* of the student, teacher and TE, as well as its prominence in Greek philosophy (especially Socrates and Aristotle).

Such a call to flourish, to reach one's full potential or personhood, is a fundamental theme evident in the biblical narratives. It appears, for example, in the call of God to Adam and Eve, including Adam's calling or naming of the first creatures (Gen. 2:19), the call of Abram (Gen. 12:1), the seeking after and rescuing of Hagar (Gen. 21:17), and perhaps the most famous call in the Hebrew Bible, the call of Moses (Exod. 3:4). In the Christian Bible, God in the person of Jesus is called and named as Son by God at his baptism (Luke 3:21-22). Jesus in turn calls the first disciples by name (Matt. 4:18), blesses peacemakers and calls them children of God (Matt. 5:9) and, in addition, calls his disciples to

---

25 Chenoweth & Ragan, '"Telos": The Destination for Higher Education', 7.
26 Division of Christian Education of the NCCC in the USA, *The Holy Bible: New Revised Standard Version*, hereafter referred to as the NRSV. Biblical references are to the NRSV unless otherwise indicated.

humility and the relinquishment of power, status and possessions (Matt. 20:25; see also the three-fold testing in the wilderness in Matt. 4:1-11). In a passage replete with overtones of 'flourishing', Jesus self-identifies as the life-giver rather than the death-dealing thief: 'The thief comes only to steal and kill and destroy. I came that they may have life, and have it abundantly' (John 10:10).

The common Greek word for happiness, or more accurately 'flourishing', is *eudaimonia*. *Eudaimonia* is a central concept in ancient Greek ethical and political philosophy. According to Bobonich, it is best translated as 'attaining one's best overall condition'.[27] He also argues that Socratic understandings of *eudaimonia*, or a rational eudaimonism, can allow for the intertwining of factors such as virtue and concern for the well-being of others. In his delineation of *eudaimonia*, Bobonich allows no place for instrumentalism. In rejecting this approach he states: 'A reasonable response to this objection is that rational eudaimonism [the desire to be happy] can allow that these things are not (merely) instrumental to my own happiness, but are themselves part of my happiness. So I do not choose, for example, virtue as a means to my happiness, but rather because a virtuous life is in itself part of what it is for me to live happily'.[28]

This call to happiness includes the presence of a strong ethical magnetism drawing people toward key values and virtues. Howard Gardner has argued for the primacy of three crucial virtues—truth, beauty, and goodness—when developments such as the Internet, new artistic expressions and art-speak, and relativistic morality, seem to have rendered them obsolete and to have shaken the foundations of many individuals' moral world-views.[29] In light of Gardner's research, all those involved in teaching and learning within TEs are obliged to ask themselves what virtues mean the most in the way I live out my life, indeed, what is of ultimate concern,[30] in today's postmodern, intercultural and globalised world.

Wolbert, de Ruyter and Schinkel take this line of thinking one important step further by deepening the concept of human flourishing (including cultivation of the virtues) as 'actualisation of human potential'.[31] Their article explores three

---

27 Bobonich, 'Socrates and Eudaimonia', 295.
28 Bobonich, 'Socrates and Eudaimonia', 330.
29 Refer to Gardner, *Truth, Beauty and Goodness Reframed: Educating for the Virtues in the Age of Truthiness & Twitter*, 1-5 and passim.
30 See for example Mackenzie Brown, *Ultimate concern*, passim; and Clarke, 'A discussion paper, passim.
31 Wolbert, de Ruyter & Schinkel, 'Formal criteria for the concept of human flourishing', 118.

sub-criteria to map the nature of this actualisation. They argue that 'flourishing as actualisation' is concerned with the whole of life, is a 'dynamic state', and presupposes there being objective goods.[32] More specifically, when they state that someone is 'flourishing', they mean that 'someone is functioning at a top level—an optimal level… [however,] how well someone's doing depends on her potential and the possibilities she gets in her life'.[33] The import of the 'flourishing' debate for educational discourse is that it forces all involved to ask what is really important in life and what matters in the end.[34] Kierkegaard stresses this same aspect of flourishing: 'the "one thing needful"… is the work of assuming the essential vulnerability of the human condition'.[35] For Wolbert et al., the ongoing challenge for educators is *not* to use the term 'flourishing' arbitrarily, but rather to put it into practice and evaluate it, and not use it as a cliché or confuse it with related terms such as well-being and happiness.[36]

Todd May also provides an analysis of 'flourishing' that is useful and relevant: 'Flourishing is the human telos. It is what being human is structured to aim at. Not all humans achieve a flourishing life. In fact, Aristotle thinks that a very flourishing life is rare'.[37] May's ultimate intention in his book, *A Significant Life: Human meaning in a silent universe,* is to make some subtle distinctions between the search for meaning, happiness, 'the good life', flourishing, values and virtue. May's understanding of 'the good life' is framed as follows:

> For Aristotle, the good life is not merely a state. One doesn't *arrive* at a good life. The telos of a human life is not an end result, where one becomes something and then spends the rest of one's life in that condition that one becomes… It is, instead, active and engaged with the world. It is an ongoing *expression* of who one is. This does not mean that there is no inner peace [or calm]. A person whose life is virtuous, Aristotle tells us, experiences more pleasure than a person whose life is not… However, a good life is not simply the possession of calm. It is one's very way of being in the world.[38]

---

32   Wolbert, de Ruyter & Schinkel, 'Formal criteria', 123-124.
33   Wolbert, de Ruyter & Schinkel, 'Formal criteria', 122.
34   Wolbert, de Ruyter & Schinkel, 'Formal criteria', 126.
35   Kangas, 'Søren Kierkegaard (1813-55), "An Occasional Discourse (Purity of Heart)"', in Holder, *Christian spirituality,* 287.
36   Wolbert, de Ruyter & Schinkel, 'Formal criteria', 126.
37   May, *A Significant Life: Human Meaning in a Silent Universe,* 4.
38   May, *A Significant Life: Human Meaning in a Silent Universe,* 5; May's emphases.

Gill and Thomson define 'flourishing' in general as 'well-being'. In their view it is characterised as '[h]aving an openness of feeling, creativity, a sense of oneself or of one's identify that is self-loving, and a strong connection to other people'.[39] They argue that spirituality and flourishing need to be considered hand in hand in order to achieve successful and integrated religious education.[40] The term 'flourishing' carries more meaning than other terms such as 'happiness' and 'well-being'. Flourishing cannot be limited to purely hedonic pursuits which might lead rather narrowly to subjective pleasures or feelings of gladness. By a similar token, 'flourishing' is more vitalising than 'well-being'. In the same text, Thomson argues that flourishing is 'more dynamic. It carries the idea that when a person's life is going well, the various parts work together in a mutually supportive way or symbiotically, such as a plant that is flowering'.[41] Flourishing is based on life-giving involvement in valuable kinds of activities, appreciation for life, and both positive self-perception and other-perception.[42]

Breadon aligns flourishing with the processes of fathoming, engaging and abiding. He links these in turn with the journey of spiritual development which is about 'the development of a sense of identity, self-worth, personal insight, meaning and purpose'.[43] According to Marshall, the educational paradigm of human flourishing 'takes into account what makes people happy and allows them the give and take that is part of successful communities. It balances justice and "rights" with compassion and responsibility'.[44] Flourishing within religious education, theological education or any form of education requires what Horthy terms the 'spiritual attitude'.

> It is sometimes called *mindfulness* and encompasses abilities like standing aside from thoughts, impartial watchfulness, awareness without ego (patience and acceptance), awareness of change (willingness to let go), and so on. I believe these abilities can be practiced, even with young children, for they make it harder for the ego and the intellect to crowd out the voice of the soul.[45]

A final compelling perspective on flourishing is drawn from the writings of

---

39 Gill & Thomson, *Redefining Religious Education*, 8.
40 Gill & Thomson, *Redefining Religious Education*, 8-10.
41 Thomson, 'A Framework for a Religious Life', 79.
42 Thomson, 'A Framework for a Religious Life', 79-82.
43 Breadon, 'Fathoming, Engaging, Abiding: The Story of the Wisdom Project', 178, citing OFSTED.
44 Marshall, 'Human Flourishing and a "Right to Education"', 46.
45 Horthy, 'Spirituality, Education, and Religion for a Human World', 69.

Harry Brighouse. In *On Education*, Brighouse states emphatically: 'The key idea in this book is that the central purpose of education is to promote human flourishing'.[46] In certain respects, compared to previous commentators on flourishing, including Socrates, his perspective is somewhat underdeveloped. Nevertheless, he does provide valuable insights into what flourishing might 'look like' within the educational domain.

Some of the aims of flourishing which Brighouse countenances are—to enable students to be autonomous and to prepare them for the labour market;[47] to have rich lives independent of participation in that economy;[48] to understand that happiness and flourishing are not identical;[49] and finally, to apprehend and prepare for aspects linked to students' long term flourishing, such as parenting, work/life balance, leisure and avoidance of consumerism.[50] He concludes: 'For somebody actually to flourish, they have to identify with the life they are leading. They have to live it from the inside, as it were'.[51]

5 The premise of a connected theology

One of the institutions at which the authors taught framed the 'what' of its theological institution in relation to a theology that is connected to the lives of students, communities, and to all academic disciplines. This theology of connection finds its full expression in the concrete praxis of staff, students and the world in which we live:

> In its scholarship, the Institute draws on the rich intellectual life of the Catholic tradition in dialogue with other faith traditions, all relevant academic disciplines, and the religious and non-religious debates that rage in the public square. Our goal is to pursue and share truth for its own sake by providing a forum for open discussion and enquiry into matters of concern for the human community wherever these concerns might be found.[52]

---

46 Brighouse, *On Education*, 42.
47 Brighouse, *On Education*, 42.
48 Brighouse, *On Education*, 2.
49 Brighouse, *On Education*, 47.
50 Brighouse, *On Education*, 54-55.
51 Brighouse, *On Education*, 16.
52 BBI-TAITE, *About Us*, www.bbi.catholic.edu.au/about-us/Our-Approach-and-Mission. Accessed 19/12/17.

Much of what is currently discussed under the heading of 'connected theology' owes its genesis to earlier discussions of 'connected knowing'. One could posit that 'connected theology' represents a type of connected knowing that can be cultivated within a theological context and TE. Connected knowing is understood here as manifold ways of knowing that eclipse the standard view of knowledge as information gained through reason. It eschews dualistic ways of knowing (mind/body, sacred/profane) and includes other often neglected forms of knowing such as silence, intuition, somatic knowing, and embodied knowing.[53] Barbour describes embodied knowledge as a type of knowing where the 'person views all knowledge as contextual and embodied. The person experiences him/herself as creator of and as embodying knowledge, valuing her/his own experiencing ways of knowing and reconciling these with other strategies for knowing as s/he lives out her/his life'.[54]

Based on theorists such as Barbour, and those she cites, a 'connected theology' not only links up individuals, groups and institutions, but privileges movement and physical expression of one's theological insights. The latter could be expressed via the arts, dance, interaction with the environment, walking and stationary meditation, *tai chi*, guided visualisation, and many other forms.[55] Other commentators such as Battle, while not always employing the expression 'connected theology', theorise that such an approach to theology/knowing is needed in order to move beyond a privatised spirituality and religion, and to connect with liturgy, prayer, and social justice, peace and activism.[56]

Still others, such as Lavallee, argue for the value and common sense of connecting divine and human realities by developing a brand of practical theology rooted in the Ignatian practice of spiritual discernment. He posits that this is one significant way of 'understanding connections among practical wisdom, habitus, research, and theological interpretation'.[57] For her part, Meek detects certain parallels between the connected knowing theories of Clinchy and Polanyi: 'Connected knowing and Polanyi's indwelling have much in common'.[58] Connected knowing in a theological context has much to recommend it such as—the pursuit of meaningfulness, exploration of cognitive and relational

---

53 Barbour, 'Embodied ways of knowing', 230.
54 Barbour, 'Embodied ways of knowing', 234.
55 For some examples, refer to Barbour, 'Embodied ways of knowing', 235.
56 Battle, 'Editorial—Social spirituality: Monastic cell or hectic street?', 393-394.
57 Lavallee, 'Practical theology from the perspective of Catholic spirituality', 203.
58 Meek, 'Cultivating Connected Knowing in the Classroom', 40.

connections, cultivation of hypothesising, questioning and imagination, as well as a necessary emphasis on attentiveness, carefulness, and empathic understanding of the other.[59]

One final but vital area of *telos* within theological institutions, namely the 'with whom' of the God who accompanies students and teachers in their learning, will include consideration of related topics such as the 'Divine Pedagogy' (the way in which God leads or guides individuals and institutions), and the associated pedagogical models of accompaniment, 'stretching' (*epektasis*), and prophetic imagination. While this warrants fuller discussion (to be developed elsewhere), space allows only brief indicators of these topics here.

Students and teachers within a theological institution are asked to reflect upon the nature and praxis of 'the Divine Pedagogy', namely the way God reveals truth to individuals and communities, leads and stretches them towards God's Self.[60] They are also asked to promote a theology/pedagogy of accompaniment. As Ospino notes: 'A pedagogy of accompaniment… defines Religious Education as a journey leading to a transforming encounter with God'. It asserts the importance of themes such as 'God with us' and 'Accompaniment as a spiritual journey'.[61]

Teachers and students within the environment of TE are also challenged to nurture a pedagogical stance of *epektasis* or the upward striving towards [straining/stretching towards] God. This straining is incremental and never ends, whether in this life or the next. Seen in this light, *theosis* expresses the understanding that people get more and more like God but without, however, attaining the fullness of God's transcendence (refer to Phil. 3:13, NRSV).[62] Finally, TE stakeholders are encouraged to develop the prophetic imagination. Brueggemann asserts: 'The task of prophetic ministry is to nurture, nourish, and evoke a consciousness and perception alternative to the consciousness and perception of the dominant culture around us'.[63] It includes a call to imagination and prophecy, pathos and amazement,[64] particularly in the face of technomania, consumerism, militarism, and media saturation.

---

59 Meek, 'Cultivating Connected Knowing in the Classroom', 40-42.
60 White, *The Way God Teaches: Catechesis and the Divine Pedagogy*.
61 Ospino, 'Theological Horizons for a Pedagogy of Accompaniment', 414, 418, 420.
62 Boersma, 'Becoming Human in the Face of God: Gregory of Nyssa's Unending Search for the Beatific Vision'.
63 Brueggemann, *The Prophetic Imagination*, 3.
64 Refer for example to the prophets Jeremiah and Isaiah, in Brueggemann, *Prophetic Imagination*, passim.

Conclusions and future directions—Towards a teleological praxis

This essay has argued that while there are traditional practices embedded within TE, perhaps the time has come for a consideration of a more radical and mature praxis and wisdom with regard to how teachers teach and how students learn. It has focused in particular on a deeper and practical understanding of the *telos* of the TE, specifically the 'what' of the theological institution engaged in that teaching.

The historical insights of Newman and others on *The Idea of the University* provide a valuable foundation for considering the *telos* of any TE. This 'what' of the TE locates its foundational integrity through an acknowledgement of Christ as the *telos* of life and education, and in the cultivation of flourishing among teachers and students, directed towards the search for truth, beauty and goodness. The latter topic, as treated in this essay in particular, represents a longer, sustained meditation on what is a crucial area of concern for all teachers and students involved in TE. The 'what' of the TE needs to be mindful of the need to promote a 'connected theology', characterised by connected knowing, which ought to move beyond strictly rational and informational approaches to knowing, and attempt to embrace intuitive, ecological, embodied and other neglected forms of knowing. As noted above, a future research article is required for the consideration of related topics such as the 'Divine Pedagogy' (the way in which God leads individuals and institutions), and the associated pedagogical models of accompaniment, 'stretching' (*epektasis*), and prophetic imagination.

One of the key challenges emerging from both Parts 1 and 2 of this study is the centrality of Christ, in relation to all discussions about the *telos* of theological education, and for the fundamental orientations of teachers, students, and institutions within that endeavour. For a Christian institution in particular, Christ is the *telos* of its vision and mission, its epistemology, its pedagogy, along with its approaches to online learning, flourishing, technology, student and faculty relationships, approaches to public theology, and so on. Christ is not a philosophy, idea or set of facts, but rather the face and person whom one *must encounter* in order to comprehend the *telos* of Christian theological education. In this sense, Christ as *telos* is constantly challenging all involved to stretch, cross frontiers, adapt, dialogue and transform. As William A. Dembski astutely observes:

> If we take seriously the word-flesh Christology of Chalcedon (i.e., the doctrine that Christ is fully human and fully divine) and view

Christ as the *telos* toward which God is drawing the whole of creation, then any view of the sciences that leaves Christ out of the picture must be seen as fundamentally deficient.[65]

Bibliography

Arndt, D.D. 'Liberal Education in Crisis', *Logos: A Journal of Catholic Thought* 19.3 (2016), 59-86.

Barbour, K. 'Embodied ways of knowing', *Waikato Journal of Education* 10 (2004), 227-238.

Battle, J. 'Editorial—Social spirituality: Monastic cell or hectic street?', *Political Theology* 8.4 (2007), 393-398.

BBI-TAITE. About Us, www.bbi.catholic.edu.au/about-us/Our-Approach-and-Mission 2020 Strategic Plan, 2. Accessed 19/12/17.

Bobonich, C. 'Socrates and Eudaimonia', in Donald R. Morrison (ed.), *The Cambridge Companion to Socrates* (Cambridge: CUP, 2011), 293-332.

Boersma, H. 'Becoming Human in the Face of God: Gregory of Nyssa's Unending Search for the Beatific Vision', *International Journal of Systematic Theology* 17.2 (2015), 131-151.

Breadon, J. 'Fathoming, Engaging, Abiding: The Story of the Wisdom Project', in Scherto R. Gill & Garrett Thomson (eds.), *Redefining Religious Education: Spirituality for Human Flourishing* (New York: Palgrave MacMillan, 2014), 177-191.

Brighouse, H. *On Education ('Thinking in Action' series)* (London & New York: Routledge, 2006).

Brown, D.M. (ed.). *Ultimate concern: Tillich in dialogue* (London: SCM Press, 1965).

Brueggemann, W. *The Prophetic Imagination* (2nd edn; Minneapolis, MN: Fortress, 2001).

Chenoweth, G.A. & B.M. Ragan (eds.). *'Telos': The Destination for Higher Education* (Kansas City, OH: Nazarene Publishing House, 2011).

Clarke, J. 'A discussion paper about "meaning" in the nursing literature on spirituality: An interpretation of meaning as "ultimate concern" using the work of Paul Tillich', *International Journal of Nursing Studies* 43.7 (2006), 915-921.

D'Agnese, V. 'The Essential Uncertainty of Thinking: Education and Subject in John Dewey', *Journal of Philosophy of Education* 1 (2016), 1-16.

Dembski, W.A. *Intelligent Design: The Bridge between Science and Theology* (Downers Grove, IL: IVP Academic, 1999).

Division of Christian Education of the NCCC in the USA. *The Holy Bible: New Revised Standard Version* (London: HarperCollinsPublishers, 1998).

---

65 Dembski, *Intelligent Design: The Bridge between Science and Theology*, 206.

Dunne, J. 'Newman Now: Re-Examining the Concepts of "Philosophical" and "Liberal"' in *'The Idea of the University', British Journal of Educational Studies* 54.4 (2006), 412-428.

Gardner, H. *Truth, Beauty and Goodness Reframed: Educating for the Virtues in the Age of Truthiness & Twitter* (New York: Basic Books, 2011).

Gill, S. & G. Thomson (eds.). *Redefining Religious Education: Spirituality for Human Flourishing.* (New York: Palgrave MacMillan, 2014).

Henrie, M.C. *The 'Telos' of a University* (2007) http://dappledthings.org/83/the-telos-of-a-university/ [accessed 25 November 2015].

Higton, M. 'Can the University and the Church Save each Other?', *Cross Currents* 55.2 (2005), 172-183.

Horthy, S.I. 'Spirituality, Education, and Religion for a Human World', in Scherto R. Gill & Garrett Thomson (eds.), *Redefining Religious Education: Spirituality for Human Flourishing* (New York: Palgrave MacMillan, 2014), 59-70.

Imbelli, R.P. 'Refashioning Catholic Imagination: Newman's writings offer a framework for a New Way of Thinking', *America* 203.7 (2010), 14-18.

Jones, N. 'The Continuous Death and Resurrection of the Liberal Arts', *Liberal Education* 101/102: 4/1 (2016), 44-51.

Kangas, D. J. (2010). 'Søren Kierkegaard (1813-55), "An Occasional Discourse (Purity of Heart)"', in Arthur G. Holder (ed.), *Christian spirituality: The classics* (London & New York: Routledge, 2010), 281-292.

Laming, M.M. *The New Inheritors: Transforming Young People's Expectations of University* (Rotterdam, NL: Sense Publishers, 2012).

Langford, M. 'Newman's *Idea of a University'*, *Prospero* 20.1 (2014), 18-19.

Lavallee, M.H. 'Practical theology from the perspective of Catholic spirituality: A hermeneutic of discernment', *International Journal of Practical Theology* 20.2 (2016), 203-221.

MacIntyre, A. 'The Very Idea of a University: Aristotle, Newman and Us', *New Blackfriars,* 91.1031 (2009), 4-19.

Marshall, K. 'Human Flourishing and a "Right to Education"', in Scherto R. Gill & Garrett Thomson (eds.), *Redefining Religious Education: Spirituality for Human Flourishing* (New York: Palgrave MacMillan, 2014), 43-58.

May, T. *A Significant Life: Human Meaning in a Silent Universe* (Chicago & London: The University of Chicago Press, 2015).

Meek, E.L. 'Cultivating Connected Knowing in the classroom', *Tradition & Discovery* 34.1 (2007), 40-48.

Ospino, H. 'Theological Horizons for a Pedagogy of Accompaniment', *Religious Education* 105.4 (2010), 413-429.

Schneider, C.G. 'Making Excellence Inclusive: Roots, Branches, Future', *Liberal Education* 102.2 (2016), 4-7.

Scruton, R. 'The End of University', *First Things* 252 (2015), 25-30.

Scruton, R. 'The Idea of a University', *The American Spectator* 43.7 (2010), 50-52.

Shrimpton, P. *The 'Making of Men'. The Idea and Reality of Newman's University in Oxford and Dublin* (Leominster, HR: Gracewing, 2014).

Thomson, G. 'A Framework for a Religious Life', in Scherto R. Gill & Garrett Thomson (eds.), *Redefining Religious Education: Spirituality for Human Flourishing* (New York: Palgrave MacMillan, 2014), 71-86.

White, J.D. *The Way God Teaches: Catechesis and the Divine Pedagogy* (Huntingdon, IN: Our Sunday Visitor, 2014).

Wolbert, L.S., D.J. de Ruyter, & A. Schinkel. 'Formal criteria for the concept of human flourishing: The first step in defending flourishing as an ideal aim of education', *Ethics and Education* 10.1 (2015), 118-129.

Peter Mudge
Australian Catholic University (ACU National)
pjpmudge@gmail.com

Dan Fleming
St Vincent's Health Australia
Daniel.fleming@svha.org.au

10 | A VISION FOR THE GOOD LIFE

SHALOM AS A *TELOS* FOR CHRISTIAN FORMATION IN TEACHING THEOLOGICAL REFLECTION

Abstract

In 2012 Ball called for theological education that is holistic and integrated. Research led learning and teaching of theological reflection (TR) as holistic Christian formation remains largely unexplored as a direct response to this challenge. This article draws on the author's current research and praxis as a theological field educator to sketch the basics of a model for TR based upon the coinherent relationship between students' spiritual, theological and ministerial formation. The case is then made for the importance of a *telos*—a vision for the good life—that helps students connect their formation to God's bigger picture through the craft of TR. The conventional *telos* of one's unique self growing into the image of Christ is surveyed, before *the walk towards shalom* is posited as a more suitable alternative for teaching TR, in light of its multifaceted, 'glocal', embodied and hopeful nature. The article concludes with some brief observations for theological educators.

Introduction

Research in recent decades highlights the enduring need for integrated, holistic

Christian formation within theological education.[1] Developing robust theology, excellent ministry skills, and/or vibrant spirituality, independently, is inadequate. As Hibbert and Hibbert argue, the 'key to enhancing theological education is the intentional integration of knowing with being and doing, of theory with practice, and of theology with life and ministry'.[2] Similarly Ball notes that:

> [t]here is a widespread and strongly expressed desire for theological education to be holistic and integrated rather than being based on sets of content that are often disconnected from one another and from life beyond the classroom. Such integration will combine cognitive, practical and affective elements… In total, it aims at a congruence of creed, conduct and character within the person of the graduate.[3]

Responses have varied, including the reassessing of aims, purposes and modes of delivery, with more *in situ*/practical learning; curriculum integration to address the siloing of disciplines; an increased emphasis upon affective/personal/spiritual domains in student learning; greater integration in life and ministry with faculty and students; problem-based learning; and learning from the medical model of education.[4] Such measures are welcome.

Still lacking, however, are models for learning and teaching the craft of theological reflection (TR) specifically developed to address this challenge. TR in this sense does not describe the general interpretation of texts and traditions, or theology on a grand scale, like systematic theology. Instead, this is TR as the engine room of practical theology. It begins with lived experience, connects this to faith, and draws out practical implications for Christian living and formation.[5] It is attuned to what Farley described as 'one of the essential components of theology itself, the theological interpretation of situations'.[6] The capacity and *habitus* for TR as a lifelong craft that fosters holistic formation, then, is surely a key graduate attribute. Wood affirms this:

---

1   E.g. Hibbert and Hibbert, 'Addressing the Need for Better Integration in Theological Education'; Farley, *Theologia*; Kelsey, *Between Athens and Berlin*; Edgar, 'The Theology of Theological Education'.
2   Hibbert and Hibbert, 'Addressing the Need for Better Integration in Theological Education', 107.
3   Ball, *Transforming Theology*, 125–26.
4   Hibbert and Hibbert, 'Addressing the Need for Better Integration in Theological Education'.
5   Kinast, *What Are They Saying About Theological Reflection?*, 1.
6   Farley, 'Interpreting Situations,' 1.

> The aim of *theological* education… is not to form Christians, but to form the habit of critical reflection on one's formation. It is not to mediate the content of the Christian tradition, but to equip one for theological reflection upon the Christian tradition. It is not to train in leadership skills, but to cultivate an aptitude for reflection on the quality of one's own and others' leadership as an instrument of the church's witness.[7]

Research led learning and teaching of TR for ongoing whole-person formation, then, is crucial. This conviction shapes my own research and praxis as a theological field educator at Tabor, a multi-denominational higher education institution in Adelaide. My approach centres on developing a theology for teaching students to reflect theologically upon the lived experience of their journeys—to 'talk their walk'—in ways that nurture their holistic formation as Christians—indeed as human beings—into God's future already begun in Christ. Holistic formation in this setting is informed by three questions.

First, *what dimensions of formation might be considered in theological reflection?* Theological anthropologies identify a variety of strands that weave together in the mysterious tapestry of our formation. For instance, Chandler names spirit, emotions, relationships, intellect, vocation, physical health, and resource stewardship.[8] Chae et al identify interiority, psychosexual and affective integration, conversation, critical thinking, universal perspective, and discerned action.[9] Willard recognises thought, feeling, choice, body, social context and soul.[10]

However, research shows that complex models used for teaching TR often bear little ongoing fruit for students within and beyond their study.[11] So any model employed needs to be accessible for students, and adaptable for their preferred learning style/s. I suggest that the aspects of *spirituality*, *theology*, and *ministry* serve well for teaching TR as holistic formation. Aside from the relative simplicity of working with just three dimensions for formation, there are many resonating threefold expressions to be found elsewhere in the theological education literature, in such examples as creed, conduct and character (Ball);[12]

---

7   Wood, 'Theological Education and Education for Church Leadership', 310.
8   Chandler, 'Whole-Person Formation'.
9   Chae SJ et al., 'Forming a Contemplative in Action', 3.
10 Willard, *Renovation of the Heart*, 36.
11 Pattison, Thompson, and Green, 'Theological Reflection for the Real World'.
12 Ball, *Transforming Theology*, 126.

intellectual, personal and pastoral formation (Mayes);[13] knowing, being and doing (Shakespeare);[14] cognitive, normative and practical knowledge (Foster et al);[15] orthodoxy, orthopathy and orthopraxy (Steele);[16] beliefs, desires and practices (Jones);[17] cognition, affects and behaviour (Shaw);[18] understanding, attitudes and practices (Banks).[19] A narrative lens provides yet another helpful locus for TR upon each dimension, by using *my story* (spirituality), *God's story* (theology), and *your story* of others/the world around us (ministry). The choice of these three is also heuristic. The claim is not that they cover every angle, nor that we can neatly segment ourselves; rather, like a 'rule of thumb', they provide a way of conceiving and reflecting upon holistic formation that seems to work. Importantly, holding these three together incorporates the role of personhood/spirituality in TR, beyond the theory-practice interface alone—something absent, at least explicitly, in many TR models.

Second, *how do these dimensions relate?* While 'balance'[20] and 'congruence'[21] have been suggested, 'integration' is certainly the most common idea. Integration, however, implies the bringing together of things that can otherwise exist independently. A closer exploration suggests the notion of *coinherence* may provide a richer understanding. Coinherence describes '[t]hings that exist in essential relationship with another, as innate components of the other'[22] (for example the two natures of Christ). In terms of Christian formation, spirituality, theology and ministry are essential dimensions of one another. No one dimension is its actual self apart from its relationship to the other two. Thus, coinherence allows consideration of various aspects of formation while affirming the essential unity of the human person. Coinherent TR, then, is like viewing an experience through a kaleidoscope. One position views it through the lens of one's own personal story (spirituality); twist the kaleidoscope a little, and it is viewed through the lens of God's story (theology); twist it again, and it is viewed through the lens of our interaction with your story—that of the others/context

---

13 Mayes, *Spirituality in Ministerial Formation*, 175.
14 Shakespeare, 'Knowing, Being and Doing'.
15 Foster et al, *Educating Clergy*, 8–10.
16 Steele, *On the Way*, 101–5.
17 Jones, 'Beliefs, Desires, Practices, and the Ends of Theological Education', 189.
18 Shaw, *Transforming Theological Education*, chapter 4.
19 Banks, *Reenvisioning Theological Education*, 226.
20 Shakespeare, 'Knowing, Being and Doing', 16.
21 Ball, *Transforming Theology*, 126.
22 Spaeth, 'The Concept of Co-Inherence In the Writings of Charles Williams'.

involved (ministry). Our perspective on each is shaped by the others. Coinherence thus provides an important contour for talking our walk in recognising the interdependence of these dimensions.

Third—and here I turn to the key focus of this paper—*what is Christian formation in these dimensions headed towards?* Reflection upon our formation is often retrospective in orientation. Contemplating prior experience is the starting point for attentiveness to the Presence and Person of God in our journey. Eschatological imagination, however, is equally critical. Kierkegaard asserted that '… life must be understood backwards … but… lived forwards'.[23] History and eschatology, together, offer insight into our present formation.

The goal or *telos* of Christian formation is important in the context of doing TR, because as Reuschling notes, '[o]ur lives will be orientated around what we love and what we view as good'.[24] Our picture of the good life, to a large degree, influences our approach to meaning making and interpretation of present experience, and hence what we are becoming in and through that reflection process. It seems strange that such an eschatological lens is largely absent from TR models, especially since this picture needs constant recalibration.

I use the term 'the good life' deliberately, even provocatively. Its popular understanding connects us with the Western cultural narrative of a frantic striving for financial security, status, sexual gratification on demand, owning the latest gadgetry, sipping a cocktail at an island resort, or always being happy. Sine terms it 'the good life of the Global Mall'.[25] As Mackay contends, it is a hollow vision.[26] But we may be surprised at how much it shapes our meaning-making. If my vision of the good life is limited to getting ahead, then that will colour my discernment towards self-centred comfort. If it is staying out of trouble and playing it safe, that will colour my discernment towards self-preservation. Equally, the good life may take other subtler, even religious forms. If it is shunning myself to try and discover God's perfect plan A for my life, that will colour my discernment towards a fearful second-guessing of the divine mind. If it is pleasing a demanding God, being noticed by others, living someone else's life and not my own, getting into heaven, being a 'good Christian'—these will colour my discernment towards a life of performance and trying to measure up. TR with a skewed vision will tend towards constriction, and most likely malformation of some sort.

---

23 Dru, *The Journals of Kierkegaard*, 89.
24 Reuschling, *Becoming Whole and Holy*, 128.
25 Sine, *The New Conspirators*, 71–92.
26 Mackay, *The Good Life*.

So in teaching TR, we need our various, prevailing notions of the good life subverted and redefined in light of a biblical eschatology, a homecoming to the 'good life of God'[27] that has already begun in Jesus. This is Jesus' 'life to the full',[28] characterised, I will argue, by the biblical notion of *shalom*. Students being introduced to TR need a theologically robust vision for this good life; one that frames reflection upon their particular and localised formation within the expanse of the divine purpose, and in turn facilitates hopeful living expressed in thought, passion and action commensurate with that purpose. While such an eschatological emphasis may be implicit in some models of TR, it needs to be brought to the fore. But before we can consider *shalom* as such a *telos*, we must first explore the two most conventional goals for Christian formation.

The *Telos* of Christian Formation?

Most authors emphasise our formation into Christ's image. Mulholland's definition is representative: '[Spiritual formation is] a process of being conformed to the image of Christ for the sake of others'.[29] Frequent emphases include character traits and the 'inner life' (for example fruits of the Spirit), the Holy Spirit's work within us, the role of community in formation, and the ultimate outcome being mission/service to others and the world. This view arises from key passages such as Romans 12:2; 2 Corinthians 3:18; Galatians 4:19; Ephesians 4:11-13; Colossians 1:28, 3:9-10; 1 John 3:2. Christian formation is the journey of becoming more fully human, and in Christ we find the *true* human being—living secure as the Beloved of God, reciprocating that love to the Father, and ministering that love in the Spirit to the world with servant-shaped authority.

This *telos* of formation into Christ necessarily points to our creation *imago Dei* and participation in the perichoretic, hospitable life of the Trinity. Reuschling explains:

> We are and will always be becoming in relationships, understanding our true selves as we understand all that God is in trinitarian relations. The wholeness and completeness of these divine relation-

---

27 Sine, *The New Conspirators*, 95–109.
28 John 10:10.
29 Mulholland, *Invitation to a Journey*, 12.

ships are settled yet open to the world without losing anything; and because they are, they provide the *telos* for what we are to become. We too can become open to the Other without losing anything in the ways that reflect the relationships of the Trinity. In fact, it is only by openness to the Other that we can gain understanding necessary for being and becoming.[30]

Reuschling surmises, then, that '[t]here is so little about me that has anything to do with me apart from others'.[31] Formation is fundamentally relational, and thus, communal. As Hall asserts, being means being-with.[32]

Others, however, also emphasize growth towards our authentic and unique selves. A focus upon our formation into Christlikeness in the context of community should not diminish the uniqueness of Christian formation. For me this tension is highlighted when students are sometimes dismissive of the invitation to ponder honestly their own desires. 'It's not about what I want, it's all about what God wants' is the reply; John the Baptist's words, '[Jesus] must increase, I must decrease', become a mantra. Such reticence may stem from fear of what such self-examination may reveal, or perhaps an embedded theology that equates self-knowledge with self-centred navel-gazing. Whatever the reason, it can engender a bland and generalised vision of Christian formation. Students are not freed to map their inner geography through the befriending of their biography, thus hindering the task of daily, *particular* living and discernment of how 'Christ-likeness' is incarnated within the unique context of *their* story. Benner comments:

> We should never be tempted to think that growth in Christlikeness reduces our uniqueness ... Paradoxically as we become more and more like Christ we become more uniquely our own true self ... [d]eep knowing of God and deep knowing of self always develop interactively. The result is the authentic transformation of the self that is at the core of Christian spirituality.[33]

This uniqueness of self is reflected in Psalm 139. The Psalmist ponders and marvels at his particular formation, from the womb right into adult life, in light

---

30 Reuschling, *Becoming Whole and Holy*, 121.
31 Reuschling, *Becoming Whole and Holy*, 121.
32 Hall, *Imaging God*, 116.
33 Benner, *The Gift of Being Yourself*, 31.

of how thoroughly he is known by God. This in turn opens him further to knowing God. God-knowledge/self-knowledge is also affirmed in Christian writings past and contemporary, including Augustine,[34] Meister Eckhart,[35] Catherine of Siena,[36] Thomas à Kempis,[37] Teresa of Avila,[38] Calvin,[39] Merton,[40] Palmer,[41] and Scazzero.[42]

Growth into both Christ in community, *and* one's unique self, reflects the paradoxical dynamics and tension between relatedness/interdependence/connectedness and particularity/autonomy/uniqueness in Christian formation. Each polarity is necessary to reinforce the other. For Balswick et al, this is expressed in *reciprocating self* as the *telos* of Christian formation, flowing from the perichoretic relations of the Trinity:

> [P]articularity and relatedness co-occur because their relatedness is characterized by perfect *reciprocity* where the three live with and for each other… [T]o live as being made in the image of God is to exist as reciprocating selves, as unique individuals living in relationship with others. We then assert that developmental teleology, the goal of human development as God intends, is the reciprocating self. To live according to God's design is to glorify God [by living and acting] as a distinct human being in communion with God and others in mutually giving and receiving relationships.[43]

The relationality of this reciprocating self is reflected, for example, in Paul's imperative, 'Do not lie to each other, since you have taken off your old self with its practices and have put on the new self, which is being renewed in knowledge in the image of its Creator'.[44] Falsehood against neighbour actually stems from falsehood in self, an acting out of the old self. This is akin to Merton's *false self*, a living in the illusion of existence 'outside the reach of God's will and God's

---

34 Cited in Pourrat, *Christian Spirituality from the Time of Our Lord Till the Dawn of the Middle Ages*, 291.
35 Cited in McGinn, *The Mystical Thought of Meister Eckhart*, 45.
36 Cited in McDermott, 'Catherine of Siena's Teaching on Self-Knowledge', 641.
37 Kempis, *The Imitation of Christ*, 5.
38 *Complete Works St. Teresa Of Avila*, 209.
39 Calvin, *Institutes of the Christian Religion*, 15.
40 Merton, *New Seeds of Contemplation*, 36.
41 Palmer, *Let Your Life Speak*, 10.
42 Scazzero, 'Know Yourself That You May Know God'.
43 Balswick, King, and Reimer, *The Reciprocating Self*, 31.
44 Col. 3:9-10.

love—outside of reality and outside of life'.⁴⁵ Conversely, formation—or in Paul's language, renewal—into the image of our Creator is the new or true self being freed to become who we uniquely already are. Formation into both Christ's image and our own skin are thus intrinsically connected. They are two sides of the same coin, and Jesus' assertion that those who lose their life for his sake will truly find it is the paradoxical pivot upon which that coin spins.⁴⁶

'The Walk Towards Shalom' as a *Telos* for Christian Formation

Christian formation, then, is God's work of our becoming our unique and true self in Christ. This is a rich teleology for Christian formation. However, when teaching the craft of TR, it needs exegeting so students can make particular connections that foster formation and hope towards that *telos*. Reflecting upon growth in Christlikeness can too easily be characterised by vague generalisations: 'How can I be more patient, more prayerful, more loving, more kind, closer to God? WWJD?!' Moreover, students' TR upon their unique selfhood can become myopic, losing sight of a more expansive vision. How does TR help them locate their reciprocating self within the thrust of God's metanarrative? TR needs to help students understand their formation beyond a mere 'me-and-Jesus' personal self-improvement project. As Smith says, 'Even if there is a centrifugal *telos* to Christian worship and formation, there is also a regular centripetal invitation to recenter ourselves in the Story, to continually pursue and deepen our incorporation'.⁴⁷ TR as formation needs a goal that is both local to us, and global, beyond us. That is, it needs a 'glocal' *telos*.⁴⁸

A *telos* for Christian formation in teaching TR must also be suitable pedagogically: rich, evocative and biblically and theologically robust, yet succinct, accessible and applicable for the purposes of teaching TR. Moreover, in correlation with the spirituality/theology/ministry model of formation outlined earlier, it needs to reflect and illustrate the coinherence between my story, God's story and your story.

---

45   Merton, *New Seeds of Contemplation*, 36.
46   Matt. 10:39, 16:25; Luke 9:24.
47   Smith, *Imagining the Kingdom*, 154.
48   'Glocal' is a neologism that describes the intimate connection between local and global contexts. See Love, 'Following Jesus in a Glocalized World: Bearers of Blessing Among Neighbors and Nations'.

The walk towards shalom meets these criteria well. While this does not explicitly appear in any TR models I am aware of, Reuschling, a Christian ethicist, does make the connection:

> *Shalom…* [as] the wholeness that God intends for all that is created in the good image of the trinitarian God… reflects a consonance between who we are, what we are becoming, what we love, and how we live. *Shalom enables us to interpret and reflect on the episodes of our lives*,[49] and it informs and directs our actions to establish 'an approved pattern of our lives'. What we care about, how we view life, what narrative we choose to live by (or which narrative chooses us), and how we perceive God's ultimate purposes are moral matters and crucial for our conceptions of wholeness. Our lives will be orientated around what we love and what we view as good.[50]

Reuschling's assertion that *shalom* provides an interpretative lens provides an intriguing invitation to rethink TR and the *telos* of formation in light of the Psalmist's and Peter's encouragement to 'seek peace (*shalom*), and pursue it'.[51] What, then, is the nature of this *telos* we are to pursue? *Shalom* is multifaceted, glocal, embodied and hopeful.

Shalom is Multifaceted

Often translated 'peace', *shalom*[52] is a multifaceted Old Testament word that means much more than just tranquillity or the absence of conflict. Rooted in notions of 'completeness' or 'wholeness' (the verb *shālēm* means 'be complete, be sound'), it can convey 'health, security, well-being, and salvation as well as peace'.[53] 'Flourishing' may be our best equivalent in the English language. '[T]he fundamental idea is totality', states Harris. '[A]nything that contributes to this wholeness makes for *shalom*. Anything that stands in the way disrupts *shalom*'.[54]

---

49 Emphasis mine.
50 Reuschling, *Becoming Whole and Holy*, 127–28.
51 Ps. 34:14; 1 Pet. 3:11.
52 שָׁלֹם, shalom.
53 Scobie, *The Ways of Our God*, 881.
54 Harris, *Shalom!*, 14.

A VISION FOR THE GOOD LIFE

As both Brueggemann[55] and Barker[56] note, however, it is not captured by a single word or idea; *shalom* carries different nuances for different biblical contexts. For instance, for the 'have nots' *shalom* carries the theme of liberation from suffering, sin, slavery and death; it is expressed as a cry for help from a precarious position of survival and desperation, and responded to by God's fidelity to save. For the 'haves', *shalom* is about the blessing of the Creator's gift of life, goodness, beauty and wholeness. This connects with Paul's command to attend to whatever is true, honourable, just, pure, pleasing, commendable, excellent and worthy of praise[57]—such things reflect the aesthetic nature of *shalom*. The appropriate response, then, is celebration, wonder and awe, gratitude and enjoyment, and obedience to God's summons to proper management and generous stewardship.[58]

Whatever the context, *shalom* is a gracious gift. It is God who declares, 'I will give you *shalom* in the land… I will remove wild animals from the land',[59] and it is God who, in the Aaronic blessing,[60] is asked to grant the recipients the divine blessing of *shalom*. Such promises and prayers reflect its covenantal nature, with the prophets Isaiah and Ezekiel even referring to a 'covenant of peace [*shalom*]'.[61] Thus, as Scobie notes, while *shalom* can be experienced by individuals,[62] the Old Testament emphasis is predominantly communal and relational rather than individual.[63] As such, reconciliation is a key facet of *shalom*, for where there are fractured relationships between individuals, communities, nations, creation or with God, there can be no peace.

A common inhibitor of *shalom* is the abuse of power. God is harsh towards those who would proclaim, 'Peace! Peace!' where there is none.[64] Brueggemann asserts that the summons to the well-off and powerful to responsible stewardship means *shalom* cannot be caged, with concern only for their own holiness and wholeness/well-being. 'They are the ones held accountable for *shalom*. The prophetic vision of *shalom* stands against… all "separate peaces", all ghettos,

---

55 Brueggemann, *Living toward a Vision*, 27.
56 Barker, 'Rest, Peace', 689.
57 Phil. 4:8.
58 Brueggemann, *Living toward a Vision*; Westermann, 'Peace (Shalom) in the Old Testament'.
59 Lev. 26:6; cf. Ps. 4:8, 29:11.
60 Num. 6:24-26.
61 E.g. Is. 54:9-10; Ezek. 34:25, 37:26; see also Num. 25:12. cf. Is. 52:7; Jer. 32:36-41.
62 E.g. Ps. 55:18; Prov. 3:2; 1 Sam. 1:17, 25:6.
63 Scobie, *The Ways of Our God*, 882.
64 Jer. 6:13-14.

that pretend that others are not there… Religious legitimacy in the service of self-deceiving well-being is a form of chaos. *Shalom* is never the private property of the few'.[65]

Thus, *shalom* is closely linked to righteousness and justice. Isaiah lays out the vision for a king who reigns in righteousness. 'The fruit of righteousness', declares the prophet, 'will be *shalom*; the effect of righteousness will be quietness and confidence forever'.[66] Conversely, where justice is absent, there can be no *shalom*;[67] hence Plantinga's definition of sin as 'culpable shalom-breaking'.[68] This means *shalom* carries with it not only attention to and promotion of God's righteousness, goodness and wholeness; it calls for active resistance against anything that disrupts well being in a person, community, nation or creation. In this sense, *shalom* is certainly neither passive nor tranquil.

Jewish scholar Abraham Heschel notes how we see this clearly in two contrasting images for justice.[69] The predominant image in the Western world is often called the 'Goddess of Justice'; a blindfolded woman holds a sword and a set of scales. In presiding, she sees neither victim nor perpetrator; impartiality demands she be protected from connection to either. Judgement is according to the precision of the law, a universal and static ideal against which evidence is weighed with clinical fairness and everybody gets their due, achieving perfect balance. 'The image of the scales conveys the idea of form, standard, balance, measure, stillness'.[70]

Contrast this to the image in Amos 5:24 (NIV): 'But let justice roll on like a river, righteousness like a never-failing stream'! Justice and righteousness are a raging, surging, unfailing torrent, with God as its source. 'The image of the mighty stream expresses content, substance, power, movement, vitality'.[71] This stream brings life, cleansing and wholeness. Nothing is at rest, because God is never at rest while *shalom* is absent or opposed. Our concept of justice might be fairness because everyone agrees it is a reasonable idea, but God's justice is entirely relational. That is because *shalom* is rooted in divine *pathos*—God's deep compassion for all creation, which compels action. God is not upset at the

---

65 Brueggemann, *Living toward a Vision*, 21.
66 Is. 32:17.
67 E.g. Jer. 6:13-14,16:5; Is. 59:8; Zech. 8:16.
68 Plantinga Jr, *Not the Way It's Supposed to Be*, 14.
69 Heschel, *The Prophets*, 271–76.
70 Heschel, *The Prophets*, 275.
71 Heschel, *The Prophets*, 275.

disruption of *shalom* because a universal law is broken, but because a person or persons are hurt.[72] God sees, and God acts.

Scobie notes the strong continuity between *shalom* and *eirēnē* in the New Testament. '[W]e must expect a strong carryover from the OT understanding with its connotations of wholeness, health, salvation, and harmonious relationships'.[73] Indeed, the LXX uses *eirēnē* to translate *shalom*. Hence the various associations of *eirēnē* with Jesus' ministry, death and resurrection affirms the reconciliation, justice, beauty and wholeness of *shalom* as ultimately Christocentric. Christ is, after all, the Davidic messiah who is the 'Prince of *shalom*'.[74] Christ 'himself is our peace', who reconciles us to himself and to each other,[75] and gives us his peace.[76] *Shalom* is also pneumatological; Jesus' gift comes through the breath of the Spirit,[77] as foreshadowed in Isaiah's vision in which the Spirit is poured from on high to bring justice and righteousness, and thus, *shalom*.[78] In this, *shalom* reflects the grand eschatological vision in Isaiah 65 of the new heavens and the new earth coming together as one, pointing forward to the eventual harmony of all things. The inclusion of all creation in this eschatology—the lamb and the lion lay down together—challenges the anthropocentricity common in much contemporary eschatology. *Shalom* is ecological. It reminds us to pair together our creation *imago Dei* (Gen. 1:27) and *imago mundi* (Gen. 2:7), for Christian formation is not just a human affair. Our future in God is with the created order: united, everlasting, and thoroughly physical.

In the meantime, God's *shalom* is given for embodiment in all relationships, including with people who do not yet know its reality. *Shalom* is missional. Surely there was surprise at Jeremiah's words to the exiled community in Babylon as recorded in chapter 29. No doubt God's people hoped for a word of deliverance from the surrounding evil. That is indeed God's promise, with plans for their 'welfare [*shalom*] and not for harm',[79] but not before seventy years as settled residents where they are to 'seek the welfare [*shalom*] of the city where I have sent you into exile, and pray to the LORD on its behalf, for in its welfare

---

72 Heschel, *The Prophets*, 275.
73 Scobie, *The Ways of Our God*, 904.
74 Is. 9:6.
75 Eph. 2.
76 Jn. 20:22; cf. Jn. 14:27.
77 Jn. 20:21-22.
78 Is. 32:15-17.
79 Jer. 29:11.

[*shalom*] you will find your welfare [*shalom*]'.[80] Similarly, Jesus sends his disciples out as bringers of peace to any house they set foot in,[81] and couples his blessing of peace with his commission to the disciples as sent ones.[82]

This brief précis suggests *shalom* is a rich, broad and malleable concept that distils and delineates the story of God. Writers have distilled such broad and rich facets of *shalom* to a few words or phrases in a variety of ways. For example, Neal utilises an acrostic developed by *Communities of Shalom* to help faith communities experience and express six 'threads' of *shalom*,[83] while Milton identifies 'regeneration, identity and destiny'.[84] However, Frost provides three words that seem to provide an accessible summary for students that reflects much of what *shalom* represents: reconciliation, justice, and beauty. To this I would add wholeness.[85] To walk towards reconciliation, justice, beauty and wholeness in our lives, is to walk towards *shalom*.

Shalom is Glocal
In what arenas does God outwork these facets of *shalom*? Here Brueggemann provides a helpful three-fold structure that connects well to the three threads of formation identified earlier: my story (spirituality), God's story (theology), and your story, that of others/world around us (ministry).

First, Brueggemann points to its most inclusive dimension: the cosmic vision of God's grand story, that of *shalom* encompassing all reality.[86] '*Shalom* is the substance of the biblical vision of one community embracing all creation'.[87] God's meta, eschatological purposes for all creation—wholeness, well-being, flourishing, right relationships, justice, compassion, reconciliation, harmony, beauty—are captured and served well by 'the controlling vision [of] *shalom*'.[88] *Shalom* reflects the overarching theme of 'God's story', the metanarrative which frames our theological understanding of God's person and action.

The second dimension is social: *shalom* is outworked at the *historical-*

---

80 Jer. 29:7.
81 Lk. 10:5-6.
82 Jn. 20:21.
83 S—systemic and sustainable change; H—healing, health, harmony and wholeness; A—asset-based community development; L—love for God, self, and neighbor; O—organized for direct action; M—multicultural, multifaith collaboration. Christensen, 'Threads of Shalom'.
84 Milton, *Shalom, the Spirit and Pentecostal Conversion*, 208.
85 Frost, 'Breathing Shalom: Bringing Reconciliation, Justice and Beauty for a Broken World', chapter 5.
86 Brueggemann, *Living toward a Vision*, 17–18.
87 Brueggemann, *Living toward a Vision*, 16.
88 Brueggemann, *Living toward a Vision*, 16.

political-communal level.[89] 'The origin and the destiny of God's people is to be on the road of *shalom*'.[90] This provides the impetus, agenda and lens of reflection for our interactions with the stories of those around us—our family, neighbours, faith communities, work colleagues, and global neighbours, and indeed, all of creation. *Shalom* is our ministerial frame of reference for engaging in 'your story'.

The third dimension—though more assumed than specifically discussed in Scripture—is individual, that of *shalom* persons.[91] The cosmic and social dimensions set the context for the unique and individual experience of *shalom*. This existential capacity for receiving and participating in *shalom* is at the heart of Christian spirituality. The lived experience of *shalom*, in all its richness, is the grounding and vision for 'my story'.

The relationship of *shalom* across each of these arenas—cosmic, social, personal—is coinherent. The primary means for God's cosmic vision for *shalom* is through human communities. Human communities experience *shalom* as it is dynamically present and expressed in persons. Individual persons, as image bearers of God, have a part to play in God's cosmic vision. As such, *shalom* exhibits the coinherent nature of Christian formation.

Thus, the *walk towards shalom* provides a *telos* for Christian formation that is faithful to the interlocking pilgrimage of God's story, your story and my story. It is richly ingrained in our remembrance and imagination of God's story for the cosmos, reflects the purposes of God in the story of the particular person/community/environment before us in any given encounter, and taps into the work of the Spirit in our own story. As a *telos* for formation *shalom* is theologically commensurate with growth towards our unique self in Christlikeness, yet perhaps offers a more expansive lens for reflecting upon experience in terms of one's spiritual, theological and ministerial formation. It keeps daily, incremental acts of participation in divine reconciliation, justice, beauty and wholeness connected to God's pleasure 'through [Christ] to reconcile to himself all things, whether things on earth or things in heaven, by making peace through his blood, shed on the cross'.[92] In this way *shalom* provides a thoroughly glocal *telos*.

---

89 Brueggemann, *Living toward a Vision*, 18–19.
90 Brueggemann, *Living toward a Vision*, 16.
91 Brueggemann, *Living toward a Vision*, 20–21.
92 Col. 1:19-20.

Shalom Embodies the Gospel of the Kingdom
How does *shalom* as a *telos* for Christian formation fit with the central biblical themes of the gospel and the kingdom of God? The gospel, as Wright contends, is the good news that *something has happened*: in the life, death and resurrection of Jesus, a new era—commonly called the Kingdom of God—has begun.[93] That reign is characterised by concrete, embodied expressions of *shalom*, in all its breadth. *Shalom* is not *an idea similar to* the gospel, but rather *the performance of* the gospel announcement of the sovereignty of Christ. For now, that reign is like a 'movie trailer', a foretaste.[94] We have been given glimpses of the new creation, a *shalom*-shaped heaven gloriously merged with our broken earth; currently the two only overlap 'fitfully, mysteriously, and partially'.[95] 'On earth as it is in heaven' is not a wish for God to wave a magic wand; it is a plea to wake us up to how we are being shaped for *shalom*, and to join in. And TR helps us wake up. Through TR we discern and participate in God's performance of *shalom* through which the new creation is being fashioned at personal, communal and cosmic levels.

This conception helps us more fully understand our formation, and indeed the gospel, in communal and cosmic levels beyond just 'Jesus and me'. If the gospel is the good news announcement that the Kingdom of God has come, performed as *shalom* in embodied reconciliation/justice/beauty/wholeness, then it *includes* the reconciliation of an individual's reconciliation with God, but is certainly not *limited to* or *only about* personal salvation. Luther's question—'How can I come before a righteous God?'—can no longer dominate the landscape of Christian formation. Though critical, surely it must be properly located within the bigger question: 'How is God's reign expressed in the performance of *shalom*, renewing the cosmos through communities of interdependent individuals—even me?'

Shalom Engenders Hope
Finally, because of its eschatological nature, *shalom* engenders hope in and towards the good life of God, the ultimate fulfilment of cosmic, communal and individual journeys. God *is* at work, we *are* headed somewhere, and *shalom* is what it looks like. This is not hope as wishful thinking, like longing for nice

---

93 Wright, *Simply Christian*, 176.
94 Frost, *Road to Missional: Journey to the Center of the Church*, 29–31.
95 Wright, *Simply Christian*, 185.

weather, or hope as optimism, based on the odds. Nor is it just holding out amidst difficulty because things will surely get better. This is Christian, eschatological hope: a certain conviction regarding God's future that shapes our daily walk. As Wright asserts, 'Our future beyond death is enormously important, but the nature of the Christian hope is such that it plays back into the present life'.[96] Hope bridges the future to the now.

Moreover, the certainty of Christian hope that shapes daily living comes from what has already occurred: the resurrection of Christ. We look forward by looking back. Peter praises God because 'he has given us new birth into a living hope through the resurrection of Jesus Christ from the dead'.[97] As Pannenberg asserts, this event is proleptic in nature.[98] Like reading a book that is out of sequence with the final chapter being placed part way through, Jesus' resurrection is a foretaste of the kingdom of *shalom*, God's new order. In it we sample the first fruits of *the* eschatological event that has already occurred and now interprets all history and gives it meaning and direction.[99] The resurrected Christ is the *goal* of history, and will be fully realised in the parousia and final resurrection where upon Creator and redeemed creation will finally experience perfect *shalom* forever.

In this sense, we are not just walking towards *shalom*, as though it is only a distant goal; *shalom* is being outworked all around us because it has begun in the Christ event. *Shalom* is both 'now and not yet'. That is why learning the craft of TR is so important; it helps us discern where in our lives, communities and world *shalom* is already coming to fruition, and where it is being resisted. Our response to that discernment becomes a participation in our individual, communal and cosmic formation towards what has already begun in the resurrected Prince of *Shalom*.

Pedagogical Application

Substantial pedagogical application remains the focus of future research and experimentation in my teaching: such is the ongoing nature of research led learning and teaching. However, some brief observations may be made.

---

96 Wright, *Simply Christian*, x.
97 1 Pet 1:3.
98 Ladd, *I Believe in the Resurrection of Jesus*, 151–52; Schwarz, *Eschatology*, 143–46.
99 1 Cor 15:20, 23.

Coinherence might not be a term we introduce to students, but it ought to influence learning and teaching in theological education. How might holistic spiritual, theological and ministerial formation in theological education be approached if we recognised these are already interrelated dimensions within each student? Educators might shift their focus from trying to bring these together, towards helping students explore the dynamics between them already operative, and work from there.

Second, if eschatology really is important in TR, then students will benefit from addressing this early in their introduction to this craft. Often TR is taught within a Supervised Theological Field Education program, or as part of an integrative studies subject. Tabor students do a whole subject on TR before doing STFE. Wolterstorff[100] and Benson[101] envisage whole curricula shaped by *shalom*. Whatever the case, educators in all disciplines may be challenged to help students to uncover their embedded (not espoused) conception of the good life—what they are *actually* hoping for—and contrast it with God's reign of *shalom* for all of creation, to explore how this reshapes their approach to meaning-making.

Shalom can also reshape models for TR that use common tools like case studies or critical incident reports. McAplin touches upon the justice dimension of *shalom* in her model when she invites reflectors to ask, 'Who benefitted in this situation? Who was burdened?'[102] *Shalom* as beauty is another intriguing lens. 'Where is there beauty? What invites celebration?' might help students learning TR, who are often pragmatically orientated, to appreciate aesthetics, gratitude and worship as important and valid aspects of this craft.

Finally, formation programs can benefit from helping students contemplate the growth of their unique self in Christ in terms of *shalom* as its *telos*. The initial response I have received from this in Tabor's formation program has been positive. One student commented, 'It's profound to think that by forming us into who we are in Christ, at the same time this brings *shalom* to communities and the world'. Such an insight can provide a helpful framework for exploring core questions of identity and vocation.

---

100 Wolterstorff and Stronks, *Educating for Shalom*.
101 Benson, 'God's Curriculum: Re-Imagining Education as a Journey toward Shalom'.
102 McAlpin, *Ministry That Transforms*.

Conclusion

Teaching TR as a lifelong craft that fosters holistic Christian formation is crucial in theological education. The coinherent dimensions of spirituality, theology and ministry—or my story, God's story, and your story—provide an accessible model of formation for students. Identifying a vision for the good life is important as it shapes how we do TR with these dimensions. While becoming our unique self in Christ is a theologically sound *telos*, the walk towards *shalom*—multifaceted, glocal, embodied and hopeful—may provide an alternative that more adequately expands students' vision beyond just personal growth in Christ. Implications exist for those teaching in field education, formation programs, and indeed in any theological education field.

Bibliography

Avila, St Teresa of. *Complete Works St. Teresa Of Avila* (London: Burns and Oates, 2002).

Ball, Les. *Transforming Theology: Student Experience and Transformative Learning in Undergraduate Theological Education* (Preston, VIC.: Mosaic Press, 2012).

Balswick, Jack O., Pamela Ebstyne King, and Kevin S. Reimer. *The Reciprocating Self: Human Development in Theological Perspective* (Downers Grove, Ill: IVP Academic, 2005).

Banks, Robert J. *Reenvisioning Theological Education: Exploring a Missional Alternative to Current Models* (Grand Rapids, MI: Eerdmans, 1999).

Barker, P.A. 'Rest, Peace', in *Dictionary of the Old Testament: Pentateuch* (ed. T. Desmond Alexander and David W Baker; Downers Grove, Ill.: InterVarsity, 2003).

Benner, David G. *The Gift of Being Yourself: The Sacred Call to Self-Discovery* (Downers Grove, IL: IVP, 2015).

Benson, Dave. 'God's Curriculum: Re-Imagining Education as a Journey toward Shalom'. Unpublished paper, Alphacrucis College, Sydney, 2017.

Brueggemann, Walter. *Living Toward a Vision: Biblical Reflections on Shalom* (Shalom Resource; New York: United Church Press, 1982, 2nd ed.).

Calvin, Jean, and Ford Lewis Battles. *Institutes of the Christian Religion* (Grand Rapids, MI: H.H. Meeter Center for Calvin Studies: Eerdmans, 1995).

Chae SJ, Joon-ho, Budi Hartono SJ, Kang-Yup Jung SJ, Deshi Ramadhani SJ, Michael Smith SJ, and Primitivo Viray SJ. 'Forming a Contemplative in Action: A Profile of a Formed Jesuit for Asia Pacific', 1–34. Ateneo de Manila University, Loyola Heights, Quezon City, Philippines: Jesuit Conference of Asia Pacific, 2011. http://sjapc.net/sites/default/files/profile_of_a_formed_jesuit_jcap_workbook_110823-2_with_appendix5.pdf.

Chandler, Diane J. 'Whole-Person Formation: An Integrative Approach to Christian Education', *Christian Education Journal* 12:2 (September 2015), 314–32.

Christensen, Michael. 'Threads of Shalom'. Communities of Shalom, 2014. http://communitiesofshalom.org/threads.

Dru, Alexander, (ed.) *The Journals of Kierkegaard* (New York: Harper & Brothers, 1959).

Edgar, Brian. 'The Theology of Theological Education', *Evangelical Review of Theology* 29:3 (2005), 208–17.

Farley, Edward. 'Interpreting Situations: An Inquiry into the Nature of Practical Theology', *Formation and Reflection: The Promise of Practical Theology* (Lewis Seymour Mudge and James N Poling, eds.; Philadelphia: Fortress Press, 1987), 1–26.

Foster, Charles R., Lisa E. Dahill, Lawrence A. Golemon, and Barabara Wang Tolentino. *Educating Clergy: Teaching Practices and the Pastoral Imagination* (San Francisco: Jossey-Bass, 2006).

Frost, Michael. 'Breathing Shalom: Bringing Reconciliation, Justice and Beauty for a Broken World', *The Road to Missional: Journey to the Center of the Church'* (Grand Ra[ids, MI: Baker Books, 2011), 101–20.

———. *Road to Missional: Journey to the Center of the Church* (Grand Rapids, MI: Baker Books, 2011).

Hall, Douglas John. *Imaging God: Dominion as Stewardship* (Eugene, OR: Wipf & Stock, 2004).

Harris, Douglas James. *Shalom! The Biblical Concept of Peace* (Grand Rapids, MI: Baker Book House, 1970).

Heschel, Abraham Joshua. *The Prophets* (New York: Harper & Row, 1962).

Hibbert, Richard, and Evelyn Hibbert. 'Addressing the Need for Better Integration in Theological Education: Proposals, Progress, and Possibilities from the Medical Education Model', *Learning and Teaching Theology Some Ways Ahead* (Les Ball and James Harrison, eds.; Eugene, OR: Wipf & Stock, 2015), 107–17.

Jones, L Gregory. 'Beliefs, Desires, Practices, and the Ends of Theological Education', in Miroslav Volf and Dorothy C. Bass (eds.), *Practicing Theology: Beliefs and Practices in Christian Life* (Grand Rapids, MI: Eerdmans, 2001), 185–205.

Kempis, Thomas à. *The Imitation of Christ* (Charleston, SC: CreateSpace Independent Publishing Platform, 2015).

Kinast, Robert. *What Are They Saying About Theological Reflection?* (New York: Paulist Press, 2000).

Ladd, George Eldon. *I Believe in the Resurrection of Jesus* (London: Hodder and Stoughton, 1979).

Love, Rick. 'Following Jesus in a Glocalized World: Bearers of Blessing Among Neighbors and Nations', unpublished paper, http://ricklove.net/wp-content/uploads/2011/03/Following-Jesus-in-a-Glocalized-World-Rick-Love-2.pdf.

Mackay, Hugh. *The Good Life* (Sydney, NSW: Pan Macmillan, 2016).

Mayes, Andrew D. *Spirituality in Ministerial Formation: The Dynamic of Prayer in Learning* (Cardiff, UK: University of Wales Press, 2009).

McAlpin, Kathleen. *Ministry That Transforms: A Contemplative Process of Theological Reflection* (Collegeville MN: Liturgical Press, 2009).

McDermott, Thomas. 'Catherine of Siena's Teaching on Self-Knowledge', *New Blackfriars: A Review* 88: 1018 (2007), 637–48.

McGinn, Bernard. *The Mystical Thought of Meister Eckhart: The Man from Whom God Hid Nothing* (New York, NY: Crossroad, 2003, First Paperback Edition).

Merton, Thomas. *New Seeds of Contemplation* (New York, NY: New Directions, 1972).

Milton, Grace. *Shalom, the Spirit and Pentecostal Conversion: A Practical-Theological Study* (Leiden; Boston: Brill, 2015).

Mulholland, M. Robert. *Invitation to a Journey: A Road Map for Spiritual Formation* (Downers Grove, ILL: InterVarsity, 1993).

Palmer, Parker. *Let Your Life Speak: Listening for the Voice of Vocation* (San Francisco: Jossey-Bass, 2000).

Pattison, Stephen, Judith Thompson, and John Green. 'Theological Reflection for the Real World: Time to Think Again', *British Journal of Theological Education* 13: 2 (January 2003), 119–31.

Plantinga Jr, Cornelius. *Not the Way It's Supposed to Be: A Breviary of Sin* (Grand Rapids, MI; Leicester, England: Eerdmans, 1996).

Pourrat, P. *Christian Spirituality from the Time of Our Lord Till the Dawn of the Middle Ages.* (London: Burns Oates & Washbourne, 1922).

Reuschling, Wyndy Corbin. *Becoming Whole and Holy: An Integrative Conversation about Christian Formation* (Grand Rapids, MI: Baker Academic, 2011).

Scazzero, Peter. 'Chapter 4: Know Yourself That You May Know God: Becoming Your Authentic Self', *Emotionally Healthy Spirituality: Unleash a Revolution in Your Life in Christ* (Nashville, TN: Thomas Nelson, 2011).

Schwarz, Hans. *Eschatology* (Grand Rapids, MI: Eerdmans, 2000).

Scobie, Charles H. *The Ways of Our God: An Approach to Biblical Theology* (Grand Rapids, MI: Eerdmans, 2003).

Shakespeare, Karen. 'Knowing, Being and Doing: The Spiritual Life Development of Salvation Army Officers', Anglia Ruskin University, 2011. http://core.kmi.open.ac.uk/download/pdf/363620.pdf.

Shaw, Perry. *Transforming Theological Education: A Practical Handbook for Integrative Learning* (Carlisle, Cumbria: Langham Global Library, 2014).

Sine, Tom. *The New Conspirators: Creating the Future One Mustard Seed at a Time* (Downers Grove, ILL: InterVarsity Press, 2008).

Smith, James K. A. *Imagining the Kingdom: How Worship Works* (Grand Rapids, MI: Baker Academic, 2013).

Spaeth, Paul J. 'The Concept of Co-Inherence In the Writings of Charles Williams', *The Inklings*, n.d. http://web.sbu.edu/friedsam/inklings/coinheretance.htm.

Steele, Les L. *On the Way: A Practical Theology of Christian Formation* (Grand Rapids, MI: Baker, 1990).

Westermann, Claus. 'Peace (Shalom) in the Old Testament', *The Meaning of Peace: Biblical Studies* (W Sawatsky, trans.; Louisville, KY: Westminster/John Knox, 1992), 16–48.

Willard, Dallas. *Renovation of the Heart: Putting on the Character of Christ* (Leicester: Inter-Varsity, 2002).

Wolterstorff, Nicholas, and Gloria Goris Stronks. *Educating for Shalom: Essays on Christian Higher Education* (Clarence W. Joldersma, ed.; Grand Rapids, MI: Eerdmans, 2004).

Wood, Charles W. 'Theological Education and Education for Church Leadership', *Theological Perspectives on Christian Formation: A Reader on Theology and Christian Education* (Jeff Astley, Leslie J Francis, and Colin Crowder, eds.; Leominster: Gracewing, 1996), 303–14.

Wright, N. T. *Simply Christian: Why Christianity Makes Sense* (San Francisco, CA: Harper SanFrancisco, 2006).

Bruce Hulme
Tabor College of Higher Education
bhulme@tabor.edu.au

11 | EDUCATION, MINISTRY AND THE NEW COVENANT

1 Introduction

This chapter argues that the terms of the New Covenant (Hebrews 8:10-11) can be used to inform the design of a learning outcomes framework for Christian education, personal development, and spiritual formation. This is grounded in the view that the internalisation of the law that is at the core of the New Covenant promise can be interpreted in virtue-based terms, and hence relates to the character required to live virtuously.

To explore this, the Scriptural theme of covenant will first be briefly outlined. The internalisation of the law on mind and heart will then be considered in both OT and NT contexts. This will involve close examinations of the centrality of the New Covenant in the rhetorical structure of the Epistle to the Hebrews, the meaning of the terms mind, heart, and law in Heb. 8:10b, and the concept of virtue. Following this the law, as addressed in the New Covenant and understood to be the Decalogue, will be related to the development of virtues.

How virtues, thus identified, may be placed in an analytical framework that addresses the graces and personal attributes specific to each virtue, and enables the development of learning outcomes or objectives will then be addressed. This will be done using Exod. 20:2 as an example of what could be done with all the precepts of the Decalogue. An excursus briefly considers learning outcomes and domains of learning. Frameworks thus developed may be used to guide and evaluate Christian ministry, identify outcomes to be attained, and assess the attainment of the outcomes thus identified.

2 Background: Theme of Covenant

The New Covenant is the culmination of the theme of covenant, which has been described as 'the backbone of the metanarrative of Scripture',[1] that which 'provides the context in which we recognise the unity of Scripture',[2] and 'God's program of revelation'.[3] Argued as beginning with Creation,[4] covenant proceeds through Adam, Noah, Abraham, Moses, and David, to the promise of the New Covenant by Jeremiah and Ezekiel and its fulfilment in and by Christ and in the outpouring of the Holy Spirit.[5] Among these, the Abrahamic, Mosaic and New Covenants contain a conditional foundational promise, is that YHWH would be the God of those in the covenant and they would be his people.[6]

The Abrahamic condition was a virtuousness or goodness variously translated with English terms denoting blamelessness, integrity, wholeheartedness, and perfection.[7] The parallel Mosaic condition was fulfilment of the law, which may be seen as a specification or expansion of the virtue required of Abraham and his descendants.[8] Both covenants were breached. The stories of Jacob, Esau, and Joseph indicate the inability of the descendants of Abraham to live virtuously. Israel's history, from the exodus to the destructions of the temples, indicates its inability to meet the conditions of the Mosaic Covenant. The destruction of the first temple and the loss of the ark of the covenant mark the end of the Mosaic Covenant. God divorced Israel. For a very long time all that was left was exile, lament and hope for the promised New Covenant.

Jeremiah and Ezekiel, declaring the utter finality of the old covenant, create

---

1. Gentry & Wellum, *Kingdom through Covenant*, loc. 238.
2. Horton, *Introducing Covenant Theology*, 13.
3. Walton, *Covenant*, chap. 2.
4. Dumbrell, *Covenant and Creation*, chap. 1.
5. For an incomplete compendium of significant recent work, see the following. Dumbrell, *Covenant and Creation*; Duncan, 'Covenant Idea in Ante-Nicene Theology'; Hahn, 'Covenant in the Old and New Testaments'; Hahn, *Kinship by Covenant*; Hillers, *Covenant*; McClean, 'Of Covenant and Creation'; Most, 'A Biblical Theology of Redemption'; Robertson, *The Christ of the Covenants*; Talbert, 'Paul on the Covenant'; Walton, *Covenant*; Williamson, 'Covenant: The Beginning of a Biblical Idea'; Williamson, *Sealed with an Oath*; Woolsey, 'The Covenant in the Church Fathers'.
6. The Abrahamic covenant is often known as the foundational covenant. This formula is consistently repeated in further covenant related declarations. See Gen. 17:1; Exod. 6:7, 19:5, Deut. 4:20, Jer 31:31-34, Ezek. 36:26-29, Heb. 8:10-11.
7. Gen. 17:1. The Hebrew word for the virtuous condition required of Abraham is *tamim* (תמים). Derived from a root that conveys the notion of completeness, a totality without diminution, words derived from this root are often used in the realm of moral and ethical assessment. For a fuller discussion see Kedar-Kopfstein, 'תמים', 699–711.
8. Exodus 20-24.

hope in their prophecies of the coming New Covenant. Both repeat the foundational promise. Both address the parallel condition of virtue. In the New Covenant, however, virtue will be provided by YHWH. Jeremiah addresses what will be attained. YHWH's action will result in the internalising of the law by writing it on mind and heart. Ezekiel addresses the means: a twofold work of the Spirit will first transform the inner person and then infill it.

3 New Covenant: Law on Mind and Heart

The Epistle to the Hebrews picks up the theme of covenant and focuses on the prophecy of Jeremiah. The centrality of the New Covenant in the message of Hebrews is made clear by its placement at its rhetorical centre.[9] The two mentions of the New Covenant form an inclusio within a larger chiasmus. In this frame, Heb. 10:16 repeats Heb. 8:10b which is drawn from Jer. 31:33b: this is:

> I will put my laws into their minds,
> and write them on their hearts.[10]

The meanings of mind, heart, and law and in this stich may be understood as follows.

3.1 Mind and Heart

Mind and heart refer conjunctively to the interiority of the whole person. Both Heb. 8:10b and its LXX equivalent (LXX Jer. 37:33b) use the same words for both mind, *dianoia* (διάνοια) and heart, *kardia* (καρδία). Like their respective Hebrew equivalents *qereb* (קרב) and *leb* (לב), both have broad and overlapping semantic ranges. Both have been used extensively to refer to the inner life of human beings. *Dianoia* is a broad and philosophically rich term that was used to address the totality of humanity's spiritual nature.[11] In Philo and several schools of Greek philosophy including Plato and Aristotle, *dianoia* is closely

---

9   Heath, 'Chiastic Structures in Hebrews', 306.
10 Heb. 8:10b.
11 For a fuller discussion and references to primary sources see Behm, & Würtheim, 'Διάνοια', 963–65.

associated with *nous* (νοῦς).¹² *Kardia* has an anatomical core meaning related to the heart as well as a broad range of metaphorical uses. The metaphorical uses address the totality of inner being.¹³ The corresponding Hebrew words in Jer. 31:33b are קֶרֶב (*qereb*), which means the inward part or midst of something,¹⁴ and לֵב (*leb*), its own gloss. These words are also used synonymously to refer to internal processes.¹⁵

3.2 Law

Law in Heb. 8:10b refers to the written commands of the law of Moses with the Decalogue specifically in view.¹⁶ The writing of the law on the mind and heart refers to this being internalised. Law must therefore be understood in terms of the non-juridical aspects of the words from which it is translated.¹⁷ These are those aspects of these words that refer to interior qualities such as character and virtue.¹⁸ The explicit association of virtue with the law and particularly the Decalogue may be found in early Patristic sources such as Clement of Rome and Clement of Alexandria.¹⁹

---

12 *Nous* is another broad and philosophically rich term, the meaning of which is centred in that which has the power of knowing and has been associated with the rational soul. In contrast to *nous, dianoia* has been related to the act of reasoning from premises to conclusions. It is therefore often seen as discursive reasoning and as a function of the *nous*. Menn, *Plato on God as Nous*, 14.

13 Fabry, Heinz-Josef, 'תּוֹרָה', 609–10.

14 See Brown, Driver, Briggs, 'BDB Hebrew: 7130. קֶרֶב (*Qereb*)—Inward Part, Midst'; Koehler, Baumgartner, & Stamm (eds.), *The Hebrew and Aramaic Lexicon of the Old Testament*, 1135. Swanson, *Dictionary of Biblical Languages with Semantic Domains: Hebrew (Old Testament)*, 7930. Rattray & Milgrom, 'קרב', 13.148.

15 Brown, Driver, Briggs, 'BDB Hebrew: 3820. לֵב (*Leb*)—Inner Man, Mind, Will, Heart'; Swanson, *Dictionary of Biblical Languages with Semantic Domains: Hebrew (Old Testament)*, 4213. Baumgärtel, F., & Behm, J., 'Καρδία', 3.606–607; Fabry, 'לֵב', 7.399–438.

16 For an extended exploration and defence of this view see Joslin, *Hebrews, Christ, and the Law*. In addition, the history of interpretation overwhelmingly identifies the Decalogue as the aspect of the Mosaic Law that continues in the New Testament.

17 These are *torah* (תּוֹרָה) and *nomos* (νόμος).

18 This is at a significant variance with current usages of 'law' in English in which this word has shed much of its connection to morality and virtue and has strong juridical tendencies. The Hebrew and Greek words translated law, *torah* (תּוֹרָה) and *nomos* (νόμος), have extensive associations with morality and virtue in both juridical and non-juridical contexts. With respect to *torah*, see Fabry, 'תּוֹרָה', 609–11, 614. See also Brown, Driver, Briggs, 'BDB Hebrew: 8451. תּוֹרָה (*Torah*)—Direction, Instruction, Law'. With respect to *nomos*, see Remus, 'Authority, Consent, Law', 13–17; Kleinknecht, 'Νόμος', 4.1032.

19 Clement of Rome, 'First Epistle to the Corinthians', 11; Clement of Alexandria, 'The Instructor', 507.

4 Virtue

The Hellenistic concepts of virtue that informed the ethics-related language of the New Testament continue to inform contemporary virtue ethics.[20] The New Testament word translated 'virtue' is *arete* (ἀρετή). While this is one of several words for moral and ethical concepts and associated qualities of character and action, *arete* and/or its derivatives have been most consistently drawn upon by theologians, philosophers and ethicists in discussions about virtue.[21] Within this usage, *arete* has developed and maintained a generic quality that encompasses almost anything related to the attainment or expression of moral and ethical ideals.

Virtue, thus conceived, relates to personal attributes that are developable, lasting, and centred on goodness.[22] They are progressively acquired as a 'second nature' through constant practice in the context of a community and are persistent drives or inclinations to act morally or ethically. As such they are habits or states of character acquired by moral work. They require skills but must be distinguished from them. They are associated with feelings but must be distinguished from them.[23]

Depending on the theory of virtue that has been adopted, the attributes of the virtuous may include skills and dispositions related to the highest aims of thought and conduct, a state of character which exercises prudence in decision-

---

[20] This has been a very active area since the publication of Anscombe, 'Modern Moral Philosophy', 1–19, which is credited as being the beginning of modern virtue ethics. A sampling of significant publications include Crisp & Slote, *Virtue Ethics*; Hauerwas, *A Community of Character*; Hauerwas, *Character and the Christian Life*; MacIntyre, *A Short History of Ethics*; MacIntyre, *After Virtue*; Wright, *Virtue Reborn*.

[21] *Arete* occurs four times in the New Testament: once in Phil. 4:8 as something upon which the mind should dwell, once in 1 Peter 2:9 as attributes of God which believers are called to exemplify through honourable behaviour, good deeds, and the control of unruly passions, and twice in 2 Peter 1:5 as the first in a list of personal qualities that believers are called upon to develop to avoid being 'ineffective or unfruitful in the knowledge of our Lord Jesus Christ'. This is a significant reconstrual of a word with an already long history and a challenge to the values expressed in that history. For a list and exposition of words that are deployed throughout the New Testament to address the concept of goodness see Louw & Nida, *Greek-English Lexicon of the New Testament: Based on Semantic Domains*, sec. 88.1-88.11. See also Barr, *The Semantics of Biblical Language*, chap. 8.

[22] Annas argues that goodness is the distinguishing factor that 'sorts out dispositions which are virtues from those that are useful and/or agreeable, but not virtues'; Annas, *Intelligent Virtue*, 108–109. Peterson and Seligman, in an attempt to clinically define positive mental health, wrote what they called a 'manual of the sanities'. In doing so they noted that they arrived at descriptions of personal attributes that were generally in accord with what philosophers and theologians had called character strengths and virtues. Peterson & Seligman, *Character Strengths and Virtues*.

[23] For discussions on the nature and constituents of virtue see Adams, *A Theory of Virtue*; Hauerwas, *A Community of Character*; MacIntyre, *After Virtue*; Zagzebski, *Virtues of the Mind*, pt. II.

making, the ability to regulate emotions, the ability to discern between that which contributes to true happiness and those things that distract from it, the motives, dispositions, or inner life of moral individuals, and the ability to identify and conform to that which is worthy of motivation.[24] Virtues may also be validly categorised into the overlapping categories of moral, intellectual and theological.[25]

Virtue-related learning outcomes must therefore be multidimensional. Development will require the acquisition of competence in moral commitment, intellectual insight, discernment, emotional regulation, habituation (second nature), skills, and motivations. Within the New Covenant context, they will also require receptiveness to those aspects of the work of grace that are related to the sanctifying inner work of the Holy Spirit in the infusing of the theological virtues in ways that are related to the precepts of the Decalogue.

5 Decalogue-related Virtues

An analytical framework has been developed to enable the attributes of character or the virtues related to the precepts of the Decalogue to be identified and described. See Table 1. This analyses each precept in terms of the theological virtues and the virtue-related personal attributes already listed.

---

[24] Theories of virtue that had influence on the Hellenistic world of the New Testament generally fall into the modern categories of the eudaimonic and the hedonic. Eudaimonic approaches included those related to Plato, Aristotle and the Stoics. For concise introductions to these, see Frede, 'Plato's Ethics: An Overview'; Kraut, 'Aristotle's Ethics'; and Baltzly, 'Stoicism'. The Epicureans held views that were both eudaimonic and hedonic. For Epicureanism see Annas, *The Morality of Happiness*, 188; Bobzien, 'Moral Responsibility and Moral Development in Epicurus' Philosophy', 229; Konstan, 'Epicurus'; O'Keefe, 'Hedonistic Theories of Well-Being in Antiquity', 29–39.

[25] Aristotle, *Nicomachean Ethics*, 2.1, 1103a-15; 2.6, 1106b-15. Aquinas, I-II Q. 59-62, and I-II Q. 62.1.

Table 1 Analytical Framework

Precept	Precept from the Decalogue
Dimension	**Description**
Graces	
Faith	The spiritual receptiveness that supports the development of a believing and steadfast relationship with the Triune God.
Hope	The spiritual receptiveness that supports the development of the confidence and assurance of the purposes and nature of God that are associated with this precept.
Love	The spiritual receptiveness that supports the development of union with and God, who is love, and whose motivations and nature are expressed in this precept.
Personal Attributes	
Moral Commitment	The determination to conscientiously build an internally consistent value system related to each precept and willingly live by it.
Intellectual Insight	The epistemological and intellectual capabilities relevant to the exercise and application of each precept.
Discernment	The prudent exercise of practical wisdom required for decision making and the resolving of dilemmas in a way that is guided by the principles of each precept
Emotionality	The emotional awareness and self-control relevant to conformity with each precept.
Habituation	The development of characteristic, fluent, and consistent responses and life-patterns aligned to and guided by each precept.
Skills	The behaviours, techniques, and other abilities essential or beneficial to the exercise of each precept.
Motivations	The inclinations and dispositions related to the embrace of each precept.

How this grid might be applied will be illustrated below by applying it to Exod. 20:2. This is the first precept in the Jewish divisions; part of the first in the Catholic, Lutheran and Orthodox divisions; and the preface in the Anglican and Reformed divisions. It is addressed indirectly in Philo.[26] It will be interpreted broadly as a 'head of the law', that is as a category heading for a domain of

---

26 Philo, 'A Treatise Concerning the Ten Commandments Which Are the Heads of the Law', 143.

ethical values. This aligns with the approach of Philo.[27] It also aligns with the interpretation and reception of the Decalogue in the writings of the early Fathers,[28] medieval and scholastic authors,[29] Reformers,[30] and modern writers.[31]

5.2 Analysis of Exod. 20:2

> Exod. 20:2
> I am the Lord (YHWH) your God (Elohim), who brought you out of the land of Egypt, out of the house of slavery.

Exod. 20:2 contains the opening words of the Sinai theophany and calls for covenant-keeping obedience. It declares YHWH's intent for Israel to be a 'treasured possession (סגלה, *segullah*) among all peoples'.[32] It was also to confront them with their need to learn to fear YHWH. Such fear is associated with godliness and the beginning of wisdom.[33] Beginning with a treaty-like statement, this develops throughout the canon into the theme of the love of YHWH for His people. Including the marriage imagery of Hosea, Jeremiah, Ezekiel, and the Song of Solomon, it culminates in the New Testament motifs of the wedding feast and marriage of the Lamb.

YHWH presents as sovereign in a way that is at odds with the constant

---

27 Philo, 'A Treatise Concerning the Ten Commandments Which Are the Heads of the Law', 140.
28 Early fathers such as Irenaeus, Athanasius, Gregory of Nazianzen, Gregory of Nyssa, and Augustine typically saw the Decalogue as foundational, universally applicable and a declaration of natural and moral law. See Irenaeus of Lyon, 'Against Heresies', 4.16.4; Athanasius, 'Letters of Athanasius, with Two Ancient Chronicles of His Life'; Gregory of Nazianzen, 'Select Orations of Saint Gregory Nazianzen', 45.17; Gregory of Nyssa, 'On Virginity'; Augustine, 'On Lying';
29 Bonaventure portrays the Decalogue as the whole of God's will in relation to humanity. Aquinas argues for a modified continuity based on the natural law. See Coughlin, *Collations on the Ten Commandments*, 6.2–3; Aquinas, 'Thomas Aquinas: The Ten Commandments: English'.
30 Luther wrote of the Decalogue as the true fountain and channel from and in which everything must arise and flow that is to be a good work, so that outside of the Ten Commandments no work or thing can be good or pleasing to God, however great or precious it be in the eyes of the world.
    Martin Luther, *The Large Catechism*, para. 311.
31 For a representative list sample of recent works see Benedict XVI, *The Ten Commandments*; Brown, *The Ten Commandments*, sec. 3; Van Harn, *The Ten Commandments for Jews, Christians, and Others*; Hauerwas & Willimon, *The Truth about God*; Mikva, *Broken Tablets: Restoring the Ten Commandments and Ourselves*; Miller, *The Ten Commandments*; Rooker, *The Ten Commandments*; and Sicker, *The Ten Commandments*.
32 Exod. 19:5. Bailey notes the similarity of usages of a related term in correspondence between a Hittite suzerain with an Akkadian vassal. Bailey, *Exodus*, 208.
33 Exod. 20:20, Deut. 4:10. For an extended exploration of the concept of fear and the fear of YHWH see Fuhs, 'ירא', 296–314.

domesticating challenges of both church and society.[34] The structure of the covenant parallels that of Ancient Near East treaties around the second millennium BCE, the time of the exodus.[35] The self-identification of the 'the LORD (YHWH) your God (Elohim)' as suzerain draws attention first to the essence of His being (YHWH), and then to His power and authority as Creator (Elohim). It also draws attention to Him as the proper object of devotion and worship. This is an unapologetic exercise of asymmetric power and an expression of loving commitment akin to a marriage.[36] The Decalogue is thus established in an authoritative and loving address from beyond the human frame of reference. It is for humanity, not from it.

The further self-identification of 'YHWH your Elohim' as the suzerain 'who brought you out of the land of Egypt, out of the house of slavery', establishes the covenant within the context of the redemption and the overarching story that goes from creation to the church. Service of YHWH will now replace service to Pharaoh.[37] This also specifies who or what God might be in a way that emphatically invalidates syncretising and diluting generalisations. It is only the one who revealed Himself as the God of Abraham, Isaac, and Jacob and the one who is the divine actor in this story that can lay claim to being the only God, the uncreated, the creator of heaven and earth.[38]

The significance of this covenant theophany is emphasised in the Epistle to the Hebrews. Comparing and integrating the establishment of the New Covenant with the Old, its author draws heavily on the Exodus and Deuteronomic accounts of the Sinai theophany.[39] Anticipating and contradicting any Marcion-like separations of the God and/or narrative the Old and New Testaments, Heb.

---

34 Cf. Hauerwas & Willimon, *The Truth about God*, 30. See also David Bentley Hart who writes: 'And so, at the end of modernity each of us who is true to the times stands thus facing [...] an abyss over which presides the inviolable authority of the individual will, whose impulses and decisions are their own moral index'; Hart, 'God or Nothingness', loc. 627.

35 In such treaties, a suzerain, or sovereign ruler, identifies by name as the first party of the covenant and then dictates its terms. The obligations and status of the second party, the vassal, whose exclusive fidelity must be pledged, are thus declared. The similarity in pattern between the Hittite and Assyrian treaties and the giving of the Decalogue was explored in the seminal article of Mendenhall, 'Covenant Forms in Israelite Tradition' and taken up by many others. A small sample includes Bright, *A History of Israel*, 150–51; Davies, *A Royal Priesthood*, 170–71; Kline, *Treaty of the Great King*, 14–16; Lane, *The Compassionate, but Punishing God*, 34. Stuart, *Exodus*, 2.450, 677; Sicker, *The Ten Commandments*, xi.

36 White, *Exodus*, 260.

37 Miller, *The Ten Commandments*, 16; Rooker, *The Ten Commandments*, loc. 384; Stuart, *Exodus*, 2:448.

38 Hauerwas & Willimon, *The Truth about God*, 28; Hazony, *The Ten Commandments*, 38.

39 Exod. 19, Deut. 4:1-24, Heb. 12:18-29.

12:18-24 apocalyptically contrasts the frightening and foreboding delivery of the covenant at Mount Sinai with the festal nature of the delivery of the New Covenant. Alluding to the shaking of the earth prophesied in Haggai,[40] Hebrews warns against refusal of the one 'who is speaking', calls for a worshipful disposition of reverence and awe and concludes with a quote from the account of the theophany in Deuteronomy:

> For our God is a consuming fire.[41]

In the history of its interpretation, Bonaventure described this verse as an address by the Trinity pointing to foundations of the faith that must be given first place: the knowledge of the Creator and the knowledge of the Redeemer.[42] Calvin described it as necessary to prepare minds for obedience, establish the rights of the legislator, prevent contempt and procure reverence.[43]

In the light of these reflections, the category label for this head of virtue will be, 'Covenant faithfulness': a disposition of faithful, diligent and covenant-focussed attentiveness. How the graces and personal attributes of virtue might be drawn from and relate to these considerations of Exod. 20:2 are summarised as 'dimensions' in Table 3.

6 Outcomes Statements

Having proposed graces and personal attributes of the virtue of covenant faithfulness, the next task is to propose learning outcomes related to them. Before doing this it will be valuable to reflect on the nature of learning outcomes and the associated domains of learning.

6.1 Learning Outcomes

Learning outcomes are statements of what a person can exhibit or demonstrate because of a learning or formational process. They are evidence of growth or change. They have been variously described as abilities, attitudes, capabilities,

---

40 Hag. 2:6.
41 Heb. 12:29, Deut. 4:24.
42 Coughlin, *Collations on the Ten Commandments*, 6:33.
43 Calvin, *Harmony of the Law*, 1.322.

competencies, knowledge, skills, understanding, and other like terms.[44] They must be distinguished from: statements of intention or aims made by teachers, trainers, or curriculum developers. Statements of aims and outcomes are both important. Aims relate to the management of learning and the presentation and delivery of learning programs and events. Outcomes relate to achievement in the learner. Aims describe intent. Outcomes describe attainment.

Outcomes-based approaches to learning first emerged in the 1960s. Since then education has shifted from being teacher-oriented to becoming learner-oriented. Three streams may be identified. The first emerged within the now largely disavowed behaviourist psychology of the 1960s. This introduced approaches such as programmed learning. The second was the 1990s development of competency-based approaches often associated with vocational education and training. Now mandatory in many jurisdictions, it has been criticised for being behaviouristic, economically driven, instrumental, technocratic, managerial, and neglectful of values, justice, aesthetics, and so on. Its defenders have argued that these criticisms are ill founded, rest on elitist assumptions about education, conceptually impoverished, and ignore the potential of key competencies to liberalise and transform the curriculum and pedagogy of general education.[45] The third stream, largely concurrent with and overlapping the development of competency-based approaches, is known simply as Outcomes-Based Education (OBE). Associated largely with school education, this exists in in several variants or models.[46] Prominent among these is that of William Spady who argues for an approach to learning that eschews rigidity and calendar driven programming, emphasises curriculum coverage over student mastery, and advocates a 'transformational' approach to OBE that necessitates a radical re-organisation of approaches to teaching and learning.[47] Spady's approach to transformational OBE culminates in what he calls the

---

44 Adam, 'An Introduction to Learning Outcomes', 2, 5; Kennedy, *Writing and Using Learning Outcomes*; Moon, *The Module and Programme Development Handbook*, 56.
45 For overviews of criticisms and defences of outcomes-based education, competency based and otherwise, see Allan, 'Learning Outcomes in Higher Education'; Gonczi & Hager, 'The Competency Model', 404; See also Moon, *The Module and Programme Development Handbook*, 52.
46 Brandt identifies three models which he refers to as the Johnson City Model, the High Success Network, and the McRel Model. Brandt, 'An Overview of Outcome-Based Education'.
47 Spady, 'Organizing for Results: The Basis of Authentic Restructuring and Reform', 4–5; Spady & Marshall, 'Beyond Traditional Outcome-Based Education', 67. Criticism of this approach to OBE has been related to the unsuitability of school environments and administrations to effectively deliver this approach to education. See Donnelly, 'Australia's Adoption of Outcomes Based Education—a Critique', 183–206.

'transformational zone' of the 'Demonstration Mountain' at which point learners are able to demonstrate 'complex role performances' involved in 'life-role functioning'.[48]

Although the language of transformational learning outcomes is most frequently associated with formal learning contexts, there is no need to restrict it to this. It may be more applicable in pastoral and other settings in which the life-long formational objectives of Christian ministry integral to the New Covenant are relevant. What have been described above as the graces and personal attributes of New Covenant/Decalogue related virtues are readily described as transformational learning outcomes. Just as outcomes-based approaches to education resulted in a shift of focus from teacher to student, it is argued that ministry may require a similar shift from leader-centred approaches to those that are more follower-centred. Formational outcomes must be distinguished from the intent or goals of ministers even though properly formed and informed intent is essential to the process of formation. Using Spady's terms, transformations involved in the acquisition of New Covenant related virtues could readily be understood as 'complex role performances' involved in 'life-role functioning', in which the virtues underlying the Decalogue are evident.

6.2 Domains of Learning

The domains of learning relate to the faculties through which the 'the process of acquiring modifications in existing knowledge, skills, habits or action tendencies' occurs.[49] Regarding virtue, three domains have consistently been identified: these are the cognitive, the affective, and the conative. Recognition of this trilogy has been persistent in various forms throughout history. It relates well to the notions of understanding, passion, and will in the writings of Aristotle, other Hellenistic philosophers who contributed to the background if the New Testament, and patristic writers to the time of Augustine.[50]

---

48   Spady, 'Choosing Outcomes of Significance', 20.
49   Gagné, 'Domains of Learning', 1; See also '"learning, n.".', : *Oxford English Dictionary Online* (Oxford University press, 2017), http://www.oed.com.ezproxy.sl.nsw.gov.au/viewdictionaryentry/Entry/106723.
50   Brett traces the trilogy to the early Greek philosophers, through the Alexandrians in the second century and eventually to Augustine who he sees as influencing the West. Brett, *A History of Psychology*, 1–20. Hilgard noted that a threefold division in the study of mind emerged in the 18th century and persisted for two centuries, traces its first mention of this emergence to Moses Mendelsohn; Hilgard, 'The Trilogy of Mind: Cognition, Affection, and Conation', 107–108.

a) Cognitive Domain

Cognition relates to those aspects of virtues that require knowledge, understanding, and insight. These are consistently valorised and called for in both Testaments.[51] The relevance of cognition to virtue is readily apparent in the emphases that may be found on intellectual virtues. Of the three domains, the cognitive is the most studied. Several writers have developed extensive taxonomies of educational objectives for this domain, the best known being Bloom's taxonomy.[52] See Table 2.

Table 2 Instructional Taxonomies for the Cognitive Domain[53]

Bloom	Gagné	Ausubel	Anderson	Merrill	Reigeluth
Knowledge	Verbal Information	Rote learning	Declarative knowledge	Remember verbatim	Memorise Information
Comprehension		Meaningful learning		Remember paraphrased	Understand Relationships
Application	Intellectual Skill		Procedural knowledge	Use a generality	Apply Skills
Analysis Synthesis Evaluation	Cognitive Strategy			Find a generality	Apply generic skills

---

51 Cf. Psa. 119:130, Prov. 1-4, Matt. 13:23, Eph. 1:17-10, Col. 1:9. Within the context of this study, this consideration must carefully be distinguished and delimited from the cognitive science of religion, in which studies religious thought and behaviour is studied from the perspective of the cognitive and evolutionary sciences. Its goal is to provide explanations for the occurrence and recurrence of religious expression in terms of cognitive structures and processes such as processing styles and the development of that are shared by all humans. Individual differences in religious belief and expression are accounted for by processing styles and the development of concepts and schemas in human development. See Barrett & Zahl, 'Cognition, Evolution, and Religion', 221–37; Boyer, 'Religion, Evolution, and Cognition', 430–33; Whitehouse, 'Cognitive Evolution and Religion: Cognition and Religious Evolution', 35–47. These approaches have been heavily critiqued as reductionistic, positivistic and naturalistic. See Nelson & Slife, 'Theoretical and Epistemological Foundations', 21–35; Hood, 'The History and Current State of Research on Psychology of Religion', 7–20.
52 Bloom et al., *Taxonomy of Educational Objectives Handbook 1 Cognitive Domain*; See also Anderson & Krathwohl, *A Taxonomy for Learning, Teaching, and Assessing*.
53 Reigeluth & Moore, 'Cognitive Education and the Cognitive Domain', 54. See also Anderson, 'ACT: A Simple Theory of Complex Cognition', 355–65; Anderson, *Rules of the Mind*, chap. 4; Ausubel, *Psychology of Meaningful Verbal Learning*; Gagne, *The Conditions of Learning and Theory of Instruction*; Merrill, 'Component Display Theory', 279–334.

b) Affective Domain

Affect relates to the emotionality associated with virtues. This refers to the awareness and self-control of emotion relevant to the expression of any virtue. It therefore relates to the experience and expression of emotion, that is of sentiments, feelings and action tendencies.[54] Issues of attitude or motivation, often seen as affect, will be carefully excluded under this heading.[55] Attitude and motivation will be addressed as parts of the conative domain. The affective domain with respect to virtues will therefore refer to the expression of congruent and appropriate sentiments and feelings.[56]

Commenting on the importance of such emotion, Orthodox theologian Edward Vacek wrote:

> Affections ground and give significance to our intellectual and volitional activity.[57] [...]
>
> Because we have emotions, we do not experience the world as devoid of value. Such an experience of value is not simply an add-on. Rather, it transforms the experience.[58]

Krathwohl, Bloom and Masia's well known taxonomy of educational objectives for the affective domain will not be used here. In this context, it is better aligned with conation.[59] Shaver's work on organising emotions around prototypes provides a better taxonomic framework for the sentiments and action tendencies that are relevant here: this is built around the six categories of love, happiness, surprise, sadness, anger, and fear.[60]

---

54 Cf. Prov. 14: 13, 15:13, 15:18, 29:11, Eccles. 3:4, Rom. 12:15.
55 This approach differs from part 2 of Bloom's taxonomy of educational objectives, which provides a hierarchy of internalisation made up of receiving (attending), responding, valuing, organising, and characterising by a value set or value complex. This addresses that which will be considered here under the heading of the conative domain. See Krathwohl, Bloom, & Masia, *Taxonomy of Educational Objectives: Book 2 Affective Domain*, 95.
56 That there could or should be appropriate emotional responses or sentiments is argued forcibly by C.S. Lewis where, speaking of the responsibility of educators, he writes: 'The right defence against false sentiments is to inculcate just sentiments'. Lewis also cites Augustine, whose definition of virtue contained the idea of *ordo amoris*, that is 'the ordinate condition of the affections in which every object is accorded that kind of degree of love that is appropriate to it'. Lewis, *The Abolition of Man*, 14, 16. See also Augustine, 'City of God', 15.22 p. 694; 9.5 p. 394; 11.28 p. 513.
57 Vacek, 'Orthodoxy Requires Orthopathy: Emotions in Theology', 19.
58 Vacek, 'Orthodoxy Requires Orthopathy: Emotions in Theology', 24.
59 Krathwohl, Bloom, and Masia, *Taxonomy of Educational Objectives: Book 2 Affective Domain*.
60 Shaver et al., 'Emotion Knowledge: Further Exploration of a Prototype Approach', 26–56.

c) Conative Domain

Conation refers to the aspects of the human psyche relevant to intentionality, volition, goal-orientation, and striving. It has been described as 'vectored energy', and is closely related to agency, self-direction, and self-regulation.[61] It may be defined as an inclination to act purposefully (such as an instinct, a drive, a wish, or a craving). It has been described as both the faculty of volition and desire, and the product of this faculty.[62] While conation has been one of three traditionally identified and studied components of psychology, reasons given for the paucity of research on it, compared with that of cognition and affect, include that conation is often intertwined with cognition and affect (emotion) and it is difficult to separate from them.[63] This is especially so with respect to affect. At times conation has been confused with affect.[64]

Conation is relevant the emphatic calls in both testaments for choosing, listening, heeding, and obedience.[65] Huitt and Cain define the conative domain as referring to that which connects knowledge and affect to behaviour. They write

> It is the personal, intentional, planful, deliberate, goal-oriented, or striving component of motivation, the proactive (as opposed to reactive or habitual) aspect of behaviour. […]

> It is closely associated with the concepts of intrinsic motivation, volition, agency, self-direction, and self-regulation [66]

In addition to words relating to motivation and intentionality, Krathwohl, Bloom, and Masia's taxonomy of educational objectives for the affective domain will be used for conative objectives.

---

61 Huitt & Cain, 'An Overview of the Conative Domain', 1–20; Atman, 'The Role of Conation (Striving) in the Distance Education Enterprise', 15.
62 'Conation, N.', *Merriam Webster Dictionary Online*.
63 Huitt and Cain, 'An Overview of the Conative Domain'; Hilgard, 'The Trilogy of Mind'; Gerdes & Stromwall, 'Conation: A Missing Link in the Strengths Perspective', 234; McDougall, 'Pleasure, Pain and Conation', 171–80; Mayer, Chabot, & Carlsmith, 'Conation, Affect, and Cognition in Personality', 31–63.
64 Aveling, 'The Psychology of Conation and Volition 1'.
65 Deut. 4:1, 7:12, 11:27-28, Prov. 2:2, 5:1, 23:12, Isa. 55:3
66 Huitt and Cain, 'An Overview of the Conative Domain', 1.. See also Militello et al., 'Conation: Its Historical Roots and Implications for Future Research', 240–47. Atman, 'Goal Accomplishment Style and Psychological Type: Cultural Variations'.

Table 3 Virtue Related Learning Outcomes for the Preface to the Decalogue

Precept	Ex. 20:2 I am the Lord (YHWH) your God (Elohim), who brought you out of the land of Egypt, out of the house of slavery.			
Virtue Category Label	Covenant Faithfulness			
	Illustrative Outcomes			
Dimension	Description	Cognitive	Affective	Conative
Graces				
Faith	A responsive openness to and embrace of the reality and character of God (YHWH) as revealed at Sinai, in Christ and the activity of the Holy Spirit. This will be manifest in expressions of both the love and the fear of God	Describe the nature of God as revealed at Sinai and in Christ. Cf. John 14:9.	Express love and reverent awe toward God as revealed at Sinai and in Christ. Cf. Deut. 6:5	Exemplify an attitude of cooperative willingness toward God as revealed at Sinai and in Christ. Cf. Psa. 110:3
Hope	An expression of confidence in the purpose of God centred upon the eternal vocation or mission of the people of God, to be a royal priesthood called to make manifest the virtues (excellencies) of God, their redeemer, in accord with what is to be in the new heavens and the new earth	Explain the eternal vocation or mission of the people of God. Cf. Heb. 11:6.	Respond joyfully toward the hope set before them (joy may be full). Cf. Psa. 103.	Set life goals in accord with eternal vocation or mission of the people of God. Cf. Phil: 3:13.
Love	A responsiveness to the being the God's treasured possession or beloved, a willing adoption of the greatest commandment to love God with the whole heart mind and strength, and a joyful embrace of the themes culminating in the marriage of the Lamb	Outline the Biblical themes relating to the love of God for His people. Cf. John 3:16.	Joyful embrace of the themes culminating in the marriage of the Lamb. Cf. Song of Solomon, Rev. 19:6-9	Commitment to wholehearted love for God as revealed at Sinai, in Christ. Cf. Psa. 17:15, Song of Solomon.

Illustrative Outcomes				
Dimension	Description	Cognitive	Affective	Conative
Personal Attributes				
Moral Commitment	A resolve to faithfully, loyally, steadfastly and reliably fulfil the covenant vow.	List and explain the content or terms of the covenant. Cf. Heb 8:10-11.	Joyfully embrace the terms of the covenant. Delight in the law of God. Cf. Psa. 1.	Resolution to faithfully, loyally, steadfastly and reliably fulfil the covenant vow. Cf. Psa 116:12-14.
Intellectual Insight	An adequate comprehension if the nature and authority of the one bringing the covenant what is means to be subject to the covenant.	Describe the nature of God as revealed at Sinai and in Christ. Cf. Dan. 11:32. Describe the place of the believer (created and infinite) relative to the Covenantor (creator, uncreated and infinite). Cf. Psalm 8, Eph 1:15-22.	Express reverence, awe and respectful fear. Cf. Prov. 9:10.	Commitment to learn hearken and understand the nature of God and His purposes. Not to be dull of hearing. Cf. Isa. 6:10, Heb. 5:11.
Discernment	The realisation that the god of the covenant is YHWH, revealed in Christ as Father, Son, and Holy Spirit, along with a watchful, prayerful vigilance committed to recognising diversions and distractions.	Critically evaluate propositions and theologies about the nature of God that accord with or differ from God as revealed at Sinai and in Christ. Cf. Psalm 14, Rom.1:18-28, Col. 4:6.	Appropriate approval and/or rejection of theologies about the nature of God that accord with or differ from God as revealed at Sinai and in Christ. Cf. Jer. 5:7, 16:20, Gal. 4:8.	Participate in or refuse expressions of faith God that accord with or differ from God as revealed at Sinai and in Christ. Cf. 1 Cor. 6:17.

Emotionality	A deeply held awe that embraces the utterly asymmetric nature of the power-relations in the covenant and the utterness of the love of God along with a humbled, awed, worshipful, loving and willing embrace of all that YHWH, the Triune God, prescribes.	Explain the utterly asymmetric nature of the power-relations in the covenant and the utterness of the love of God toward His people and His creation. Cf. Isa. 45:9, Rom. 9:20-21.	Express love, adoration, awe and respectful fear of God as revealed at Sinai and in Christ. Psa. 103, 116, Song of Solomon.	Participate in or refuse expressions of devotion toward God that accord with or differ from God as revealed at Sinai and in Christ. Cf. Psa. 115.
Habituation	The development of life-patterns that worshipfully express spiritualities associated with watchfulness, attentiveness and regular prayer and worship	Identify and evaluate life patterns and activities that foster watchfulness, attentiveness and regular prayer and worship. Deut. 17:9, Josh. 1:8, Psa. 55:17.	Express zeal to become conformed to the ways of God. Cf. Rom 12:1-2.	Participate regularly in activities that foster watchfulness, attentiveness and regular prayer and worship. Cf. Psa. 133, Heb. 10:25.
Skills	The development of intellectual and discernment skills related to recognising the nature and authority of God and covenant along with the emotional awareness and regulation related to the fear and love of God, watchfulness, attentiveness, and regular prayer and worship.	Identify and evaluate to acquire covenant and related regulatory skills. cf. Psa 119, Prov. 4:7.	Express eagerness to acquire covenant and related regulatory skills. Cf. Psa. 25:4.	Commitment to acquire covenant and related regulatory skills. Cf. 1 Sam 3:10.
Motivations	The development of a persistent disposition, inclination or drive to live a loyal, devoted life that is marked by paying heed to God and obedience to the covenant	Describe and explain the disposition, inclination or drive to live a loyal, devoted life that heeds God and covenant. Cf. Psa. 40:7.	Express enthusiasm toward living a loyal, devoted life that heeds God and covenant. Cf. Psa. 40:8	Adopt the disposition, inclination or drive to living a loyal, devoted life that heeds God and covenant. Cf. Psalm 119:11, 16, 24, 47, 92.

7 Conclusion

Interpreting the law in virtue-based terms provides a way by which its internalisation on mind and heart can be understood in terms of Decalogue-related learning outcomes relevant to personal development and spiritual formation. This internalisation is the core promise of the New Covenant and may be seen as the means by which the condition of virtue or blamelessness first required of Abraham is met as a result of the transforming work of YHWH, God Himself, in the believer. This is central to the prophetic hope declared by Jeremiah and Ezekiel and the emphatic declaration of its inception in the Epistle to the Hebrews.

Analysis of the precepts of the Decalogue, as illustrated in the analysis of Exod. 20:2, by addressing the graces and personal attributes specific to each precept and relating them to appropriate domains of learning, enables the development of learning outcomes or objectives. This provides a means by which frameworks can be developed to guide and evaluate Christian ministry, identify outcomes to be attained, and assess the attainment of the outcomes thus identified.

Bibliography

Behm, J., & E. Würtheim. 'Διάνοια', G. Kittel & G.W. Bromiley (eds.), *Theological Dictionary of the New Testament: Λ - N* (Grand Rapids: Eerdmans, 1967), 4.963–65.

Baumgärtel, F., & J. Behm. 'Καρδία', in G. Kittel & G.W. Bromiley (eds.), *Theological Dictionary of the New Testament: ϑ -K* (Grand Rapids: Eerdmans, 1966), Vol. 3.605–13.

Swanson, J., קרב in J. Swanson, *Dictionary of Biblical Languages with Semantic Domains: Hebrew (Old Testament)*, 7930.

Adam, Stephen. 'An Introduction to Learning Outcomes', in Eric Froment et al. (eds.), *EUA Bologna Handbook: Making Bologna Work* (Berlin: Dr Josef Raabe Verlag: Raabe Academic Publishers, 2006), chap. B 2.3-1.

Adams, Robert Merrihew. *A Theory of Virtue: Excellence in Being for the Good* (Oxford; New York: Oxford University Press, 2009).

Allan, Joanna. 'Learning Outcomes in Higher Education', *Studies in Higher Education* 21.1 (1996), 93–108. doi:10.1080/03075079612331381487.

Anderson, John R. 'ACT: A Simple Theory of Complex Cognition', *American Psychologist* 51.4 (1996), 355–65.

Anderson, John R. *Rules of the Mind* (New York & London: Psychology Press, 2014).

Anderson, Lorin W., & David Krathwohl (eds.), *A Taxonomy for Learning, Teaching, and Assessing: A Revision of Bloom's Taxonomy of Educational Objectives* (New York & London: Longman, 2001).

Annas, Julia. *Intelligent Virtue* (Oxford & New York: Oxford University Press, 2011).

Annas, Julia. *The Morality of Happiness* (Oxford & New York: Oxford University Press, 1993).

Anscombe, G. E. M. 'Modern Moral Philosophy', *Philosophy* 33.124 (1958), 1–19.

Aquinas, Thomas. *Summa Theologica* (The Fathers of the English Dominican Province, transls.; Complete American edition; Claremont: Coyote Canyon Press, 2010). Kindle edition.

Aquinas, Thomas. 'Thomas Aquinas: The Ten Commandments: English' (Joseph B. Collins, trans.; Dominican House of Studies,). http://dhspriory.org/thomas/TenCommandments.htm.

Aristotle, *Nicomachean Ethics* (W. D. Ross, trans.; London: Aeterna Press, 2015). e-Book.

Athanasius, 'Letters of Athanasius, with Two Ancient Chronicles of His Life', in Philip Schaff, Henry Wace, and Archibald Robertson (eds.), *Athanasius: Select Works and Letters* (CCEL edition, vol. 4; Nicene and Post-Nicene Fathers 2; Grand Rapids: Christian Classics Ethereal Library, 1890). www.ccel.org/ccel/schaff/npnf204.pdf.

Atman, Kathryn S. 'The Role of Conation (Striving) in the Distance Education Enterprise', *American Journal of Distance Education* 1.1 (1987), 14-24 doi:10.1080/08923648709526568.

Atman, Kathryn S. 'Goal Accomplishment Style and Psychological Type: Cultural Variations', in *Proceedings of Psychological Type and Culture – East and West: A Multi-Cultural Research Symposium* (Gainesville: University of Hawaii: Center for Applications of Psychological Type, 1993), 207-220. www.researchgate.net/profile/Kathryn_Atman/publication/260299264_Goal_Accomplishment_Style_and_Psychological_Type_Cultural_Variations/links/55e5ff4c08ae-cb1a7ccd6299.pdf.

Augustine, 'On Lying', in *On the Holy Trinity, Doctrinal Treatises, Moral Treatises* (Philip Schaff, ed.; H. Browne, trans.; CCEL edition, vol. 3; Nicene and Post-Nicene Fathers 1; Grand Rapids: Christian Classics Ethereal Library, 1887).

Augustine, 'City of God', in *City of God and Christian Doctrine* (Philip Schaff, ed.; CCEL edition, vol. 2; Nicene and Post-Nicene Fathers 1; Grand Rapids: Christian Classics Ethereal Library, 1887). http://www.ccel.org/ccel/schaff/npnf102.pdf.

Ausubel, David Paul. *Psychology of Meaningful Verbal Learning: An Introduction to School Learning* (New York: Grune & Stratton, 1963).

Aveling, F. 'The Psychology of Conation and Volition1', *British Journal of Psychology. General Section* 16.4 (1926), 339-353. doi:10.1111/j.2044-8295.1926.tb00394.x.

Bailey, Randall C. *Exodus* (The College Press NIV Commentary; Joplin, Missouri: College Press, 2007).

Baltzly, Dirk 'Stoicism', in Edward N. Zalta (ed.), *The Stanford Encyclopedia of Philosophy* (Stanford, California, Stanford University, 2014), 1-46. http://plato.stanford.edu/archives/spr2014/entries/stoicism/.

Barr, James. *The Semantics of Biblical Language* (Eugene, Oregon: Wipf & Stock, 2004).

Barrett, Justin L., & Bonnie Poon Zahl, 'Cognition, Evolution, and Religion', in K. I. Pargament, J. J. Exline, and J. W. Jones (eds.), *APA Handbook of Psychology, Religion, and Spirituality: Context, Theory, and Research* (APA Handbooks in Psychology 1; Washington, DC: American Psychological Association, 2013), 221–37. doi:10.1037/14045-012.

Benedict XVI, *The Ten Commandments*, ed. Giuliano Vigini, Kindle edition, Catholic Foundation Stones 6 (London: St Pauls Publishing, 2014);

Bloom, B. S., et al., *Taxonomy of Educational Objectives Handbook 1: Cognitive Domain* (London: Longman, 1956).

Bobzien, Suzanne. 'Moral Responsibility and Moral Development in Epicurus' Philosophy', in Burkhard Reis (ed.), *The Virtuous Life in Greek Ethics* (Cambridge: Cambridge University Press, 2006), 206-229.

Boyer, Pascal. 'Religion, Evolution, and Cognition', *Current Anthropology* 45.3 (2004), 430–33. doi:10.1086/420914.

Brandt, Ron. 'An Overview of Outcome-Based Education', *ASCD: Learn, Teach, Lead: Curriculum Handbook* (Alexandria, Virginia; ASCD, 1998). www.ascd.org/publications/curriculum_handbook/413/chapters/An_Overview_of_Outcome-Based_Education.aspx.

Brett, George Sidney. *A History of Psychology* (London: G. Allen, 1912). http://archive.org/details/cu31924031036761.

Bright, John. *A History of Israel* (Louisville & London: Westminster John Knox Press, ⁴2000).

Brown, Francis, S.R. Driver, and Charles A. Briggs, 'BDB Hebrew: 3820. לֵב (Leb)—Inner Man, Mind, Will, Heart', *Brown-Driver-Briggs Hebrew and English Lexicon, Unabridged, Electronic Database.* (Glassport, Pennsylvania: Biblesoft, Inc., 2006). http://biblehub.com/bdb/3820.htm.

Brown, Francis, S.R. Driver, and Charles A. Briggs, 'BDB Hebrew: 7130. קֶרֶב (Qereb)—Inward Part, Midst', *Brown-Driver-Briggs Hebrew and English Lexicon, Unabridged, Electronic Database.* (Glassport, Pennsylvania: Biblesoft, Inc., 2006). http://biblehub.com/bdb/7130.htm.

Brown, Francis, S.R. Driver, and Charles A. Briggs, 'BDB Hebrew: 8451. תּוֹרָה (Torah)—Direction, Instruction, Law', *Driver-Briggs Hebrew and English Lexicon, Unabridged, Electronic Database.* (Glassport, Pennsylvania: Biblesoft, Inc., 2006, http://biblehub.com/bdb/8451.htm.

Brown, William P., (ed.), *The Ten Commandments: The Reciprocity of Faithfulness* (Louisville, Kentucky: Westminster John Knox Press, 2004).

Calvin, John. *Harmony of the Law* (Charles William Bingham, trans.; CCEL Edition, vol. 1; Grand Rapids: Christian Classics Ethereal Library, 1852). www.ccel.org/ccel/calvin/calcom03.pdf.

Clement of Alexandria, 'The Instructor', in Alexander Roberts & James Donaldson (ed.), *Fathers of the Second Century: Hermas, Tatian, Athenagoras, Theophilus, and Clement of Alexandria* (CCEL edition, vol. 2; The Ante-Nicene Fathers; Grand Rapids: Christian Classics Ethereal Library, 1885). www.ccel.org/ccel/schaff/anf02.pdf.

Clement of Rome, 'First Epistle to the Corinthians', in Alexander Roberts & James Donaldson (ed.), *The Apostolic Fathers, Justin Martyr, Irenaeus* (CCEL edition, vol. 1; Ante-Nicene Fathers; Grand

Rapids: Christian Classics Ethereal Library, 1885). www.ccel.org/ccel/schaff/anf01.pdf.

Coughlin, F. Edward, (ed.), *Collations on the Ten Commandments. Works of Saint Bonaventure*, vol 6 (Paul J. Spaeth, trans.; New York: The Franciscan Institute, St. Bonaventure University, 1995).

Crisp, Roger, & Michael Slote (eds.), *Virtue Ethics* (Oxford & New York: Oxford University Press, 1997).

Davies, John A. *A Royal Priesthood: Literary and Intertextual Perspectives on an Image of Israel in Exodus 19.6* (London & New York: T&T Clark, 2004).

Donnelly, Kevin. 'Australia's Adoption of Outcomes Based Education—a Critique', *Issues in Educational Research* 17.2 (2007), 183–206.

Dumbrell, William J. *Covenant and Creation: An Old Testament Covenant Theology* (Milton Keynes: Paternoster, 2013 [Revised Kindle edition]).

Duncan, Jennings Ligon. 'Covenant Idea in Ante-Nicene Theology' (Edinburgh: University of Edinburgh, 1995). www.era.lib.ed.ac.uk/handle/1842/10618.

Fabry, Heinz-Josef. 'לב', in G. Johannes Botterweck, Helmer Ringgren, & Heinz-Josef Fabry (eds), *Theological Dictionary of the Old Testament* (D.E. Green, trans.; Grand Rapids & Cambridge, UK: Eerdmans, 2003 [Revised]), 7.399–438.

Fabry, Heinz-Josef. 'תורה', in G. Johannes Botterweck, Helmer Ringgren, & Heinz-Josef Fabry (eds), *Theological Dictionary of the Old Testament* (D.E. Green, trans.; Grand Rapids & Cambridge, UK: Eerdmans, 2003 [Revised]), 15. 609–47.

Frede, Dorothea. 'Plato's Ethics: An Overview', in Edward N. Zalta (ed.), *The Stanford Encyclopedia of Philosophy* Stanford, California, Stanford University, 2013), 1-67. http://plato.stanford.edu/archives/fall2013/entries/plato-ethics/.

Fuhs, H. F. 'ירא', in G. Johannes Botterweck, Helmer Ringgren, & Heinz-Josef Fabry (eds), *Theological Dictionary of the Old Testament* (D.E. Green, trans.; Grand Rapids & Cambridge, UK: Eerdmans, 2003 [Revised]), 6.296–314.

Gagné, Robert M. *The Conditions of Learning and Theory of Instruction*. Fourth edition (New York: Wadsworth, 1985).

Gagné, Robert M. 'Domains of Learning' (Annual Meeting of the American Educational Research Association; New York: American Educational Research Association, 1972), 1-21 http://files.eric.ed.gov/fulltext/ED054853.pdf.

Gentry, Peter J., & Stephen J. Wellum, *Kingdom through Covenant: A Biblical-Theological Understanding of the Covenants* (Wheaton: Crossway, 2012).

Gerdes, Karen E., & Layne K. Stromwall, 'Conation: A Missing Link in the Strengths Perspective', *Social Work* 53.3 (2008), 233–242. doi:10.1093/sw/53.3.233.

Gonczi, Andrew, & Paul Hager, 'The Competency Model', *International Encyclopedia of Education* 8 (2010), 403-410.

Gregory of Nazianzen, 'Select Orations of Saint Gregory Nazianzen', in *Cyril of Jerusalem, Gregory Nazianzen* (Philip Schaff & Henry Wace, eds.; Charles Gordon Browne & James Edward Swallow, transls.; CCEL edition, vol. 7; Nicene and Post-Nicene Fathers 2; Grand Rapids: Christian Classics Ethereal Library, 1893). www.ccel.org/ccel/schaff/npnf207.pdf.

Gregory of Nyssa, 'On Virginity', in *Gregory of Nyssa: Dogmatic Treatises, Etc.*, (Philip Schaff ed.; William Moore & Henry Austin Wilson, transls.; CCEL edition, vol. 5; Nicene and Post-Nicene Fathers 2; Grand Rapids: Christian Classics Ethereal Library, 1893).

Hahn, Scott. 'Covenant in the Old and New Testaments: Some Current Research (1994-2004)', *Currents in Biblical Research* 3.2 (2005), 263–92. doi:10.1177/1476993X05052433.

Hahn, Scott. *Kinship by Covenant: A Canonical Approach to the Fulfillment of God's Saving Promises* (Yale University Press, 2009).

Horton, Michael. *Introducing Covenant Theology* (Grand Rapids: Baker Books, 2009 [Reprint edition]).

Hart, David Bentley. 'God or Nothingness', in Carl E. Braaten & Christopher R. Seitz (eds.), *I Am the Lord Your God: Christian Reflections on the Ten Commandments* (Grand Rapids: Eerdmans, 2005). Kindle edition.

Hauerwas, Stanley, & William H. Willimon, *The Truth about God: The Ten Commandments in Christian Life* (Nashville: Abingdon, 1999). Kindle edition.

Hauerwas, Stanley. *A Community of Character: Toward a Constructive Christian Social Ethic* (Notre Dame: University of Notre Dame Press, 1991). Kindle edition.

Hauerwas, Stanley. *Character and the Christian Life: A Study in Theological Ethics* (Notre Dame: University of Notre Dame Press, 1994).

Hazony, David. *The Ten Commandments: How Our Most Ancient Moral Text Can Renew Modern Life* (New York: Scribner, 2014 Reprint edition).

Heath, David Mark. 'Chiastic Structures in Hebrews: A Study of Form and Function in Biblical Discourse' (University of Stellenbosch, 2011).

Hilgard, Ernest R. 'The Trilogy of Mind: Cognition, Affection, and Conation', *Journal of the History of the Behavioral Sciences* 16.2 (1980), 107-117. doi:10.1002/1520-6696(198004)16:2<107::AID-JHBS2300160202>3.0.CO;2-Y.

Hillers, Delbert R. *Covenant: The History of a Biblical Idea* (Baltimore: Johns Hopkins University Press, 1969).

Hood, Ralph W., Jr., (ed.), 'The History and Current State of Research on Psychology of Religion', in *The Oxford Handbook of Psychology and Spirituality* (Oxford Handbooks of Psychology; Oxford: Oxford University Press, 2013 [Reprint edition]), 7–20.

Huitt, William, & S. Cain, 'An Overview of the Conative Domain', *Educational Psychology Interactive* (2005), 1–20.

Irenaeus of Lyon, 'Against Heresies', in Alexander Roberts & James Donaldson (ed.), *The Apostolic Fathers, Justin Martyr, Irenaeus* (CCEL edition, vol. 1; Ante-Nicene Fathers; Grand Rapids: Christian Classics Ethereal Library, 1885). www.ccel.org/ccel/schaff/anf01.pdf.

Joslin, Barry C. *Hebrews, Christ, and the Law: The Theology of the Mosaic Law in Hebrews 7:1-*

10:18 (Milton Keynes: Paternoster, 2015).

Kedar-Kopfstein, Benjamin. 'תמים', in G. Johannes Botterweck, Helmer Ringgren, and Heinz-Josef Fabry (eds.) *Theological Dictionary of the Old Testament* (D.E. Green, trans.; Grand Rapids & Cambridge, UK: Eerdmans, 2003 [Revised]), 3.699–711.

Kennedy, Declan. *Writing and Using Learning Outcomes* (Cork: University College Cork, 2007). https://cora.ucc.ie/bitstream/handle/10468/1613/A%20Learning%20Outcomes%20Book%20D%20Kennedy.pdf?sequence=1&isAllowed=y.

Gutbrod, W., & Kleinknecht, H. 'Νόμος', in G. Kittel & G.W. Bromiley (eds.), *Theological Dictionary of the New Testament: Λ - Ν* (Grand Rapids: Eerdmans, 1967), 4.1022-1085.

Kline, Meredith G. *Treaty of the Great King: The Covenant Structure of Deuteronomy: Studies and Commentary* (Eugene, Oregon: Wipf & Stock Publishers, 2012).

Koehler, Ludwig, Walter Baumgartner, and Johann Jakob Stamm (eds.), *The Hebrew and Aramaic Lexicon of the Old Testament* (Leiden: E. J. Brill, 1994 [electronic edition]).

Konstan, David. 'Epicurus', in Edward N. Zalta (ed.), *The Stanford Encyclopedia of Philosophy* (Stanford, California; Stanford University, 2014), 1-37 http://plato.stanford.edu/archives/sum2014/entries/epicurus/;

Krathwohl, D. R., B. S. Bloom, & Bertram B. Masia, *Taxonomy of Educational Objectives: Book 2 Affective Domain* (London: Longman, 1964).

Kraut, Richard 'Aristotle's Ethics', in Edward N. Zalta (ed.), *The Stanford Encyclopedia of Philosophy* (Stanford, California; Stanford University, 2016), 1-68 http://plato.stanford.edu/archives/spr2016/entries/aristotle-ethics/.;

Lane, Nathan C. *The Compassionate, but Punishing God: A Canonical Analysis of Exodus 34:6-7* (Eugene, Oregon: Pickwick Publications, 2010).

Lewis, C. S. *The Abolition of Man* (San Francisco: HarperOne, 2015).

Louw, J.P., & Eugene Albert Nida (eds.), *Greek-English Lexicon of the New Testament: Based on Semantic Domains* (New York: United Bible Societies, ²1989).

Luther, Martin. *The Large Catechism* (CCEL Edition; Grand Rapids: Christian Classics Ethereal Library, 1529). www.ccel.org/ccel/luther/largecatechism.pdf.

McClean, John. 'Of Covenant and Creation: A Conversation between Systematic Theology and Biblical Theology', in John A. Davies (ed.), *An Everlasting Covenant: Biblical and Theological Essays in Honour of William J. Dumbrell* (Reformed Theological Review: Supplement 4; Doncaster, Victoria: Reformed Theological Review, 2010), 187–227.

McDougall, William. 'Pleasure, Pain and Conation', *British Journal of Psychology. General Section* 17 (1927), 171–80. doi:10.1111/j.2044-8295.1927.tb00421.x.

MacIntyre, Alasdair. *A Short History of Ethics: A History of Moral Philosophy from the Homeric Age to the Twentieth Century*, Second edition, Kindle edition (London: Routledge, 1998).

MacIntyre, Alasdair. *After Virtue: A Study in Moral Theory* (Notre Dame, Indiana: University of Notre Dame Press, ³2007 [1981]).

Mayer, John D., Heather Frasier Chabot, & Kevin M. Carlsmith, 'Conation, Affect, and Cognition in Personality', Gerald Matthews (ed.), in *Advances in Psychology* vol. 124, Cognitive Science Perspectives on Personality and Emotion (Amsterdam & New York: North Holland, 1997), 31–63. http://www.sciencedirect.com/science/article/pii/S0166411597801197.

Mendenhall, George E. 'Covenant Forms in Israelite Tradition', *The Biblical Archaeologist*; 7,3 (1954), 50–76.

Menn, Stephen Philip. *Plato on God as Nous* (Carbondale, Illinois: Southern Illinois University Press, 1995).

Merrill, M. David. 'Component Display Theory', in Charles M. Reigeluth (ed.), *Instructional-Design Theories and Models: An Overview of Their Current Status*, vol. 1 (Hillsdale, NJ & London: Lawrence Erlbaum Associates, 1983), 279–334.

Mikva, Rachel S., (ed.). *Broken Tablets: Restoring the Ten Commandments and Ourselves* Woodstock, Vermont: Jewish Lights Publishing, 2001).

Militello, L.G., et al., 'Conation: Its Historical Roots and Implications for Future Research', in *International Symposium on Collaborative Technologies and Systems (CTS'06)*, (Wright-Patterson, Ohio, Air Force Research Laboratory Logistics Readiness Branch), 2006), 240–47, doi:10.1109/CTS.2006.31.

Miller, Patrick D. *The Ten Commandments* (Interpretation: Resources for the Use of Scripture in the Church; Louisville, Kentucky: Westminster John Knox Press, 2009).

Most, William G. 'A Biblical Theology of Redemption in a Covenantal Framework', *The Catholic Biblical Quarterly* 29.1 (1967), 1–19.

Moon, Jennifer. *The Module and Programme Development Handbook: A Practical Guide to Linking Levels, Outcomes and Assessment Criteria* (London: Routledge, 2002).

MWDO 'Conation, n.', *Merriam Webster Dictionary Online* (Merriam Webster Incorporated). www.merriam-webster.com/dictionary/conation.

Nelson, James M., & Brent D. Slife, 'Theoretical and Epistemological Foundations', in Lisa J. Miller (ed.), *The Oxford Handbook of Psychology and Spirituality* (Oxford Handbooks of Psychology; Oxford University Press, 2013 [Reprint edition]), 21–35.

OEDO, 'Conation, n.', *Oxford English Dictionary Online* (Oxford: Oxford University Press, 2017). http://www.oed.com.ezproxy.sl.nsw.gov.au/viewdictionaryentry/Entry/38030.

OEDO, 'learning, n.', *Oxford English Dictionary Online* (Oxford: Oxford University Press, 2017). http://www.oed.com.ezproxy.sl.nsw.gov.au/viewdictionaryentry/Entry/106723.

O'Keefe, Tim. 'Hedonistic Theories of Well-Being in Antiquity', in Guy Fletcher (ed.), *The Routledge Handbook of Philosophy of Well-Being* (London & New York: Routledge, 2015), 29–39.

Peterson, Christopher, & Martin Seligman, *Character Strengths and Virtues: A Handbook and Classification* (Washington, DC & New York: American Psychological Association & Oxford University Press, 2004).

Philo, 'A Treatise Concerning the Ten Commandments Which Are the Heads of the Law', in *The Works of Philo Judaeus, the Contemporary of Josephus* 3 (Charles Duke Yonge, trans.; London:

Henry G. Bohn, 1855). https://archive.org/details/theworksofphiloj03yonguoft.

Rattray, S., & Jacob Milgrom, 'קרב', in G. Johannes Botterweck, Helmer Ringgren, & Heinz-Josef Fabry (eds.), *Theological Dictionary of the Old Testament* (D.E. Green, trans.; (Grand Rapids & Cambridge, UK: Eerdmans, 2003 [Revised]), 13.148-152.

Reigeluth, Charles M., & Julie Moore, 'Cognitive Education and the Cognitive Domain', in Charles M. Reigeluth (ed.), *Instructional-Design Theories and Models: A New Paradigm of Instructional Theory* (New York and London: Routledge, 2009), 51-68.

Remus, Harold E. 'Authority, Consent, Law: Nomos, Physis, and the Striving for a "Given"', *Studies in Religion/Sciences Religieuses* 13.1 (1984), 13–17.

Robertson, O. Palmer. *The Christ of the Covenants* (Grand Rapids: P & R Publishing, 1987).

Rooker, Mark. *The Ten Commandments: Ethics for the Twenty-First Century* (New American Commentary Studies in Bible and Theology; Nashville, Tennessee: B&H Academic, 2010). Kindle edition.

Shaver, Phillip et al., 'Emotion Knowledge: Further Exploration of a Prototype Approach', in W. Gerrod Parrott (ed.), *Emotions in Social Psychology: Essential Readings* (Philadelphia: Psychology Press, 2001), 26–56.

Sicker, Martin. *The Ten Commandments: Background, Meaning, and Implications: From a Judaic Perspective* (Lincoln, New England: iUniverse, 2007).

Spady, William G. 'Organizing for Results: The Basis of Authentic Restructuring and Reform', *Educational Leadership; Alexandria* 46.2 (1988), 4-8.

Spady, William G., & Kit J. Marshall, 'Beyond Traditional Outcome-Based Education', *Educational Leadership; Alexandria* 49.2 (1991), 67-72.

Spady, William G. 'Choosing Outcomes of Significance', *Educational Leadership; Alexandria* 51.6 (1994): 18-22.

Stuart, Douglas K. *Exodus* 2 (The New American Commentary; Nashville: B&H Publishing Group, 2006).

Swanson, J. *Dictionary of Biblical Languages with Semantic Domains: Hebrew (Old Testament)* (Oak Harbor: Logos Research Systems Inc., 1997 [electronic edition]).

Talbert, Charles H. 'Paul on the Covenant', *Review & Expositor* 84.2 (1987), 299–313.

Vacek, Edward Collins. 'Orthodoxy Requires Orthopathy: Emotions in Theology', *Horizons* 40.2 (2013), 218-241. doi:10.1017/hor.2013.79.

Van Harn, Roger, (ed.). *The Ten Commandments for Jews, Christians, and Others* (Grand Rapids: Eerdmans, 2007).

Walton, John H. *Covenant* (Grand Rapids: Zondervan, 1994 [Kindle edition]).

White, Thomas Joseph. *Exodus* (R. R. Reno, ed.; Brazos Theological Commentary on the Bible; Grand Rapids: Brazos Press, 2016).

Whitehouse, Harvey. 'Cognitive Evolution and Religion: Cognition and Religious Evolution', *Issues in Ethnology and Anthropology* 3.3 (2016), 35–47.

Williamson, Paul R. 'Covenant: The Beginning of a Biblical Idea', *Reformed Theological Review* 65.1 (2006), 1–14.

Williamson, Paul R. *Sealed with an Oath: Covenant in God's Unfolding Purpose* (Downers Grove, Illinois: IVP Academic, 2007).

Woolsey, Andrew A. 'The Covenant in the Church Fathers', *Haddington House Journal* 5 (2003), 25–52.

Wright, Tom. *Virtue Reborn* (London: SPCK, 2010)

Zagzebski, Linda Trinkaus. *Virtues of the Mind: An Inquiry into the Nature of Virtue and the Ethical Foundations of Knowledge* (New York, NY, USA: Cambridge University Press, 1996).

Peter Carblis
University of Newcastle/ Sydney College of Divinity
petercarblis@gmail.com

12 | ACADEMIC FREEDOM IN THE THOUGHT-POLICED UNIVERSITY

CHALLENGES FOR CHRISTIAN EDUCATORS TODAY

Abstract

The contemporary university in Western societies has become the captive of politically-correct ideology and of processes for policing and restricting freedom of thought and speech. Especially in the domains of the study of history and of the literary heritage of Western civilisation in English literature, which is substantially of Christian provenance, the imposition of theories about such as race, class and gender, have demanded either that such works be distorted to be read in accord with those principles, or simply disposed of—in such as the dismantling of the study of the 'canon' of English texts. This enforced cultural suppression and forgetting poses particular challenges for educators committed to the study of texts of Christian origin or character and to nurturing the appreciation of them by students.

> There is no greater heresy and no more offensive notion than that the loss of Christian faith might have a downside [...]. The task of community leaders was once to uphold the values of [Christian] civilisation; now, more often than not, it is to dismantle them.[1]

---

1   Kelly, 'Blessed be the egoistic individuals'.

The secular university in Western societies has undergone an unexpected and astonishing revolution in the last generation or so. The radical upheavals of the 1960s—conducted in the name of liberation, including freedom from all censorship—have, perversely, produced a caste of university administrators and academics committed to the suppression of freedom of thought and speech, unprecedented in the history of the academy. Linked to this, and assisting its enforcement, is the 'infantilisation' of the university (as Frank Furedi has recently described it),[2] whereby undergraduates are perceived (strategically, for the ideologues' purposes) as endangered, fragile children needing protection—in a 'safe space'—from ideas or opinions that might challenge or contradict such as the orthodox Marxist-Feminist-Postmodernist positions on race, gender and class. This phenomenon poses particular challenges for an academic who would promote teaching and learning from a Christian perspective and in the study of Christian texts. The greatest literary works of Western civilisation, such as Dante's *Divine Comedy* or John Milton's *Paradise Lost*, depend for their intelligent appreciation on readers' willingness, at least, to entertain a degree of openness to their biblical and doctrinal content—the suspension of disbelief, in Coleridge's phrase. The abolition of the 'canon' in the study of English literature, and the disappearance of such texts as Milton's (central to that canon) from curricula, lead us to ponder the question: what does the future hold for Christian educators and for the maintenance and promotion of works of Christian provenance in the university, and indeed for the university, so-called, itself?

For all modern Humanities academics' relentless rhetoric and invective against colonisation, their faculties and departments have been very successfully colonised by leftist orthodoxy of thought, to the point where that orthodoxy is the pervasive, taken-for-granted position. Long ago, students learnt that their success depended upon reproducing the 'right' views on anything and everything: any argument that appeared to question, let alone set out to demolish, that correctitude of analysis would be a reckless and imprudent departure that, certainly, no student ambitious for academic success would hazard. A zombie generation has been produced, by school and university syllabi, for which independent thought is frowned upon, counter-cultural ideas and opinions are suppressed or even denounced, and freedom of thought and speech seriously compromised. This is the totalitarian ideal. The aptly-surnamed Bernardt Rust, Adolf Hitler's Reichminister of Culture and Education, stated in *Education and*

---

2   Furedi, *What's Happened to the University?*

Instruction, that 'No individual must think himself more brilliant than his fellows: we must have no intellectuals. Each mind is of equal importance'.[3] In other words, minds must be ground down until all that remains is flat conformity to the authorities' precepts. The ancient conception, that it is of the essence of a university that it should be the forum for catholicity of thought, has been seriously undermined in our day, as a result of these principles.

This degradation of what a university should be (and what the very word itself means)—a commonwealth of learning, in which any and every opinion can be aired for free and respectful discussion; an intellectual adventure for probing and testing any proposition imaginable—has been copiously documented and commented on in numerous publications, over several decades. Classics of the genre include Allan Bloom's *The Closing of the American Mind*, published as long ago as 1987, where Bloom argued that (as the book's subtitle indicates) 'higher education has failed democracy and impoverished the souls of today's students'. The impoverishment has proceeded apace over the subsequent thirty years, to our present nadir. Students have been brainwashed into believing that the highest virtue consists in being resolutely and relentlessly at daggers drawn with the Western civilisation that they have inherited and which produced the university wherein they are engaged in its disposal. The sustained attack on Western culture in universities is the most conspicuous and influential cause of the death of that civilisation, the subject of Douglas Murray's latest monograph, *The Strange Death of Europe*, in which he describes 'a continent and culture caught in the act of suicide'. Murray asks 'why anyone, let alone an entire civilisation, would do this to themselves?'[4] The answer is not far to seek: the Left, who have taken absolute control of educational systems and, almost to the same extent, of the media in the West—a project in which they have been very successfully engaged for some fifty years—take, as axiomatic, the suppression and destruction of all that Western, Christian civilisation has taught and stands for.

A more recent and local contribution to the analysis of the dismantling of the idea of a university is Keith Windschuttle's presentation of what has happened to the teaching of modern history in the Australian academy, entitled *The Killing of History*, a closely-argued analysis of 'how literary critics and social theorists are murdering our past' (to quote its subtitle). This annihilation of a once-respected discipline has the motive of bringing that past into line with current

---

3   Quoted by Sitwell in *Taken Care Of*, 39.
4   From the book's blurb.

acceptable opinion, stretching it on the Procrustean bed of race, gender and class correctness. Speaking of its effects on literary study, Emeritus Professor Michael Wilding has referred to 'the surrender of history':

> One of the most worrying aspects of the post-modern, and of current institutional practice in the universities, in particular in departments of history and literature, is the surrender of history; even more than that, the rejection of history, the denial of history.[5]

The past, wrong about everything, by the standards of our enlightened times, having nothing of value to teach us, must be suppressed, denounced or re-written in our terms. In W.B. Yeats's words, 'The past had deceived us: let us accept the worthless present'.[6] That past, in Western civilisation, with reference to the commitment to liberty of thought and speech, presents us with the wisdom of giants, through several centuries: there is John Milton, in the seventeenth, with his great tract, *Areopagitica*, in rejection of censorship; Voltaire in the eighteenth century, with his conviction: 'I wholly disagree with what you say and will defend to the death your right to say it'[7] and John Stuart Mill, in the nineteenth, with his essay 'On the Liberty of Thought and Discussion':

> If all mankind minus one, were of one opinion, and only one person were of the contrary opinion, mankind would be no more justified in silencing that one person, than he, if he had the power, would be justified in silencing mankind[...]. But the peculiar evil of silencing the expression of an opinion is, that it is robbing the human race; posterity as well as the existing generation; those who dissent from the opinion, still more than those who hold it. If the opinion is right, they are deprived of the opportunity of exchanging error for truth: if wrong, they lose, what is almost as great a benefit, the clearer perception and livelier impression of truth, produced by its collision with error.[8]

One would like to put this statement for comment to such as Monash University which, this year, appointed officials to conduct surveillance for trigger warnings

---

5   Wilding, *Growing Wild*, 219.
6   Yeats, 'Modern Poetry'.
7   The statement is usually attributed to Voltaire and would certainly be in accord with his intellectual principles, but there is ongoing debate about the accuracy of the attribution to him.
8   Mill, 'Of the Liberty of Thought and Discussion'.

to be applied to unacceptable or inappropriate ideas that might be confronting for students—the first fatal step to eliminating *any* idea or opinion that does not conform. No doubt some other Australian universities will mulishly follow suit; but elsewhere, distinguished academies have refused to succumb to this assault on freedom of thought and the free play of ideas. The Dean of Students at the University of Chicago, John Ellison, made this comment to incoming freshmen last year:

> You will find that we expect members of our community to be engaged in rigorous debate, discussion and even disagreement. At times this may challenge you and even cause discomfort. Our commitment to academic freedom means that we do not support so-called 'trigger warnings', we do not cancel invited speakers because their topics might prove controversial, and we do not condone the creation of intellectual 'safe spaces' where individuals can retreat from ideas and perspectives at odds with their own.[9]

And the President of the University, Robert Zimmer, tellingly observed: A university should not be a sanctuary for comfort but rather a crucible for confronting ideas.[10]

The scandal of the active destruction of the idea of the university as the nurturer of liberty of thought and the unflinching protector of dissent has only been exceeded, in our day, by the silence and complicity of many academics, in the contemporary version of the *trahison des clercs*. 'Intellectual disgrace', W.H. Auden wrote, at the time of burgeoning totalitarianism in Europe, 'stares from every human face'[11]; while, Yeats, again, foreseeing the decline of the West in his apocalyptic poem, 'The Second Coming', wrote:

> The best lack all conviction, while the worst
> Are full of passionate intensity.[12]

One might have supposed, after the oppressive, punitive regimes of Stalinist, Hitlerian and Maoist tyranny, that the lessons of comparatively recent history about such restrictions of intellectual freedom would have been well and truly learnt, but such is the suppression and denial of history by the Left, that we are

---

9   Ellison, 'So you like the University of Chicago's rejection of safe spaces'.
10 Zimmer, 'Free speech is the basis of a true education'.
11 Auden, 'In Memory of W.B. Yeats'.
12 Yeats, 'The Second Coming'.

now doomed to repeat these lessons.

With regard to the study of English literature, George Orwell—that acute visionary and hammer of tyranny—foresaw this phenomenon of cultural forgetting, suppression and outright denial, as long ago as 1949, in his dystopic novel, *Nineteen Eighty-Four*—enjoying renewed popularity today as people recognise that the nightmare society that Orwell so brilliantly describes is the very one which we have allowed to prosper and which has now engulfed us:

> By 2050—earlier, probably [he was right about that, too]—all real knowledge of Oldspeak will have disappeared. The whole literature of the past will have been destroyed. Chaucer, Shakespeare, Milton, Byron—they'll exist only in Newspeak versions, not merely changed into something different, but actually changed into something contradictory of what they used to be[…]. The whole climate of thought will be different. In fact there will be no thought, as we understand it now. Orthodoxy means not thinking—not needing to think. Orthodoxy is unconsciousness.[13]

That unconsciousness now prevails in what is left of the study of literature in English in the 'Colleges of Emotional Engineering (Department of Writing)', in Aldous Huxley's similarly dystopic and prophetic terminology,[14] the social conditioning institutes into which many universities are allowing themselves to be degraded, and indeed in such pre-university curricula as the New South Wales Higher School Certificate English syllabus (where clever students know, and have long acknowledged, that saying the 'right' thing about texts is a game that has to be played, and daring to proffer a creative and sceptical reading of any set text would be a mug's game). Policed thought is, by definition, non-thought.

What the theologian, E.L. Mascall, noted of the Churches in the West in the latter half of the twentieth century applies equally to universities: 'The Church, in all its branches, has been subjected to a widespread and many-faced process of erosion [to which its leaders] have often helplessly capitulated'. He saw this, in 1992, as 'the first wave of a storm which is breaking upon the Church as a

---

13 Orwell, *Nineteen Eighty-Four*, chapter 5. Aldous Huxley foresaw it a generation before Orwell, in *Brave New World*: 'There were those strange rumours of old forbidden books hidden in a safe in the Controller's study. Bibles, poetry […]', 41.
14 Huxley, *Brave New World*, 71.

whole'.¹⁵ In the case of the universities, the storm, then, has turned into a totally destructive tsunami today. Even leading radical thinkers of the past can get caught up in the firestorm of today's campus political correctness for daring to entertain views that fail the test of strict conformity to the Commissars' approved thought. Last year, Germaine Greer contended that transgender women were not 'real' women. Immediately, the now-predictable barrage of personal and foul abuse of anti-social media and the nitwits of the Twittersphere descended upon Greer—and, on cue, her own university, Cambridge, which was preparing to confer an honorary degree on her, rescinded the offer, and Cardiff University, where she was due to deliver a public lecture, told her that it would be unwise for her to attend the campus, as she could be physically assaulted for the offence that she had caused—for speaking her mind; now, a prohibited activity, especially at a university. 'I was expressing an *opinion*!' Greer expostulated, in an interview in the wake of the uproar. 'I was accused of inciting violence against transgender people. That's nonsense. I've been accused of things I've never done or said'. Reflecting on what has become of the university culture in the West, Greer observed that people had commented they were astonished at the way she had been treated by Cambridge. 'Not me', said Greer, ruefully recognising that this was only what you could expect if you dared to give voice to an incorrect thought in the modern university.¹⁶

In December, 2017, eminent Oxford professor of theology, Nigel Biggar, who wrote an opinion piece suggesting that there might be something positive to be said about colonisation and the British Empire, was denounced as a 'racist bigot' by students and more than fifty of his colleagues wrote a letter rejecting his views, preferring, as Biggar reflected, not to address him directly and collegially but to engage in 'collective online bullying... They do not have the right to control how I, or anyone else, thinks about these things'.¹⁷ 'They', no doubt, would beg to differ. To its great credit, and very unusually these days, the authorities of the professor's university refused to be cowed by the campus student and staff Gestapo who would repress a scholar's freedom to express his ideas, and invite discussion of them, issuing this statement:

> We absolutely support academic freedom of speech. The history of empire is a complex topic and it is important that universities

---

15 Mascall, *Saraband*, 380.
16 Greer, 'Transgender women are "not women"'.
17 Harding, 'Eminent Oxford professor is branded a bigot'.

consider our global history from a variety of perspectives. This is a valid, evidence-led academic project and Professor Biggar, who is an internationally-recognised authority on the ethics of empire, is an entirely suitable person to lead it.[18]

What is disconcerting, however, is that such a statement had to be issued at all.

So much for the broad and dismal setting which poses formidable personal and professional challenges for educators of Christian persuasion and those who would introduce students to the vast wealth of human experience and its expression in Western civilisation which had the Christian faith as its source and inspiration through two millennia, and would not have come into existence without that faith.

Christian educators—that is, teachers or lecturers of Christian faith themselves, or, more generally, educators committed to advancing the understanding of and a degree of empathy towards texts of Christian provenance—are, by that very commitment, set in opposition to all that the contemporary ideologically-driven secular academy stands for and would enforce. The deep embedding of the suppression, in the study of literature, of texts of Christian character has been cunningly achieved through two processes, both resolutely and very successfully advanced by the Left: the progressive undermining and dismantling of the study of the 'canon' of English literature (to the point, now, where it has completely disappeared and its recovery is unimaginable) and, second, and more broadly, the concomitant transformation of the discipline into a branch of cultural studies, where texts are no longer to be read (let alone valued) as masterpieces of thought and expression, but as evidence to be adduced in advancing or condemning various cultural practices and beliefs. So, just to give a brief example of the latter: a student I know has been told that she must read Jane Austen's *Pride and Prejudice* in terms of the radical feminist theories of Austen's contemporary, Mary Wollstonecraft (even though there is no evidence that Austen had even heard of Wollstonecraft, and nowhere in any of her writings does she refer to her). No time at all, in this student's classroom study of the novel, has been devoted to what a student of English literature used to be (and ought to be) doing: analysing and appreciating Austen's wondrous mastery of the language, her intricate plot construction and development, the evolving subtlety of her characterisation and its insight into human nature, and so on—

---

18 Turner, 'Oxford academics criticise professor who suggested people should have "pride" about aspects of British Empire'.

once the bedrock of the discipline's study of a novel. Now, the text is of value only as evidence of the subduing of women by the phallocentric, masculinist patriarchy in order that some statement or scene can be wrenched from its context to be manipulated into the construction of Austen as a proto-feminist campaigning against the oppression of her gender. And then we wonder that students are turned off the study of literary works! This particular student recognises that the entire miserable enterprise is fraudulent, but she also realises that she must go along with it as it is the only 'acceptable', mark-gaining approach. Tyranny and totalitarianism—the enemies of freedom and liberty—have always thrived on such dishonesty and distortion, and are especially committed to securing submission to correct ideas by young minds.

The so-called 'canon' of English literature borrowed its name from the canon of approved books of the two Testaments: the authoritative collections of texts to be read. While the canon of English texts has never been as fixed as those of scripture, the very concept of an authoritative, time-honoured group of works in poetry, the novel, non-fictional prose, and drama to be studied by anybody seeking mastery of the discipline is immediately offensive to the Leftists' general distaste for authority—other than their own, of course, which is ruthlessly and comprehensively enforced. The resonance of this idea of a canon of texts with the Christian notion of a list of approved reading only adds to the secularists' determination to be rid of it. Moreover, the generally-accepted canonical texts of literature in English were written, through the centuries since the Renaissance (the extensive time period which English literature study used, systematically, to attempt to encompass) by men and women who were steeped in Christian texts and practice (even if they had, in adulthood, abandoned belief) and who assumed such familiarity on the part of their readers. Bertrand Russell is an example of this. More particularly, in the study of English literature, such sources as the Authorised ('King James') version of the Bible (1611) and The Book of Common Prayer (going through various editions, from 1549 to 1662) and texts like John Bunyan's *Pilgrim's Progress* (1678), nurtured the literary and linguistic, in addition to spiritual, sensibilities of countless readers and writers for generations. Dictionaries of quotations will show this, to this day. The King James Bible was the most important—enriching, 'for centuries to come, English language, English character, essential English life, with a treasure beyond price'.[19] And, we would add to that list, English literature.

---

19 Brook, 179.

Virtually any poet or author in English you care to think of, up to the midtwentieth century, was steeped in such texts in childhood—whether it was Jane Austen's upbringing in her father's parsonage, D.H. Lawrence at the Congregationalist chapel in Eastwood with his devout mother ('the influence of the Bible, its imagery, language and symbolism, did much to form his style and shape his vision of man and the cosmos'[20]) or W.H. Auden, with his particular devotion to the Prayer Book, deriving from his own childhood experiences of Anglo-Catholicism—both his grandfathers were priests. This kind of background was by no means confined to England or Anglicanism. The greatest Modernist novel, James Joyce's *Ulysses*, begins with the opening versicle of the Latin Mass, deriving from the psalms: *Introibo ad altare Dei*: I will go to the altar of God (Ps. 43:4), and our contemporary Australian novelist, Tim Winton, draws effortlessly and inevitably from his faith and its hymnody. His best-known novel, *Cloudstreet*, has, as its epigraph, lines from the nineteenth-century hymn: 'Shall we gather at the river / Where bright angel-feet have trod', and Winton employs various words with Christian symbolic resonance in the book—as in the character, Fish Lamb. Winton recognises that his 'orthodox Christian point of view' is 'very much against the current' of modern Australia: 'Not only is it a post-Christian age, it's an anti-Christian culture in many respects. I think that's one reason why I am read. I'm an oddity'.[21]

Such examples could be multiplied a hundredfold—and, indeed, the further back we go in the history of English literature, especially to the sixteenth and seventeenth centuries, long regarded as its golden age, the more concentrated and richer the debt to Christian faith, practice and foundational texts is found to be, in the writings (for example) of John Donne, George Herbert and Milton. Arguably the greatest and certainly the most influential of poets in the twentieth century, T.S. Eliot, is, in his poetry and plays, deeply immersed in Christian language and thought. In 1927, Eliot declared himself to be 'royalist in politics, classicist in literature, and anglo-catholic in religion'[22]—a triple disqualification by today's standards; so he, too, is languishing in the shades.

It is impossible to enter into the worlds and minds of such writers and their creativity without a knowledge of, and a degree of sympathy with (and certainly not with an implanted and mandated hostility to) this vast and complex religious

---

20 Kalnins, 'Introduction', 3.
21 Sigley, *OzLit Guide*, chapter 44, 'Tim Winton'.
22 Eliot, 'Preface', *For Lancelot Andrewes*, 7.

culture, in word, sacrament, theology, imagery, music, architecture and so on, from which it derived its abundant riches. For this is the overwhelming heritage in which literature in English is steeped—from Shakespeare to Wordsworth, Faulkner (*Absalom, Absalom!, Go Down, Moses* and so on) to Muriel Spark, and on to Les Murray. But the educational system we have allowed to flourish, unimpeded and largely uncriticised, has set itself in fierce opposition to all that Christianity has contributed to Western civilisation—and, thereby, to that discredited civilisation itself. The result is a cultural forgetting of staggering dimensions.

Eliminate such masterworks as *Paradise Lost*—the greatest of English poems, which was eliminated long ago—with its multitude of incorrect ideas about the divine origin and purpose of life and human existence, men's and women's relationship to each other and to God—and you have struck a decisive blow for the revolution. It bothers the iconoclasts not at all that in doing so they have produced the absurdity of English study—even by students at honours, master's and, believe it or not, doctoral level in English literature—who have never read a word of Milton (the equivalent, in Italian, of not having read Dante, or in German, Goethe, or in Latin, Virgil, or in Greek, Homer). That the integrity of the discipline has thereby been wilfully and risibly eroded under submission to ideologically-correct thought, rendering it intellectually bankrupt, is not merely of no account but a process to be celebrated—a great leap forward to the brave new world. Such is the success of this disastrous devolution of the discipline that what would have been regarded, fifty years, ago as a ludicrous lacuna in a student's study of English at university is now taken for granted[23] and, moreover, anyone who promoted the restoration of *Paradise Lost* not only to the curriculum but to a core syllabus of mandated study of canonical texts (which until the 1970s was universally available in universities) would be roundly denounced with the now-usual campus pillory-litany as racist, sexist, homophobic, Zionist, anti-Islamic, and so on—the *acceptable* hate speech of the modern university.

Milton is the most obvious example, not only because of his stature as the epic poet of genius in the English language (and virtually all of his poetry is on Christian and biblical themes) but because his influence—whether in imitation

---

23 About twenty years ago, one of my PhD students, who was writing a thesis on English poetry, came to me from another university with First Class Honours and the University Medal in English literature. He had not read a line of Milton in the four years of his study of the subject. I sent him off to read *Paradise Lost*.

or determined development away from his principles and poetics—was momentous, across the centuries. So it is not merely a matter of the neglect of the extensive corpus of his poetry, but the consequent misunderstanding of later poets—such as Pope (who parodies *Paradise Lost* in *The Rape of the Lock*), Wordsworth, Tennyson, Hopkins, even T.S. Eliot—who cannot be read aright without prior knowledge of their response to Milton.

Gerard Manley Hopkins was one of the required authors for study in the core course of English I in my undergraduate years, nearly 50 years ago, just before English as a recognised and recognisable discipline in the universities began to be subjected to the white-anting processes of the Silly 'Sixties' ideologues.[24] A year later, in our English II, George Herbert was there, along with Donne, Milton and so on. Like Milton, Herbert (from earlier in the seventeenth century) and Hopkins, from the later nineteenth century, are poets who write entirely within the framework of Christian faith and practice and they are amongst the greatest poets in the language. Both have, like Milton, been 'disappeared'; put on the Index of Prohibited Works by the Orwellian Ministry of Truth. Numerous other examples could be given.

What does the future hold for up-and-coming academics of Christian faith, or those with a more general commitment to teaching and researching the great works of Western civilisation—such as we find in the glorious treasury of poetry in English—in this environment of civilisational self-loathing?[25] I have always warned any aspiring academics amongst my students, who share this faith and/or pedagogic commitment, that unless they have a sure vocation to martyrdom, the very last place to which they should apply their talents and hard work is the modern academy and the cultural studies departments within it into which English has been disintegrated and dissolved. I suspect that, in some form of other, there will, in time, be a reaction to all the damage that has been done to our culture and civilisation. Already, 'Great Books' courses in various famous universities, such as the University of Chicago which (as we have seen) has held out commendably against the rot that has ruined so many other institutions, plus the establishment of small liberal arts colleges, such as Campion College in Sydney, which are not ashamed of the Christian faith or embarrassed to commend and teach works which are steeped in it and which are fundamental to an understanding of the Western mind, are giving people a little hope. But all

---

24 The phrase, 'the Silly 'Sixties', was coined by A. L. Rowse, the historian and Fellow of All Souls' Oxford.
25 The phrase is Mark Steyn's.

the big battalions remain steadfastly opposed to such developments and, worse, they are now on the alert, having discerned that their hegemony, secured by their triumph over an opposing worldview they imagine that they had utterly quelled, may be under threat.

Eliot, who foresaw, in the middle of the twentieth century, the future which has now all but consumed us in the twenty-first, gives us the wisest counsel, as we address and do what we can to resist what is nothing less than a catastrophe for civilisation:

> The World is trying the experiment of attempting to form a civilized but non-Christian mentality. The experiment will fail; but we must be very patient in awaiting its collapse; meanwhile redeeming the time: so that the Faith may be preserved alive through the dark ages before us; to renew and rebuild civilization, and save the World from suicide.[26]

Bibliography

Auden, W.H. 'In Memory of W.B. Yeats' https://newrepublic.com/article/113208/wh-auden-poems-september-1-1939-and-memory-wb-yeats [accessed 16/7/17].

Bloom, A. *The Closing of the American Mind: How Higher Education Has Failed Democracy and Impoverished the Souls of Today's Students* (New York: Simon & Schuster, 1987).

Brook, V.J.K., *Whitgift and the English Church* (London: Hodder and Stoughton, 1964).

Eliot, T.S., 'Preface', *For Lancelot Andrewes* (1928; London: Faber and Faber, 1970).

Eliot, T.S., 'Thoughts after Lambeth', in *Selected Essays* (1932; London: Faber and Faber, London, 1951).

Ellison, J. 'So you like the University of Chicago's rejection of safe spaces' www.washingtonpost.com/news/answer-sheet/wp/2016/08/30/so-you-like-the-university-of-chicagos-rejection-of-safe-spaces-for-students-consider-this/?utm_term=.4db7dd6337d1 [accessed 2/1/17].

Furedi, F. *What's Happened to the University? A sociological exploration of its infantilisation* www.kent.ac.uk/news/society/10981/frank-furedi-asks-what-has-happened-to-our-universities [accessed 30/3/17].

Greer, G. 'Transgender women are "not women"'—BBC Newsnight, www.youtube.com/watch?v=7B8Q6D4a6TM [accessed 14/7/17].

---

26 Eliot, 'Thoughts after Lambeth', in *Selected Essays*, 387.

Harding, E. 'Eminent Oxford professor is branded a bigot' www.dailymail.co.uk/news/article-5181631/Eminent-Oxford-professor-branded-bigot-students.html [accessed 8/1/18].

Huxley, A. *Brave New World and Brave New World Revisited* (New York: Harper, 2004).

Kalnins, M. (ed.), *The Cambridge Edition of the Works of D.H. Lawrence: Apocalypse and the Writings on Revelation* (Cambridge: Cambridge University Press, 1980).

Kelly, P. 'Blessed be the egoistic individuals' www.theaustralian.com.au/news/inquirer/blessed-be-the-egoistic-individuals/news-story/49de39a232f038a03100cb967a4f4967 [accessed 15/7/17].

Mascall, E.L. *Saraband: The Memoirs of E.L. Mascall* (Leominster: Gracewing, 1992).

Mill, J.S. 'Of the Liberty of Thought and Discussion' www.bartleby.com/130/2.html [accessed 3/4/17].

Murray, D. *The Strange Death of Europe* www.amazon.co.uk/Strange-Death-Europe-Immigration-Identity/dp/1472942248 [accessed 5/7/17].

Orwell, G. *Nineteen Eighty-Four* https://ebooks.adelaide.edu.au/o/orwell/george/o79n/chapter1.5.html [accessed 23/1/17].

Sigley, T. *OzLit Guide*, chapter 44, 'Tim Winton' https://sites.google.com/a/ozlitguide.com/www/Home/ch-44-Tim-Winton [accessed 15/7/17].

Sitwell, E. *Taken Care Of: an autobiography* (London: Hutchinson, 1966).

Turner, C. 'Oxford academics criticise professor who suggested people should have "pride" about aspects of British Empire' www.telegraph.co.uk/education/2017/12/20/oxford-academics-criticise-professor-suggested-people-should/ [accessed 8/1/18].

Wilding, M. *Growing Wild* (North Melbourne: Australian Scholarly Publishing, 2016).

Windschuttle, K. *The Killing of History: How Literary Critics and Social Theorists Are Murdering Our Past* (San Francisco: Encounter Books, 1996).

Yeats, W.B. 'Modern Poetry' https://books.google.com.au/books?id=4j-xCwAAQBAJ&pg=PA177&lpg=PA177&dq=Yeats+the+past+and+deceived+us,+let+us+accept&source=bl&ots=BT_OfPAZc4&sig=WTapFipoGcXbPuqP8c-qoNV604M&hl=en&sa=X&ved=0ahUKEwju8cntge_UAhXE2LwKHdTJDHcQ6AEIMTAC#v=onepage&q=Yeats%20the%20past%20and%20deceived%20us%2C%20let%20us%20accept&f=false [accessed 4/7/2017].

Yeats, W.B. 'The Second Coming' www.poetryfoundation.org/poems/43290/the-second-coming [accessed 16/7/17].

Zimmer, R. 'Free speech is the basis of a true education' www.wsj.com/articles/free-speech-is-the-basis-of-a-true-education-1472164801 [accessed 2/1/17].

Barry Spurr
Formerly Professor of Poetry, Department of English, The University of Sydney
profspurr@gmail.com

13 | EXPLORING THE NEXUS BETWEEN ACADEMIC FREEDOM AND ECCLESIAL EXPECTATIONS

Abstract

Most denominational ministry training today is carried out in a higher education context. Such a context requires college leaders to adhere to a policy on academic freedom. Faculty and students must be able to enjoy the freedom to explore ideas even if those ideas do not align with a denomination's confessional stance. While the idea of academic freedom is mostly encouraged in theological colleges, anecdotal evidence suggests that there are points of tension where the desire to uphold academic freedom clashes with ecclesial expectations that candidates for ministry be strongly formed in a confessional ethos. In this paper, we will explore this tension from the perspective of the College Principal and Academic Dean who usually live in this space and thus face the many challenges found therein. We will also suggest that confessional formation and training need not be at odds with a policy of academic freedom. Rather, this tension, if understood, can provide a space for deeper formation and commitment to one's denominational distinctives.

Introduction

Most denominational ministry training today is carried out in a higher education context. Such a context requires College Principals and Academic Deans to adhere to policies on academic freedom as laid down by accrediting authorities. Faculty and students must be allowed the freedom to explore ideas even when those ideas are not in harmony with a denomination's confessional stance. While academic freedom is recognised as an important principle by theological institutions of higher education, anecdotal evidence suggests that there are points of tension where the desire to uphold academic freedom clashes with ecclesial[1] expectations that candidates for ministry be strongly formed in a confessional ethos. In fact, according to McConnell, it is in religious institutions that the tension between individual and institutional academic freedom is 'most extreme'.[2]

In an attempt to move beyond the anecdotal by introducing a documented case study, this paper will explore the tension that may arise when theological colleges of higher education seek to maintain their right to a confessional stance while adhering to policies on academic freedom. In laying the groundwork for this exploration, we will first define terms and clarify the focus of our argument before going on to discuss and analyse in more detail the tension between academic freedom and ecclesial/denominational expectations by way of a particular case study. We will end our paper by drawing a few tentative conclusions and providing some measured suggestions.

Defining the Situation

'Academic Freedom' (or 'Free Intellectual Inquiry') in the higher education sector has been and continues to be an important topic of discussion and concern in both private and public colleges and universities around the world. Within this context, academic freedom has been broadly defined as 'the freedom to conduct research, teach, speak, and publish, subject to the norms and standards of scholarly inquiry, without interference or penalty, wherever the search for truth and understanding may lead'.[3]

In Australia, the Tertiary Education Quality Standards Agency (TEQSA) has highlighted the importance of Academic Freedom in the *Higher Education Standards Framework 2015* (*HES*). Therein, under criteria for Higher Education Providers (§B1.1.2), we read: 'The higher education provider has a clearly articulated higher education purpose that includes a commitment to and support for free intellectual inquiry in its academic endeavours'; and in the Governance

---

1 In the context of the argument advanced in this paper, the terms 'ecclesial' and 'denominational' are interchangeable.
2 McConnell, 'Academic Freedom', 303–324.
3 GCUP, *Statement on Academic Freedom*.

and Accountability section (§6.1.4), it states: 'The governing body takes steps to develop and maintain an institutional environment in which freedom of intellectual inquiry is upheld and protected'.[4] The Sydney College of Divinity (SCD) has created a *Free Intellectual Inquiry Policy*, which is very much in line with *HES*, adding that students undergoing studies through SCD or its Member Institutions 'may pursue patterns of study required by their sponsors, but their learning and completion of assessment tasks will be carried out with due regard for the principle of free intellectual inquiry in pursuit of academic excellence, and they will not be penalized for expressing particular opinions'.[5]

The definition and policies referenced thus far focus primarily on the academic freedoms of faculty and students. However, this phenomenon also applies to the institution. The National Tertiary Education Union (NTEU) emphasises the importance of institutional autonomy as a 'key requirement of academic freedom'.[6] Furthermore, the Global Colloquium of University Presidents (GCUP) has produced a statement that notes: 'This autonomy includes the right of the university to determine for itself, on academic grounds, who may teach, what may be taught, how it shall be taught, and who may be admitted to study'.[7]

Policies and statements such as these are important for a variety of reasons. However, their implementation in the private sector and especially in theological colleges of higher education, which are often denominationally owned and/or governed, is both complex and challenging.[8] To speak from our own particular contexts, like many other denominations, the Church of the Nazarene and the Salvation Army in Australia began educating pastors using a variety of unaccredited training models. These were directly run by the denominations and allowed for greater control of the formation of ordination candidates with little to no outside interference. However, in the past few decades, both groups have formed theological colleges of higher education that have become stand-alone entities required by law to comply with a great many governmental policies and procedures, including those pertaining to academic freedom. This has often led to significant tension between the denominations and the academic institutions. Furthermore, since the Principal and Academic Dean are almost always accountable to the denomination, there is a significant strain on these two people to

---

4   TEQSA, *Higher Education Standards Framework*.
5   Speed, *Free Intellectual Inquiry Policy*.
6   NTEU, *Inquiry into Academic Freedom*.
7   GCUP, *Statement on Academic Freedom*.
8   Williams, 'Academic Freedom'; Burgess and Sedlacek, 'Academic Freedom'.

adhere to denominational expectations while simultaneously meeting the needs of their other stakeholders and this has sometimes resulted in struggles between administrators and faculty.

A significant part of the latent tension between the denomination and the higher education provider is a direct result of the differences in identity and mission between these two entities as well as the differing approaches for accomplishing the mission. Denominational identity is often founded and grounded in its distinctive theological positions and practices and a large part of the denomination's mission is to perpetuate said distinctives by attracting and shaping adherents, a task best accomplished through 'well-trained' pastors and lay leaders. Therefore, most denominations expect their theological college to produce 'work-ready' pastors who embrace the orthodoxy, ethos, and framework of the denomination, with many believing this is best done by adhering to a predetermined set of outcomes. While theological colleges may share much in common with their affiliated denomination, nevertheless, higher education institutions have an identity and mission that is heavily committed to the pursuit of knowledge, critical thinking, and free exploration and exchange of ideas. They believe that these values help them accomplish the mission in more lasting and significant ways than simply the transmission of information or teaching towards set outcomes. On the one hand, it is these differences in identity, mission, and approach that account for denominational expectations that may be unreasonable, even untenable. On the other hand, the banner of academic freedom has sometimes been engaged too liberally by academic institutions, which has inevitably hurt the denomination and increased the discord.

Illustrating the Tension

To illustrate the tension that can exist between academic freedom and denominational expectations, and in an attempt to move beyond the anecdotal, we will give attention to a documented and well-publicised case in which a tenured professor teaching in the USA at Northwest Nazarene University (NNU) was laid off on the pretext of economic cutbacks.[9] However, other evidence

---

9 Due to paucity of evidence from the Australian context we have chosen a well-documented case from the USA that has denominational ties to the authors. However, there are many other cases we could have used. See, Pashman, 'Wheaton College Seeks to Fire'; Banks, 'Professor Fired from Atlanta Seminary'; Bailey, 'Westminster Theological Suspension', just to name a few.

(including but not restricted to the report of the professor himself) suggests that the reason behind the sacking of Reverend Professor Thomas Oord was that he had, in the view of the University President, pushed the boundaries of Nazarene belief too far.[10] Oord is a popular writer and spokesperson for a theological view that has come to be known as Open Theism, which emphasises, among other things, God's unknowingness and God's uncontrolling nature. This view, however, has not been well or widely received amongst the broader evangelical movement with which the Nazarenes have traditionally found connection.[11]

The basics of the story are as follows. In November 2010, the then President of NNU, David Alexander, wrote a letter to Oord raising concerns about his teaching. He said Oord was a 'polemic' with a 'penchant to shock' and was focusing on 'nonessentials'.[12] This resulted in Oord's being pulled from teaching introductory course in theology and assigned to teach only postgraduate courses. In 2013, Alexander informed Oord that the university had continued to receive significant 'concerns, criticisms and questions' about his theological stances.[13] In that same year, Alexander informed Oord that he had set in motion an administrative inquiry into Oord's theological perspectives,[14] a rare occurrence in the Church of the Nazarene. After being provided with a list of sixty-eight questions to answer, Oord returned a written response of some eighty pages. In January 2014, he appeared before church officials at the Nazarene headquarters in Kansas to discuss his responses.

In a letter of response to Alexander, Jesse Middendorf (then one of six General Superintendents of the Church of the Nazarene) and Ray Dunning (a leading Nazarene theologian) stated that many of Oord's positions were 'well within' the bounds of Nazarene belief. However, they did note that '[t]here are positions he holds that raise serious questions of compatibility with the doctrines of Scripture and interpretation as understood within our church'.[15] They also

---

10   Oord provided us with a 170 page packet that includes all the email and letter correspondence between Oord, Alexander, and other connected parties, which we have titled 'Supporting Documentation from Oord'. For the sake of research, this has been bound and is held in the Nazarene Theological College library in Brisbane. For the sake of clarity, we will reference each document separately throughout this essay.
11   For example, see the eleven articles in Piper et al. *Beyond the Bounds*. Also, in 2002, The Evangelical Theological Society devoted a whole issue of their Journal to this issue with six articles arguing against open theism—*Journal of the Evangelical Theological Society* 45.2.
12   Alexander to Oord, 16 November 2010.
13   Roberts, 'Northwest Nazarene Professor'.
14   Alexander to Oord, 1 October 2013.
15   Middendorf and Dunning to Alexander, 24 February 2014.

recommended that the university work with Oord to alter those particular positions stating that:

> [i]f that is not possible, we would hope that the university could find a way to provide a graceful and meaningful exit for him to exercise his gifts and graces in places more compatible with the positions and approaches to examining the faith and expressing his grasp of truth as he understands it.[16]

Oord emphasised that the letter stopped short of accusing him of a breach of faith saying that 'their list of concerns—as important as they may be—does not place me out of step with the denomination's stated beliefs or at odds with the creeds'.[17]

In April 2014, Alexander asked Oord to resign and offered him a severance package. However, Oord said that he did not wish to leave NNU and therefore gave a counter offer, which was quickly rejected.[18] In March 2015, while on holiday, Oord received an email from Alexander with a letter that informed him that he would be let go effective May 2015 citing finances and declining enrolment as the reasons.[19] This action ignited a storm of angry students, alumni, and lecturers from all over the country.[20]

While Alexander later apologised for informing Oord by email, he denied that it had anything to do with Oord's teaching or theological views.[21] However, the backlash of Alexander's actions led to a faculty vote, in which 77% said they had lost confidence in Alexander's leadership.[22] They articulated that their vote was not based solely on the Oord issue, but that there was a need for '"shared governance" of the university in which faculty are asked for advice on issues facing the university and a clearer definition of academic freedom'.[23] Soon after,

---

16 Middendorf and Dunning to Alexander, 24 February 2014.
17 Oord to Alexander, n.d.
18 Alexander to Oord, 22 April 2014.
19 Alexander, 'Checking In', email to Oord, 30 March 2015; Alexander to Oord, 31 March 2015.
20 For Example, sixty scholars from eighteen different colleges, universities, and districts across the USA sent a signed document to Alexander expressing their support of Oord—McCormick, et al to Alexander, 16 April 2015; Brown, 'Petition Sent to NNU', reported another petition sent to the NNU board from 123 faculty members of the Council for Christian Colleges & Universities. Also, a Change.org petition was started by a then current NNU student named Amina Chinnell-Mateen that received 596 supporters.
21 Alexander to Faculty, 11 April 2015.
22 Carrim, 'Faculty Statement', email to Alexander and Craker, 15 April 2015.
23 Roberts, 'Northwest Nazarene'. See also Carrim, 'Faculty Statement'.

Alexander resigned his position.[24]

Reflecting on these events, Oord wrote: 'Christian universities have always wrestled with questions of academic freedom. I hope my situation will be used as a tool to teach Christians that the Church must support its brightest scholars. […] My colleagues at NNU and the leadership must work now to shore up the university's commitment to academic freedom'.[25]

Discussion and Analysis on the Question of Academic Freedom

We begin our discussion by questioning two major assumptions informing contemporary debate around academic freedom. The first is the idea that academic freedom entails some form of the modern epistemological stance of disinterested objective enquiry as supposedly modelled in the pure sciences. For many schooled during the second half of the twentieth century, the difference between private—often religious—schools and public schools was that the curriculum delivered by religious schools was considered by many to be ideologically driven while public schools supposedly delivered their curriculum from an ideologically/value-neutral position. Of course, such a position of value neutrality—Thomas Nagel's view from nowhere[26]—has largely been discredited.[27]

In bringing this point home, the philosopher of science Thomas Kuhn argued that scientists are formed or trained within a distinct paradigm and constrained by the rules and methods of that paradigm.[28] Additionally, the philosopher and ethicist Alastair MacIntyre has argued that there is no such thing as rationality that is not the rationality of some tradition.[29] It is therefore not a question of whether we are ideologically formed within a particular tradition or paradigm but rather in which tradition or paradigm we are formed. The point is that whether a lecturer in a secular university or in a theological college, we all speak, teach, and write from a confessional/ideological standpoint and freedom has to be understood as freedom within that confessional stance, whether that

---

24 Lee, 'Christian College President Quits'.
25 Oord, 'My Response to NNU Announcement'.
26 See Nagel, *The View from Nowhere*.
27 See Macintyre, *Whose Justice?*; Kuhn, *The Structure of Scientific Revolutions*.
28 Kuhn, *The Structure of Scientific Revolutions*, 167.
29 Macintyre, *Whose Justice?*

stance be Christian, Marxist, reductive materialist or some other. Nicholas Wolterstorff states in his paper 'Ivory Tower or Holy Mountain? Faith and Academic Freedom' that, 'those who have taught at secular institutions would have to have their heads in the sand not to be aware of the extent to which ideological considerations, as distinct from considerations of competence, enter into hiring, promoting, and firing'.[30]

The second assumption that needs to be recognised and addressed is that academic freedom works against confessional identity and formation because it opens the possibility of challenge and critique and is therefore likely to unsettle the beliefs of those undergoing formation. To respond to this assumption, we will draw upon the insights of James Fowler and MacIntyre who take the critical stance to be vital for the proper development of both individuals and traditions. Fowler identifies the important role that critique plays in the psycho-spiritual development of an individual. Stage 4 faith development, which Fowler refers to as the Individuative-Reflective stage, most appropriately takes form in young adulthood but for a significant group it emerges only in the mid-thirties or forties.[31] According to Fowler:

> for this stage to emerge, two important movements must occur, together or in sequence. First, the previous stage's tacit system of beliefs, values and commitments must be critically examined. [...] Evocative symbols and stories by which lives have been oriented will now be critically weighed and interpreted. Second, the self, previously constituted and sustained by its roles and relationships, must struggle with the question of identity and worth apart from its previously defining connections. This means that persons must take into themselves much of the authority they previously invested in others for determining and sanctioning their goals and values.[32]

In similar fashion, MacIntyre argues in *Whose Justice? Which Rationality?* that the health of any tradition in terms of making epistemic progress is measured by the health of its critique. A tradition that fails to critique itself in seeking for greater coherence will inevitably cease to make rational progress and will in the end be the loser if and when it fails to make sense to those who inhabit the

---

30 Wolterstorff, 'Ivory Tower', 22
31 Fowler, *Stages of Faith*, 182.
32 Fowler, *Faithful Change*, 62.

tradition. Healthy critique is a mark of a tradition that is making progress. According to MacIntyre, 'the test for truth in the present, therefore, is always to summon up as many questions and as many objections of the greatest strength possible; what can be justifiably claimed as true is what has sufficiently withstood such dialectical questioning and framing of objections'.[33] These observations highlight the fact that while maintaining a confessional stance and adhering to principles of academic freedom may elicit tension at times, the two are ultimately not incompatible.

Having addressed these two assumptions, we now turn to consider another issue raised by Wolterstorff, namely that freedom in the academic context has always to be understood as qualified freedom. 'Academic freedom is no more absolute than the civil liberty of free speech. The formulation concerning free speech in the U.S. Bill of Rights is absolute, but if one looks at the law that emerges from judicial decisions having to do with free speech, it's clear that free speech is a qualified liberty'.[34] In like manner, Wolterstorff acknowledges that 'although it's never a good thing to infringe on academic freedom, every educational institution does and should attach qualifications to that freedom. The issue will always be which qualifications are appropriate'.[35]

To the question posed by Wolterstorff on which qualifications are appropriate, we will consider three qualifications to academic freedom particularly as they relate to faculty and students. First, faculty have a responsibility to teach according to their institution's theological ethos. If a lecturer has been hired to teach in a Wesleyan college, for example, it is reasonable to suppose that that lecturer will teach according to the standards and methods of that socially embodied paradigm.[36] However, it is perfectly reasonable to suppose that in the process of exploring ideas within that paradigm, academic freedom would allow the exploration of alternative views as developed within a Reformed, Catholic, Orthodox, or progressive perspective. Nevertheless, there should be no doubt by teacher and student alike what the Wesleyan position is in relation to these competing frameworks.

Second, the encouraging of creativity and forward-thinking engagement with the wider culture means that research-active faculty must be allowed to reach beyond the received (or perceived) certainties of their tradition if that

---

33 MacIntyre, *Whose Justice?*, 358.
34 Wolterstorff, 'Ivory Tower', 18.
35 Wolterstorff, 'Ivory Tower', 18.
36 We are using the terms tradition and socially embodied paradigm interchangeably.

tradition is to continue to develop. This is where risks must be managed carefully. Some of the difficulties for academics and institutions arise when there are disputes as to whether certain ideas are consonant with a particular paradigm, whether Wesleyan, Arminian, Reformed, Catholic, or Orthodox, often before those ideas have been fully explored. It seems reasonable to suppose that one cannot know before significant research is carried out whether a new idea or set of ideas can be successfully incorporated into one's traditional paradigm. By way of example, Oord is committed to an open view of God. Now opinions differ among Wesleyans and Arminians as to whether Open Theism represents a radical modification of these traditions or is in harmony with them.[37] However, since Open Theism is a relative newcomer on the theological scene, one cannot know beforehand all the possible implications of this or any other 'new view' for the traditional paradigm. All it takes for trouble to emerge for a lecturer in Oord's position is for those opposed to this or any other 'new view'—students, church leaders, or other stakeholders (often without having explored the view in any depth)—to agitate for disciplinary action based on a claim of 'teaching unorthodox ideas'. Were such action to be taken, we could say that this would run counter to the spirit of academic freedom. New ideas should be explored and often it takes quite some time to follow these through to their logical conclusions, to the point where one can determine whether they are fundamentally compatible with one's overarching socially embodied paradigm or tradition. In the case of Oord, if after a thorough exploration of Open Theism there was a general consensus that the new theory was incommensurable with classical Wesleyanism, then perhaps it would be clearer that Oord had something to answer for. But a much more thorough investigation would need to be undertaken before any such judgement were made. And given the relatively 'new' status of Open Theism, it would not be unreasonable to suggest that we are far from a consensus on this matter.

Third, there are good reasons why academic freedom must be constrained to some degree by the pastoral imperative. It has been acknowledged that academic freedom means that both students and faculty alike must be free to explore ideas within the context of a traditional frame of reference. As highlighted by developmental theorists like Fowler, since people all develop through different stages of faith, there needs to be a sensitivity on the part of educators to the needs of students still in the process of this development. The fact is that while

---

[37] Sanders, 'Open Theism'; Wood, 'Divine Omniscience'; Hicks, "Classical Arminianism and Open Theism'.

presenting new ideas should be part of any higher education ethos, not all students are at the same stage of faith development. Faculty should recognise that, since theology is about matters of ultimate concern, students are not just playing with detached ideas, but they are exploring very deep foundations of faith with implications not only for belief but for emotional and psychological well-being. It is therefore imperative that faculty consider academic freedom in combination with pastoral responsibility. While a case might be made for students to be encouraged freely to explore certain ideas, given pastoral sensitivities, it might legitimately be considered inappropriate that a student be exposed to them in the early stages of their study. Presumably this kind of thinking lay behind Alexander's initial decision to assign Oord only to postgraduate teaching. Perhaps in terms of pedagogy, it may be perfectly compatible with academic freedom that the emphasis in the early stages of a student's higher education experience should be on formation within a particular tradition; that is, learning the contours of a particular socially embodied paradigm with greater competency in the knowledge of that framework bringing greater freedom in the development and skills of critique as the course develops throughout the program.

In returning to our case study above, with regard to the current topic of this paper, the point is not who is right and who is wrong. Rather, we could argue that both parties had reasons for why they did what they did and that these reasons may or may not appear valid depending on the position and perspective from which one approaches this case. Alexander represents a denominational perspective that seeks to safeguard the identity and integrity of the sponsoring church. It is entirely appropriate for a University president to address stakeholders' concerns and legitimate to fear the potential loss of students and revenue that may result from this situation. In other words, he represents a person who acts to protect the viability, stability and integrity of the institution and, ultimately, possibly also the denomination. His misstep was failing to balance these concerns with the demands of academic freedom, thereby limiting honest exploration of thought and reducing the potential for students to think critically about their own beliefs. Ironically, for such a denominational champion, the lack of such freedom will ultimately, according to MacIntyre, be a loss and not a gain to the denomination sponsoring the institution of higher education.[38]

---

38 For MacIntyre, there can be no progress in a tradition without vigorous critique, and critique implies freedom including academic freedom. See *Whose Justice?*, 358

Oord, on the other hand, represents the perspective of a professor teaching in the context of higher education and committed to academic freedom in its pursuit of truth and the advancement of knowledge. He also represents the academic who is trying to challenge students, stretch the church's thinking, and further his own career, all the while honestly believing himself to be within the bounds of both orthodoxy itself and his original commitment to the faith statements of the denomination and the university. In the end, the question may be raised as to whether Oord unknowingly overextended his individual freedom without taking full account of his responsibility to students, institution, and denomination.[39]

Both parties, it could be argued, sought to be faithful to their missions, but in the process failed to understand the other's perspective with the view to perhaps reaching a compromise. With this idea in mind, denominations need to understand the importance of academic freedom and of the critical thinking and long-term sustainability it is meant to produce in its students. Likewise, theological college or university administrators and faculty must have a clear understanding of their responsibility to uphold the confessional ethos of the institution and of the denomination. Both entities must seek to understand each other and to appreciate why they need one another to be successful. When these two entities trust each other and work together, there is potential for the strengthening and well-being of both.

Tentative Conclusions

First, if anecdotal reports and the documented case of Oord endorse McConnell's claim that in religious institutions the tension between individual and institutional academic freedom is 'most extreme', no doubt the tension will always be a factor to negotiate. To ensure the tension is healthy—if not creative—requires honest and ongoing communication between denominational leaders and theological college/university principals around the identity and mission of both, and about how they can better collaborate for the good of the church. In some instances, minimal contact between Church leaders and College leaders

---

[39] Here, it should be strongly noted that we are not trying to make a judgement call on Alexander's or Oord's positions or actions. While we have our own opinions on this case, this is not the purpose of sharing the story. Rather, Alexander and Oord are used representatively to provide a picture of the tensions that can and often do exist between these two sides.

and faculty can lead to dangerous misunderstandings and decisions being made on questionable evidence. If Church leaders are to avoid acting on hearsay without knowing all the facts, regular, honest, and open communication is a necessity.

Second, in many cases real tensions between denominational expectations and academic freedom can be mitigated with appropriate policies and procedures. Many of the tensions emphasised in this paper can be lessened or even avoided with well thought out and articulated policies and procedures. In presenting the tension between academic freedom and faith in the American context, Wolterstorff states:

> My own view, then, is that the best service the AAUP (American Association of University Professors) can continue to render to this teeming multitude of American institutions of higher education is to compose and recommend model codes of procedure for resolving issues of academic freedom. Almost always, it is in the procedure, not in the qualifications [placed on academic freedom] as such, that the injustice lies.[40]

In the Australian context, the policies put forth by governmental and accrediting bodies may be too broad to encompass the complexities of the theological college and its relationship to a denomination. Theological colleges must therefore strengthen these existing polices with the following:

1) development of a confessional statement that accurately represents the Christian ethos of the college and its distinctives and which takes into account its denomination's essential confessional elements;
2) policies which clearly define academic freedom and comprehensively outline the rights and responsibilities of both institution and faculty;
3) clear procedures on how alleged breaches of academic freedom and breaches of the college's confessional statement are to be reported and dealt with;
4) clearly stated procedures for orienting new faculty and refreshing existing faculty about these policies and procedures; and
5) procedures in place for regular review of all these elements with all stakeholders involved.

---

40 Wolterstorff, 'Ivory Tower', 22.

Third, where tensions are unable to be resolved, Christian grace and due process should characterise any disciplinary action by administrators and leaders. From the Oord case study, we can perhaps draw the conclusion that in the end it is unlikely that the tension would have been resolved through normal processes. In looking at the evidence, it appears that while Oord was left grieved at being treated poorly, the University nevertheless had policies and procedures relating to academic freedom. Perhaps we have to acknowledge that there are times when an academic's theological stance or direction cannot be accommodated by a particular denominational body. In Oord's case, it may be that he is now working, to use Kuhn's language, within an incommensurable paradigm. Just as in science, the possibility of paradigm change is most likely during times of conceptual revolutions and it could be argued that we have entered such a period when many of the classical certainties are coming under question.

There can be no doubt that in Oord's case the final separation from NNU was marked by hurt and disappointment. And while it may well be the case that blame can be levelled on both sides, what is clear is that the termination process itself was not marked by Christian grace. It is certainly hoped that, with appropriate and comprehensive policies and procedures surrounding the question of academic freedom, what happened in Oord's case would not be repeated in an Australian context.

Final Thoughts

This paper highlighted the tension that exists between academic freedom and ecclesial expectations, and the consequent risks for scholarship. Like Christopher Columbus setting out for the new world, the researcher in the spirit of free enquiry can never know exactly where the journey will take them. The nature of academic freedom is such that the dangers ahead either for individual scholars or denominational bodies are never known in advance. In a risk-averse culture the wonder of learning can be lost as academics trim their sails to a risk-averse setting. Ultimately, though, we all will be the losers for it. There always have been, and always will be, martyrs for the cause of truth. Likewise, denominational responsibility demands that orthodox norms are maintained for the good of the many. Although this tension is inherent in a denominational college operating within a Higher Educational environment, the balancing act is often not achieved well.

However, not knowing all the possible scenarios in advance should not prevent an institution from developing good policies and procedures to safeguard both the denominational body and the individual scholar. There is no doubt that from time to time tensions will erupt along the fault lines of academic freedom and ecclesial expectations. But carefully protecting both the responsibilities of the individual scholar to engage in free enquiry in the pursuit of God's truth, and the integrity of the denominational higher education body is something we all need to work hard at to maintain for the sake of the primary stakeholders—the students.

Bibliography

Alexander, David. 'Checking In', email to Tom Oord, 30 March 2015.

Alexander, David. Letter from David Alexander to Tom Oord, 16 November 2010.

Alexander, David. Letter from David Alexander to Tom Oord, 1 October 2013.

Alexander, David. Letter from David Alexander to Tom Oord, 22 April 2014.

Alexander, David. Letter from David Alexander to Tom Oord, 31 March 2015.

Alexander, David. Letter from David Alexander to NNU Faculty, 11 April 2015.

Bailey, Sarah Pulliam. 'Westminster Theological Suspension', *Christianity Today* (2008) www.christianitytoday.com/news/2008/april/114-24.0.html [accessed 5 March 2018].

Banks, Adelle M. 'Professor Fired from Atlanta Seminary over Evangelical Beliefs?', *Christianity Today* (2012) www.christianitytoday.com/ct/2012/august-web-only/professor-fired-from-atlanta-seminary.html [accessed 5 March 2018].

Brown, Ruth. 'Petition Sent to NNU Board on Oord Layoff', *Idaho Press-Tribune* (2015) www.idahopress.com/members/petition-sent-to-nnu-board-on-oord-layoff/article_fc92e20c-e326-11e4-9615-6776a1a49d0a.html [accessed 5 March 2018].

Burgess, Aaron and James Sedlacek. 'Academic Freedom in Christian Church (Independent) Institutions of Higher Education: Critical Matters Regarding Academic Freedom', *Stone-Campbell Journal* 18 (2015), 13-25.

Carrim, Rhonda. 'Faculty Statement', email to David Alexander and Randy Craker, 15 April 2015.

Chinnell-Mateen, Amina. 'Call to a Careful Reconsideration and Reinstatement of Dr. Thomas Jay Oord to His Faculty Position', Change.org (2015) www.change.org/p/to-the-president-and-board-of-trustees-at-northwest-nazarene-university-call-to-a-careful-reconsideration-and-reinstatement-of-dr-thomas-jay-oord-to-his-faculty-position-2 [accessed 5 March 2018].

Cooper, John W. *Panentheism: The Other God of the Philosophers* (Nottingham, England: Apollos, 2007).

Fowler, James W. *Faithful Change: The Personal and Public Challenges of Postmodern Life* (Nashville: Abingdon Press, 1996).

Fowler, James W. *Stages of Faith: The Psychology of Human Development and the Quest for Meaning* (San Francisco: HarperCollins, 1995).

Global Colloquium of University Presidents (GCUP), *Statement on Academic Freedom* (2005) www.columbia.edu/~md2221/academicstatement.doc [assessed 5 April 2017].

Hicks, John Mark. 'Classical Arminianism and Open Theism: A Substantial Difference in Their Theologies of Providence', *Trinity Journal* 33.1 (2012), 3-18.

Kuhn, Thomas. *The Structure of Scientific Revolutions (*Chicago: The University of Chicago Press, 2012).

Lee, Morgan. 'Christian College President Quits After Attempted Layoff of Pro-Evolution Professor', *Christianity Today* (2015) www.christianitytoday.com/gleanings/2015/may/christian-college-president-resigns-tom-oord-evolution.html?paging=off [accessed 20 April 2017].

MacIntyre, Alasdair. *Whose Justice? Which Rationality?* (Indiana: University of Notre Dame Press, 1988).

McConnell, Michael W. 'Academic Freedom in Religious Colleges and Universities', *Law and Contemporary Problems* 53.3 (1990), 303–324

McCormick, K. Steve, et al. Letter from K. Steve McCormick, et al. to David Alexander, 16 April 2015.

Middendorf, Jesse C. and H. Ray Dunning. Letter from Jesse C. Middendorf to David Alexander, 24 February 2014.

Nagel, Thomas. *The View from Nowhere* (Revised 3rd edn; Oxford: Oxford University Press, 1986).

National Tertiary Education Union (NTEU), *Inquiry into Academic Freedom* (2008) www.nteu.org.au/library/view/id/4816> [accessed 5 April 2017].

Oord, Thomas Jay. 'My Response to NNU Announcement' (2015). http://thomasjayoord.com/index.php/blog/archives/my-response-to-nnu-statements-about-my-being-laid-off-for-enrollment-reasons [accessed 20 April 2017].

Oord, Thomas Jay. 'Supporting Documentation for Oord Narrative' (unpublished document received from author on 31 May 2017).

Oord, Thomas Jay. Letter from Tom Oord to David Alexander, n.d.

Pashman, Manya Brachear. 'Wheaton College Seeks to Fire Christian Professor Over View of Islam', *Chicago Tribune* (2016) www.chicagotribune.com/news/local/breaking/ct-wheaton-college-professor-fired-20160105-story.html [accessed 5 March 2018].

Piper, John, Justin Taylor, and Paul Kjoss Helseth, (eds.), *Beyond the Bounds: Open Theism and the Undermining of Biblical Christianity* (Wheaton, IL.: Crossway Books, 2003).

Roberts, Bill. 'Northwest Nazarene Professor Shares Views on God, Loses Academic Freedom', *Idaho Statesman* (2016) www.idahostatesman.com/news/local/education/article95597627.html [accessed 20 April 2017].

Sanders, John. 'Open Theism: A Radical Revision or Miniscule Modification of Arminianism'. *Wesleyan Theological Journal* 38.2 (2003), 69-102.

Speed, Diane. *Free Intellectual Inquiry Policy*, SCD Policies (2017) http://scd.edu.au/about/#policy-procedures-manual [assessed 4 April 2017].

Tertiary Education Quality Standards Agency (TEQSA), *Higher Education Standards Framework (Threshold Standards)* (2015) www.legislation.gov.au/Details/F2015L01639 [assessed 4 April 2017].

Williams, L. Bryan. 'Academic Freedom in Church-Related Academic Institutions: The Management of Tension', *Didache: Faithful Teaching* 7.2 (2007): 1-19.

Wolterstorff, Nicholas. 'Ivory Tower or Holy Mountain? Faith and Academic Freedom', *Academe* 87.1 (2001), 17–22.

Wood. Laurence W. 'Divine Omniscience: Boethius or Open Theism?', *Wesleyan Theological Journal* 45.2 (2010), 41-66.

Dean G. Smith,
Nazarene Theological College
dsmith@ntc.edu.au

Rob A. Fringer
Nazarene Theological College
rfringer@ntc.edu.au

14 | THE PERILS OF ACADEMIC FREEDOM

THE AUSTRALIAN COLLEGE OF THEOLOGY AS AN AUSTRALIAN UNIVERSITY OF SPECIALISATION

Abstract

The essay advances a definition of academic freedom that emphasises the responsibilities as well as the (more usually touted) rights involved in the concept. It augments the perils inherent in balancing these rights and responsibilities by identifying additional hazards to academic freedom encountered by theological educators in particular as they negotiate the socio-political context in which they operate. The essay goes on to consider what this might mean at the institutional level by taking as a case study the application of the Australian College of Theology (ACT) for registration by the Tertiary Education Quality and Standards Agency (TEQSA) as an Australian University of Specialisation. As the first Higher Education Provider to lodge such an application, the ACT adumbrates the issues that arise for all private 'identity institutions' seeking recognition in the higher education system. The essay shows how the ACT is seeking to reconcile its openly Christian identity (its rights) with the obligation to comply with the Higher Education Standards (2015) (its responsibilities). It concludes with some suggestions for how Christian institutions might maintain their integrity and uphold academic freedom in an increasingly unfavourable social setting.

At first sight a consideration of academic freedom is an odd inclusion in a sustained discussion around the theme 'wondering about God together: research-led learning and teaching in theological education'. Such discussion is of course the essence of theology and might be supposed to arise out of its own mystery and to be allowed to proceed untrammelled by external controls. Yet even a cursory knowledge of the history of Christianity signals that exercising academic freedom can cause trouble. In this quincentenary year of the beginning of the Reformation, the speculations of Martin Luther immediately come to mind as an example of disruption within the church. More broadly, theology, often prophetic and counter-cultural, can also unsettle the community context of the wider society and lead to attempts to curb the freedom to wonder out loud. The eve of the centenary of Karl Barth's *Epistle to the Romans* is a reminder of the part played by theological reflection in the German church struggle of the 1930s. The matter of academic freedom arises when we think about the practical consequences in church and society of wondering about God, and indeed of the conditions that favour or hinder such wondering.

It also arises when we think about the place of Theology in the academy. Ever since the rise of the modern university there have been those who have said that Theology has no place in this domain. Wondering about God, the argument goes, is inherently irrational on the grounds that no such being can be shown to exist. 'Faith seeking understanding' can never amount to anything more than a pious hope at best and rank superstition at worst. It follows that Theology can have nothing to say to modern society with its need of empirical consideration of its many and varied issues and problems, and should not be allowed a voice. The defence of Theology in the academy has a long history,[1] and will need to continue if theologians expect to be allowed to speak in this space.

A particular social context that further problematises academic freedom for academic theologians and providers of theological education is furnished by the accrediting regimes of the states in which they operate. Ten years ago, in the wake of the promulgation of the National Protocols for Higher Education Approval Processes in Australia by the Ministerial Council on Education, Employment, Training and Youth Affairs (MCEETYA), Neil Ormerod, Professor of Theology at Australian Catholic University, highlighted the issue of academic freedom and predicted that 'we can expect theological colleges seeking accreditation as Higher Education Providers (HEPs) to face close questioning

---

1 Two recent accounts are: Zachhuber, *Theology as Science;* and Inman, *The Making of Modern English Theology.*

on the issue, particularly if such colleges are assessed for (specialist) university status'.[2] If anything, the issue has intensified in the intervening decade. The advent of the Tertiary Education Quality and Standards Agency (TEQSA) in 2011 dramatically reversed the Federation settlement by centralising regulation of the higher education sector.[3] Publication in October 2016 of a draft Guidance Note on Equity and Diversity seemed to portend the difficulties for institutional autonomy that comprehensive centralisation had brought.[4] At the same time, several providers of theological education have reached a level of maturity at which they might reasonably apply for registration either as an Australian University of Specialisation (AUS) or as a University College. The first of these actually to apply is the Australian College of Theology (ACT) which is therefore offered as a case study of a theological provider navigating the requirements of the regulatory system while seeking to maintain its institutional integrity and academic freedom as it prepares for registration as an AUS.[5]

The Nature of Academic Freedom

The discussion should begin by trying to establish some understanding of academic freedom as a concept.

In general, academic freedom may be regarded as the right to unrestricted learning, teaching, research and communication. Purportedly authoritative definitions are not hard to find. The Academic Freedom Statement of the Global Colloquium of University Presidents held in 2005 may be taken as indicative. According to this body, academic freedom is 'the freedom to conduct research, teach, speak and publish, subject to the norms and standards of scholarly inquiry, without interference or penalty, wherever the search for truth and understanding may lead'.[6]

Nor is it difficult to find statements about its importance. For example, the claim that academic freedom is a condition of effectiveness in higher education

---

2 Ormerod, *Academic Freedom in a Theological Context*, 1.
3 On the significance of TEQSA and its impact on the theological sector, see Treloar, 'From the Martin Report to TEQSA'.
4 Available at www.teqsa.gov.au/sites/default/files/GuidanceNote_DiversityandEquity1.0.pdf. Following a strong reaction, the draft Note 1.0 was withdrawn.
5 For an account of the history of the ACT which posits the AUS application as the next stage in its evolution, see Treloar, 'The Three (or Four) Identities of the Australian College of Theology, 1891-2016'.
6 GCUP, 'Academic Freedom Statement (2005)'.

is not unusual. One instance will suffice. The National Tertiary Education Union—no friend of conservative academic causes—states that academic freedom is 'vital to the process of gaining and disseminating knowledge as one of the central defining characteristics of a university'.[7]

Academic freedom is also protected in Commonwealth legislation. Subdivision 19-G of the Higher Education Support Act (2003) states that universities 'must have a policy that upholds free intellectual inquiry in relation to learning, teaching and research'. In Australian institutions of higher education at least, academic freedom is tantamount to a basic human right.

Less often highlighted but no less important are the obligations that go with academic freedom. The International Association of Universities 1998 statement on 'Academic Freedom, University Autonomy and Social Responsibility' asserts that it entails a commitment to academic excellence and open communication: 'Academic Freedom engages the obligation by each individual member of the academic profession to evidence, to innovation, and to advance the frontiers of knowledge through research and the diffusion of its results through teaching and publication'. It also entails commitment to ethical responsibility and public defence: 'the University has the obligation to uphold and demonstrate to Society that it stands by its collective obligation to quality and ethics, to fairness and tolerance, to the setting and upkeep of standards'.[8]

At the same time the exercise of academic freedom involves risks of unpopularity, marginalisation, and even persecution. The statement of the International Association of Universities goes on to maintain: 'the expression of views which follow from scientific insight or scholarly investigation may often be contrary to popular conviction or judged as unacceptable or intolerable'. The reality of this risk incurs an obligation on the part of institutions to protect their employees: 'agencies which exercise responsibility for the advancement of knowledge [...] must recognise that such expressions of scholarly judgment and scientific inquiry shall not place in jeopardy the career or the existence of the individual expressing them nor leave that individual open to pursual for *delit d'opinion* on account of such views expressed'.

The following list summarises the salient features of academic freedom arising from this brief review:

i. It is a powerful and multi-faceted concept.

---

7   NTEU, 'Intellectual (Academic) Freedom'.
8   IAU, 'Academic Freedom'.

ii. It covers teaching, learning, inquiry, and communication.
iii. It is said to be a condition of the effectiveness of higher education institutions.
iv. It is a legal requirement of higher education institutions (at least in the Australian context).
v. The exercise of academic freedom is risky.

Most importantly, however, as a sixth feature, academic freedom establishes a complex field of rights and responsibilities. The right to free expression might well be in tension with the obligation to ethical and wise expression. Ideally this tension will be creative, but striking the balance between the two is difficult. Its very nature is such that the commitment to academic freedom is perilous.

Adding to the difficulty operationally are the three levels at which academic freedom works. There is first the personal. Here we are talking about the rights and obligations of the individual. The individuals are students and academics. Then there is the institutional. Here we are talking about the rights and obligations of the institution. In general, institutions want three things in relation to academic freedom: i) freedom to select staff and students, and to determine the conditions on which they stay; ii) freedom to determine curriculum content and set standards; and iii) freedom to allocate funds according to their own objectives and priorities. Thirdly, there is the contextual. Persons and institutions function as part of communities and a society which establish the legal framework and set the cultural norms.

As these operational dimensions come together as part of a social system they present particular dilemmas for what we might call 'identity institutions' such as providers of theological education which have tended historically in this country to be denominational and partisan. Identity institutions are organisations that stand for a particular viewpoint and/or interest with an inescapably discriminating effect. The basic issue becomes: how to reconcile the integrity of the institution with the claims of academic freedom? In navigating this terrain, the following specific questions arise: What level of identification with that viewpoint or interest is consistent with the ideal of academic freedom? To what extent does the identity institution as the employer have the right to determine the lines of inquiry and the expression of the employee? To what extent does it have the right to control access to the institution and to determine the curriculum and its limits? And how far can it expect the students who study this curriculum to embrace its distinctive standpoint?

Providers of theological education are also subject to the demands of their own discipline. The obligations of Theology as a form of public knowledge are succinctly adumbrated by David Ford who proposes an 'ecology of responsibility' with three dimensions.[9] The first is the responsibility to other academic disciplines to research and teach according to the highest standards of probity and truthfulness, and to subject its own perspectives and values to rigorous scrutiny. The responsibility to the churches is to commend scholarship and informed believing to communities of faith and to provide theological literacy to all who seek it. To society at large Theology has a responsibility to engage with contemporary social and political concerns, listening attentively to what others have to say and making a respectful and informed contribution to community conversation. In these three ways, Christian theology itself sets out the responsibilities it should observe as a condition of the freedom it claims to go about the legitimate business of wondering about God and the implications for religion and life, matters to which it will want to give public expression.

Academic Freedom in Practice

In addition to the difficulties inherent in the concept, there is any number of pressures at work in contemporary society to limit academic freedom and add to its perils.

Academic freedom is affected by conflicts over the nature and effects of knowledge. Disputation has always arisen over these impacts and gives rise to warring factions and campaigns to promote some knowledge and repress other knowledge.[10] The case of Bjorn Lomberg at the University of Western Australia is instructive. Establishment of his Australian Consensus Centre was blocked by the combined protest of students and staff alike because of his views on global warming, an outcome condemned by the Human Rights Commissioner at the time as a form of 'soft censorship'.[11] Whatever the merits of the particular situation, the point is that knowledge is a social phenomenon and functions in a sociological framework which brings out how, for human reasons, academic

---

9   Ford, *Theology: A Very Short Introduction*, 17-18. Ford's three dimensional web of responsibility might be regarded as the obverse of the theological account of higher education as concerned with the ideals of intellectual virtue, sociality and service of the common good in Higton, *A Theology of Higher Education*).
10 For an orientation, see Burke, *A Social History of Knowledge*.
11 Taylor, 'Bjorn Lomborg confident of getting host for his Consensus Centre'.

freedom is limited.

Second, academic freedom is subject to shifts in ideology. Itself an ideology arising from the Enlightenment, academic freedom is vulnerable to changes in culture which generate new, and possibly rival, ideologies.[12] At present, academic freedom is being affected by the depredations of what we might call 'welfarism'. What's happening is illuminated by insights from moral psychology, especially the work of American social psychologist Jonathan Haidt.[13] Moral Framework Theory holds that in society at large there are underlying moral foundations which function as continuums between opposites. Two of these continuums are 'care/harm' and 'liberty/oppression'. It does appear that at this moment there is a widespread feeling that care is more important than liberty, a priority which gives rise to empathy for perceived victims in spite of inconsistencies and conflict with other principles and rights such as free speech and academic freedom. For want of a better term (and well aware of likely confusion with the phenomenon of dependence on welfare payments through the social security system), I have called this priority in the moral sphere 'welfarism'. Things cannot be said because they are offensive, hurtful, threatening—uncaring—and deleterious to the welfare of 'the other'.

Third, the priority of the care foundation—'welfarism'—has overlapped with the emergence of identity politics. The last two decades have seen the rise of the strong advocacy of the interests and perspectives of socio-cultural groups based on such factors as race, religion, and sexual orientation, usually including some claim to oppression and victimhood. Proponents of identity politics have typically evinced a marked tendency to absolutism. They are not content to dialogue, reasoning their way to success, but seek to shut down viewpoints at variance with their own. In other words, they deny to others what they seek for themselves, replacing perceived privilege with a new privilege—their own. A recent example is the banning of the documentary 'The Red Pill' on campuses and other venues on the spurious grounds that it evinces a perspective sympathetic to males and is therefore *ipso facto* threatening to females.[14] Identity politics has rightly been condemned as a new totalitarianism which, ironically, suppresses diversity in the quest for recognition of diversity. What is truly

---

12 See the defence of the Enlightenment ideal by former Labor Minister Peter Baldwin, 'Regressive Left Puts Bigotry on a Pedestal'.
13 Beginning with *The Righteous Mind*.
14 See Akerman, 'The Red Pill'. Reported under the headline 'Men's Rights Film Canned. Feminist Protests Black Out Cinemas'.

disturbing is how the higher education sector has become an incubator of identity politics and made academic freedom problematic in the very place it ought to be not only safe but championed.

The second and third developments coincide with a tendency to make academic freedom itself the issue. By this I mean the frequent trumping of a claim to academic freedom with a counter claim to be the true academic freedom. That is, a claim that mine is the authentic academic freedom and yours is bogus. A very good example is the response to the intellectual diversity movement which emerged as a protest against the dominance of 'progressive-left' viewpoints and consequent bias on university campuses. It attracted a strong reaction from Katherine Gelber of UNSW, who argued with some vehemence that hers was the genuine academic freedom.[15] Again, whatever the merits of the particular argument, the claim to academic freedom is used to curb others seen to inhabit a lower order of academic freedom.

Within this cluster of forces we should also note an anti-Christian turn in our day which seeks to silence the Christian voice. It is evident in the attempt to arraign the Catholic Archbishop of Hobart before the Tasmanian anti-discrimination board for circularising the traditional church teaching on marriage. It is evident in the recent attempt by an LGBT lobbyist to discredit Stephen Chavura, a lecturer in Politics at Macquarie University, because of his membership on the Board of the Lachlan Macquarie Institute, a private organisation intended 'to foster a greater appreciation of the relevance of a Christian worldview to public policy'.[16] Until recently it was possible to be a citizen and a Christian in Australian society. The compact between church and state that created this possibility is presently under attack from what journalist Paul Kelly calls a fundamentalist secularism.[17] The attack involves the demonisation of Christianity and seeking to limit the enunciation of the Christian standpoint.

These developments constitute a very interesting feature of the contemporary Australian socio-political landscape and could be discussed at much greater length. But the point is that academic freedom, particularly for Christians, is at this moment being subverted by unprecedented historical and social forces that compound the tensions inherent in the rights-responsibility binary inherent in the concept of academic freedom with additional elements of peril. While it

---

15 Gelber, 'Academic freedom and the "intellectual diversity" movement in Australia'.
16 See www.lmi.org.au/purpose. It may not be without significance that the Staff page on the Institute's web site has been 'temporarily closed'.
17 Kelly, 'A New Secularism Trashes Tradition'.

exists as an ideal, the reality is that academic freedom is not an operating condition of academic life on which providers of theological education can depend. Christians operating in the higher education sector are justified in proceeding with a sense of vulnerability and fear that their academic freedom will not be respected.

The Australian College of Theology as a Case Study

Against this background, the ACT has applied to TEQSA for registration as an Australian University of Specialisation (AUS). It is the first Higher Education Private Provider (HEPP) to do so.

The ACT has made this application for two main reasons. First, it is the next step in its evolution. The ACT was granted self-accrediting status by the NSW Department of Education and Training in 2010. It has served its five-year apprenticeship as a self-accrediting body and established a record of a sustained research culture. It is now ready to move to the next stage. Second, the ACT recognises that without AUS status it will become increasingly uncompetitive in the higher education market place. In evolutionary terms, the application is an adaptation to the rapidly changing environment in the interests of survival and prosperity.

Although these reasons have been persuasive, the application for AUS status has not been made without misgivings. This is because the move is fraught with the peril associated with academic freedom. Concern about a new future is inherent in the nature of the institution. The ACT is a consortium of affiliated colleges. As with all such bodies, there is tension between the administrative centre and the teaching bodies around the country which deliver the courses. The basic issue is the location of power. Where does it lie: in the ACT or in the colleges? The tension is no longer so acute as it once was, but it remains a factor in the life of the consortium. How much autonomy does a college have to give up in order to be a member of the larger organization? What happens if the ACT in pursuit of registration by a secular authority promulgates a policy on academic freedom which is unacceptable to an affiliated college which serves other stakeholders (such as churches) as well?[18]

---

18 See the issues raised by the case study in the previous chapter in this volume, Smith & Fringer, 'Exploring the Nexus'.

Retention of Christian identity is another consideration. Through its affiliated colleges the ACT has become conservative theologically. It is far from being fundamentalist, but collectively the ACT does presently represent a conservative expression of Protestant Christianity. That is, it is decidedly an 'identity institution'. As it approaches AUS registration, the ACT faces the question of how to retain its Christian identity. This is a key issue for two reasons. One is that, historically, Christian institutions tend to secularise when they become universities: that is, in rising to the expectations of universities, they lose their Christian identity.[19] The other, as already indicated, is that the times are not favourable to open Christian profession. To what pressures will the ACT and its member colleges be subject as a publicly recognised embodiment of Christian higher education? Will the wider society acquiesce in the existence of a distinctly Christian university? Will it allow, at a time when the main cultural flows are distinctly hostile to Christianity, true academic freedom for Christian learning and teaching?

To manage its dilemmas the ACT has adopted two strategies. The first is the declaration of its Christian identity through such mechanisms as its constitution, educational philosophy, Graduate Attributes, course rationale statements and learning outcomes. That is, it is using the apparatus required by the state and the higher education sector to affirm the legitimacy of its place in the sector and the compatibility of Christian means with the ends of public education. The objects of the ACT Ltd are stated in the constitution as: 'to foster and direct the systematic study of theology and other disciplines related to Christian ministry by teaching and research in a manner and at a level comparable to the standards of Australian universities'. The effects of these objects are to: i) claim a place for ACT courses in the higher education sector; ii) state the nature of the ACT's specialisation; and iii) align the ACT with community standards for Higher Education institutions, including academic freedom. And then, importantly for students, the Graduate Attributes specify the aspiration of all ACT courses. They say clearly, openly, up front, fairly and legally what ACT courses seek to achieve—Christian people, Christian scholars, Christian professionals and Christian leaders. No student has to be a professing Christian in order to pass a course but the intent of the courses is there for all to see. Hopefully this candour supports a process of self-selection. The presumption is that only those who accept the Christian ethos and aspiration of the ACT will be interested in

---

19 See, for example, the essays in Hart & Mohler, *Theological Education in the Evangelical Tradition*.

taking its courses. In any case, a clear statement of Christian identity has been made and nobody will be able to claim deception.

Second, the ACT is clarifying what it means by 'Christian'. A working group has developed a statement on the Christian foundations of the ACT. The proposal is that the ACT should build on some of the 'Fundamental Declarations' at the start of the constitution of the founding body, the Anglican Church of Australia, especially the first two:

> 1. The Anglican Church of Australia, being part of the One Holy Catholic and Apostolic Church of Christ, holds the Christian Faith as professed by the Church of Christ from primitive times and in particular as set forth in the creeds known as the Nicene Creed and the Apostles Creed.
>
> 2. This Church receives all the canonical scriptures of the Old and New Testaments as being the ultimate rule and standard of faith given by the inspiration of God and containing all things necessary for salvation.

The numerous advantages of this approach are its ecumenism, inclusiveness and affirmation of diversity, its continuity with the past—the Australian and longer history of Christian civilization—and its invocation of the rich tradition of Christian intellectual culture and learning, especially the New Testament warrants for free intellectual inquiry.

Third, the ACT is starting to engage with epistemological questions in a new way. What are the conditions of knowledge? What is the place of theological knowledge in the broad field of human inquiry? In what ways is theological knowledge similar to and different from other forms of inquiry? As James Dalziel points out, 'worldview studies have a particular role to play here',[20] and I would add that the perspectives of the sociology of knowledge also warrant exploration. Here the benefits to the ACT are self-awareness and openness, and, in line with its responsibility to other participants, genuine engagement with the rationality of the discourse of the academy.

Fourth, the ACT is reviewing its policies and procedures with a view to identifying their implications for academic freedom. It is not entirely clear at this stage where this process is heading. I anticipate that all potentially gratuitous

---

20 Dalziel, 'Universities, Christian Higher Education and Ideological Diversity'.

causes of offence will be removed; the requirements of the Higher Education Standards will be satisfied; and every effort will be made to ensure that the ACT can exist and function legally as what it is, a provider of Christian higher education. I also anticipate that risk management strategies will be devised for dealing with the extraordinary cases that are sure to arise.

Fifth, the ACT has reviewed the affiliation agreement with the colleges of the consortium. It would have to be conceded that this is the point of greatest vulnerability for the ACT, as the affiliated colleges as uncontrolled entities have their own distinctive identities and functions to which they are perfectly entitled. So the affiliation agreement acknowledges that:

1. While all affiliated colleges within ACT are required to be Christian, ACT does not impose any denominational or religious restrictions in relation to enrolment in any ACT course; and

2. The College and other affiliated colleges are free to require enrolling students to:
    i. Give an account of their Christian commitment
    ii. Express their willingness to conduct themselves in accordance with the affiliated college's Christian ethos;
    iii. Affirm the affiliated college's statement of faith; and/or
    iv. Show evidence of prior experience in Christian leadership.

In relation to academic staff, the affiliation agreement requires that:

> the staff of affiliated colleges shall be of such number, quality and diversity as to provide the context in which there is vigorous learning and interchange of ideas. In addition to moral, religious and intellectual depth, excellence in teaching and concern for ministry should characterise the members of the academic staff of each college.

Finally, the ACT affirms its commitment to freedom of inquiry and expression in an area where such freedom has not always been encouraged.

The College:

1. Supports the view that, while adopting a point of view, students should have an understanding of other perspectives that Christians hold on topics that are taught. One prevailing presupposition is that the Christian world-view is not just a theoretical framework of beliefs but is something which is related to and guides all that we do; and

2. Accepts that students should be able to work in accordance with standards of critical scrutiny and academic freedom which guide this community, including being able to look critically at their own presuppositions as well as those of others.

Proposals for Reconciling Academic Freedom with Institutional Integrity

From what the ACT is doing I have developed a framework for managing the perils of academic freedom as they arise from an unfavourable setting and from the peculiar nature of our institutions (see the table below). Its ten points are envisaged as a check list for theological providers as they seek to navigate the regulatory and social environment.

First, state clearly and repeatedly who you are in terms of vision, mission and values and ensure that this identity permeates policy and practice. Be up front.

Second, if you do not have one, produce and parade a statement or policy on academic freedom as it is intended to operate in your organisation. Be transparent.

Third, a policy statement positions you to carry out a systematic review of internal arrangements, policies and procedures to identify and resolve perspectival and practice issues. Be consistent.

Fourth, achieve and evidence alignment with the Higher Education Standards (2015), especially in relation to 'equity and diversity'. Be compliant.

A fifth strategy would be to work out and state what is expected of staff. It may be wise to take a whole of institution approach here, so that all staff, not just academic staff, know what is expected of them perspectively and practically as employees. Be proactive and fair.

Sixth, promote an awareness of and a commitment to what the institution contributes to the public good, viz. the academic, social and economic well-being of the community. In other words, make it clear that losing the institution will entail loss to society and that its continuation will bring benefits. Be confident and assertive.

Seventh, undertake appropriate risk management. Identify what could happen in relation to academic freedom and work out how likely scenarios will be dealt with. Be ready.

Eighth, develop the case for religious freedom and (more broadly) freedom of speech. In other words, be in a position to defend your institution in terms of the rights and values the community at large is supposed to ensure. Be prepared.

Ninth, cultivate epistemological awareness. By this I mean include and support on the staff somebody who has a capacity to articulate how knowledge functions as a social activity so that its pretensions and limitations can be exposed as required. Be informed.

Finally, engage with the sector, so that the existence and nature of our institutions are seen to be a valuable part of the higher education scene. Misrepresentation and dismissiveness are harder to sustain when identity institutions are actually present; understanding and appreciation are facilitated. The Higher Education Private Provider Quality Network (HEPPQN) is an outstanding model of what can be achieved by strategic engagement.[21] It has become the informal peak body to which TEQSA occasionally refers in relation to private providers. Be a presence.

---

21 See www.avondale.edu.au/about/heppqn/.

Academic Freedom Management Framework		
Step	Action	Disposition
1	Clearly articulate your identity	Be up front
2	Produce and parade a statement on academic freedom	Be transparent
3	Review internal arrangements, policies and procedures to identify/resolve perspectival and practice issues	Be consistent
4	Achieve and evidence alignment with the Higher Education Standards (2015)	Be compliant (inoffensive?)
5	Work out and state expectations of staff	Be proactive and fair
6	Promote contribution to academic, social and economic capital	Be confident and assertive
7	Appropriate risk management	Be ready
8	The case for religious freedom and (more broadly) freedom of speech	Be prepared
9	Cultivate epistemological awareness	Be informed
10	Engage with the sector	Be present

Conclusion

In these ten points I see the leading requirements for the management of academic freedom by a Christian higher education provider. They exhibit the ACT seeking to function as a legitimate participant in the sector. They also show the ACT carrying out the tasks of Theology as public knowledge. At a moment of some jeopardy from the wider society, the ACT is claiming its freedom to 'do Theology' in an open and defensible manner. At the same time it is endeavouring to fulfil its responsibilities to the academy, the church and society at large. The approach of the ACT presumes that the host society will live up to its claim to be free, secular, pluralistic, tolerant and inclusive. It also claims to be a model of the conduct required by society of the identity institutions that feed its diversity. Whether Australian society at large has the eyes to see and ears to hear what the ACT is attempting remains to be seen. In the meantime, its approach is no more than a particularisation at an historically critical moment of the broader mandate to be a Christian in the world—always prepared to give an account of the hope that is within us, and all the while being as wise as serpents but innocent as doves (1 Peter 3:15; Matt. 10:16, cf. Rom. 16:19). Taking every step that wisdom suggests and waiting to see how it all turns out under Providence is part of 'wondering about God'.

Bibliography

Akerman, T. 'The Red Pill. Feminist Protests Black Out Cinemas', *The Australian* 19 April 2017, 3. www.theaustralian.com.au/arts/film/red-pill-film-feminist-protests-black-out-cinemas/news-story/e259601260bcb8bdea0df3fe7fe53e36.

Baldwin, Peter. 'Regressive Left Puts Bigotry on a Pedestal', *The Weekend Australian* 17-18 September 2016, 19.

Burke, Peter. *A Social History of Knowledge: From Gutenberg to Diderot* (Cambridge: Polity, 2000).

Dalziel, James. 'Universities, Christian Higher Education and Ideological Diversity: Insights from Moral Foundations Theory, unpublished paper presented at Christian Heritage College Research Symposium "Learning and Loves: Re-imagining Christian Education".

Ford, David F. *Theology: A Very Short Introduction* (Oxford: Oxford University Press, 2013).

Gelber, Katharine. 'Academic freedom and the "intellectual diversity" movement in Australia', *Australian Journal of Human Rights* 14.2 (2009), 95-114.

GCUP [Global Colloquium of University Presidents] 'Academic Freedom Statement (2005)' www.columbia.edu/~md2221/academicstatement.doc.

Haidt, Jonathan. *The Righteous Mind: Why Good People are Divided by Politics and Religion* (New York: Pantheon Books, 2012).

Hart, Darryl G. & R.A. Mohler, Jr. (eds). *Theological Education in the Evangelical Tradition* (Grand Rapids: Baker Books, 1996).

HEPPQN [Higher Education Private Providers Quality Network] www.avondale.edu.au/about/heppqn/.

Higton, Mike. *A Theology of Higher Education* (Oxford: Oxford University Press, 2012).

Inman, Daniel. *The Making of Modern English Theology: God and the Academy at Oxford 1833-1945* (Minneapolis: Fortress Press, 2014).

IAU [International Association of Universities]. 'Academic Freedom, University Autonomy and Social Responsibility (1998)'. http://archive.www.iau-aiu/he/af/.

Kelly, Paul. 'A New Secularism Trashes Tradition', *The Weekend Australian*, 15-16 April 2017, 15, 18.

Lachlan Macquarie Institute. www.lmi.org.au/purpose.

NTEU [National Tertiary Education Union]. 'Intellectual (Academic) Freedom', www.nteu.org.au/policy/workforce_issues/intellectual_freedom.

Ormerod, Neil. *Academic Freedom in a Theological Context* (Australian College of Theology Occasional Paper No. 4; Sydney: ACT, 2008).

Taylor, Paige. 'Bjorn Lomborg confident of getting host for his Consensus Centre', *The Australian* 11 May 2015.

TEQSA. 'Guidance Note: Diversity and Equity', www.teqsa.gov.au/sites/default/files/GuidanceNote_DiversityandEquity1.0.pdf. Note that only 1.2 is available now.

Treloar, Geoffrey R. 'From the Martin Report to TEQSA: Church and State in Australian Theological Education, ca. 1965-2015', *Interface Theology* (forthcoming).

Treloar, Geoffrey R. 'The Three (or Four) Identities of the Australian College of Theology, 1891-2016', in Andrew Bain and Ian Hussey (eds). *Theological Education: Foundations, Practices and Future Options* (ACT Monograph Series; Eugene, OR.: Wipf & Stock, 2018), 101-118.

Zachhuber, Johannes. *Theology as Science in Nineteenth-century Germany: From F.C. Baur to Ernst Troeltsch* (Oxford: University Press, 2013).

Geoffrey R. Treloar
Australian College of Theology
gtreloar@actheology.edu.au

15 | WINDOWS, MIRRORS AND ICONS AS WAYS INTO THE CONTEXT, CONTENT AND CALL OF SACRED NARRATIVES

Abstract

In Biblical Studies we have become familiar with the diachronic and synchronic analyses which have added much to our understanding of texts and the traditions that created them. However, in the most recent past a new form of analysis has emerged and Reimund Bieringer is at the vanguard of advancing this new method. His term for it is meta-chronic analysis, a method that is rooted in the past, formed in the present and focused on the future. This method may help to counter what Franz Niehl calls 'bible fatigue' which results from a lack of connection between the sacred texts and people's own lives. The method utilises a future oriented eschatology that provides a living bridge between past, present, and future based in fundamentals established by Ricœur and Schneiders. As such it is important to use a mixed approach when reading biblical text to engage fully with the totality of the narrative: an approach that understands the context from which the text comes, and disentangles its sacred content from the social mores that restrain it, to hear the call of world the text seeks to bring into being—to move beyond the past and the present into a future the text will help to create. But how is this concretely achieved in an educational setting? Wolfgang Klafki, a German educationalist, has a useful method to enable the creation of 'buy-in' among students. Could his method move biblical studies out of its self-created ghetto and serve the real problems in the real world? Could the approach proposed herein be extended to all the disciplines of theology?

Introduction

This essay works from a confessional theological approach, understood as a deliberate admission of theistic bias much along the lines of *fides quaerens intellectum*, in which the love of God is the motivation for seeking a deeper knowledge of [and relationship with] God.[1] Thus understood, the intellect is brought to bear on the experience of faith. In his analysis of effective historical consciousness, Hans-Georg Gadamer observes: '[e]xperience is not science itself, but it is a necessary condition of it',[2] In other words, there is no science without experience. And faith is of its very nature experiential. The approach taken herein does not seek to defend faith as a form of apologetics but uses science and reason to ask questions of the text with a view to eliciting the comfort of and the challenges to an authentic faith-filled life and ethic. It makes the case that exegesis—holistically developed and applied—leads to a theocentric eschatological ethic, one that makes real demands in the real lives of real people. If the bible is read as 'churchy' and removed from the ordinariness and messiness of everyday life, exegesis may lead to that which Franz Niehl calls 'bible fatigue' (in German *Bibel Ermüdungen*), a lack of connection between the sacred text and people's own lives.[3] How can biblical educators combat this very real problem to show the bible—and by extension, theology—to be relevant to people's lives?

For centuries, the method for interpreting sacred scripture was the *Quadriga*. Originally a name for a Roman chariot drawn by four horses, this fourfold method of interpretation, after beginning in the early church with Clement and Origen of Alexandria, was completely developed by the Middle Ages. Focusing on the meanings that are to be found in the sacred text, the four-fold method was applied as follows: the first is the literal (or plain/ obvious) meaning of the text; the second is a moral meaning in the text, one which instructs people how they should live; the third is the allegorical meaning to be derived from the text, which reveals doctrinal content; and finally the analogical meaning to be discerned in the text and is expressive of some future hope. The often cited example is that of the phrase 'to go up to Jerusalem' which could mean ascending

---

1 Williams, 'Saint Anselm', says that, 'Faith for Anselm is more a volitional state than an epistemic state: it is love for God and a drive to act as God wills. In fact, Anselm describes the sort of faith that "merely believes what it ought to believe" as "dead" (*Monologion*, 78). So "faith seeking understanding" means something like "an active love of God seeking a deeper knowledge of God"'.
2 Gadamer, *Truth and Method*, 314–379.
3 Niehl, *Bibel verstehen: Zugänge und Auslegungswege*.

to the earthly city (literal meaning), souls going to a place of moral excellence (moral meaning), people should be going to church (allegorical meaning), or the hope of heaven in the future (analogical meaning). With the advent of the grammatico-historical method of Renaissance Humanism, with its flowering in both Reformation and Enlightenment forms, this particular way of exegesis became used less frequently, as philosophy underwent a paradigm shift and the rise of rationality gave birth to the empirical method in science. This had consequences for understanding the sacred texts.

The Three Worlds of the Text

Paul Ricœur's interpretative theory has proven to be a decisive turning point in how to understand and deal with texts.[4] His literary theoretical framework has been put to the service of biblical studies by Sandra Schneiders[5] and it is their combined approach that will form the outline for this chapter, which utilises the 'three worlds' approach to the text.

The first world is the world behind the text which, according to Riemund Bieringer, functions as a *window* on the past. The rise of the historical-critical method, which developed as a result of the Enlightenment in Europe, led to an almost cultic pursuit for scientific objectivity which sought to counter the overly dogmatic approach which had come to characterise biblical interpretation. This approach is pre-eminently diachronic and focuses on how the text was formed, changed and developed through time. In short, the diachronist treats the bible as books with histories.[6] However, the approach is not without its flaws—the sole focus on the history of the text meant that there were areas of the text that were neglected. John Barton notes that prior to 1970 the vast majority of historical-critical scholars 'ask questions about the origins and development of the text, the intentions of its author or authors and its connection with other, similar [ancient] texts'.[7] Indeed, as one commentator says, the 'books of the Bible were often treated more as resources for historical reconstruction than as

---

4   Ricœur, *Interpretation Theory*, 87–94.
5   Schneiders, *The Revelatory Text*.
6   Examples of diachrony are form criticism, tradition criticism and redaction criticism to mention just three of the most frequently used methods.
7   Barton, 'Historical-Critical Approaches', 14.

works of literature in their own right'.[8] In this way, the text can often become an almost secondary consideration as the 'quest' for its historicity is pursued. Barton favours the view that this has put the historical critical method 'under a cloud', since there has been a paradigm shift such that many scholars are unconcerned 'with the historical context and the meaning of the text'.[9]

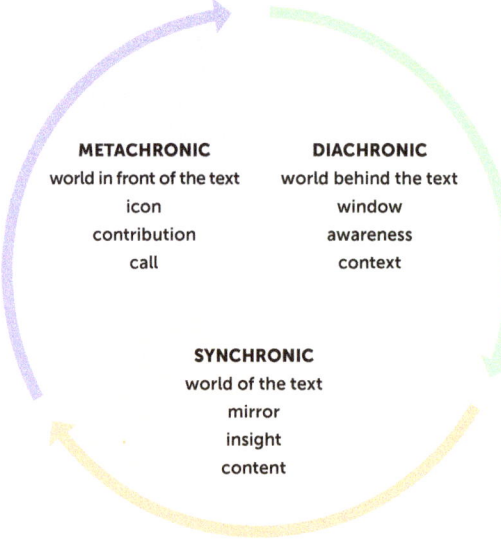

But this is rather an over-statement, as historical-critical concerns are still commonplace in exegesis, as, for example, in feminist biblical criticism.[10] What has changed is the particular concerns, commitments, and identities of the interpreters of the biblical texts, which has led to different questions being asked of ancient historical contexts and of the close readings of the sacred text. As one example, an examination of the diverse range of scholarship and textual studies that may be loosely gathered under the term 'feminist' shows that there is no singular 'feminist perspective' or identity, and no 'feminist method' *per se*, save an openness to the many different sensitivities that have been previously

---

8 Powell, 'Narrative Criticism', 239, following the original observation of Frei, *The Eclipse of Biblical Narrative*.
9 Barton, 'Historical-Critical Approaches', 9.
10 Clines, 'Historical Criticism: Are Its Days Numbered?', 542–58, and Nissinen, 'Reflections on the Historical-Critical Method', 479–505.

ignored by academic biblical scholarship.[11] Indeed, the historical-critical methods used to examine the world behind the text remain constant, tried, tested, and sound and much used by said feminists! It would be more accurate to say that the recent changes in biblical scholarship have more to do with the identity of the modern reader. This is married with a realisation that the world in front of the text will always inform the way one attempts to reconstruct the world behind the text and to understand the text itself. There has always been, and will always be, an element of subjectivity in scientific study. That said, it would be an error not to point out the blatantly obvious, as James Muilenburg pointed out long ago, that the victim of an exclusively rationalistic diachronic approach is usually the text itself.[12]

As early as 1969, William A. Beardslee[13] advocated a more literary approach to the Gospels. By the 1980s there had been an important shift to a text-immanent approach to the New Testament.[14] Synchronic approaches to the text[15] treat the bible as a finished product; as a coherent, logical, unified whole; as a textual world in its own right (the world of the text). Such approaches treat the bible as literature.[16]

> The treatment of Biblical literature as literature was practiced during the ages, e.g., by the medieval commentator Abarbanel. Nevertheless, in modern times, after two hundred years of research immersed in literary criticism, emphasizing the 'criticism', while largely neglecting the 'literary', a literary approach seems something new and fresh.[17]

In such an approach, co-text becomes the key to interpretation, that is, the examination of other biblical passages that include a discussion of the topic

---

11 Newsom, 'Women as Biblical Interpreters before the Twentieth Century', 11–26.
12 Muilenburg, 'Form Criticism and Beyond'. James Muilenburg's 1968 presidential address to the Society of Biblical Literature demonstrated an interest in what the New Criticism had called 'the text itself'. Rather than reading and dissecting biblical texts primarily to find information about the ancient genres and historical milieux in which the texts were formed, Muilenburg asked biblical critics to pay close attention to how particular biblical texts functioned as works of literature.
13 Beardslee, *Literary Criticism of the New Testament*.
14 Snyman, 'A Semantic Discourse Analysis of the Letter to Philemon', 86.
15 Among the synchronic approaches are discourse analysis, narrative criticism, and ideological criticism.
16 Talshir, 'Synchronic and Diachronic Approaches in the Study of the Hebrew Bible', 12–13. Indeed, Talshir (citing a study by Zakovitch) goes on to say that many scholars in Israel choose the synchronic approach (against the diachronic approach) as their religious beliefs inhibit them from participating in the critical analysis of the bible.
17 Talshir, 'Synchronic and Diachronic Approaches', 12.

under investigation in the primary study text.[18] This method sees the text as both source and resource and as a confrontation with the self and the narrative of the text. Thus, the world of the text functions as a *mirror* on the present, to use a category Bieringer has usefully exploited. This mirroring happens in different ways but each is an expression of one's own feelings and/ or experiences. The first mirroring is one of *substitution* which involves inserting oneself into the text. The second is in the form of an *anticipation* of what one may be in the future. The third mirror is a form of transference and counter-transference wherein one transfers one's own experience onto the story. And finally is the mirror of *empathy* in which one is differentiated from the text but develops deep understanding and participation through the text.

However, the diachronic and synchronic approaches share a perspective on the text as 'promise and past'; seeking to understand the promise immersed in the text, and in the pursuit of objectivity, interpreters remain focussed on the past, with many studies stopping at the intent of the original human authors and their human audience. Such scholarly engagement with the biblical text is critical and has provided the Church with much to contemplate. However, an overly rationalistic approach to biblical texts does a disservice to the text itself and to its origins. To take one example from diachrony and another from synchrony in the field of biblical studies, an overly rationalistic approach may be seen in the work of Rudolf Bultmann in the mid-twentieth century and, more recently, in the work of Gerd Theißen.[19]

Pre-eminent among form critical scholars Bultmann believed, according to Mournet, that '[t]he aim of form-criticism [*sic*] is to determine the original form of a piece of narrative, a dominical saying or a parable. In the process we learn to distinguish secondary additions and forms, and these in turn lead to important results for the history of the tradition'.[20] Seeking to demythologise the New

---

18 Lewis, *The Lexical Approach*, 103, as follows: 'Contextualisation means noting the **situation** in which the word may occur, but most importantly noting **the co-text with which it can regularly occur**. If context is seen as situation + co-text, it is the latter—co-occurring language—which is more important for language learning' (author's emphasis). As such we may distinguish 'co-text' (the linguistic environment of a word) from 'context' (the non-verbal environment in which a word is used). However, here I would extend the use of the term to include to concept of topic of the text and in particular other biblical passages that speak to the topic in a given text. Therefore, co-text looks at the intertextual layers to discerning the meaning in a pericope or textual unit. Thus, it is my deliberate intention to extend the meaning of co-text beyond Lewis's original use such that it includes the examination of other inter-textual elements.
19 Theißen, *Urchristliche Wundergeschichten*, 48.
20 Mournet, *Oral Tradition and Literary Dependency*, 56.

Testament, Bultmann called on interpreters to replace 'traditional supernaturalism' with temporal and existential categories and rejected doctrines such as the pre-existence of Christ.[21] By stripping it of the 'mythical world picture' of the first century, which had the potential to alienate modern people from Christian faith, Bultmann sought to make the Christian message more palatable to the modern reader. In doing so, he succeeded in calling the historical value of the Gospel narrative into question.

Working with the quasi-synchronic approach of psychological transformation, Theißen explains away the feeding miracle as a trick. Jesus did not work the miracle, rather the rich women who support him provided the food, but their efforts go unnoticed by the poor. Thus, for Theißen, this becomes a 'gift miracle' with a rational explanation of how such 'miracle' occurs.[22] Both scholars use rationalism to the detriment of the sacred texts. There is a need for something more. Could the world in front of the text provide the 'holy grail'?

In 1967 Roland Barthes declared that, 'writing is the destruction of every voice, of every point of origin. Writing is that neutral, composite, oblique space where our subject slips away, the negative where all identity is lost, starting with the very identity of the body writing'.[23] In doing so, he asserted the 'death of the author' and the 'birth of the reader':[24]

> We are now beginning to let ourselves be fooled no longer by the arrogant antiphrastical (*sic*) recriminations of good society in favour of the very thing it sets aside, ignores, smothers, or destroys; we know that to give writing its future, it is necessary to overthrow the myth: the birth of the reader must be at the cost of the death of the Author.[25]

Barthes reasoned that readers were freed to advance their own meaning concerning the text, independent of, and indeed, in opposition to, any need to

---

21 Bultmann, 'New Testament and Mythology', 328.
22 Theißen, *The Shadow of the Galilean*.
23 Barthes, 'The Death of the Author', 142.
24 Barthes, 'The Death of the Author', 142–148.
25 Barthes, 'The Death of the Author', 148. On page 147 he writes, 'Once the Author is removed, the claim to decipher a text becomes quite futile. To give a text an Author is to impose a limit on that text, to furnish it with a final signified, to close the writing. Such a conception suits criticism very well, the latter then allotting itself the important task of discovering the Author (or its hypostases: society, history, psyche, liberty) beneath the work: when the Author has been found, the text is "explained"—victory to the critic. Hence there is no surprise in the fact that, historically, the reign of the Author has also been that of the Critic, nor again in the fact that criticism (be it new) is today undermined along with the Author'.

reconstruct the human author's original intent in writing.[26] This then is the world in front of the text which focuses on how individual readers and/ or communities of readers construct their own meanings of the text, disregarding the meaning these texts may have had in their original contexts.[27] The approaches to the text that take this world-view as their hermeneutical paradigm all share an interest in the particular positions of readers/users of the texts and how the same text, read in different contexts and through time, manifests different potential meanings and effects. However, Brendan Breed has identified fundamental problems with this approach, when applied to biblical texts.[28] It divides the world behind the text—that is, the original context of the text and hence the original meaning—from later contexts, later readers, and later meanings. But how does one decide where the original context ends and the later context begins, since it is only thanks to the historical-critical approaches that we understand how the texts themselves were gathered, formed, and redacted over time—sometimes across centuries? How does one decide when redaction becomes corruption? On the positive side, this method raises awareness that texts really do create alternative worlds, beyond their original context.

> If texts are supposed to function outside their context, perhaps we should then assume that the natural habitat of a text is, in fact, living in the wild, and as a result, we should spend time studying how biblical texts function in a variety of [contemporary] contexts. Perhaps we should no longer ask 'What does this text mean', or 'How should we read this text'—but rather, 'How has this text functioned? What can it do? Of what is it capable? What capacities does it have, and how might these capacities reveal themselves in a variety of contexts?'[29]

---

26 Breed, 'What can Texts do?'.
27 An example of this type of approach is reader-response criticism wherein in a critic/interpreter theorises a potential reader or studies the responses of particular readers of the texts. An example of the reader-response approach is found in Iser, *The Implied Reader*; for an early example of a survey of actual responses, see Fish, *Surprised by Sin*. Another form this approach has taken is called reception history which focusses on the tracing of how a particular text has acquired meaning through interactions across different communities and through time; see Breed, *Nomadic Text*. More recently still is the work of Beal, 'Beyond Reception History', who is developing what he calls a 'cultural history' approach that focuses on the particular ways that biblical texts are produced and/ or reproduced within a particular culture, instead of focusing on the text's meanings or uses across cultures.
28 Brendan Breed, 'What can Texts do?'.
29 Brendan Breed, 'What can Texts do?'. This line of questioning derives from Gilles Deleuze's reading of Spinoza; see Deleuze, *The Fold*, 20–22.

Such questions demonstrate that the sacred texts need a mixed approach. Bieringer asserts that doing so reveals that texts have a future dimension, projecting alternate worlds as can be seen in the book of Revelation's vision of a new heaven and a new earth.[30] But this is true not only of the book of Revelation but of all biblical books since, he contends, these books are more than their historical or literary worlds—which focus on the author and the author's world, or the text and its world respectively. They have a future dimension also, and this future is transformative, proposing a utopian world. Access to this world requires a radically different perspective to the text, one that transcends the deficiencies of both diachrony and synchrony! Bieringer terms this different perspective a meta-chronic perspective. By meta-chronic he means that texts 'are rooted in the past, formed in the present, but transcend both of them into the future'.[31] Viewed in this way religious texts function as symbols (in a sacramental sense of the word), in that, in and through them readers encounter God and God, in turn, summons all God's creatures to fullness of life. Without question revelation has both past and present dimensions; however, revelation itself is future-oriented, with an eschatological perspective where texts of the past function, in essence, as *icons*, revealing the mysterious reality of the future, the coming kingdom of God. This future-oriented eschatology forms a living bridge between the past, the present, and the future.

This approach to biblical texts enables communities to understand their identity in terms of the realisation of the future embodied in the text. This is a future that is already in process, since the text itself is the first stage of bringing it about. Such an approach is both text immanent (synchrony) and text transcendent (metachrony) and becomes a form of eschatological hermeneutics. What is required of the reader/interpreter is both openness and receptiveness.

Even if the word of God is written in human language and contains traces of human sin within,[32] or as the Portuguese proverb puts it, 'God writes straight with crooked lines',[33] for all Paul's supposed misogyny, it is the same Paul who wrote: 'for in Christ Jesus you are all children of God through faith. As many of you as were baptised into Christ have clothed yourselves with Christ. There is no longer Jew or Greek, there is no longer slave or free, nor male and female; for all of you are one in Christ Jesus' (Galatians 3:26-28). With Bieringer, this

---

30   Rev. 21:1ff. *Cf.* Isa. 65:17.
31   Bieringer, 'Texts That Create a Future', 105.
32   *Dei Verbum*, § 13 and *Verbum Domini*, § 42.
33   Portuguese proverb which means that strange events become clear with time.

is an example of normativity of the future, which, as Hans-Georg Gadamer has posited, requires the surpassing of their horizons of understanding[34] to achieve the goal of the biblical text and recover the traces of 'God's dream for creation' —a dream of transformation and inclusivity. In this way one may build a dialogue with the biblical text, which will combat 'bible fatigue'.[35]

According to Bieringer, the future unfolded by the texts is an alternative world with the building blocks for a better understanding of God's ultimate dream for humanity expressed as 'a vision of a just and inclusive community'.[36] One must remain aware that 'ideological distortion may still be present in one's understanding of a biblically inspired future' and further, that one is cognisant that this future is not necessarily superior to the present or the past, yet this future dimension makes certain ethical and theological claims on the present.[37] The value of this approach is that it ensures that texts have a paradigmatic value. This happens in such a way that the reading community has the task of reading and internalising the ancient text as the first chapters in a chain novel. They then write the next chapter in light of what they have discerned as the Normativity of the Future, which has a certain hermeneutical privilege over the present and the past because of its association with God's vision for humanity.[38] This means that any conflict of values encountered in the historical and literary dimensions of the text are abrogated by the biblical text's horizon of a future of inclusive justice, the life-giving values of the kingdom of God.[39] As such, rather than a closed canon, the bible becomes an open narrative to which each generation has a contribution to make, and all authors, past and present, must take responsibility for the consequences of their writings including any effects it may have on others since '[s]cholarship is a political act'.[40] This approach to the text is positioned in the borderlands of a theocentric vision of inclusive-pluralism. But how is it attained? By means of education.

---

34 Gadamer, *Truth and Method*, 302.
35 Niehl, *Bibel verstehen: Zugänge und Auslegungswege*.
36 Bieringer & Pollefeyt, 'Prologue', 13.
37 Bieringer & Elsbernd, 'Introduction', 6–9.
38 Bieringer & Elsbernd, 'Introduction', 10.
39 Bieringer & Elsbernd, 'Introduction', 12.
40 Bieringer & Elsbernd, 'Introduction', 27 and also Bieringer & Pollefeyt, 'Prologue', 14.

Awareness, Insight, Contribution

Wolfgang Klafki, a German educationalist, argued that the school had to open the child to the world and give the child the necessary tools to take part and share responsibility in the world in order to develop new values and competences.[41] He proposed four important elements that are relevant to education. First, Klafki made clear that education must integrate self-determination, co-determination, and solidarity, enabling students to become autonomous. Second, he argued that teaching has to be problem-based and must address the core problems of the present time and the foreseeable future, enabling students to work out authentic problems (whatever they may be). This student-based problem-solving approach gives rise to the third element, namely, that a larger part of school teaching had to be multi-disciplinary since authentic problems are cross-curricular by nature and must be approached using a wide variety of tools and methods. Finally, learning processes must be directed towards themes and social competences so that students understand their co-responsibility to create a solution and are ready and able to contribute to the formation of a solution. By enabling students to become active in their own education, Klafki seeks to bring them to the point of *awareness, insight* and *contribution*, thus creating a 'buy-in'. This buy-in means that students become *actively engaged* in their own learning, *critically aware* of authentic problems, *develop insights* to possible solutions and so have readiness to *make a contribution* to the formation of a solution.

Context, Content, Call

What can biblical studies learn from following Klafki's lead in regard to creating 'buy-in' in the theological endeavour? Biblical studies must move out of its self-created ghetto and serve the real problems in the real world. Arguing over the historicity of miracles is no longer tenable. Holding the privileged position of custodians of the sacred texts, biblical scholars must make their work relevant to the authentic problems their global communities face. With Gadamer, they must confront unnecessarily narrow approaches that claim, either implicitly or explicitly, to be the sole arbiters capable of leading others to the highest forms

---

41 Klafki, 'Didaktik Analysis as the Core of Preparation of Instruction', 139–159. See also Klafki, *Neue Studien zur Bildungstheorie und Didaktik*.

of truth.[42] The theoretical pursuits of understanding that shape modern epistemology and which have become lionized in philosophical, and by extension, literary methodologies are contrary to the nature of biblical texts. Theory will take the interpreter so far, but it is practical reasonableness that may take them the rest of the way.[43] Engagement with the texts is not the exclusive domain of scientists or of the literary scientific approaches, as vital and necessary as they may be. However, re-imagining a theological anthropology will facilitate a deeper, spiritual engagement. This re-imagining makes use of science, but continues above and beyond it—moving from original praxis to modern practicality, a practicality which is, more often than not, culturally subversive, and eschews appropriated cultural norms, since it is designed to influence the religious and social structures of thought of the day.

What is needed to help re-image the current theological anthropology is a tri-partite approach[44] to engage fully with the totality of the narrative. The *context of the text* must be properly grasped in order to understand what of it may rightfully be left behind. The *content of the text* must be disentangled to discern what 'crooked lines' may be therein, and the *call of the text* and the vision of the world it wants to bring into being must find a response. Indeed, to extend Breed's metaphor, we must become theocentric eschatological nomadologists, not just following the text 'from the ancient Near East to the present day',[45] but moving beyond the past and the present into a future the text will help to create. This is so because, as Louis-Marie Chauvet points out, if the scriptures are sacramental in the concreteness of their letter, they are so from an iconic perspective. The letter can be the mediation of the revelation of God only to the extent that it forms *figures*. For the letter is not revelatory except as a witness after the fact of something completed. The letter arises as figure (and thus as a sacramental mediation of revelation) only by splitting itself into two: a witness to the 'has been' of the creation, the Exodus, or the manna, and at the same time a witness to the 'must be' of a new creation, a new exodus, a new manna, and so forth. As figure, it is an *in-between*, a passage, a transit toward something other than itself, which is the other side of itself: the Jordan is the Jordan crossed by Joshua, then Elijah; for John the Baptist, and because of this,

---

42 Porter & Robinson, *Hermeneutics: An Introduction to Interpretive Theory*, 82.
43 Gadamer, 'The Ethics of Value and Practical Philosophy', 117.
44 Bieringer, 'Texts That Create a Future', 91–116.
45 Brendan Breed, 'What can Texts do?'

it awaits Jesus.[46]

Meta-chronic analysis is not without its own tensions and difficulties. The biblical text must be consciously interpreted by an explicit mediation, wherein one gives up independent authority in order to bridge the gap between the explicit word and the spirit of the gospel, thus enabling a real encounter with the numinous to take place in the form of a dialogical conversation.[47] Interpreters can often be painfully aware of their inevitable distance from the original text, since dealing with even a small pericope requires effort to understand the human author's bias. Bridging the gap from the explicit text to an eschatologically-oriented future interpretation[48] can at times prove daunting. Indeed, the best solution is often found in the to-ing and fro-ing of the dialogue that weighs possibilities and considerations against each other to bridge that gulf, one that clearly shows the reciprocal relationship that exists between the interpreter and the text, as the written marks are changed back into meaning. In so doing, a communicative event takes place, 'that is more than mere adaptation', which is, in essence, 'a fusion of horizons [...] in which something is expressed that is not mine or my author's, but common'.[49] The result is that the interpreter engages 'with the Spirit who transcends the text, to go beyond the limitations of the biblical text and "write their own fifth gospel"'.[50] One way to do this is to create dialogue partners between the biblical narratives and modern literature/culture.[51]

---

46 Chauvet, *Symbol and Sacrament*, 218.
47 *Dei Verbum* 2. *Verbum Domini* 56, 'Reflection on the performative character of the word of God in the sacramental action and a growing appreciation of the relationship between word and Eucharist lead to yet another significant theme which emerged during the synodal assembly, that of the *sacramentality* of the word. Here it may help to recall that Pope John Paul II had made reference to the "*sacramental* character of revelation" and in particular to "the sign of the Eucharist in which the indissoluble unity between the signifier and signified makes it possible to grasp the depths of the mystery"'. 'We come to see that at the heart of the sacramentality of the word of God is the mystery of the Incarnation itself: "the Word became flesh" (John 1:14), the reality of the revealed mystery is offered to us in the "flesh" of the Son. The Word of God can be perceived by faith through the "sign" of human words and actions. Faith acknowledges God's Word by accepting the words and actions by which he makes himself known to us. The sacramental character of revelation points in turn to the history of salvation, to the way that word of God enters time and space, and speaks to men and women, who are called to accept his gift in faith'. *Cf.* Encyclical Letter *Fides et Ratio* (14 September 1998), 13: AAS 91 (1999), 16. Original emphasis.
48 Bieringer & Elsbernd, 'Introduction', 5.
49 Gadamer, *Truth and Method*, 350.
50 Bieringer, & Pollefeyt, 'Prologue', 13. *Cf.* Bieringer, 'Biblical Revelation and Exegetical Interpretation According to *Dei Verbum* 12', 25–59, esp. 52. See further Bieringer & Elsbernd, 'Introduction', 4ff.
51 An example being the film 'Rabbit Proof Fence' and the narrative of the Exodus.

In order to achieve this, one must approach the text dialogically, all the while aware of, and endeavouring to avoid, the twin extremes of objectivity and subjectivity to explore how meaning and truth are mediated through language, which is itself thoroughly historical in nature.

> Every conversation presupposes a common language, or, it creates a common language. Something is placed in the centre, as the Greeks said, which the partners to the dialogue both share, and concerning which they can exchange ideas with one another. Hence agreement concerning the object, which is the purpose of the conversation to bring about, necessarily means that a common language must first be worked out in the conversation. This is not an external matter of simply adjusting our tools, nor is it even right to say that the partners adapt themselves to one another but, rather, in the successful conversation they both come under the influence of the truth of the object and are thus bound to one another in a new community. *To reach an understanding with one's partner in a dialogue is not merely a matter of total self-expression and the successful assertion of one's own point of view, but a transformation into a communion, in which we do not remain what we were.*[52]

The interpreter's present horizon (their knowledge and experience) is a productive ground for understanding, since truth is an event in which there is both a revealing and a concealing. What is known and believed to be true in the present will often change as cultural beliefs and values shift. Understanding is a perpetual working through of the hermeneutical circle wherein new presuppositions and prejudgements are challenged as the interpreter waits for the disclosure of glimpses of truth. According to Gadamer, to embrace this basic truth is to become able to partially transcend the potentially vicious circle of objectivism, which fails to take into account that historical and cultural conditioning can never be completely erased.[53] The interpreter accepts their own limitations and submits their work to the academy for scrutiny.

Is it possible that such an approach might move beyond biblical studies and become normative for all theological disciplines? And if so, what would theology look like?

---

52 Gadamer, *Truth and Method*, 341. Emphasis added.
53 Gadamer, *Truth and Method*, 341–379.

Bibliography

AAS 91 (1999). *ACTA APOSTOLICAE SEDIS* 91 An. et vol. XCI 7 Ianuarii 1999 N. 1. URL = http://passthrough.fw-notify.net/download/935259/ www.vatican.va/archive/aas/documents/AAS-91-1999-ocr.pdf

Barthes, Roland. 'The Death of the Author', in Roland Barthes, *Image-Music-Text: Essays selected and translated by Stephen Heath* (New York: Hill and Wang, 1977), 142–148.

Barton, John. 'Historical-Critical Approaches', in *The Cambridge Companion to Biblical Interpretation* (J. Barton, ed.; Cambridge: Cambridge University Press, 1998), 9–20.

Beal, Timothy. 'Beyond Reception History: Toward the Cultural History of Scriptures', *Biblical Interpretation* 19 (2011), 357–372.

Beardslee, W.A. *Literary Criticism of the New Testament* (Guides to Biblical Scholarship, New Testament Series; Philadelphia, Penn.: Fortress, 1969).

Benedict XVI. Post-synodol Apostolic Exhortation *VERBUM DOMINI* (30 September 2010). URL = http://w2.vatican.va/content/benedict-xvi/en/apost_exhortations/documents/hf_ben-xvi_exh_20100930_verbum-domini.html

Bieringer, Reimund. 'Texts That Create a Future: The Function of Ancient Texts for Theology Today', in Reimund Bieringer & Mary Elsbernd (eds.). *Normativity of the Future: Reading Biblical and Other Authoritative Texts in an Eschatological Perspective* (Leuven: Peeters, 2010), 91–116.

Bieringer, Reimund, & Didier Pollefeyt, 'Prologue: Wrestling with the Jewish Paul', in idem. (eds.), Paul and Judaism: *Crosscurrents in Pauline Exegesis and the Study of Jewish Christian Relations* (London: T&T Clark, 2012), 1–14.

Bieringer, Reimund, & Mary Elsbernd, 'Introduction: The "Normativity of the Future" approach: Its Roots, Development, Current State and Challenges', in Reimund Bieringer & Mary Elsbernd (eds.), *Normativity of the Future: Reading Biblical and Other Authoritative Texts in an Eschatological Perspective* (Annua Nuntia Lovaniensia, 61; Leuven: Peeters, 2010), 1–25.

Bieringer, Reimund. 'Biblical Revelation and Exegetical Interpretation According to Dei Verbum 12', in Matthias Lamberigts and Leo Kenis (eds.), *Vatican II and its Legacy* (BETL 166; Leuven: Leuven University Press—Peeters, 2002), 25–59.

Breed, Brennan. 'What can Texts do? A Proposal for Biblical Studies', *@thispoint* 10.1 (Winter 2015), Main Article. Available at http://www.atthispoint.net/articles/what-can-texts-do-a-proposal-for-biblical-studies/262/. (Accessed on April 26, 2017).

Breed, Brennan. *Nomadic Text: A Theory of Biblical Reception* (Bloomington: Indiana University Press, 2014).

Bultmann, Rudolf. 'New Testament and Mythology: The Problem of Demythologizing the New Testament Message', in Craig A. Evans (ed.), *The Historical Jesus: Critical Concepts in Religious Studies* (New York: Routledge, 2004), 323–358.

Chauvet, Louis-Marie. *Symbol and Sacrament. A Sacramental Reinterpretation of Christian Existence* (Collegeville, Minn.: Liturgical Press, 1995; [French: 1987]).

Clines, David J. 'Historical Criticism: Are Its Days Numbered?', *Teologinen aikakauskirja* 6 (2009), 542–558.

Deleuze, Gilles. *The Fold: Leibniz and the Baroque* (T. Conley, trans.; Minneapolis: University of Minnesota, 1993).

Fish, Stanley. *Surprised by Sin: The Reader in Paradise Lost* (Cambridge: Harvard University Press, 1967).

Frei, H.W. *The Eclipse of Biblical Narrative: A Study of Eighteenth and Nineteenth Century Hermeneutics* (New Haven, Conn.: Yale University, 1974).

Gadamer, Hans-Georg. 'The Ethics of Value and Practical Philosophy', *Hermeneutics, Religion and Ethics* (Joel Weinsheimer, trans.; New Haven, Conn.: Yale, 1999), 103–118.

Gadamer, Hans-Georg. *Truth and Method* (G. Barden and J. Cumming, transls.; New York: Seabury, 1975).

Iser, Wolfgang. *The Implied Reader* (Baltimore: Johns Hopkins University Press, 1974).

John Paul II. Encyclical Letter FIDES ET RATIO (14 September 1998). URL = http://w2.vatican.va/content/john-paul-ii/en/encyclicals/documents/hf_jp-ii_enc_14091998_fides-et-ratio.html.

Klafki, Wolfgang. 'Didaktik Analysis as the Core of Preparation of Instruction', in Ian Westbury, Stefan Hopmann & Kurt Riquarts (eds.), *Teaching as a Reflective Practice: The German Didaktik Tradition* (Mahwah, New Jersey: Lawrence Erlbaum Associates, 2000), 139–159.

Klafki, Wolfgang. *Neue Studien zur Bildungstheorie und Didaktik: Zeitgemäße Allgemeinbildung und kritisch-konstruktiver Didaktik* (Weinheim und Basel: Beltz Verlag, 21991).

Lewis, M. *The Lexical Approach: The state of ELT and a Way Forward* (Boston, Mass.: Global ELT, 2002 reprint, [1993]).

Mournet, Terence C. *Oral Tradition and Literary Dependency: Variability and Stability in the Synoptic Tradition and Q* (WUNT 195; Mohr Siebeck, 2005).

Muilenburg, James A. 'Form Criticism and Beyond', *JBL* 88 (1969), 1–18.

Newsom, Carol A. 'Women as Biblical Interpreters before the Twentieth Century', in C. Newsom, S. Rindge, J. Lapsley (eds.), *Women's Bible Commentary* (Louisville: Westminster John Knox, 2012), 11–26.

Niehl, Franz W. *Bibel verstehen: Zugänge und Auslegungswege. Impulse für die Praxis der Bibelarbeit* (München: Kösel-Verlag, 2006).

Nissinen, Martti. 'Reflections on the Historical-Critical Method: Historical Criticism and Critical Historicism', in J. LeMon & K. H. Richards (eds.), *Method Matters: Essays on the Interpretation of the Bible in Honor of David L. Petersen* (Atlanta: Society of Biblical Literature, 2009), 479–505.

Porter, Stanley E., & Jason C. Robinson, *Hermeneutics: An Introduction to Interpretive Theory* (Grand Rapids, Mich.: Eerdmans, 2011).

Powell, M.A. 'Narrative Criticism', in J.B. Green (ed.), *Hearing the New Testament: Strategies for Interpretation* (Grand Rapids, Mich.: Eerdmans, 2010), 239–255.

Ricœur, Paul. *Interpretation Theory: Discourse and the Surplus of Meaning* (Fort Worth: Texas Christian University, 1976).

Schneiders, Sandra M. *The Revelatory Text: Interpretating the New Testament as Sacred Scripture* (New York: Haper Collins, 1991).

Snyman, A.H. 'A Semantic Discourse Analysis of the Letter to Philemon', in P.J. Hartin and J.H. Petzer (eds.). *Text and Interpretation: New Approaches in the Criticism of the New Testament* (*NTTS* 15; Leiden: Brill, 1991), 83–99.

Talshir, Z. 'Synchronic and Diachronic Approaches in the Study of the Hebrew Bible: Text Criticism within the frame of Biblical Philology', *Textus* 23 (2007), 1–35.

Theißen, Gerd. *The Shadow of the Galilean: The Quest of the Historical Jesus in Narrative Form* (John Bowden, transl.; Minneapolis, Minn.: Fortress Press, 2007 [German: 1986]).

Theißen, Gerd, Urchristliche Wundergeschichten. *Ein Beitrag zur formgeschichtlichen Erforschung der synoptischen Evangelien* (StNT 8; Gütersloh: Mohn, 1974). English edition: *The Miracle Stories of the Early Christian Tradition* (Francis McDonagh, transl.; Minneapolis, Minn.: Fortress Press, 1983).

Vatican Council II. Dogmatic Constitution on Divine Revelation *DEI VERBUM* (18, November 1965). URL www.vatican.va/archive/hist_councils/ii_vatican_council/documents/vat-ii_const_19651118_dei-verbum_en.html.

Williams, Thomas. 'Saint Anselm', in Edward N. Zalta (ed.), *The Stanford Encyclopedia of Philosophy* (Spring 2016 Edition). URL = https://plato.stanford.edu/archives/spr2016/entries/anselm/ (Accessed on April 26, 2017).

Debra Snoddy
Catholic Institute of Sydney
dsnoddy@cis.catholic.edu.au

16 | IN MY FATHER'S HOUSE

THE PLACE OF WONDER IN PROVERBS' VISION OF EDUCATION

Abstract

The interest in wonder has been a welcome trend in theological education. Curiously, though, it has happened without much reference to the Bible's own witness on schooling. This essay seeks to address the gap, therefore, by looking at a key text in the study of Israelite education: the book of Proverbs. It does so is by locating wonder within Proverbs' vision of education. Since metaphors are central to this vision, the study especially considers the ones that are foundational. What it finds, though, is that the usual suspects—the 'way' and the father/son relationship—do not provide a truly governing metaphor for education. Instead, such a metaphor may be found in the idea of the 'house' and 'house-building'. Viewed through this lens, wonder takes on new significance. It becomes the animating spark that connects the two 'houses' of education: the 'house' of the father and the 'house' of God. If humans are to 'build' their homes like God built the cosmos, they must imitate Woman Wisdom; and the ideal portrait of Woman Wisdom, in Proverbs 8, characterises her chief attribute as wonder (vv 29-31). The governing ethos of wisdom education, therefore, is divine hospitality: God has made the world as our 'playhouse' and he invites us to learn through wonderment.

Introduction

Wonder has become the darling of education, with teachers from a variety of disciplines recognising its value and seeking to weave it into their curriculum. This is a healthy response to the situation in which we now find ourselves, which is to say, the 'disenchantment' of education.[1] It is even more heartening to find it in the halls of theological education, where the disenchantment has at times been severe. Yet the theological discussions, for all their merit, have featured a curious gap: they have developed largely without reference to the Bible's own witness on education. That is, they have tended to ask questions of pedagogy, theology, and philosophy without asking, directly, whether ancient educators envisioned wonder within education. The goal of this essay, therefore, is to ask that question, especially looking at a key educational text from ancient Israel: the book of Proverbs.

As is well known, the exact practice of education in ancient Israel remains elusive and much debated.[2] Yet what is often lost in the debate is that practice is only one side of the educational coin. The other is educational *vision*. The question how education actually worked is just as important as the question how it was *meant* to work. Fortunately, this question is more accessible to us in regard to Proverbs.

Proverbs' vision of education may be understood, generally, within the wisdom tradition: its fundamental aim was to train children to be wise. By listening to their parents' instruction in the home, children learned to perceive wisdom and folly in the world outside. This provided them with the skills to navigate life successfully. Yet Proverbs aimed to do more than train children in rudimentary wisdom. It ultimately aimed to create in them a worldview, 'a view of reality that made sense of the world and guided human existence'.[3]

Such 'world-building' was rooted in Israel's creation theology: that the world was created by God and for people, and that he infused his handiwork with wisdom so that it might be discovered by those who seek it. Thus biblical wisdom naturally began in acknowledging God as Creator (Prov. 9:10) and

---

1 The classic treatment of this in regard to Western culture was Weber, *Sociology of Religion*, who borrowed the term 'disenchantment' (*Entzauberung*) from Friedrich Schiller.
2 There are a number of helpful summaries available, such as Millard, 'Sages' and Chalmers, *Exploring Religion*, 67–88.
3 Perdue, *Wisdom and Creation*, 49. For an excellent discussion on the wisdom literature as world-building, see Bartholomew and O'Dowd, *Wisdom Literature*, 47–72.

proceeded by seeking out his 'secrets hidden in nature and human behavior'.[4] Yet to stop here is to stop short:

> the wisdom experience is to be described as a faith experience [...] done in an ambience of faith, and was characterized by trust and reliance upon God [...] God drew the people, through their daily experience of themselves and creation, into the mystery of God's dealings with each individual human being.[5]

The goal of wisdom education, therefore, was to train children not only to master life, but to discover its source. Here we see how education in the wisdom tradition complemented salvation history the other main tradition: salvation history focused on knowing God through the *magnalia dei*, the mighty acts of God (e.g. Deut. 6), while the wisdom tradition focused on finding God's wisdom 'hidden within the universe' as 'God's gift to those who bore the Creator's image'.[6] In this way all education, Proverbs included, sought to accomplish a singular aim: to teach children to 'walk in the way of the Lord' (Gen. 18:19).[7]

Education as House Building

To discern whether wonder played a role in this vision involves, first, considering Proverbs' metaphors. The wisdom writings, more than others, 'depended on the power of language to create a world view that stimulated the imagination of those they addressed', and, since 'metaphors provoked the imagination to conceive of and experience reality in compelling ways [...] they became the organizing centers for ethical life and moral discourse'.[8] But when we ask about the 'organizing' metaphors for education, we find something interesting: a metaphor that governs education as a whole is yet to be named.

---

4   Crenshaw, *Wisdom*, 88 n.1.
5   Murphy, *The Tree of Life*, 125.
6   Crenshaw, *Wisdom*, 61.
7   Andrew Hill, 'Education', 193.
8   Perdue, *Wisdom & Creation*, 339. Elsewhere Perdue offers a most helpful discussion of the importance of metaphors in the wisdom literature (pp. 325–342).

The 'Way'

One of the most important metaphors in Proverbs is the 'way', which, since Norman Habel's seminal work, has been seen as a 'nuclear symbol' around which other 'satellite symbols' orbit.[9] Essentially, this means the 'way' characterises life as a journey with two divergent paths: the way of life and the way of death (Prov. 4:10-19).[10] Two things determine the path a person follows: 1) one's heart and 2) one's pursuits. For this reason, Habel labeled the so-called two hearts (Prov. 4:20-27; 6:12-15) and two women (Prov. 4:1–7:5) as supporting, or 'satellite', metaphors for the 'way'.[11] Thus the wise person has a righteous heart and pursues Lady Wisdom, which leads down the path of life; the foolish person has a wicked heart and pursues Dame Folly, which leads down the path of death.

Although whether the 'way' does in fact serve as a foundational metaphor is beyond the scope of this essay, what is important here is to note the effect of the view's prevalence. Because many have seen the 'way' as a nuclear metaphor, they have likewise assumed other ideas revolve around its orbit. Education, being one such idea, is seen along these lines. The 'way' becomes the de facto governing metaphor for education.

Yet this does not reflect the text itself. It is true that the 'way' appears often and in key places to summarise education, both in the salvation history and wisdom tradition. And it is also true that the 'way' serves as an important metaphor in Proverbs 1–9, whose focus is on education. Yet this does not mean the metaphor represents education as a whole. It may only represent an aspect *of* education.

Indeed, that is precisely what the texts suggest. In both traditions, the language connecting education to the 'way' is teleological: education is meant to accomplish something, namely, to enable people to walk in the 'way' of the Lord (e.g. Gen. 18:19; Prov. 5:21). And Michael V. Fox says much of the same for Proverbs 1–9.[12] It is important to point out, therefore, that even if the 'way'

---

9 Habel's influential work, 'Symbolism of Wisdom'. For an analysis of the words used for 'way', see Kim, *Coherence*, 5–8. Two other proposals for ground metaphors in Prov 1–9, which, while tenable, have not garnered as much of a following, include Woman Wisdom (Camp, 'Woman') and 'liminality' (Leeuwen, 'Liminality') For a helpful but brief critique of Van Leeuwen, see Fox, *Proverbs 1–9*, 129 fn 115.

10 According to Michael V. Fox, *Proverbs 1–9*, 130, the characterisation of life as polarities, that is, as two ways to live, is unique to Proverbs among ancient literature. The closest parallel of Egyptian literature only features the way of life.

11 Habel, 'Symbolism'.

12 According to Fox, 'Education in wisdom is needed to enable a person to [...] classify each path and deduce its end point from its quality at point of entry' (*Proverbs 1–9*, 131).

is a root, or nuclear, metaphor in Proverbs 1–9, it is not necessarily a root metaphor for education. Perhaps it is better to say that the 'way' is a metaphor for life[13] and that education, the focus of Proverbs 1–9, aims to prepare people for life. As such, the 'way' is not so much a metaphor for education itself as for the *goal* of education.

The Father and Son

The second common metaphor is that of the father-son relationship. Proverbs uses the language of 'father' and 'son' to represent the roles within education: teacher and student. Some have taken this to mean that 'father' *means* 'teacher' and 'son' *means* 'student', but this is not quite true.[14] The root idea here is not that of teaching or studying but that of being a father or being a son. To be sure, teaching and studying are important responsibilities of fathers and sons, and ones that are foregrounded in Proverbs, but they are still only part of a larger picture for each role. We shall speak more to this in a moment. For now, it is important to note that the family, or the 'house of the father', is the primary context in view, and teaching/learning serve within this. That is why mothers are characterised as teachers and daughters as the crown jewel of education (Prov. 1:8; 4:3; 6:2; 31:1-2, 10-31). The language of 'father' and 'son', therefore, is shorthand for the calling upon parents to teach their children in the home.

Yet there is another teacher in the book of Proverbs: Wisdom herself. Just as parents teach children in the home, so Woman Wisdom teaches them outside the home. The relationship between the two spheres of teaching emerges in Proverbs 1–9, where the ten 'lectures' of the father are interspersed with five 'interludes' of Woman Wisdom.[15] In the lectures, the father exhorts his son to

---

13 Waltke is perhaps closer to this idea when he summarises 'way' as having three interrelated meanings: 'course of life', 'conduct of life', and 'consequences of that conduct': 'In sum, "way" is a metaphor for the deed-destiny nexus upheld by God, the knowledge of which is necessary for wisdom' (*Proverbs 1–15*, 194).

14 Fox, 'Social Location', 230–232. Often the equating of father/son with teacher/student is attributed to parallels in Egyptian wisdom texts, but Fox shows that it is not true there, either.

15 The language of 'lectures' and 'interludes' is from Fox, 'Ideas of Wisdom', 614. He prefers the term 'lecture' to 'instruction' to keep from confusing the specific material from the genre, which is typically called 'instruction'. Whybray was the first to identify the ten lectures in *Wisdom in Proverbs*. But Fox includes more verses in the ten lectures than Whybray did: 1:8–19; 2:1–22; 3:1–12; 3:21–35; 4:1–9; 4:10–19; 4:20–27; 5:1–23; 6:20–35; 7:1–27. The interludes are: 1:20–33; 3:13–20; 6:1–19; 8:1–36; 9:1–18.

'listen' to his instruction. His chief aim, however, is not merely to make his son hearken to his voice, but to teach him to pursue something greater: Wisdom herself (Prov. 4:7).

In this way the father's instruction is outwardly oriented, pointing out through the door of the home into the world beyond. And that is where the interludes pick up. They contain the voice of Woman Wisdom, calling in through the doorway for the child to come out into the world and find her. Yet when she invites people to 'listen' to her, it is a slightly different kind of listening: it is listening with the eyes. Since Wisdom is the architect of creation, it is in observing the workings of creation—both in the natural and social worlds—that a person 'listens' to her (3:19-22). In essence, then, the father and Woman Wisdom serve as complementary teachers. The father learns by observing Woman Wisdom and this forms the substance of his instruction. The child, by listening to this instruction, learns to do the same for himself (e.g. 7:1-7).

The House

There are metaphors for the goal of education (the 'way') and for its participants ('father' and 'son'), but where is the metaphor for schooling itself? Recent research has highlighted the importance of the 'house-building' metaphor to Israelite thinking in general and Proverbs in particular. It is therefore worth exploring its relationship to education.

Ray Van Leeuwen has been most helpful in illuminating the metaphor's influence on scripture.[16] He has shown, in the first place, that the 'house' was a foundational metaphor for Israel's overall thinking: the "house of the father' functioned materially and culturally to organize the life world of ancient societies'.[17] That is, the ancients envisaged the cosmos itself as a 'house', God's house, and all other domains as 'houses' that fit within God's 'house'. Israel envisaged these different 'houses' fitting within each other like Russian dolls: the family (the 'house' of the father) was the smallest 'house', fitting within the next biggest house, typically the kingdom (the king's 'house'), which fit within

---

16 Ray Van Leeuwen, 'Cosmos, Temple, House'; see also Van Leeuwen, 'Building God's House'.
17 Van Leeuwen, 'Cosmos', 68. The 'house of the father' typically included a father and mother and their unwed children, along with their son's wives and children. It would also include the father's unwed aunts and sometimes unwed uncles, not to mention everybody's cattle and servants. All such people lived together on one property and often under one roof, hence the term 'father's house'.

God's 'house' the cosmos.

This was more than conceptual, for it also carried with it an ethos. It implied a certain kind of behaviour, which may be called a 'form of *imitatio dei*'.[18] Because God's cosmos was the 'house' in which all other 'houses' dwelt, it stood as the model. Or perhaps more accurately, God himself stood as the model builder. Whenever a person set about 'house-building', therefore, it was meant to be done according to the model given by God. The extent to which it achieved this goal determined the goodliness and sustenance of the 'house'.

But how exactly were people to imitate God's manner of building? By building 'with wisdom'. Wisdom was the defining feature of the building of God's own house, and wisdom would allow others to do likewise. This principle was especially visible in an ancient convention known as the 'wisdom statement'. Most of the archeological evidence for this comes from royal building projects, where kings inscribed on buildings a declaration of their wisdom. The inscription, in essence, was evidence the king had followed the divine model and his building was rooted in the cosmic order. There are two close parallels in the Old Testament, found in the building accounts of the tabernacle (Exod. 31:3) and temple (1 Kgs. 7:14).

Yet it has become clear the convention, and the ethos it represented, extended to common homes as well.[19] And this is where Van Leeuwen makes his chief contribution. He argues the book of Proverbs applies the same thinking to the house of the father, as the building block of Israelite society. He points to two passages in support:

> The Lord founded the earth *with wisdom*,
>   *With skill* he established the heavens.
> *With his knowledge* the deeps broke open,
>   and the clouds drop down the dew (Prov. 3:19-20).

> *With wisdom* a house is built,
>   and *with skill* it is established
> *With knowledge* the rooms are filled
>   with all precious and pleasant riches. (Prov. 24:3-4).

---

18 Van Leeuwen, 'Cosmos', 81.
19 Van Leeuwen, 'Cosmos', 82, cites the example given by Richard Ellis, *Foundation Deposits*, 163–165, which points out the striking example of a building statement of wisdom in the private home. Van Leeuwen's work especially leverages Ellis'.

The repetition between the passages is meant to highlight the connection between the two builders: the builder of the family home is to imitate the builder of the cosmos.

This suggests that Proverbs is to family what the tabernacle/temple passages (Exod. 31:3; 1 Kgs. 7:14) are to royalty: a text modeling 'house-building'. Each models how the builders are to go about constructing the 'houses' for which they are responsible. Proverbs stands apart, however, in that it is also considered an educational text. What we have called modeling in house-building usually goes by the name of wisdom education. This in itself suggests the house metaphor is important to the idea of education.[20] But can something more be said?

Returning to the house-building passages in Proverbs 3:19-20 and 24:3-4, we see that both appear immediately before instructional passages. To some this simply represents a seam in the text, where one type of wisdom saying has been stitched to another,[21] with the telltale sign being the difference in mood: the house-building passages appear in the indicative, describing how things are built, while the instruction passages appear in the imperative, exhorting people how to behave. What could be more different than a description and a command?

Ironically, that difference may be the very thing that binds the passages together. Bruce Waltke has argued that the house-building texts actually represent 'the typical introductory educational saying', which 'marks itself as an introduction' by following certain conventions.[22] The move from description to exhortation is central among these conventions, for, in wisdom thinking, what God's world *is* (description) determines how humans *ought* to live (imperative). In other words, the placement of the passages is not accidental but intentional, even necessary, because it represents the very essence of the wisdom pursuit: how observation of the world leads to right living. And the fact that in each case the foundational idea is in the form of a house-building metaphor, suggests the metaphor itself might be foundational to Proverbs' vision of education. It portrays God's creation as the great schoolroom after which parents model their own.

---

20   Van Leeuwen does not himself make the connection, though it is difficult to discern his perspective since his most sustained work on the metaphor has come after his work referencing education. For example, see 'Liminality' and 'Building God's House'.
21   E.g. see Fox, 'Ideas of Wisdom', 615; R. Whybray, *Composition*, 19; and McKane, *Proverbs*, 7, 397.
22   Waltke, *Proverbs: 15–31*, 270. See p. 271 for the particular conventions. See also Waltke, *Proverbs: 1–15*, 263.

Wonder in Education

This provides a path to wonder, for it brings us into conversation with William Brown's seminal work on wonder in the wisdom literature. Brown has sought to develop wonder as the engine of the wisdom pursuit, seeing it as the essential desire motivating children to pursue wisdom in the first place. In this he speaks to a longstanding question in Proverbs study: How exactly does Proverbs, as an educational text, cultivate a desire for wisdom?[23]

Brown's view is that Proverbs is a 'manual of desires'.[24] Its purpose is not merely to train children *in* wisdom, but to cultivate an appetite *for* wisdom. In this prologue in Proverbs 1–9 plays a key role through its depictions of Woman Wisdom, which are meant to whet the appetite. Brown particularly highlights how food imagery assists, with chapter 9 portraying two banquet tables: one set by Woman Wisdom and one by Madam Folly. Wisdom's food is nourishing and life-giving, while Folly's is alluring but lethal. The role of these images, therefore, is to characterise wise sayings as 'edible words': 'the metaphor of Wisdom's lavish banquet marks each proverb as a nugget of nourishment. Proverbs, varied as they are, provide the rich nutrients for developing and sustaining right character'.[25] By feasting on proverbs a person feeds character and nourishes his life.

Yet as Brown recognises, there is still the question of how to find wisdom in the world. To consume a proverb one must be available in the first place. This is fine for children, who are given wisdom on a platter during their parents' instruction. But what about parents, where do they get these morsels of wisdom? As already noted, adults find wisdom by observing the workings of God's 'house'. They listen with their eyes and distill their learning into proverbs, which their children consume with their ears. At this point the question of hunger arises again: if this is how people find wisdom in the world, what motivates them to pursue it in the first place?

For Brown, Proverbs 8 provides the answer. Just as Wisdom's banquet (Prov. 9) whets the appetite for *listening* to instruction, so her depiction in Proverbs 8 kindles a desire for *looking* for wisdom. Proverbs 8 is well known, of course, as the definitive portrait of Woman Wisdom, but Brown draws attention to the character of Woman Wisdom as the 'ideal inquirer', the model for people to

---

23 For example, see Fox, 'Ideas of Wisdom', 621.
24 Brown, *Wisdom's Wonder*, 66, quoting Anne Stewart.
25 Brown, *Wisdom's Wonder*, 58. See, for example, Prov. 10:21, 31; 16:24; 18:20. Brown develops this idea more fully in 'Didactic Power'.

imitate (vv. 29b-31).[26] For the current discussion, the passage also contains a rather interesting figure:

> When [YHWH] inscribed the foundations of the earth,
>   I was beside him growing up.
> I was his delight day by day,
>   playing before him every moment,
> playing in his inhabited world,
>   my delighting in the offspring of *adam* (8:29b-31)

What might be expected is the figure of a serious sage, furrowed in the contemplation *of* creation, but what we find instead is a frolicking child 'delighting' and 'playing' *in* creation. What is it, then, that the passage commends?

Brown suggests there are two elements in view.[27] Firstly, the heart of the wisdom pursuit is portrayed as a childlike 'delighting' in God's handiwork and 'playing' before him. The language implies an act of worship, but rather than a restrained kind,[28] it is the kind that is carefree and self-abandoned, the kind that might offend those with certain sensibilities, such as David's wife Michal (2 Sam. 6:14-23). It is no small irony that Proverbs portrays a childlike disposition as the key to children maturing into adulthood (8:30).

Secondly, the passage commends a unique perspective of creation, for in place of a wild and alien landscape, stands a 'playhouse'.[29] Humans are not introduced as 'complete stranger[s]'[30] but as children in their father's home, which he has built with them in mind. Indeed, the 'playhouse' has been created so that they might take up Wisdom's invitation to explore and discover the manifold mysteries hidden within. As such, the overarching sense of the portrait is '*familial* belongingness':

> The intensely personal relationship between Yahweh and Wisdom is first and foremost the fruit of an inviolable familial relationship. Wisdom's play is the natural and appropriate response to the formation of the cosmic domicile, the *bet YHWH* [house of Yahweh][31]

---

26 Brown, *Wisdom's Wonder*, 51. See his discussion in footnote 62 about the textual difficulties in this passage.
27 Brown developed this previously in *Ethos*, 271–280.
28 The word pair 'delight' and 'play' only occurs in the context of worship. See Waltke, *Proverbs 1–15*, 421–422, and Brown, *Ethos*, 278–279.
29 Brown, *Ethos*, 277.
30 Von Rad, *Wisdom in Israel*, 3.
31 Brown, *Ethos*, 279.

Thus, the disposition of the ideal inquirer depicted here is to view God's world as a playhouse and to delight and play in it.

Brown identifies this disposition as wonder.[32] He sees it, in essence, as one of humanity's basic instincts taking shape in Israel's unique worldview.[33] That instinct might be understood generally as curiosity that grows from twin impulses: 'inquisitive awe', which sparks interest in the unknown, and the '*eros of inquiry*', which draws a person toward discovering more about the unknown.[34] In Israel's worldview, and Proverbs in particular, the curiosity becomes inherently personal and theological. Inquisitive awe grows out of a disposition of worship, and the *eros* of inquiry out of a desire to know more of God and his world. And this is done at the invitation of Wisdom herself.

Conclusion

Although aspects of Brown's view can be critiqued,[35] it nevertheless helps to locate wonder within Proverbs' vision of education. Firstly, it shows an important point of connection between the two houses—argued above to be the core educational environments. The house of the father (family home) is the foundational environment, where children learn to listen to wise instruction. But such listening only prepares children to *receive* wisdom, not to *find* it for themselves. As such, it points children toward the world outside: God's 'house', where they meet Woman Wisdom, the architect of God's house, who takes them by the hand and teaches them how to find wisdom. Yet there is one more step in their education: not merely to find wisdom, but to *embody* it. Woman

---

32 It is interesting that O'Donovan, in a passing comment, once said the book of Proverbs 'remains poised at the point of wonder'. See O'Donovan, 'Response', 114. Thanks to Craig Bartholomew for bringing this to my attention.
33 Brown, 'Wonder of it All', 35.
34 Brown, *Wisdom's Wonder*, 24.
35 To my mind, two major concerns exist. One is that his description of wonder is similar to another central wisdom concept: the fear of the Lord. Traditionally, this has been understood as growing out of two impulses as well: mystery that frightens (*mysterium tremendum*) and mystery that fascinates (*mysterium fascinosum*). Not only that, but Brown's own summary of wonder is 'fear seeking understanding' (*Wisdom's Wonder*, 24). We might also raise the related, broader question of how Brown's notion of wonder relates to the classic notion of the sublime. The second concern is in ascribing so much influence to something that leaves such little linguistic trace in the text. There are but a handful of instances in the wisdom literature, and only in Proverbs and Job at that, for the word related to wonder (*pala'*: Job 5:9; 9:10; 10:16; 37:5; 37:14; 42:3; Prov. 30:18). Neither of these necessarily undermines Brown's view, but they do show some need for further clarity moving forward.

Wisdom's goal is to train children in a unique form of *imitatio dei*, where they observe God's house-building in order to build their own homes in a similar manner. After all, that is the goal of wisdom education in Proverbs: to train children in house-building. Wonder is important, because it serves as the animating spark in the *imitatio dei*. Woman Wisdom is the ideal enquirer (8:29-31), whom children are to imitate in pursuing wisdom, and her chief attribute is wonder. If children are to find wisdom in the world and embody it in house-building, they must be wonderers.

Secondly, Brown's view provides a way of understanding wisdom education as a faith experience. To begin with, the call to wisdom is not a quest out onto an alien landscape but an invitation *into* the Father's house. Everything is personal, nothing is abstract. The animating spark of wonder rises up from worship of God, and its pursuit happens before God and in hopes of finding him. Indeed, the whole pursuit begins in the invitation to frolic and delight in God's playhouse.

Implications for Theological Education

One quickly realises that Proverbs' view of wonder cannot be plucked from its context and put within another, at least not without some work. It is too interwoven within the book's vision of education. The intricate relationship between houses (schooling environments), builders (teachers), and inhabitants (students) essentially requires that wonder remains *in situ*. But how then can it be brought to bear on contemporary theological education at all? The best way, it seems, is to work at the level of ethos. This allows the preservation of the integrity of Proverbs' vision of education while bringing it into conversation with other curricula.

Proverbs' ethos of education is *divine hospitality*.[36] The God of the cosmos invites humanity into his house, beckoning, like the Ghost of Christmas Present, 'Come in and know me better!'[37] This frames theology as invitation: God's invitation to come to know him by wondering at his handiwork. Framing theological study in this way would affect its educational ethos in at least three ways:[38]

---

36 Brown suggests something similar: *Ethos*, 297–300; *Wisdom's Wonder*, 53–54.
37 Dickens, *A Christmas Carol*.
38 For a discussion of some of these things from a more philosophical angle, see Fiddes, *Seeing the World*.

1. Closure versus openness: Traditionally, as most would acknowledge, theological education has been shaped by doctrinal concerns. But what often goes unnoticed is how the implied values, or ethos, of the doctrinal pursuit have also shaped theological study itself, especially in its underlying view of the path of progress toward knowing God: to move from openness to closure.[39] Here openness signals rudimentary or unclear thinking, and closure the pinnacle or goal. This ethos surfaces at curious times, such as when students are given space for creative thinking, but they simply want the 'right' answer. This is not necessarily students being lazy or mercenary, but a case of their living out the values they have absorbed. While it would take some thought to implement, introducing the idea of divine hospitality would add a helpful corrective. Students would learn that a certain kind of openness, sacred wonder, is in fact necessary for maturity in faith. Like the ancient Israelites, we would thus hold in tandem both exploration *and* systemisation as modes of knowing God.
2. Observation versus participation: The Enlightenment is another force that has shaped theological education, but which has not been adequately challenged is. In particular, the subject-object distinction is assumed, in that the role of students, as subjects, is to observe and analyse their object of study. But this notion is difficult to maintain, for all learning is inherently participatory.[40] To separate students from their object of study is like teaching surfing on the shore. It is woefully incomplete. Nowhere is this truer than in theological education, where the object of study is a God who calls people into relationship with himself. Ironically, scripture itself would seem to see the Enlightenment learner as a failed learner: one who knows about God without knowing God. Reframing theological inquiry as divine invitation would help change this culture.
3. Disenchantment versus enchantment: The state of theological education, in North America at least, is often summarised in a play on words: it is said that 'seminaries' are 'cemeteries'. This refers to number the students who enter theological study with enthusiasm and curiosity but leave with disinterest and bewilderment. Exactly why this is true has been the matter of much debate, but one reason that has not received due attention is the

---

39 Fiddes, *Promised End*, 7.
40 Michael Polanyi has argued this most persuasively. In recent times, the work of Polanyi has been parlayed into religious studies. For example, see Ferrer & Sherman, *The Participatory Turn*.

'disenchantment' of theological study. Students believe they are entering a Narnian land where Aslan roams and at any moment might turn up; but upon entry they learn they have come to Narnia in a time that is 'always winter, but it never gets to Christmas'.[41] They feel caught in a land where there is little hope of Aslan turning up, and many choose to leave instead. Yet this need not be true. Proverbs' vision of the world is Israel's version of 'a great enchanted garden' (*Zaubergarten*).[42] God has built it with marvels and mysteries, and he invites us to discover these by delighting and playing before him in his playhouse.

Bibliography

Bartholomew, Craig, Ryan O'Dowd. *Old Testament Wisdom Literature: A Theological Introduction* (Downers Grove, IL: Intervarsity, 2011).

Brown, William. *Wisdom's Wonder: Character, Creation, and Crisis in the Bible's Wisdom Literature* (Grand Rapids, MI: Eerdmans, 2014).

Brown, William. 'The Wonder of It All: Faith, Creation, and Wisdom', *Journal for Preachers* 34/4 (2011), 33–38.

Brown, William. 'The Didactic Power of Metaphor in the Aphoristic Sayings of Proverbs', *Journal for the Study of the Old Testament* 29.2 (2004), 133–154.

Brown, William. *The Ethos of the Cosmos: The Genesis of the Moral Imagination in the Bible* (Grand Rapids, MI: Eerdmans, 1999).

Camp, Claudia. 'Woman Wisdom as Root Metaphor: A Theological Consideration', in Kenneth G. Hoglund, E. F. Huwiler, J. T. Glass, and R. W. Lee (eds.), *The Listening Heart: Essays in Wisdom and the Psalms in Honour of Roland E.Murphy* (Sheffield: Sheffield Press, 1987), 45–76.

Chalmers, Aaron. *Exploring the Religion of Ancient Israel: Prophet, Priest, Sage & People* (Downers Grove, IL: InterVarsity, 2012).

Crenshaw, James. *Old Testament Wisdom: An Introduction* (Louisville: Westminster John Knox, 2010).

Dickens, Charles. *A Christmas Carol* (London: Chapman & Hall, 1843).

Ellis, Richard. *Foundation Deposits in Ancient Mesopotamia* (New Haven: Yale University Press, 1968).

Ferrer, Jorge, & Jacob Sherman. *The Participatory Turn: Spirituality, Mysticism, Religious Studies* (Albany, NY: State University of New York, 2008).

---

41 Lewis, *The Lion*, 43.
42 Weber, *Sociology of Religion*, 270.

Fiddes, Paul. *Seeing the World and Knowing God: Hebrew Wisdom and Christian Doctrine in a Late-Modern Context* (Oxford: Oxford University Press, 2013).

Fiddes, Paul. *The Promised End: Eschatology in Theology and Literature* (Oxford: Blackwell, 2000).

Fox, Michael V. *Proverbs 1–9* (New York: Doubleday, 2000).

Fox, Michael V. 'Ideas of Wisdom in Proverbs 1–9', *Journal of Biblical Literature* 116.4 (1997), 613–663.

Fox, Michael V. 'The Social Location of the Book of Proverbs', in Michael V. Fox, Victor Avigdor Hurowitz, Avi M. Hurvitz, Michael L. Klein, Baruch J. Schwartz, and Nili Shupak (eds.), *Texts, Temples, and Traditions: A Tribute to Menachem Haran* (Winona Lake, IN: Eisenbrauns, 1996), 227–239.

Habel, Norman. 'The Symbolism of Wisdom in Proverbs 1–9', *Interpretation* 26 (1972), 131–157.

Hill, Andrew. 'Education in Biblical Times', in Walter Elwell (ed.), *Evangelical Dictionary of Biblical Theology* (Grand Rapids, MI: Baker, 1996), 192–196.

Kim, Seenam. *The Coherence of the Collections in the Book of Proverbs* (Eugene, OR: Pickwick, 2007).

Leeuwen, Ray Van. 'Cosmos, Temple, House: Building and Wisdom in Mesopotamia and Israel', in Richard Clifford (ed.), *Wisdom Literature in Mesopotamia and Israel* (Atlanta: Society of Biblical Literature, 2007), 67–90.

Leeuwen, Ray Van. 'Building God's House: An Exploration in Wisdom', in J.I. Packer and Sven Soderlund (eds.), *The Way of Wisdom: Essays in Honor of Bruce K. Waltke* (Grand Rapids, MI: Zondervan, 2000), 204–211.

Leeuwen, Ray Van. 'Liminality and Worldview in Proverbs 1–9', *Semeia* 50 (1990), 111–144.

Lewis, C.S. *The Lion, the Witch, and the Wardrobe* (New York: Harper Collins, 1994).

McKane, William. *Proverbs: A New Approach* (London: SCM, 1970).

Millard, A.R. 'Sages, Schools, Education', in Peter Enns & Tremper Longman III (eds.), *Dictionary of the Old Testament: Wisdom, Poetry, & Writings* (Downers Grove, IL: InterVarsity, 2008), 704–710.

Murphy, Roland. *The Tree of life: An exploration of Biblical Wisdom Literature* (New York: Doubleday, 1990).

O'Donovan, Oliver. 'Response to Craig Bartholomew', in Craig Bartholomew, Jonathan Chaplin, Robert Song & Al Wolters (eds.), *A Royal Priesthood? The Use of the Bible Ethically and Politically: A Dialogue with Oliver O'Donovan* (Grand Rapids, MI: Zondervan, 2002), 113–115.

Perdue, Leo. *Wisdom & Creation* (Nashville: Abingdon, 1994).

Rad, Gerhard von. *Wisdom in Israel* (J.D. Martin, transl.; Nashville: SCM, 1972).

Waltke, Bruce. *The Book of Proverbs: 1–15* (Grand Rapids, MI: Eerdmans, 2004).

Waltke, Bruce. *The Book of Proverbs: 15–31* (Grand Rapids, MI: Eerdmans, 2005).

Weber, Max. *The Sociology of Religion* (Ephraim Fischoff, transl.; Boston: Beacon, 1963 [1922]).

Whybray, R.N. *Composition of the Book of Proverbs* (Sheffield: Sheffield Press, 1994).

Whybray, R.N. *Wisdom in Proverbs* (London: SCM, 1965).

A.J. Culp
Malyon College
aj.culp@malyon.edu.au

17 | TEXT AND INTERPRETATION

FROM CLASSICAL MUSIC TO BIBLICAL STUDIES

Abstract

Classical musicians and biblical scholars have the reading and interpretation of texts in common. The fundament of both disciplines is facility in basic techniques followed by interpretative skills. As a professional violinist and lecturer in Biblical Studies this chapter reflects on my experience of the teaching of Biblical Studies influenced by a musician's training. My training as a musician is presented in terms of—technique, immersion, and encounter with major concepts. The three aspects then become the paradigm for presenting the teaching of Biblical Studies in the later part of the essay. A range of examples is given to demonstrate ways that students can receive an experience of the Bible.

The Sydney College of Divinity organised a conference in April 2017 with the title 'Wondering about God Together: Research-Led Learning and Teaching in Theological Education'. Two phrases used to describe the theme of the conference were 'creative activity' and 'multi-perspectval approach'. This essay started as a response to those two phrases. I work as a professional violinist with the Auckland Philharmonia Orchestra—a creative arts environment. I also teach undergraduate Biblical Studies at Good Shepherd College, the tertiary theological formation institution of Aotearoa New Zealand in the Catholic tradition—an educational environment. As I have trained in two different fields and work in them, this, I believe, allows me to write on multi-perspectival approaches to learning.

This essay is anecdotal, based on my own experience of practising the violin and performing, and also on my research of biblical texts, writing and teaching. It does not build on educational or pedagogical theories. How I became and continue to be a musician, interpreting and performing musical compositions, influences how I teach Biblical Studies. My teaching of Biblical Studies focuses on text—learning to read and interpret text. The biblical text is the primary source. It is the biblical text that has inspired communities and their leaders for hundreds of years in different traditions. What wise people and scholars have written about biblical texts can be insightful but these learned writings are secondary sources. The disciplines of Biblical Studies and the Performing Arts have the interpretation of texts in common.

Many students at Good Shepherd College have completed tertiary studies and worked in various fields but as regards theology studies they are undergraduates. My teaching aims at giving a foundation in Biblical Studies on which students can build. If they continue in the field of Biblical Studies as their particular area of theological talent or interest, then a biblical base is in place.

Before proceeding, two working definitions are necessary. Firstly, interpretation is understood as making sense of, or facilitating the meaning of a text. Secondly, text refers to good editions of primary sources. In the context of Biblical Studies good editions are extant Hebrew and Greek texts or a translation of those texts such as the New Revised Standard Version (NRSV) which aims to render closely the sense of the original languages. In the context of classical music a good edition is an *Urtext* (original) edition such as Henle or Bärenreiter.[1]

'Text' consists of written words or notated music, the means by which writers or composers communicate their ideas. Notation is an attempt by an author, or authors, at a written rendition of the idea they want to communicate. However, notation is limited. Not every aspect of an idea can be notated—gaps, inconsistencies and ambiguities are sometimes apparent in texts. Experience and interpretation allow one to read into gaps and deal with ambiguities. However, interpretation primarily draws on standard skills or technique.

---

1   Urtext editions are renditions of the original musical composition. The choice of what exactly goes into the text is supervised by an editor chosen by the publishing company of the music. The editor often has access to the hand written composer's manuscript, or a facsimile, and in some instances the parts which were used by musicians for the first performance of the composition. Parts used for the first performance may incorporate changes requested by the composer (or conductor, or performers) during rehearsals for the first performance. Henle and Bärenreiter are examples of two companies based in Germany that publish Urtext editions.

Good training and facility in the standard techniques of a discipline provide the basis of interpretation. The first part of this essay therefore addresses training. Three points are taken from my life and development as a musician—technique, immersion, and encounter with major ideas. These points become the paradigm for the second part of the essay, which elaborates on the three points with examples from my teaching of Biblical Studies.

The Classical Musician

Technique

The first point regarding training as a musician concerns technique. I completed my undergraduate violin studies at the University of Auckland, knowing in the 1970s that New Zealand was distant from Europe—the origin of classical music composition and performance. I went to Vienna, Austria, for post-graduate music studies. A violin technique in which both left and right hand function effortlessly is essential. The intricacies of violin technique cannot be dwelt on here. It is taken as understood that a good training in violin technique and continuing to practise is essential to stay in form for performance. As a professional sportsperson must daily train the body, so too must a performing artist.

Technique is the medium through which musical ideas are expressed. It can be said that musical interpretation is only as advanced as the degree to which one has the means to express a musical idea. In other words, the sophistication of interpretation is allied with technical means. However, it is also true that the intention of interpretation can be stronger and greater than what may be called the mere means. Great compositions such as J. S. Bach's St Matthew or St John Passion, or Mozart's 'The Magic Flute', have a drama and artistic force that carries beyond the means of the interpreter.

Immersion

The second point is the concept of immersion as part of training. In Vienna, I was exposed to a music smorgasbord, to a wide variety of music in many settings. I worked in the Austrian Radio Orchestra where in addition to standard repertoire, a lot of contemporary and twentieth century Austrian compositions were played. I also gigged (musician's speak for extra part-time work) at the Viennese Chamber Opera, playing the early operas of Mozart, written in his teenage years, for example, *Bastien und Bastienne* or *La finta Semplice*. Sunday mornings were busy playing Haydn, Mozart, and Schubert Masses at various churches for services. Then I played baroque violin in Melkus' *Capella Academia*. Summers were full of music festivals. One particularly noteworthy festival was at the *Universitätskirche* where music dramas composed by Austrian emperors of the Baroque period were performed.

Immersion in life in Vienna gave me a music education via osmosis. With the passing of time, natural inculturation occurred. I learned German and started to read Austrian literature. I ate Austrian food, visited historic sites and hiked in the mountains. The speed of life in a city is related to the tempi (speeds) of its music.

Think of dance forms in triple time. Minuets by Wolfgang Amadeus Mozart (1756-1791) and Joseph Haydn (1732-1809), or waltzes by Johann Strauss II (1825-99) may come to mind. Gustav Mahler (1860-1911) uses yet again another dance form in triple time, the Ländler, in his 'First symphony'. Though the dance forms—the Minuet, Ländler, and Waltz—are all in triple time, they are different. The Ländler is slower than the Waltz. Its origins were in the village where it was danced with the stomping of feet, hence it is heavy-ish. The stylised symphonic Minuet is associated with the royal court and nobility. The Waltz is associated with ballroom dancing and can therefore not be played too fast. The speed of each of the three dance forms is a little different. Each dance in triple time with its particular spice and sound conjures up different associations. It is easier to learn the feeling of the dances with their characteristic lilt and emphases in their country of origin. The dances were appropriated from a folk setting then morphed into something new with different instruments for a new context.

The flavour of different dances in triple time is not learned from a book, but by working in the world of music. Some things are learned through immersion in an environment, as an apprentice learns hands-on training with a person skilled in the craft.

Encounter with Major Ideas

The third point is encounter with major ideas. In Vienna a significant person for me was a violinist, Eduard Melkus. Studying with him was my encounter with major concepts that continue to influence me today and make me think:

- the nature of baroque violin playing versus the modern violin;

- the relationship between music and architecture;
- the relationship between words and music.

The significance of all these concepts and their ramifications cannot be demonstrated. However, the importance of the relationship between words and music is addressed. In English there are hard consonants such as d and t and soft consonants such as p and f. In violin playing the difference between these consonants is rendered with a harder or softer touch in the right arm into the violin bow. The ability to start the bow moving with different consonantal sounds is related to the words of a language. The lines and forms that Bach gives to a musical instrument often imitate the consonants and vowels, shapes and sentences of the German texts in his vocal music. As Western languages have a wide range of consonantal sounds—hard to soft with a direct to less direct beginning of the sound—so too use of a violin bow requires a wide range of expressive suppleness.

Another example pertaining to words and music is the difference between two forms of church music—chant and song. In the case of chant, music serves the words, that is, the words have priority. If notated music is given for the chant with X number of beats to a bar you will generally find that the composer has tried to transliterate the natural rhythm of the words into notated format. In praxis the correct rhythm is not the notated rhythm.[2] It is the rhythm that results when the words are spoken as natural delivery—with local accent and emphases. One of the psalm refrains used by a New Zealand composer, Douglas Mews (1918-1993) is 'The Lord has become my defender; in him I put my trust'. When the words of the refrain are spoken aloud as though proclaiming them, it shows where syllables are stressed or appear to have more weight. Likely the rendition resembles the following where the stressed or longer syllables are italicised, 'The *Lord* has be*come* my de*fen*der; in *him* I *put* my *trust*'. A natural break or breath, linked with meaning, occurs after the words defender and trust. Mews' composition gives the required space for a breath at these two points. Note too that '*come* my de-' and '*fend*-er in' fall into a unit with three parts so a 3/8 or 6/8 compound time signature suits the refrain better

---

2   The difference between notated (printed) rhythm and realised (when sung in communities) rhythm can be observed with songs such as Dan Schutte's 'City of God' or 'Though the Mountains May Fall', and John Foley's 'One Bread, One Body', found in the song collection, *As One Voice*. Congregations tend to sing their own rhythmic version and not the syncopated or swung-rhythms going over bar lines as printed.

than a simple time such as 3/4. Mews' music for the refrain supports the rhythm and natural stresses of the text when spoken.

The above two examples, on consonants and chant, demonstrate some of the links between music and words though many more examples are possible. I thank Melkus for setting me off thinking about the never-ending links between words and music.

Different elements that made up my early adult education as a violinist were—developing technique, immersion in the music world and encounter with major concepts. It is easy to be young, have potential, and if lucky have transforming encounters. However, it takes the rest of one's life to develop the potential and the art. The professional musician is faced with having to work at technical exercises every day they play. This never stops. Exercising is part of on-going daily discipline.

The Mentor in Biblical Studies

These three points—technique, immersion and major ideas—can now be applied to the teaching of Biblical Studies, drawing upon examples used for the course: 'Introduction to Biblical Studies'.

Technique

Students are expected to prepare a set biblical text for each week of the semester. As there are twelve weeks in a semester this means the exercise of text preparation is practised at least twelve times.

Preparing a text involves techniques such as:

- reading the text several times, preferably aloud;
- breaking the text down into units of meaning and giving each unit a title;
- listing the different characters, or voices;
- listing different places, locations;
- noting the social and historical world suggested by the text;
- noting any words/phrases/places that are not understood;
- noting references, explicit and implicit, to God;
- recording questions.

The above points are technical, skills learned through practice. Further preparation involving factors outside the text are:

- thinking about the genre (style or category or kind of writing);
- considering the possible original audience;
- considering the possible dating of the text.

Some points can be researched via the biblical text alone. Other points require reading secondary sources. The set text for the course is *The New Oxford Annotated Bible* (NOAB). As the NOAB is a study Bible in addition to the biblical text there are introductory articles and commentaries. This means a student is not left to struggle with what may perhaps be taken for an incomprehensible biblical text. The NOAB commentaries offer reputable guidelines for understanding the text.

Exercise in the field of Biblical Studies is firstly, reading the biblical text and reflecting on its meaning. When queries arise, answers may be found in secondary sources. Then one needs to return to the biblical text. A further round of questioning, research, and understanding may ensue. The cycle continues—biblical text to secondary sources, then back to the biblical text. The constant is the biblical text even as understanding of the text changes.

In addition to grappling with and researching various aspects of a text, interpretation involves insight or the sixth sense. Interpretation is an unending mix of basic technique with the addition of insight but basic reading techniques cannot be bypassed. For students taking an introductory course on the Bible there are a lot of firsts—reading the Bible (not reading about the Bible), learning to use biblical examples and explain them, trying out the concepts of the field, and using newly learnt terms. Practice, lots of writing practice, means that writing techniques can improve. Why should academic writing be different from violin playing? Every day I pick up my violin, I have to practise basic technique. I aim to teach students good techniques for reading biblical texts. How they interpret biblical texts for themselves and for their apostolic work into the future is their own journey.

Immersion

Immersion in a discipline is about soaking-up its environment, participating in its world, and having experiences. To have an experience the senses need to be activated. Active arts such as drama and music engage the senses as they require use of the voice and the body. Two forms of drama suited to enacting biblical texts are the voice-drama which uses different voices, and the biblio-drama, where various characters speak and act. Texts such as Amos 5:1-27 or Psalm

22:1-31 with their changing moods and tones are well suited to voice-dramas. The narratives 'David and Goliath (1 Sam 17:1-57)' and 'The Samaritan Woman at the Well (John 4:5-30)' lend themselves to biblio-dramas. Different characters, the narrator included, are involved in the action. The stories have a beginning, middle and end—tension builds within the plot that is then resolved.

The human voice has a broad expressive range from speaking and singing to producing voluntary or involuntary sounds, thereby enabling the expression of a wide range of emotions. A joyful voice can induce laughter. A sad voice can lead to weeping. Volume adds to the emotional character of singing which can range from loud (as in a rage) to soft (as in a whisper). An individual is a single voice but many voices become a chorus, perhaps standing for a people, nation, or assembly. Drama also requires use of the body—movement with different gestures and postures. Voice and body possibilities are mentioned because students have bodies and voices with which they can get involved in a text.

Different forms of music voice production range from chant to song. Chant is text sung at natural spoken speed to a tone. Important words can be embellished with melisma (several notes sung on one syllable). Song is melodic and tuneful. In song, the climax or chosen parts of a sentence can be highlighted with harmony, that is, several different pitches sung together. The hymn-like structure of Genesis 1:1–2:3 with its refrains of praise is well suited to a rendition with all mentioned sung features—chant, chant with melisma, melody, and melody harmonised.

Drama is an active art as opposed to a passive art (e.g. watching a DVD or listening to music via ear-plugs). For voice and biblio-dramas, students have to actively use their voices and bodies, which can lead to an experience. Three examples follow to demonstrate use of the voice and body as a form of active involvement in biblical texts.

The first example is with a sung version of the *Shema*, a prayer found in the Pentateuch. The *Shema* allows an introductory taste of the Hebrew Bible with its Semitic world and theology. The first sentence of the prayer is the most important faith statement of the Hebrew Bible and the most important prayer for Jews, '*Shema Yisrael: Adonai Eloheinu, Adonai echad*', or, 'Hear, O Israel: The Lord is our God, the Lord alone'.[3] A song by Dan Nichols lends itself to easy learning of the *Shema*. The first line is the Hebrew as above then the opening words are repeated with a small music variation. After a short middle

---

3   Complete *Shema* is Deut. 6:4-9; 11:13-21; Num. 15:37-41.

section, the opening section is repeated so all in all the major phrase is sung four times.

In the closing section of Nichol's song, the interval of a fifth and the words *Shema Yisrael* are used to imitate the sound of the *shofar*, the ram's horn. Strictly speaking the *shofar* is only blown at the synagogue during special seasons but Nichols adds the *shofar* effect to his *Shema* composition. If you hear the *shofar* you know it is a time of change or an important announcement is going to be made. The importance of the sound of the *shofar* is similar to that of a fire department siren calling fire-fighters to their trucks. Nichols draws attention to the text of the *Shema* by imitating the sound of the *shofar*.

The word God is not spoken in the *Shema*. Instead an honorific word, Lord, is used to refer to God. I get students to sing the *Shema* standing and facing to the west as Jerusalem by the most direct route is west of Auckland. The Jerusalem temple was where God had an earthly place to dwell. Vestiges of respect for God's name are reflected in the Christian tradition with the words in the Lord's Prayer—'Hallowed be your Name'. The *Shema* is meant to be prayed twice daily.

Through learning a sung version of the *Shema*, in Hebrew, students encounter the significance of the statement '*Adonai eloheinu, Adonai echad, The Lord is our God, the Lord alone*'. The song opens them to an experience of the Semitic world through the Hebrew language and joins them with a tradition that has recited the prayer for over 2500 years. The prayer imbues one with faith in a single God and with respect for words that are used to speak of God. Jesus was a Jew. He would have prayed the *Shema* at least twice a day.

The second example to enable a Hebrew Bible experience is with the 'David and Goliath (1 Sam 17:1-57)' narrative which, as previously mentioned, lends itself to biblio-drama. The geographical location of the scene is the Valley of Elah. Opposed groups of fighting men are camped on hills on either side of the valley. Teaching space can easily be transformed into two camps with desks pushed to either side of the room, the Philistine camp seaward towards the Mediterranean at Sucoh and the Israelite camp more inland at Azekah. The desks represent the Shephelah, or Judean hills approximately 150-200 metres above sea level. Place names and orientation are mentioned as through biblio-drama geographical awareness can be developed.

Several characters have speaking roles—Goliath, David, Eliab (David's oldest brother), Abner (the commander of the Israelite army), and Saul (the king). Sub-plots are David's interaction with his father, Jesse, at Bethlehem away from the fighting location, and David's interaction with the Israelite fighters on the front. Some of the obvious acting scenes are Goliath marching backwards and forwards before the Israelite lines taunting the Israelites, Saul dressing David with his armour, David choosing stones for his sling-shot. Sometimes I get the narrator to stand on a chair to read, outside the action as the narrator's role is nearly omnipotent—being everywhere, knowing everything, and organising the unravelling of the plot. This can open discussion on the role of the narrator in the art of narrative.

The third example to develop the idea of immersion in the context of Biblical Studies is Psalm 22, from the perspective of voice-drama and reception history (how biblical texts are received and read by a community). In the Jewish tradition Psalm 22 is associated with the exile and is read at Purim, a festival commemorating the freeing of Jewish people during the Persian period (sixth to fourth century BCE). In some Christian traditions Psalm 22 is associated with the suffering of Jesus and read on Good Friday, the day when Christ's death on the cross is remembered.

Psalm 22 is structured in two parts—a lament section (verses 1-21a) and a hymn of praise (verses 21b-31). The second section, the hymn of praise, lends itself to song with harmony. Music instruments and anything that can be used to express praise, such as dance or hand gestures, are appropriate.

The first section, the lament, is particularly dramatic. It is interpreted very differently in the two traditions—Jewish and Christian.[4] The three voices in the lament section are those of the psalmist, the enemy and God.[5] The psalmist stands for the voice of the individual or the community (verses 1-2, 6, 14-15, 20-21a). The enemy ('the wicked') is the people or the nation who oppresses the psalmist (verses 7, 12-13, 16-18). The third voice is the one that speaks of God (verses 3-5, 8-11, 19).

In the Jewish tradition, the 'ravening and roaring lion' of verse 13 is often read as a metaphor for Nebuchadnezzar, the Babylonian king who destroyed the first Jerusalem temple and forced Judeans into the Babylonian exile.[6] The 'dogs all around' of verse 16 are the Babylonians, perceived as hostile to the exiled Judeans captured in the land of Babylonia. I get students to speak the words referring to the enemy with an angry voice.

---

4 Wallace, *Psalms*, 53-59.
5 Clifford, 'Introduction to Psalms', 773-75.
6 Gruber, *Rashi's Commentary*, 256-62; *Tehillim: New Translation*, 269-85.

The voice of the psalmist or the exiled Jewish community opens the lament with the cry, 'Why have you abandoned me'. 'You' refers to God whose presence has departed from the people of Israel as they go into exile filled with shame. Chant tones that are mournful and with minor intervals are appropriate for the verses that suggest the voice of the psalmist. Positive or major sounding chant tones are suitable when the psalmist, despite lamentation, speaks of the divine as 'holy, enthroned on the praises of Israel (Ps 22:3)' and as 'not far from me (Ps 22:1)'. The differing chant tones highlight the difference between verses that relate to the lamenting community and verses that relate to trust in the divine.

After an exegesis of Psalm 22 and finding the different voices I set as a possible historical scene, a settlement of exiled Judeans on one of the canal systems in Babylonia in the fourth century BCE. This is a form of historical reconstruction but it allows a Jewish rendition of the psalm and an experience of immersion. The two chant tones are practised then the psalm is performed with its three voices.

On a different day I return to Psalm 22 for a reading from a Christian perspective. The voice of the psalmist is then an individual—Christ. The setting is Jesus' suffering on the cross at Golgotha. Jesus cries 'My God, my God, why have you forsaken me (Ps 22:1)', and 'My mouth is dried up like a potsherd, and my tongue sticks to my jaws (Ps 22:15)'. The laments offer insight into Christ's suffering—physical and emotional. The same variety of tones is used for the Christian as for the Jewish reading of Psalm 22 lament tone for the voice of the psalmist, praise tone for the voice which refers with trust to the divine, and an angry voice for reading the words relating to the enemy.

The *Shema* prayer, the 'David and Goliath' story and Psalm 22 are examples of ways in which an experience of immersion in a biblical text is possible.

Encounter with Major Ideas

Major ideas are about big concepts. They are often sown when large brush strokes of a field are offered, something John Barton does in his book *The Bible: The Basics*. Often awareness of major concepts is not immediately apparent. Awareness of concepts may grow years after formal studies have finished. What is a major idea or thinking break-through for one person may not be a major thinking break-through for another person. Examples of possible major ideas in the field of Biblical Studies follow.

Take a Bible. Open at the contents page and look at the lists of books. The Old Testament (OT) list is more extensive than the New Testament (NT) list—simply because there are more books in the OT. The varying length of the OT and NT lists is the first general observation to be made. The second observation concerns an overview of genres or kinds of writing. On the contents page the biblical books may be listed under section headings such as Historical Books, Prophetic Books, Gospels, or Letters, as in the NOAB. The same NRSV translation printed by Thomas Nelson gives headings for the biblical books in a 'Subject Index' at the back of the edition. The headings indicate that writing styles are more varied in the OT than in the NT—genres such as laws, historical-theological writings and poems in the OT in contrast to Gospels and letters in the NT. The headings permit a beginning discussion on genres, and also on texts as prose or verse.

The third general observation concerns history. The contents of the OT texts cover centuries of social change in comparison to the writings of the NT which cover approximately a hundred years. The differing length of historical periods covered in the OT and the NT is significant. Social structures suggested by the writings of the OT range from the supposedly semi-nomadic kinship structure of the matriarchs and patriarchs to David and kingship—involving the beginnings of a central royal city and administration in Jerusalem (tenth century BCE). Then under Solomon, a temple is built and some kind of formalisation of Israelite cult occurs. Jumping forward to the sixth century BCE, Judah no longer has self-determination in the political sense. Judeans who return from the Babylonian exile to Jerusalem, especially those based in Babylon, experienced the sophistication of a large imperial city and urbanisation. The general time frame for the OT is ca. 2100 to 300 BCE, over 1800 years, or in archaeological terms from the middle Bronze Age to the Hellenistic period. The NT writings—Paul's letters to the early Christian communities in several Graeco-Roman cities, Christ's ministry in the region of Galilee, and the Apocalypse of John written under the influence of Roman oppression—are set in a comparatively short period, all in the first century CE. The various biblical writings stem from very different social, historical and political settings.

Another big picture idea relates to language and the influence of a language on thought patterns. The original language of the OT is Hebrew and the original language of the NT is Greek. Hebrew and Greek are linguistically two very different languages—Hebrew is from a Canaanite or Semitic family of languages and Greek from the Indo-European family of languages. How ideas are expressed is influenced by the language in which the ideas are communicated. To over-simplify, Hebrew can be described as concrete and Greek as abstract. In Hebrew, adjectives, adverbs and abstract nouns are sparse. If abstract ideas are expressed in Hebrew it tends to be done using a concrete form. Godfrey Driver gives the example of Hebrew words stemming from the lexical form *k-b-d*.[7] In one verbal form it can mean 'to be heavy' (e.g. Ps. 32:4), and in another verbal form it can mean 'to honour' (e.g. Ps. 91:15). In one substantive form *kābēd* means liver (e.g. Lev. 3:10), sometimes regarded as the heavy organ. In another substantive form with different pointing it can mean abundance, glory, or honour (e.g. Isa. 22:23). The example of the liver, as something concrete and the centre of weight, is linked with the abstract attribute, honour. In Greek however, abstract concepts are not expressed in terms of the body or what can be called anthropological philosophy.[8] Plato did not regard the soul as dependent on the body. Hence body and soul can become separated. The apostle Paul wrote in Greek. He grew up in Tarsus, a centre of Greek philosophy. His writings reflect Greek cultural thought, differentiating between flesh and spirit thereby creating the idea that the human is separable. In short, despite differences in genre and historical period, even in English translation the cultural difference between for example a Hebrew psalm and a Greek Pauline letter can be perceived.

A very general look at the writings within the Bible, historical periods covered in the Bible, and the difference between Greek and Hebrew thought are three examples of possible major concepts in the context of Biblical Studies.

Returning now to text and interpretation, to sum-up, the absolute essential for interpretation of texts, musical or biblical, is practice. Regular, even daily, exercising is the basic technique of the disciplines. Insights grow out of daily practice. Insights are also related to creative activity which is nourished through exposure and immersion. The lecture room can be a place of exposure and immersion in the biblical writings. When students enact out the biblical texts in some creative manner in the lecture room they are open to a possible movement of the spirit, or Spirit. The spirit may be creative, or playful, leading to an arts experience; or, the Spirit may be inspirational, offering a taste of the divine. This is "Wondering about God Together" in the context of the lecture room.

To finish, a verse from a poem by an American Jewish Poet, Marge Piercy, from 'Meditation before Reading Torah' is appropriate. It reflects the fascination

---

[7] Driver, 'Hebrew Language', 279-84.
[8] Schroer & Staubli, *Body Symbolism*, 1-39.

of those of us who cannot resist being drawn into the texts of the Bible:

> *"We are the people of the book*
> *And the letters march busy as ants*
> *Carrying the work of the ages through our minds".*

Bibliography

Bates, Kevin et al. *As One Voice Vol 1* (Manly Vale, NSW: Willow Connection, 1995).

Barton, John. *The Bible: The Basics* (London: Routledge, 2010).

Clifford, Richard. 'Introduction to Psalms', in *The New Oxford Annotated Bible: NRSV with the Apocrypha* (Michael D. Coogan, ed.; Oxford: Oxford University, 2010).

Coogan, Michael D. (ed.). *The New Oxford Annotated Bible: NRSV with the Apocrypha* (Oxford: Oxford University, 2010).

Gruber, Mayer I. *Rashi's Commentary on Psalms* (Philadelphia: Jewish Publication Society, 2007).

Driver, Godfrey Rolles. 'Hebrew Language' in *Encyclopaedia Britannica* (Sydney: William Benton, 1971) 11:279–284.

Catholic Publications Centre. *Mass and Psalm Book* (Auckland, NZ: Catholic Publications Centre, 1995).

Nichols, Dan. 'Sh'ma. Hear, O Israel'. SheetMusicDirect.com. www.youtube.com/watch?v=WYlB-3KcgI0w [Accessed 03 July 2017].

Piercy, Marge. *The Art of Blessing the Day* (New York: Alfred A. Knopf, 1999).

Schroer, Silvia, & Thomas Staubli. *Body Symbolism in the Bible* (Collegeville, MN.: Michael Glazier, 2001).

Feuer, Avrohom Chaim. *Tehillim. A New Translation with a Commentary Anthologized from Talmudic, Midrashic and Rabbinic Sources Vol 1* (New York: Mesorah, 2010).

Thomas Nelson Publishers. *The Holy Bible NRSV* (Nashville, TN.: Thomas Nelson, 1990).

Wallace, Howard N. *Psalms* (Sheffield: Sheffield Phoenix, 2009).

Sarah L. Hart
Good Shepherd College–Te Hepara Pai, Auckland, New Zealand
Sarahhart324@gmail.com

18 | THE PEDAGOGY OF BIBLICAL FICTION

WHERE RESEARCH AND CREATIVITY COLLIDE

Abstract

Partly inspired by the recent popularity of fan fiction, fictional short stories based on the Bible can be set as assessment tasks in theological education. A number of different story types can be utilised: recontextualisation ('missing scenes'), refocalisation ('alternative perspective'), genre emulation, and (possibly) expansion ('prequels and sequels'). The creative process involved in coming up with a fictional viewpoint actually encourages the student to function at the higher levels of Bloom's cognitive domain, particularly synthesis. In contrast with traditional theological essays, Bloom's affective domain will also be involved. From personal experience the results of research conducted using this method are long remembered and have a definite impact on the writer. These are, of course, the hallmarks of deep learning. Some assessment considerations will also be discussed.

Introduction

The traditional assessment tool of theological education is, without doubt, the essay. Essay writing requires students to research a given topic, at first widely, then more specifically as they hone their thesis, and then to organize their thoughts into a coherently argued written piece. It is hoped that as the student goes through this process, deep learning, that is learning that is life-changing and long-remembered, will occur.

However, the essay is not the only way to achieve such deep learning. Creative writing, if suitably focused, can also achieve this aim. Without suggesting that we replace the thematic essay completely, this chapter proposes that theological students should be given creative writing choices where appropriate, which will encourage students to bring together theological research and their own creativity. This will result in pedagogical benefits that are more than commensurate with having them produce traditional essays.

But how can creative writing be utilised in theological education? As a springboard into answering this question, let's begin by looking at the recent explosion in popularity of fan fiction.

Fan Fiction

Juli J. Parrish defines fan fiction as 'writing 1) by amateur fans of a particular media text or texts (television program, book, film, role-playing game, anime, cartoon, etc), 2) commencing from (but not limited to) some of the characters and sometimes premises of that text or those texts'.[1] Fan fiction, then, is a *derivative* work, one that takes a media text as its source and then expands on that source material in some way. Parrish goes on to comment: 'Critical opinion more or less agrees on the fact that fan fiction is written not by casual viewers, readers, or players but by *fans*, people who generally have an extensive and expansive knowledge of the specific text about which they are writing'.[2] In addition, most fan fiction is only of interest to *other fans*. One of the first popular culture inspirations of fan fiction was the television series *Star Trek*. When it was cancelled—after only three seasons—fans of the show were unwilling to abandon the characters and the narrative universe they inhabited. So they began writing their own stories, some of which were even distributed via magazines which came to be known as fanzines.

However, it was with the arrival of the internet that the writing of fan fiction truly took off. The internet has made the distribution of fan fiction easy, with

---

1   Parrish, *Inventing a Universe*, 11. She includes two additional points: '3) explicitly calling attention to itself as fan fiction, and 4) published on the internet'. But these are not integral to the concept of fan fiction when taken in a more general sense.
2   Parrish, *Inventing a Universe*, 11.

fans of particular sources being able to come together virtually to share their own literary creations whilst also reading (and commenting on) the literary creations of others. The largest fan fiction website is fanfiction.net. As of April 2017, this website's list of the top five books (or series of books) in terms of having generated items of fan fiction is: 1) Harry Potter, 2) Twilight, 3) Percy Jackson, 4) Lord of the Rings, and 5) The Hunger Games. In particular, it should be noted that the Harry Potter series has generated more than 762,000 individual works.[3] While the occasional piece of fan fiction might achieve wider distribution[4] most of this material is only read by fans of the original source.

Not surprisingly, the Bible too has fans who utilize the biblical text as the source or springboard for their own writings. On fanfiction.net's book list, the Bible comes in at number 27 with nearly 4,100 items.[5] While this demonstrates that fan fiction authors are far more interested in writing about Harry Potter, it shows that there are still people out there wanting to write their own stories about the characters and events found in the Bible.

Actually, fiction based on the Bible is not a new development at all and it is not limited to internet fans, either. A number of serious published works have been based on the Bible. John Milton's *Paradise Lost*, Lloyd C. Douglas's *The Robe*, and Elizabeth George Speare's *The Bronze Bow*, are three works that readily come to my mind. However, there is a Goodreads page that lists over 1,800 books that have been shelved by users of the site as 'Biblical Fiction'.[6]

In fact, there is rather a long tradition of material that expands on the Jewish scriptures in some way. Nehemiah 8.8 speaks of the Levites orally translating the text into Aramaic for the benefit of those who no longer spoke Hebrew, giving the sense of the text but also explaining it when necessary. This process was later formalised into the Targums: written translations of the Hebrew Bible into Aramaic that occasionally went beyond a strict translation of the original text.[7] Similarly, the Midrashim are documents containing exegesis of Scripture, sometimes in the form of synagogue sermons. These show significant additions

---

3   www.fanfiction.net/book/, as of 3rd April 2017.
4   One notable example of fan fiction achieving wider popularity is a series entitled *Master of the Universe* involving the characters from the Twilight books that was reworked by its author into *Fifty Shades of Grey* and sequels.
5   See www.fanfiction.net/book/Bible/, as of 3rd April 2017.
6   See www.goodreads.com/shelf/show/biblical-fiction, as of 3rd April 2017.
7   F.F. Bruce in *The Books and the Parchments*, 129–135, provides some fascinating examples from the Targums where the translator-exegetes have added significant amounts of additional material to Gen. 3:21-24, Ruth 1:1-22 and Isa. 52:13–53:12.

to and explanations of the biblical text, referred to as *midrash*, from which the documents get their name.[8] Scholars have even gone so far as to identify a genre of ancient texts known as 'rewritten Bible'.[9] For example, Moshe J. Bernstein describes two such works as follows:

> Jubilees covers Gen 1 through Exod 12, retelling the biblical story with the addition of 'midrashic' details to the narrative and, of equal if not more significance, with the insertion of biblical laws whose commandment and/or observance has been retrojected to the period of the patriarchs [...] The Genesis Apocryphon, one of the original seven [Dead Sea] scrolls from Cave 1, contains within its fragmentary surviving 22 columns narrative material belonging to the stories of Lamech, Noah, and Abraham, some of it close enough to the biblical text to perhaps merit the appellation targum, some responding to exegetical stimuli within the biblical text and more analogous to rabbinic midrash, and some apparently constituting freely composed additions.[10]

As will be seen shortly, explication and expansion of the original source material are two of the hallmarks of fan fiction.

Fan Fiction Story Types

An examination of the various types of fan fiction actually provides us with a framework within which to set our own creative writing questions.[11] While not all fan fiction story types will be entirely suitable for applying to the Bible, the following are those that might work well.

Recontextualisation

The first is Recontextualisation, otherwise known as 'missing scenes'. This is where the writer describes scenes that are not in the original story but that

---

8   McNamara, *Targum and Testament Revisited*, 30.
9   Cf. Porton, *Understanding Rabbinic Midrash*, 72.
10 Bernstein, 'Rewritten Bible', 174.
11 Wright, *Imitation, Not Limitation*. See also Shamburg, 'When the Lit Hits the Fan in Teacher Education'.

would fit appropriately in it. It might be something that the original story makes reference to but never describes in detail. A good example of this is John Milton's *Paradise Lost,* which takes the opening chapters of the book of Genesis and significantly adds to them.

Refocalisation

The second is Refocalisation, or 'alternative perspective'. This is where the writer tells the story from the point of view of another character, perhaps a secondary character in the story. For example, Frank Viola's book *God's Favorite Place on Earth* tells the story of Jesus' visits to Bethany from the viewpoint of Lazarus.

A combination of these two fan fiction types can produce eminently suitable springboards for creative, yet contextually integrated, works of biblical fiction. This is particularly the case with those books that consist of narrative, such as the Gospels, which contain a wealth of possibilities for the biblical fiction writer. For example:

> You are a member of the Sanhedrin. Describe the events of Passion week from your perspective.

Answering such a question will involve the student in reconstructing the events of Passion week, including scenes that are only alluded to in the Gospels, yet portraying them from the perspective of someone opposed to Jesus. Or a student may choose to write as Joseph of Arimathea or Nicodemus, both secret followers of Jesus, which would bring its own level of interest and complexity to the story. Or:

> Based on Luke 7:18-23, write a first-person account of Jesus' early ministry from the perspective of John the Baptist.

This would allow the writer to discuss the messianic expectations of the time—no doubt shared by John himself as Luke 3:16-17 suggests—and to contrast this with the reality of Jesus' words and deeds.

Similarly, the book of Acts also has a lot of scope for questions involving recontextualisation and refocalisation. For example:

> Choose one person who attended the Council of Jerusalem (Acts 15) and write their perspective of what happened.

Students could choose Paul, who was very happy to welcome gentiles into the church with no strings attached, James who seemed to want to include quite a lot of strings, or Peter who, as we can surmise from his behaviour as reported in Galatians 2, was somewhere in-between.

This type of question need not be limited *only* to books of the historical genre. The New Testament epistles are rooted in a wider narrative, even if we are not always privy to that wider narrative. Yet by reading the epistles—and in the case of the Pauline epistles, the book of Acts—we can make educated guesses about the context in which those epistles were written. For example, a close reading of Paul's letter to the Galatians and the book of Acts might be the spur for the following question:

> You are a Gentile believer living in Antioch at the time Paul and Peter are both ministering in the church. Describe what happened when Jewish Christians from Jerusalem came to Antioch from your point of view including how you felt about Peter's actions and the subsequent disagreement between Peter and Paul.

Similarly, the book of Revelation has a historical contextual narrative: it was written at a particular time (arguably late first century) to a particular audience (the churches of Asia Minor) for a specific purpose (that is, to encourage the believers to hold firm in the face of persecution arising from pressure to conform to the Emperor Cult). Consequently, a question could be set as follows:

> Choose one of the seven churches mentioned in Revelation 2–3. The scroll of Revelation has just arrived in your church and the section written specifically about your church has just been read out. How does the church react? What do you personally think about what was said?

Short stories of this nature can also be employed in other theological subjects. The necessary criterion is the presence of narrative. If there is a narrative then there is the opportunity for a short story that springs from, or intertwines with, that narrative. Church history is full of exciting narratives and since theology often involves dealing with the historical context of particular theologians, narrative is present there, too. By setting a short story for these subjects, we are therefore asking students to write their own historical fiction. For example,

> You have just been handed a copy of Luther's 95 theses. Who are you and what is your reaction to reading it?

The open-ended nature of this question allows the student to choose their central character: it could be someone in the hierarchy of the church, perhaps even Pope Leo X himself; it could be one of Luther's friends; or it could be a German commoner with a newly translated printed version. The tone of the story will greatly depend on this choice, as will the discussion of the relevant theology.

Genre Emulation

A third story type, one not strictly taken from the realm of fan fiction however, is 'Genre Emulation'. This approach allows those biblical genres that are not historical narrative to be utilised. Essentially, after studying a particular genre type, the student is asked to write their own exemplar. In the Old Testament, this could be usefully applied to Psalms[12] and prophetic texts. For example,

> What might an Old Testament prophet say if God gave them a vision of 21st century Australia?

The student's answer would then be modelled on the *form* of Old Testament prophetic texts, utilising similar language and style, yet the message would be contextually applicable to the sins and excesses of Australian society.

In the New Testament, students could be asked to write their own parable,[13] epistle,[14] or even their own apocalyptic material:

> Use apocalyptic imagery to describe the groaning of creation (Rom. 8.19-22) in light of the current ecological crisis.

Or:

> Write an apocalyptic or dream-visionary response to modern consumerism in the way that John does with respect to the Roman economic world in Revelation.

Such questions will involve the student in matching the *style* of the original

---

12 See, for example, Jacobson, 'Creative Writing and Interpreting Biblical Poetry', in Roncace & Gray, *Teaching the Bible,* 194–195.
13 Cf. Cukrowski, 'How to Write a Parable', in Roncace & Gray, *Teaching the Bible,* 303–304, in which the author asks students to contextualize one of Jesus' parables in a modern setting.
14 See Reimer, 'Epistle for Today', in Roncace & Gray, *Teaching the Bible,* 349–350.

genre, yet applying it to a new context. It will also require them to think about contemporary issues from a biblical perspective. For example, in Mark Roncace & Patrick Gray's excellent resource book *Teaching the Bible*, Raymond H. Reimer talks about students writing their own Pauline epistle, one addressed to the community to which they belong:

> each student is encouraged to wrestle with and articulate the 'essence' of Paul's thought and how it pertains to the student in his or her present life situation. While the narrative of all such reports is expected to 'retell' Paul's understanding of the gospel in some way, the decisions each student makes concerning presentation, organization, focus, symbol, and vocabulary reflect personal interpretation—and then, of course, linkage of the message to particular contemporary issues makes the epistle their own.[15]

Expansion

However, not all types of fan fiction in popular usage can be appropriately applied to the Bible. It is *possible* that questions involving prequels or sequels, also known as Expansion,[16] could be set in which students are asked to describe events that would come either before or after events described in the Bible. For example:

> If archaeologists were to find a fifth chapter of the book of Jonah, what might it say?

However, it could well be argued that adding a fifth chapter significantly lessens the impact of the sudden ending of Jonah in its current form. Perhaps worthy of greater attention is the following:

> Some scholars believe that the original ending of Mark's Gospel has been lost and that subsequent copyists have added their own endings. Assuming that Mark's Gospel did in fact continue beyond 16:8, what might it have said?

---

15 Reimer, 'Epistle for Today', 350.
16 Wright, *Imitation, Not Limitation*, 36.

However, assessment considerations suggest that prequels and sequels will be much harder to mark, given that there is potentially less to anchor the resulting story to the source material.

Other, Less Applicable, Story Types

There are other, even less applicable fan fiction story types:

1. 'Alternate universe', where a major character or event in an existing narrative is changed so that the story becomes a 'what if…' story;
2. 'Alternate realities', also known as crossovers,[17] in which characters from one story enter the world of another story;
3. And finally, if you spend even a short amount of time looking through fan fiction on the Internet, you'll find that a substantial proportion of it would be classed as erotica.

Now, Song of Solomon aside, it is difficult to envisage these story types as fitting within the scope of theological education.[18]

Bloom's Cognitive Domain

What of this chapter's previous claim that deep learning will occur in the writing of suitably focused short stories. Having provided some examples of what is meant by 'suitably focused' in the previous section, it is now appropriate to examine that earlier claim, which will be done by reference to Benjamin Bloom's domains of learning.

The first of these, the cognitive domain, 'includes those [educational] objectives which deal with the recall or recognition of knowledge and the development of intellectual abilities and skills'.[19] The levels of learning in the cognitive domain have been deliberately arranged hierarchically from simple to complex such that 'the objectives in one class are likely to make use of and be

---

17 Wright, *Imitation, Not Limitation*, 37.
18 However, there is no stopping a dedicated fan from writing such fan fiction: see, for example, teh gr8 arthur's short story 'Jesus Goes to Hogwarts' (https://www.fanfiction.net/s/1560633/1/Jesus-goes-to-Hogwarts) a Bible/Harry Potter crossover, as of 3rd April 2017.
19 Bloom, *Cognitive Domain*, 7.

built on the behaviors found in the preceding classes'.[20] In the original taxonomy of 1956, the levels were as follows: knowledge, comprehension, application, analysis, synthesis and evaluation.[21] Without going into details, it is not hard to see how a good theological essay would involve most, if not all, of these levels. A good essay will demonstrate that a student has taken a body of knowledge, understood it, and then applied it appropriately to the essay question. The student would need to show that they have analysed their sources, both primary and secondary, evaluated those sources, and synthesised their own thinking so as to provide an ordered, well-argued response to the question.

However, in practice, this does not always happen. Students often submit essays that are essentially a pastiche of quotes from secondary sources, strung together without an appropriate demonstration of analysis and synthesis. In the worst cases, it is not even apparent that the student has comprehended what they have researched.

How will writing a fictional short story be any different? The creative process involved in coming up with a fictional viewpoint actually *encourages* the higher levels of learning, particularly synthesis. In preparing to write a short story, the student will still need to do the same amount of research as for a theological essay and, clearly, they will need to understand that research and apply it appropriately to the given question. So far, so much the same. However, the analysis and synthesis of that body of research is *essential* in coming up with the background context of the short story, if that context is to be historically accurate and believable to the reader. The creative writing process is therefore more likely to be holistic, rather than piecemeal, if the end result is to be both internally and externally consistent. The author will need to immerse themselves deeply in the historical events and then describe what happens from that viewpoint. To do this successfully, they will definitely need to work at those higher levels of learning.

The role of *creativity* is especially perceived at the level of synthesis, as Bloom himself recognised:

> This is a process of working with elements, parts, etc., and combining them in such a way as to constitute a pattern or structure not clearly there before. Generally this would involve a recombination of parts of previous experience with new material, reconstructed into a new

---

20   Bloom, *Cognitive Domain*, 18.
21   For a good summary of these levels of learning, see also Yount, *Created to Learn*, 140–145.

and more or less well-integrated whole. This is the category in the cognitive domain which most clearly provides for creative behaviour on the part of the learner.[22]

Bloom also noted the intrinsic motivational benefit of synthesis activities: 'Such tasks can become highly absorbing, more so than the usual run of school assignments. They can offer rich personal satisfactions in creating something that is one's own. And they can challenge the student to do further work of a similar sort'.[23]

Interestingly, when Bloom's taxonomy was updated in 2001,[24] the level descriptions in the cognitive domain were changed from nouns to verbs. But even more interesting was the swapping of the top two levels, in recognition of the greater importance of synthesis, now renamed 'create'. Consequently, the creating level is now seen as the highest cognitive level of learning, and this is so for both scholarly *and* creative writing. In other words, the act of creation provides the student with the opportunity to incorporate all of the lower learning levels into one finished piece of work.

Bloom's Affective Domain

Bloom's affective domain will also be involved in the creative writing process. The affective domain 'includes [educational] objectives which describe changes in interest, attitudes, and values, and the development of appreciations and adequate adjustment'.[25] It involves receiving and responding to stimuli of affective behaviour, such that the individual forms values which are then organised into a value system which thereby shapes the individual's character.[26] A coverall term for this process is 'internalization'.[27]

How does this relate to creative writing? Essentially, as the author creates believable characters for their short story, they will need to *inhabit* those characters, putting themselves into their characters' shoes (or sandals, as the case may be!) such that they see the world through their eyes. This will involve

---

22   Bloom, *Cognitive Domain*, 162.
23   Bloom, *Cognitive Domain*, 167–168.
24   Anderson et al, *Taxonomy for Learning, Teaching, and Assessing*.
25   Bloom, *Cognitive Domain*, 7.
26   Bloom, *Affective Domain*, 34–35. See also Yount, *Created to Learn*, 145–148.
27   Bloom, *Affective Domain*, 28.

appreciating the characters' motivations and values, thereby giving the author the opportunity to evaluate and then (hopefully) appropriate those values that are worthy of emulation whilst avoiding those that are not. As Pillow Wright puts it:

> The writer may be able to see in the experience of his subject some solutions that will be helpful to him. Or he may be able to use the life experiences of his subject as a trial-and-error testing ground [...] Creative writing has endless possibilities for making the 'gospel learned about' into the 'gospel acted out'. The writer's reaction when he sees his thoughts on paper may even create a desire to change.[28]

Clearly then, the student's imagination is a necessary component of this process. As Marisa Crawford and Graham Rossiter put it: 'Imagination is the capacity to see things differently—new possibilities in contrast with what exists now [...] *Imaginative rehearsal* of future possibilities is a "pathfinder" for personal change [...] imagination is a potent mechanism of human learning'.[29] Later in their book, these authors go on to say:

> *Imaginative identification* is a natural and commonly used learning process through which individuals empathise with the situation of others; it involves imaginatively 'standing in their shoes', seeing things as they see them. It can lead to the acquisition of new attitudes and values; one can learn vicariously by identifying with others.[30]

The authors say this in the context of role-playing, but the point applies equally well to the writing of compelling fictional characters.

Creativity

The process of researching for and then utilising creativity to write a short story will involve the student in deep learning. The student will certainly learn about the particular biblical narrative (or genre) that forms the background of the story, but there are other lessons to be learned. When badly done, Theology is

---

28 Wright, 'Creative Writing', in Minor (ed.), *Creative Procedures for Adult Groups,* 54, 56.
29 Crawford and Rossiter, *Reasons for Living,* 35–36.
30 Crawford and Rossiter, *Reasons for Living,* 292.

often reduced to static propositions, and biblical exegesis can become so atomistic that the overall thrust of a narrative is lost. But salvation history is a grand *story*, one that deserves to be retold in many and various ways. And God is a *creative* being. By more purposefully utilising their own creativity, students will be mirroring God's own creative work, such that as they go through the process of writing fiction, students will actually learn more about the nature of God.

In fact, there appears to be a growing appreciation of the role of creativity in theological circles. For example, N.T. Wright uses an intriguing analogy to describe how the Bible can be considered authoritative.[31] He describes a Shakespearean play that is missing its last act. The actors performing the play need to immerse themselves in the first four acts and then improvise the last act in a way that is consistent with what came before. Applying this analogy, Wright argues that Christians need to immerse themselves in the Bible and then be *creative* in the way they go about life and ministry in the current context whilst remaining consistent with what has preceded and keeping an eye on the hints in the text concerning how the story will end.

In a similar fashion, Samuel Wells has written about how *improvisation* is a helpful way to understand the nature and purpose of Christian ethics:[32]

> The Bible is not so much a script that the church learns and performs as it is a training school that shapes the habits and practices of a community. This community learns to take the right things for granted, and on the basis of this faithfulness, it trusts itself to improvise within its tradition.[33]

Biblical fiction, then, turns that creativity and improvisation back onto the text of Scripture itself, thereby engendering a new appreciation for and exploration of those earlier acts of the divine drama of salvation history. Indeed, what Trevor Hart says about enacting stories from the Bible on the stage is also true for biblical fiction:

> Biblical texts will often 'come to life' in a wholly new way if we attend to them with the expectation born of faithfulness to a Word who is himself known only as he 'takes flesh', and an imagination

---

31 Wright, *The New Testament and the People of God*, 140–143.
32 Wells, *Improvisation*, 11. Wells also gives a critique of Wright's five act model and makes some appropriate modifications to it on pp. 51–57, and provides a comprehensive list of comparable treatments in note 11 on p. 225.
33 Wells, *Improvisation*, 12.

primed and open to receive new meanings rather than resting content with the imagined *textus receptus*.[34]

My Personal Experience

One of the main reasons why I think it is worth giving students creative writing options stems from my own personal experience. Writing biblical fiction is a particular interest of mine and I have found that the process of combining research and creativity has forced me to engage very deeply with the text and with different scholarly perspectives on that text. As such, I can confirm that deep learning does occur.

During my own undergraduate studies, whilst researching for a traditional thematic essay on 1 Samuel, I came across a scholarly article that I found fascinating and extremely helpful for understanding why Saul was rejected as king over Israel.[35] I also utilised a book that provided an excellent overview of two of the overarching theological concerns of the Deuteronomist.[36] A couple of years after finishing my studies, I thought back to these two works and, inspired by Peter Shaeffer's play *Amadeus*, I decided to try and write a play of my own that would put that content into a more accessible form—more accessible in the sense that the average church attender does not read journal articles or scholarly books all that often. The resulting play, *Saul, First King of Israel*, was originally self-published on Smashwords but has since been reissued by MST Press.

Somewhat more recently, in response to the Left Behind series, I wrote a novel entitled *The Ephesus Scroll* that utilises G.B. Caird's commentary[37] to provide an alternative exegetical approach to the book of Revelation, that is, a non-dispensational/premillennial one. A sequel, *The Corinth Letters*, is a fictional account of Paul's dealings with the church in Corinth (as reconstructed from 1 & 2 Corinthians and the book of Acts), interwoven with a modern-day plotline involving romance, document forgery, archaeology, and descriptions of delicious Greek cuisine. Finally, the third book in this series, *The Rome Gospel*, is a historical novel that deals with the writing of Mark's gospel in Rome during

---

34 Hart, 'Beyond Theatre and Incarnation', in Vander Lugt & Hart (eds.), *Theatrical Theology*, 40.
35 Dragga, 'In the Shadow'.
36 Gerbrandt, *Kingship*, especially 140–158.
37 Caird, *Revelation*.

the period of intense persecution that followed the Great Fire of AD 64, with extended flashbacks into the book of Acts.[38]

These works took quite a lot of time and effort to write. I am therefore not suggesting we ask students to write plays or full-length novels! But coming at the text from the perspective of writing fiction forced me to grapple with the original biblical context and the meaning and application of the text and what I learned in the process has stayed with me far more than the content of any of my undergraduate theological essays.

Assessment Considerations

This essay aims to inspire others to include creative writing options in their classes. However, for those with lingering reservations, particularly concerning how to go about assessing such a piece, the following five considerations could be used to develop a suitable marking rubric.

First, how well does the story cohere with the original text? Stories that fill in missing scenes or provide an alternate perspective need to fit as naturally as possible with the narrative as originally presented in the Bible. As H. Maxwell Butcher puts it:

> Imagination and faithfulness to the text need to be kept in a disciplined balance [… A] novel that sets out to tell God's story dare not contradict that story as it is already recorded there. It can expand, it can interpret, but it should never distort the original.[39]

However, the writer may also draw on historical-critical research that suggests events were not always exactly as described.[40] Consequently, revisionist or 'against the grain' readings[41] are by no means impossible and may well add a certain amount of depth and emotional impact to the story. But significant departures from the biblical text would need to be explained and justified in a footnote.

---

38 A chapter from this novel, one that incidentally provides a response to the question on the Jerusalem Council given earlier in this article, can be found at www.ephesusscroll.com/2017/04/03/the-jerusalem-council/. This excerpt explores the possibility that this meeting occurred in John Mark's mother's upper room.
39 Butcher, *Story as a Way to God*, 131–132.
40 For example, the Israelite conquest of the land of Canaan may not have been as complete as it is described in the book of Joshua.
41 Or as Clines calls it, 'reading from left to right', cf. Clines, 'The Ten Commandments'.

Second, how accurate is the description of the historical context? A good writer of historical fiction will attempt to avoid anachronisms as much as possible. However, the key phrase here is 'as much as possible' since avoiding anachronisms completely would be impossible. The thing to be avoided is allowing something to intrude into the text that will cause the reader to be jolted out of the story, such as anachronistic items, behaviours and language. This will clearly require a certain amount of general research into the wider historical context of the particular time period in which the story is set.

Third, how much does the story show an awareness of scholarly opinion? A story that merely retells the original source material will not be desirable. In the same way that a good piece of historical fiction will flesh out the bare bones of the known historical facts, a story based on the Bible will need to supply additional socio-cultural background material so as to root the story in its original historical context. This will definitely require research. A good piece of biblical fiction should therefore demonstrate that the author has interacted with relevant scholarship. This would best be done through the use of footnotes, used for example to support particular events in the story, character motivations and interesting historical details.

Fourth, how well does the story help to *explain* the original text? I can see this being perhaps a bone of contention for some. After all, does every work of fiction need to have a pedagogical function? Not necessarily. However, while biblical fiction could be created for sheer artistic merit, in the context of theological education it should still have an explanatory function. In the same way that a traditional theological essay needs to argue a particular case, such a work of fiction needs to implicitly argue for a specific way of understanding the original text. In other words, it *should* provide the reader with insight into that text.

Fifth, and finally, how much creativity has been displayed? This will, of course, be quite subjective on the part of the marker and may be rather hard to quantify. But subjectivity is always difficult to avoid, even when marking a traditional theological essay (especially when a student argues for a position diametrically opposed to one's own!). Generally speaking, though, just like an experienced marker knows a well-researched and well-reasoned essay, the same will be true of a good short story.

One caveat to these considerations is that writing fiction can be difficult.[42]

---

42 Again, I say this from personal experience. Whether it is harder than writing a more traditional theological essay, though, I remain undecided.

Sometimes, in order to make a story work one must utilize artistic licence. Perhaps where the writer employs artistic licence it could be noted in a footnote.

The above discussion referred to the use of footnotes to provide explanations and comments. An alternative is requiring students to submit a supplementary document describing the process *behind* the creation of their creative writing. This shorter piece of writing could describe the research employed, the thinking and planning that occurred, and the rationale for artistic decisions made. This would allow the student to demonstrate that they have wrestled with the original text and that they have considered differing scholarly perspectives other than the one they went with in their creative writing. This approach may well be preferable in that the creative writing will thereby be unencumbered by scholarly footnotes which would otherwise weigh down the flow of the story. It will also *provide evidence of the depth of research that went into the story, also reflected in an included bibliography.*

And After...

There is clearly an appetite for fan fiction, as those earlier figures from fanfiction.net clearly demonstrate. As such, students should be at liberty to share their short stories on fan fiction websites, if they so desire. Alternatively, the theological institution might even consider self-publishing an anthology of students' stories through a site like Smashwords. The anthology could be released as a free ebook, or sold at a low price.[43] Students will be excited to see their stories available online. They will also be able to read the stories written by the other students in their class and thereby gain an appreciation for alternative viewpoints or approaches to the same question they answered. Students can tell their family and friends about it, and as these stories are shared more widely, this would also serve as an advertisement for their institution.[44] Perhaps depending on how well the stories fit the assessment criteria listed above, the anthology could also spread the institution's ethos and some of its teaching content to the wider church in a more accessible form.

---

43   However, the aim should not be to make a profit but to share the content!
44   To read about one school in the US that did this with an anthology of poetry, see http://blog.smashwords.com/2014/05/ebook-publishing-in-classroom-los-gatos.html, as of 3rd April 2017.

Conclusion

Rather than proposing theological institutions abandon the thematic essay as a primary form of assessment, this chapter suggests that students could be given more creative options where appropriate. Providing students the opportunity to use their creative abilities in conjunction with their critical-thinking abilities, affords an opportunity to experience deep and memorable learning—the goal of every assessment task.

Bibliography

Anderson, L.W., Krathwohl, D.R., Airasian, P.W., Cruikshank, K.A., Mayer, R.E., Pintrich, P.R., Raths, J., Wittrock, M.C. *A Taxonomy for Learning, Teaching, and Assessing: A Revision of Bloom's Taxonomy of Educational Objectives* (New York: Pearson, Allyn & Bacon, 2001).

Bernstein, Moshe J. '"Rewritten Bible": A Generic Category Which Has Outlived its Usefulness?', *Textus* 22 (2005), 169–196.

Bloom, Benjamin (ed.). *Taxonomy of Educational Objectives: 1. Cognitive Domain* (London: Longman, 1956).

Bloom, Benjamin (ed.). *Taxonomy of Educational Objectives: 2. Affective Domain* (London: Longman, 1964).

Bruce, F.F. *The Books and the Parchments* (London: Marshal Pickering, rev. 1991).

Butcher, H. Maxwell. *Story as a Way to God* (San Jose: Resource Publications, 1991).

Caird, G.B. *The Revelation of Saint John* (Peabody, MA: Hendrickson Publishers, 1993 [repr.]).

Clines, D. 'The Ten Commandments, Reading from Left to Right', in Davies, Harvey and Watson (eds.), *Words Remembered, Texts Renewed: Essays in Honour of John F. A. Sawyer*, 97–111.

Crawford, Marisa, & Graham Rossiter. *Reasons for Living: Education and Young People's Search for Meaning, Identity and Spirituality* (Melbourne: ACER Press, 2006).

Davies, Jon, Graham Harvey, & Wilfred G. E. Watson (eds.). *Words Remembered, Texts Renewed: Essays in Honour of John F. A. Sawyer* (JSOTSup 195; Sheffield: Sheffield Academic Press, 1995).

Dragga, Sam. 'In the Shadow of the Judges: The Failure of Saul', in *Journal for the Study of the Old Testament* 38 (1987), 39–46.

Gerbrandt, Gerald Eddie. *Kingship According to the Deuteronomistic History* (Atlanta, Georgia: Scholars Press, 1986).

McNamara, Martin. *Targum and Testament Revisited: Aramaic Paraphrases of the Hebrew Bible* (Grand Rapids: Eerdmans, 2010).

Minor, Harold D. (ed.). *Creative Procedures for Adult Groups* (Nashville: Abingdon Press, 1966).

Parrish, Juli J. 'Inventing a Universe: Reading and Writing Internet Fan Fiction' (Unpublished PhD Thesis, University of Pittsburgh, 2007).

Porton, Gary G. *Understanding Rabbinic Midrash: Texts and Commentary* (Hoboken: Ktav, 1985).

Roncace, Mark, & Patrick Gray (eds.). *Teaching the Bible: Practical Strategies for Classroom Instruction* (Atlanta: Society of Biblical Literature, 2005).

Shamburg, Christopher. 'When the Lit Hits the Fan in Teacher Education', http://blogs.slj.com/connect-the-pop/2012/11/comics/guest-post-by-christopher-shamburg-when-the-lit-hits-the-fan-in-teacher-education/ [accessed 3rd April 2017]

Vander Lugt, Wesley, & Trevor Hart (eds.). *Theatrical Theology: Explorations in Performing the Faith (Eugene: Cascade Books, 2014).*

Wells, Samuel. *Improvisation: The Drama of Christian Ethics* (Grand Rapids: Brazos Press, 2004).

Wright, Molly. 'Imitation, Not Limitation: Fan Fiction in the Classroom' (unpublished BA Hons Thesis, Columbus State University, 2006).

Wright, N.T. *The New Testament and the People of God* (London: SPCK, 1992).

Yount, William R. *Created to Learn* (Nashville: Broadman & Holman, 1996).

Examples of Biblical Fiction Cited

Chenoweth, Ben. *Saul, First King of Israel* (Melbourne: MST Press, 2016 repr.).

Chenoweth, Ben. *The Corinth Letters* (Melbourne: MST Press, 2015).

Chenoweth, Ben. *The Ephesus Scroll* (Melbourne: MST Press, 2016 repr.).

Chenoweth, Ben. *The Rome Gospel* (Melbourne: MST Press, 2017).

Douglas, Lloyd C. *The Robe* (Boston: Houghton Mifflin, 1942).

Milton, John. *Paradise Lost* (London: Samuel Simmons, 21674).

Speare, Elizabeth G. *The Bronze Bow* (Boston: Houghton Mifflin, 1961).

Viola, Frank. *God's Favorite Place on Earth* (Colorado Springs: David C. Cook, 2013).

Ben Chenoweth
Melbourne School of Theology
bchenoweth@mst.edu.au

19 | IS THE GOD OF THE BIBLE AN UGLY BULLY?

HELPING BIBLE STUDENTS COME TO TERMS WITH VIOLENCE IN THE BIBLICAL TEXT

Abstract

Biblical studies should not ignore the reality of violence in the Bible in their teaching, but should instead address it honestly and in the process help their students towards coming to terms with it. This essay reflects on the author's own teaching practice. It offers some pedagogical strategies for tackling this challenge and shows how the spiritual and pastoral needs of students can be attended to as part of the academic learning process. The focus of attention within Scripture in this study is on violent Old Testament texts, especially those dealing with the conquest of Canaan. Consideration is also given to why addressing biblical violence is important, to designing and teaching a segment of a course directed specifically at the issue, and to helping students to be able to lead their own students well in relation to this issue. Through the essay, key principles are presented for effective learning around biblical violence wherever it appears within biblical studies courses.

Background

I was eighteen when I first faced head-on the issue of God as a bully. It was the first year of my initial theology degree and preparation for ordination, and when I was also the enthusiastic leader of a Lutheran parish Sunday school in Adelaide, South Australia. My unease at that time was prompted by the scheduled biblical focus in a coming lesson on the fall of Jericho. To use a line from a Rachel Held Evans video presentation, it was dawning on me that this hitherto cute tale of a glorious victory over evil was actually a story about genocide and, to make it much worse, genocide ordered by God: 'It turns out these Bible stories aren't happy, feel-good fairy tales; no they're much darker than that'.[1]

My unease also arose in response to another layer of interpretation over the top of the biblical tradition itself, namely that from my own Lutheran tradition, which offered an explanation of, and an apologetic for, the issue of divine violence in Scripture. In some respects, at times this was helpful for me, as it has been for Bible readers from other Christian traditions, but in some instances it has only served to deepen and strengthen my own and others' sense of unease. This layer can include sources from very early in the tradition. For example, in commenting on Deuteronomy 7, Martin Luther wrote: 'First he (God) commands them to destroy the makers of the images (The Canaanites), and then the images themselves, because it is useless to remove the images if their makers and proponents are left behind to worship them'.[2] The layer from one's tradition will often be thickened by more contemporary sources found in books, video resources and Bible study materials, along with declarations from pastors, priests, family members, and others.

I served as pastor of a rural NSW Lutheran parish for five years and as a religious education teacher and coordinator in Lutheran schools for twenty-three years. As far as I can recall, I never addressed this issue in those roles in any more than an incidental way. This is in part because the issue was rarely, if ever, raised by people to whom I ministered, or taught—people who ranged in age from young children to seniors. How could it be that the violence of stories and images which were central to the biblical narrative never prompted my students to raise questions with me? Low levels of biblical literacy? The church's lectionary would have helped by omitting much of the discomforting biblical material from the readings. Perhaps the human ability to hear and see only what we want helped some Bible readers to edit out the difficult bits? Perhaps

---

1   Held Evans, 'Testaments'.
2   Luther, 'Lecture on Deuteronomy 7'.

shock, horror, disbelief got in the way of some readers' enquiring into what they saw in Sacred Scripture. Or perhaps the fear that to question what offended their sense of right and wrong would amount to questioning the authority of Scripture at the very least, and maybe even challenging God? Or, in some Christians, perhaps, it was fear of having to reassess the core of their faith if they had to confront something so antithetical to their values. This last point has certainly operated in me as I have mostly opted for the safer approach of avoiding teaching others about issues which I have not worked through sufficiently myself. Early in my teaching role at Australian Lutheran College based in the School of Education at the Australian Catholic University in Brisbane, I became very intentional about addressing this. I was studying ACU's Graduate Certificate in Higher Education and the final unit involved a research project, one outcome of which was a public lecture and a journal article entitled 'God is big enough for our questions: introducing students to a critical approach to reading the Bible'.[3] One outcome of that research was a decision to include in my introductory biblical studies units a module addressing the issue of a violent God in the Bible. What follows is a description of that module and critical reflection on its value and effectiveness.

What I Do in the Module

The module aims to help Bible students to come to terms with violence in the biblical text, especially the violence which the biblical texts tell us God perpetrated or commanded. The focus is especially on Old Testament texts, though the New Testament is implicated as well, both as a source of the issue[4] and as a means for coming to terms with it.

What does it mean to help students to 'come to terms with' the violence? More will be said about this later in this essay, but at this point it is enough to make clear that the goal is not to provide a neat resolution of the issue at either

---

3 Jaensch, 'God is big enough', 190–194. The major findings of that project were (1) a critical approach to study of the Bible is good educational practice because it fosters desire for further and deeper learning; (2) a critical approach can lead to a stronger and more resilient faith in Christians and create the environment in which faith might be born in others; (3) a critical approach promotes good health, including and especially spiritual health, because at its core it is honest and allows the learner to be fully, honestly human; (4) a critical approach allows the learners to find in Scripture the foundation of a just worldview and a just way of life.

4 E.g. Matt. 18:23–35.

the academic or the pastoral level. This would not be theologically possible for any Christian (or Jew) who was unsatisfied with simplistic explanations of difficult biblical material. Nor is it an educationally valid objective, unless one jettisons an enquiring and critical approach to learning. The coming to terms with divine violence in Scripture which this essay has in mind has at its core the willingness to live within the tensions of an issue for which complete academic or theological resolution is not possible. Therefore the objective of the learning described in this essay is, more than anything else, to help learners towards coming to terms with the violence by helping them to live within its tensions. Rachel Held-Evans refers to Bible readers being 'presented with the challenge of making sense of the Old Testament in the light of Jesus, of celebrating the harmony between the Testaments when we find it, and living in the tension when we don't'.[5]

The module in question is called: 'Is the God of the Bible an ugly bully?' It is included in four introductory biblical studies units, three undergraduate and one postgraduate. In all of these units the basic approach to learning is reading the Bible well as literature, within its historical context including the history of the text itself, and with a view to discerning its theology for its original context and for today. The module both addresses the issue of God and violence and serves as a case study in reading the Bible well.

My thinking around and practice with this module has been significantly influenced by the work of Eric Seibert, whose research and writing, as well as his reflection on his own practice in teaching about the issue, have challenged and informed me on the one hand, and also given me the impetus to do something intentional about it in my teaching. In particular I am indebted to his article 'When God smites: talking with students about the violence of God in Scripture'.[6]

Why I Do It

I was initially prompted to include the study of violence in the Bible in my units because of my own discomfort with these texts from my youth, especially discomfort as a Christian whose faith has at its core a God of love revealed in

---

5   Held Evans, 'Testaments'.
6   Seibert, 'When God smites'.

Jesus. More recently the proliferation of scholarship in the area has reinforced my conviction that the issue should not be avoided in introductory Bible units.

Reflecting on his own teaching practice in regard to this issue, Eric Seibert lists several reasons for including the issue.[7]

- There is a lot of violence in the Bible.
- Many people are perplexed by the references to violence.
- There is need to help Christians to respond to ridicule of the Bible prompted by the violence.
- It can help people to read Scripture non-violently and to live non-violently.

Alongside these reasons, such a module supports the development of critical thinking in theological education. To illustrate from two of the University of Divinity's Graduate Attributes:[8]

1. 'Learn: Graduates are equipped for critical study, especially of Christian texts and traditions'. While helping students to address a key issue within Scripture, intentional study of the issue of divine violence supports their critical thinking in general.
2. 'Serve: Graduates are prepared for the service of others'. If working critically with the issue of violence in Scripture can help people to read Scripture non-violently and to live non-violently, then it will be preparing them for their service of others, shaping their view of others as precious.

How I've Been Doing It

The focus in what follows is a single semester undergraduate unit taken by education students as part of their initial teacher education degree. Until now I have provided a single session of about an hour close to the end of the Old Testament-focused part of the unit, i.e. with the New Testament 'just over the horizon'. I lead this face-to-face within a three-day workshop context, and also offer a recorded video version of that in an online module. This has been for optional study by online students.

Right at the beginning of the unit an activity establishes a goal for the

---

7   Seibert, 'When God smites', 325–327.
8   www.divinity.edu.au/study/graduate-attributes/

students' learning. The idea for this comes from David Clines. He calls it 'the pub test'. This is what is presented to students.

> Imagine you're at a party and you hear one of these remarks about the Bible from someone:
>
> - *'The Bible is full of myths and legends'*.
> - *'The Bible is sexist'*.
> - *'The God of the Bible is an ugly bully'*.
> - *'If you are studying the Bible you must be a very religious person'*.
>
> How confident would you be in responding well? Practise a response now.[9]

These 'remarks from the pub' are revisited from time to time through the unit, and in a planned way at the end of the unit. They are also offered as topic suggestions for an essay assessment task (due nine weeks into the unit) which requires students to develop their own topics from an area of interest.

Here now is a walk-through of the module as it takes place within a three-day workshop.

The issue is introduced with a cartoon image of a school yard bully accompanied by the question 'Is the God of the Bible an ugly bully?' I briefly explain that this session addresses questions and concerns of Bible readers about instances in the Bible where God is associated with violence. Students are invited to comment on whether, where, and how this has been an issue for them. I then present my purpose for including it in the unit, quoting Siebert's four reasons referred to earlier in this essay.

I introduce the idea of textual blindness, where in our reading of the Bible we edit out problematic images. This happens in much the same way as our loss of awareness of everyday things such as the colour of our bathroom walls—we visit the bathroom so often that we stop noticing. Siebert likens this to what happens for many people who encounter presentations of violence in the Bible.

> They have heard certain Old Testament stories so many times they fail to notice how violent and bloody they really are. Since the way these stories are often retold focuses on "positive" aspects of the text (such as God's great deliverance), their more violent dimensions

---

[9] Clines, 'Learning, Teaching and Researching', 25.

tend to get ignored. This conditions people to see these stories from a particular angle of vision, one that does not really pay attention to the violence contained within them.[10]

I illustrate the idea of textual blindness through the account in Joshua 6 of the conquest of Jericho. Students are given time in class to read that and to note what they are seeing in the text as well as their feelings about it. Students are then invited to share responses with the class. I then extend the class's reflection on textual blindness by presenting two contrasting pieces of art relating to the conquest of Jericho, one brutal, the other a cartoon image prepared for children depicting the conquest almost joyously as a victory with no victims.

I then read a brief imaginary piece in which, in the late afternoon of the day before the army of Israel destroys the city, a woman of Jericho is showing hospitality to one of the Hebrew soldiers. She shows him her home and family and then says to him:

> But look at the sun, time is running out. You have to hurry to join Joshua again and leave before the gate is closed [...] Tomorrow, when the sun rises, the wall will fall down. The city will be burnt. You know, the God of Joshua has no mercy at all, not even for the old ones or the children. Joshua will take all the silver and gold for his God. So go now, and tomorrow we will meet again—and then you will kill me.[11]

I then provide time for the students to process what they have seen and heard and to select a response from across a continuum, suggested by Seibert,[12] which matches their feeling about what they have just read and heard:

DEEPLY DISTURBING—UPSETTING—A WORRY—OK—COMPLETELY FINE

I follow this with encouragement for the students to read the biblical text from the victims' perspective and not only from the perspective of the victors. The remainder of the session provides possible ways for Bible readers, especially Christian readers, to come to terms with the issue.

I explain that there are different forms of violence in the Bible which are

---

10 Seibert, 'When God smites', 328.
11 Epp-Tiessen, 'Conquering the land', 64–65.
12 Seibert, 'When God smites', 331.

associated with God, naming some of these, and pointing out that each requires a different theological response. These include the violence that is a consequence of being part of God's good creation, such as when gravity is a cause of suffering, or when people's own sin or the sin of others results in violence.

Following Seibert again,[13] I use humour to highlight the confronting nature in biblical texts, especially texts which are commonly used in arguably dishonest ways in teaching children. For this I employ a video clip of American comedian Tim Hawkins in which he satirises presentations of the Genesis flood for children.[14]

I then return to the Joshua 6 context and move to proposals for addressing and coming to terms with the issue of God's role in the violence within the narrative. I offer a set of responses to God's violence in the Bible in the context of holy war, as proposed by Terence Fretheim:

- God works in and through human beings to achieve God's purposes.
- God does not perfect humans before working through them.
- Humans will never have a perfect perception of how to serve as God's instruments in the world.
- Israel's rationale for waging war was:
  - So they would not be led astray by their neighbours' religious practices
  - As instruments of divine justice against wickedness.
- God's action is cause for hope because God does not give people up to violence but works for good purposes.
- God himself gets caught up in the violence.[15]

In developing Fretheim's last point, I move into theological reflection, highlighting Luther's theology of the cross, especially God's own redemptive experience of human violence in the person of Christ.

I conclude the session with two activities which invite the learners to live within the tensions of an issue for which complete academic or theological resolution is not possible. The first activity uses Testaments, a ten minute video presentation from Rachel Held Evans addressing the question 'what are we to do with the Bible's dark side?', which concludes with the hope of being able to

---

13   Seibert, 'When God smites', 329.
14   www.youtube.com/watch?v=YVxRddVYYig
15   Fretheim, 'About the Bible', 135–137.

live within the tension around this issue.[16]

I return to the question I began with ('Is the God of the Bible an ugly bully?') to help the students to identify what they have learned and what they are still wrestling with.

> If someone suggested to you that the God of the Bible is an ugly bully,
>
> - How would you respond?
> - What uncertainty of your own would you need to admit to with them?

Students are given time to reflect, write, and then share with a partner or the group depending on what time is available. They are also asked to hand in a copy of their written response to me. This provides useful feedback on the learning process, and a prompt to offer pastoral support to particular students, if necessary. I encourage the students to seek support from someone if the session has raised troubling feelings for them, and then I conclude with prayer, which acknowledges the tension and which hands it to the God of love in Christ.

What Has Been Effective

Feedback on my practice to date has come from two sources: comments and questions from students in a workshop context, and results from an online survey conducted with a group of ten participants in a workshop which included the 'Is the God of the Bible and ugly bully?' module.[17] The responses are small in number but consistent in tone.

One consistent theme in the feedback is that attention to this issue in an introductory biblical studies unit is necessary. Almost all students indicate having been concerned about the issue before they came to the unit. Seibert argues for its inclusion in spite of compelling reasons to include other topics in place of it, given that time is always limited.[18] Most of my students are preparing for teaching in schools, are already teachers, or are preparing for ministry in some other form which will also require them to stretch their students through

---

16   Held Evans, 'Testaments'.
17   www.surveymonkey.com/r/XDYLFXW.
18   Seibert, 'When God smites', 323–324.

their teaching of the Bible. Having ventured into the hermeneutically and spiritually challenging territory of this issue themselves, they will be better equipped as teachers to guide expeditions of their own students into the same territory.

Reflected in the students' overall positive feedback is their apparent ability to handle the kind of 'adult content' which this module contains and also their engagement in the task of constructing their own learning. The presentation in the module of multiple 'solutions' to the issue is a necessary aid for them in that process, as is the challenge to live in the tension that must inevitably remain.

It is important that the approach to learning in the module allows a voice for victims. This can prompt Bible students to resist textual blindness and so recognise the victims within the biblical text and then also in the world around them.[19] This supports students' growth in respect to the University of Divinity's Graduate Attribute 'Serve: Graduates are prepared for the service of others.' The timing of the module within the unit and the workshop supports effective academic and spiritual growth objectives. Seibert advocates for a timing which allows for sufficient trust to be built between students and teacher, and also for some hermeneutical foundations to be established which can provide solid ground for consideration of a very difficult issue and some 'solutions' to it which can be confronting in themselves for people of faith.[20]

The learning and teaching approach attends to the emotional and spiritual safety of the learners in a number of ways, although observations in the next session of the essay also highlight areas which need addressing. I encourage the students in the workshop session to get in touch with their feelings, and to express them, both in pairs and within the full group. I am also honest and vulnerable with the learners myself in sharing my own struggle as a human being and a Christian with the issue, intending to demonstrate among other things that it is possible 'to live in the tension'. Within this, even as I speak honestly and critically about the humanness of Scripture, I also communicate respect for it and for the Jewish and Christian faiths.

I am pleased that feedback from Christian students who have been troubled by this issue indicates that they are grateful to have received some help with it. All survey respondents indicated that the module had provided them with some useful tools for responding to the claim that the God of the Bible is a bully. My

---

19   Seibert, 'When God smites', 330.
20   Seibert, 'When God smites', 335–336.

own research referred to above into learners being supported in approaching Scripture critically has shown that being honest about something dear to you like Scripture is good for your health. In the survey all students expressed appreciation for the opportunity to learn to read the Bible with their eyes open to some of its difficult content.

What Needs Adjusting

The standout point here is the amount of time set aside for the module within the workshops. For the goals of the session to be achieved as completely as they can be, more time is required, though not a lot more. It is also not just a matter of more time within class itself, if we are thinking of face-to-face mode. Space also needs to be provided between when the issue is introduced and when it is concluded. If more time is provided, then it becomes possible to include other strategies which can make the goals of the module more achievable. These include pre-reading of strategically selected biblical texts and/or background material in the way of a flipped classroom approach. For example, Seibert asks students in advance of the first of two sessions on the issue to read a chapter from Christopher Wright's *The God I don't understand*, because it represents an evangelical attempt to deal with God's decree to slaughter the Canaanites.[21] With more time available the students would be able to engage in a focused study of a text such as Joshua 6–11 in which they could practise reading the biblical text as literature, as history, and as theology.

An honest approach to difficult issues in Scripture is good for the kinds of learners I work with, and such honesty requires a certain level of confrontation.[22] However, it is important to avoid unnecessary bluntness, something which is more likely to occur when time is short and the learning process rushed. I need to remind myself that I have had many years to work through this very challenging issue myself. The unit needs to be a safe space for those just beginning their consideration of the issue. The survey results indicated a wish among most responders for increased attention to the learners' faith in teaching about the issue. Personal faith is an area of vulnerability and sensitivity and so the importance of a safe space for exploration of this cannot be overstated. A student

---

21 Seibert, 'When God smites', 336–337.
22 Jaensch, 'God is big enough', 190.

remark at a 2017 workshop session on the issue illustrated this. Near the close of the workshop session I sensed a real heaviness in the room, and this was underlined by one discerning mature age student asking that we close the session with prayer before breaking for lunch.

At this point the module has been required for those participating in the workshop/intensive, but is optional for online students. Given that the feedback from students reflects strong support for the inclusion of the issue in the unit, consideration needs to be given to making the module a required area of study for online students as well and then also to the provision of appropriate academic and personal support through that study.

Some form of 'assessment' is essential for the sake of the students' emotional and spiritual welfare, as well as for their learning and the learning of future cohorts. The Survey Monkey tool has allowed me to gather some anonymous feedback and this is a start, but it is crucial that I provide for more opportunity within the learning process as a group as well as individually. This can include providing opportunities to write down questions and feelings. For example, Eric Seibert asks students to write a two page paper at the conclusion of the whole unit which invites them to comment on the impact of the course on their faith.[23] As well as helping to clarify and deepen the students' learning, this strategy also allows the teacher to follow up with students on academic and pastoral levels.

Conclusion

The focus of this essay is supporting learners in their 'wondering about God' when the images of that God they are confronted with in the biblical text are very confronting. 'Wondering' is a core driver of all learning, but it involves additional challenges for learners who are people of faith or on a journey towards faith. The research of Clines and Seibert referred to above is especially valuable for educators seeking to provide the best possible support for such learners. Many others involved in research-led learning and teaching are contributing to this field. In 'Teaching Oppressive Texts' (2013), Camp, Webster and Thelle present teaching strategies for exposing oppressive elements in the biblical text and showing how the oppression operates. In 'Faith in the

---

23 Seibert, 'When God smites', 338–339.

Classroom: the Perspective of a Pastor Called to College Teaching' (2008), Martin proposes that faith development can deepen pluralism, autonomy and critical thought in the learning process. Solvang's 'Thinking Developmentally: the Bible, the First Year College Student, and Diversity' (2004) explores ways of teaching and applying critical thinking within the context of an introductory Religion course. A factor behind her research is her awareness of the non-Western nature of the Bible along with its potential for both constructive and destructive interpretations and applications.

Through 'Is the God of the Bible an ugly bully?' in my own small way I am making a choice not to consign a difficult issue in my own faith to the 'too hard basket', but instead to support the learners in constructively 'wondering' about that God. When other Bible teachers do that, they too are refusing to take the easy path of passing on textual blindness (with all that entails) to another generation of Bible students. In making these choices teachers are also making it possible for their students to support their own students in the same ways.

Bibliography

Camp, Claudia V, Janes S. Weller & Rannfrid Thelle. 'Teaching Oppressive Texts (2004)', *Teaching Theology and Religion* 16.3 (2013), 256–273.

Clines, David. 'Learning, Teaching and Researching Biblical Studies, Today and Tomorrow', *Journal of Biblical Literature* 129.1 (2010), 5-29.

Drane, John. *Introducing the Old Testament* (Oxford, UK: Lion, 2011).

Epp-Tiessen, Esther. 'Conquering the land', in Alain Epp Weaver (ed.), *Under Vine and Fig Tree: Biblical Theologies of Land and the Palestinian-Israeli Conflict* (Telford: Cascadia Publishing House, 2007), 62–74.

Everts, Don. *God in the Flesh: What Speechless Lawyers. Kneeling Soldiers, and Shocked Crowds Teach Us about Jesus* (Downers Grove, ILL: Intervarsity Press, 2005).

Held Evans, Rachel. 'Testaments: One Story, Two Parts', Video recording. In Carla Barnhill and Paul Soupiset (ed.), *Animate Bible* (Sparkhouse Minneapolis, MN, 2013). See www.wearesparkhouse.org/store/product/22248/Animate-Bible-Starter-Pack.

Fretheim, T. *About the Bible* (Minneapolis, MN: Augsburg Books, 2009).

Jaensch, Andrew. 'God is Big Enough for Our Questions: Introducing Learners to a Critical Approach to Study of the Bible', *Lutheran Theological Journal* 48.3 (2014), 186–197.

Lockwood, Peter. 'Massacre and mayhem in the Old Testament: twelve exit strategies'. Address to the *Queensland District Pastors' Conference*. Brisbane, 2008.

Luther, Martin. 'Lecture on Deuteronomy 7 (1519)', *Luther's Works. Vol. 9: Lectures on Deuteronomy* (E. Theodore Bachman & Helmut T. Lehmann, eds.; Minneapolis, MN: Fortress Press, 1986), 3–22.

Martin, Thomas W. 'Faith in the Classroom: the Perspective of a Pastor Called to College Teaching', *Teaching Theology and Religion* 11.4 (2008), 213–221.

Seibert, Eric A. 'When God smites: talking with students about the violence of God in Scripture', *Teaching Theology and Religion* 17.4 (2014), 323--341.

Seibert, Eric, A. *The violence of Scripture: overcoming the Old Testament's troubling legacy* (Minneapolis, MN: Fortress Press, 2012).

Seibert, Eric A. *Disturbing divine behavior: troubling Old Testament images of God* (Minneapolis, MN: Fortress Press, 2012).

Solvang, Elna K. 'Thinking Developmentally: the Bible, the First Year College Student, and Diversity (2004)', *Teaching Theology and Religion* 7.4 (2008), 223–229.

Wright, Christopher J. H. *The God I don't understand: reflections on tough questions of faith* (Grand Rapids, MI: Zondervan, 2008).

Andrew Jaensch
Australian Lutheran College
andrew.jaensch@alc.edu.au

20 | AN APPROACH FOR DEEP THEOLOGICAL LEARNING IN RESEARCH METHODOLOGIES

Abstract

Theology students embarking on higher degree research are met with the task of having to critically evaluate key research methodologies, in order to identify and articulate those that are most relevant to their research topic. This paper is informed by research-led learning and teaching in theological education and offers pedagogical and theological insights through implementation of enquiry-based and deep learning strategies for the delivery of transformative learning. The work suggests that learnings contextualised through scaffolding activities such as collaborative learning, modelling, and problem solving, facilitate a process of enquiry. With a focus on 'learning relationships' and contextualised assessment and evaluations, students are supported in their deep levels of thinking about the strategies for developing research design in theology. Forming a matrix of ideas with the students demonstrates how key ideas about the workings of various epistemologies, theoretical perspectives, methodologies, methods, data analyses and theological interpretation support and deliver solutions to new theory. This learning practice of enquiry explores how students become familiar with the content and process frameworks theologians may use for designing research, and encourages understandings about the research design options relevant to their research of topic. This learning activity also informs students in making meaning of research methodologies for critique and review of scholarly literature. An example of a matrix of ideas illustrating these qualities suggests the process of 'learning to learn' is guided by the pedagogical tools and are indicative of transformative learning.

An Approach for Deep Theological Learning in Research Methodologies

Principles of 'transformative learning' applicable for adult learning sensitivities,[1] and 'deep learning' for assessment,[2] find coherence with practical strategies and techniques offered through 'enquiry-based learning'.[3] Enquiry-based learning approaches can enhance students' learning by incorporating scaffolding activities such as modelling, collaborative learning techniques, and providing appropriate resourcing opportunities.[4] Assessment guided by these approaches can encourage students to navigate their personal learning with confidence, through independent application of research techniques previously practised during the unit delivery. To this end, an assessment task was planned for students to review the methodology of various pieces of theological scholarship. This task called for exploration of theological research and the nature of various methodologies, and for students to identify and analyse theological problems, questions and their solutions, given different theological fields. The provision of clearly stated objectives and outcomes was a significant part of this process, supported by relevant and meaningful guidelines.

Background

A set of activities was aimed at exploring teaching and learning approaches for accommodating a theologically diverse group of students in the field of research methodologies. One challenge was how to cater for each separate theological field, which oftentimes had indigenous ways of articulating its research design. For example, practical theological studies encompassing social science disciplines can speak to epistemologies, theoretical perspectives, methodological approaches, methods and data analyses in ways foreign to research in other disciplines such as biblical, church history and or systematics studies. An example in practical theology may describe the following qualitative research design, where its epistemology operates within a social constructionist domain, and where its hermeneutic is phenomenological.[5] Compatible with these func-

---

1 Mezirow, *Transformative Dimensions*.
2 de Jongh, 'Theories of Multiple Intelligences'.
3 Bruner, *The Process*.
4 Goodwin, 'A Practical Approach'.
5 Gergen, 'Social Construction',

tions, an action research methodology may utilise focus groups methods for its interview techniques.[6] The data gathered can then be analysed according to content analysis[7] and a mutual critical correlation method appropriate to its theological reflection.[8] A biblical study, on the other hand, may appropriate a feminist hermeneutic, adopting literary criticism, with socio-historical and cultural methodologies and utilise a sociology of narrative and contextual worlds taken from various texts to focus analyses of women from a specific biblical culture.[9] In this way, theoretical perspectives form a picture through a feminist lens. Designs offering methodologically complex theological and philosophical approaches require practised observation and learning through modelling activities in research design, facilitation of purposeful peer group discussion and think tank collaborative sessions around designing example research projects. Ideally content would differ to meet the methodological needs of the various theological disciplines. These scaffolding activities promote peer group cohesion and help develop personal confidence in students. Ultimately the outcome for these activities would be for students to critically evaluate key research methodologies and review the scholarly work of others. It is important to note that, while critical evaluation and review of such work is the metric for measuring success in this learning area, the efficacy of the assessment task lay in the planning and facilitation of appropriate scaffolding activities.

Research Design for Theology

When asked about the methodology for their research project, potential research students often offer a one term response to describe their approach. They may say auto-ethnography, historical critical method, action research, critical realism, grounded theory, liberation theology or theology of redemption, to name a few examples. What they offer is a design element or mechanism that drives a study in part and not the whole. Academic research requires robust design, and sound theology exacts no less. The provision of a design framework used to support students' systematic planning of methodology offers guidance

---

6   Bloor, et al., *Focus Groups* and Litosseliti, *Using Focus*.
7   For content analysis applicable to qualitative studies, see Berg, *Qualitative Research*; Hijmans, 'The Logic of Qualitative Media', 93–109; and Gillham, *Research Interviewing*.
8   Swinton & Mowat, *Practical Theology*.
9   van Eck, 'Socio-rhetorical Interpretation'.

in research design. A research design matrix used to map methodological ideas for theological projects was presented to the student cohort with the aim that they identify, examine and critique a theological discipline's epistemology, theoretical perspective, methodology, methods, types of analysis and theological interpretation. This was done to assist learning by deconstructing the relationship between the methodological assumptions and its approaches, and for developing an appreciation of the range of design elements that can assist in their critical review of scholarship.

Knowledge may exist as scientific information generated from empirical evidence (the Earth exists as a planet within a solar system), or human experience (human emotion around the experience of death and dying affect people from different cultures and their funeral practices variously). Epistemologies for these can assume objectivist or subjectivist approaches, having positivist or relativist positions for research. The epistemology situates the principle of understanding how knowledge is to be conceived within a research study. From the research methodologies unit, students required input about research design elements, to philosophically account for and justify their theological thought. The genesis of the knowledge articulated in a research project's theory, solutions or interpretations requires a sound basis in methodology to support its theoretical perspectives. For example, a hermeneutic of phenomenology can support relativist positions of understanding, challenging positions of positivism, because analysis and interpretation based on 'lived experience' of phenomena invite the source of a human perception as a viable datum for scientific interpretation.

Various theoretical perspectives provide the opportunity for researchers to interpret knowledge given different hermeneutical lenses. Students' learning for understanding in the methodologies unit revolves around the type of questions they wish to resolve concerning their research problem or hypothesis. As an example of an interpretive lens, a researcher's questions involving feminist and social theory might ask, 'Why did Paul name the women Phoebe, Prisca, Junia, Tryphaena and Tryphosa as singular identities in Romans 16:3-12?'; 'Why does he name Prisca before Aquila in Romans 16:3?'. To name a woman as a single identity without relational projection to a male was possibly counter-cultural, and to precede the naming of a woman, linked to a male partnership was counter-cultural. Presenting questions of this nature around the naming of women in Paul offers a feminist hermeneutic.

Methodology assumes a theoretical approach for the study of a system of methods, applied to a field of research or activity. 'It implies a family of methods that have in common particular philosophical and epistemological assumptions'.[10] An understanding of these theoretical assumptions is important to the research learner, since it seeks to promote their working knowledge of the terms and approaches used in research literature, and offers examples or precipitates questions for how or what they may use in their own research design. Knowledge of methods highlights the ethical use of specific techniques which are undertaken to develop a line of enquiry towards gathering and analysing data for the purposes of seeking plausible solutions to a problem, or justifiable support for a hypothesis. The matrix activity and the review of a piece of research literature support, guide and inform students, helping them to identify how research methodologies work. They learn about the significance of a research problem or hypothesis being debated, about underlying assumptions for what is measured or argued, the techniques or arguments used to conduct the measure/s or deliver debate, and whether the measures or debate deliver plausible recommendations or solutions.

Learning Outcomes

The subject for this paper was the teaching and learning practice given to a research methodologies assessment task. The task called for a written review of one thousand words, examining the methodology of a piece of theological scholarship. A stated objective prescribed in the student's unit handbook was the critical review of scholarly literature relevant to their own research topic. For students to undertake this activity with comprehension and confidence in explaining the methodological subject matter, 'sound preparatory guidance, material and personal support, and appropriate resourcing'[11] are required. Proposed outcomes for the delivery of the stated objective are to:

- Identify the problem or thesis stated in a piece of theological scholarship relevant to their own theological field
- Articulate the research question/s the work is investigating
- Distinguish the design elements in that piece of scholarly literature
- Interpret the relationship between the methodological assumptions and its approaches

---

10   Swinton & Harriet Mowat, *Practical Theology*, 75.
11   de Jongh, 'Theories of Multiple Intelligences', 210.

- Critically review a piece of scholarship relevant to their own research topic
- Develop an appreciation of the range of terms, assumptions and approaches for research that are current in selected theological disciplines.

Literature

Two fields of literature support and inform the delivery of this exploration into learning and teaching research methodologies in theology. The first identifies its design elements and provides a rationale for the methodological approaches chosen. The second area informs pedagogy and the educational premises that underlie its delivery.

Presented as a qualitative study, students' written understandings about various methodologies and approaches applicable to their different theological field were analysed through general discussion and the completion of a group work activity. The collective meaning of these was contextualised in a matrix of ideas or framework, identifying design elements for research methodology in theology. Student perceptions about their learning performance and the contributions of others were offered during group work activities. For this small study, social constructionism was chosen as an epistemic element, because it could describe the position for what can be known about students' perspectives on a specific topic within research methodologies and, broadly speaking, how they evaluated their learning in the context of their student culture.[12] The learning process is informed by drawing from student academic experiences, questions and assumptions about the purpose of research methodologies, what each offers theological enquiry, and how they may go about designing their own research. It does this by offering the lecturer a means to interpret students' learnings from the collective set of responses and understandings. As a theoretical perspective, the hermeneutic of 'students' lived experiences' provides the opportunity to cultivate a student's and lecturer's learnings, engaging positive agency in the process of adult education.[13]

The epistemic terms and assumptions support the methods used in the online and face-to-face case studies. This multi-site methodology incorporating aspects

---

12 Gergen, 'Social construction and the Educational Process'; Gergen, 'Social Construction and Theology'.
13 van Manen, *Researching Lived Experience*.

of action research generated information from the students' group work sessions, via face-to-face activities, online forums and chat sessions.[14] The action research component delivered cyclic feedback via focus groups, with the purpose of questioning the methodological assumptions of the theological disciplines and their respective scholarship. Other methods harnessed perspectives from tutorial and forum sessions, as well as the discussion responses that explored each student group's research design findings for a set text. These responses were drafted into a research design matrix.

The final copy of the research design matrix offered a synthesis of students' research methodological understandings and produced new learning foci belonging to the face-to-face and online groups. In effect the group work activities produced diagnostic and formative assessments without penalty for the cohort. They informed the lecturer's unit evaluation and supported students by capturing their understandings for further research in areas they needed, providing them direction and confidence before executing summative assessments.

Literature informing pedagogy situates teaching and learning perspectives in educational theory and practice. Transformative learning, enquiry-based learning, and deep learning educational theories reflect and capture synchronic constructivist pedagogical perspectives.[15] Constructivist learning principles suggest that humans construct knowledge and meaning from their own experience, and by processes of personal ongoing interpretation.[16] Theory and practice situating adult psychological learning frameworks, strategies for developing confident, independent learners, and deep learning assessment principles ground the purpose and aims of the curriculum and deliver specific learning outcomes. These learning perspectives generate various questions and posit seeds for best practice in adult learning. Transformative learning asks, 'How do adults learn best?' It highlights the importance for applying the appropriate pedagogical approach to assist adults in becoming independent learners. It identifies the importance of enhancing transformational meaning structures in adult learning, delivering supportive and purposeful learning content, and providing the premise and process reflection types for engaging

---

14 Patton, *Qualitative Evaluation*; Grundy & Kemmis, 'Educational Action Research'; Grundy, 'Three Modes'; and McCutcheon & Jurg, 'Alternative Perspectives'.
15 Mezirow, 'An Overview of transformative Learning'; Bruner, *The Process*; Goodwin, 'A Practical Approach'; and De Jongh, 'Theories of Multiple Intelligences'.
16 Taber, Constructivism as Educational Theory, 2011.

personal experiences in deep consideration of new information.[17] 'Enquiry-based Learning' asks, 'What skills and techniques are required for an adult learner to become proficient in learning how to learn in the constructivist approach?' Principles for learning here are premised on developing knowledgeable, independent and confident students who, when faced with new problems, can draw on previous learning frameworks and schemas to assist them to systematically work through problems and gain credible solutions. 'Deep Learning' enquires, 'Where does assessment of outcomes offer best practice for adult learners?' It does this by envisioning assessment within the whole of its course design, where student centred learning activities take account of the learner's achievement, and where objectives of the course of study are differentiated to make known its specific learning outcomes. Assessment requirements are explicit. They offer care and support for students' achievements and deliver prepared, practised and well-resourced learners, who have received prompt supportive feedback.[18]

Constructivist Learning Perspectives

Transformative Learning

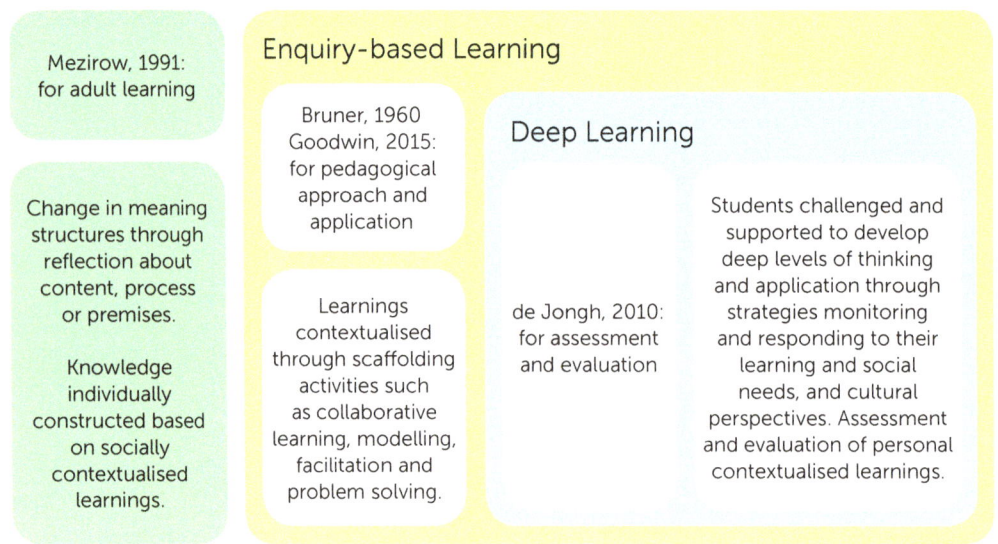

Diagram: Relationship of Constructivist Learning Perspectives

---

17   Jack Mezirow, *Cognitive Processes: Contemporary* 1998, 5-12.
18   De Jongh, Theories of Multiple Intelligences, 2010, 210.

The data collection: the tutorial focus group activities

Face-to-face and online students were invited to share their field of interest with their group and then choose one of four readings relevant to their own theological discipline. Before coming together in discussion, they were asked to read and examine their chosen article, and make notes around the headings of:

- Identifying the research problem
- Research question/s author is investigating
- The means to a solution is attempted
- What 'might have been' if the author had taken a different approach.

The readings students could choose from represented the cohort's theological disciplines of church history, systematics, biblical study and ministry and pastoral studies. The four readings presented for scholarly review for the tutorial practice groups were:

> Alison, James. *Knowing Jesus* (Illinois: Template, 1994), 31–58.

> Cotter, Wendy. 'Women's Authority Roles in Paul's Churches: Counter-cultural or Conventional'. *Novum Testamentum* 36, 4 (1994). 350–372.

> Australian Catholic Bishops Conference, 'Catholics Who Have Stopped Attending Mass', Final Report. Australia: Pastoral Projects Office, 2007.

> Massam, Katherine, 'Cloistering the Mission: Abbot Torres and changes at New Norcia 1901–1910'. *The Australian Catholic Record* 89 (2012), 13–25.

These readings were chosen to encourage an appreciation for the variety of design elements available for use in theological research, illuminating the use of a range of terms, assumptions and approaches that are current in selected theological disciplines. It is important to note that presenting only four readings is limiting, in so far as these offerings provided some examples, not all, of the methodological terms, approaches and assumptions for students to gain familiarity in their theological field. Catering for a wider range of methodologies for each discipline was beyond the scope of this study. Given the use of four texts as study examples, the scope of study could nevertheless demonstrate a range and variety of methodological elements across the theological fields.

Group discussions were arranged during face-to-face classes and in online forums. There were six students in the face-to-face group and eleven students online. There were four homogeneous theological disciplines across the delivery modes. Online delivery had cohorts belonging to pastoral and ministry, scripture, systematics and church history. Face-to-face delivery had cohorts belonging to pastoral and ministry, scripture and systematics. The aim was to facilitate student learning through the identification of a research problem, the discernment of relevant research questions and their hermeneutic appropriation, in order to develop an awareness of how the implementation of different methodological components can change the direction and solution of a given project or thesis. Both face-to-face and online groups were given the opportunity to share their thoughts and opinions about these perspectives from their article, by referring to the notes they had taken previously.

A collaborative learning approach was implemented to guide and prepare students, since it provided scaffolds to help explore the parameters of theology's research methodologies. Lectures from guest lecturers previously covered the methodologies of the theological disciplines, to provide examples of the operations of methodology in those fields. Through shared examination of text, personal research and group discussion, face-to-face and online students were given the opportunity to navigate new areas of study in the initial stages of learning, with their peers. This was staged to engage robust discussion, encourage networking amongst the group and develop personal confidence within each student. A leader was nominated within each group to collate and write up the consensus of findings. They presented their written deliberations during class and via online forum respectively. Findings, identifying terms and approaches that had been presented in authors' solutions for the various disciplines, were collected as data, analysed and configured in a matrix presentation, displaying a synthesis of elements representative of the various research designs.

In a concluding session, and after the matrix had been configured, students were asked to read, comment and ask questions about the collated information. This process of learning invited students to engage with the methodologies and hermeneutics of theology across the disciplines and broaden their awareness of the depth and breadth of the subject matter. It also aimed to develop skills and competencies for them to present a review of methodology within their chosen discipline, and assist them later in the formulation of their research proposal. See Figures 1 and 2 for matrices showing the synthesis of face-to-face and online groups' findings. The figures also indicate diagnostically the areas of research design that required further teaching and learning.

These constructivist learning perspectives also informed the overall learning approach. Within the transformative learning paradigm, student reflection was aimed at building structures of meaning for how to process their learning activity. Awareness involved understandings about problem solving in the review of research methodologies. Based on students' contextualised learnings from lectures and tutorials, the design elements of a given study could be approached systematically by asking questions about a study's problem or hypothesis, exploring its questions, examining the way a solution was attempted and deliberating on other possible outcomes attributable to creative research design. Enquiry-based learning offered guidance and support in reviewing literature, through a practice of deconstructing research design elements that were articulated in the texts. Examination of the synthesis of ideas presented in the matrix offered deep learning opportunities for assessment and evaluation, for students had been practised and well-resourced to execute a review of methodology confidently on their own. Preparedness gained from articulating modelled frameworks in collaborative social settings helped them develop an understanding of the various terms, as well as interpret the relationship of methodological assumptions within different approaches.

Analysis of student responses

An analysis of students' written responses from the initial tutorials and focus group work provided the information for framing the matrix of ideas. These responses aimed at identifying the epistemology, theoretical perspectives, methodologies, methods, analysis and interpretation or theology of a scholarly text.

For the reading of the pastoral and ministry text, both face-to-face and online students correctly identified the study as qualitative. The branch of knowledge was not known, nor were the theoretical perspectives applicable for this type of study. The methodology and methods of the study were correctly identified from the reading. The link between the interview method and the need for data analysis was not recognised in either group, even though the term 'content analysis' was used in the context of analysis for participant interviews. For those who were intending to undertake a qualitative study in this discipline area, the social science elements of its research design were not a strong part of their academic vernacular. In both groups, learning and resourcing was provided to inform the relevant theoretical perspectives and data analysis.

In the groups belonging to the systematics reading, there was uncertainty about, and in some cases, error in assuming the reading as a qualitative work, apropos of the vein study of a social science project, where ontology can assume a subjectivist epistemology. The online student group incorrectly posited the epistemology of social constructionism, which is an epistemology that assumes a subjectivist ontology. It was noted in discussion that the confusion was linked to the student's interpretation of the word 'qualitative', viewing it as a measure of value given to the actual content of the text. Both groups correctly identified the methodology as a type of literary criticism. While questions about the applicability of social constructionism were initially considered by the face-to-face group, a consensus was reached that the text was objectivist in approach, though they were unsure how to name its branch of knowledge. The Christological hermeneutic was clearly identified by both groups, as was its theology. A design element to identify the type of analysis used was not readily distinguished in the text by either group.

In biblical study, conflicting ideas about the nature of qualitative study and deductive reasoning prevailed in the online group. This cohort presented uncertainty about the nature of qualitative studies, attributing the sociological, historical and cultural dimensions contained in the reading as a descriptive nuance, imparting quality to the hypothesis about conventional or counter-cultural authority existing among the women in St. Paul's early churches. In articulating the epistemology, they identified a rationalist research study, assuming an objectivist approach, which contradicted a qualitative study's characteristic subjective approach. Once again, confusion existed in the students' interpretation of the word 'qualitative', viewing it as a measure of value to be given to the content of text. The face-to-face students belonging to the biblical group correctly identified the epistemological position of the text, though they were unsure how to name its branch of knowledge. Both face-to-face and online students identified the text's methodology as belonging to socio-historical criticism, with online students including the cultural dimension in their understanding. The feminist hermeneutic was clearly identified and understood in both groups. The methodology was thoroughly explored and articulated, with notable examples given to various social groupings of women and the demarcation of conventional and counter-cultural spheres of influence for women's authority roles. Both online and face-to-face groups correctly interpreted the main contention belonging to this biblical study.

Online members examining the church history text were not clear about the nature of what was meant by a qualitative study. This group correctly posited the research project as rationalist, which did contradict the qualitative approach they assigned to the study. Their review of methodology clearly identified literary criticism and historiography as operatives, and use of credible primary and secondary sources for historical analysis was noted. Students discussed appropriate ways to conduct an analysis of the data and interpreted the historical significance of the text correctly. They described the relations involving a series of errors made in the appointment of clergy to the mission, and observed that eventually it led to decisions that detrimentally changed the nature of the mission.

Students' Matrix of Ideas and Research Design Elements in Theology

Figure 1. Synthesis of face-to-face group findings in black text and projected learning focus in blue

Theological Discipline	Epistemology	Theoretical Perspective	Methodology	Method	Analysis	Interpretation and / or Theology
Pastoral/Ministry Australian Catholic Bishops Conference. Catholics Who Have Stopped Attending Mass, Final Report. 2007	Qualitative research study assuming subjectivist approaches E.G. Social Constructionism, where the collective generation of meaning as shaped by the conventions of language and other social processes occur, and where culture is the medium for publicly transmitting their system of intelligibility.	Phenomenological Hermeneutic Interpretivist: where the phenomena of human experience is interpreted	Multi-site case study conducted in six dioceses	Life-history interviews	Content analysis: Technique focussed on formation of theory from observation of messages and coding of messages. (see Hijmans' typology of qualitative content analysis in Hijmans, Ellen. The Logic of Qualitative Media Content Analysis: A Typology Communications. 21, 93-109, 1996.	Theological perspective provided by theologian separate from the research team
Systematics The Intelligence of the Victim in Alison, James O.P., Knowing Jesus. Illinois: Template, 1994.	Uncertainty about the nature of subjectivist and objectivist studies Contextual Theology presenting a theology of redemption, taking contexts of past experience from scripture, and finding contextual meaning and value for present day experience.	Christological The Translation Model in Bevans, Stephen. *Models of Contextual Theology*. Orbis Books. Maryknoll NY, 1994	Literary narrative criticism	Study of contextual and narrative world's focussing Jesus' crucifixion and resurrection Explication of narrative: 'The Beatitudes'	Socio-rhetorical analysis: analysis and interpretation via social / historical constructed reality of symbolic universe, vis 'The Intelligence of the Victim' vis 'The Intelligence of the Victim' (see Ernst van Eck on Socio-rhetorical interpretation. (HTS 57(1 &2) 2001)	Identification of Jesus and 'the intelligence of his victimhood' as humankind's model for standing in solidarity with world's marginalised and gaining closeness to God

Figure 1. Synthesis of face-to-face group findings in black text and projected learning focus in blue

Theological Discipline	Epistemology	Theoretical Perspective	Methodology	Method	Analysis	Interpretation and / or Theology
Biblical Study Cotter, Wendy. "Women's Authority Roles In Paul's Churches: Countercultural or Conventional." Novum Testametum XXXVi, 4 (1994). 350-372	Rationalist research study assuming objectivist approach Narratology	Feminist hermeneutic	Socio-historical criticism Social scientific criticism: engaging sociological analysis Elliot, J H. *A Home for the Homeless: A Sociological Analysis of 1 Peter, its situation and strategy.* Minneapolis: Fortress Press, 1991	Sociology of narrative worlds in Phil 2, 1 Cor 1:11, 16:19, Rom 16:3,4; Phil 4:2, Rom 16:1-2) Study of women in St Paul's letters Cultural anthropology	Socio-historical and rhetorical analysis: Study of women's authority roles in his churches, and interpreted through cultural and social activities for ascertaining conventional or counter-cultural identification	The women in Paul's churches had both conventional and counter-cultural authority. For the context of politics it was counter-cultural and for social and family, it was conventional

Figure 2. Synthesis of online students' findings in black text and projected learning focus in blue

Theological Discipline	Epistemology	Theoretical Perspective	Methodology	Method	Analysis	Interpretation and / or Theology
Pastoral/Ministry Australian Catholic Bishops Conference. Catholics Who Have Stopped Attending Mass, Final Report. 2007	Qualitative research study assuming subjectivist approaches E.G. Social Constructionism, where the collective generation of meaning as shaped by the conventions of language and other social processes occur, and where culture is the medium for publicly transmitting their system of intelligibility.	Phenomenological Hermeneutic Interpretivist where the phenomena of human experience is interpreted	Multi-site case study conducted in six dioceses	In depth, 'Life-history' Two categories of inquiry: Church-related reasons for non-attendance and participant-related reasons	Content analysis Technique focussed on formation of theory from observation of messages and coding of messages. (see Hijmans' typology of qualitative content analysis in Hijmans, Ellen. *The Logic of Qualitative Media Content Analysis: A Typology.* Communications, 21, 93-109, 1996.	Project addressed a gap in previously conducted empirical studies by using qualitative methodology to supplement and extend existing data
Systematics The Intelligence of the Victim in Alison, James O.P., Knowing Jesus. Illinois: Template, 1994.	Social-constructionist epistemology incorrectly chosen for this reading Contextual Theology presenting a theology of redemption, taking contexts of past experience from scripture, and finding contextual meaning and value for present day experience	Christological The Translation Model in Bevans, Stephen. *Models of Contextual Theology.* Orbis Books: Maryknoll NY, 1994	Historical literary criticism	Study of narrative world: telling the story of the apostle's witness of Jesus crucifixion and resurrection Explication of narrative 'The Beatitudes'	Socio-rhetorical analysis: analysis and interpretation via social / historical constructed reality of symbolic universe, vis 'The Intelligence of the Victim' vis 'The Intelligence of the Victim' (see van Eck, E. *Socio-rhetorical Interpretation: Theoretical Points of Departure.* HTS 57(1 and 2), 2001	Christ's resurrection open up a new level of understanding for disciples about Christ's identity: Assuming the nuanced 'intelligence of victim' Jesus shapes our present understanding of what it means to stand in solidarity with the marginalised and advocate for their well being.

Figure 2. Synthesis of online students' findings in black text and projected learning focus in blue

Theological Discipline	Epistemology	Theoretical Perspective	Methodology	Method	Analysis	Interpretation and / or Theology
Biblical Study Cotter, Wendy. "Women's Authority Roles In Paul's Churches: Countercultural or Conventional." Novum Testametum XXXVI, 4 (1994). 350-372	Qualitative approach, incorrectly posited Narratology	Feminist hermeneutic	Literary criticism Socio-historical and cultural methodology Social scientific criticism: engaging sociological analysis Elliot, J H. *A Home for the Homeless: A Sociological Analysis of 1 Peter, its Situation and Strategy.* Minneapolis: Fortress Press, 1991.	Sociology of narrative worlds in Phi 2; 1 Cor 1:11 ; 16:19; Rom 16:3,4; Phil 4:2; Rom 16:1-2) Use of primary and secondary sources Women's leadership in context of church, home and politics	Socio-historical and rhetorical analysis: Women's authority roles in Paul's churches... Interpretation of regular, recurrent, routinised behaviour, systematic relations and structured patterns of behaviour	Pauline churches in mainly Roman contexts deduction that women played conventional role. Political nuancing of role in context of *Ekklesia* sees role of women here as counter-cultural
Church History Massam, Katherine, "Cloistering the Mission: Abbot Torres and changes at New Norcia 1901-1910." The Australian Catholic Record: 89 (2012). 13-25.	Qualitative approach incorrectly posited Narratology	Institutional History	Literary criticism Historiography	Study informing of the changes Abbot Torres made after Abbott Salvado at the mission of New Norcia, Australia Primary/Secondary sources: Government policies; Chronicles of the abbey, diaries, correspondence of abbot; articles/letters from newspapers	Sociology of narrative world: Analysis and interpretation of social grouping focussing on systematic relations	A series of errors made in appointing clergy to the mission caused much frustration and eventually led to decisions that significantly changed the nature of the mission

Using the Matrices as a Resource for Assessment Preparation

From an analysis of the students' written responses provided in group work, the lecturer diagnostically assessed the academic needs of the students. The matrices indicated the methodological areas and approaches (shown in magenta), which would support the cohorts in their preparation to successfully review the methodology of a piece of scholarship in their chosen theological discipline. This approach to learning demonstrates evidence based practice that coheres with deep learning assessment principles, engaging students' personal and contextualised learnings in their field. Using the matrices as background information, a tutorial session and forum for face-to-face and online learners respectively, were organised to develop a better informed understanding of research methodologies. A precis of these sessions follows.

Analysis of discussions for the reading 'Catholics Who Have Stopped attending Mass' developed insight into the nature of qualitative research study finding that the epistemology of the study assumed a subjectivist approach. The reasons for this noted that, in interviewing people, reliable knowledge could be gained from a collective generation of their perceptions. These perceptions were understood to be shaped by the conventions of language and the social process that occurred within a selection set, where Catholic culture pre-set a dialogue for transmitting their intelligibility about falling numbers in Mass attendance. Assuming knowledge generated from language and culture in this way identified social constructionism as the study's epistemology.

The asking of interviewees for comment about their personal experiences in church attendance focused a theoretical perspective around the interpretation of their personal 'lived experience'. The study of a collective phenomenon (i.e. Catholics who have stopped attending Mass) cites the presence of a phenomenological hermeneutic. The researcher's undertaking to conduct interviews in the dioceses identifies a multi-site case study. Choosing life-history interviews identified the method for gathering data for the research study, and content analysis measured data via observed recurrence of themes and the coding of messages.[19] In response to the data analysis, interpretation was offered in the form of responses, which were gathered from a sociologist, theologian, religious educator, liturgist and a bishop. The theological perspectives for this study drew correlation to communal theologies of Church. Eucharistic communion in surrender to faith was offered as a solution to arrest perceived authoritarian, non-compassionate views of Church held by the growing number of non-attenders of Mass. In terms of the 'what might have been' perspective, discussions with the students considered possibilities for incorporating the separate responses presented in the text, as one theological import, through the mutual-critical method.[20] In this approach it was viewed that the theological ramifications of the study questions, its themes of communal theology and expressions of new evangelisation could be considered in the light of the sociological and religious education perspectives explored in the report.

Discussion of the systematics reading, 'The Intelligence of the Victim', delivered complexity around ontology and the epistemology it assumed. Students were unsure about what it meant for a written work to be a qualitative

---

19   Hijmans, 'The Logic of Qualitative Media', 93–109.
20   Swinton & Mowat, *Practical Theology*.

study. The students noted that Alison's text delivered new meanings and values about standing in solidarity with victims, attributing incorrectly that the rhetoric given for exploring Christ's humanity and divinity was qualitative. Further resourcing of students in practice and theory about the nature of qualitative studies was required. Information about indicators belonging to qualitative studies highlighted that interviews, surveys, focus groups and the like are conducted with human participants to explore their perceptions about aspects of their personal experience. It was stated that these indicators were not present in the set reading. Students were aware that social constructionism was an epistemology that referenced qualitative studies but incorrectly applied it to Alison's research methodology. This epistemology intrinsically assumes a subjectivist ontology, where Alison's work did not. A face-to-face and online tutorial was delivered to examine why various epistemologies assumed subjectivist ontology and others assume objectivist ontology.

The Contextual Theological Approach was suggested as a way of holding together the contextual nature of the human experience presented in Alison's work, in tension with the scriptural contexts presented about Jesus' crucifixion, resurrection and the author's understandings for redemption.[21] With the Christological lens guided by Steven Bevan's Translation Model, the theoretical perspectives explored a theology involving the activity and process for assuming Jesus' modelling of 'The Intelligence of the Victim'.[22] Methodologically the text presents a literary narrative criticism, and its methods articulate study of a contextual world leading to Jesus' crucifixion and resurrection. In the text, an explication of the Beatitudes narrative, Matthew 5:1-12, calls readers to solidarity with the marginalised. Socio-rhetorical analysis underpins interpretation of the social and historical construction of reality contained in a 'symbolic universe' where Jesus is the model of right relationship for existence in the Kingdom of God.[23] This theological interpretation was articulated and understood in both groups.

The biblical group examined the reading 'Women's Authority Roles in Paul's Churches: Countercultural or Conventional'. Presented as narratology, its feminist theoretical perspective posed questions through the naming of female co-workers who were not referenced to male family members operating in Paul's early church, with differentials occurring between Roman and Mediterranean

---

21 Bevans, *Models of Contextual Theology*.
22 Bevans, *Models of Contextual Theology*.
23 van Eck, 'Socio-rhetorical Interpretation'.

cultures. Having a social-scientific methodology, sociological analysis informed methods of examination into the nature of women's roles in Paul's letters, and the study of women's narrative worlds in Phil. 2; 1Cor. 1:11; 16:19; Rom. 16:3, 4; Phil. 4:2, and Rom. 16:1-2. The complementary methodology, method and analysis approaches cited for this reading in Figures 1 and 2 studied the various women's authority roles in Paul, and interpreted their significance through their cultural and social activities. The conclusion and theological perspective showed the women exercising both conventional and counter-cultural authority: counter-cultural activities were exhibited by women in the context of Ekklesia, and conventional authority roles in social and family matters.

Presenting as a narrative, 'Cloistering the Mission' articulated an institutional history, examining the New Norcia Mission. It asked questions about the causal effects for the changed nature of mission and treatment of the Aborigines as a coincidence of changed leadership. Its methodology involved a historiography, studying the changes Abbot Torres made after Abbot Salvado. Analysis and interpretation of the data in relation to the social groupings operating within the monastery focused on the special physical barriers that were built in its surrounds, and the consequential disbanding of inclusive social interactions between the monks and indigenous Australians, as having a detrimental result. Theological reflections noted the effects of these decisions as significantly changing the nature of the mission in New Norcia.

Recommendations for Teaching and Learning Research Methodologies in Theology

a) Students need to be empowered to learn

Constructivist learning found in transformative, enquiry-based and deep learning approaches provides robust pedagogy for developing sound learning relationships between students, their peers and the lecturer. The findings of this research-led study highlight the value for implementing contextualised learning processes, such as the matrix of ideas approach, to effectively assist the delivery of stated outcomes, and provide trustworthy evaluation of a unit of work. Higher research degree students need to be encouraged and valued for their commitment to ongoing study. Their academic learning needs to teach them learning processes, and not just theory, to instil in them confidence in their adroit abilities.

b) Students need specialist workshops to practise skills in collaborative settings

The diagnostic nature of contextualised learning and assessment activities is meant to demonstrate gaps in student knowledge and understanding, without stigma. In this study, an outcome to develop and appreciate the range of terms, assumptions and approaches in research current in selected theological disciplines was given, and findings related to this suggest that separate specialised workshops for the various theological disciplines would benefit learners. It is important to note that students need to know the discipline in which they envisage doing research, so that they may critically evaluate key research methodologies and identify those that are most relevant to their own.

c) Deep learning comes from assessment processes with earnest learning mechanisms for students

Educators understand diagnostic, formative and summative assessments, and that listening, speaking, reading and writing play an integral part as mechanisms of learning. This research has begun to touch the surface of what can be done in areas where earnest learning mechanisms are tested. Earnest learning mechanisms build on and layer processes of learning, with more sophisticated layering delivering enhanced theological learning. The layered activities of listening, speaking, reading and writing contained in the matrix of ideas approach, when contextualised and layered with scaffolding, modelling, collaboration, and problem-solving for example, offer degrees of earnest intent, which readily hear the voice of the students in the process of their learning. In coherence with deep learning and assessment, this study found that earnest learning mechanisms served diagnostic, formative and summative assessment, which kept the students informed of their progress during the learning process.

d) Further evidence-based research is required in teaching and learning

There were several encouraging aspects which have come from this research-led learning activity. The prospect for building on constructivist approaches in adult education, which can support and promote academic rigour, requires further onsite practice and research. Strategies in the lecture and tutorial room need to be tested for currency and cogency, and further research in this area with larger cohorts would benefit the field of learning research methodologies in adult education more broadly.

Bibliography

Alison, J. *Knowing Jesus* (Illinois: Template, 1994), 31–58.

Australian Catholic Bishops Conference, 'Catholic Who Have Stopped Attending Mass', Final Report. Australia: Pastoral Projects Office, 2007.

Berg, B. L. *Qualitative Research Methods for the Social Sciences* (Needham Heights, MA: Allyn & Bacon, 1995).

Bevans, S.B. *Models of Contextual Theology* (Maryknoll, NY: Orbis Books, 2004).

Bloor, M., J. Frankland, M. Thomas, & K. Robson. *Focus Groups in Social Research* (London: Sage Publications, 2002).

Bruner, J. *The Process of Education* (Cambridge, MA: Harvard University Press, 1960).

Cotter, W. 'Women's Authority Roles in Paul's Churches: Countercultural or Conventional', *Novum Testamentum* 36.4 (1994), 350–372.

de Jongh, C. 'Theories of Multiple Intelligences and learning Assessment for Deep Learning in Higher Education', (PhD dissertation, University of Johannesburg, Faculty of Education, 2010).

Elliot, J.H. *Home for the Homeless: Sociological Analysis of 1 Peter, its Situation and Strategy* (Minneapolis: Fortress Press, 1991).

Gergen, K. J. 'Social Construction and the Educational Process', in L.E. Steffe & J. Gale (eds.), *Constructionism in Education* (Mahwah, NJ: Lawrence Erlbaum, 1995), 17–39.

Gergen, K. J. 'Social Construction and Theology: The Dance Begins', in C. A. M Hermans, G. Immink et al (eds.), *Social Constructionism and Theology* (Leiden: Brill, 2002).

Gillham, B. *Research Interviewing: The Range of Techniques* (England: Open University Press, 2005).

Goodwin, D. 'A Practical Approach for teaching Foundational Theology: Enquiry-Based Learning and the Matrix of Ideas', in L. Ball & J.R. Harrison (eds.), *Learning and Teaching Theology: Some Ways Ahead* (Northcote, Vic: Morning Star Publishing, 2012).

Grundy, S. & S. Kemmis. 'Educational Action Research in Australia: The State of the Art', in S. Kemmis & R. McTaggart (eds.), *The Action Research Reader* (Geelong: Deakin University Press, 1981).

Grundy, S. 'Three Modes of Action Research', *Curriculum Perspectives* 2 (1981), 23–34.

Hijmans, E. 'The Logic of Qualitative Media Content Analysis: A Typology', *Communications* 21 (1996), 93–109.

Litosseliti, L. *Using Focus Groups in Research* (London: Continuum, 2003), 93–109.

McCutcheon, G. & B. Jurg. 'Alternative Perspectives on Action Research', *Theory into Practice* 24 (1990), 144-151.

Mezirow, J. *Transformative Dimensions in Adult Learning* (San Francisco: Jossey-Bass, 1991).

Mezirow, J. *Cognitive Processes: Contemporary Paradigm of Learning* (San Francisco: Jossey-Bass, 1998).

Mezirow, J. 'An Overview of Transformative Learning', in P. Sutherland & J. Crowther (eds.), *Lifelong learning: Concepts and Contexts* (New York: Routledge, 2006), 24–38.

Patton, M. *Qualitative Evaluation and Research Methods* (Newbury Park, California: Sage, 1990).

Swinton, J. & H. Mowat. *Practical Theology and Qualitative Research* (London: SCM, 2006).

Taber, K. S. 'Constructivism as educational theory: Contingency in Learning, and Optimally Guided Instruction', in J. Hassaskhah (ed.), *Educational Theory* (New York: Nova, 2011), 39–61.

van Eck, E. 'Socio-rhetorical Interpretation: Theoretical Points of Departure', *HTS* 57 (1 & 2), 2001.

van Manen, M. *Researching Lived Experience: Human Science for an Action Sensitive Pedagogy* (London: Althouse Press, 1990).

Denise Goodwin
Catholic Theological College, Melbourne
Denise.Goodwin@ctc.edu.au

21 | THE RELATIONAL TEACHER

SHARING LIFE AS VOCATIONAL ESSENCE

Abstract

The essence of a theology teacher's vocation is about 'sharing life' as a 'relational teacher'. Andrew Root in *The Relational Pastor* argues that relationships are not merely a tool of ministry but its very goal. He contends that ministry grounded in 'place-sharing' and being with and for others is especially appropriate for our dawning new age, as well as consistent with the essence of Christianity as sharing in the life of others and the life of Christ. This chapter builds on Root's analysis of ministry to explore the practice of teaching theology as 'sharing life' in several directions—sharing life with God in cultivating authentic spirituality, sharing life with faculty colleagues as team and sharing life mutually with students. It also considers how teaching serves to foster sharing life with the communities our students will serve as the ultimate point of evaluation. This is an exercise in reflective practice—establishing a theological basis for 'The Relational Teacher: Sharing Life as Vocational Essence' while reflecting personally on how I share life with God, colleagues, students and the world.

In expressing my philosophy of teaching as being a relational teacher, and viewing the vocational essence of my teaching as 'sharing life', I am influenced by Andrew Root's pastoral theology in *The Relational Pastor*.[1] He upholds a high view of personhood, critiques idolatry of individualism and argues that

---

1   Root, *The Relational Pastor.*

relationships are not merely a tool of ministry but its very goal. Root draws on Jeremy Rifkin's analysis in *The Empathic Civilization* of how new energy regimes lead to new communication forms, and new ways of understanding ourselves, others and God.[2] The current oil regime is at its limit and needs a new system, to help all of us not just to consume but to produce and share. Root comments that ministry empathically grounded in 'place-sharing' and being with and for others is especially appropriate for this dawning new age. It is also consistent with the essence of Christianity as sharing in the life of others and the life of Christ.

This essay builds on Root's analysis of ministry, as well as James K. A. Smith's teaching on formation practices and Parker Palmer's philosophy of teaching, to explore the practice of teaching theology as 'sharing life' in several directions— with God in cultivating authentic spirituality, with faculty colleagues as team, with students as a mutual learning community, and with the world that we are preparing students to serve. It thus focuses on the theological imperative and divine calling to relationships. I am exploring elsewhere the metaphor of 'shared life' as a framework for missional leadership.[3] Here I want to explore what it means for my teaching. Wonder at the works of God cannot be caught and taught apart from relationships. Thus, this is an exercise in reflective practice, exploring my calling and practice of being a relational teacher and sharing life as the essence of my vocation.

Spirituality with God

My role as a relational teacher begins with God in cultivating authentic spirituality. I echo the heart of a great teacher Saint Augustine, who famously said: 'You have made us for yourself, and our gut will rumble until we feed on you'.[4] John 15 reminds me that as I abide in Jesus, Jesus abides in me and I will be fruitful. Andrew Root reminds me that the essence of the incarnation is not just a model of ministry, but the mystery of Jesus' very person, communicating and *sharing* of the life of God's self; and inviting us to share in God's life, to be together.[5] Kathryn Tanner continues this theme in writing:

---

2   Rifkin, *The Empathic Civilization*.
3   Hammond and Cronshaw, *Shared Life*.
4   As paraphrased in Smith, *You Are What You Love*, 58.
5   Root, *The Relational Pastor*, 114-115.

> God does not so much want something of us, as [yearn] to be with us… An incarnation-centred Christology emphasizes the fact that God does not so much require something of us as want to give something to us. Our lives are for nothing in the sense that we are here simply to be the recipients of God's good gifts.[6]

That receptivity to God's generosity of sharing life with us is a foundational part of how I want to function as a teacher, and how I want to see my students grow.

Among my most formative moments as a learner have been when teachers made space for me to engage with God directly. These times did not usually involve much information transfer but were worshipful class episodes. A biblical teacher, Rikki Watts, once invited us to stay after class and pray in thanks for the richness of faith in the passage we had been studying. That fostered more of an attitude of appreciation and respect for the Bible than the previous three hours of lecturing. A spiritual formation teacher, Jill Manton, later challenged me to go beyond merely doing my assignments for passing the unit and to reflect authentically on where God was inviting and encountering me.[7] I appreciated teachers who drew my attention back to attentiveness to God, and I know that is where I function best as a teacher.

One of the main obstacles to cultivating my inner life, however, is busyness. I know I let myself become dysfunctionally driven to overwork when I am trying to make an impression on others, or striving to be someone other than what God calls me to be.[8] The word of grace from God is that who I am, and what I have done, is 'enough'. A 'busy teacher', just like a 'busy pastor' whom Eugene Peterson critiques, is an oxymoron or a betrayal—two words that should not go together just like 'embezzling banker' or 'adultrous husband'.[9] Dallas Willard has sage advice for me in saying, 'You must ruthlessly eliminate hurry from your life, for hurry is the great enemy of spiritual life in our world today'.[10] Finding stillness in the midst of busy demands and sharing life with God who loves and calls me are essential for the health of my soul. This is also what I want to embody and model for my students.

---

6 Tanner, *Jesus, Humanity, and the Trinity*, 68, 69, cited in Root, *The Relational Pastor* 115, 116.
7 Previously discussed in Cronshaw, *'Desiring the Kingdom* (book review)', 199.
8 Fryling, *The Leadership Ellipse*.
9 Peterson, *The Contemplative Pastor*.
10 Cited in Ortberg, *The Life You've Always Wanted*, 78.

James Smith, Professor of Philosophy at Calvin College, urges exegeting the culture of churches and society, to see what we really value and what our culture fosters. For example, Smith unveils the spin and idolatry of the shopping mall and the not-so-subtle messages of shopping to accumulate belongings in order to match up to others, to feel good, and to appear successful. He also identifies the liturgies of university that prioritise rational learning and promote workaholism. Reading Smith reminded me of a learning moment at college when our Vice Principal, Bruce Searle, maintained students should not need to study and work 60+ hours every week, a workload pattern that was establishing unsustainable work patterns for ministry. Rituals that students practise and expectations they adopt shape them just as much as what they learn in a classroom. Smith urges us to be attentive to what culture shapes us for: 'habit-forming, identity-shaping, love-directing rituals that capture our imagination and hence our desire, directing it towards a *telos* that is often antithetical to the *telos* envisioned as the kingdom of God'.[11]

Smith also suggests that sharing life with God and cultivating authentic spirituality does not come from accumulating more knowledge or confessing certain beliefs, but from adopting new habits or practices that recalibrate what we love: 'Jesus is a teacher who doesn't just inform our intellect but forms our very loves. He isn't content to simply deposit new ideas into your mind; he is after nothing less than your wants, your loves, your longings'.[12] I encourage my students to adopt practices that help form their longings and spirituality, but I need formative practices too.

This year I have adopted the spiritual practices of *examen* and journaling. The *examen* is about discerning what in my day has been life-giving and what has been life-draining. Our family practises it in a simple form over the dinner table—asking one another what was the best part of our day and the hardest. I also use this approach as I journal some evenings. Since the essence of my vocation is 'sharing life', it helps to pay attention to where I find life flowing at its best, and where God is moving. I resonate with the scene from Narnia where Lucy sees Aslan and says to her companions, 'He wanted us to follow him'. Peter asks, 'Why wouldn't I have seen him?' Lucy replies, 'Maybe you weren't looking'.[13] Thomas Merton wrote: 'The Christian life—and especially the contemplative life—is a continual

---

11 Smith, *Desiring the Kingdom*, 126.
12 Smith, *You Are What You Love*, 1.
13 Lewis, *Prince Caspian*, 119-134.

discovery of Christ in new and unexpected places'.[14] The *examen* and journaling help me to look attentively and discover what Jesus is doing around me.

Another practice I am re-adopting this year is fruit-tree gardening. As I nurture my garden and its twenty-two assorted fruit trees, I remind myself I want to nurture my soul, and nurture those closest to me in my family, church and classroom. When I notice that leaves are wilting from neglect, I am reminded I cannot just plant and forget my trees, and I need to nurture them attentively and feed them with what they need—just as I need to feed my soul, and nurture the congregation where God has planted me.

I need these practices to direct my posture towards attentiveness to God—to share life with God and let God share life through me with others.

Team with Faculty Colleagues

> One of the privileges (and sometimes challenges) of theological education is sharing life with faculty colleagues as a team. The etymology of the word 'college' relates to a faculty organising together with the aim, duty and privilege of teaching. In this vocation, our colleagues are, in fact, a gift of God to us. They sharpen our thinking. They watch our backs. Our vocation that begins with sharing life with God is something we share with one another as colleagues. We share in the privilege of our calling—to walk with God as God's friends and to serve God in the world.

Parker Palmer explores education as a spiritual journey in his book *To Know As We Are Known*. He suggests many faculty feel disconnected from their students and colleagues, and from their own hearts. The love of our subject and the desire to share what is so life-giving for us with others draw us into the vocation. But when institutional expectations foster combat rather than community, or when debates of the intellect alienate us from those we debate, the heart of teaching evaporates and there is no team to sustain us.[15]

> When we spend time with faculty colleagues it can be helpful to watch for metrics of 'sharing life' together. Do we enjoy eating

---

14 Merton, journal entry March 3, 1950, in *The Sign of Jonas*, 275.
15 Palmer, *To Know as We Are Known*, x.

together? How much do we laugh together? When do we take time to play together? What is the quality of our prayer together?

In another Narnia story, the warrior mouse leader Reepicheep has his tail cut off. He asks Aslan to grow it back. Aslan initially refuses, but Reepicheep's mouse friends offer to cut their tails off in sympathy. Aslan says: 'Not for the sake of your dignity, Reepicheep, but for the love that is between you and your people… you shall have your tail again'.[16] That is a lovely image of team solidarity being affirmed.

I am inspired to seek to embody the kind of love Paul urged the church in Rome to have: 'Don't just pretend to love others. Really love them. Hate what is wrong. Hold tightly to what is good. Love each other with genuine affection, and take delight in honoring each other'. (Romans 12:9-10, NLT)

Mutuality with Students

Sharing life is also a helpful framework for my relationship with students.

Theological colleges used to teach ministers-in-training 'don't expect to be friends with your parishioners'. The concern was to maintain appropriate boundaries, and not preference any one set of people in a congregation. But denying the possibility of friendship sets up ministers for an unhealthy lack of mutuality in ministry.

Our default hierarchy in the classroom, furthermore, is for the teacher to be the expert sage-on-the-stage and the student to be there to have their empty jug filled with knowledge. There is an unstated (or perhaps sometimes stated) assumption that teachers and students cannot be friends. Again, there is concern for appropriate boundaries and avoiding favouritism. As teachers, we cannot expect to have all our emotional or spiritual needs filled from sharing life with our students. But I suggest there is room for more mutuality in our classrooms. This mutuality may extend to include friendship as well as exchange of learning and encouragement between teacher and students, as well as among students.

Adult education methods are recognising that students, especially mature-age students, bring a wealth of experience. In my recent missional leadership

---

16 Lewis, *Prince Caspian;* cf. 'A Tale of Tall Tails'.

classes I realised early that many of my students had years and sometimes decades of experience in diverse settings. It benefits us as teachers, and other students, when we can draw out and learn from that level of experience. Students and teachers, furthermore, are more likely to learn fruitfully in the context of a class that functions as a supportive community.

Unfortunately, our systems often default to lectures, readings and assessment. Many teachers hold on to the power of controlling the curricular agenda. Many students resist alternative approaches, as Palmer bemoans:

> Students themselves cling to the conventional pedagogy because it gives them security, too, a fact well known by teachers who have tried more participatory modes of teaching. When a teacher tries to share the power, to give students more responsibility for their own education, students get skittish and cynical. They complain that the teacher is not earning his or her pay, and they subvert the experiment by noncooperation. Many students prefer to have their learning boxed and tied, and when they are invited into a more creative role they flee in fear.[17]

In one of my recent Missional Leadership classes, I started by inviting the small group of students to introduce themselves and their context extensively. I explained the class was very much for reflective practitioners and that I would expect a lot from them in terms of transparently sharing and reflecting on their experience, and relating that to Scripture and literature from the unit readings. The class thus started with their experience of faith and leadership and grappling with the challenges of their context, in conversation with the background reading and missional leadership literature, rather than as a class where I would offer a lot of spoken input with traditional lectures. With a 'flipped classroom' format, I distributed sections of some of the material I had prepared to different students, inviting them to rework and add to it and prepare to present it to the class for us to discuss. Yet one student after two classes said he would like to withdraw, since he found he 'did not like my style' and found it too haphazard and not well prepared. It prompted a crisis of confidence for me. I responded by saying perhaps the class would prefer more content from me. Perhaps I was less prepared than I could have been. But I decided I would persist in my 'flipped classroom' experiment, convinced that sharing life and experience as a community of

---

17   Palmer, *To Know as We Are Known*, x.

learners would foster deeper learning.

Palmer's words have inspired me to persevere in my attempts to foster community and shared life. He commented that people find it threatening when leaders or teachers refuse to tell people how to do things, let alone do it for them—and this is because people have a wound of inadequacy.[18] Palmer helped me realise that the vocation of a teacher is to maintain the space for mutual inquiry, not revert to lecturing and rule-making even if that is what students are demanding:

> It takes a deeply grounded leader—a leader with a source of identity independent of how popular he or she is with the group being led—to hold a space in which people can discover their resources while those same people resist angrily accusing the leader of not earning his or her keep.[19]

We do not need to fill empty space in the classroom with our own words and deeds and egos as teachers.[20] Stepping back from a presupposition that a teacher's role is to transmit knowledge helps create space for a true community of learning from one another's experience to emerge.

Palmer describes community as a spiritual disciple in itself. Community has worked since monastic times—alongside studying sacred texts and prayer and contemplation—in ways that sustain a spiritual journey. Palmer comments on how sharing life in community enhances spiritual formation:

> In the gathered life of the spiritual community, I am brought out of the solitude of study and prayer into the discipline of communion and relatedness. The community is a check against my personal distortions; it helps interpret the meaning of texts and gives guidance in my experience of prayer. But life in community is also a continual testing and refining of the fruits of love in my life. Here, in relation to others, I can live out (or discover I am lacking) the peace and joy, the humility and servanthood by which spiritual growth is measured. The community is a discipline of mutual encouragement and mutual testing, keeping me both hopeful and honest about the love that seeks me, the love I seek to be.[21]

---

18 Palmer, 'Thirteen Ways', x.
19 Palmer, 'Thirteen Ways', xi.
20 Palmer, 'Thirteen Ways', xii.
21 Palmer, To Know as *We Are Known*, 18.

As teachers, we invite students together not for pedagogical convenience, but to engage together in searching for wisdom and reflecting on faith and ministry.[22]

We could benefit from learning more communal values from sisters and brothers from non-Western cultures. I find my Western individualism challenged as I get to know friends from non-Anglo cultures that value communal over individual interests. Communal cultures can have their own downsides with group conformity, and hierarchy and patriarchy that marginalise youth and women. But I am attracted by a culture that encourages the next generation to value serving family and community rather than just the dream of making their own way in the world. I saw this in a Karen youth worker intern at Werribee Baptist Church, Mi Doh Htoo. While doing studies in youth work, he developed a community project on how Karen young people can help their community access community services. He then did a work placement with Wyndham Youth Services and spent part of his week serving as a community liaison helper or driver for his community—many of whom are very new in Australia.[23] That sort of moving beyond individualism and living for others is a value I would love my children to adopt. It is a posture I would be proud to see in my students.

Unfortunately, the academic system can foster individualism and competitiveness, at a time when people training for ministry need more interdependence and collaborative skills. We need more team players and less lone rangers in ministry. Let's begin fostering a more cooperative approach to ministry by reshaping the 'hidden curriculum' in our courses to value cooperation and teamwork more than achieving individual results. James Smith suggests that a story of scarcity robs us of community:

> We have a 'feel' for the world that is informed by stories that dispose us to inhabit the world as *either* a bounteous but broken gift of the gracious Creator *or* a closed system of scarcity and competition; and as a result, either I will just 'naturally' be disposed to see others as neighbors, as image-bearers of God, whose very faces *call* me in a way that is transcendent, or I will have a 'take' on others as competitors, threats, impositions on my autonomy.[24]

Despite theologically valuing community, our assessment systems tend to

---

22 Palmer, To Know as *We Are Known*, 36-37.
23 Cronshaw, 'Training Next Generation', 120.
24 Smith, *Imagining the Kingdom*, 36.

encourage students to default to competitiveness and individualism. One of my online students commented that they struggled with not having as much access to their teacher or class, and transparently confessed that when other students were not initiating much online interaction they hesitated too:

> I got to the point of thinking if they weren't interacting on line then I was not going to give them all my ideas and thoughts and they could passively take it in. I know that this sounds selfish but those who did interact on line we did keep it up via email too, for the same reason.

Even with online possibilities for sharing life, this student was functioning with perceptions of scarcity and competitiveness.

Rifkin's analysis of how society is changing is that we are entering a new consciousness, flowing from new energy regimes and communication systems.[25] We share files and information on unprecedented scale through the internet. Rifkin believes we are also on the verge of producing and distributing energy in wholly new decentralised ways. We are potentially entering a new era of sharing and seeing others anew as persons:

> The increasing connectivity of the human race is advancing personal awareness of all the relationships that make up a complex and diverse world. A younger generation is beginning to view the world less as a storehouse to expropriate and possess and more as a labyrinth of relationships to access.[26]

However, there is also a tendency towards narcissism. We are drawn between sharing life and cooperation on the one hand, and narcissistic self-involvement on the other. Rifkin comments:

> The shift into a Third Industrial Revolution and a new distributed capitalism is leading both to a greater sense of relatedness… as well as a more fractured sense of self, and increased narcissism… The likely reality is that a younger generation is growing up torn between both a narcissistic and empathic mind-set, with some attracted to one and some to the other.[27]

---

25 Rifkin, *The Empathic Civilization*; discussed also in Root, *The Relational Pastor*, 42-43.
26 Rifkin, *The Empathic Civilization*, 594.
27 Rifkin, *The Empathic Civilization*, 575, 589.

Our classes will best form our students if they can steer away from individualism and narcissism, and instead foster empathy and sharing life.

Theologically, we are sisters and brothers before and after we are also teachers with students. In Matthew 23, Jesus critiqued the Pharisees and religious scholars of his day for their pretentious show of hierarchy and failing to practise what they preach. He urged his followers in fact not to be called rabbis or instructors, and not celebrate titles or positions of honor. The position of teacher and instructor belongs ultimately to Jesus before whom we are all students in the one classroom, as the Message translation suggests:

> Don't let people do that to *you*, put you on a pedestal like that. You all have a single Teacher, and you are all classmates. Don't set people up as experts over your life, letting them tell you what to do. Save that authority for God; let *him* tell you what to do. No one else should carry the title of 'Father'; you have only one Father, and he's in heaven. And don't let people maneuver you into taking charge of them. There is only one Life-Leader for you and them—Christ. (Matthew 23:8-10, MSG)

As people tasked with the role of teacher, we are still sisters and brothers with one another, and fellow students of the one teacher. Jesus called his disciples 'friends' (John 15:15). This is not a functional relationship, but a person-to-person relationship of mutuality. Surely if the Son of God could call his disciples friends, then we can be friends with our students.

Root suggests that pastoral ministry is not primarily a utilitarian relationship for the pastor to get people to fulfil certain interests or achieve selected tasks. A pastor is called to open their spirit to the spirit of the people in their congregation—through sharing life and being present in prayer, worship and the stories of their people. Root suggests: 'Pastoring is the brave action of leading by opening your person to the person of others so that together we might share in the life of God'.[28] That is a delightful image of pastoral ministry that also has resonance for me as a teacher. Teaching is a brave process of opening our self to others, and together sharing life with God, and one another, and the world around us.

---

28 Root, *The Relational Pastor*, 68.

Mission in our Neighbourhoods

Sharing life is a metaphor that frames my approach to learning and teaching in the classroom. But it also flows on to what I hope will be its product, in terms of students sharing life with the communities they will serve. This is the ultimate point of evaluation for learning and teaching.

Universities that teach teachers are best evaluated by examining the learning that happens in the school classrooms of the trained teachers. Similarly, our training of people for ministry is best evaluated by examining the quality of sharing of life that happens in the local communities where our students serve.

Sharing life is a helpful framework for vocation. Part of what I want to fulfil as a teacher is helping my students connect with what is most life-giving for them. Part of my role as teacher is to help students discern how they can best share life and the fullness of what really is good news about Christianity with their world. Regarding vocational discernment, Frederick Buechner counsels, 'The place God calls you to is the place where your deep gladness and the world's deep hunger meet'.[29] Parker Palmer expands on Buechner's wisdom and urges people to 'let your life speak', and make your contribution based on the gifts and passions God has given you, rather than what others think you 'ought' to do.[30]

The lesson of following not someone else's expectations but one's own passion for contributing to the world was learned (or not) by the students in the story 'Dead Poets Society'. The new English teacher John Keating, played by Robin Williams, inspires his students through teaching poetry. He urges them to 'make your lives extraordinary', and teaches them the Latin phrase *'carpe diem'* or 'seize the day'. It is not just the teacher but the class that supports one another in dreaming and following their dream. They re-form 'The Dead Poets Society' and meet in a cave to recite and create poetry in ways that tap into their creative potentials.

James Smith upholds a high view of worship as part of education; not in the sense of being overly formal, but being important for forming people and inviting them into union with God. Notably he urges making the most of the arts, metaphor, and especially story to captures people's imagination in Kingdom of God directions:

---

29 Buechner, *Wishful Thinking*, 95; cited in Palmer, *Let Your Life Speak*, 16.
30 Palmer, *Let Your Life Speak*.

> We don't just need teachers and preachers and scholars and "doctors" of the church to *tell* us what to do; if the gospel is going to capture imaginations and sanctify perception we need painters and novelists and dancers and songwriters and sculptors and poets and designers whose creative work *shows* the world otherwise, enabling us to imagine differently.[31]

This essay is an exercise in reflective practice—establishing a theological basis for the relational teacher but also reflecting on my experience of sharing life with God, colleagues, students, and the world. It is unfortunate if students are so preoccupied with the demands of study (or teachers are so focused on the mechanics of teaching and learning), that they spend little time fostering shared life with God, with their classmates, and with their church and neighbourhood community their studies are designed to serve. Wonder at the works of God cannot be caught and taught apart from relationships. This chapter thus explores my calling and practice of being a relational teacher and sharing life as the essence of my vocation.

Bibliography

'A Tale of Tall Tails (An occasional paper inspired by the movie *Prince Caspian*)', 20 February 2008, https://www.vermande.us/tim/302.html, accessed 20 May 2017.

Buechner, F. *Wishful Thinking: A Theological ABC* (New York, NY: Harper & Row, 1973).

Cronshaw, D. '*Desiring the Kingdom: Worship, Worldview and Cultural Formation,* by James K. A. Smith (book review)', *Journal of Adult Theological Education* 8.2 (Dec 2011), 199.

Cronshaw, D. 'Training Next Generation Culturally and Linguistically Diverse Baptist Leaders for Mission', *Charting the Faith of Australians: Thirty Years in the Christian Research Association* (P. Hughes, ed.; Melbourne: CRA, 2016), 118-133.

Fryling, R.A. *The Leadership Ellipse: Shaping How We Lead by Who We Are* (Downers Grove, IL: IVP, 2010).

Hammond, K. and D. Cronshaw. *Shared Life* (Downers Grove, IL: IVP, forthcoming).

Lewis, C.S. *Prince Caspian: The Chronicles of Narnia* (New York, NY: HarperCollins, 2002).

Merton, T. *The Sign of Jonas* (New York, NY: Harcourt, Brace & Co, 1953).

---

31   Smith, *Imagining the Kingdom*, 163.

Ortberg, J. *The Life You've Always Wanted: Spiritual Disciplines for Ordinary People* (Grand Rapids, MI: Zondervan, 2002).

Palmer, P. *Let Your Life Speak: Listening for the Voice of Vocation* (San Francisco, CA: Jossey-Bass, 2000).

Palmer, P. 'Thirteen Ways of Looking at Community (… with a fourteenth thrown in for free)', July 10, 2014.

Palmer, P. *To Know as We Are Known: Education as a Spiritual Journey* (New York, NY: HarperOne, 1993).

Peterson, E. *The Contemplative Pastor: Returning to the Art of Spiritual Direction* (Grand Rapids, MI: Eerdmans, 1993).

Root, A. *The Relational Pastor: Sharing in Christ by Sharing Ourselves* (Downers Grove, IL: IVP, 2013).

Rifkin, J. *The Empathic Civilization* (New York, NY: Jeremy P. Teacher/ Penguin, 2009).

Smith, J.K.A. *Desiring the Kingdom: Worship, Worldview and Cultural Formation* (Grand Rapids, MI: Baker Academic, 2009).

Smith, J.K.A. *Imagining the Kingdom: How Worship Works*. Volume 2 of *Cultural Liturgies* (Grand Rapids, MI: Baker Academic, 2013).

Smith, J.K.A. *You Are What You Love: The Spiritual Power of Habit* (Grand Rapids, MI: Brazos, 2016).

Tanner, K. *Jesus, Humanity, and the Trinity* (Minneapolis, MINN: Fortress, 2009).

Darren Cronshaw
Australian College of Ministries, Sydney
dcronshaw@acom.edu.au

22 | DEEP LEARNING FROM A SHALLOW SURFACE?

ENCOURAGING GOOD RESEARCH IN THE INTERNET AGE

Abstract

The internet presents learners with ready access to a vast amount of information, and a vast number of potential conversation partners. The internet has inevitably affected student learning and will continue to do so. Despite creating an enormous shallow surface it nevertheless presents opportunities for 'deep learning'. However, not all 'deep learning' is '*worthwhile* deep learning', which ought to be the desirable educational outcome—especially for theological education. In order for this outcome to be achieved through learning led by internet-assisted research, certain pitfalls need to be avoided.

Informational challenges have previously been identified, but conversational challenges also need to be addressed. The internet opens up the potential for a vast number of social learning experiences, but certain pitfalls need to be avoided: the recency effect, the loss of expertise, being in the hands of machines, or in the hands of one's peers, 'bubble and hype', and the difficulty of rediscovering those with genuine expertise. The chapter closes by offering some maxims to help students avoid the informational and conversational pitfalls of research in the internet age, in order to engage in deep learning that is worthwhile.

Introduction: A Generation with the Internet

After twenty-five years, the Internet now provides the researcher with a 'virtually infinite'[1] amount of *information* and potential *conversations*. After being around for a generation, it has changed the way society learns and thinks. But this is not always positive. If the Internet is to assist the worthwhile deep learning that is necessary to transform people into better human beings engaged in building a better society, certain pitfalls of research in the internet age need to be avoided.

A metaphor of depth is often utilised to describe desirable learning strategies that will achieve desirable learning outcomes. Students can adopt a *shallow* approach to learning that will result in undesirable poorer learning outcomes, whereas a *deep* approach to learning is beneficial for desirable better learning outcomes.

Sometimes discussions of deep learning are purely in terms of approaches, rather than outcomes.[2] Certain principles will be listed, such as the learning being internal, integrative into existing knowledge, relative to the learner's present or future life, with responsibility for learning assumed by the learner.[3] Such discussions may then focus on learning activities, including assessments, which are deemed to encourage the exercise of such deep learning strategies. So, for example, within a constructivist paradigm, 'the deepest learning is achieved through (1) exposure to rich experiences, (2) opportunity to practise, (3) conversation and exchanges with others, and (4) reflection on action'.[4]

But what does deep learning look like in terms of its outcomes in the life of the learner? Descriptions of the results of deep learning might focus upon the knowledge learned, to speak of it being remembered, lasting, transferable to contexts outside the classroom, integrated into the learner's life, issuing in a life-long learning stance, and so on. But once these results are described, it becomes clear that deep learning is not so much focused upon approaches or strategies or activities of the learning process, but on the *person being transformed* by the learning.

---

1   Ball, 'Where are we going?', 13.
2   E.g. Briggs, 'Deeper Learning'.
3   Ball, 'Principles of Deep Learning', summarises that deep learning is part of an outcomes-based education; an integrative process in which new knowledge is connected to old; and promoted by learning activities that connect with existing frameworks of reference, relate to learners' aspirations; and engage learners in assuming responsibility for their own learning.
4   Smith & Healey, 'On the Frontiers of Change', 158.

> While effective learning will always prize critical analysis and academic rigour, it will also focus on being *holistic* (respecting the psychological, social, intellectual, physical, and spiritual dimensions of the learner) and *deeply transformational* (producing deep personal change evident in improved practice).[5]

Deep learning brings the subject matter deep within the person to effect transformation of life.

However, one important addition not often discussed—perhaps because it is assumed—is the notion that deep learning needs to be *worthwhile*, in that it transforms the learner for their good, and for the good of society. Neither education in general, nor deep learning in particular, should be treated as if it is morally neutral. With the wrong subject matter, amongst the wrong conversation partners, deep learning may indeed effectively transform a person, but towards life outcomes that are far from worthwhile. The apostle Paul warned the Corinthians that 'bad company corrupts good character' (1 Cor. 15:33), and just like a literary work can be either life-enhancing or life-corrupting,[6] so can an entire education—depending upon what has been learned. Just as there are good lessons learned badly, there are also bad lessons learned well. Deep learning in a medical school about how to heal leads to a very different kind of life-transformation than deep learning in a terrorist training camp about how to kill.

Since Higher Education turns out future society leaders, it ought to be concerned about *worthwhile* deep learning. Since theological educators aim to turn out future society leaders who spread the fragrance of the knowledge of God, they ought to be even more concerned.

But taking place in the Internet Age, the internet poses challenges for worthwhile deep learning of at least two kinds. There are *informational* challenges and *conversational* challenges.

---

5   Smith & Healey, 'On the Frontiers of Change', 147.
6   I allude here to the life-project expressed in Wayne Booth's works, from *The Rhetoric of Fiction*, via *Don't Try To Reason With Me* (specifically with the US Education system in target), *A Rhetoric of Irony*, *Modern Dogma & the Rhetoric of Assent*, and *Critical Understanding*, through to the volume whose title is taken from the apostle Paul, *The Company We Keep*.

Informational Challenges from Internet-led Research to Worthwhile Deep Learning

Knowledge about the learning process of the brain rapidly advanced in exactly the same decades as the Internet was defining the present Age.[7] For effective deep learning to occur, learning needs to be in tune with the way the human brain works. Unfortunately, aspects of post 1960s educational theory dispensed with methods now recognised by brain scientists to be extremely brain friendly. Speaking of 'neuroplasticity-based techniques' with great potential for improving our weak brain functions, Norman Doidge notes that:

> The irony of this new discovery is that for hundreds of years educators did seem to sense that children's brains had to be built up through exercises of increasing difficulty that strengthened brain functions. Up through the nineteenth and early twentieth centuries a classical education often included rote memorization of long poems in foreign languages, which strengthened the auditory memory (hence thinking in language) and an almost fanatical attention to handwriting, which probably helped strengthen motor capacities and thus not only helped handwriting but added speed and fluency to reading and speaking. Often a great deal of attention was paid to exact elocution and to perfecting the pronunciation of words. Then in the 1960s educators dropped such traditional exercises from the curriculum, because they were too rigid, boring, and "not relevant". But the loss of these drills has been costly; they may have been the only opportunity that many students had to systematically exercise the brain function that gives us fluency and grace with symbols.[8]

The effects of these changes in educational theory were compounded by the arrival of television in the same period.

> About twenty years after the spread of TV, teachers of young children began to notice that their students had become more restless and had increasing difficulty paying attention. [...] When those

---

7   Smith & Healey, 'On the Frontiers of Change', 148, 149–154. For an accessible digest and popularisation of the recent advances in brain research see N. Doidge, *The Brain that Changes Itself*, and *The Brain's Way of Healing*; Radin, 'Brain-Compatible Teaching'; Rowland, 'The brain that changes itself'.
8   Doidge, *The Brain that Changes Itself*, 41–42.

children entered college, professors complained of having to "dumb down" their courses each new year, for students who were increasingly interested in "sound bites" and intimidated by reading of any length. Meanwhile, the problem was buried by "grade inflation" and accelerated by pushes for "computers in every classroom", which aimed to increase the RAM and gigabytes in the class computers rather than the attention spans and memories of the students.[9]

After the Internet was switched on to be readily channelled through those high gigabyte class-room computers, problems in student learning were compounded. For many of the ways that information is gained from the internet are exactly what the human brain *does not* need for effective learning, that is, they are counter-productive. At a Sydney College of Divinity Learning & Teaching Conference, Charles de Jongh drew attention to five 'challenges to learning in the age of the internet', which all relate to the way *information* was acquired.

a) The medium has become the distraction[10]

Whereas good learning requires the brain to be focused and attentive, the Internet offers opportunities for constant distraction, through such things as hypertext and multimedia, which distract the attention, diminishing the ability to focus, and so to process the information.[11]

Smith and Healy therefore rightly highlight the need for attention: 'While the internet has given many more people access to searchable information, it has not necessarily taught those users how to think and learn effectively'. With the distraction of the ever-present hyperlink and need for multitasking, the constant availability of more information causes people not to do the focused work necessary for memory formation, whereas 'concentration and contemplation are crucial to building the rich mental models of complex knowledge necessary to develop expertise in any given field'.[12]

---

9   Doidge, *The Brain that Changes Itself*, 307, drawing on the work of Jane Healy, *Endangered Minds*.
10 De Jongh, 'Challenges to Learning', 117.
11 De Jongh, 'Challenges to Learning', 115–117, 124. Contrast: 'The importance of technology is to personalise education. Multimedia is a real hook in the digital age. It makes kids the co-creators of knowledge', Briggs, 'Deeper Learning'. For the effects of media on the brain, see 'A Vulnerable Brain— how the Media Reorganizes it', in Doidge, *The Brain that Changes Itself, 306–311*
12 Smith & Healey, 'On the Frontiers of Change', 152–153.

b) More information has narrowed the Field of Vision[13]

Perhaps paradoxically, the expanded amount of available information has not broadened students' horizons: 'while valuable in certain ways, the problem is that students, while having access to "more", do not access more'.

> It is arguable that the quantity of data and material, together with ease of access, demands that students need tools to access that material. However, ironically, the use of the tools—the key one being search engines—undermines access to the vast quantity of material available, which ultimately undermines the quality of the material accessed.

Dependent upon the internet aggregators and pressured by a consequent increase in speed with which the material needs to be dealt with, both student and teacher have suffered a narrowing of the field of vision.

c) Breadth is greater than focus[14]

For a good deal of their time in research, students simply trawl through the incredible width of information the internet makes available, much of it useless, without the time needed to examine it properly. This also diminishes their focus, and also encourages a superficial reading in which 'quantity is elevated over quality', and 'countless bits' of information are grasped, without being integrated by context. The 'F-shaped pattern' of online reading also decreases focus and so absorption and understanding of information.

d) Surface is greater than depth[15]

This lack of focus 'results in students who find that they are increasingly unable to plumb the depths of the material and find themselves "trapped" on the surface'. With a decreased ability to get the connotations, or to concentrate on anything much, even a blog post of three or four pages becomes a challenge. Thus, 'students may have a grasp of what is on the surface of the material, but are unable to both appreciate and interact with the depth of that material', because their 'brains are engaged less directly and more shallowly in the synthesis

---

13   De Jongh, 'Challenges to Learning', 117–119.
14   De Jongh, 'Challenges to Learning', 119–121.
15   De Jongh, 'Challenges to Learning', 121–123.

of information when we use research strategies that are all about "efficiency", "secondary (out of context) referencing", and "once over, lightly"'.[16]

The brain works best if it concentrates on one thing only: '[as] we plunge into a new world of infinitely connectible and accessible information, we risk losing our means and ability to go beneath the surface, to think deeply'[17]—and, presumably, to *learn* deeply, towards worthwhile ends.

(e) Information is not understanding[18]

Information retrieval has replaced knowledge formation, and students are finding it difficult to process the vast quantities of information available. Their 'lack of authentic engagement' correlates with a consequent loss of comprehension.

But as well as such *informational* challenges, as outlined by De Jongh, the internet also presents *conversational* challenges to worthwhile deep learning.

Conversational Challenges to Deep Learning from Internet-Led Research

a) Deep Social Learning

There is no doubt the internet presents a wealth of information. However, the longer the internet has been with us, the clearer it has become that the vast opportunities it affords have not been accompanied by a correspondingly vast improvement in internet age learners.[19] In order for it to be an effective tool for worthwhile deep learning, the challenges to learning faced by the internet age must continue to be identified and addressed, even if it is difficult to do so in the

---

16   De Jongh, 'Challenges to Learning', 122–123, citing Carr, *The Shallows*, 137.
17   Jackson, *Distracted*, 155; cited by De Jongh, 'Challenges to Learning', 123.
18   De Jongh, 'Challenges to Learning', 123–125.
19   See the summary of concerns raised by Greenfield (2003), Bauerlein (2009), Carr (2011), and Williams (2011), in De Jongh, 'Challenges to Learning', 113–115.

face of the loud voices shouting in its favour[20]—and often with a volume unmatched by quality of evidence and argument, or even awareness of previous research.[21]

Certainly the internet offers greater potential opportunities for activities noted in connection with strategies of deep learning, namely, 'exposure to rich experiences', and 'conversation and exchanges with others', if not also 'opportunities to practise' and 'reflection on action' as the learner adds their own input online, for example.[22] But connecting does not automatically guarantee good learning, especially if the cost of connection is a less efficient usage of the brain. And, to put the contrary case, when the deeper learning requirements of the brain are taken into account, 'technological advances to date have favoured the streamlined delivery of explicit knowledge rather than deep learning that comes with emphasising tacit knowledge'.[23]

In fact, the development of such tacit (and transformative) knowledge may be linked less with the *activities* or *strategies*, and more with the *social context* in which deep learning is facilitated—less with *information* and more with *conversation*. As such, the secret to success would lie in the interaction between technology and pedagogy.

> Learning is rooted in relationships, and supportive relationships can unleash the potential of every student. […] The future of teaching may ultimately center in deeper relationships built between teachers and students, developed through creative, collaborative, socially connected and relevant learning experiences. Technology can enable and accelerate these deep learning relationships—both

---

20 Since educational technology is big business, the quest for profits can make the technological tail wag the educational dog. In such an environment, those who raise legitimate educational questions can be written off as luddites. It is instructive that both De Jongh and Baggaley feel obliged to explain the positive purpose behind their criticisms. De Jongh, 'Challenges to Learning', 115, insists that his 'bias should not be seen as antagonism, but rather as an endeavour to encourage deliberate consideration of and reflection on the nature of learning in the age of the Internet'; Baggaley & James, 'The fog of online learning', 128, assert that 'the current article has neither a technocentric message nor a technophobic one, for good and bad teaching is to be found in all types of education'.
21 See, for example, Baggaley's discussion of the ignorance of previous research in reports from the Global Learning Council (*Technology-Enhanced Learning*) and MIT (Wilcox, Sarma, & Lippel, *Online Education*). He also notes Downes' 'rancorous' (p.367) response ('Preparing for the digital university') to the more academically rigorous report sponsored by the Gates Foundation (Siemens, Gasevic, & Dawson, *Preparing for the Digital University*); Baggaley, 'Sandcastle Competitions'.
22 Smith & Healey, 'On the Frontiers of Change', 158.
23 Smith & Healey, 'On the Frontiers of Change', 157.

between teachers and students and between students and other "learning partners" such as peers, mentors, and others with similar learning interests. Technology as a platform for more connected social learning experiences is a far cry from the notion of technology supplanting teaching.[24]

However, as with its vast amount of information, so too the internet opens up a vast number of possible 'social learning experiences', and so, alongside its *informational* challenges, the internet also brings *conversational* challenges to worthwhile deep learning. For with the vast mass of information now available, the need for good conversation partners who prove to be reliable guides has become paramount.

b) The Challenges to Learning in Online Communities
The Recency Effect
The 'Recency Effect' contains a cluster of internet-fuelled problems. In various ways, internet knowledge has a very short life-span and so the internet researcher tends to focus on 'the now'. The rapid advances of technology create the illusion that while the future cannot be known, the past has nothing to say. The traditional was wrong, because its day is over, and nothing is worth knowing if it cannot be described with the adjective 'innovative'. In this environment, as opinions are announced as innovative, they can be accompanied by proposals that issues already addressed in previous research but overlooked or ignored ought to be items for future research.[25]

However, claims to originality should be justified. To overlook past research is to deprive present advances in knowledge from a solid foundation, and to open up present opinion-makers to errors of analysis, conclusion, and action.[26] Citing Target's loss of billions through attempting to set up in Canada, but ignoring previous research, Baggaley finds that, in education,

> similar mistakes were made in the emergence of the MOOC from marshy blogland origins. When their warnings went unheeded, experts in fields including distance education were unable to prevent

---

24 Fullan & Langworthy, *Towards a New End*, 14.
25 Baggaley, 'Sandcastle competitions', 369, of the MIT report.
26 Baggaley, 'Sandcastle competitions', 369.

the wastage of millions on ill-conceived MOOC projects.[27]

This semi-deliberate stance taught by some, caught by others, has led to a profound ignorance of the past, which just as surely breaks the contemporary world from its steadying heritage. This occurs in many areas, and—perhaps ironically—it is certainly not new.[28] It is especially present in educational theory and practice which makes claims to novelty for practices that have been around for a very long time. In a unique kind of plagiarism, old practices and ideas are 'reframed' for a new day, as if the new label totally transforms the practice into something entirely different from what it used to be when it was practised under a different name.[29]

As an example, Baggaley cites the notion of the 'Flipped Classroom'. Claimed to be invented in 2007 by two Colorado High School teachers, it was fuelled by 'bubble and hype' to take the world by storm as a 'radical innovation'.[30] But this reversal of teaching procedure has been used by Distance Educators for decades, and even the term itself has been utilised before.[31] The identification of 'flipped learning' as 'a breakthrough':

> reveals how in the Internet age years of scholarly theory and research can be eclipsed literally overnight, and work in fields such as distance education marginalized by groundless press and blog claims, and by journals and institutions that accept them.[32]

The Loss of 'Expertise'
After decades of interacting with the scholarship of and trends in distance and online education, Jon Baggaley points to a decline in the quality of research associated with online learning, not only amongst students, but also amongst

---

27 Baggaley, 'Flips and flops', 444.
28 See, for example, Hamilton, *To Turn From Idols*, Ch. 4, who sounded an alarm against the drive for 'relevance' as early as 1973. To go back even earlier, the apostle Paul appears to have encountered the same problem in Athens and Ephesus (Acts 17:21; 2 Tim. 4:3).
29 Baggaley, 'Sandcastle competitions', 370, 371.
30 Baggaley, 'Flips and flops', 437.
31 Baggaley, 'Flips and flops', 438–444; 'Sandcastle competitions', 369.
32 Baggaley, 'Flips and flops', 438.

academics.[33] This does not portend well for the future, for not only will problematic academics model problematic research behaviours to students producing another generation of sloppy academics, but, worse still, it is a further corruption of society, since sloppy research methods contribute to gross ignorance amongst graduates, who then become societal leaders.

The internet has also contributed to the democratisation of 'expertise' and the demise of the 'social gatekeepers'. According to Nichols, the day is over when participation in public debate

> required submission of a letter or an article, and that submission had to be written intelligently, pass editorial review, and stand with the author's name attached.
>
> We are witnessing the "death of expertise": a Google-fuelled, Wikipedia-based, blog-sodden collapse of any division between professionals and laymen, students and teachers, knowers and wonderers—in other words, between those of any achievement in an area and those with none at all.[34]

In the Hands of Machines

With a mass of internet information to domesticate, usually in the midst of an already busy life, the time-poor researcher is hungry for a quick fix. This can be delivered by the most basic guide to what is out there: internet aggregators. However, the search engine is not a thoroughly reliable guide. Aggregators give access only to about 15% of available material, and then only to the popular and commercial portion of it.[35] In addition, using their own in-built 'deep learning' algorithms, they also deliver content based on the user's previous search history, further narrowing the results. Inexperienced users also lack the skills to design more than the simplest searches, further restricting the results they are served. But it is not simply the students, for even academics once trained

---

33 Baggaley, 'Sandcastle Competitions', 372: The GLC (2016) and MIT (2016) reports 'contain numerous flaws and false premises, and ignore the theory and practice accumulated in distance education, educational technology and other disciplines over 50 years' and 'should be regarded as major embarrassments to the institutions that sponsored them'. 'Sadly, [their] problems [...] are symptomatic of those observed in modern society generally', citing the US Presidential campaign of 2016, 'in which incorrect statements are being made almost daily, plagiarisms are denied, proved and still denied, and libellous insults are issued of the most extreme kind'.
34 Nichols, 'The Death of Expertise'.
35 Jackson, *Distracted*, 163; cited from De Jongh, 'Challenges to Learning', 120.

in the finest research skills during their PhD, now tend to rely on aggregators, with a consequent narrowing of range in the works consulted and cited in their writing.[36]

The search engine guides, therefore, lead to a 'narrowing of vision' whereas good research should open it out as widely as possible. In addition, as De Jongh has already pointed out, the same pressure that leads researchers to use the aggregator, namely, the combination of a vast amount of information and a limited amount of time, also means that they do not give adequate time to evaluating search results, or to giving them the due consideration that will result in worthwhile deep learning.

At the Institutional level, rather than employing an expensive faculty of well-trained teachers, the need for a quick fix leads to institutions pushing educational methods that are cheaper to run—and more impersonal. This becomes one of the causes of 'the fog of online learning' identified by Baggaley:

> Anxious to save on costs, many educational institutions are encouraging learner-based approaches and exhorting their teachers to develop MOOCs as their platforms. The first type of fog arises from institutional priorities and disciplinary trends of this kind, which lead established practices to be abandoned and cost-saving but flawed approaches to be applied in their place.[37]

In the Hands of one's Peers

The same economic pressures also favour a learner-centred education that is largely driven by the learners themselves, supplemented by peer-group interactions. Good educational theory endorses both these things as good practice, of course, and both are part of deep learning strategies. But peer-learning is not without its own problems in this Internet Age.

In an interesting experiment in an online 'learning community', noting that a family-history online community has similarities to MOOCs, Baggaley compared online family trees with a family tree constructed pre-internet and from the old-fashioned slog work of tracking down records in archives all over the country—many of which still cannot be found online. The online trees clearly showed that about half were constructed by *leaders*, who claimed to

---

36 See the research of James Evans, cited by De Jongh, 'Challenges to Learning', 118.
37 Baggaley & James, 'The fog of online learning', 125.

have checked other sources, and half by *followers*, who were content to simply accept one of the trees offered by a leader. Further checking then revealed that only 30% of the leaders had actually done any real checking and, furthermore, that even if they had the facts basically correct, they still made errors of interpretation, thus leading to flawed conclusions.[38] These errors were further compounded as the trees were copied by the followers. The fog of 'negative emergence' descended, that is, 'when a mass of errors gathers around knowledge that re-emerges in confused situations and goes unchallenged'.

> The fog thickens as coats of jargon are applied to poor conclusions in order to protect them from scrutiny and to unoriginal ones to make them seem new. [...] With each new flawed set of conclusions that emerges the fog around the fact increases, until, with luck, its contradictions and conclusions are discredited.[39]

But often the outcome is not so positive. In terms of peer-group learning, the experiment illustrates that to rely on a peer-group often means relying on those unskilled in good research practices; insufficiently experienced to have research hunches that aid interpretation of data; unused to drawing fitting and sensible evidence-based conclusions; and so quite unsuitable to act as *reliable* guides for others. They can certainly act as guides, given the propensity for 50% of this sample to simply follow, and the followers may indeed follow with a deep learning approach that ensures they deeply learn what the leader has to impart. But ultimately, because of the inherent deficiencies in the peer-guide, the deep learning is not worthwhile, and so the guide is proven to be unreliable. 'The confused conclusions that can be generated by online peer instruction are not an acceptable alternative to the kind of knowledge that emerges from reliable facts and tuition'.[40]

Research by Numbers and 'Bubble and Hype'
The internet provides a vast number of potential peers to act as guides on the learner's journey, and choices need to be made about 'the company we will keep' (1 Cor. 15:33). But how does the learner select the peer group they will invite to guide them through the maze? One tried and true method in a

---

38 Baggaley & James, 'The fog of online learning', 124.
39 Baggaley & James, 'The fog of online learning', 125.
40 Baggaley & James, 'The fog of online learning', 127.

democratic society is to follow the numbers. But the numbers can be followed in at least two directions.

Some learners will be content to go with the majority. But in the internet age, what does 'the majority' mean? Huge numbers of pages saying the same thing may well derive from just one source, and whether or not that source is a reliable guide is a question that needs to be decided by weighing rather than counting.[41] Anyone who has done a footnote chase through printed materials will recognise that this problem is not new in kind, but the internet has intensified its magnitude.

From the other end of the scale, other learners will go with a minority. This may be because, for whatever reason, they simply cannot trust the dominant paradigm (research by protest), or it may be because they prefer to be part of an echo-chamber in which the other voices sound very much like their own (research by tribalism, or shared ideology).

And once we have descended from the majority to the minority end of the numerical scale, it raises a third way of choosing a peer-group by numbers. For through social media the internet age has developed incredibly powerful means to generate 'bubble and hype'. Any mere opinion, once stated, can be 'liked' by a couple of thousand Face Book followers, shared, tweeted, and reshared and retweeted, until a new majority is generated with all the persuasive force, manipulation and pressure—along with, of course, the vitriol for which social media has become infamous.[42] With the evil presence of internet trolls potentially lurking under any seemingly innocent posting, this is a peer group that, for some, is almost impossible to resist.

But, once again, even if through 'bubble and hype' the old minority manages to give the impression that it has become the new majority, this still says nothing about the reliability of the peer-guidance it provides. Opinion expressed on a blog, or a Face Book post, or Tweet, even if it attracts a large number of followers, is still only the opinion of the blog writer, or social media poster. The 'bubble and hype' possible now through declarations on social media can certainly be

---

41 This lesson from the family tree experiment in Baggaley & James, 'The fog of online learning', is already well-known in New Testament Textual Criticism.

42 Noting Millbank's claim that social media displays people 'clubbing each other to death', Michael Jensen is thoroughly familiar with the fact that 'there is a brutality about the verbal jousting that internet community fosters. At its worst, people can forget that there is a flesh-and-blood human being at the other end of the line. The disembodied, the defaced, too easily becomes the depersonalised'; Jensen, 'The Challenge of Virtual Community', 60.

powerful, even subversive, but large numbers may mean nothing in terms of worthwhile deep learning.

This is the phenomenon Baggaley has called 'Blogfuscation', that is 'when an issue becomes hidden behind a hundred inane blog posts'. Quoting a line from Battleship Galactica: 'You have an amazing capacity for self-deception. How do you do that?', he notes that:

> the more web site and blog strongholds one can build, the more likely one is to emerge as the apparent leader in a field, since web sites and blogs typically do not require their writers to verify their sources and originality. The larger the number of blogging collaborators one can gather together, the more they can go forth and multiply one's personal version of history far and wide.[43]

This is an environment often not conducive to 'social learning experiences':

> useful responses to learners' questions are regularly eclipsed by a welter of unhelpful comments, frequently inaccurate and condescending and at worst downright rude. This is a further aspect of the fog that is a significant reality of the 21st century online learning environment.[44]

Thus—and returning full circle—exactly as the internet dispenses with the expert, it brings a greater need to rediscover one:

> Teachers may prove to be even more essential in this context, as experts, guides, and arbitrators, than in face-to-face situations. Expert input is still needed.[45]

The Problem of Rediscovering the Expert

In one sense the Internet Age makes everyone an expert. Devices to access knowledge are constantly in our hands. A whole generation has grown up tech-savvy, internet natives, with claims to be far more technologically advanced than preceding generations. But apparently these technological skills have not extended them much further. Despite the ready access to digital tools, 'young

---

43 Baggaley, 'Flips and flops', 443–444. He is referring, in particular, to the 2010–15 Flipped Learning era. See also his 'Sandcastle competitions', 366.
44 Baggaley & James, 'The fog of online learning', 128.
45 Baggaley & James, 'The fog of online learning', 128.

Americans are no more learned or skilful than their predecessors, no more knowledgeable, fluent, up-to-date, or inquisitive, except in the materials of youth culture' and—of special note for this chapter—'their technology skills fall well short of the common claim, too, especially when they must apply them to research and workplace skills'.[46]

The explosion of information on the internet creates the need for reliable guides through the maze. The explosion of the number of potential conversation partners forces choices to be made about guidance, and peer groups are simply not good enough. But the internet also offers its own expert guidance in a variety of forms. For example, despite its inherent risks (e.g. of articles being distorted by the enthusiast without real knowledge, or by those with vested ideological interests), the grand and largely successful experiment of Wikipedia has its checks and balances, including the 'Talk' section in which the merits of articles are discussed, debated, and improved. The MOOCs that arose dramatically in 2012 to decline just as dramatically by 2014 relied for their credibility on the fact that it was major US schools, such as MIT, who put their courses online, so learners were riding on the capital of their long history of good teaching. Even the connectivist theory of online education conceives of learners connecting around 'nodes' that provide some expertise as they construct their own education. It is not just simply everyone who has their blog, so do the experts. If the learner is motivated to find it, the expert discussion in the world of blogs is out there, and sometimes (but not always!) this is where the leading-edge discussion is taking place.

But even the experts may not be the reliable guides needed to lead the potential researcher through the maze to worthwhile deep learning. After all, *everyone*, including the expert, is affected by the internet. Problems of learning linked to the internet have been identified not only for students, but also amongst educational leaders—such as the MIT and GLC reports into online learning which suffer from the recency effect, by showing no awareness of decades of relevant educational literature into distance education.[47] Ignoring what has been done previously means new work is not built on solid foundations, but is like castles built on sand.[48]

---

46 Bauerlein, *The Dumbest Generation*, 8–9; cited by De Jongh, 'Challenges to Learning', 119.
47 See Baggaley, 'Sandcastle competitions', passim. Baggaley passes the tongue-in-cheek remark that 'it appears that online education began with the online publication of MIT's curricular materials in 2002' (p.367).
48 Baggaley, 'Sandcastle competitions', 371.

But surely the need to find reliable teachers has always been incumbent on the student, whether in oral or print-based learning environments. As society moved into the hyper-print learning environment of multi-media, and then on into the internet age, the quest is nevertheless the same in kind, even if much more acute in magnitude.

Avoiding the Pitfalls and Encouraging Good Research Conversations in the Internet Age

Because Higher Education produces future leaders of society, Higher Educators need to do all they can to promote worthwhile deep learning that transforms students into better human beings, to build a better society. Entrusted with the weighty task of passing on the knowledge of God which transforms humanity into God's own image, perhaps this task is incumbent on Theological educators all the more so.

To avoid the *informational* threats to deep learning, at least as a start, de Jongh's observations can simply be reversed to give a series of maxims that students should be encouraged to live by:

1. Pay attention to your task, don't get distracted by other possibilities that arise as you use the internet. You need to remain in control of your research at all times. Use the internet to serve your research—do not let it take charge and move you away.
2. Open your field of vision. Good research wonders about all possibilities, so move beyond your own small circle. Do not get caught in an echo-chamber in the blogosphere. Wisely utilise the information potential of the internet.
3. Allow the precise focus of your research to determine what information you gather.
4. Plumb the depths of the topic, do not stay on the surface. Think critically, pressing beyond the opinion or conclusion of a writer, to the quality of the argument, and of the evidence at its foundation. Do not simply parrot opinion, but learn to think critically for yourself, even in the company of others.
5. Understanding through engagement is better than acquisition of information. Quality is better than quantity.

It is also best to utilise the internet (and other) resources within learning strategies that are brain friendly and, as brain science develops, there is an increasing amount of resources available to assist in this.[49] But brains always come packaged in people, and learning should never be isolated from the relational networks in which it flourishes. As well as the informational challenges of learning in the internet age, therefore, the conversational challenges also need to be addressed and overcome if worthwhile deep learning is to occur. Perhaps a further set of maxims is a start:

1. Education is a relational activity, and even through the internet students should strive to experience deep *social* learning. The internet is one tool amongst many, and is best utilised as part of a relationship between learners and teachers. Remember that there is always a person behind any information. A book is the product of a person. A blog, or a website, despite being situated in a virtual world, is also the product of a person. A blogger may be committed to the age-long quest for truth, or they may be committed to building a fan-base to serve their own purposes. Behind the web lies vested interests that are not always out for the greater good. On the other hand, there are good people with good resources out there as well.

2. It is therefore important to be careful about the company you keep.[50] The internet age requires users to be as wise as serpents and innocent as doves. As in the real world, the virtual world offers the user all types along the spectrum of friends, fellow travellers, timewasters, and enemies. At any point the student can be in positive or negative company, which is either enriching or diminishing their life. If they find themselves in bad company, wisdom says cut losses early. If the company is good, wisdom says travel further in the journey.

3. Learning is best done in the company of peers, but peer learning has its limitations. Peers can also be good company or bad. Rather than sharing opinions or conclusions, perhaps the best things peers can do for each other is to share good analytical questions that assist the discovery of

---

49 For an early work encouraging brain-friendly education, see Caine & Caine, *Teaching and the Human Brain*. More recently, see Radin, 'Brain-Compatible Teaching and Learning'; and, for a recent summary, see StateUniversity.com, 'Brain-Based Education'.

50 I am thinking, once again, of the work of Wayne Booth (see note 6 above). Booth also co-authored a very successful book on research, successive editions of which take into account the impact of the internet. See Booth, Colomb, & Williams, *The Craft of Research*. For a taster, see their author Interview (listed on bibliography).

good evidence, the honing of good arguments, and the formulation of conclusions that are built upon good evidence-based arguments and whose relative strengths are always in proportion to the evidence and argument. With vitriol being ubiquitous in the virtual (under)world, it is imperative that peer groups self-regulate online language to redeem the space for respectful conversation designed to produce worthwhile human transformation. Peers can also help each other to find the expertise they all need, even if only some might recognise that need.

4. Learning requires expertise, because students need guidance in the art of research. If a student cannot exceed their teacher, a commitment to life-long learning is a commitment to finding the next teacher. The word 'scholar' means 'learner', and so even a recognised 'scholar' needs to be an expert in learning, in order to help others to learn too. This means that, even though seeking always to take knowledge into new areas, an expert is someone who will not fall prey to 'the recency effect', but who values being anchored in the tradition of their discipline.

One of the greatest opportunities of the internet is the ease of access to many potential teachers, but one of its greatest challenges is to find the expert guides that are worthwhile. To find the genuine expert, a student will definitely have to push beyond their own echo-chamber, through the empty rhetoric of the envy-driven nastiness of the social media, and ignore the 'bubble and hype' of the blogger who makes the most noise. In the end, the expert will be the person who seeks to explain real evidence by mounting good arguments towards proportional conclusions, as the latest attempt in the age-long quest to discover and clarify what is real about the world, for the greater good of their fellow-human being. The guidance of such an expert will play a part in the student's deep learning that leads towards their worthwhile transformation into a larger and better humanity.

Bibliography

Baggaley, J. 'Sandcastle Competitions', *Distance Education* 37.3 (2016), 366–375.

Baggaley, J. & S. James. 'The fog of online learning', *Distance Education* 37.1 (2016), 121–129.

Baggaley, J. 'Flips and flops', *Distance Education* 36.3 (Nov 2015), 437-447.

Ball, L. 'Where are We Going?', in L. Ball & J.R. Harrison (eds.), *Learning and Teaching Theology. Some ways ahead* (Northcote, Vic.: Morning Star, 2014), 11–20.

Ball, L. 'Principles of Deep Learning', *Transforming Teaching* 1.3 (July 2013), 1–2. http://scd.edu.au/learning-teaching-theology/scd-newsletters/.

Bauerlein, M. *The Dumbest Generation: How the Digital Age Stupefies Young Americans and Jeopardizes our Future* (New York: Tarcher, 2008).

Booth, W.C. *The Company We Keep: An Ethics of Fiction* (Berkeley, CA: University of California Press, 1992).

Booth, W.C. *Critical Understanding: The Powers and Limits of Pluralism* (Chicago: University of Chicago Press, 1979).

Booth, W.C. *Modern Dogma & the Rhetoric of Assent* (Chicago: University of Chicago Press, 1974).

Booth, W.C. *A Rhetoric of Irony* (Chicago: University of Chicago Press, 1974).

Booth, W.C. *Now Don't Try to Reason with Me: Essays and Ironies for a Credulous Age* (Chicago: University of Chicago Press, 1970).

Booth, W.C. *The Rhetoric of Fiction* (Chicago: University of Chicago Press, 1961, 1983).

Booth, W.C., G.G. Colomb, J.M. Williams, J. Bizup, & W.T. FitzGerald. *The Craft of Research* (Chicago: Chicago University Press, ^{4}2016 [1995]). See also 'An interview with Wayne C. Booth, Gregory G. Colomb, and Joseph M. Williams, authors of *The Craft of Research, Third edition*', www.press.uchicago.edu/Misc/Chicago/065685in.html.

Briggs, S. 'Deeper Learning: What Is It and Why Is It So Effective?', *InformED*, 7/3/2015. www.opencolleges.edu.au/informed/features/deep-learning/

Caine, R.N. & G. Caine. *Teaching and the Human Brain* (Alexandria, VA: ASCD, 1991).

Carr, N. *The Shallows: What the Internet is Doing to Our Brains* (New York: Norton, 2011).

De Jongh, C. 'Challenges to Learning in the Age of the Internet', in Y. Debergue & J.R. Harrison (eds.), *Teaching Theology in a Technological Age* (Cambridge: Cambridge Scholars, 2015), 113–126.

Del Vicario, M., A. Bessi, F. Zollo, F. Petroni, A. Scala, G. Caldarelli, H.E. Stanley, & W. Quattrociocchi. 'The spreading of misinformation online', *PNAS* 113.3 (January 19, 2016), 554–559.

Doidge, N. *The Brain that Changes Itself* (Brunswick, Vic.: Scribe, 2008, rev. 2010, repr. 2015).

Doidge, N. *The Brain's Way of Healing* (Brunswick, Vic.: Scribe, 2015).

Downes, S. 'Preparing for the digital university: a review of the history and current state of distance, blended, and online learning [Blog post]', *Knowledge, Learning, Community*. www.downes.ca/cgi-bin/page.cgi?post=63823.

Fullan, Michael & Maria Langworthy. *Towards a New End: New Pedagogies for Deep Learning* (Seattle, Washington: Collaborative Impact, June 2013). http://npdl.thumbtack.co.nz/wp-content/uploads/2015/08/Towards-a-New-End-New-Pedagogies-for-Deep-Learning-Invitation.pdf.

Global Learning Council. *Technology-Enhanced Learning: Best Practices and Data Sharing in Higher Education* (2016). www.globallearningcouncil.org/full-text-technology-enhanced-learning-best-practices/.

Greenfield, S. *Tomorrow's People: How 21st Century Technology is Changing the Way We Think and Feel* (London: Penguin, 2003).

Hamilton, K. *To Turn From Idols* (Grand Rapids: Eerdmans, 1973).

Healy, Jane *Endangered Minds. Why Our Children Don't Think* (New York: Simon & Schuster, 1990).

Jackson, M. *Distracted: The Erosion of Attention and the Coming Dark Age* (New York: Prometheus, 2008).

Jensen, M.P. 'The Challenge of Virtual Community: Benefits and Deficits', in Y. Debergue & J.R. Harrison (eds.), *Teaching Theology in a Technological Age* (Cambridge: Cambridge Scholars, 2015), 51–61.

Nichols, T. 'The Death of Expertise', *The Federalist* (17 Jan 2014). http://thefederalist.com/2014/1/17/the-death-of-expertise/.

Radin, J.P. 'Brain-Compatible Teaching and Learning: Implications for Teacher Education', *Educ. Horiz.* 88.1 (2009), 40–50. https://files.eric.ed.gov/fulltext/EJ868337.pdf.

Rowland, D.R. 'Book Review: The Brain that Changes Itself: Stories of Personal Triumph from the Frontiers of Brain Science', *J. Academic Language and Learning* (2010), B1–3. http://journal.aall.org.au/index.php/jall/article/view/121/87.

Siemens, G., G. Gasovic, & S. Dawson (eds.) *Preparing for the Digital University: A Review of the History and Current State of Distance, Blended and Online Learning* (2015). http://linkresearchlab.org/PreparingDigitalUniversity.pdf.

Smith, S. & S. Healey. 'On the Frontiers of Change: Designing Bespoke Learning Architecture', in Y. Debergue & J.R. Harrison (eds.), Teaching Theology in a Technological Age (Cambridge: Cambridge Scholars, 2015), 147–166.

StateUniversity.com. 'Brain-Based Education – Summary Principles of Brain-Based Research, Critiques of Brain-Based Education', http://education.stateuniversity.com/pages/1799/Brain-Based-Education.html. Brain-Based Education – Summary Principles of Brain-Based Research, Critiques of Brain-Based Education.

University of Chicago Press. 'An interview with Wayne C. Booth, Gregory G. Colomb, and Joseph M. Williams, authors of *The Craft of Research, Third edition*', www.press.uchicago.edu/Misc/Chicago/065685in.html.

Willcox, K.E., S. Sarma, & P.H. Lippel. *Online Education: A Catalyst for Higher Education* (Boston: Massachusetts Institute of Technology, 2016). https://oepi.mit.edu/?s=Online+Education%3A+A+Catalyst+for+Higher+Education.

Williams, R.B. 'Is the Internet Making Us Dumber?', *Psychology Today* (2014). www.psychologytoday.com.

Peter G. Bolt
Sydney College of Divinity
PeterB@scd.edu.au

23 | MAKING GOOD PRACTICE AFFORDABLE

UNDERSTANDING YOUR STUDENTS WITH LEARNING ANALYTICS

Abstract

How might a teacher move an 'average student' to the top of the class? What investment would be needed to achieve this? Could the typical teacher afford the time, effort, and finance required?

Bloom's analysis of a wide range of educational models showed mastery learning together with one-on-one tutoring had results two standard deviations better than the control group (a traditional classroom lecture). Although clearly effective, Bloom deemed this model financially unfeasible. He raised the challenge for educators to find ways to reproduce this impact in an affordable and scalable format. He dubbed this *the two-sigma problem.* Improving education was not primarily a *theoretical* challenge, but an *economic* one.

This ssay argues that technology can help solve Bloom's two-sigma problem by making mastery learning and tutoring more economically feasible. The benefits of all technology are essentially economic, since it increases productivity and lowers costs. Educational technologies can improve teaching and learning by making good practice affordable. Specifically, learning analytics make it feasible to inform both students and tutors of progress, maximising the value of tutoring. Additionally, analytics of students' formative quizzes help develop mastery learning.

This essay presents applications of learning analytics in a theological college.

First, monthly 'progress feedback emails' provide students details of their online activity, important dates, and suggestions for next steps. Second, phone coaches are provided with a report on an individual student to help them optimise their 20-minute call. Last, the 'Online Greek Intensive' implements a 'flipped classroom' model, allowing new students to learn Greek fundamentals at their own pace, leading up to a face-to-face intensive where the teachers can use analytics to support each student with their individual needs. In each of these cases, learning analytics are making mastery learning and student support more economical, thus helping solve the two-sigma problem. More strategically, learning analytics helps make research a core operational facet of teaching, by enabling the teacher to continually learn from students' behaviour.

Introduction

Over thirty years ago, Benjamin Bloom set out to compare the effect of different educational models, in the hope of finding the best one.[1] The clear winner was a combination of mastery learning and one-to-one tutors. This model would catapult a student in the middle of a normally distributed class to the top two percent—that is, a two-standard deviation improvement.

Why is this model not more common in education today, given such a clear finding several decades ago? Bloom himself anticipated the problem. Although the technique was powerful, it was also too expensive:

> The tutoring process demonstrates that most of the students do have potential to reach this high level of learning. I believe an important task of research and instruction is to seek ways of accomplishing this under more practical and realistic conditions than the one-to-one tutoring, which is too costly for most societies to bear on a large scale. This is the '2 sigma' problem. Can researchers and teachers devise teaching-learning conditions that will enable the majority of students under group instruction to attain levels of achievement that can at present be reached only under good tutoring conditions?

In other words, mastery learning with personal tutors is too expensive to be used on any significant scale. First, mastery learning requires a bank of assess-

---

1 Bloom, 'The 2 Sigma Problem'.

ments that students can repeatedly attempt by themselves. Writing, and especially marking repeated assessments with helpful feedback, takes time and effort. This cost only increases if individual students are given control of the number and timing of assessments they could attempt. Feedback such as where the student needs to revise and when mastery is achieved is both critical and expensive. Second, a tutor needs to spend significant time with a student to gauge their progress and needs. This time costs the same as when teaching a full class of students, making it hard to justify.

Learning Analytics

Learning analytics is defined as 'the collection and analysis of data generated during the learning process in order to improve the quality of both learning and teaching'.[2] This essay proposes that educational technology, and learning analytics specifically, resolve Bloom's 2-sigma problem. Learning analytics makes mastery learning and personal tutoring more affordable at scale. Three examples will be presented on how learning analytics has been used to make mastery learning and/or personal tutor support more affordable at Moore College, Sydney. It concludes with some of the lessons learned.

Unbundling Strategy for a Distance Course

Moore College's Preliminary Theological Certificate (PTC) is a correspondence course covering biblical studies, doctrine, and history. It is aimed for lay Christians and has been running for several decades with students enrolling from many countries. In 2009, an Online Learning Environment was launched to provide additional resources such as discussion forums, eReadings, and quizzes.

Technology's impact on education gained significant enthusiasm and attention at the start of the decade, with the growth of MOOCs and the 'flipped classroom' model.[3] During this time, Moore thought carefully about how technology was changing the economics of education, and how our business model

---

2   Siemens, Dawson, and Lynch, 'Improving the Quality and Productivity of the Higher Education Sector'.
3   Christensen, Horn, and Johnson, *Disrupting Class*; Khan, 'Let's Use Video to Reinvent Education'; Khan, 'Year 2060: Education Predictions'; Thompson, 'How Khan Academy Is Changing the Rules of Education'; The Economist, 'Electronic Education: Flipping the Classroom'.

should adapt. The considerations included how scale, affordability, and educational quality could be balanced. Moore reasoned that our courses offered three core benefits to students:

- *access* to a curated set of quality educational resources;
- *interaction* with peers and educators; and
- *a credential*, flowing from a valid assessment. This credential offers the student a formal acknowledgement and feedback on their learning.

Although these were traditionally offered as a single bundle for a single enrolment fee, digital technologies were changing the economics of each of these areas in different ways. While the cost of producing educational content was significant, it was an upfront cost. Distributing the digital content now had a zero marginal cost. The offering of quality interaction and a credential still carried a variable cost, however. Moore College therefore *unbundled* its offering into two: Moore Access and a subject enrolment.

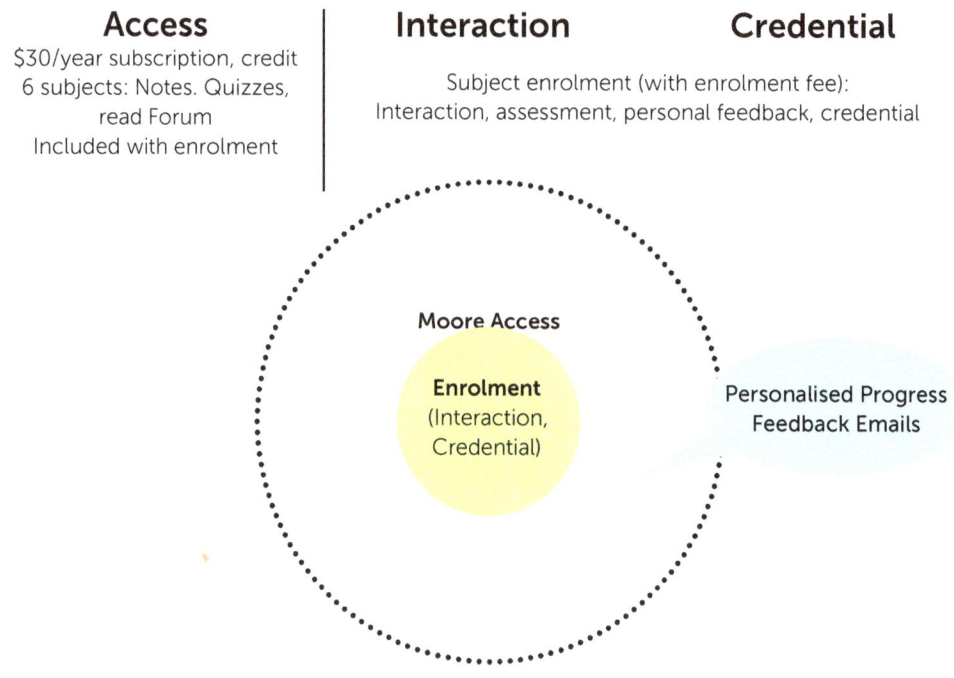

Figure 1: Unbundled Model

Moore Access is a 12-month online subscription to the content and resources of the first six subjects in the PTC. Critically, this is not an enrolment, but rather a flexible and affordable first step towards an enrolment. The subscription fee is credited towards the first enrolment after the subscription, ensuring the student doesn't see the subscription fee as 'wasted'. It was designed to change the decision architecture that students typically go through when considering an enrolment. Questions such as which subject to study, what is the quality and difficulty of the content, and when to attempt the exam can block a student from studying. Moore Access was designed to remove these blocks and allow students to start immediately. They can sample the content, look at different subjects, with no immediate deadline and at little cost.

A subject enrolment offers interaction and a credential. Moore Access is included at no extra charge to provide online access to the content of several subjects. Interaction is with peers and moderators in online discussion forums. For an optional fee, students can also have personal support of a coach with four 20-minute phone calls. A credential is offered via a supervised examination and supported via a detailed feedback report on the student's performance. It gives students the formal recognition of their learning, which is lacking in Moore Access (and MOOCs at the time).

These two offerings were designed to work together, with learning analytics used to inform and encourage students to progress through their learning. A student can join the online learning community (see the wider circle in the figure above) via subscribing to Moore Access. Enrolling in a future term also grants immediate access to this wider circle. Once there, students start receiving feedback emails with feedback and encouragement to enrol and/or prepare for the exam. During the term of enrolment, students join the inner circle where they enjoy additional interaction. Once a subject enrolment is complete, students remain in the outer circle for nine months as part of the Moore Access subscription included in their enrolment. During this time, they have access to other subjects which they can start studying at no extra cost. They continue to receive feedback emails informing them of their learning and their readiness for their next enrolment.

By adapting our business model to the new digital economies, we were able to escape the tension between scale, affordability, and educational quality. Moore Access is an affordable and very scalable offering that helps students learn in a flexible way. This freed Moore to offer an enrolment with a higher level of support, such as coaches.

The obvious risk in this strategy was that students would only pay for the online subscription, and avoid the subject enrolment fee. After all, the fee for six subject enrolments prior to this unbundling model was eighteen times the Moore Access subscription fee.

The expectation was that, as often happens, new technology would create new abundances and scarcities, thus shifting where value is perceived. The dramatic cost reduction of reproducing and distributing content would lead to an abundance of digital content. In turn, access to content would be seen as a commodity, valued very little. Value (and the willingness to pay a fee) would shift towards more personal feedback, moderated interaction with peers, support from coaches, and a credible credential from a trusted institution. This proposal was implemented during a period where MOOCs and the idea of 'free education' were being discussed heavily. In hindsight, MOOCs are free because of two reasons: it is very cheap to provide access to online content, and few would pay much for it anyway.

Learning analytics played an important role in this strategy. It would be used to keep students informed and engaged once they entered the Moore Access circle. It would let them know when they were ready to enrol and sit the exam for a subject. On the other hand, learning analytics would identify at-risk students, and offer specific resources and tips. This would shift the student's experience from a transactional one to a more relational one; from a simple exchange of printed content for a fee, towards an ongoing connection to an online learning community that offered feedback and support.

Impact of Moore Access on Enrolments

Given the risks about this strategy, the relationship between a Moore Access and subsequent subject enrolments was analysed closely. During its first year in 2014, Moore Access was an optional extra that students paid for. Thus, the number of enrolments of those who subscribed versus those who did not can be compared. The chart below follows students who enrolled in term one in 2014 (abbreviated as '1/14') and segments them by whether they got Moore Access in that term or not (as at 20 June 2016). It then shows the percentage of students in each group who enrolled in only one or more subjects in the following terms.

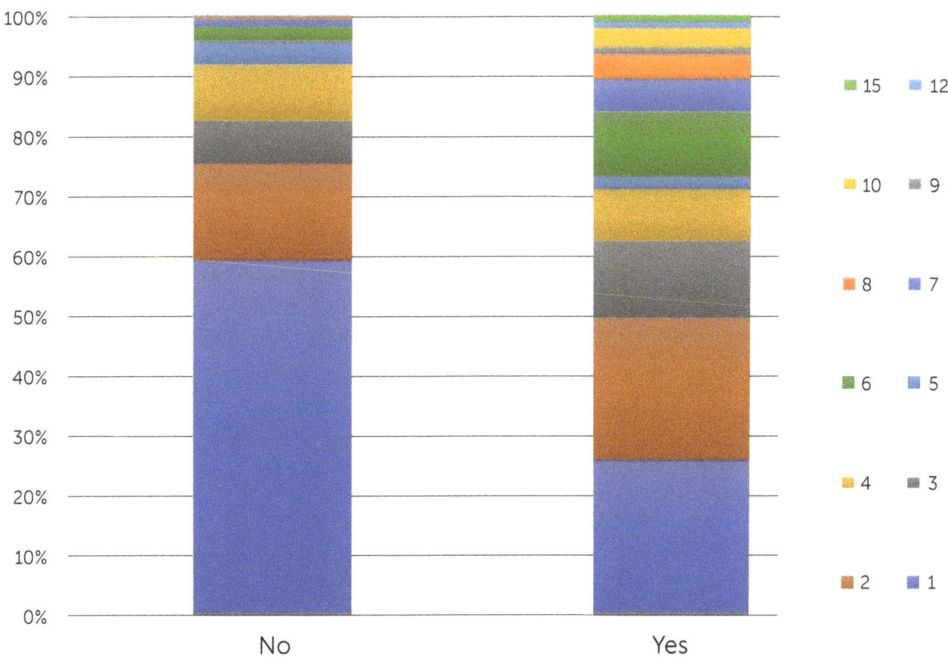

Figure 2: Percentage of students who enrolled in only one or several subjects. 'Yes' had Moore Access, 'No' didn't.

Clearly, those students who did subscribe to Moore Access enrolled considerably more after the initial enrolment. Only a quarter of students with Moore Access stopped at one enrolment, versus 60% of those who did not.

The table below shows the mean number of enrolments per student. Those with Moore Access had 1.67 enrolments more than those without:

Got Moore Access?	No	Yes	Total
Mean Enrol/Student	1.98	3.65	2.43

Note that students who did not subscribe in term 1/14 *but subscribed later or enrolled from 2015* would have had Moore Access for a period, but still fall under the 'No Moore Access' segment. Thus, the enrolments for students who have never had Moore Access would be even lower than stated.

It may seem counter-intuitive that students with Moore Access enrolled more, given they already had access to all the content of six subjects. However, the premise behind the unbundling strategy was that students would value the interaction, feedback, and credential sufficiently to enrol. These students did not think of Moore College as booksellers, but as educators, and so wanted more than just content. They wanted the personal feedback, interaction, and formal recognition that an enrolment and credential offered.

Progress Feedback Emails

These are regular emails sent to the wider community of students to inform, engage, and encourage them. They are sent about monthly, in weeks one, four, and eight of the term. A different template is used depending on whether the student has a past, current, or future enrolment (or none). Further, much of the content is programmatically generated for each student, with details of their own activity. Figure 2 shows an example of an email to a highly engaged student.

Your activity

Activity level	**High.** Great, you're using the OLE a lot, which will help you prepare to sit an exam.
Time since last visit	**A few days.** Great! Keep using it regularly to make the most of your learning.
Quiz Attempts	141
Forum	Why not **gpost a question or comment** nin the discussion forum? You could post your response to one of the exercises and get others' feedback, for example.

Progress: Subjects and Lessons

Subject	01	02	03	04	05	06	07	08	09	10
ECH	94	96	86	110	132	125	132	127	117	142
NT2	60	66	60	60	60	60	60	60	0	0
RCH	96	98	99	99	99	97	100	98	95	99
ROM	17	35	31	24	22	24	26	26	0	0

The table below shows the number of correct question attempts per subject and lesson. Getting **20 or more** correct question attempts in each lesson will prepare you well for sitting the exam.

Figure 3: Feedback email example

The emails typically included:

- General, quiz, and forum activity comments. If no activity was recorded, a link to the technical helpdesk was offered in case of difficulties.
- General timing information in term (e.g. exam window).
- Progress via quiz attempts: this was the central summary of learning. It shows the number of correct quiz questions in each subject and lesson. The student was encouraged to get 20 or more questions correct in each lesson, after which they were well prepared for the exam.
- Current enrolment status (exam date and mode, supervisor status): this simple reminder aimed to prepare students for the exam.
- Active forum discussions: links to specific forum discussions that might be helpful, even if in subjects other than their enrolment.
- Time left in subscription: this was critical to encourage past students to remain within the learning community by enrolling in their next subject.
- Next subject suggestion: For students with no current or future subject enrolments, a suggestion for their next subject is made depending on their entire enrolment history. This includes a link to the online subject, with a reminder that they already have free access under their Moore Access subscription.
- College news and events: these were meant to include students in the wider community of the college.

The emails were progressively rolled out from October 2014, with all students receiving them from the start of the 2015 academic year. During the two years since the full introduction in 2015, the two key metrics improved significantly. The percentage of students who enrolled in a subject but did not sit the exam started decreasing on the initial rollout of the emails (see figure 4, dashed grey line), and had the lowest level on the term when all students started receiving them (solid grey line). No other significant changes were made in this period to this course. Additionally, the percentage of students in each term who enrolled in the following term also increased (see Figure 5, where the term labelled '15 T1' represents term one in 2015). This metric is seasonal, as enrolments overall are heavily influenced by the calendar year. However, comparing the equivalent terms shows a marked improvement. Over all, it seems clear that as more students persevered and sat the examination, more of them passed and then returned for the next subject.

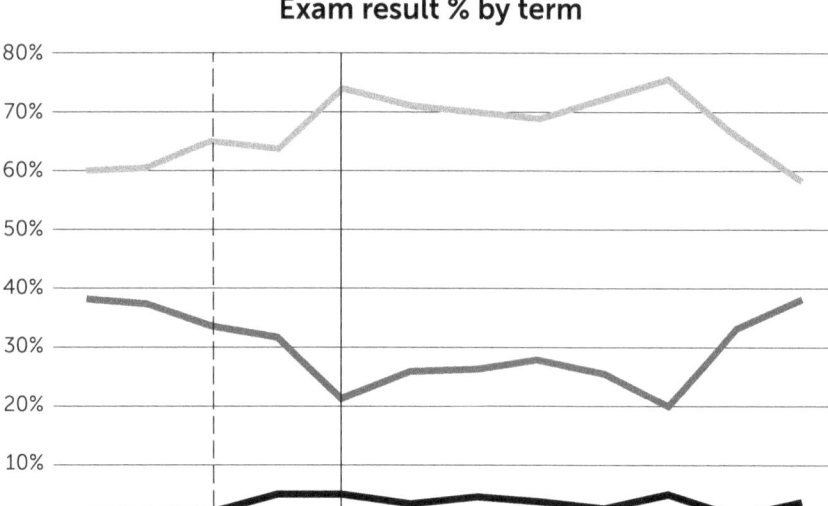

Figure 4: Dropout rates per term decreased

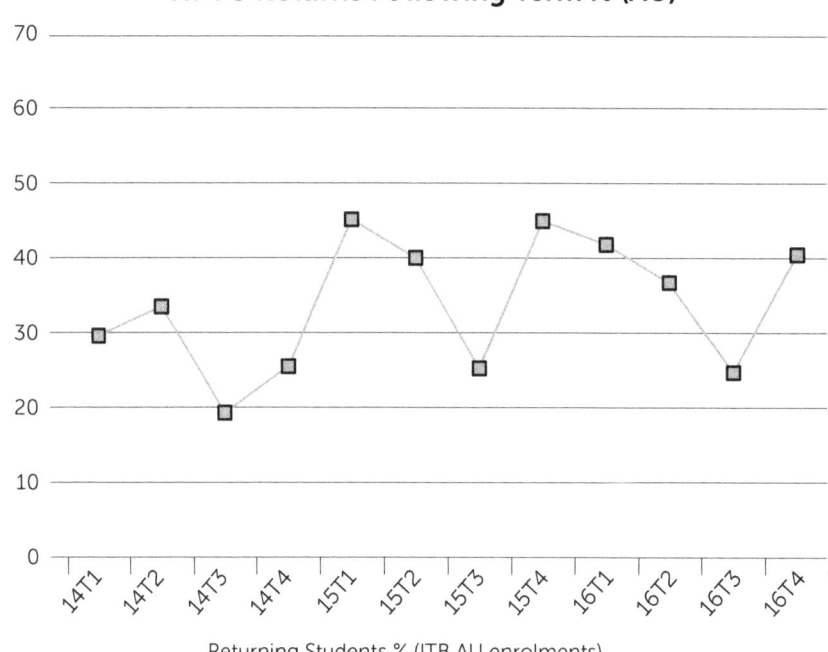

Figure 5: Return rates after each term increased

Well over 62,000 emails have been sent. A key part of these is emails is what happens after they are sent. Activity and enrolments following the emails are tracked to gauge the response from each segment. Further, split testing helps experiment and improve the emails. The students with a current term might be randomly split, with one segment sent a variation of the email and the other remaining a control sent the standard email. For example, half of current term students were sent emails with a subject line including the words 'Exam Tips' close to the exam period. This group had a higher increase in quiz attempts and overall activity, as well as a higher level of new enrolments. This technique allows for monthly experiments, which leads to small but continuous improvements. It grows an operational research capability to the organisation, by continually learning from students' behaviour.

There is considerable potential for future improvements. Just under three million individual question attempts have been recorded in our database. This allows Moore to report to students their performance across time and subjects. Further, this information is used to report overall performance by subject and section in the content, which in turn can inform content review. Lastly, Machine Learning, a field of Artificial Intelligence, is being used to develop predictive models from this large volume of data, so that at-risk students can be identified and offered further support (perhaps by personal coaches).

Coach Calls

As part of the unbundled strategy, Moore College introduced optional coaches who give support over four calls of 20 minutes each throughout the term. They are designed to offer the one-on-one tutoring support encouraged by Bloom. In order to make the most of the students' time with coaches, and therefore make them more affordable, student reports were developed. These reported on the activity of a specific student, with the coach as the audience. Given Moore could train the coaches, and given interpreting these reports would be a common task for them, Moore could afford to make these reports more extensive and sophisticated. The reports were generated daily as PDF files, and coaches would view each just before the call was made.

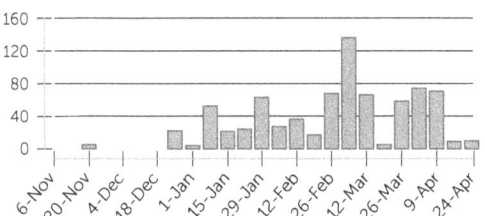
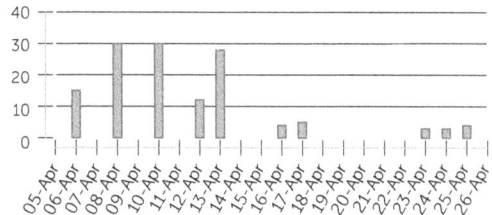

Weekly Test Results

	1	2	3	4	5	6	7	8		10
JN	8.33	7.00	7.17	7.67						7.50
OT3	9.33	4.50	8.33	6.67	7.17	5.03	5.57	4.67		7.92

Test Scores are indicative only. Final marks are calculated at the end of term. Attempt details listed below.

Question Attempts

Lesson	01		02		03		04		05		06		07		08		09		10	
Subject	✓	%	✓	%	✓	%	✓	%	✓	%	✓	%	✓	%	✓	%	✓	%	✓	%
EPH	4	67%	4	67%	4	67%	5	83%	3	50%	5	83%	4	67%	4	67%	5	83%	4	67%
JN	102	90%	93	86%	103	85%	102	86%	87	89%	65	78%	52	76%	64	88%	48	80%	55	83%
NT1	9	75%																		
OT1	23	100%																		
OT3	48	92%	60	88%	72	94%	45	92%	76	95%	72	91%	78	88%	60	86%	72	96%	70	91%

Figure 6: Selections from student activity report for coaches

The coach report included the following content:

- A summary of activity, including number of forum views, posts, quiz attempts, and resource views.
- Weekly and recent daily activity.
- Previous and current subject enrolments, including the mark, examination supervisor status, and whether they studied in a group or not. The coach could check that the examination supervisor had been nominated and confirmed, a necessary but sometimes forgotten step.
- Weekly test scores.

- Forum posts (highlighting any posts that had not yet been answered).
- Flagged quiz questions. Students could flag individual questions in any of the online quizzes for follow up with a coach.
- Correct and incorrect answers, grouped by subject, lesson, difficulty level, and question outcome. This offered coaches a more detailed view of the student's performance.

Further, students were asked to fill out simple forms before and after each call, noting their levels of confidence and any questions they would like to discuss. The pre-call survey asked for students' confidence about the exam. The post-call survey asked the degree to which the pre-call survey questions were addressed. All surveys included a free-text field which allowed the student to make any other comments.

The questions in the surveys varied slightly depending on the week in the term. The consistent questions about the student's confidence and the call's helpfulness were asked in all weeks, allowing further analysis. Although this remains to be done, it may prove predictive when combined with activity data. For example, a student whose confidence is not increasing and whose online activity is dropping may be highly predictive of a student at risk.

Students with coaches had very good educational outcomes. The passing and returning rates were both much higher than students without a coach.

Online Greek Intensive

The third and last example of using learning analytics to make good education more affordable is an implementation of the 'flipped classroom' model to teaching Greek to incoming students, which is reported in more detail by Olmos.[4]

All students of Moore's accredited degree programs learn Koiné Greek, which causes considerable anxiety in many. In late 2011, Moore College released an online resource called the 'Online Greek Intensive' (OGI) for the incoming 2012 cohort. It aimed to offer students a way of preparing ahead of the academic year and building their confidence.

The OGI implements a flipped classroom model, where engaging online

---

4   Olmos, 'The Greek Flip: Old Language, Online Learning'.

material is used by students to learn at their convenience, followed by more interactive class work reviewing and discussing exercises. The OGI contains forty-six instructional videos, supported by several online quizzes and digital resources such as readings and audio vocabularies. Students were provided access on their enrolment confirmation, and could start learning Greek immediately, even up to six months prior to the academic year. Students may watch each video and complete the paired quiz as often as they wish, until they feel confident enough to move to the next one. They could also introduce themselves in the online forum, to start forming relationships with their future classmates ahead of time. A two-week face-to-face class intensive was then conducted at the start of the academic year. Thus, the videos and quizzes formed a 'mastery learning' phase, with the class time being the personal supportive phase.

There are two broad challenges to this model. First, how could the student be engaged and encouraged to complete the units, as well as informed of their progress? Second, how could the faculty member know which students needed support (or extension) and what content areas needed to be revised during the class intensive?

Learning analytics has functioned as the glue between the mastery learning and the class intensive. Just prior and during the intensive period, faculty are provided with a summary of students' quiz scores by quiz and by student (see Figure 7). Although this is not one-on-one tutoring as recommended by Bloom's research, it allows for adapting the content presented and an earlier allocation to a smaller high-support group for students who need it.

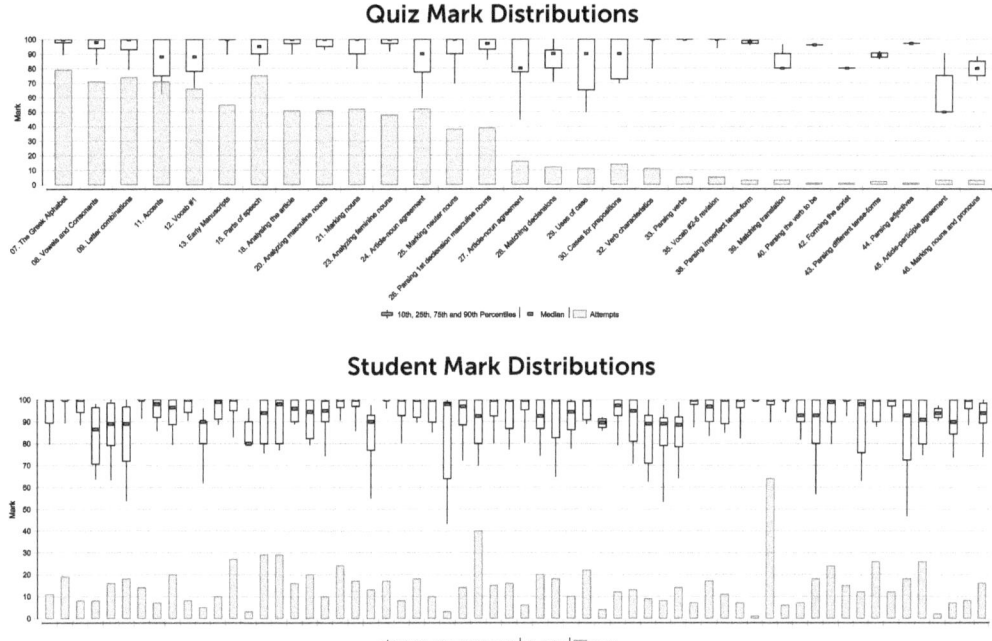

Figure 7: Sample OGI report for faculty

Additionally, progress feedback emails similar to those described above for Distance students have been recently introduced for the OGI. These emails inform students of their progress with a simple checklist format (see Figure 8). The quizzes are listed in an email, with a checkbox against each. A grey tick mark is shown when students have attempted the quiz, and a green one when they achieve a perfect score in at least one of their attempts (signifying mastery). Additionally, these emails include more general details about the student's online activity and instructions prior to the intensive weeks.

Topic 5: Analyzing nouns

Quiz		Attempts	Best Score
☑ 23.	Analyzing feminine nouns	2	100
☑ 24.	Article-noun agreement	1	100
☑ 25.	Marking neuter nouns	2	100
☑ 26.	Parsing 1st declension macsuline nouns	1	100

Continue through these other topics as you are able.

Topic 6: Memorizing vocab and paradigms

Quiz		Attempts	Best Score
☑ 27.	Analyzing feminine nouns	1	70

Topic 7: Pronouns

Quiz		Attempts	Best Score
☑ 28.	Matching declensions	0	0

Figure 8: Sample of OGI feedback email

Lessons Learned

Moore College has learned several lessons from these three experiences. A summary of these is offered below.

Economics is a powerful lens to understand technology's impact on education. Educational technology does not create excellent education. It simply makes it affordable. When a new technology is developed, the existing business models will be affected because they are founded on the old economics. Digital technologies disrupted the economics of education, with different areas affected in different ways. The unbundling strategy was Moore's attempt to adapt its business model for distance education to these changes.

Learning Analytics can make Bloom's ideal model of mastery learning with personal tutoring much more practical, and there it can improve educational outcomes at larger scales. More specifically, learning analytics provides a glue between the student's growing mastery and the personal support they receive. It helps the student with questions such as, 'How am I doing? What should I do next?', while helping the tutor with questions such as 'Who needs help? Where are they struggling?'.

It takes a cross-disciplinary team and iterative approach. The design of learning analytics involves skills in teaching and learning, technology, and design. If these areas are not able to work together well, the likely result is a sub-optimal solution. Without solid teaching and learning representation, a technology-driven solution might report on existing data without addressing the real needs of students and teachers. Without technologists' involvement, hazy requirements that are difficult to implement might never be delivered. Last, without information design and usability, the solution might well report data that is helpful and accurate but difficult to understand and therefore to act on. In order to address this need, the author has developed a tool for a consulting client called the 'Analytics Design Canvas' that brings these different areas together and scaffolds a team through the key considerations. Starting small and iterating quickly as a learning process is also critical. Basic charts showing existing data to early adopters is a good way to grow momentum.

Developing a data culture takes time. Using evidence for decision-making often requires both a development of organisational capabilities and a cultural change. These processes cannot be realised by the purchase of a technology product. The organisation needs to commit to the slow work involved.

Beware the treachery of images. 'The treachery of images' is the title of a painting by Belgian painter René Magritte, which shows a pipe with the words, 'This is not a pipe' below it. This reminder that a representation of an object is not an instance of that object is very helpful in this field. Creating analytics involves first encoding student behaviour in a database, which is typically only a subset of their total learning activity. This data is then grouped, summarised and aggregated. Last, this processed data is represented visually via various charts. At each of these steps, a pipe is painted. Each of these steps involve assumptions and choices, often hidden, which can be misleading if misunderstood. This is known as the 'map and territory' relation. This raises a warning to educational leaders in particular, who might see learning analytics without a close experience of the actual learning. They need to complement abstract visualisations with direct conversations with teachers and students. They need to use analytics *shrewdly*, appreciating their value with a dose of scepticism towards their potential treachery.

The interplay between map and territory is fertile ground for insights. Perhaps paradoxically, the person who can benefit the most from learning analytics is the one already intimately familiar with students' behaviour. The person who understands the land the best, and therefore the person who can have the richest insights about it, is the explorer with their hands on the map and their feet on the territory. This gives them both the abstract whole and the concrete particular. At Moore, the combination of summary reports with the personal student-coach interaction enabled abstract pattern and direct personal confirmation.

Don't replace teachers, liberate them. Given the above point, it is critical that learning analytics are not seen as replacing teachers, but rather empowering them to support students more personally. As Khan puts it regarding the flipped classroom model, 'by removing the one-size-fits-all lecture from the classroom and letting students have a self-paced lecture at home, and then when you go to the classroom, letting them do work, having the teacher walk around, having the peers actually be able to interact with each other, these teachers have used technology to humanize the classroom'.[5]

Analytics as a question-generator. While analytics can provide answers to many important questions of the 'what', 'when', 'how many' kind, perhaps its most powerful role is in *generating questions*, especially of the 'why' type. While the data might not answer these questions, knowing they need to be answered is itself helpful progress.

Conclusion

Over 30 years ago, Bloom[6] wistfully envisioned a world where the two-sigma problem had been solved:

> If the research on the 2 sigma problem yields *practical methods* […], it would be an educational contribution of the greatest magnitude. It would change popular notions about human potential and would have significant effects on what the schools can and should do with the educational years each society requires of its young people.

---

5   Khan, 'Let's Use Video to Reinvent Education'.
6   Bloom, 'The 2 Sigma Problem', 4-16.

This essay has argued that learning analytics offers great promise in resolving Bloom's two-sigma problem, by drastically reducing the costs of delivering mastery learning together with personal tutor support. It offered three examples of how Moore College has implemented learning analytics to facilitate educational models closer to Bloom's recommendation. These models have in turn led to better educational outcomes.

This is not to say that the improved outcomes could not have happened without learning analytics. Online formative quizzes and personal coaches, for example, would have been helpful in their own right. Rather, learning analytics played an enabling role, by making these tools more affordable and practical. In particular, learning analytics enabled mastery learning and personal support to work together, acting as a glue between them.

Technology has a humble role in education: make good practice more affordable. Addressing the two-sigma problem would, however, be very significant. In Bloom's words, this would be 'an educational contribution of the greatest magnitude'.[7]

Bibliography

The Economist. 'Electronic Education: Flipping the Classroom', *The Economist* 17 (September, 2011). www.economist.com/node/21529062 [accessed 25 June 2013]

Bloom, B. S. 'The 2 Sigma Problem: The Search for Methods of Group Instruction as Effective as One-to-One Tutoring', *Educational Researcher* 13.6 (1984), 4–16.

Christensen, C. M., Michael B. Horn, and Curtis W. Johnson. *Disrupting Class: How Disruptive Innovation Will Change the Way the World Learns* (New York: McGraw-Hill, 2010).

Khan, S. 'Let's Use Video to Reinvent Education'. March 2011. www.ted.com/talks/salman_khan_let_s_use_video_to_reinvent_education.html [accessed 10 June 2011]

Khan, S. 'Year 2060: Education Predictions'. 27 December 2011. www.khanacademy.org/talks-and-interviews/our-vision/v/year-2060--education-predictions [accessed 28 June 2013]

Olmos, M. 'The Greek Flip: Old Language, Online Learning'. In *ASCILITE-Australian Society for Computers in Learning in Tertiary Education Annual Conference*(Australasian Society for Computers in Learning in Tertiary Education, 2013), 661–670. http://ascilite.org/conferences/sydney13/program/papers/Olmos.pdf.

---

7   Bloom, 'The 2 Sigma Problem', 5.

Siemens, G., Shane Dawson, and Grace Lynch. 'Improving the Quality and Productivity of the Higher Education Sector'. *Policy and Strategy for Systems-Level Deployment of Learning Analytics. Canberra, ACT: Society for Learning Analytics Research for the Australian Office for Learning and Teaching*, 2013. https://pdfs.semanticscholar.org/d307/34019734c219f6ab83af3dcebfa39c9e8b84.pdf.

Thompson, C. 'How Khan Academy Is Changing the Rules of Education'. *WIRED* 15 (July 2011). /www.wired.com/magazine/2011/07/ff_khan/all/1 [accessed viewed 13 April 2012]

Martin Olmos
Moore Theological College
martin.olmos@moore.edu.au

24 | THEOLOGICAL EDUCATION IN CONTEXT

EXPLORING THE DELIVERY OF THEOLOGICAL EDUCATION IN A MULTI-CULTURAL SETTING

Abstract

This chapter is a reflection on the recently implemented Culturally and Linguistically Diverse (CALD) program delivered into Fiji by Nazarene Theological College in Brisbane. The different cultural setting gives opportunity to examine challenges in pedagogy, curriculum, culture, and language from a different perspective. Using the Jerusalem model articulated by Das, these challenges are explored in the light of a missional approach to theological education that keeps contextuality as an important element alongside content, character and competency. Lessons learned as well as questions raised for further exploration are presented in the light of this experience.

Introduction[1]

Rupen Das has summarised several approaches to theological education in his

---

1   This chapter is the result of reflection with Rev Leilani Roqara (Fiji CALD Facilitator), and Major Dr Dean Smith (teacher of two of the four units taught in Fiji). I express my thanks and appreciation for both scholars.

useful booklet, *Connecting Curriculum with Context*.[2] Using his summary, I have identified Nazarene Theological College (NTC) in Brisbane as following a 'Jerusalem' or 'Missional' model. This designation forms the broader context for a consideration of theological education in the Church of the Nazarene, which is NTC's major stakeholder. Each of the models described by Das brings its own set of philosophical and theological parameters for curriculum development in the preparation of clergy.

The purpose of this paper is not to consider the appropriateness of the model followed, but rather, to take this as part of the context in which the Culturally and Linguistically Diverse (CALD) program, developed at NTC, can be used as a vehicle for bringing the issue of local context to this model.

The Church of the Nazarene, with its emphasis on education, compassionate ministry and discipleship, has grown to be a denomination in over 160 countries with approximately two and a half million members. Education is a part of the DNA of the denomination that now has 53 educational institutions around the world. Not surprisingly, adapting to different contextual constraints has been part of an ongoing conversation in several different areas of church life—mission, leadership, and of course education (ministry preparation).

The current statement in the Manual for the Church of the Nazarene states:

> 527.2 Cultural Adaptations for the Educational Foundations for Ordained Ministry.
>
> **The variety of cultural contexts around the world makes one curriculum unsuited for all global areas.** Each region of the world will be responsible for the development of specific curricular requirements for providing the educational foundations for ministry in a way that reflects the resources and the expectations of that global area. Approval of the International Course of Study Advisory Committee, the General Board and the Board of General Superintendents (527.5) will be required before implementing a regionally designed program. Even within global regions there are varieties of cultural expectations and resources. As a result, **cultural sensitivity and flexibility will characterize regional provisions for the educa-**

---

2   See Appendix Das, *Connecting Curriculum with Context* 17-18. Das's representation is based upon Brian Edgar's 'The Theology of Theological Education'. For a summary explanation of the various models see Das, 'Relevance and Faithfulness'.

tional foundations for ministry, which shall be directed and supervised by the District Ministerial Studies Board. Cultural adaptations of each region's program for providing educational foundations for ministry will be approved by Global Clergy Development and the International Course of Study Advisory Committee in consultation with the regional educational coordinator.[3]

This process attempts to bring context into the ordinary milieu of the education conversation.

However, a declared position can be more aspirational than actual. While the 'missional model' of theological education appears to consider context, historically, there has been movement back and forth along the spectrum of a contextualised to a decontextualized approach within the Church of the Nazarene. The denomination has steadfastly held to a position of being a global denomination with a group of six General Superintendents guiding the denomination. This, in one sense, minimises contextualisation at least in the jurisdictional arm of the denomination. The Global Mission Department has historically been tasked with making Christ-like disciples in the nations, and their efforts have resulted in the Church of the Nazarene having a global reach. An unintended consequence of a passionate drive for mission can sometimes be not 'hearing' well from the contexts in which mission and education is to be conducted. It is this perception that has prompted me to look for ways of giving context a stronger and more intentional voice.

Contextual engagement

Das says that 'leadership formation and theological education is most effective when theory and practice, action and reflection are combined'.[4]

> Theology must be critical reflection on the community's faith and practice. Theology is not simply reiteration of what has been or is currently believed and practiced by a community of faith [... W]hen this responsibility for critical reflection is neglected or relegated to a merely ornamental role, the faith of the community is invariably

---

3   *Manual 2013-2017, Church of the Nazarene,* 202. Emphasis mine.
4   Das, *Connecting Curriculum with Context.* 14.

threatened by shallowness, arrogance and ossification.[5]

According to Das's 'Jerusalem' model, context and formation both require contextual engagement. This focus of engagement is two-fold:

1. The context within which the education takes place is the community in which the students find themselves, so this is no education in isolation.
2. The content of the curriculum is found within the context so that the education itself is understood as part of mission.

This second perspective is illustrated by Meyers as she relates corporate worship and mission.[6] Using Schattnauer's description, Meyers speaks of corporate worship being understood as one of three perspectives:

1. 'Inside and out'—distinguishes sharply between worship that takes place inside the church, and mission that occurs outside;
2. 'Outside in'—the activities of mission become part of worship, for example, the seeker sensitive worship style;
3. 'Inside out'—the worshipping assembly is the locus for the missio Dei. 'In this approach, worship itself is mission, not in the instrumental sense of enabling mission activity, but as a place where God's reconciling love for the world is manifest'. [7]

When applied to education rather than worship, the 'Jerusalem' model reflects the 'inside out' perspective. The teacher 'is not removed from practice [and] teaching involves sharing lives as well as truth'.[8] This has implications for both curriculum development and pedagogy.

The diversity found within many different contexts can result in a confusing array of foci. Robert Woodruff argues strongly for a single focus in an educational program to avoid program tension points.[9] Amid the diversity, Woodruff says that a single focus can be determined from the expectations placed upon the student by educational stakeholders, perhaps in this case, the global denomination.

---

5 Das, *Connecting Curriculum with Context*, 5 quoting Migliore.
6 Meyers, 'Missional Church, Missional Liturgy', 37.
7 Meyers, 'Missional Church, Missional Liturgy', 38.
8 Das, *Connecting Curriculum with Context*, 18.
9 Woodruff, *Education on Purpose*, 8-10.

> [A]n arguably appropriate purpose for an educational program that leads directly into early ministry or mission would be READINESS FOR EARLY PRACTICE OF THE MINISTRY. This focus would not only influence every subject in its inclusion, but would also affect the manner in which the same materials were treated within even the cognitive knowledge areas.[10]

As such, educational outcomes such as academic content, spiritual formation, and ministerial skill are subject to that single focus of the program. If these three become foci in their own right, there is a high risk of confusion, competition or tension.

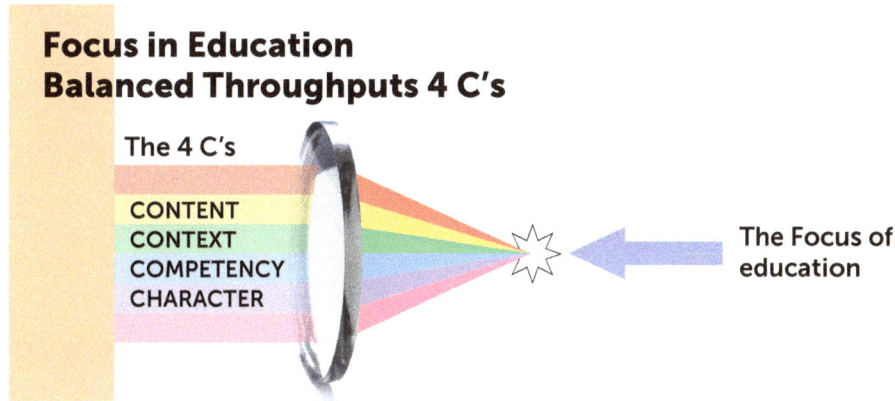

Figure 1: Adapted from Robert L Woodruff, *Education on Purpose: models for education in world areas*, 10.

Smith and O'Flynn's concept of 'capability' could be substituted for competence in Woodruff's 4 Cs of content, context, competency, and character (Figure 1) to provide broader input for focusing. On this basis, the beginner practitioner develops the capacity for competence in a variety of contexts. Even so, the need to focus these outcomes through a single lens still exists.

Context does not necessarily influence the focus of the program (we still want effective beginning practitioners), but it will influence, firstly, the answer to the question, 'What should a beginning ministry practitioner look like in this particular context?' and thus influence the content of the curriculum. Secondly, the context can provide the laboratory in which the learning takes place. Thirdly,

---

10 Woodruff, *Education on Purpose*, 12. See also Ault, 'Assessing Integrative Learning and Readiness for Mission'.

context will influence the delivery (pedagogy) of the educational exercise. It is with these aspects of context in mind, that I turn to a specific vehicle that holds the potential to address contextual issues intentionally.

The NTC Experience

NTC Brisbane has historically been involved in a multi-cultural context with its delivery of theological education. There has been a collegial connection between NTC with the South Pacific Nazarene Theological College and its campuses in Suva, Apia, Honiara, Port Villa, as well as with Melanesia Nazarene Bible College in Papua New Guinea. Students have come from Korea, PNG, Solomon Islands, Samoa, India, Netherlands, USA, and elsewhere.

With good connections in the South Pacific, NTC has moved into the provision of the CALD program. This program has been developed through the Sydney College of Divinity. The benefits are at least:

1. the provision of an accredited undergraduate award through a facilitated on-line program into areas of the world where such programs are difficult to access;
2. students remain in their ministry setting, thus not disadvantaging the church by losing personnel for long periods of time. Likewise, the student does not face issues of re-entry into the ministry setting after an extended absence;
3. it is financially accessible;
4. the students' current ministry experiences become part of the educational resource.

An important feature for the CALD units offered in Fiji is the 5-day facilitation sessions. A locally based facilitator was trained by modelling the facilitation process in the first unit undertaken. All notes and resources were delivered via the Google Classroom platform on-line. The facilitator ensured smooth operation of the video conference, gave students an orientation to student life at NTC, and taught students how to access the NTC library and do basic research. The format of the facilitation has been replicated for all four units delivered in Fiji. The local facilitator is a Fijian herself, who can facilitate discussions that focus on the local issues. Facilitation can be done by those who are effective in the contexts of the students. Values and character forming processes can be modelled through times of discussion.

Response from a student and facilitator in Fiji

Care is taken to listen well to students to ensure that the vehicle used in delivering the classes is appropriate. Formal and informal student feedback is gathered regularly. An example of some of the feedback is:

> Overall the students have managed well with the course content, readings, assignments and especially the group assignments. About 90 percent of the students are involved in full-time ministry and a handful are bi-vocational. It has not been an easy transition and students are still adapting to the higher education requirements. However, the program is challenging the students in areas of theology and learning in ways they have not been challenged before. In session discussions, many students have experienced new ways of thinking, beginning to think analytically and critically. It has helped students to think about things around us here in Fiji and how they have an impact on us.
>
> The facilitated online learning is a brand-new experience for all of us in Fiji. The students have all felt that the openness of the teachers and encouragement during discussions have given us the confidence to speak up. The Fijian culture is one where respect for elders is highly important, including that of the teacher. Students have had to work through this and it has been helpful that our teachers are open and welcoming of students as they speak up and share their thoughts.
>
> The one-week intensive facilitation followed by a portion of two Saturdays later in the semester has worked well. The teachers are available as well for us to be able to be in contact with them.
>
> The theological language has been a stretch for most of the students, especially at this level of learning. However, there are students who are more vocal than others and this helps the less vocal students. They listen in on the conversations and, when it is break time, students are able to ask each other for help in understanding terms. It is good that here in Fiji we have students translate and explain in the Fijian language so that the Fijian student can have a better grasp of discussions or conversations that they may find difficult during the discussion time. The teachers have provided times for free discussion whilst they listen in. This is helpful toward

the classroom learning. The language challenges will be a work in progress as new students join from various educational experiences.[11]

Lessons and Questions Along the Way

Firstly, it is possible to overreach in our expectations that this program is genuinely contextual. Simply using the word 'contextual' frequently is not sufficient. Faculty members come from very different contexts from that of the students, and our Course Unit Booklets come with embedded Western cultural expectations. While listening well is a priority in our pedagogy, it is arrogant to suggest that we can be fully contextual. At best, this approach is a vehicle for a conversation between contexts. It builds into the fabric of the program an orientation that encourages contextual considerations to be acknowledged and addressed. However, the danger is we may acknowledge the presence of different contexts and cultures, but in practice, not bring these differences into conversation with each other. For example, Boyung Lee draws a distinction between 'multi-culturalism' and 'inter-culturalism'. In her experience of working as a Korean in America, she encounters deep-seated cultural assumptions. She claims that multi-culturalism is an 'individualistic and colonial way of engaging with different racial and ethnic communities'.[12] The term 'inter-culturalism' is a preferred term, in her opinion, for it allows for diversity but does not bring assimilationist assumptions, or alternatively, 'silos' of different cultures that exist in isolation from one another.

Lee illustrates the subtlety of these assumptions by drawing a distinction between the cultural assumptions found in the term 'communalism' of the West and those of the East. Gathering in small groups is certainly a significant movement now in most congregations of all denominational persuasions. This has prompted some to suggest that Westerners are becoming communalists, and no longer can be defined as 'alienated individualists'.[13] However, Lee writes:

> If one looks closely at the nature of small groups, one easily sees that small groups typically exhibit what I call 'collectivism', rather

---

11 Rev Leilani Roqara, Chancellor, Nazarene Theological College, South Pacific Nazarene Theological College.
12 Lee, *Transforming Congregations Through Community,* loc. 114 in 3179.
13 Lee, *Transforming Congregations Through Community,* loc. 181 in 3179.

than communalism. The sense of community undergirding the current American trend in small groups is far different from the communalists for they lack solidarity and kin-ship relationships; rather the notion of community in mainline small groups is more like a gathering of individuals in reciprocal relationships.

Members (of these small groups) are not disproportionately oriented toward community or toward fitting in, helping others, bending their interests toward the will of the group. They are strong individualists who bring their individual needs and interests to the group.[14]

Individualism and communalism are two completely different cultural patterns that lead people to view the world and life through different lenses—even though they may use the same English words to describe what they are experiencing.[15]

The first question then, is, 'What are the contextual blind spots within the syllabi?' Some of the blind spots are easy to note, e.g. are bibliographic references included that are culturally specific for the student's context; are the unit objectives relatable to the student's context; how do word counts in assessments relate to a story-telling culture; what are the students' understanding of plagiarism; does our curriculum relate to the context of the student? Other questions are probably much less obvious but nonetheless significant.

Secondly, there is the understanding of the teacher's role in class. While we in the West tend to take a student-centred approach to learning and teaching, this is not the case in many other cultures. Some would argue that even in the West theological educators have not made this shift well,[16] but Fernandez points to a shift that needs to be made if context is to be taken seriously:

> Theological education must be based on the affirmation that knowledge is constructed, not transmitted. New knowledge cannot be just 'transmitted' or 'absorbed' from one person to another. When students receive new information they must process that information, based on their previous knowledge, before they can try to make sense of it. In other words, they must construct a new perspective of reality by assimilating or adapting that new knowledge… The

---

14 Lee, *Transforming Congregations Through Community,* loc 1.81-182 in 3179.
15 See Kiki and Parker, 'Is There a Better Way to Teach Theology to Non-Western Persons?' for further discussion of the community and the role of learning in communal cultures.
16 See Fernandez, 'Engaging Contextual Realities in Theological Education', 339-349.

richest learning experiences occur when new knowledge is socially constructed—when that knowledge is discovered through intentional interaction with the main actors of the context in which that learning is taking place... When education is confined to the individual struggle with bibliographic material, without the corporate assessing of the implication of that material for cultural transformation, its value is very limited.[17]

We have discovered that the facilitation sessions that accompany these units are vital. In class discussions, there is a specific pecking order to the contributions. Even though the more senior (in age) students verbally gave permission for all students to contribute, the junior members of the class wait for the senior students to contribute first. There was a growing courage by the younger students to contribute more spontaneously as time progressed. The eagerness of the teacher to hear from all students, the willingness of the teacher to be challenged in graceful ways, and the teacher affirming countering views being expressed have been important ways of changing the understanding of the teacher's role.[18]

The content of the class was accessible on-line via Google Classroom so the facilitation times were focused on processing the content, not delivering it. This requires dialogue between students and between students and teacher to be effective. A helpful process was asking a question related to the content and having the class divide into small groups to discuss this. The results of the discussions were brought to the whole group so that all could learn from their peers. Teachers found that these break-out times, and the resultant plenary conversations, were very helpful in coming to terms with the students' own contexts.

An initial challenge was the way the conversational tone of most of the teachers was received. Australian egalitarianism is strong at NTC, and very few personal titles are used by students and faculty alike. Classes are usually held 'in the round' and there is plenty of discussion and interruption as students think aloud, explore new ideas, and challenge what is said. This is a very different approach from the experiences of students in Fiji. At times, it was important to show that the low key conversational tone of the teacher held deep, insightful wisdom to the same degree as one who might present in a more formal way.

---

17   Fernandez, 'Engaging Contextual Realities in Theological Education', 342.
18   See Horder, 'Encouraging Vulnerable Learning' and Marshall, 'Learning from the Academy', 185-204 for discussion of the effectiveness of peer learning and vulnerabilities of teachers in modelling learning.

Student feedback indicated that they sensed the teacher's eagerness to assist each student. They feel connected with the teacher (only an email away) and do not feel isolated in the process of working out the unit requirements.[19]

Thirdly, peer learning through informal opportunities is a strength in the highly relational society of Fiji. The informal processing of content that occurred over meal and small break times was conducted in languages other than English. Teachers found it helpful to take time for questions after each break since the students had further worked through class material with their peers. It appeared that processing concepts in students' first language gave them the confidence to ask questions or make comments in English later in class. The process of having intensive facilitation sessions face to face (among the students) certainly enhanced learning in this case.

A question from this experience is whether this peer learning can be conducted asynchronously, through discussion pages on Google Classroom. Currently, this is not part of the culture of the Fijian students, but perhaps it can be.[20] The issue of synchronous engagement in peer discussions and the relative proximity to the ministry context may be two competing facets to learning. The larger pedagogical issue is that asynchronous engagement may address the aspect of ministry context proximity, but the synchronous social engagement, so much a strength of the Fijian culture, appears to be lost in such asynchrony.

Fourthly, assessments create challenges when considering diverse contexts. The highly-individualised orientation embedded in our syllabi may set artificial barriers. Often it is easier to set a book review, an essay, and perhaps a quiz early on, as the default decontextualised assessment rubric. Taylor says,

> One hypothesis being generated in the e-learning arena is that the closer a student is to their context, the more likely they are to begin to experience transforming theology, as they seek to integrate content with their current lived experience… the face to face class removes a student from their context, while e-learning allows them to stay in context, increasing their range of connections they, as a 'living library', are likely to make.[21]

---

19 Feedback from student Feb 2017 conducted as part of the formal student feedback mechanism.
20 Taylor, 'Embodiment and Transformation in the Context of e-Learning', 174. In considering the themes of *embodiment, participation, praxis, and community* in e-learning, Taylor suggests that these are not only theological necessities but entirely possible through extending our perspective on 'living libraries' as resources for learning.
21 Taylor, 'Embodiment and Transformation in the Context of e-Learning', 175.

If context is where the learning takes place and where curriculum is formed, then assessments should reflect this. In our case, students are all involved in vocational ministry assignments and have a rich context in which to do their learning. This integrative learning does introduce a degree of complexity not found in a decontextualised approach.[22]

The Fijian context makes group projects a 'natural'. The criteria for assessing the group, as well as the individual's contribution within the group, are critical to the process. Currently the assessment suite has involved one group assessment (with a common mark for the individuals of the group), usually the middle of three, and the other two assessments have been individually based. The first assessment piece, placed early in the semester, has been either a book report or a quiz. This gives both student and teacher an indication of the context.

One student in Fiji took the initiative to use the video conference facility to connect synchronously to the other students to discuss the assessments (a book review and a group project). All the students found the synchronous meeting an encouragement and minimised feelings of being overwhelmed. This student made two points as he invited interaction: firstly, he acknowledged they were adult learners and not there to compete, but rather to learn from one another; secondly, they sought to grow as effective disciples of Christ and ministers for God's glory. This promoted student engagement and has improved the quality of the work presented.

A key question regarding assessments is, 'What is the assessment actually assessing—content, the ability to write, the ability to memorise or synthesise, the ability to adjust to the culture of the teacher etc.?' While this question is universal for all educators, it appears that the multi-cultural context intensifies the issue considerably.

Fifthly, the facilitator has a key role in the success of the class. The term 'facilitator' here is used in a different way from that often used in a 'flipped classroom' setting.[23] In that situation, the facilitator is often the qualified teacher, helping students to process the material. In the CALD setting, the facilitator is

---

22 See Ault, 'Assessing Integrative Learning and Readiness for Ministry' and Hibbert, 'Addressing the Need for Better Integration in Theological Education'. One such assessment piece used was a group project reporting on a theological reflection of a pastoral encounter. The initial reflection was conducted within the assigned group, and then each member of the group presented a part of the group report to the whole class. The cohort gathered in one location for the presentations and the teacher observed them via video conference.

23 Mangan 'Inside the Flipped Classroom'.

not necessarily academically qualified, but brings the credibility of cultural understanding and often ministry expertise. Close supervision and oversight by the qualified teacher continues. The facilitator does the typical work of ensuring enrolment, registration, and the physical logistics of the meeting room. However, familiarity with the IT requirements and the facility to use Google Classroom and e-book borrowing etc. are essential for a positive student experience. The facilitator becomes the first point of contact for both student and teacher.

As each of the facilitator's responsibilities is done well, the learning experience is given every opportunity to be positive and constructive. As with all new technology and models, it takes only one bad experience in the initial stages to make this approach appear to be unviable. It helps to keep the process as simple as possible, even though one could add to the technical delivery systems with all kinds of nuanced facilities. It must be easily maintained. Goodwill and determination on the part of the teacher, facilitator and students keeps the focus on the outcomes.

Sixthly, the model must remain flexible and dynamic for it to respond well to changing contexts. Our scheduled facilitation sessions have not been without their physical challenges. Two cyclones at the very time of scheduled facilitation sessions, an unexpected death of a church leader leading to extended times of mourning, transport issues for students getting to facilitation sessions, internet reliability issues, electricity blackouts, teachers' overloaded schedules, all have demanded a nimbleness in response to ensure a class is successfully completed. Expect the unexpected. Those with missionary experience can attest to this, I am sure.

Seventhly, time spent articulating learning and teaching outcomes for the program in contextual ways is time well spent. This is a way of keeping the big picture before the facilitators and introduces conversations about the contextual expressions of these outcomes. The document, 'Teaching and Learning Outcomes for a Bachelor's Degree in Theology agreed to by the Council of Deans in Theology' in April 2016 has helped in this process. It is interesting to note that of the five outcomes, context is explicitly mentioned in three of them and implied in a fourth. While these outcomes are expressed within mainly academic priorities, the 'articulation, relevance, and implications of Christian belief'[24] could be considered within the focus, 'function as a competent beginning practitioner'. Listening well to students who live and work in very different

---

24 Point 4 of the TLOs Council of Deans of Theology, April 2016.

contexts will be an ongoing challenge.[25] Ball suggests that teachers may not necessarily be very well versed in this skill.

> While many faculty teach using illustrations and applications related to life experience, there is the challenging question [...] as to whether faculty are connecting in the classroom with their own prior life and ministry experience or with the students' life experience. Hence there is a need to make such connections intentional and systematic.[26]

Working cross-culturally and over distance amplifies the contextuality gap.

Conclusion

The student body at NTC is culturally diverse and reflects the growth of a global denomination that is its major stakeholder. Contextual issues are amplified by the multi-cultural context of NTC's vision and student body. The CALD program shows itself to be a promising vehicle that gives context an intentional voice in the provision of theological education. While the focus of this paper has been on the Fijian context, many more questions will arise as there is engagement in further cultural contexts. Several of the challenges and lessons learned are generic to on-line and distance education; others are unique to each setting and strike at the heart of the issue of contextualisation. As this conversation continues intentionally, a shaping of the CALD program will be possible. I am confident that as we move ahead in humility, with a spirit of hospitality, and the courage to ask hard questions of ourselves and different contexts, we will embrace a diversity of cultures and settings within the SCD community of learners and scholars.

Bibliography

Ault, Nancy. 'Assessing Integrative Learning and Readiness for Ministry', *Learning and Teaching Theology: some ways ahead* (Les Ball & James R. Harrison, eds.; Preston, Vic: Morning Star, 2014), 81-90.

---

25 See Lawson, 'The Unprecedented Educational Challenge', 373, regarding the challenges of an education irrelevant to a students' context.
26 Ball, *Transforming Theology*, 56.

Ball, Les. *Transforming Theology: student experience and transformative learning in undergraduate theological education* (Preston, Vic: Mosaic, 2012).

Blevins, Dean et al (eds). *Manual 2013-2017 Church of the Nazarene* (Kansas City, MO: Beacon Hill, 2013).

Clarke, Thomas. 'A Critique of the Anglo-American Model of Corporate Governance', *Comparative Research in Law & Political Economy* (Research Paper No.15/2009; http://digitalcommons.osgoode.yorku.ca/clpe/129 accessed Dec. 2, 2016).

Das, Rupen. *Connecting Curriculum with Context: a handbook for context relevant curriculum development in theological education* (Carlisle, UK: Langham Global Library, 2015).

Das, Rupen. 'Relevance and Faithfulness: Challenges in Contextualising Theological Education', *Insights Journal for Global Theological Education* 1. 2 (May 2016), 17-29.

Edgar, Brian. 'The Theology of Theological Education', *Evangelical Review of Theology* 29.3 (2005), 208-217.

Fernandez, Enrique. 'Engaging Contextual Realities in Theological Education: Systems and Strategies', *ERT* 38.4 (2014), 339-349.

Hibbert, Richard & Evelyn. 'Addressing the Need for Better Integration in Theological Education', *Learning and Teaching Theology: some ways ahead (*Les Ball & James R. Harrison, eds.; Preston, Vic: Morning Star, 2014), 107-117.

Horder, John. 'Encouraging Vulnerable Learning: student responses to groupwork experience', *Journal of Adult Theological Education* 7.2 (2010), 60-77.

John, Eeva; Michael Volland & Robin Barden. *Context-based Learning for Discipleship and Ministry: introducing the PC3 approach* (Cambridge, UK: Grove Books, 2017).

Kiki, Gwayaweng & Ed Parker. 'Is There A Better Way to Teach Theology to Non-Western Persons? Research from Papua New Guinea that Could Benefit the Wider Pacific', *Australia eJournal of Theology* 21.2 (August 2014).

Lawson, Michael. 'The Unprecedented Educational Challenge:... Make Disciples of All Nations...', *Christian Education Journal,* Series 3, 13.2 (2016), 361-375.

Lee, Boyung. *Transforming Congregations Through Community: faith formation from the seminary to the church* (Louisville, KY: Westminster John Knox, 2013).

Mangan, Katherine, 'Inside the Flipped Classroom', *Chronicle of Higher Education* 95982 10/4/2013 Vol 60, Issue 5 http://web.a.ebscohost.com/ehost/detail/detail?sid=2232ce7b-2323-4b1d-ad5f-8737 237276c9%40sessionmgr4010&vid=7&hid=4207&bdata=JnNpdGU9ZWhvc3QtbGl2ZQ%3d %3d#AN=90544338&db=rlh Accessed April 7, 2017.

Marshall, Brian. 'Learning from the Academy: From Peer Observation of Teaching to Peer Enhancement of Learning and Teaching', *Journal of Adult Theological Education* 1.2 (2004), 185-204.

Meyers, Ruth A. 'Missional Church, Missional Liturgy', *Theology Today* 67 (2010), 36-50.

Ritchey, Jeff. 'Decentralised Theological Education in Europe', *Christian Education Journal*, Series 3, 13:2 (2016), 391-405.

Smith, Stephen & Leon O'Flynn. 'Responding to complexity: moving from competence to capability', *Learning and Teaching Theology: some ways ahead* (Les Ball & James R. Harrison, eds.; Preston, Vic: Morning Star, 2014), 119-128.

Taylor, Steve. 'Embodiment and Transformation in the Context of e-Learning', *Learning and Teaching Theology: some ways ahead* (Les Ball & James R. Harrison, eds.; Preston, Vic: Morning Star, 2014), 171-183.

Woodruff, Robert. *Education on Purpose: models for education in world areas* (Brisbane, Qld: QUT, 2001).

Appendix: Models of Theological Education

Symbol	Athens	Berlin	Geneva	Jerusalem	Auburn	New Delhi
Model	Classical	Vocational	Confessional	Missional	Contextual	Spiritual
Context	Academy	University	Seminary	Community	Parish	Ashram
Goal/Purpose	Transforming the individual	Strengthening the church	Knowing God	Converting the world	Planting locally	Engaging other world views
Emphasis	Personal formation: knowing who...	Interpretive skills: knowing how...	Information, enculturation: knowing what...	Mission, partnership: knowing for...	Local community: knowing where...	Multi-cultural, pluralistic: knowing others
Formation	Individualised and focussed on inner personal, moral and religious transformation	Clarify vocational identity as the basis for Christian practice	Discursive analysis, comparison and synthesis of beliefs	Learning has to have reference to all dimensions of life, family, friendships, work and neighbourhood	Learning how to be relevant locally	Learning to co-exist respectfully while retaining one's identity
Theology	Theology is the knowledge of God, not about God	Theology is a way of thinking, applying theory to life. Theology is applied: spiritual, missiological, vocational	Theology is knowing God through a specific tradition	Missiology is the mother of theology. It involved action - mission.	Theology is about being spiritual relevant locally	Theology is about understanding the revelation of God in other religions and world views
Teacher	Provider: of indirect assistance through intellectual and moral disciplines to help students undergo formation	Professor: the teacher is a researcher whom the students assist	Priest: knowledge of tradition, lives and exemplifies it as well as knows it	Practitioner/missionary: the teacher is not removed from practice; teaching involves sharing lives as well as truth	Pastor: the teacher leads by being relevant in the community	Apologist: where the teacher not only defends the faith but also builds bridges
Student	Cultivates his mind, character and spirit	Becomes a theoretician able to apply practice	Initiated into the tradition, beliefs, vocation and ministry	Discipled to become a disciple-maker	Learns to serve the community	Learn to build bridges and defend the faith

Rupen Das, *Connecting Curriculum with Context,* 17-18, adapted from Edgar, 'The Theology of Theological Education'.

Bruce G Allder
Nazarene Theological College, Brisbane
ballder@ntc.edu.au

25 | INTEGRATING THEOLOGY IN A QUESTIONING AGE

Abstract

This essay presents a case for the need to develop an intentional platform for the integration of theological learning in the face of an increasingly questioning and confrontational age. It takes as a base some established principles of practical theology as expounded by Browning and Osmer in particular and expands them into a more general application to the broader ambit of theological studies. In doing so, it constructs a practical paradigm for integrating theological education and offers a number of pedagogical approaches that facilitate such integrative learning.

Keywords: theological education, integrative learning, practical theological principles, pedagogical approaches

The need for theological integration

Confronting a Questioning Age

Contemporary western (and, increasingly, other) society does not accept, but always questions. Traditional values are simply rejected if not convenient. A solid education and a professional skill set are no longer guarantees of recognised authority if what is presented is not conducive to the recipient. Unpalatable medical diagnoses provided by a physician are rejected if a more pleasing version can be found by recourse to Dr Google. Police officers are constantly under challenge by armchair critics and self-appointed bush lawyers, with a resultant decline in their social respect and operational authority. School classrooms are microcosms of this phenomenon. At a Secondary Principals conference in June 2015, Associate Professor Rob Nairn spoke of how the traditional school, with the teacher as the font of all knowledge, has no chance of survival in the twenty-first century, since classes now contain 'kids that are questioning and [who] learn differently—that "I know it all or I can find it out" idea'. The teacher, he says, no longer merely informs, but needs to create a 'collision of ideas' in the classroom.[1] Society at large challenges authority and resists its imposition.

But so too do Christian communities closer to our home. Congregations question authority: things need to make sense, not just sound authoritative. During a school staff room conversation around the time of a papal visit, a good friend of mine expressed a thought which was warmly endorsed by all, when she said, 'I'm a good Catholic, I go to Mass every Sunday, but I don't let my religion affect my life' . Lest I be charged here with sectarian bias, let me add a further example of a polite, conservative young gentlemanly student in a theology class in an evangelical college where I once taught, who was moved to respond exasperatedly to a contentious point being expounded by the lecturer, 'Oh, we don't have to believe this garbage, do we?'. The days of passive reception have been replaced by a new dawn of aggressive confrontation.

There is of course always the matter of resistance to such developing trends, especially in the interest of preservation of what we value or what has served us well. Jeff Astley cites the following extract from *Angela's Ashes*:

> Never mind what is Sanctifying Grace, Quigley. That's none of your business. You're here to learn the catechism and do what you're told. You're not here to be asking questions. There are too many people wandering the world asking questions and that's what has us in the state we're in and if I find any boy in this class asking questions I won't be responsible for what happens.[2]

While traditionalists may bemoan such a seemingly narcissistic societal trend, individual challenging of authority is none the less a reality that ministry practitioners and other theological graduates constantly encounter in our questioning age and thus it is imperative that theological education equips them for so doing.

---

1   Nairn, 'Teachers lead the way', 6 June 2015.
2   McCourt, *Angela's Ashes*, 13. Astley, *Ordinary Theology*, 13.

Guiding Motif

The overarching motif of this paper derives from the ideal of the integration of theory and practice to attain a desired praxis which in turn issues in an integrated person in ministry and life, who is well equipped to provide answers to real (even unanticipated) questions in a real world. As I look back over my forty years of engagement with theological education, as either student or teacher, I find myself questioning the permanent worth of much of what has been delivered, especially in terms of how it relates to my present world. The aim of my questioning is not to reject or to devalue, but to discern what has been of permanent worth, and more importantly, how I can factor into my current teaching those things which retain intrinsic value. For example, the ministry training I received in the late 1970s featured Christian education, in which I had a passionate interest. The teaching methodology taught included such cutting edge skills as the use of the overhead projector, in which I was quite competent. The need for that particular skill mastery was of course short-lived. What was of more lasting value was the confirmation of the centrality of the learner in the educative process: 'You are not teaching religion; you are teaching people'. This is a philosophy that has strongly influenced—I dare say shaped—my teaching for many years, in both secular and theological teaching, and has been the main basis of any success I have had in that career. But it is not just antiquated technology that becomes quickly obsolete. I recently pondered the question, 'Could ministry training delivered as recently as ten years ago answer questions of the impact of social media in today's world?'. It is increasingly self-evident that, in a rapidly changing and increasingly questioning world, theological education needs to be more than a compendium of theological and biblical dogma and more than the acquisition of vocational ministry skills. This article advocates an educational approach which revolves around a cohesive and interdependent interplay of theology-informed practice and practice-informed theology, expressed coherently in and through a practical-theologically integrated person in a real world setting.

A practical paradigm for theological integration

Practical Theology as a Base

For thirty years, I have been engaged in delivering theological education, primarily in the classical areas of Historical Theology and New Testament. In the last ten years, I have been working in the area of Practical Theology, with a particular focus on educational research and the integration of theological concepts and ministry practice. In the last few years, I have noticed something of a pedagogical transformation in my own development as I have consciously sought to bring into a harmony the broad range of my academic passions: Bible, theology, history, practical ministry, transformative learning. This process has been stimulated by grappling with the potential provided by some leading writers in practical theology, designed essentially for ministry praxis, but which I have found to be most adaptable to an enrichment of the entire gamut of theological education. Such a paradigm offers an effective means of developing not only a theologically informed graduate, but also a theologically integrated graduate, which is what this paper explores.

'Practical Theology' is not a simple term to define. Astley avoids what he calls 'the rather obscure and slightly embarrassing label of "practical theology"' by using the expression 'ordinary theology'. However, his audience is 'ordinary' Christians who have received little or no theological education.[3] For the purposes of theological educators, a more useful discussion is provided by Bonnie Miller-McLemore in *Christian Theology in Practice: Discovering a Discipline*.[4] She treats the 'multivalent nature of practical theology' with reference to four distinct categories with different audiences and goals: a discipline among scholars; an activity of faith among believers; a method for studying theology in practice for theological educators; and a curricular area of subdisciplines in the seminary.[5] The focus of this chapter is her third area (a method for studying theology). Within these categories, however, all share in common a focus on local, concrete, religious expression and its transformation; all are concerned with the embodiment of religious belief in the day-to-day lives of individuals and communities; and all seek to understand and to influence religious wisdom or faith in action. Thus, practical theology not only describes how people live as people of faith, it also considers how they might do so more fully, and to do so within a coherent integration of thought, action, and personhood.

In investigating such 'lived theology', practical theology differs from pastoral theology, which has a primary focus on reflection on pastoral care and counselling. It also differs from systematic or doctrinal theology, with its traditional

---

3   Astley, *Ordinary Theology*, 1, 56.
4   Miller-McLemore, *Christian Theology*, 100–110.
5   Miller-McLemore, *Christian Theology*, 101.

focus on proclaimed beliefs. Practical theology is ultimately a normative project guided by the desire to make a difference in the world.[6] It involves not just theological knowledge applied via ministry competencies. Rather, it involves *theological praxis*: that is, value-directed and value-laden action, incorporating a circular movement from practice to theologically informed critical reflection and back to corrected practice, even to radically transformed practice. It requires a coherent and dynamic correlation between tradition (theology) and experience (practice).[7]

A Starting Point: Supervised Field Education

The mention of 'practical' learning leads immediately to the topic of supervised field education. There are many possibly self-evident reasons why supervised field education should become an arena for integrating theology, but I will focus on just two. First, the entrenched myth of the academic/practical, scholar/practitioner false dichotomy needs to be dispelled. Practically integrated theology intentionally challenges the conventional divisions between classical and practical disciplines, between academy and congregation, between theory and practice. It strategically counters the misperception of theological education as being based on either the clerical paradigm (the acquisition of technical pastoral skills) or the academic paradigm (the acquisition of cognitive knowledge of doctrine).[8] Classical theological courses are frequently criticised for their fragmented compartmentalisation, where separate disciplines of Bible, Theology, History, and Ministry do not engage in conversation with one another, let alone with the lived practice of students or graduates. Yet the classroom is typically set up in ways that could well facilitate the learning of theory and dialogically processing ways in which the theory may be worked out in practice. Accordingly, the arena of *in situ* field education provides an ideal locus for the actual implementation, refinement and further consolidation or even remediation of such theoretical considerations.

It is important to note that field education disconnected from theological development is no more valuable than theological development without lived engagement: while both may have merit, such merit does not necessarily translate to value. Field placements have at times been typified by an erroneous assumption of (meritorious) learning by 'doing stuff' or what I call 'theological

---

6   Miller-McLemore, *Christian Theology in Practice*, 103–106.
7   Astley, *Ordinary Theology*, 2–3.
8   Miller-McLemore, *Christian Theology in Practice*, 108.

osmosis'. It is still not uncommon for field education placements to be not much more than a convenient construct to assume practical skills development. In recent years, I have reviewed many field education programmes and processes and interviewed numerous students and supervisors. While there has been a marked development of vocational and performative skills in the field, there has been little evidence of integrative reflection on the field practice 'back in the classroom'. Reflection is typically focused on how to perform better, rather than a penetrating theological integration in either field location or classroom. The most common plaint voiced by missions directors and denominational superintendents during my recent research[9] is the lack of integration of theology in the lives of theological graduates, who know their doctrine well and have good skills, but who, when faced by problems, resort to pragmatic expedience rather than a theological frame of operation. Many final year students and recent graduates have noted the gap between intellectualized theological theory and practical life and ministry: 'We tend to be more academic. We are very content driven'.[10] If active learning is not grounded in a coherent theological frame of reference, how can we assure that effective learning is taking place? If our teaching of theology is not furnishing an operational frame of reference, does that teaching need to be reviewed and refined? Is it good enough to manage an ever changing and constantly questioning world if we lack an appropriately integrated theological world-view?

So, in short, supervised field placements are an appropriate first place to consider the potential for practically integrated theology, to ensure that theology is not divorced from practice and that practice is not isolated from theology. Yet while we need to promote theologically informed practice, we also need to develop practically framed theology.

Integrated Theology: A Dialogue

The first step in initiating an integrative dialogue is the creation of an ethos of *facilitation*.[11] Facilitation involves a gathering of students with a leader (typically,

---

9   Ball, *Transforming Theology*, 81-85.
10 See Ball, *Transforming Theology*, 61.
11 The Australian College of Ministries (ACOM) has developed a thoroughgoing and highly successful system of facilitation as a central plank in its extensive online and distance learning delivery in all subject areas. I am indebted to my colleagues at ACOM for the general ideas expressed in this paragraph.

though not necessarily, a faculty member) as an element in a specific unit of study. It may be scheduled for anything from an hour to five days. The purpose of this time is not to 'teach' new material, nor to cram information into students in the form of a lecture or an intensive, but to help students to:

- process what they have been learning in the unit
- apply their learning to their individual lives and ministries
- question, challenge and explore confronting ideas
- seek clarification on difficult issues
- grow through healthy interaction with fellow students and a competent facilitator.

The role of a facilitator is not to be the 'font of all knowledge' who dispenses wisdom to the grateful students. Instead, a facilitator helps students to understand, develop, refine and apply their learnings to their own real world context through leading a peer learning experience.[12]

Within such a facilitative ethos, we need then to establish a *strategy* for the creation of a continuous pedagogical dialogue that constantly reviews, refines and enhances theological understandings, practical applications and personal appropriation. This will incorporate both effectual reflection and implementation. A helpful starting point is provided by Don Browning's critical hermeneutics, a system of integrated theological reflection based on a circle of four stages: Descriptive Theology; Historical Theology; Systematic Theology; Strategic Practical Theology.[13] In approaching Browning's system, theological educators need first to discern just what is their own fundamental approach to practical theological hermeneutics. Is it foundational (based on normative texts and systems), pragmatic (what works), pastoral (caring for people)? What is our starting point, what shapes our hermeneutics? Is it normative texts/theology as the basis of objective truth? Is it inherited historical traditions as the way our tradition has developed? Is it pragmatics—what works for me and my people in our particular context? Is it compassion—what is best for my people in their need? Perhaps it is even ambition — how can I establish a position of influence? While there is arguably nothing inherently wrong with any of these approaches, paradoxically there may well be something inherently wrong with all of these

---

12 ACOM, *Facilitator Handbook 2017*, 3-20 provides a detailed treatment of that college's distinctive facilitation.
13 Browning, *Equality*, 3–30 gives a summary of his seminal book, *A Fundamental Practical Theology*.

approaches, since a dominant focus on the strength of one approach tends to reject the strengths of all others. Whatever our fundamental approach to hermeneutics might be, it will shape very much our approach to a practical theology of ministry.

The pedagogical genius of Browning's critical hermeneutics lies in its starting point, which embeds it squarely in the spirit of transformative learning. It involves an epistemology that prioritises *understanding* over *explanation* and that leads one to take seriously the effective history of the past as it moves forward to strategic practical action in the future. It begins with the description of concrete questions; it moves backward to the interpretive concerns of historical theology; it goes on to systematic theology as ordered reflection on this interpretive process; and, finally, it moves forward to strategic practical theological reflection about ways to proceed with concrete and faithful action.

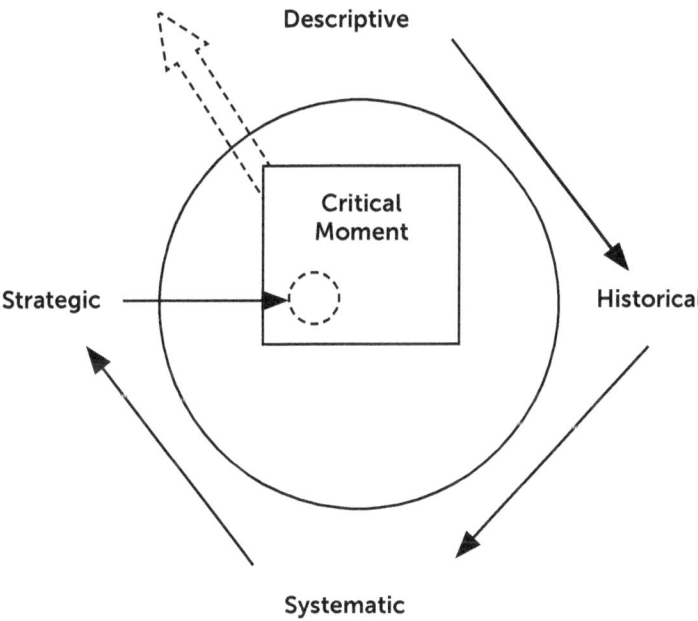

Figure 1. Browning's critical hermeneutics

Browning's ideas have been progressed by Richard Osmer, who proceeds to the step of strategic implementation of the principles of practically integrated theology.[14] In effect, he translates Browning's stages of theological reflection into four applied tasks of practical theology. He begins with four basic questions:

- What is going on?
- Why is this going on?
- What ought to be going on?
- How might we respond?

Accordingly, he constructs four corresponding core tasks of practical theology:

- The *descriptive-empirical* task: gathering information to discern patterns and dynamics in current situations or contexts (*Priestly Listening*);
- The *interpretive* task: drawing on theories of the arts and sciences to understand and explain why these patterns are occurring (*Sagely Wisdom*);
- The *normative* task: using theological concepts to interpret particular situations or contexts, constructing ethical norms to guide responses, and learning from 'good practice' (*Prophetic Discernment*);
- The *pragmatic* task: determining strategies of action that will influence situations in ways that are desirable and entering into a reflective conversation with the 'talk back' emerging when they are enacted (*Servant Leadership*).[15]

A significant aspect of Osmer's method is that the tasks are not linear but interpenetrative, constantly re-visiting tasks that have already been explored, and adjusting progressively in light of such re-visiting. While there is of necessity an initial order in their execution (we should not start a four lap race at lap three), as they proceed, each task is in ongoing dialogue with each of the other tasks. As a pragmatic outcome is enacted, it resumes the dialogue with interpretive and normative analysis. It is this continuous interaction and mutual influence of all four tasks that is at the heart of his method.[16] Thus, not only is pragmatic action conditioned by theological parameters and traditional processes, that very undergirding theology and its traditions of being understood and communicated may come to need review and modification in the light of

---

14 See Osmer, *Practical Theology*.
15 Osmer, *Practical Theology*, vii, 4.
16 Osmer, *Practical Theology*, 10.

that pragmatic outcome. This is a true marriage of theology, practice and personhood, wherein ministry is shaped by theology, theology is refined by ministry, and a theologue is formed within a cohesive and real world-view. While the observation is commonly made of the need to infuse practice with theological principles, another consideration is whether many theological educational institutions have a forum for theological refinement.

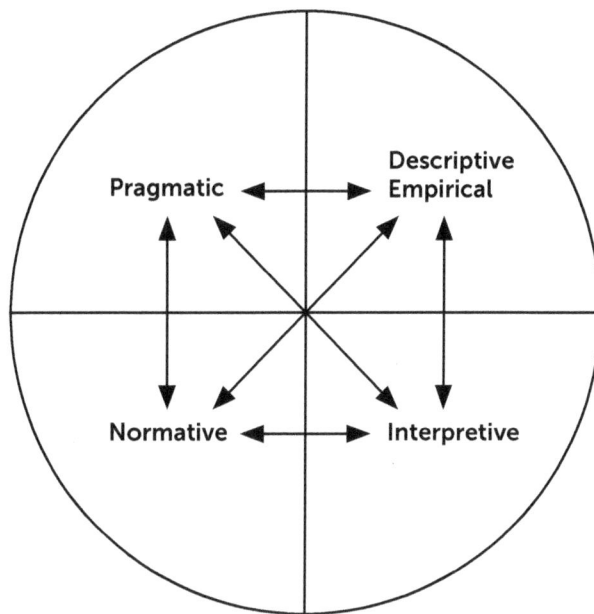

Figure 2. Tasks of Practical Theological Interpretation[17]

Fostering the Dialogue

There are basic ways in which the educator may initiate and foster such a dialogue: by astute field placements; by the promotion of peer learning; and by actively employing and intentionally teaching the principles of critical hermeneutics in both methods and curriculum. Such a pedagogic approach by a committed body of teachers will sustain and develop a culture of integrated theological thought, action, and life.

Traditionally, practical education is structured around an individual placement of a student in a local church or associated setting under the

---

17   Based on Osmer, *Practical Theology*, 11.

supervision of a local minister, which has potential for developing performative skills and the integration of theology and practice and personhood. This potential can be realised in various ways, including such simple strategies as promoting forums including multiple faculty, supervisors, and students in integrative exercises. But the church is not the only locus for such placements, especially as the church is not (and perhaps even should not be) the world in which most theological graduates will live and work for the majority of their lives. The non-church world—even the non-Christian or non-Christendom world—may well provide an expanded, albeit more challenging, and realistic context for valid theologically integrated learning. Such opportunities would take the learner's theology beyond the cocoon of church into the more challenging domain of 'the world', thus requiring a more refined conceptualisation and implementation of embodied theology. In all such scenarios, the higher domains of empirical analysis, interpretive understanding, and the critical interplay of theology and practice need to be prominent, so local supervisors and teaching faculty need to combine to promote such learning.

Yet most theological education is centred on the campus, either physical or virtual, and the teachers and students are the core of the human face of the enterprise. In today's questioning age, individual learners need to operate within a social context, where such questioning by others will realistically hone the individual's concepts and practices. One method of achieving this within the framework of due care for the welfare of the learner is the creation of a 'community of practice', with an emphasis on peer learning and processing.

Steve Taylor of Flinders University recently reported on his theology programme's community of practice, which includes an important element of repetitive questioning and feedback.[18] His approach involved asking the same four questions at the start, at the middle, and at the end of various topics, an approach which could well be adopted in the field education program.

- What are you most interested in learning?
- What resources will best support your learning?
- How valuable is it to have choice?
- What aspects of the topic are you concerned about (if at all)?

At the start, students' focus was on the content of the subject and their excitement about choice. At the mid-point, the focus shifted from a 100% anticipation of

---

18   Taylor, 'A class above'.

content to a 50/50 split between content and how they were learning, especially the learning dynamic of the class and the diversity of their peers. There was a strong feeling of support in their learning by the resources and through the lecturer engagement. Choice continued to be seen as positive, in extending learning and enhancing motivation. By the end of the course, responses maintained appreciation of content but also included reflection on how they were learning. In particular, the role of fellow students remained significant with the diversity of the class named as a significant factor in learning. Choice continued to be perceived to increase engagement and to have a positive impact on learning.[19]

While learners, both individually and communally, are central to the integrative process, the role of the teacher in fostering an integrative dialogue is vital. First, the teacher needs actively to *employ* the principles of critical reflective theology in the classroom or another learning setting. By so doing, the pedagogic approach of an empirically researched examination of current beliefs and practice, the interpretive analysis of their development, the critical appreciation of the normative base of concepts and practice, and the strategic action for realistic implementation will provide an operational model for practically integrated theological thought and action. Second, as a natural adjunct to such modelling, intentional *teaching* of such principles can be incorporated into the standard curriculum of any course—in systematic theology just as well as in field education. This whole approach to analytical inquiry and review of received knowledge leads students not only to examine beliefs and practices already held, but also to appreciate how they came into being, what are the normative bases for their continuation, and the 'so what now?' questionings that emerge. Accordingly, it has clear application to the whole range of Bible, theology, history and ministry units that comprise theological curricula. To train learners in the processes of critical reflective theology in both demonstrated action and didactic words will help to produce graduates who can appropriate such principles and take them into their ministry and general life.

Pedagogical approaches to theological integration

We turn now to some samples of the kinds of pedagogical approach which may prove useful in the generation of an integrated theological ethos. There is of

---

19   Taylor, 'A class above', 11–14.

course no limit to the creative ways in which teachers may lead students into theological integration, many of which are born of the very personality of the teacher or the culture of the college. However, there are several established teaching approaches which are by their nature conducive to the sort of integration we have been exploring. Each of these approaches is driven by an underlying educational assumption regarding the learner or the learner's situation, which has a profound impact on the starting point of the learning activity and the pedagogical method adopted. This paper concludes by a brief reference to three such approaches.

Problem Based Learning (PBL)[20] has its roots in practical ministry and other applied areas of education (medicine, social work and law being some prime examples). It starts from the assumption of an existing problem to be resolved and systematically works to a realistic resolution. In this process, a learner runs the gamut of possibilities that may arise in a critical situation and is required to integrate all relevant facets of knowledge and skills with an application to a specific setting.

Inquiry Based Learning (IBL)[21] starts from a different assumption and is very appropriate for transformative theological learning. Rather than assuming the existence of a problem, IBL emphasises positive progress in the learner's knowledge or capacities. It seeks to develop a person as a continuing 'work in progress'. It leads a learner to discover new things and to process them as they are encountered, with no pre-determined outcome in view, but rather it seeks a growth in knowledge, understanding and personal development. Appreciative Inquiry is one form of IBL, wherein a learner celebrates and analyses personal strengths and past victories as a platform for devising and building future successes. It has the potential for developing embodied personal convictions and world-view, a legitimate goal of theological integration.

Group Project Based Learning (GBL)[22] combines aspects of both PBL and IBL. It is based on the assumption that the communal aspect of working to a solution or reaching a successful point in development maximises the energies of the collective group. Accordingly, it provides an effective platform for team development and cohesion, a particularly suitable outcome of ministry education in particular—and a noted deficiency listed in many student evaluations of courses.

---

20   See Walker et al, *Essential Readings in Problem-Based Learning*.
21   See Pedaste et al, 'Phases of inquiry-based learning'.
22   See Boss and Krauss, *Reinventing Project-Based Learning*.

The following table summarises the assumptions and methodological stages involved in these three approaches.

Problem Based Learning (PBL)	Inquiry Based Learning (IBL)	Group Project Based Learning (GBL)
Basic Assumption: Person Has/Organization Is a problem to be solved	Basic Assumption: Person is a Continuing Work in Progress with past/existing successes that can be built on	Basic Assumption: Group Dynamic Maximises Energies with potential to incorporate PBL and IBL
'Felt Need' Identification of a Problem ↓ Analysis of Causes ↓ Analysis of Possible Solutions ↓ Action Plan (Treatment of Problem)	'Appreciating' Valuing the Best of 'What is' or 'Where I have come from' ↓ Envisioning 'What might be' or 'What I might become' ↓ Dialoguing 'What should be' or 'What I should become' ↓ Innovating 'What will be' or 'What I will become'	'Defining a Possibility' Articulating aspirations ↓ Establishing a Working Group ↓ Analysis of Situation and Resources ↓ Establishing Possibilities ↓ Establishing Course of Action ↓ Implementation of Action

Table 1. Pedagogical assumptions and methods

Finally, the overarching goal of establishing any platform of theological integration is to respond to the demands of an increasingly questioning age, where conceptual knowledge and task competency are no longer sufficient. Rather, ministry and any other arena of lived theology will need the capability to address complex emergent issues with increasing integration and constant refinement of both theologically held positions and traditionally practised methods.[23]

Bibliography

Astley, J. *Ordinary Theology* (Aldershot, Hants: Ashgate, 2002).

Australian College of Ministries. *Facilitator Handbook 2017*.

Ball, L. *Transforming Theology: Student Experience and Transformative Learning in Undergraduate Theological Education* (Preston, Vic: Mosaic, 2012).

Boss, S. & J. Krauss. *Reinventing Project-Based Learning: Your Field Guide to Real-world Projects in the Digital Age* (Eugene OR: International Society for Technology in Education, 2014, 2nd ed.).

Browning, D. S. *Equality and the Family: A Fundamental, Practical Theology of Children, Mothers, and Fathers in Modern Societies* (Grand Rapids, Michigan: Eerdmans, 2007).

Browning, D. S. *A Fundamental Practical Theology* (Minneapolis: Fortress, 1991).

Cronshaw, C. & Andrew Menzies. 'From Place to Place: A Comparative Study of 5 Models of Workplace Formation at 2 Colleges on 1 Campus', in Les Ball & James R. Harrison (eds.), *Learning and Teaching Theology: Some Ways Ahead* (Preston, Vic: Morning Star, 2014), 217–227.

Dalziel, J. 'Developing Scenario Learning to Theological Education', in Yvette Debergue & James R. Harrison (eds.). *Teaching Theology in a Technological Age* (Newcastle, UK: Cambridge Scholars, 2015), 17–29.

McCourt, F. *Angela's Ashes: A Memoir of a Childhood* (London: HarperCollins, 1997).

Miller-McLemore, B. J. *Christian Theology in Practice: Discovering a Discipline* (Grand Rapids, Michigan: Eerdmans, 2012).

Miller-McLemore, B. J. (ed.) *The Wiley-Blackwell Companion to Practical Theology* (Malden, Mass: Wiley-Blackwell, 2012).

Nairn, R. 'Teachers lead the way', *The Courier-Mail* (Brisbane, Qld: 6 June 2015).

Osmer, R. R. *Practical Theology: An Introduction* (Grand Rapids/Cambridge: Eerdmans, 2008).

Pedaste, M. et al. 'Phases of Inquiry-based Learning: Definitions and the Inquiry Cycle', in *Educational Research Review* 14 (February 2016), 47-61.

---

23 Smith & O'Flynn, 'Responding to Complexity', 119–128.

Smith, S. & L. O'Flynn. 'Responding to Complexity: Moving from Competence to Capability', in Les Ball & James R. Harrison (eds.), *Learning and Teaching Theology: Some Ways Ahead* (Preston, Vic: Morning Star, 2014), 119–128.

Taylor, S. 'A class above: Evidence based action research into teaching that is connected, mobile and accessible in a higher education context' (HERGA Conference, Adelaide: September 2015).

Walker, A., H. Leary, C. E. Hmelo-Silver & P. A. Ertma (eds.). *Essential Readings in Problem-based Learning* (West Lafayette, IN: Purdue University, 2015).

Les Ball
Australian College of Ministries, Sydney
les.j.ball@gmail.com

26 | CURIOSITY AND DOUBT IN RESEARCHING THE FUTURE

THE CONTRIBUTION OF FLIPPED LEARNING TO SOCIALITY IN THEOLOGICAL INNOVATION

Abstract

Wonder is a verb, involving actions of curiosity and doubt. Research suggests that class time in higher education offers little opportunity for active student participation. This has particular consequences for theological education, given the motivations, experiences and investments of our students. Curious about ways to increase student participation, five innovations in teaching are outlined. These include attention to classroom interaction, industry-shaped assessment, tutorial design, curricula development and flipped learning. Student feedback suggested these innovations enhanced learning by increasing sociality. Doubtful about the place of technology in learner-centred teaching, a survey of recent literature on technology and education is brought into conversation with the results of a small action-research project, which implemented flipped learning into a theology class. Student feedback again provided evidence that teaching is a profoundly social activity. The argument is technology enables the delivery of better learning, increasing student participation and the sociality of learning.

Introduction

Come, let us wonder together about our teaching. Wonder is a noun. As a naming word, it speaks to feelings of amazement and admiration, caused by something beautiful. Wonder is also a verb. It speaks to actions, including those of curiosity and of doubt.[1] So this essay examines learning and teaching as verb: as actions of wondering curiosity and wondering doubt. In relation to curiosity: how might increased class participation impact on student learning? In relation to doubt: that new technology that my teenagers are using, could it really be a worthwhile part of our teaching practice?

This essay thus invites us to wonder—to be full of curiosity and doubt about learner-centered education. Curious about learners, we begin with an outline of a learning cohort in theological education and examine the interplay between motivation, maturity and investment in their learning. We outline one recent teaching journey that in five innovations wrestled with enhancing active student participation. Doubtful about the role of technology in enhancing learner-centred teaching, we conduct a survey of recent literature.[2] This is brought into conversation with the results of action-research on introducing flipped learning into a theology class. We argue that teaching is a profoundly social activity. While attention to our learners and their active participation demands increasing the sociality of our class, especially between and among students, technology is actually an essential innovation in attending to this dimension of teaching. Such are the conclusions when we wonder together, full of curiosity and doubt in the actions of teaching.

Curious About Learners

We begin with our learners. An experience in 2015 brought home the uniqueness of the theological cohort. I (Steve) took an early draft of my Vice Chancellor's Excellence in Teaching application into the Teaching and Learning office at Flinders University. I witnessed the staff being called out of their offices and invited to gather around my application, because it was so interesting. I was

---

1   'Wonder', www.google.co.nz/search?q=definition+wonder&ie=utf-8&oe=utf-8&client=firefox-b&gfe_rd=cr&dcr=0&ei=clqvWYGjHMHr8Afcuotw.
2   This research has been made possible by funds form Flinders University, allocated as part of the Vice Chancellor's Award for Excellence in Teaching, which was awarded to Steve Taylor in 2015 and conducted by Rosemary Dewerse.

surprised. Theology. Interesting? In a secular University? 'Yes', they said, 'your cohort is so unique. You work mainly with older students. There are very few career paths for this degree. People do it because they want to. You have a very unique set of learners'. Theological education is shaped by our students and the particularity of their *motivations, experiences* and *investments.*

There is significant diversity with regard to the *motivations* of those who study theology. Some students study for personal interest, others with vocational intentions. There are those wanting to develop professionally or to pursue an academic career. This brings a complex range of motivations into our classes, arguably more than in other sectors of higher education.

Students are more likely to be part-time and mature in age. This means they bring *experience* which, if cultivated, can significantly enhance the learning experience both for themselves and for the class. At the same time, they often have concerns about returning to higher education. They bring memories of traditional approaches to education and theology. This requires educators to manage adult learners with significant anxieties about education, while ensuring they are exposed to the critical processes expected in higher education.

In regard to *investment,* we are dealing with 'matters of the heart', to quote singer, Tracy Chapman.[3] Theology attracts students shaped by multiple investments, including in personal matters of faith, belief and worldview, in denominational stories and identity and in vocational pathways. These generate a deeply felt (in the heart) set of 'investment' questions: Will I still have faith as the class ends? Will I be accepted, and acceptable, as a minister? Do I have to believe what my denomination believes at the end of this course?

Teaching theology to such a cohort requires considerable pedagogical sensitivity and skill. Students need to find ways to own their investments. At the same time, they need to be exposed to diverse and counter perspectives. Higher education requires a commitment to teach in ways that are critical and pluralist, creating a space in which students participate in ways that are neither pietistic nor dogmatic.

Such commitments are to be applauded, for they are a significant public good. In a global context of rising religious intolerance, higher education should provide a cultural space in which critical conversations can occur. Teachers play an essential societal role: cultivating, nurturing and protecting these spaces, growing in students the capacity to work confidently in diverse environments,

---

3   Chapman, *Matters of the Heart.*

able to deal with subject matter in which they, their peers and diverse communities, remain potentially highly invested. This is the context in which we teach theology: among adults who are motivated, experienced and invested. What might 'learner-centred' education look like in this context?

Curious About Teaching[4]

When we turn from learning to teaching, the reseach in higher education poses some significant challenges. Maryellen Weimer, in *Learner-Centered Teaching*, argues that only five percent of university class time involves active student participation. During the other ninety-five, students are passive learners, recipients of the lecture as monologue.[5] Coming from a discipline (theology) that historically has valued content, Weimer's work is a significant challenge. Could her strategies, honed as an educator in American universities, help theology students in Australia? What would be the result of increasing active student participation during class time?

As part of my professional development, I (Steve) took these wonderings into my teaching. Curious, I worked on a range of ways to increasing active learner-participation. In what follows, five actions are outlined: the active facilitation of all voices, re-designed assessment, tutorials to enhance personalisation, developing indigenous Christology curricula to facilitate contextualisation and integration of Bloom's taxonomy into content delivery. In order to maintain learner-centred focus, I will also draw from student comments in Student Evaluation of Teaching (SET) forms. SET forms are a fairly blunt instrument of assessment, shaped by a set of power dynamics. Nevertheless, they are a source of data that ensures student voice and establishes a link between learning and teaching. They provide feedback regarding the specific context of actions of wondering about teaching in ways that increase student participation in higher education.

---

4   This section is based on an application by Steve Taylor, in 2014 and again in 2015, for the Flinders University Vice Chancellor's Award for Excellence in Teaching. My application, which was successful in 2015, was awarded for leading sustained innovation in theological pedagogy over six years, implementing quality improvements that ensure the embedded diversity of the student body is a resource in contextualising, personalising and deepening the overall teaching and learning experience.
5   Weimer, *Learner-Centered Teaching*.

Learner-centred in Active Class Facilitation

Theological teaching has historically tended to be delivered in lecture mode. Interaction is based on individual question and answer and summative assessment. My observation is that this suits a certain sort of learner. Certain voices become dominant. In order to increase student participation, I sought to better structure the class room time.

In my lecture preparation, I took time to craft questions that would invite participation and to design a range of activities that used different sized groups to encourage participation. I began by asking students to share in pairs rather than to the whole class. I encouraged students with invitations like, 'Who heard something in a group they found helpful?'. I actively monitored class interaction, noting if perspectives were missing. (For example, 'I have not heard from any younger people', 'I want to provide a space for anyone who hasn't spoken to contribute'). Feedback on these approaches to facilitation was positive. Students expressed an appreciation for the 'intentional engagement and interaction' (THEO 3341, 2015), because it gave them 'the ability to hear what I'm saying, reflect on it and build on the conversation' (THEO 3336, 2014). This feedback suggests learning is a social activity, facilitated by the opportunity to test ideas with peers.

I engaged the diversity that exists among adult learners by intentionally offering a range of learning experiences. Students affirmed that these diverse approaches inspired and motivated them. 'The variety of teaching methods multimedia / small groups / worksheets / class tutorials helped maintain energy and interest and focus on what we were studying'. Using a variety of learning experiences and modes of learning resulted in 'reinforcement through [group] project and journaling' (THEO 1502, 2011, 2012).

I discovered that my actions of carefully structured participation resulted in more students finding their voice. This had individual benefit, as students clarified their thinking and found themselves linking with the wider theological discipline. Anxious students were able to test ideas in contexts that were formative, not summative. More importantly, as multiple individual voices speak, the sociality of the classroom experience was enhanced. Students were exposed to the diversity of their peers. This added to the classroom experience.

Learner-centred in Assessment Design

To be learner-centred in teaching includes being curious about the contexts in which graduates will implement what they are learning in the classroom. Very few of our students will be required to write 3000 word essays in their vocations beyond our classrooms. So why do we assess in this way?

In seeking to help students contextualise class learning in the real world, I shifted in one class from individual essays to industry-based case studies. Students were given a case study and required to work in groups, imaging themselves giving advice to their local industry partner, i.e. church Council.

This brought inevitable resistance. Students do not like group work. My response was to note the reality of ministry and how it tends to include group work, in settings like church councils with membership already defined. So students need to get used to working with people with differing motivations. Despite the initial resistance, student evaluation affirmed the value of active participation in groups. 'The group project really helped me and all the explanation that was done in class really help me a lot'. '[I valued] The opportunity to learn in a supportive community. The group approach to learning' (2011, 2012). Actively facilitating group work provided support. It provided a formative process in which ideas could be tested.

Seeking to extend this from one class to the wider student body, the Faculty where I then taught (Uniting College for Leadership and Theology/Adelaide College of Divinity) took this industry focus a step further. The Faculty identified eight core skills our students would need to be workplace ready. These included academic skills of referencing and thinking logically. It also included industry skills of using powerpoint and social media. Thus began a key skills matrix for our first year core topics. Each skill was distributed to a different first year topic. Each topic developed a tutorial which taught the specific skill, for example how to use a library catalogue or build a power point. Each topic also developed a piece of assessment which drew on that skill. This brought a greater degree of 'real world' realism into the design of assessment.

Learner-centred in Tutorial Design

Higher education is based on developing critical thinking. This requires care, given that students often arrive already invested in a favoured method for doing theology. In order to equip students to think about the theological methods they use, I redesigned tutorial activities in an upper level undergraduate theology class.

In the first class, I introduced five different questions that would be discussed in tutorials. In addition, each student was given five cards that represent five theological resources essential for critical theological thinking—Scripture, tradition, reason, experience, culture. Over the five class tutorials, each student was allowed to use each theological resource once in answering the set tutorial question. This meant that once they had shared their resource (for example, a Scripture to address a question about baptism) I would collect that (Scripture) card. This meant that in the next tutorial, they then had to draw from their remaining, and thus different, theological resources. Over the five tutorials, each student was required to utilise all five theological resources as part of their participation in the tutorial.

At the end of each tutorial, the collected cards were placed in the middle. Students reflected together on the shape of that particular tutorial discussion in light of the particular resources used in that specific discussion. Inevitably, a rich set of reflections on the processes of communal theological reflection was generated. We saw the impact when Scripture was prioritized at the expense of experience; when culture was elevated above tradition.

Student evaluation affirmed the value of this approach to active student participation. 'Using cards to reason from various perspectives extended me'. 'It helped me to think differently and in a way I wasn't used to'. 'I was really challenged to think about my personal theology and this provided some great learning experiences for me' (THEO 3336, 2012, 2014). This innovation enhanced critical thinking about theological thinking, both individual and in a group settings. Again we see the impact in tutorial design of the social in the way that the theological resources others share shapes communal theological thinking.

Learner-centred in Creating Curricula: Indigenous

Being learner-centred and paying attention to the social involves attending to the voices, both present and absent. This involves not only individual participants in the sociality of the classroom, but also the voices in our curricula.

Teaching 'Jesus Christ' (THEO 2314) in 2014, I was concerned at the limitations of existing readings. A pre-occupation with historical theologies from Europe, combined with a lack of published resources from other contexts, has resulted in a lack of contextual readings in theology. In response, I initiated a project that worked in mutual dialogue with indigenous women to produce indigenous theology curricula. These indigenous resources were presented to students in the same format as existing readings, resulting in a more global reading list.

This significantly impacted student learning. One student wrote in their final essay that they would be 'exploring Christology in light of [their] Filipino identity, which was inspired by the presentations of [indigenous Christologies]' (THEO 2314, 2014). It is striking that it was contextualisation from one culture (hearing indigenous Christologies) that encouraged contextualisation in another. Being learner-centred requires us to attend to diversity, in the class and in the curricula.

In each of these four examples, the focus has been on increasing the active participation of the learner. This began with small beginnings, in paying attention in preparation to the crafting of questions and the structuring of group activities. It was extended to include the redesign of assessment, a reworking of tutorials and the creation of new curricula. Student feedback in every case indicated that the sociality of the class was an important factor in learning.

A fifth and final example, that of flipped learning, involved a much more significant shift into active student discussion, with the entire class time turned into active student participation. I want to outline a key resource—Bloom's taxonomy—that was used to garner student participation and repeatedly structure the class experience.

Learner-centred in Blooms Taxonomy (Flipped Learning)

In 2014, I set out to 'flip' a core upper theology Christology class. This involved asking students to engage the course content, including readings, video clips and lecture notes in their own time, with lecture time given over to activites chosen by the students.[6] My wondering, a mix of curiosity and doubt, was whether students would demonstrate higher levels of personalisation and

---

6   The introduction of indigenous voices to encourage personalised learning, the use of Bloom's Taxonomy to scaffold activities in class time and digital participation to cultivate the learning culture address all four pillars (Flexible Environment, Learning Culture, Intentional Content, Professional Educator) of flipped learning. "The Four Pillars of F-L-I-P™".

become more aware of their own role in the teaching and learning experience.

Flipping the class would require a major shift in student behaviour. Lecturer input—through course notes, spoken explanations and readings—remains, but is shifted from class time to individual time. Such a change requires students to read in their own time. In order to inspire this change, in the first week Bloom's Taxonomy was introduced, related to flipped learning and to how individual and class time would be structured. It was noted that if students spent their own time remembering and understanding, then the class time would be spent moving up the taxonomy to analyse, apply and create. My time as lecturer in class would then be spent resourcing learning in these upper areas of the taxonomy. The class was invited to consider what types of behaviours would support this flipped learning approach. Their responses became the basis for a shared class contract.[7]

The following weeks involved the offering of more personalised learning. Monologue lectures were replaced by a range of activities, from which students could choose. Each activity was linked to a different part of Bloom's taxonomy. I kept track of student participation by analysing questions and class interaction against Bloom's Taxonomy and offering this as feedback to the class. For example, 'The questions you asked last week were located mainly in the analysing category of Bloom's Taxonomy. There were two questions in the creating category, which I share with you as an example of what it means to be learning in this part of Bloom's Taxonomy'. The result was a remarkable learning experience. The entire class kept pace with the readings. There were some wonderful examples of student learning. For example, in evaluating my teaching, one student drew on Bloom's taxonomy. 'I cannot really learn unless I'm applying, analysing or creating. This is so apparent from past subjects where I've only got content' (THEO 2314, 2014). This incorporation of categories from Bloom's taxonomy is evidence of a depth of reflection on their own (student) role in learning.

Flipped learning is a fifth and final example of ways that I have sought to pay attention to learning-centred teaching. My journey began with the challenge, that studies suggest only five percent of class time in higher education involved active student participation. These five strategies were ways I sought to change the percentage, with flipped learning being a complete one hundred percent

---

[7] What type of individual behaviours enhance group learning? *Listening, openness, humility; active involvement; do your home work; come with thoughts; respect differences; receptive to other ideas.*

shift. For each of these five innovations, student feedback pointed to the significance of their peers, the sociality of the class, in learning. These examples invite us to wonder together, to be full of curiosity—about what learner-centred teaching might look like. They also provide concrete examples of teaching in ways that increase active student participation.

However, wondering together also includes actions not only of curiosity but also of doubt. In using the example of flipped learning, I am aware that it raises questions about the impact of technology upon our students' ability to rememember, understand, apply, analyse, evaluate, create. In the face of both curiosity and doubt, let us move from lived experience to a wider survey of the recent literature on educational theory and technology.

Educational Theory: Doubtful About Innovation for Transformation

In 2012, Les Ball published the results of a comprehensive study of 'transformative learning in theology in the Australian context'.[8] Among the conclusions was the observation that undergraduate programs in Australia had changed very little over thirty-five years. They continued to emphasise content and to be focused on lecturer-centred delivery. Ball called for a redesign of curricula to 'maximise learning activity and discovery… and… promote relational integrity'[9] so that personal transformation born in the crucible where *life experience meets theology* might be empowered.

Technology

At the same time as Ball was noting stable content and calling for student-centred, transformative curricula, the wider world of education was responding to significant advances in technology. This included its simplification and thus accessibility to more than the tech-savvy, along with the availability of open-source software and thus the provision of low or no-cost options for creating resources. Consider the range of technologies that did not exist in 2006:

---

8   Ball, *Transforming Theology*, 1. The findings of this work were engaged with also in Taylor, 'Embodiment and transformation in the context of e-learning', 171-184.
9   Ball, *Transforming Theology*, 2.

> Iphone
> Ipad
> Kindle
> Uber
> Airbnb
> Android
> Oculus
> Spotify
> Nest
> Stipe
> Square
> Instagram
> Slack
> Snapchat

We all now have at our disposal e-readings, weblinks, podcasts, prezi and powerpoint presentations, videos and animation, webinars, Twitter feeds, and apps for mobile phones facilitating revision. Tools to evaluate understanding are available, including quizzes of varying kinds, forum discussions and Edpuzzle.

More powerfully, collaborative creation of new content with students can also be served by a range of options.[10] Such innovations make it possible to experiment with how, what, why and when content is offered across intelligences and learning styles, and in what space. They also create opportunities to ask how best to spend face-to-face or synchronous time given content can be accessed independently and at any time. Might technology provide room for learning activity and transformative discovery in different configurations and in ways that still encourage sociality in learning?

In contemplating redesigning for learner-centred curricula it is important to acknowledge the perennial chestnut of theological education that appears whenever technology is brought into the conversation, namely a belief that (trans)formation occurs best in a solely face-to-face environment (despite Ball's observation that theological education, at least in Australia, has much to

---

10   These include forum discussions, eportfolios and collaborative options such as wikis or Google Docs, as well as multi-media possibilities. Other resources available online for content include The Global Church Project https://theglobalchurchproject.com/, Bible Odyssey www.bibleodyssey.org/ and The Bible Project https://thebibleproject.com/.

improve on in this regard).[11] This issue creates, firstly, rifts with distance education where technology has become crucial in facilitating learning for those doing so from home and, secondly, problems for experiments in blended learning, where possibilities created by technology are combined with the traditional classroom but time online might be underutilised as a result of prejudice and/or ignorance.[12]

In regard to the *rifts with distance education*, Mark Nichols used mixed methods research to compare the learning experiences of students on-campus with those at distance. Nichols defined 'distance' as involving a combination of printed, video and online material alongside online discussion.[13] He discovered that transformational learning occurred in equal measure. '[T]here was no significant difference across the spiritual maturity profiles and propensity for further growth between on-campus and theological distance education students'.[14] Transformation is not more likely face to face. Nor is it less likely at distance.

Interestingly, for distance students, the *life experience meets theology* crucible affirmed by Ball occurred as they remained connected to church and community contexts while studying. In contrast, there were on-campus students who expressed a loss of connection to church and community contexts.[15] The research affirmed the crucial need to be *in situ*, grounded in reality, for transformation to occur.

In regard to the *blending of technology with the traditional classroom*, Norman Vaughan, Martha Cleveland-Innes and Randy Garrison argue that blended learning offers an invitation to step into innovation, inquiry, reciprocity and collaboration via 'the organic integration of thoughtfully selected and

---

11 Mark Nichols recalls an instance in 'A Comparison of Spiritual Formation Experiences', v. He notes objections from literature across pages 63-90, particularly pages 66-68 in regard to formation. See also Nichols, 'The *akadameia* as paradigm for online community in theological distance education', 5-23.
12 'Distance Learning' refers to learning methods that involve no face-to-face engagement. 'Blended Learning' (or 'Hybrid Learning') refers to a combination of face-to-face and, mostly these days, online learning.
13 Nichols, 'A Comparison of Spiritual Formation Experiences', 193.
14 Nichols, 'A Comparison of Spiritual Formation Experiences', iv. Nichols used the Christian Spiritual Participation Profile Instrument and semi-structured interviews to obtain his data. It is important to note that Laidlaw College, the institution featured in Nichols' study, had invested significantly in specialist course design, media creation, and student support services for distance students. At its height, eight people were working for the Centre for Distance Learning (EFT=6).
15 Nichols, 'A Comparison of Spiritual Formation Experiences', 195. There is also some research that points out the value of contextual community for those studying online, particularly from a distance. Taylor, 'Embodiment and transformation', 171-184.

complementary face-to-face and online approaches'.[16] Blended learning invites students to 'extend thinking and discourse over time and space'.[17] It offers a number of access points, increases the variety of learning opportunities for students and has the potential to teach across life for everyone involved. The role of teaching as part of a sociality remained important. For blended learning to be effective, teachers need to practise presence that is profoundly engaged in the learning process

Far from impoverishing opportunities for transformation, technology can open new pathways for facilitating it. Already within wider education circles there exists a model that provides a response to Ball's call for redesign towards student-centred curricula, which employs technological tools alongside sound pedagogies.

The Inverted or Flipped Classroom

In the year 2000, Glenn Platt and Maureen Lage from Miami University published their work on inverting their classroom, the result of wanting to empower transformative learning and increase access for as many students as possible.[18] Aware that personal time with students was limited, they came to believe that spending class time in delivering a traditional lecture, while leaving students to try to process and apply the content in their own time, was not serving their students nor their hopes well. Using the technology then available, they inverted the experience, leaving students to view, listen to and read content in their own time and to spend face-to-face time in class with the lecturer-expert and their peers. This involved actively engaging the lecture content together via a variety of methods. Platt and Lage found that it became much easier to offer real-time advice to conundrums, encourage skills growth, and monitor success across the levels of Bloom's taxonomy.[19] Platt and Lage were before their time.[20] YouTube was not yet available and video creation—a key means for transferring content—was for the experts. But by 2007, technology had significantly advanced and

---

16 Vaughan, Cleveland-Innes and Garrison, *Teaching in Blended Learning Enviornments*, 8.
17 Vaughan, Cleveland-Innes and Garrison, *Teaching in Blended Learning Enviornments*, 9.
18 Lage, Platt and Treglia, 'Inverting the Classroom', 30-43. Arguably it was approached even earlier by Walvoord and Anderson in their book *Effective Grading* where they argued for students gaining 'first exposure learning' before class and processing of learning within class.
19 See Armstrong, 'Blooms' Taxonomy'.
20 Noonoo, 'Flipped Learning Founders Set the Record Straight'.

Bergmann and Sams would pioneer the Flipped Classroom.

Bergmann and Sams began with in a concern 'to help students become learners who can learn for themselves and by themselves'.[21] They were working with high school students and were keen to instill skills and dispositions that would serve them well for life. Class-time spent focusing on teacher delivery of content, they felt, was not delivering on this. So they flipped their classrooms, bringing in discussion, experimentation, experiential, problem-solving, project-based and inquiry learning, and turning homework into content transfer—largely via video. Education was thus not simply about transferring knowledge or ideas but evidencing the ability to explore, apply and use ideas to address situations and/or create new responses. A 2014 definition offered by members of the Flipped Learning Network describes the change thus:

> Flipped Learning is a pedagogical approach in which direct instruction moves from the group learning space to the individual learning space, and the resulting group space is transformed into a dynamic, interactive learning environment where the educator guides students as they apply concepts and engage creatively in the subject matter.[22]

What is being described is a commitment to learner-centred teaching, one now evident across a number of higher education providers worldwide.[23]

Flipping learning, it can be argued, is not unfamiliar in the Humanities where the use of tutorials to engage student thinking has long been a standard pedagogy. The Oxbridge model, where students in their own time read material and then come to tutorials prepared to defend and critique their ideas as well as those of others, is an example of a longstanding institutional commitment to the idea. Further, libraries have always been available for research and knowledge acquisition in the student's own time. So what is the difference here?

First, flipped learning takes advantage of the full range of teaching tools now available to educators, including those offered by technology. The delivery of content and the work of the lecturer exist in service to a greater goal, the

---

21 'The Flipped Classroom'. In this video Aaron Sams is speaking.
22 'What is Flipped Learning?' For more on Flipped Learning see http://flippedlearning.org/
23 There is indirect evidence of flipped learning's ability to improve student learning but not yet research to conclusively prove this. For a recent review of flipped learning in higher education see O'Flaherty and Phillips, 'The Use of Flipped Learning in Higher Education', 85-95. It should be noted that Flipped Learning has to date been most popular amongst the sciences. Bergmann and Sams, for example, are chemistry teachers.

deepening of learning. This results in a willingness to understand and use a variety of pedagogy to include and empower as many students as possible in the learning enterprise.[24] The ability to intelligently operate, synthesise, and evaluate these for any given scenario, as well as to create within them, invites lecturers to be expert educators as well as subject matter experts. This is a modelling that augurs well for training engaged and engaging leaders for society (and the church).

Second, flipped learning invites inclusion as delivery is diffused from the one to the many as real world scenarios are introduced and ideas are applied in class with others.[25] Cultural intelligence is required. So is the awareness that not all activities will work for all people. Multiple opportunities are offered to everyone to listen to, discover, and be heard by a wider range of people and disciplines. In theological education where community—being formed into the body of Christ—is so important, flipped learning offers a way for relational integrity to be promoted as students and their teacher, and any invited others, collaborate, create and reflect together.[26] In Aotearoa New Zealand, flipped learning further enables the realisation of the Maori notion of *ako*, a word which recognises that 'teaching and learning are two interactive parts of the whole education experience'.[27] A central concept in tertiary education in Aotearoa New Zealand, *ako* also lies deep within church discipleship as a fellowship of equals.[28]

Third, in regard to the role of libraries, Joyce Valenza has argued that flipped learning provides opportunity and impetus for a much closer relationship between lecturers, students, and librarians, (and a more empowered role for the librarian than currently exists). Librarians become 'trusted tech scouts'. They are recognised as expert curators of the resources on offer, employed to evaluate what is available and recommend resources for given topics. They provide professional development in regard to copyright and content creation. In terms of availability, librarians can be more accesible than lecturers in guiding students through content. Valenza also suggests that library instruction is eminently

---

24 A blog series across 2013 from the Wabash Center detailed a creative variety of pedagogies being employed across the theological disciplines: '12 Surprises When Lecturing Less (and Teaching more!)'.
25 Cultural inclusivity comes more naturally to constructivist oriented models of learning, according to Freschette, Layne and Gunawardena, 'Accounting for Culture in Instructional Design,' 57.
26 Cf Esterline and Kalu (eds), *Shaping Beloved Community*.
27 https://akoaotearoa.ac.nz/ako-aotearoa.
28 Palmer, 'An Educational Approach Towards a Discipleship of Equals in a Socially Prophetic Church'.

ready to be flipped.[29]

In sum, there is considerable attention in the wider educational world to flipped learning, as a way to enhance learner-centred teaching. Technology as a tool to enable flipped learning is driven not by market concerns for more students nor by the geographic challenges of distance. Rather, it emerges from a desire to offer genuinely transformative learning by making the learner central. These are the same motivations as Ball's call for transformative learning in theology. Hence this essay invites theological education to wonder together about the contribution of flipped learning.

Children coming through primary schooling are learning collaboratively, via project or inquiry-based learning that operates most often across the disciplines in ways that cater to different learning needs while making use of available technology. High schools are beginning to adopt similar priorities and it behoves higher education institutions to pay attention.[30] There is a profound commitment to formation for meaningful contribution to glocal settings embedded within the education of young people today. If theological education continues to offer anachronistic approaches to adult education, it is in danger of losing an emerging generation of learners.

Flipped learning is one way to respond. To implement effectively will require changes in teaching and learning habits, along with a willingness to invest in developing educational and technological expertise. It demands that we wonder, appreciatively and critically: about ourselves as teachers—who we are, what we know and do not know, our openness to new ideas and methods, our willingness to learn; about others as learners—their stories and perspectives, their commitment to and desire for understanding and its outworkings, their confidence and willingness to embrace the teaching mantle; and about our God who gifts curiosity, imagination, faith and risk, community and transformation.

---

29 Valenza, 'The Flipping Librarian'. Valenza works in higher education. Her article begs the question: Are theological libraries in a position to agree?

30 See http://nzcurriculum.tki.org.nz/Key-competencies for documentation from the Ministry of Education detailing key competencies across schooling. The Australian Curriculum has seven general capabilities: www.australiancurriculum.edu.au/generalcapabilities/overview/introduction. For an article discussing the uptake of Flipped Learning in New Zealand classrooms see from the Education Review Office, 'Flipped Learning in Kiwi Classrooms'.

Researching Flipped Learning in Theological Education

Let me draw the threads together. We have examined doubts in theological education about the place of technology in realising transformation by conducting a literature survey of technology in higher education. We turn now to action research of flipped learning in a theology class. This returns us to where this essay began, focused on the practice of teaching and in particular, of being learner-centred in flipped learning.

I have described already my wondering—my curiosity—as I ventured in flipped learning. As I began, I also had doubts. How would flipped learning impact on student learning? In order to attend to both curiosity and doubt, I participated in a (2014) Flinders University Community of Practice. This involved undertaking research on student experience as I introduced pedagogical change in a compulsory undergraduate Christology topic. In order to research learning, students completed a four question written survey at the start, middle and end of the topic.[31]

The results indicated a significant shift. At the start, every participant was eager to learn about content: in this case about Jesus. By the end, half of the participants were eager to learn from the diversity inherent among their peers. This was a profound shift, in which the sociality of the entire class became of value in learning. Students affirmed a preference for choice, collaboration and diversity and expressed ways in which flipped learning had enhanced their ability to learn. Some students gave evidence of a depth of reflection upon their learning, including drawing on Bloom's Taxonomy to describe their learning.

This data can be theorised using the notion of learning as a social act, shaped by learner agency. Preston ('Braided Learning,' 2008) observed that students fill different roles in an on-line learning community. Some act as e-facilitators, others as braiders or accomplished fellows. Each of these roles depends on agency being given to, and received by, fellow learners. Student assignments from this 2014 Christology class provided evidence that these roles were present during in-class time and further, that flipped learning was essential in inviting students into these roles.

How might this work? I would suggest that it is easier to voice a first, tentative, critique of a new learning among peers than in direct question and

---

31 What are you most interested in learning? What resources will/have best support your learning in this topic? How valuable is it to have choices about what and how you learn in a topic? How have your initial concerns about aspects of this topic been addressed?

answer with a lecture. In the small group context, students can participate by adopting roles as facilitators, braiders and accomplished fellows. In other words, student learning is profoundly social. When teachers structure ways to facilitate the voice of student peers, these dimensions of students-as-teachers are made possible. Flipped learning enhances these opportunities for peer sociality and thus the learner-centred experience.

At the same time, some feedback in the Student Evaluation of Teaching was negative. While, overall, people affirmed flipped learning, some expressed a desire to return to traditional lecture modes. Again, this can be theorised using Preston. Participants who expressed concern about flipped learning were reluctant to trust their fellow learners. They remained committed to the notion of lecturer as expert and remained unwilling to trust their peers as facilitators, braiders and accomplished fellows.

This suggests that flipped learning is an important way to encourage learner-centred teaching. However, success depends not on the technological ability to produce videos. Rather, it depends on pedagogical strategies, including those that help learners appreciate agency in their peers. In sum, respect for good pedagogy and sociality was essential to learning. In using technology, teaching remains at the core of the educative experience.

Conclusion

To conclude, we have wondered about learning and teaching in actions of curiosity and doubt. Given our context is theological education, we began with curiosity about learners and outlined motivation, experience and investments of theological students as adult learners. In response to research that revealed that only five percent of higher education classroom interaction involves active student participation, changes in teaching practice were outlined. These include attention to classroom interaction, industry-shaped assessment, tutorial design, curricula development and flipped learning.

Given that our wider social context includes significant changes in technology, we have wondered full of doubt. Could the technologies that our teenagers play with enhance learning? A literature survey of research into higher education and technology demonstrates that technology has potential for formation as it is harmonised with the sociality of the class. This was reinforced by the results of action research into flipped education in teaching Christology. We embrace technology not because it helps us survive economically. We embrace technology because it enables the delivery of better learning. And as teachers, our vocation is to explore every possible avenue in the encouragement of learning that transforms.

Bibliography

Armstrong, P. 'Bloom's Taxonomy', https://cft.vanderbilt.edu/guides-sub-pages/blooms-taxonomy/ [accessed 13 March 2017].

Ball, L. *Transforming Theology: Student experience and transformative learning in undergraduate theological education* (Preston, Vic: Mosaic Press, 2012).

Chapman, T. *Matters of the Heart* (Album, Elekta, 1992).

Education Review Office, 'Flipped Learning in Kiwi Classrooms', www.educationreview.co.nz/magazine/march-2014/flipped-learning-in-kiwi-classrooms/#.WL4efjuGPb0 [accessed 7 March 2017].

Esterline, D. & O. Kalu (eds.). *Shaping Beloved Community: Multicultural Theological Education* (Louisville: Westminster John Knox Press, 2006).

Freschette, C., L. Layne, & C. N. Gunawardena. 'Accounting for Culture in Instructional Design', in Insung Jung and Charlotte Nirmalani Gunawardena, *Culture and Online Learning: Global Perspectives and Research* (Stirling, Vir: Stylus, 2014), 54-66.

Lage, M. J., G. J. Plat, & M. Treglia. 'Inverting the Classroom: A Gateway to Creating an Inclusive Learning Environment', *The Journal of Economic Education* 31.1 (Winter 2000), 30-43.

Nichols, M. 'The *akadameia* as paradigm for online community in theological distance education', *Journal of Christian Education* 54.1 (May 2011), 5-23.

Nichols, M. 'A Comparison of Spiritual Formation Experiences between On-Campus and Distance Evangelical Theological Education Students' (Ph.D. dissertation, University of Otago, Department of Theology and Religion, 2014).

Noonoo, S. 'Flipped Learning Founders Set the Record Straight', 20 June, 2012 https://thejournal.com/articles/2012/06/20/flipped-learning-founders-q-and-a.aspx [accessed 14 March 2017].

O'Flaherty, J. & C. Phillips. 'The Use of Flipped Learning in Higher Education: A Scoping Review', *The Internet and Higher Education* 25 (April 2015), 85-95.

Palmer, D. 'An Educational Approach Towards a Discipleship of Equals in a Socially Prophetic Church' (PhD dissertation, Boston College, 1989).

Taylor, S. 'Embodiment and transformation in the context of e-learning,' *Learning and Teaching Theology: Some Ways Ahead*, in Les Ball and J. Harrison (eds.), (Northcote, Vic: Morning Star, 2012), 171-184.

'The Flipped Classroom' (16 December 2010), www.youtube.com/watch?v=2H4RkudFzlc [accessed 14 March 2017].

'The Four Pillars of F-L-I-P™', (12 March, 2014) https://flippedlearning.org/definition-of-flipped-learning/ [accessed 13 March 2016].

Valenza, J. 'The Flipping Librarian' (12 August 2012), http://blogs.slj.com/neverendingsearch/2012/08/14/the-flipping-librarian/ [accessed 21 March 2017].

Vaughan, N. D., M. Cleveland-Innes, & D. R. Garrison. *Teaching in Blended Learning Environments: Creating and Sustaining Communities of Inquiry* (Athabasca University: AUPress, 2013).

Walvoord, B. & V. J. Anderson. *Effective Grading: A Tool for Learning and Assessment* (San Francisco: Jossey-Bass, 1998).

Weimer, M. *Learner-Centered Teaching: Five Key Changes to Practice* (San Francisco: Jossey-Bass, 2002).

'What is Flipped Learning?', https://flippedlearning.org/wp-content/uploads/2016/07/FLIP_handout_FNL_Web.pdf [accessed 14 March 2017].

'Wonder', www.google.co.nz/search?q=definition+wonder&ie=utf-8&oe=utf-8&client=firefox-b&gfe_rd=cr&dcr=0&ei=clqvWYGjHMHr8Afcuotw [accessed 6 September 2017].

'12 Surprises When Lecturing Less (and Teaching more!)', http://wabashcenter.typepad.com/12_surprises_when_lecturi/ [accessed 22 March 2017].

https://akoaotearoa.ac.nz/ako-aotearoa [accessed 21 March 2017].

APPENDIX: LEARNER-CENTRED PRINCIPLES IN ACTION

1 Learner-centred in assessment design (a)

Each of you will be presented with a local community. This assignment will be in groups of three or four. In the final week, each group will present to the class what they have learnt in addressing the case study question.

Your task is to prepare a "sociology for ministry" presentation for a church leadership team. You need to:

- outline the key sociological factors you see at play in the context
- name their implications for ministry
- suggest <u>one</u> ministry metaphor that might be fruitfully applied in this context

You will be assessed on your class presentation. Creativity is encouraged. The mark will be allocated based on the overall group project (50%) and each person's individual contribution (50%). With regard to individual contribution, each person will also be asked to assess both themselves and their group members.

Group project Assessment (handed out in week 2)

CLASS ASSESSMENT

                                               Weak Pass Credit Distinction H.Distinction

My effort in the group _____
                          (NAME)

Effort in the group of _____
                          (NAME)

Effort in the group of _____
                          (NAME)

LECTURER ASSESSMENT

                                               Weak Pass Credit Distinction H.Distinction

Ability to explore issues at the interface of society, ministry

Analysis, critique of the interactions between church, society

Ability to see ministry from a sociological perspective

Research undertaken

COMMENTS:

SUMMATIVE GRADE: _____

    (average of self-assessment _____ + group _____ + lecturer group assessment _____)

2 Learner-centred in assessment design (b)

Aim: to strengthen the skills required for academic achievement. First, we prioritise key entry level academic skills. Second, lecturers select one skill to each of the eight first year topics. The lecturer will focus on this skill, offering training, seeking to find a way to integrate into the assessment. The selection of key skills was agreed at Ministry Studies Committee, May 2013.

Core units	Key skill focus	Responsibility re distance?	Date for Action
Interpreting OT	Referencing and bibliography Reading and note taking		
Interpreting NT	Writing an essay including generic good writing skills		
Intro to Christian Leadership	Verbal communication, including speaking, presentations		
Sociology for ministry	Group work, collaborative learning		
Intro to Christian Thought	Use of library, introduction, advanced		

3 Learner-centred in tutorial design

The tutorials will have the following format:
- each tutorial the lecturer will offer a case study statement/question, along with some readings and resources. All of these readings are on ACD Online.
- each tutorial the lecturer will stand at the board and prepare to take notes on the student discussion
- each tutorial discussion will evolve using the following framework. Each student will be given a set of cards and be expected to play <u>one</u> of their cards (an experience, or a Scriptural reflection, or an insight from tradition, or some reason, or an artifact from creation/culture) per tutorial. All must be in relation to the case study question and should expect discussion and interaction by all the class. (The cards is based on a 'modern' Wesleyan Quadrilateral, offering a model for our theological reflection).
- in the last 20 minutes the class will switch from discussion to reflection on the overall process. Overall, how do the 'cards' integrate? Are there

missing or overabundant parts? What are the implications for our processes as ministers and leaders in theological reflection?
- Student will write up <u>one</u> of the (four) tutorials. This will involve providing a 500 word response to the case study statement/question. This should be in the form of a 'Pastors' paragraph'—a communication from a minister to a congregation in a regular newsletter. While references are not expected in this, a separate Bibliography is expected. This is to be handed in 7 days <u>after</u> the tutorial (and thus no later than Thursday 27 February, 5 pm). Students will gain extra marks if they show evidence of extra research over and above the set readings and class discussion. In other words, if a class finds a weakness in one tutorial in, say, tradition or Scripture, and the student goes away and does extra work in this area, more marks are gained.

Further resources, including a list of readings and some Scriptures you might like to read/exegete/lectio/commentary. It is intended you will read this prior to the tutorials. Note that this will enable you to better 'play' your 'Scripture', or 'tradition', but not 'experience', or 'reason', or 'an artifact from creation/culture' cards. Some of your preparation time should be spent reflecting on these resources.

4 Learner-centred in Bloom's taxonomy: class handout, 2014

Aim: To influence students to reflect on their learning and inspire students in their commitment to flipped learning. The traditional face to face lecture is replaced with a set of activities. Students choose their activities as part of personalising their learning. Each activity is linked to Bloom's Taxonomy, which encourages students to consider the level at which they are choosing to operate within the class.

Week 2 in the flipped classroom: let's work

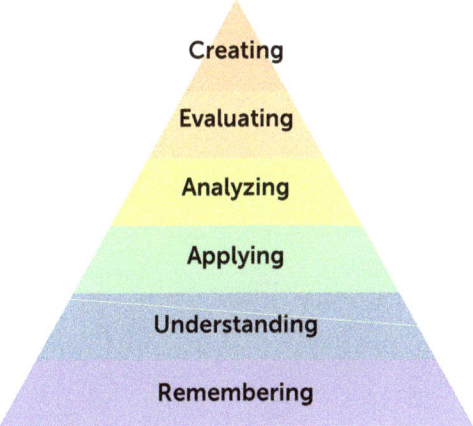

I have designed activities at three of the stages on Bloom's taxonomy.

(i) Understanding

a) what questions do you have about the reading?

b) comprehension—try to summarise the main points of [reading reference] in your own words.

c) Count up how many different original sources are used? Are there any implications for how we understand Jesus?

(ii) Applying

Let us use Fredriksen and see how it helps us understand three stories in Mark...
a) Jerusalem power groups (Fredriksen, 167, 171 ff)
Imagine you are either a worker in Herod's temple or a priest serving with the High Priest in the temple or a soldier. One day, on the way to work, you find yourself watching the events of Mark 11:8-11. Drawing on Fredriksen, what is the significance of what you see for your 'boss'?

b) How might the systems of tax described in Fredriksen (170-1) help you understand Mark 12:14-15?

c) How do the festival patterns described in [reading reference] help you understand Mark 11:12?

(iii) Analysing – Using a frame (John Drane, *After McDonaldisation*). Use A3 butchers paper around walls

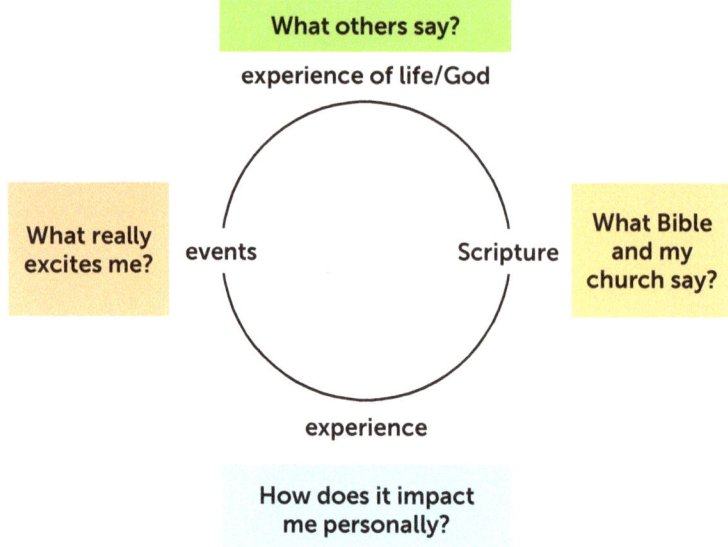

5 Learner-centred in creating curricula

i) Bio

As a Fijian teenager, Helper A[32] won a scholarship to train as a kindergarten teacher in Australia. She returned home to Fiji with not just a qualification but also an Australian husband. As a young family they returned to Australia in 1987, uprooting from a country she loved. Helper A and her husband now live in a country town, where both work as church ministers. Helper A is passionate about weaving together her Christian faith and her Fijian heritage: a task that finds an expression through creating ecclesial stoles which blend Fijian Tapa style with Christian symbolism. She sees her cultural heritage as the basic formation of who she is: providing her identity, her story and her history. Helper A is the chairperson of her denomination's multi-cultural reference committee.

ii) A Reflection

Helper A is with us to reflect on who Jesus was, and is, for her Fijian people. We are here to learn from her as she 'does' Christology with us. What light will her

---

32 Helper A and Helper B were both asked to present to a Christology class. Their verbal presentations to the class were summarised by a researcher. This summary was submitted to both helpers for their approval, which was given by return email. Ed. Note: The helpers' names have been removed to allow them anonymity.

shared wisdom shed on our own context, on our own culture? What can we learn from her of the process by which she reflects theologically?

Now a minister, Helper A speaks of how the Preamble to the Constitution of the Uniting Church encouraged her to think about her own culture. She was inspired (and resourced) by the theological reflection of others to engage in theological work on her own cultural heritage. She draws our attention to Paragraph 3 of the Preamble:

> 3. The First Peoples had already encountered the Creator God before the arrival of the colonisers; the Spirit was already in the land revealing God to the people through law, custom and ceremony. The same love and grace that was finally and fully revealed in Jesus Christ sustained the First Peoples and gave them particular insights into God's ways.

Helper A reminds us that the Fijian context is different than that of the First Peoples in Australia. The first outsiders to come to Fiji, were missionaries. Not colonisers and convicts. Thus her story is different from the Australian one.

As well as embracing the Preamble, Helper A draws on the Basis of Union of the Uniting Church in Australia. She sees Paragraph 11's encouragement to 'confess the Lord in fresh words and deeds' as an invitation to hold the old and the new together. The traditions of the Christian faith and of her people, expressed in new ways.

Like Helper B, Helper A speaks of Jesus being present before the outsiders came. She wonders how this was expressed, how this could been seen in the story of her land, her people. She sees a crucial task as being uncovering what is already there.

In reflecting on her own heritage, Helper A was reminded of a 'forgotten thing' from her childhood. A framing or explanation of her culture's leadership hierarchy, learnt at school, in which she could see points of connection with the story of Jesus. Things that resonated for her, and could resonate with others of her culture. In traditional Fijian culture there are seven statuses, seven families into which one is born, each with different roles and responsibilities:

	Role in Fijian culture
Chief	Highest level of status
Chief upholder	Tends the chief
Priest	Communicates with God (and back to chief)
Spokesman	Speaks on behalf of the Chief, and back to the Chief

Club carriers (warriors)	Protects the Chief; different kinds of clubs for different jobs
Woodcutters	Carpenters
Fisherman	Catching fish

For Helper A, and for us as we listened, there is a deep sense of affirmation, of incarnation, as we are introduced to a Jesus who entered into the world, into all categories.

	Role in Fijian culture	Jesus Christ
Chief	Highest level of status	King of the Jews. King of Kings
Chief upholder	Tends the chief	Came to do the will of the Father
Priest	Communicates with God (and back to chief)	High priest; prays, "Father forgive them"
Spokesman	Speaks on behalf of the Chief, and back to the Chief	Sharing stories eg Beatitudes, other teachings of Jesus
Club carriers (warriors)	Protects the Chief; different kinds of clubs for different jobs	Carries the cross; the weapon that banished death
Woodcutters	Carpenters	Jesus was born into this family
Fisherman	Catching fish	Directed Peter to let down nets on other side, make fishers of people, etc

Helper A thus invites us to do Christology within our own contexts; to remember the forgotten things; to make the links; to consider how and where Jesus is evident in the stories of our past and our present.

Steve Taylor
Knox Centre for Ministry and Leadership, Dunedin/Flinders University, Australia
principal@knoxcentre.ac.nz

Rosemary Dewerse
Knox Centre for Ministry and Leadership, Dunedin
rosemary.dewerse@knoxcentre.ac.nz

EPILOGUE: WONDERING ABOUT GOD TOGETHER

At the end of a lifetime of theological reflection, Karl Barth gave 'wonder' a pre-eminent place for those who wish to be theologians. To close this volume, this chapter meditates on theological education in company with Barth.

Socratic Wonder

The role of wonder in generating wisdom has been long a part of the philosophical tradition. Perplexed by the words of the Delphic oracle that he was the wisest of all people, yet knowing he knew nothing, Socrates began testing what others thought they knew, in order to show that they didn't know anything at all. The famous maxim inscribed in the Temple of Apollo at Delphi, 'Know yourself' (Pausanias 10.24.1), added further cause for perplexity, but because 'the unexamined life is not worth living' (Plato, *Apology* 21a and 37e), he launched himself on his most irritating task. However, as his life-journey continued, Socrates experienced how productive wonder-as-perplexity could be: 'Wisdom begins in wonder' (see Plato, *Theaetetus* 155c-d; *Meno* 84). For Socrates, sharing his perplexity with others in the pursuit of knowledge cost him his life. But in the next generation, Aristotle agreed that wonder is a first step towards escaping ignorance, for the person 'who is perplexed and wonders believes [themself] to be ignorant' and takes 'to philosophy to escape ignorance' (Aristotle, *Metaphysics*, 982b). With the blood of its famous martyr behind, Philosophy's pathway to critical inquiry was now open.

With such a philosophical tradition lying behind it, critical inquiry has been a *sine qua non* of a Western Higher Education. If the educational vision is firmly centred on the student learning experience, it is fair to say that all the curriculum design and development, the multiplicity of class-room activities, the ever present student assessment, as well as the monitoring, moderation, and governance systems essential for quality improvement and assurance, properly exist to move a student from ignorance to knowledge by creating a sufficient amount of wonder-as-perplexity to bring about an education—but, perhaps preferably, without the irritation the great Socrates managed to create!

Theological Wonder

Twentieth century theologian Karl Barth honoured the Greek philosophical tradition by noting that 'Socratic amazement is the root of all true science'.[1] When a person 'encounters a spiritual or natural phenomenon never met before',[2] it evokes a general kind of wonder, 'an astonished and receptive desire to learn'.[3] But, he asked, what happens when the unfamiliar becomes familiar? Then the wonder passes and the person can move on and begin to wonder about some other unknown. After a time, this next object too, 'although at first astonishing, would certainly sooner or later cease to be so'.[4] Socratic perplexity gives rise to an endless quest for objects of inquiry, a thirst for a lifetime of learning, involving many lives, and across many lifetimes.

Without at all diminishing the importance of this scientific inquiry into the world around us, Barth contrasts this ignorance-born human perplexity with that wonder which strikes the theologian. For theological wonder has an entirely different character.

Standing firmly in the theological tradition of 'Faith seeking Understanding',[5] and exemplifying his famous Christocentricity, Barth affirms that the theologian does not so much wonder about God from a distance, as they wonder about God who has come close. Theological inquiry is a quest to know the One who

---

1 Barth, *Evangelical Theology*, 64.
2 Barth, *Evangelical Theology*, 64.
3 Barth, *Evangelical Theology*, 65.
4 Barth, *Evangelical Theology*, 65.
5 Barth took Anselm's expression *fides quaerens intellectum*, which he used to describe his own posture to his inquiry about God's existence, to reflect the key posture of theological inquiry; Barth, *Fides Quaerens Intellectum*. Some have disputed the adequacy of the motto as a description of the theological enterprise, e.g. Norman, 'Abelard's Legacy', noting that Abelard introduced an approach based more on 'the principles of methodological doubt'—which, for Barth, would be a continuation of the Socratic inquiry. Despite Aquinas following Abelard, in 2009, Pope Benedict XVI commended Anselm's 'famous words [...] regarding healthy theological research that are directed to those who desire to study in depth the truths of the faith [which] remain relevant to this day'; Benedict XVI, '"Faith Seeking Understanding"'.

has already made himself known in Jesus Christ. The wonder evoked by this grand miracle—to which all other miracles point as signs—is not a perplexity at our own ignorance, but a wonderment at being confronted by the living God, over and over and over again:

> Another kind of wonder assumes control over a [person] when [they take] up the subject of theology. Certainly this amazement also obliges a [person] to wonder and compels [them] to learn. But in theological wonder it is a sheer impossibility that [they] might one day finish [their] lessons, that the uncommon might become common, that the new might appear old and familiar, that the strange might ever become thoroughly domesticated. [… Human beings are] never dismissed from the wonder that forms the sound root of theology.[6]

In the biblical tradition, a person's quest for wisdom begins not (only) by recognising that they are ignorant, but by recognising that the source of all wisdom is God. This leads to a wonder, not of perplexity, but of reverential awe: 'the fear of the Lord is the beginning of wisdom' (Psalm 111:10; Proverbs 1:7; 9:10). Operating from—and indeed, embodying—that premise, Jesus had his own set of questions which, as in the case of Socrates, proved sufficiently irritating to provoke his opponents to get rid of him. However, wisdom is recognised by her children (Luke 7:35) and, in word and deed, he constantly moved the crowds to wonder, that is, to be awestruck at what God was doing through his Christ: 'Nothing like this has ever been seen in Israel' (Matt. 9:33).

It is not that theological inquiry is unscientific. With its own object of inquiry, it is simply 'a special science, a very special science, whose task is to apprehend, understand, and speak of God'.[7] For, its proper 'object' is actually a 'Subject'—the living God who has revealed himself in Christ.[8] Studying the 'object' of theology is therefore like following 'a bird in flight':[9]

> The object of theology never encounters a [person] routinely as does an ordinary object of the world. Instead, it constantly hovers on the edge

---

6 Barth, *Evangelical Theology*, 65. Throughout this chapter, I have changed Barth's language to gender-neutral.
7 Barth, *Evangelical Theology*, 3.
8 That is, the God of the gospel. See, for example, Barth, *Evangelical Theology*, 12: 'Evangelical theology is concerned with Immanuel, God with us! Having this God for its object, it can be nothing else but the most thankful and *happy* science!'.
9 Barth, *Evangelical Theology*, 10.

of [their] circle of reflection, however large the circle may be. Progress in science, at this point, can only mean that theological hesitation and inquiry, in the face of the object of theology, more and more gain the upper hand. This captivation by the object will by no means ever lose its hold on [humanity]. If [a human being] becomes ever newly surprised then [they become] entirely and irrevocably a [person] who wonders.[10]

Wondering Together

Theological inquiry must be done in company with others. The apostle Paul, of course, was well aware of the biblical wisdom tradition that reached its climax and centre in the one who was the source of all wisdom (Col. 2:3). He was also sufficiently aware of the Greek maxim—and presumably of Socrates' life-task—to put his own spin on Delphi, when he told the Corinthians: 'If anyone thinks he knows anything, he does not yet know it as he ought to know it. But if anyone loves God, he is known by Him' (1 Cor. 8:2-3). Wisdom comes from God, and from being known by him. Wisdom comes to the one known by him, as they avoid the way of puffed up pride, and embrace the way of love (8:1). Proper knowing is anchored in rich and harmonious relationships, created and maintained by love. The pursuit of the knowledge of God is not an individualistic task. Since the knowledge of God in Jesus Christ shines the light of the incarnation on our fellow human beings, knowing God occurs delightfully in the midst of human relationships. 'When theology confronts the Word of God and its witnesses, its place is very concretely in the *community*, not somewhere in empty space'.[11] Theological education is best done together.

Wondering and Transformation of the Person

Such theological inquiry is transformative of the whole person. In the Reformed tradition, the famous opening sentence of John Calvin's *Institutes of the Christian Religion*[12] is honed on the Delphic maxim, but filtered through the

---

10   Barth, *Evangelical Theology*, 65.
11   Barth, *Evangelical Theology*, 37.
12   Barth, *The Theology of John Calvin*, 162, also notes that the impulse for Calvin's sentence came from Zwingli, but Calvin much more fully embraced it, deriving the whole of his doctrine from the angle of this dual knowledge.

apostle Paul, and thoroughly grounded in an epistemology which worked outwards from the incarnation of the God-man:[13] 'Nearly all the wisdom we possess, that is to say, true and sound wisdom, consists of two parts: the knowledge of God and of ourselves' (*Ins.* 1.1.1). And this is exactly the correct order. The pursuit of the knowledge of God results in the finding of ourselves. Once again, wonder-as-awe is part of the mix. Catching up both sides of what Christian piety often attributes to the 'fear' of God, Calvin noted the result of the pursuit of this dual knowledge: 'hence the dread and wonder with which Scripture commonly represents the saints as stricken and overcome whenever they feel the presence of God' (*Ins.* 1.1.3).

But, for Barth, 'dread' seems hardly an appropriate companion to the wonder associated with the 'happy science' of theology. Although deeply indebted to Calvin, Barth prefers to accent the freedom and joy of theological wonder:

> Christ the Saviour is here! In a real and decisive sense, therefore, *he* is the miracle, the miracle of all miracles! Whoever takes up the subject of theology finds [themselves] inevitably confronted with this miracle. Christ is that infinitely wondrous event which compels a person, so far as [they experience and comprehend] this event, to be necessarily, profoundly, wholly, and irrevocably astonished.[14]

Building further on Calvin, Karl Barth recognized that, with such an epistemology, the 'theologian' (by which he means any Christian person),[15] is inevitably and inescapably struck with wonder, and as appropriate for its particular branch of science, theology has a particular character. It is wonder-as-astonishment:

> A quite specific *astonishment* stands at the beginning of every theological perception, inquiry, and thought, in fact at the root of every theological word. This astonishment is indispensable if theology is to exist and be perpetually renewed as a modest, free, critical,

---

13 See Barth, *The Theology of John Calvin*, 164: 'Christ is the original unspoken presupposition'. See also p.166 for his observation that Calvin's first thought about Christ is that he is One with the Father, and that he assumed flesh for our sake. This provokes wonder for Barth: 'there takes place here the wonderful participation that we are [...] a new creation'.
14 Barth, *Evangelical Theology*, 71.
15 See, for example, Barth, *Evangelical Theology*, 40: 'Since the Christian life is consciously or unconsciously also a witness, the question of truth concerns not only the community but the individual Christian. [The Christian] too is responsible for the quest for truth in this witness. Therefore, every Christian as such is also called to be a theologian. How much more so those who are specially commissioned in the community, whose service is pre-eminently concerned with speech in the narrower sense of the term!'.

and happy science. If such astonishment is lacking, the whole enterprise of even the best theologian would canker at the roots. On the other hand, as long as even a poor theologian is capable of astonishment, [they are] not lost to the fulfillment of [their] task. [They remain] serviceable as long as the possibility is left open that astonishment may seize [them] like an armed [person].[16]

As a reflex of the wonder at God in Christ, in the midst of the wonder of human fellowship, the theologian—whether the junior scholar [learner] learning for the first time, or the senior scholar [learner] learning for a life-time—cannot cease to wonder at themselves:

No one can become and remain a theologian unless [they are] compelled again and again to be astonished at [*themselves*]. Last but not least, [they] must become for [themself] an enigma and a mystery. [...] After all, who am I to be a theologian? [...] Who am I to have put such trust in myself as to devote myself even remotely to the task of theology? Who am I to co-operate in this subject, at least potentially and perhaps quite actively, as a minor researcher, thinker, or teacher? Who am I to take up the quest for truth in the service and in the sense of the community, and to take pains to complete this quest? I have put such trust in myself as soon as I touch theology with even my little finger, not to speak of occupying myself with it more or less energetically or perhaps even professionally. And if I have done that, I have without fail become concerned with the new event and the miracle attested to by the Bible.[17]

The Wonder of Theological Education

The special science and the special wonder yields a special kind of person. For the confrontation with God in theological inquiry creates a kind of 'indelible quality', that of a person 'who has been afflicted and irreparably wounded by theology and the Word of God'.[18]

---

16 Barth, *Evangelical Theology*, 64.
17 Barth, *Evangelical Theology*, 71.
18 Barth, *Evangelical Theology*, 72.

> To become and be a theologian is not a natural process but an incomparably concrete fact of grace. This is so, precisely from the viewpoint of the radical and fundamental astonishment in which alone a [person] can become and be a theologian. While looking only at [themselves], a [person] can *not* recognize [themselves] as a recipient of grace, and consequently [they] cannot take pleasure and pride in [themself]. As the recipient of grace, a [person] can only become active in gratitude. If anyone supposed [they] could understand [themself] as such a receiver of grace, [they] would do better to bid theology farewell and devote [themself] to some other sort of activity. There [they] might shut [their] eyes to the wonder of God (if [they] can) and would also not need to wonder at [themselves] (if [they are] able). But perhaps [they] will find no other activity in which [they] might effectively and definitively elude theology, the wonder of God, and, consequently, [their] astonishment at this wonder and at [themselves].[19]

For those involved with theological education, life-long learning is inescapable, communal, transformative, and infused with wonder:

> I have become involved in the *reality of God* [...] who reveals himself in his Son through the Holy Spirit, who desired to be the God of [human beings] so that [human beings] might live as *his* [human beings]. I have become involved in the wonder of this God, together with all its consequences for the world and for each and every [human]. And whatever, however, and whoever I may be in other respects, I have finally and profoundly become a [human being] made to wonder at [themselves] by this wonder of God. It is another question whether I know what self-wonderment means for me, whether I am ready and able to subordinate my bit of research, thought, and speech to the logic of this wonder (and not in reverse order!). But there can be no question about one fact: I find myself confronted by the wondrous reality of the living *God*.[20]

Come, let us wonder about God together!

---

19 Barth, *Evangelical Theology*, 73.
20 Barth, *Evangelical Theology*, 72.

Bibliography

Barth, K. *Evangelical Theology: An Introduction* (Edinburgh: T.&T. Clark, 1963).

Barth, K. *The Theology of John Calvin* (G.W. Bromiley, transl.; Grand Rapids: Eerdmans, 1995 [Original: 1922]).

Barth, K. *Fides Quaerens Intellectum. Anselm's Proof of the Existence of God in the Context of His Theological Scheme* (London, SCM Press, 1960).

Benedict XVI '"Faith Seeking Understanding", Pope Benedict XVI's weekly catechesis (September 23, 2009), *National Catholic Register* www.ncregister.com/site/article/faith_seeking_understanding.

Calvin, J. *The Institutes of the Christian Religion* (LCC 20; F.L. Battles, transl.; Philadelphia: Westminster Press, 1960).

Norman, R. 'Abelard's Legacy: Why Theology is not Faith Seeking Understanding', *Australian eJournal of Theology* 10 (May 2007). http://aejt.com.au.

Peter G. Bolt
Sydney College of Divinity
PeterB@scd.edu.au

www.ingramcontent.com/pod-product-compliance
Lightning Source LLC
Chambersburg PA
CBHW042034100526
44587CB00030B/4423